A **N**

Student Handbook

ADMINISTRATION

Carol Carysforth
Maureen Rawlinson

Heinemann Educational Publishers
Halley Court, Jordan Hill, Oxford OX2 8EJ
a division of Reed Educational & Professional Publishing Ltd

Heinemann is a registered trademark of Reed Educational & Professional Publishing Limited

OXFORD   FLORENCE   PRAGUE   MADRID   ATHENS
MELBOURNE   AUCKLAND   KUALA LUMPUR   SINGAPORE   TOKYO
IBADAN   NAIROBI   KAMPALA   JOHANNESBURG   GABORONE
PORTSMOUTH NH (USA)   CHICAGO   MEXICO CITY   SAO PAULO

First published 1997
2001 2000 99 98 11 10 9 8 7 6 5 4 3 2 1

A catalogue record for this book is available from the British Library on request.

ISBN 0 435 451332

Designed by Ken Vail Graphics Design

Typeset by Tech-Set Limited, Gateshead, Tyne & Wear

Printed and bound by Biddles Ltd, Guildford

Acknowledgements

Our grateful thanks are due to all those who have made contributions and assisted us in the production of this book. In particular we would like to thank those friends and colleagues who so freely and willingly gave of their time to offer practical advice and suggestions. Special thanks in this regard must go to Sharon Harper, Alison Henderson, Sue Knights, Carolyn Lee, Peter Nangle and Chris Wainwright. We are also indebted to Jonathan Turley, Cathryn Higham and the auditing team at Freeman Rich Chartered Accountants for their expertise.

Thanks must also go to our Heinemann colleagues who helped in the production of this book. Margaret Berriman, our editor, for her constant encouragement and patience when deadlines were stretched, Jan Nikolic, whose attention to detail with such a lengthy book was absolutely invaluable and Roger Parker for his meticulous editing ability and forbearance over our sense of humour! We should also like to acknowledge the contribution of our typesetters, Tech-Set, whose professionalism considerably reduced much of the tedium we normally associate with the checking stage of the production process.

Finally, thanks to Mike for his invaluable contribution to the preparation of the index during a particularly hectic time.

Dedication

This book is dedicated to our comrades-in-arms in our early years of teaching, who provided us with a fund of rich memories which are treasured ever more with each passing year. Particularly, in memory of LMP and MS and our friends and ex-colleagues from D34 as was – Shelagh Millward, Audrey Thorpe, Muriel Eccles and Susan Heap – who will always be remembered for their own unique contributions to our experiences!

Authors' note

This book has been designed and written to fulfil the knowledge and understanding requirements of the NVQ4 Administration award. For ease of reference we have therefore used the same headings as the NVQ4 scheme for each particular unit/chapter. Because of this, readers may find there is a certain amount of repetition between headings and some duplication of content. This has been essential to conform to the scheme but, where possible, we have inserted appropriate cross-references to minimise the problem. Readers will also find that the information provided has been specifically written to relate to the particular unit. Therefore the 'slant' is rather different even if the topic is not. This correlates with the requirements of the award and links with the type of knowledge and understanding evidence that candidates must provide.

In choosing this format, we have also borne in mind that not all readers will work through the book quickly, or indeed, will read every chapter. It is therefore important that relevant information is provided in each chapter, particularly if a candidate is only seeking unit accreditation rather than attempting to achieve the full award.

Readers may also be interested to know that a companion book, *Support Pack to NVQ4 Administration*, has been written to provide candidates with all the information they need to produce a professional portfolio and relevant evidence to meet the scheme requirements. It also presents the NVQ4 standards in a clear and easy-to-read format as well as explaining the NVQ criteria and requirements to new candidates. This pack is intended for photocopying and is therefore particularly useful for advisers and assessors who may wish to select relevant pages to issue to their candidates.

Contents

Introduction

This book has been written to assist all those who are employed in administration who have taken the decision to augment their existing skills and qualifications with an NVQ level 4 award in Administration. It is also the result of a number of requests from advisers and facilitators for a student handbook, in a similar format to that for level 3, which covers the knowledge and understanding requirements of the award.

The Administration award at level 4 offers natural progression from level 3 in the way it has been designed and structured. However, at this level the award is appropriate only for those administrators who work at a level and in a role wherein they have responsibilities in the following areas:

- the achievement of team activities and team performance
- the organisation and maintainance of productive working conditions
- action planning to meet work objectives
- liaising and communicating with colleagues and contacts outside the organisation
- organising and leading meetings and discussions and obtaining information to inform management decisions
- designing, implementing and evaluating organisational systems and procedures.

Beyond these areas, candidates have a choice of three optional units from which they must select one. They can concentrate on Unit 8 relating to negotiating contracts for the supply of resources, Unit 9 which relates to financial planning and resourcing, or Unit 10 which relates to legal and regulatory requirements. Much will depend upon the exact area in which the candidate operates and his/her specialisms.

The rewards for successful candidates have already been documented. According to *The Economic Returns to Graduates*, a survey commissioned by the government and carried out by the Policy Studies Institute in 1996, non-graduates with an NVQ level 4 qualification earn between £895 and £1500 more a year than graduates in their early to mid-20s. The qualification also provides a route into traditionally graduate employment for those who chose to obtain an award based on practical experience and the application of knowledge, rather than traditional academic routes. These are therefore useful incentives to potential candidates.

Whilst all NVQ awards are competence based, and appropriate only for those who are working in a job which closely relates to the scheme and who have commensurate responsibilities to those outlined in the scheme, it would be inaccurate to assume that all potential candidates automatically have the broad range of knowledge and understanding they must later demonstrate to obtain the qualification. Many jobs, even though challenging, can be extremely task specific and repetitive. In other cases, the techniques which are adopted or are standard practice for the candidate may have been developed through trial and error. An introduction to other ways of thinking, and examples of good practice, can usefully inform job performance and be an invaluable source of help and reference. There is also the strong suggestion that, when NVQ schemes are revised following the Beaumont report, knowledge and understanding may be tested by external assessment rather than through inclusion in the portfolio of evidence.

To assist candidates to link the theory with the NVQ level 4 award, each element follows the knowledge/understanding headings used in the scheme itself. However, the text has been written to give candidates the information they require to enable them to address each of the performance criteria and all aspects of the range statements. Readers will also notice that the chapters relating to the optional units are more concise than those relating to the mandatory units, given that it is understood this should be a specialist area with which the candidate is already familiar. This is particularly the case for option Units 9 and 10. Option Unit 10 may be used as a default option unit for many candidates operating on a broad basis and not intimately concerned with purchasing or financial issues. Given the legal nature of this unit and the fact that many candidates may be non-legal generalists, the text has been designed to allow for this and to consolidate many of the legal and regulatory aspects covered in earlier chapters.

Even after competence has been achieved and accredited it is hoped that the book will be retained for its informative value and the practical guidance it gives to practising administrators.

Assessing competence

NVQ accreditation at level 4 is likely to be achieved either in the workplace or through attending part-time workshops or advisory sessions at a college or training organisation. APA (Accredited Prior Achievement) and APLE (Accredited Prior Learning and Experience) are two terms used for candidates who gain the award, with the help of an adviser, by assembling evidence from the workplace.

Because the NVQ award is a work-based qualification, it will be expected that the vast majority of evidence will originate from the candidate's day-to-day role in the workplace. In a few cases, candidates may be able to choose from a wide range of evidence for each element. This may include documentary evidence, assessor observation reports, witness testimonies from colleagues or other contacts, and records of discussions (written and oral). These are then compiled in a portfolio and clearly cross-referenced when they relate to two or more areas of the scheme.

After assessment, the portfolio is first verified by an internal verifier and then by an external verifier who is employed by the awarding body to ensure quality standards are maintained. The areas for concern are usually:

- the degree to which the candidate's own work role is established and *personal* evidence submitted (as opposed, for instance, to company documentation and policies)

- the degree to which *all* areas of the scheme (i.e. all performance criteria and range statements) have been covered
- the degree to which the knowledge and understanding requirements have been demonstrated.

The standard way for identifying personal evidence and experience is through the writing of a storyboard which clearly links the work undertaken by the candidate to the requirements of each element (see also Chapter 1, page 5). In some cases, awarding bodies supply additional recording and tracking documentation and/or cumulative assessment records. Where these are compulsory they must be used in addition to a storyboard – in each case the candidates should check with their own adviser as to the specific requirements of the awarding body, and ensure that these are followed from the outset.

In some cases, candidates find difficulty in providing the range of evidence required. If their job role does not normally cover that area then the first preference is job rotation to broaden skills and experience. The second is for top-up training to be given, possibly linked to a simulated activity (e.g. an in-tray exercise) to contribute towards the evidence. However, the degree to which simulation can be used is very limited and must be checked carefully through the internal or external verifier. It is usually better if any simulation contains specific tasks linked to a work-based project or assignment which is carried out on an independent basis to meet that candidate's particular needs. If the candidate attends a workshop or assessment session then his/her performance can be observed and noted in addition to the production of documents as evidence.

To assist candidates, advisers and facilitators, a companion book to this text, *Support Pack to NVQ4 Administration*, can be used to help portfolio building and to give useful ideas and suggestions for bridging any gaps between the scheme and the actual job role. It also provides guidance on the type of evidence which can be used to claim competence as well as questions specifically designed to enable candidates to demonstrate their knowledge and understanding.

Our aim is to provide all those involved with the NVQ4 Administration scheme with a comprehensive resource which will be equally useful no matter which route is being followed to achieve the award.

Carol Carysforth-Neild
Maureen Rawlinson

September 1997

1 Facilitate the improvement of individual and team performance

Element 1.1

Develop self and individuals to improve performance

This element focuses upon you, your immediate colleagues and the organisation for which you work. Its aim is to examine how you can identify and implement development activities for yourself and your colleagues which correspond to the objectives of your section and the strategic aims of your organisation. Because most people today wish, or need, to develop a broad portfolio of skills and qualifications which will enable them to move onwards and upwards (or even sideways) in their career, this aspect of individual development is also considered.

1996 was designated as the European Year of Lifelong Learning – although you may not have noticed! The aim was to promote the benefits of continued training and development to individuals and to organisations. As an example, one company, Co-Steel Sheerness, benefited from an 80 per cent productivity increase after investing £5.5 million in training and development. At an individual level, the Institute of Fiscal Studies report, *The Determinants and Effects of Work-Related Training in Britain*, identified that employer-provided work-related training, leading to accredited qualifications, can add 5 per cent to an individual's earnings. It has also been demonstrated by various gurus that even companies involved in cost-cutting should *increase* their training budgets to get the most out of their staff. Unfortunately, in many instances, the opposite occurs.

Other studies, such as that carried out by the Institute of Employment Studies, have demonstrated that it is not the staff who have been trained who are the main beneficiaries but the organisations themselves – through increased productivity, better service or production quality and a greater recognition of business needs. Training and development is both valuable and beneficial – provided it is targeted accurately and resources are used wisely.

The changes which are affecting organisations today are diverse in many ways, but similar in that they all create pressure for changing skills and knowledge in order that organisations can be in a position to reap the benefits of a competitive marketplace. The increase in flexible working practices and more diverse career paths for individuals have resulted in people making more career transitions through their working life – from full-time to part-time to self-employed, from employment to unemployment to planned career break, from one occupation to another or from one industry to another. Any method which better equips organisations and individuals for continual change and development should therefore be welcomed.

A survey of corporate Barclaycard holders, carried out in 1996, found that 49 per cent of senior managers are more likely to offer a job to applicants who take part in active sport than those who don't. Only 25 per cent of executives feel that sporting activities are completely irrelevant to recruitment and selection.

Before you decide to switch from your NVQ4 to aerobics or squash, or update your CV rapidly, you may like to know the reason for this apparently unlikely finding. Senior managers justify their views by claiming that those involved in sports are better at working in a team, are self-disciplined, have a keen desire to win and have better social skills. You may like to bear the last claim in mind next time you witness an altercation between rival fans at a football match!

Your own work role and responsibilities

Defining your own work role is often more difficult than it sounds. Yet doing this as precisely as possible not only helps you to formulate your own position more objectively, it is also useful for your NVQ adviser or facilitator, as he or she will be more clearly aware of the areas of work you cover and the type of evidence you could contribute for accreditation. In addition, it may be some time since you sat down and thought about *yourself* in some detail.

Most medium-sized and large organisations issue their staff with *job descriptions* stating the range of tasks which relate to a particular job and the degree of responsibility accorded to the job holder. Ideally these should be issued to prospective employees who apply for a job within the company. If you have always worked for a small firm you may never have even heard of job descriptions – let alone received one. If you have worked for any organisation for some time – especially in the same job – you may find that your official job description bears only a passing resemblance to the work you actually do at the moment. In any case, there is usually a 'catch-all' phrase which says something like 'and undertake any other duties of a commensurate nature which may be required' which may, to all intents and purposes, appear to refer to the work you undertake for about 95 per cent of an average week! However, the biggest single criticism of job descriptions (apart from the fact that they are seldom updated) is that they are rarely, if ever, written by the job holders themselves – who may not even be consulted when they are updated! Your job description therefore may be a senior manager's perception of your job, rather than your own.

The fact that you are taking an NVQ level 4 award means that you are working at a responsible level within your organisation. You should have a reasonable degree of autonomy in certain areas and the ability to make decisions on your own and implement them. The most common difficulty for many administrators working at this level is the *fragmentation* of their jobs. It is relatively easy for the switchboard operator of any company to define his/her job content. It is far more difficult for the sales manager and even more complex for the MD. Whereas at junior level you are expected to perform a relatively small number of tasks to a specific skill level, as you rise through the ranks the range of tasks you are expected to monitor or perform and the number of staff with whom you are expected to relate increases considerably. You may work hard all day but then find it difficult to put into words exactly what you have achieved. Rosemary Stewart's description of the work of managers, in *Management Today and Tomorrow*, may strike a strong chord with many practising senior administrators.

'The picture that emerges ... is of someone who lives in a whirl of activity in which attention must be switched every few minutes from one subject, problem and person to another, of an uncertain world where relevant information includes gossip and speculation. Management work becomes less clear and more disorganised.'

One thing is certain, it is doubtful that this type of comment is included in your job description!

Defining your work role and responsibilities

Whilst it is possible simply to list the tasks you do every day, this is unlikely to give anyone (including you) a clear insight into your work role or your responsibilities. The degree of responsibility and accountability you have may also vary from one area of your job to another.

When jobs are being formulated or described – or pay rates devised – a range of techniques are used including job analysis and job evaluation. These relate to dividing a job into different segments and then identifying the degree of skill or complexity required for each segment. This type of analysis can be used to define more precisely your own job or career path to date. To help you, Figure 1.1.1 gives the *suggested* headings which may be appropriate to a high-level administrative job and shows the types of indicators which signify complexity. You are obviously free to customise the chart for your own use but it should prove a useful starting point to help you to map out a job description which more precisely reflects your actual activity than the official version.

THEORY INTO PRACTICE

Undertake the following tasks to create an in-depth job description which evaluates the key aspects of your work role *as you perceive them*. Discuss your findings with your adviser.

1 Start by giving your job title and then identify the key aim or purpose of your job.
2 List all the key areas for which you are responsible. If these are not clearly defined, think of those areas where the results are critical to your own success, i.e. areas where you would least like something to go wrong!
3 Grade each component of your job given in Figure 1.1.1 using the indicative measures as a guideline.
4 Add any further components or comments you feel give a more accurate 'flavour' of the work you perform.

Job component	1	2	3	4	5
● Overall task complexity (1 = low, 5 = high)					
● Overall task continuity (1 = continuous, 5 = highly fragmented/discontinuous)					
● Degree of autonomy (1 = low, 5 = high)					
● Degree of uncertainty/change (1 = low, 5 = high)					
● Range of internal contacts (1 = few/similar levels, 5 = many/variety of levels)					
● Range of external contacts (1 = few/limited influence, 5 = many/high influence)					
● Performance standards required (1 = general competence, 5 = highly prescribed/exacting/specified)					
● Type of information handled (1 = general/basic, 5 = highly complex/technical)					
● Amount of information handled (1 = low, 5 = high)					
● Overall organisational culture (1 = stable/cooperative, 5 = highly competitive/pressured)					
● Overall management style (1 = open/trusting, 5 = secretive/blame culture)					
● Management style of own line manager (1 = autocratic, 5 = laissez faire)					
● Degree of freedom to manage – own time – own workload (1 = low, 3 = variable, 5 = high)					
● Level of authority to make/implement decisions relating to key tasks (1 = low, 3 = variable, 5 = high)					
● Type of subordinates for whom you have direct line responsibility (1 = few/similar job roles, 5 = several/disparate job roles)					
● Opportunities for delegation (1 = low, 5 = high)					
● Degree of influence over organisational/ departmental policies (1 = low, 5= high)					

Figure 1.1.1 Work role indicators

Your work role and NVQ4

You are likely to find it useful if you now map the work you carry out against the NVQ level 4 scheme, which you will be given by your adviser or facilitator. Although a low score in the preceding exercise will not necessarily preclude you from undertaking the award, you may be counselled to consider taking a level 3 Administration NVQ if your responsibilities are not commensurate with those expected for level 4 candidates. Broadly, the level 4 award equates to middle management level.

At this point it is also important that you identify any areas in the scheme which you consider you do not normally cover as part of your work role. Obviously you also need to consider the option unit which would most likely suit you and the work you do. You should also be aware that a key requirement for the award of an NVQ is the production of evidence linked to the **performance criteria** for each element of the scheme across *the whole* of the range statements. It is worth mentioning now that this must be work that *you* carry out – all NVQ assessors and verifiers are familiar with the portfolio which would enable the organisation but not the candidate to gain the award! To help you, the key terms used in 'NVQ-speak' are given in Figure 1.1.2. It is worth discussing these with your adviser or facilitator *at the outset* to make sure you have no misconceptions which may create problems or even cause you extra work obtaining appropriate evidence.

One criticism of NVQ awards has been that, because they are awarded in recognition of what you can actually do, little personal development is inherent in the scheme. It is argued that if you are a poor administrator with few skills in relation to managing your work team or liaising with other people, then an NVQ will not help you to develop these. If this is the case, then there is something seriously wrong with the way in which you are being assessed! The **knowledge/understanding** section of each unit is designed to cover the theoretical aspects of these areas of your work – and your ability to put your knowledge into practice is a key part of assessment under each performance criterion. Unless it can be clearly demonstrated that you have put your knowledge into practice, then your assessor must ensure that you have acquired this (or already know it) before accrediting you with a particular unit.

This book concentrates particularly on those aspects of the award with the aim of helping you develop your own knowledge and skills. Used properly it should help you to develop new ideas, challenge some of your existing perceptions and become a more knowledgeable and competent administrator.

A key difficulty for many mature candidates taking NVQs is their reluctance to state their achievements in writing, claim credit for any innovative ideas they have implemented – or even to write the word 'I' at all! Unfortunately, many candidates suffer from a deeply held belief, usually firmly inculcated into their heads by school teachers, that formal communications must always be written in the third person. Yet if you do this on your **storyboard** or **cumulative assessment record** then the assessor will be unable to distinguish your own activities from those of other people in the organisation.

Figure 1.1.2 'NVQ-speak' – key terms

Accreditation of prior learning (APL)
The process of accepting relevant evidence for accreditation regardless of how it has been acquired. It may comprise prior evidence from the workplace or previous workplace, from a temporary job or a voluntary activity.

Accreditation
The process of confirming that competency has been achieved, either in a specific area or for the whole award.

Adviser
The person who guides a candidate through an NVQ award and helps him/her to compile evidence and build a portfolio. All advisers must have undertaken TDLB training and accreditation themselves to a specified standard (known as D36).

Assessment
The process of checking that the evidence submitted is to the specified standard, meets the performance criteria and covers all the range statements.

Assessor
A qualified person who checks and evaluates your evidence to confirm that it proves you, personally, are competent in all the areas covered by the award. TDLB awards D32 and D33 are required by all assessors.

Authenticity
All the evidence you provide must relate to you and you alone. If any relates to other people then your own role must be clearly identified.

Awarding body
The body which will give you official accreditation, e.g. BTEC, RSA, City & Guilds.

Competence
This relates to your ability to perform consistently a variety of tasks according to the criteria laid down for the award.

Cumulative assessment record (CAR)
Issued by some awarding bodies to record and track actions taken and related evidence against PCs, range statements and knowledge and understanding requirements.

Elements of competence
These apply to a particular aspect of the work role – normally a subset of a key area which has been identified (see Units of competence).

External verifier
A verifier appointed by the awarding body to check that all assessment has been carried out correctly and that quality standards have been applied. The external verifier is also qualified to TDLB (D35) standards.

Knowledge and understanding
This refers to the areas that have been identified as underpinning competent performance for the award. The candidate must prove he/she has the knowledge and understanding defined for each unit.

Figure 1.1.2 'NVQ-speak' – *continued*

Internal verifier
The role of an internal verifier is to check that assessment has been undertaken correctly by random sampling units across a range of portfolios. All internal verifiers must be trained to a TDLB (D34) standard.

Lead Body
The public body designated by the government to be representative of a particular occupational sector. This body is responsible for setting, maintaining and reviewing national standards of competence within these occupations. The Administration Lead Body has defined the role of administrators as 'the establishment, operation, maintenance and evaluation of systems, procedures and services to assist organisations to achieve their objectives'.

Qualifications and Curriculum Authority – QCA
Scottish Qualifications Authority – SQA
The first is the accrediting body for all NVQs in England, Wales and Northern Ireland. SQA is the sole awarding body for SVQs (Scottish Vocational Qualifications)

Performance criteria (PCs)
The outcomes which must be achieved to demonstrate competency by the candidate.

Portfolio
The file in which evidence is presented for the assessor.

Range statements
These cover the circumstances to which evidence of competency must relate. In the Administration award they are all compulsory and must all be covered by appropriate evidence.

Storyboard
A personal report, usually written for each element, which clearly outlines the job holder's activities relating to the award and identifies the activities for which evidence is included.

Supplementary evidence
Evidence which supports a claim for competence but which would not, *on its own*, enable accreditation to be given. Typical examples are copies of company policies and procedures.

Training and Development Lead Body (TDLB)
Sets national standards for all concerned with advising, assessing and verifying NVQ awards.

Units of competence
Identify the key areas which cover a particular role.

Witness testimony
Used to support documentary evidence or to provide evidence when no documentary evidence is available. Typically may take the form of a letter, memo or statement from a manager, colleague, customer or contact which confirms a particular action or behaviour. Witness testimony should be specific and used to support specific claims made in the storyboard.

Which of the following statements is acceptable to an NVQ assessor, and which is not?

A The company operates an appraisal scheme through which individual training needs can be included in a departmental staff development plan. This links to the strategic plan of the organisation. Appraisal is carried out in line with organisational procedures and training is mapped to inform the departmental plan. The employees' needs are fully discussed and, if required, referred to a line manager for agreement. Company appraisal policy and a copy of all relevant company documentation are given as evidence 1.1.1 to 1.1.6.

B In my job, I am responsible for appraising three staff according to standard company procedures. Their individual training needs are discussed at length. I then produce a summary which links these to our department's staff development plan which I write in liaison with my line manager. This in turn links to the strategic plan of the organisation. It is my job to negotiate any training requests which would not be relevant to the needs of the organisation and, if required, refer these to my own line manager. Attached as evidence are witness testimonies from one of my staff and my line manager (1.1.1 and 1.1.2), summary staff development document written May 199- (1.1.3), departmental development plan (1.1.4). As supplementary evidence I also include a copy of the strategic plan for the current year (1.1.5) and a copy of the organisation's appraisal policy document (1.1.6).

Coping with a mismatch

If you identify areas where you may have difficulty providing evidence, do not worry. Sometimes it can be difficult to provide 'real' evidence across the whole of the range. For instance, when you start Unit 4, you can hardly instigate a major conflict or disagreement with your colleagues just to demonstrate how you act when one occurs! In such cases, however, you will be expected to say what you *would* do if one *did* occur – and this is where the knowledge and understanding you gain from this book becomes invaluable. For instance, it will help you to evaluate the range of behaviours which would be appropriate under different circumstances. This is far more acceptable to your assessor than a simple statement saying you would sort it out!

Even if you do not cover a particular unit or element as part of your normal job role, this does not mean that you cannot undertake the award (unless there are too many – in which case a different occupational NVQ may be more suitable). A variety of techniques can be used to solve the problem.

- *Career path evidence or career profile.* If you have only recently started in your present job then you may have covered other areas of the award in your previous jobs. Unless you have a problem contacting your ex-employers you could ask them to provide witness testimony for any aspect with which you were keenly involved in then, but which is not part of your current job. (Do be aware, however, that there is a limit to how far you are allowed to track back – more than three years is not normally acceptable!)

- *Additional or voluntary activities.* Many people undertake other activities in their spare time besides those that they are paid to do. You may run the local Scouts or be the Membership Secretary at your golf club. Evaluate the activities you carry out in any of these roles and discuss opportunities for evidence with your adviser.
- *Job rotation and job enrichment.* In the first you swap jobs (or tasks) with someone else for a while. In the second you develop the skill to take on a new task (possibly by delegating an old one if time is at a premium).

However, do not take these routes until you have talked through any mismatches with your adviser. An experienced adviser will often see links between your work role and the scheme which you cannot, and will understand from the outset the wide range of evidence which can often be submitted. Flexibility and imagination, together with a determination to succeed, are usually all that are required – plus the ability to identify *minor events* which can contribute just as effectively as major ones. For instance, for Element 1.2, team performance monitoring can be formal or informal – there is no requirement for candidates to introduce a formal monitoring system to produce acceptable evidence – which may be outside their remit or area of responsibility. You may simply have regular discussions with your team and evaluate outcomes. If you record these discussions and attach any action plans then these documents would be just as relevant – and less likely to disrupt your colleagues or irritate senior management!

A companion book to this is the *Support Pack to NVQ4 Administration*. This contains forms on which you can map your work role against the scheme and identify any gaps or mismatches quickly and easily. It also provides ideas for evidence, questions you can answer (verbally or in writing) to demonstrate your knowledge and understanding, as well as suggested in-tray exercises which you can use to provide evidence by simulation if you have absolutely no other alternative. You should note, however, that the amount of evidence you can produce in this way is very limited on an NVQ level 4 scheme (currently to a maximum of between 15 and 20 per cent). Above all, the evidence should be *work-based* across the whole of the award.

THEORY INTO PRACTICE

1 To the detailed job description you drew up earlier (see page 3) attach your official job description as well as information on any other relevant tasks you have carried out in a previous career or during your spare time. It is also helpful if you can provide a brief description of your organisation, the work it carries out and the way it is structured, together with an organisation chart which shows *clear* links between yourself and your colleagues (see below) as well as an indication of the regular contacts you have which are external to the organisation.
2 If it would be helpful, draw up a career profile which gives your adviser details of other sources of evidence you could use.

Facilitate the improvement of performance

3 Make sure you have your own copy of the NVQ level 4 Administration scheme and examine this in relation to the work you personally undertake. Discuss with your adviser the links you have made between the scheme and your work role – and any gaps which still concern you.

Work roles and responsibilities of colleagues

Your colleagues, in this sense, may be your subordinates, your peer group and even your line manager (or other managers) to whom you relate. Basically, to accord with the scheme, they must comprise:

- those individuals with activities related to your own in the workplace
- those who are nominated by the organisation for development purposes.

Ideally, if the organisation which employs you is well structured and work roles are clearly delineated, the whole resembles a jigsaw, with the pieces fitting together neatly to provide a clear picture of the department, section or organisation. Without being cynical, in many establishments staff are apt to be more than a little surprised if this type of 'best fit' occurs! Indeed, overlap and duplication of work roles and tasks, with no-one to do some jobs and people getting in each other's way in relation to other duties, will occur even in the best organisations. There can be a variety of reasons for this. Rapid growth (or financial cuts) mean that, for a time, there are insufficient people to cope with all the work roles. Rapid change can mean that one area of work grows very quickly and requires more staff or that new systems and procedures have been introduced which affect everyone. It usually takes some time for the formal structure to 'catch up' with what is really taking place – which is when a restructuring exercise may be required, either on a small or large scale. At this stage a complete rethink of work roles is required – sometimes for a whole section. This will need monitoring to check that the original ideas for job allocation actually work in practice.

Even if your organisation has gone through such an exercise, unless there was careful consideration of the key aims and objectives of the section in which you work, and a relatively open organisation culture in operation which allows frank discussion on the best way to reorganise the work, you may still find anomalies. These may be caused by a variety of factors – from organisational or power politics, to basic misconceptions of work roles, or autocratic management.

In your job, you will deal with colleagues who have the ability to impact upon your own work role in a variety of ways. In some cases, their own work role may be such that they can severely affect your own productivity and performance. People with a high impact potential are not always those with whom you are in contact frequently or those who are senior to you. It is an old adage that before you plan a key event out of hours you should check the idea with the custodian of the building before you ask the MD! Generally, however, the people who have the most power to affect your own performance are those with whom you have regular contact and upon whom you depend for accurate information and a speedy response.

If you work in a large organisation and department and relate to very many different people on a constant basis, you may need to narrow down your focus to a small number of key individuals to keep this part of the scheme manageable. You are advised to start by identifying those individuals with whom you work closely and whose performance in their job can severely affect your own.

If you work as part of a team, obviously the other members of the team are those who should have top priority when you start to define your colleagues' work roles and responsibilities. In this case, even if your section or department seems to comprise a disparate set of individuals, your team should not be so – otherwise it is hardly likely to achieve its objectives. This is extremely important to you if you are in any way responsible for the performance of the team as a whole as, in this case, the successful functioning of the team is crucial to your own job performance (see also Element 1.2, page 77).

THEORY INTO PRACTICE

Identify the individuals in your own organisation who have activities related to your own and who have the most potential to affect your own job performance. Bear in mind you should look upwards, sideways and downwards! Then identify those individuals for whom you have any responsibility for training and development (either formal or informal).

Try to obtain job descriptions for each of the persons you identify. If you cannot obtain the official job descriptions then write these yourself from observation and, if possible, check their accuracy with each person concerned. Do be aware that, unless you do this, it will be only your own perception of their work roles and responsibilities that you are devising. However, you may have to tread warily if one of the people you have identified is your own line manager!

Reams of paper have been produced by management writers discussing the importance of developing human resources. Peter Drucker has defined staff as the one uniquely flexible resource. Tom Peters has a more robust line of comment (see below). Despite this, the reality in many organisations is still that 'staff development' refers to the list of external courses circulated around the company once a year – with a note attached stating which would be suitable for each level of staff.

'You have to ask yourself what you see, what you really see, when you look into the eye of a front-line employee. Do you see a ne'er-do-well that needs that span of control of 1 to 10 prevalent in your organisation, that'll rip you off if you turn your back for more than 3 or 4 seconds? Or do you see a person that could literally fly to the moon without a face-mask if only you would just train the hell out of them, get the hell out of their way and give them something decent to do?' (Tom Peters – *Business Matters*, BBC TV, 1989)

Identifying development needs in self and others

The biggest obstacle for staff development is the confusion between 'training' and 'development' in the minds of many managers. The key difference is that training is something which is traditionally 'done to you' whereas development is something you owe to yourself. The modern emphasis, therefore, is away from large, impersonal training centres and customised or standard courses towards greater flexibility which incorporates a wide range of objectives – from the company strategic plan to the needs of different individuals.

That said, it is likely that the perception of appropriate development needs for individuals may vary between different members of the organisation.

- The senior management are concerned with organisational objectives and the strategic plan. They are likely to take the 'global view' across the organisation and pursue objectives with the future needs of the organisation as a whole to the fore.
- Departmental managers are more concerned with tactical plans and meeting targets. They are concerned about the key areas of growth and change in their own area and any skill shortages which have been identified. These may, or may not, accord with development areas identified at senior level.
- Team leaders are concerned with operational objectives and productivity. They are interested in the *combined* skills of the team as a whole and the development of positive team dynamics (see Element 1.2, page 79).
- Individuals are as likely to be concerned with their own personal interests and career development as with organisational objectives – particularly if they have little faith in top management or a high level of job insecurity.

If all these areas coincide then identifying development needs is a relatively simple matter. However, the chances are that they won't – and you may find yourself in the difficult position of trying to persuade key staff with strongly held ideas that they should be following the dictates of senior management (or even your own manager) with which they do not agree. Your negotiation skills may be critical in this situation (see Chapter 4, pages 307 and 380, also Chapter 8, page 603). A key task will be to try to find some common ground, to persuade your line manager to change his/her mind or to 'sell' your manager's idea to your subordinates. In the long run, you are paid to carry out instructions, but if you are confident you can handle your boss or are fortunate enough to work for one who is consultative and open-minded, then you may be able to influence a change of mind. Much depends upon the suggestions made by your colleagues, the organisational culture and predominant management style in operation, staff perception of the organisation and management and, in the end, whether any actual benefits would accrue *in the long term* to the team, department or organisation. Many an organisation has found that, if it takes too shortsighted an approach to development, it misses out on useful areas which would give it a leading edge in the future.

The term *Learning Organisation* has been given by management gurus such as Tom Peters to organisations which focus and foster continual change and development. Garratt defined this as 'an organisation which facilitates the learning of all its members and continuously transforms itself' (*Creating a Learning Organisation*, 1990). Key aspects of a learning organisation culture include:

- group and team working encouraged – often complemented by SMTs (self-managed teams) which set their own goals and targets and monitor their own performance
- open communication at all levels and networking across the organisation
- employee welfare high on the list of corporate objectives – but expectations of performance also high
- a healthy respect for the customer with a strong emphasis on product quality and customer service
- continual staff training and development
- a holistic approach to problem solving – favouring collaboration and coordination over internal segmentation, competition and individual rivalry
- new ideas and experimentation welcomed – solutions to problems sought from all levels with success rewarded and failure openly tolerated, mistakes treated as 'positive learning experiences'
- bureaucracy detested and the structure as decentralised and simple as possible, with all employees encouraged to share in the decision-making processes of the organisation
- change viewed as an opportunity not a threat
- the culture is one of pride in organisational achievements to date.

In 1987 a project called 'Developing the Learning Company' was carried out by Pedler, Boydell and Burgoyne. They identified eleven characteristics of a learning organisation and a summary of these is given in Figure 1.1.3.

THEORY INTO PRACTICE

To what extent does your organisation foster a culture where it is keen to learn? Is there an open culture where staff can openly discuss their needs and contribute to the decision-making process? Is there a history of confidence or discontent in senior management? To what degree does your own line manager foster a participative culture?

You may like to consider how the culture of your organisation and the way in which it reacts to staff suggestions, comments and mistakes is likely to influence

- the range of suitable development activities which would be allowable
- the degree to which staff are likely to want to participate in their own self-development.

Learning approach to strategy
Clear feedback loops are incorporated into the process so that there is continuous improvement through experience.

Participative policy-making
Company policy is shared with all stakeholders (employees, suppliers, customers and community) with the aim of 'delighting customers'. Differences of opinion are viewed as productive tensions.

Informating
Technology is widely available to inform employees about what is occurring in the company. The focus is on stimulating learning and not rewarding, punishing or controlling staff. 'Bad news' (e.g. why a customer was lost) is seen as positive information, rather than an excuse for criticism.

Formative accounting and control
Accounting, budgeting and reporting systems are designed to assist staff learning and delight the internal customer.

Internal exchange
All internal departments, sections or units are seen as each other's suppliers or customers. The focus is on collaboration and co-operation – not competition.

Reward flexibility
Pay awards/scales/rates are a matter of open debate. Money is not seen as the only possible reward.

Enabling structures
Work roles are flexible to allow for personal growth and experimentation, e.g. project groups across departments to help to spread new ideas and encourage change.

Boundary workers as environmental scanners
All workers who have contacts with stakeholders to have as a key part of their role the collection of relevant data from outside the organisation.

Inter-company learning
Linking with customers and suppliers in training, research and development and work shadowing/job exchanges. Learning from competitors by observing 'best practice' (known as *benchmarking*).

Learning climate
The encouragement of experimentation and learning from experience. Importance of continuous improvement fostered and feedback encouraged. Constructive criticism and ideas welcomed. Mistakes allowed because it is seen as better to have tried and failed than never to have tried – and not all new ideas will work.

Self-development opportunities for all
Resources and facilities accessible to all levels of employees to provide coaching, mentoring, peer support, counselling, feedback to support individuals whilst they are learning.

(Adapted from *The Learning Company* by M. Pedler, J. Burgoyne and T. Boydell, McGraw-Hill, 1991)

Figure 1.1.3 Characteristics of a learning company

Matching development needs – the options available

Various techniques can be used to identify development needs. Ideally these should link organisational, departmental, team and personal needs together. *Top-down (formal) options* which do this include:

- the company appraisal scheme
- performance management systems
- succession planning
- needs analysis
- skills audits.

In all these cases the technique is likely to be undertaken or instigated by senior managers, be part of company policy and then discussed with staff. The degree to which staff are actively expected to participate to inform the process (in reality rather than in theory) can be critical to its success.

Supervisory techniques include:

- personal observation
- work sampling and evaluation.

In these cases evaluation of training needs is usually carried out by line managers, supervisors or administrators. In both techniques the focus is likely to be more on current *tasks* and standards of performance – and the needs of the organisation or department – than on the *people* and their individual development needs. One way of balancing this is to allow staff members themselves an input in informing the staff development plan.

Bottom-up techniques are usually more informal and include:

- informal discussions
- team meetings
- feedback from staff.

Ideally there should be a mix in operation so that all concerned feel that their needs are being taken into consideration.

Top-down options

Appraisal schemes

Almost 50 per cent of UK organisations today have some type of appraisal system in operation where interviews are held – usually annually – between employee and line manager, regarding job performance and the future needs of the organisation and the individual. The content of all discussions is confidential – and this means that you cannot use appraisal documents as evidence (apart from your own!) without the express consent of the person involved. In cases where the employee feels he/she might not obtain a fair interview with his/her line manager it is usually possible to nominate a different person to be the appraiser.

Appraisal interviews are nothing new – they were around in one form or another in America for the best part of this century. However, it took until the

1970s before they were introduced in Britain – initially for middle and junior managers in the private sector. Later they were adopted by the public sector.

Staff appraisal schemes usually have a variety of aims. Initially they concentrated upon employee traits – such as loyalty and commitment. The focus then changed to concentrate more upon job performance – what people did rather than how they acted. Today research undertaken by the Institute of Personnel and Development (IPD) has shown that 65 per cent of appraisals are used to identify training requirements. Generally appraisal interviews involve:

- reviewing past performance (often linked to success in meeting previous targets)
- reviewing – and hopefully improving – job performance
- setting new targets or performance objectives for the coming year
- assessing training and development requirements – linking the needs of the individual with the organisation's strategic plans
- assessing future potential or promotability
- assisting the employee to plan his/her career.

Good appraisals are carried out in a positive way by managers who have received some training in how they should be undertaken. Three styles have been identified:

- the 'tell and sell' approach – where the appraiser does most of the talking (this is generally the wrong approach to take)
- the 'tell and listen' approach – where the appraiser opens the interview and the appraisee then takes over
- the problem-solving interview – where there is a frank and open discussion on the strengths and weaknesses of the appraisee followed by an agreed plan to move forwards.

Appraisal training helps to prevent managers from falling into the common traps experienced by those with less experience, such as:

- being overly influenced by recent events or the long service of the appraisee
- allowing a good or poor rating in one area to affect judgement in other areas
- 'playing safe' by giving a middle score to everyone
- over-rating employees if a pay award is linked to the appraisal (see below) to avoid bad feeling afterwards
- avoiding discussion on sensitive areas or poor performance
- wanting perfection and making unfair criticisms and evaluations (this can destroy staff morale and motivation).

The main aim of the appraisal interview should be to maintain and increase staff motivation. An IPD survey found that 60 per cent of employees were motivated by the experience. A well structured appraisal is only part of the relationship between a manager and his/her staff – it should not be the only time the two ever meet or talk about what is going on. However, it may be the only occasion they have time to step back from day-to-day problems and tasks and look at the big picture together.

Most appraisals today involve some type of review against targets. It should be emphasised that this can only be done fairly if external factors are taken into account – as well as those aspects of the job which cannot be measured quantitatively.

The success and value of appraisals depends to a large extent on the skill of the appraiser and his/her management style. If the appraisal ends in confrontation then this is an indication that there is something far more serious taking place than poor appraisals. Adequate time should be allowed for appraisals – between one and two hours per person is fairly normal – and there should be no interruptions. The support of top management is essential – if appraisals are loathed or feared by staff they will not serve their purpose.

Successful appraisals aim to:

- enable the organisation to identify where rewards (including promotion) should be allocated
- discover the work potential of the employees and, collectively, each section or department
- identify the training needs which are required and link these to strategic planning
- control and monitor performance
- assist individuals with their own self-development (see below)
- improve employee motivation by understanding and recognising their needs
- check the effectiveness of current practices, e.g. recruitment and training.

A 360-degree appraisal system is one where performance is assessed by a person's manager, peers and subordinates. Peers and subordinates are usually asked for their contribution through an anonymous questionnaire which may then be evaluated at an assessment centre. It is usually the case that the person being appraised can specify those peers and subordinates from whom opinions can be sought. Glaxo Wellcome and BP are two British companies to have introduced the scheme.

This system is considered to give a better all-round picture of the appraisee – although there can be obvious problems. Peers are hesitant to give their views in case they are considered to be criticising colleagues. Negative feedback can also severely disrupt good team working (see Element 1.2, page 53). Subordinates will have a narrower view of their manager's performance but will be capable of giving feedback on management style and 'people' skills. Both, however, are likely to be unduly influenced by recent events and by the degree of perceived confidentiality which exists within the system. There is, of course, also the fact that no-one is likely to identify a subordinate or colleague to be asked for an opinion if they have a particularly contentious relationship or if negative feedback may be a strong possibility!

Recent research by the Institute for Employment Studies in Brighton has indicated that three conditions need to be met for 360-degree appraisal to operate successfully. The first is care taken over giving feedback, over receiving it and over following up any problems. Otherwise, according to Polly Kettley, author of the report *Personal Feedback: Cases in Point*, people feel vulnerable and criticised. However, being secure enough to introduce the system is considered a sign of confidence.

THEORY INTO PRACTICE

1 Identify the strengths and weaknesses of implementing a 360-degree appraisal system in your organisation.
2 A variation on this system is to include other stakeholders in the process – notably customers. How do you consider customers could be asked their views of individual employees, and what would be the advantages and disadvantages of this idea?

An IPD survey on appraisals carried out in 1996 showed an increase in the number of people motivated by their appraisal. Sixty per cent of those interviewed felt positive about the experience and over 75 per cent felt they could talk freely in the session. Most people felt the most objective appraisal would be carried out by their immediate line manager, though 25 per cent would have been happy to be appraised by colleagues and peers. However, only 1 per cent considered that they would receive an objective appraisal if it were carried out by their subordinates!

One other problem with appraisals appears to be cultural. Those who work for Japanese employers struggle with cultural differences between what they expect to be told and how – and what actually happens. The Japanese are not keen to commit themselves to paper (for job descriptions or anything else) and prefer to drop subtle hints (preferably out of hours) rather than give specific statements in scheduled interviews. Even getting a pay rise is no indicator of good performance – Japanese companies are more likely to reward staff because of good organisational performance rather than for individual merit or achievements.

Performance management systems

These systems link the objectives of the organisation to employee performance. In a survey by Bevan and Thompson in 1992, entitled *An Overview of Policy and Practice* (IPD), 20 per cent of organisations surveyed had introduced this type of system. Performance management systems are usually designed in-house to suit the needs of an individual organisation. However, there are some features common to most systems.

- Organisational objectives are clear and communicated downwards – often through the mission statement, strategic plan and operating statement. Job descriptions, which link to these objectives, are regularly reviewed.
- Individual performance objectives are agreed by appraiser and appraisee. The objectives are specific and concentrate on task achievement and methods of assessing performance. The writing of the objectives is critical as, unless these are closely defined, performance cannot be accurately assessed (see also page 28 and Element 1.2, page 81). The acronym SMART is often used to describe the type of targets which must be set, i.e.
  - specific
  - measurable
  - agreed
  - realistic
  - time-related.
- A development plan is agreed which identifies the type of support and/ or development activities required to support the individual during the period.
- Performance is assessed both on a formal basis (e.g. annually) *and* on an ongoing basis. In some schemes successful achievement is linked to a pay award.

Not all experts take a positive view of appraisals or performance management systems. Tom Peters was quoted as saying 'performance appraisal is the number one American management problem. It takes the average employee six months to recover from it.'

Whilst this may seem unduly negative, research by the IPD shows that about one-third of companies use appraisals to decide pay awards and yet others use them to decide redundancies. Generally, the experts consider that pay should be separated from the appraisal process. It goes without saying that, in this case, employees will feel honour-bound to defend or justify their performance – and only agree to low targets which they know they can achieve. However, others take the view that appraisal is only taken seriously when pay issues are involved and that those who are high performers are 'disadvantaged' when the review does not include a reward for their achievements.

Experts also criticise appraisals and performance management systems which measure targets in unsuitable areas. A hospital doctor who has achieved the fastest 'throughput' of patients is an obvious example – as doctors may be tempted to send people home early to meet their 'targets'. In the late 1980s and early 1990s, many people were sold inappropriate pensions by financial advisers trying to meet sales targets.

The main area where appraisals are considered successful is in the identification of training and development needs – provided, of course, that the organisation is then prepared to support or assist with the training and link personal development with new performance goals.

---

1. A study undertaken by Garland and Price found that the success of female managers was attributed to luck or an easy task whilst the success of male managers was attributed to skill and hard work *by the majority of appraisers*.
   a. What do you think caused this view?
   b. What action could an organisation take to overcome findings such as this?
   c. To what extent do you think such views can ever be totally eradicated?
2. What is your view in relation to
   a. linking appraisals to pay awards (note that both advantages and disadvantages are mentioned above!)
   b. the difficulty (and dangers) inherent in setting performance targets for certain types of jobs, e.g. police constables.
3. What is your own experience of appraisals? Are they carried out in your current organisation? To what degree do you feel your appraisal interview gives you the opportunity to identify your own training and development needs?

Succession planning

Whilst appraisal interviews help to identify possible promotion candidates, alongside this there is usually some form of succession planning being undertaken within most organisations. Succession planning is concerned with the future of the organisation – where it wants to be or in what situation or markets it will operate in a few years' time. Imagine you are the management accountant in a large department. Your assistant is due to retire long before you do. In this case you would be sensible if you were assessing other members of staff to see who would be the likely future contenders for the job. There is likely to be a considerable gap between the career point reached at present by any possible candidates, and the skills and abilities they would need to be able to submit an application. You should therefore try to encourage them to bridge the gap by taking additional qualifications. Or you may find that one or two are well-qualified but hopelessly lacking in people skills – again you should look to remedy the problem. Obviously any potential promotee who refuses your support and encouragement takes the inevitable consequences, but it is better to find out about their attitude now rather than after appointment.

At an organisational level a system of management development may be in operation to encourage ambitious managers to develop their skills and abilities. This not only improves the level of management in the organisation but also provides for career progression and succession – so that key people are nearly always replaceable quickly. Additionally, the organisation may have plans for expansion and growth, or a change of product line or process development, or be about to modify all its computer systems. Again staff profiles may be studied to see who would be suitable to relocate, change job, transfer and so on – and training may be given to facilitate this where necessary. If you are renowned for your fluency in languages, don't be too surprised if you find yourself suddenly transferred to Marketing when the company decides to put 'increasing international sales by 20 per cent' at the top of its strategic plan!

Needs analysis

This technique is used to identify the gap between expertise the company needs to have and what it actually has. To be of value, it should allow for changing circumstances and future plans. It is usually a cost-effective exercise because it concentrates on developing existing staff rather than just hiring new staff. Needs analysis is usually carried out at organisational level and comprises all types of training and qualifications, in contrast with the technique below, which concentrates purely on skills.

Skills audit

This is an exercise carried out to ascertain the skills currently 'owned' by the organisation. It can be carried out throughout the company but is often done departmentally – given that some duplication of key skills is essential. For instance, in most organisations computer literacy is a basic requirement of all administrative staff. However, if one department found it had eight word-processor operators but only one person who could use a spreadsheet package, something would need to be done – and fast! A lack of key skills can seriously hamper growth and development – and reduce flexibility. It can also increase costs as staff with the necessary skills need to be employed. Either that, or an entire operation may be considered more suitable for outsourcing or contracting out to save money.

In addition, the department obviously needs to identify the skills which are needed for the department as a whole to operate effectively – and provide cover for holidays, sickness and personal leave entitlement. In this case the staff are being considered as a departmental team – it is the combined skills which are important rather than individual attributes. To improve flexibility, many organisations have concentrated on promoting *multiskilling*, where people steadily work towards achieving a range of skills related to their jobs. This can have the added benefit of making individual jobs more interesting provided the strategy is properly planned from the outset.

An alternative strategy now being adopted in more and more organisations is that of contracting out non-core or peripheral activities to external providers and suppliers. This is believed to be both beneficial and cost-effective for the organisation, which is then free to concentrate on its core profit-making business. All other requirements, such as security, catering, payroll and computer services, are outsourced to service providers. Today virtually nothing is considered unsuitable for outsourcing – from customer service to human resources development.

As an example, all BP's accounting is now contracted out to Arthur Andersen. All accounting staff, still sitting at their old desks, are now employees of Arthur Andersen. In a recent survey, accountants said that they now made more money through contracted out services than through undertaking their traditional accounting roles.

Employees of public sector organisations, particularly local authorities, will find this nothing new. The advent of CCT – compulsory competitive tendering – forced such organisations to put services up for tender. Unless such organisations can prove that they can provide the service more cost-effectively internally, then they have no option but to outsource their requirements.

It may appear to be something of an anomaly for organisations that are moving towards flatter, more egalitarian structures to pursue staff development and appraisal activities – given that career progression upwards is severely constrained. Not so, according to the Institute of Personnel and Development, which has published a report on *broadbanding*. This is a system of lateral career development and flatter pay scales where increments are given for developing additional skills and qualifications rather than being 'promoted' in the traditional sense. The IPD also foresees a clear link between appraisal and broadbanding given that appraisals are concerned with skill development. Broadbanding emphasises the need for this throughout a person's career with clearly specified rewards for personal development and additional qualifications.

Supervisory options

These are the techniques most likely to be instigated and used by you, as an administrator.

Personal observation of competency

Observation can be carried out as an ongoing technique by good administrators or happen through pure accident by poor ones! If the newest member of staff takes two hours to key in the simplest document then it is fairly obvious to anyone that some basic training is required. However, if he/she is struggling to cope with customers satisfactorily, or deal with telephone calls or file documents accurately, you may know nothing about it until a barrage of complaints arrives on your desk!

Keeping your eyes open and listening to casual remarks should not be undervalued. Simply seeing who sits around the most gossiping – and doing something about it – will give you credibility with your team. Spotting the 'willing horse' who is being constantly overloaded and therefore cannot be expected to cope, is also important. Finding that the most junior person is being given all the routine or boring jobs because the office staff want rid of these duties should also make you take action – if only to rescue the poor junior! He or she will hardly improve if that is the current limit of the work role.

A rather more organised system of observation can be carried out if you are aware of the *competencies* required for a job and whether these are being achieved. Identifying *standards of competence* takes away the vagueness from any feedback about performance you might give to staff. You should be interested in competence – as this is the fundamental criterion upon which your NVQ awards are based. As you saw on page 6, competence relates to the key tasks which have to be covered in a job, the level of achievement required and the range across which this should be demonstrated. Quite obviously, all these variables will change as greater levels of responsibility are given to a person. The tasks will be broader, the achievement levels higher and the range more diverse. Identifying the level of competence required is quite a skilled operation – and NVQs were originally instigated to provide national standards and avoid variations from one organisation to another.

However, whilst NVQs are excellent for giving information on the competencies identified for a particular job, you may be trying to assess an individual whose job does not relate to one specific NVQ. What you are trying to ascertain in this case is whether or not the person can perform the key tasks of the job, in a variety of situations, to an appropriate standard over and over again.

THEORY INTO PRACTICE

Identify the key skills required by a switchboard operator of a large organisation. These would relate to the units and elements of an NVQ for this occupation – if one existed. Now decide the level of performance you would expect and what duties the operator must be able to perform *consistently* to be classed as competent. These are your performance criteria. Finally, decide the range of circumstances which might apply in each case. For instance, if you are concentrating upon the communication aspects you may identify a range of callers – those who know to whom they want to speak and those who don't, callers from the UK and overseas, those who speak English well and those who don't. You may decide to include the disabled – such as those who are hard of hearing or speech-impaired who may communicate with the switchboard through the Typetalk relay service.

There has been a move by experts towards defining *organisational competencies* rather than *individual competencies*. Organisational competency is the next logical step from defining 'core business' but, to be useful, must relate not only to the overall mission and strategy of the organisation but also to its future plans. The aim is then to unite organisational competencies and individual competencies to maximise organisational performance through the skills and abilities of the staff who work there. Flexibility and constant updating is then vital if the range of competencies is clearly to reflect the skills which are required within the organisation. Consistency in relation to the method of specification is also necessary if the system is to be understandable to the workforce and provide a method through which change can be managed and controlled.

Work measurement systems

You may wish to check work on a more systematic basis than just personal observation. A variety of work measurement systems can be used to check quality and quantity of work produced by your staff. The simplest is a basic log of jobs received and completed with the name of the person alongside. If this would be too heavy-handed or time-consuming, then simply making sure you know who has responsibility for what – and checking output in these areas – will tell you a considerable amount.

In some areas, of course, work measurement is more formalised. Many computer systems can measure key strokes per hour, some word-processor operators are monitored by the number of documents produced each day. Provided that targets are realistic and take account of factors such as task complexity and number of interruptions or distractions, any noticeable discrepancy between planned output and actual performance should be investigated.

Nowhere is training more stringent and targets more closely monitored than in direct-line telephone selling. Telesales staff in many organisations undergo an intensive training course which lasts a week or longer, are monitored consistently throughout their first month (by their supervisor listening in to their calls at random) and are given sales targets from the outset. The calls are controlled and monitored by computer and if targets are not met over any period then the staff member is scheduled for a remedial training course.

Perhaps the remedial course should also include an input on dealing with stress!

Bottom-up options

It is a reckless organisation which ignores the needs and wishes of its staff. This is not only because staff will often become discontented and disaffected, but also because many employees often have some very insightful perceptions of the organisation and what it needs – and no manager can afford to ignore their suggestions.

Informal discussions

These can take place at any time and anywhere! Often the best ideas are those you hear in passing or on occasions when some of your colleagues are discussing a problem or situation. Two creative people together can spark off a whole host of ideas. One member of your team may have read about a new development in a newspaper or journal and want to tell you. Do bear in mind that it is always easier to talk a member of staff into learning something new if they have been the one to discover it in the first place! If you can link the idea to organisational objectives (or give feedback to inform your organisational objectives) then this is probably the best technique of all.

Team meetings

This is normally a more controlled environment than the one above – unless all your team meetings usually take place in the local pubs! On these occasions the focus of attention should be on the needs of the team, rather than the needs of individuals or the organisation. Each member will have his or her own perception of what is required – and it may take some firm leadership to tease out the key issues and guide the discussion towards fruitful channels.

(See Element 1.2 for identification of team needs.)

Feedback from staff

Feedback can be formal or informal. Formal feedback is normally requested through questionnaires or reports, informal feedback is given in meetings and discussions. Simply asking a question 'how easy is that new package?' and *listening* to the answer equals feedback. The key point is not to ignore unwelcome feedback! Staff will usually be very willing to give you feedback about objective issues (the new computer, photocopier, the last training course they went on). They are usually less keen to talk about themselves or their colleagues in a similar way. They will hesitate to discuss their own shortcomings if they feel this will be held against them – or do not know what you have in mind when you ask the question. They will be very reluctant to talk about their colleagues if they feel that any individual may be penalised as a result. If you are therefore trying to find out whether someone is suited to a job or needs additional development – and decide to ask one of his/her colleagues – do be aware that other staff will often be very wary of making even an implied criticism. Only if you can convince them that your aims are positive and that any information will be kept strictly confidential are you likely to succeed. However, you are not wise to make a habit of trying to keep abreast of developments by this method!

THEORY INTO PRACTICE

1 Write a short questionnaire which would ascertain your colleagues' views on the skills they have and the skills they would like to have. Make sure that it gives some guidance on key areas you think are relevant. Try to include questions which relate both to 'task' skills they need to have to perform their job, and 'people' skills which means they can work effectively with other people (see below and also Element 4.1, page 262). Remember to include space for their suggestions. Check your draft with your adviser.
2 Issue the questionnaire to your colleagues and analyse the results.
3 Write a short report which links your colleagues' perceptions of their development needs with your company's organisational needs as evidenced by your strategic plan. Can you suggest reasons for any differences?

Now what about you?

Your own development needs may have been identified through any of the formal methods discussed above – appraisal, needs analysis – or simply through informal discussions with your own line manager. However, turning the spotlight on yourself to identify areas where you may have development needs is really up to you. It can also be a difficult process. It is quite possible to find individuals who have areas they should develop but, given that everyone is prone to 'blind spots' about their own limitations (or to putting their heads in the sand), it is usually more difficult to evaluate analytically our own abilities and needs than other people's.

Self-evaluation is always a difficult exercise. It involves looking at yourself almost as a separate person. Broadly it relates to identifying and assessing:

- what you have done in the past
- what you want to do in the future
- the routes you can take to get there
- the qualifications, skills and abilities you will need
- the constraints which may operate to prevent you
- what you can do to overcome these
- who can help you
- over what timespan you intend to achieve your goal(s)
- how you will know whether you have achieved your goal(s).

To achieve your goals you need support. Whilst financial support is always helpful (see below) there are other types of support you will need. Critical to your success is likely to be the support of key individuals in your life – particularly your partner and your line manager. This does not mean that they simply tacitly agree, but actively support your plans.

Your partner can

- provide active encouragement when you are experiencing difficulties
- remove some of the pressure of day-to-day problems and chores
- even help to support you financially and emotionally.

Best of all is the partner who will discuss and comment on your ideas (positively!).

Your line manager can

- give you information and assistance on areas in the organisation where you have only sketchy knowledge
- help you to expand and develop your work role to try new ideas and put your learning into practice
- challenge you by giving you more complex work assignments to complement your development
- take a counselling and advisory role when you need it.

The wise manager realises that by managing your own learning you will be more committed and more motivated. You will also become more effective in your job, which has a spin-off effect for both your manager and your organisation.

In some organisations, self-managed learning has developed to the degree that employees design their own *personal development plans, development contracts, learning agreements* or *career plans*. If you want to start your own, then a useful place to begin is with the points given above. You should then concentrate on the key areas of your job, of which the following are examples.

- *Task-based skills* – the range of jobs you carry out at work and your degree of competence in each area. Have you always kept well away from statistics? Have IT developments left you behind? Are your communication skills debatable? Are you lost without a spellcheck and do you regularly struggle to put what you mean into words?
- *People skills* – your ability to deal with your boss, colleagues and subordinates. Can you 'read' them well or are their reactions a constant

surprise? Are you a good listener? Can you be assertive without being aggressive? Do you know how to say 'no' and not offend anyone?

- *Coping skills* – your ability to manage your own problems. Are you a good time manager or always on the last minute? Are you stressed out most of the time? How do you react in a crisis?
- *New developments* – your ability to manage change, for yourself and others. Do you welcome new challenges and situations – or shy away from them? Are you easily bored? Do you have an enquiring mind or are you at your happiest with well-known systems and procedures you have been following for years?
- *Administrative and management skills* – can you honestly say that your skills are excellent in the key areas of your job – such as communicating and negotiating, delegating and fostering teamwork, decision-making and problem-solving, planning and controlling activities? Would you confidently apply for promotion or feel that you are not yet ready or not good enough?

Financial help with external training may be available from a range of sources. Whilst you may start with expecting your employer to contribute, you should be aware that on many programmes either you or your employer can receive financial help from your local Training and Enterprise Council (depending upon who pays the bill and the course you want to study). A further source of funds is a Career Development Loan – details of which are available from your local Jobcentre or by telephoning 0800 585 505.

Young employees may be recruited on a Modern Apprenticeship programme where they can study up to NVQ level 3 free of charge.

Finally, if no other source of funding is available, you could persuade your employer to register to become an Investor in People. Investors in People is a national scheme to encourage staff training and development in organisations both large and small and financial support is available for all companies who commit themselves to achieving this objective. Again, further information is available from your local TEC.

THEORY INTO PRACTICE

1 Using each of the headings given above (and adding to or amending these if you wish), write a brief evaluation of your own accomplishments at the moment. Consider carefully the key areas which you would like to develop and link these to your future aspirations. Then identify how you would like to develop each of these areas. You may like to read the following sections before you complete your evaluation.

2 Given that you obviously wish to be considered an effective line manager yourself, select *one* individual who would relate to you for his/her development and identify the ways in which you could support his/her self-managed learning.

Management visionaries such as Charles Handy and others have proclaimed the probable end of the traditional career structure and organisational methods of training and development. They argue that new, flexible organisations with flat structures are keen to develop self-managed training and development with their staff – often termed as *empowered learning*. This takes the responsibility for training and development away from the organisation and puts it firmly in the hands of individual employees. This is important because, in a flat structure, there are fewer opportunities for promotion. In a delayered structure there are likely to be greater 'jumps' between each rung on the ladder. Empowered learning removes the need for traditional methods of training identification – such as appraisal, succession planning and management development – and replaces it with other self-managed techniques such as mentoring, networking and self-development activities – all of which contributes to a *learning culture* in the organisation. Theoretically, this gives staff the ability to take more decisions about their own learning and introduce innovations such as action planning workshops, lunchtime training debates and problem-solving project groups – rather than sending people on traditional training courses.

However, in case you are concerned about your own future, investigations by the Career Research Forum, set up to look at the impact of organisational change on people's career prospects, has found that despite many interesting innovations the traditional career still survives in most organisations in the UK, and that some of those which had introduced new practices had found them costly and time-consuming.

Agreeing and setting development objectives

Once development needs have been identified then the next stage is to formulate realistic and achievable objectives against which progress can be measured. These need updating regularly so that they act as a continual development tool for staff (or yourself) – as well as clearly showing what has already been achieved. They also must be both achievable and realistic in relation to the individual, his/her current abilities and work role and future potential.

When you are setting development objectives you have six key headings to consider:

- *who* is being developed
- *what* they know or have achieved already and now need to learn or achieve (the aim should be for steady progression or an extension of skills across a related area)
- *how* development can be achieved
- *when* it must be accomplished by
- *who* could facilitate this development
- *where* it could be carried out.

Much of this information can be gleaned from the personal development plan discussed above. Your own knowledge of the individual concerned and opportunities available will further inform the objectives.

The additional factors you may need to consider under each heading are shown in Figure 1.1.4. Do note that these are not exclusive considerations – there could easily be others you could include which are relevant to your own organisation, facilities available and recommended procedures for development.

Who	Job role and range of responsibilities Previous experience and qualifications Motivation Learning style Strengths/weaknesses Career aims and ambitions
What	Previous experience and qualifications Development needs identified Level of skill or ability required
How	Range of opportunities possible – formal and informal
When	Dates for partial/complete accomplishment and constraining factors (work and personal commitments, current ability level) Dates of availability of staff/course, etc.
Who	External/internal Professional tutor, trainer or professional exponent or practitioner, or mix of these
Where	In-house or external environment Training or working environment

Figure 1.1.4 Development objectives – additional relevant factors

Whereas a developmental goal is a general aim, each objective is usually a statement of intent which leads to that end-point or goal. By definition it is therefore usually more specific and may even be broken up into performance standards or competencies to be achieved.

Do bear in mind that the key considerations when writing any objectives equally apply to training objectives.

- Quantitative statements are preferable to qualitative judgements – which are harder to assess in terms of achievement.
- Dates for accomplishment should be identified.
- Overall performance objectives should be broken down into basic components (or competencies) which act as 'staging posts' for total achievement.

- If possible the objectives should include or encompass the personal objectives of the trainee as well as clearly identify the link with organisational or departmental objectives.

Bear in mind, too, the SMART acronym discussed on page 19. If your organisation operates a performance management system then it is likely that the development objectives will be linked into the performance objectives of the appraisal system.

Quite obviously, writing a series of objectives which link to a specific training course is likely to be considerably easier than planning a series of development activities for an individual. As an example, your objectives for this course may read:

- obtain information on NVQ4   July 199–
- commence programme   August 199–
- complete first unit   Sept 199–
- complete second unit   Oct 199–
  (etc.)
- achieve award   March 199–

It is then a simple matter to log your progress against these objectives to see whether you are keeping to target or falling behind. Note that the objectives may have to be revised if there are external circumstances which prevent you from achieving an objective (such as having to work overtime for a month in December or a family crisis in January). Just as you would expect your own problems to be taken into consideration when revising your own objectives, so you should be prepared to take into account other people's difficulties – unless they occur too frequently for comfort!

However, if you are trying to improve the communications ability of one of the junior staff who has been identified as needing staff development, then writing the objectives may be more difficult. You would need to revert to thinking about competencies to ask yourself:

- what key tasks does he/she undertake?
- what range of communications skills are required?
- to what level?
- in what circumstances?

You then need to consider the various ways in which these standards could be achieved. It may be that a simple course in written communications would suffice. However, if his/her problem is because he/she cannot use e-mail or talk fluently to visitors, then this would hardly be appropriate. Only by accurately defining the objectives, therefore, can you decide the best way(s) to achieve the required standards of performance.

It goes without saying that you will usually have more success and staff will normally be more motivated if they are involved in this process. At two opposite extremes, you could ask the staff member concerned to write his/

her own objectives (something you would expect to do, at your level) or write them out and then 'sell' the idea. In between these extremes is the sensible compromise of making some notes based on your own ideas and then discussing and agreeing these with the person concerned.

Types and resource requirements of development opportunities

There are two ways in which development activities can be measured:

- *by their efficiency* – how much they cost, what resources were used. In other words, did you do things right?
- *by their effectiveness* – what was covered, how much was learned, retained and applied. In other words, did you do the right thing?

You may like to note that Rosemary Stewart, in *Management Today and Tomorrow*, considered effectiveness the most important of the two – in that, if you don't do the right thing, how you do it is almost irrelevant!

One of your key aims when deciding upon a suitable method of training or development is to assess the options which are feasible in this instance and which would be the most cost-effective to deliver. This does not necessarily mean the most inexpensive! A cheap training course which bores everyone and which no-one can remember the following day is extremely expensive in terms of staff time wasted. Cost-effectiveness simply means that it has the greatest chance of success for each pound spent. However, the resources don't just relate to the direct cost of development. You must also take into consideration:

- *Time*. How much staff/trainer time will be involved? Are staff expected to learn in their own time? How long will it take for the objectives to be achieved?
- *Physical resources*. What facilities, equipment and training aids will be required? Are these available in-house? Can equipment be rented or hired for large-scale use?
- *Money*. What would be the comparative cost of informal/formal and in-house/external methods? What financial benefits could be quantified as a result of the training or development?
- *People*. How many people will be involved? Would it be more cost-effective to develop or train them simultaneously or is this impossible? What range of skills and abilities do they possess and what common areas are involved?
- *Expertise*. Is there the internal expertise to train or develop staff in house? Do the proposed trainers need any training? Do they have a range of methods at their fingertips plus good communication skills *in addition to* subject or skill expertise?

You can decide the most appropriate method only if you have information on all the different types of opportunities available, the type of activities which are appropriate to suggest in each particular case, and understand the benefits and drawbacks of the different ways of delivering training.

Identifying development activities

If your organisation has its own training section then your first point of contact should be with the Training Manager to discuss your needs. However, in these days of decentralised human resource management it is quite possible that you or your line manager are expected to suggest or recommend staff development opportunities and your proposals are then evaluated at senior level and then approved or not, as the case may be. If you work for a small organisation you may find that your manager considers that staff development is your remit and it is up to you to investigate and evaluate the various options. Don't forget, however, that in these days of empowered learning the potential trainee should also be involved in this process. Participating in identifying and agreeing the activity involves a degree of commitment from the employee and will help motivation (see page 63). For a very young or very junior employee this participation can form part of the learning and development process.

The opportunities available for staff development today are extremely diverse. The main alternatives are given in Figure 1.1.5, but you may wish to add to these with any other types of training you have experienced yourself or which you know exist in your own organisation.

Try to think small! A wide range of informal and impromptu opportunities will exist which you can use to develop different individuals. These can be as simple as showing a member of staff how to use a new piece of equipment, to giving feedback quickly on inappropriate behaviour (which may be through laziness or lack of knowledge of company procedures). An example would be the receptionist who is obviously indifferent to the needs of a customer. You can also use tasks you have to carry out yourself as an opportunity to develop your staff – as you will see in the next section.

THEORY INTO PRACTICE

1 If you are studying for your NVQ as part of a group, in a tutorial or workshop session, you may find it useful to debate the range of development activities given in Figure 1.1.5 to find other methods experienced or used by other people in your group.
2 Contact your local TEC and your local college for details of training opportunities available in your area.
3 Make a list of training opportunities available in-house in your company, or from external providers who have been hired by your organisation.

On-the-job

Asking for help to do a new job
Observation
Following a manual or handbook
Discussion groups
Work shadowing
Appraisal interviews
Undertaking work-based projects and assignments and making presentations
Job rotation

Off-the-job

Reading (books, newspapers, journals)
Videos
Audio cassettes (e.g. language tapes)
Attending a short course
Distance learning
Attending a college, university or business school
Outdoor activity training
Taking a correspondence course
Away-days
Action learning
Secondments

Applicable to either

Attending a workshop
Using a CD–ROM, computer-based training package (CBT) or multimedia package

Figure 1.1.5 (above) Development opportunities

If you are trying to persuade an individual to attend an external training course, you may wish to bear in mind the results of a MORI poll on learning that surveyed 5000 adults and children about their attitudes to training and learning. Although 75 per cent said they would work much harder at school if they had their time again, and 95 per cent believed 'you are never too old to learn new things', only 4 out of 10 thought they would take any type of course over the next 12 months.

Eighty-two per cent felt they needed to learn new things to do well at work, and 93 per cent wanted the opportunity to study whilst at work. However, 98 per cent thought staff should be supported by their employers, especially on work-related courses, whilst only 33 per cent actually received backing by their employers.

The Campaign for Learning, launched as the first step to create a 'learning society' in the UK by the year 2000, categorised people into four groups based on their motivation for training:

- *improvers* (who value learning and are receiving training)
- *strivers* (who value learning but aren't doing enough)

- *drifters* (who are dissatisfied with their achievements but aren't doing anything to change the situation)
- *strugglers* (who see no point in learning and aren't doing anything either).

Those who completed the survey said their reasons for not furthering their ambitions at present included personal responsibilities, lack of time, and apathy.

Management research into this area has found that the main factors which affect the motivation of employees include:

- the structure and culture of the organisation
- the way the work is organised
- the style of management in general and their own manager in particular
- their past experiences of learning.

In addition, Vroom and Lawler found that people's behaviour is affected by their perception of the world and how they see the link between effort, performance and rewards. They termed this *expectancy theory*. People are motivated when they believe that effort will lead to effective performance and that this will lead to attractive rewards (see also page 68).

Selecting appropriate development activities

The development activities which are selected for or by an individual must be objectively analysed to ensure that:

- they are cost-effective and utilise available resources where possible
- they will contribute towards meeting the development objectives which have already been agreed.

However, the development activity must also relate to the needs, abilities and perceptions of the learner. This is not just a case of ensuring that everyone who goes on an external course must select one which is at an appropriate level – although this is obviously important. It also means that the *type* of development activity must be appropriate to:

- the current experience and skills of the individual
- his/her preferred learning style
- the time he/she has available and take into consideration any constraints identified
- the type of development required – whether it is simple or complex, practical or academic, short-term or long-term, etc.

Various techniques are available by which you can identify the type of activities that would be most suitable or appropriate for either yourself or your colleagues.

Learning styles

The way in which people learn has been the subject of many studies. The first to develop a theory of experiential learning was Kolb, who developed a four-stage learning cycle. This incorporated the characteristics of both learning – normally a passive activity – and problem-solving, which usually requires active involvement. The cycle involves:

- understanding the theory – or theory building
- deciding how to put it into practice
- undertaking the activity
- reflecting upon the activity, i.e. evaluating one's own performance and strengths and weaknesses.

Few people are good at all of these stages. Some are better with practical tasks, others enjoy the theory. Some enjoy the planning, others are good at reflection. Based on this, Honey and Mumford identified four styles of learning which are displayed by learners.

- *Activists* are those who are the practical adventurers. They prefer to 'have a go' and learn by experience. They have little time for planning and preparing.
- *Reflectors* enjoy listening and working out what happened. They are good at observation and keen analysts. They will think carefully about what to do and how to do it.
- *Theorists* enjoy building up a body of knowledge about a topic upon which they can develop models or explore concepts. They enjoy academic studies and reading different approaches to a subject.
- *Pragmatists* like to have a practical application for the information they receive – otherwise they are apt to see it as pointless. They will want to put suggestions into practice as quickly as possible.

Honey and Mumford compiled their *Learning Styles Questionnaire* so that any learner can assess his or her own style of learning. This not only enables people to choose learning activities which will appeal to their own individual styles, but also helps them to improve any areas in which they are lacking.

THEORY INTO PRACTICE

1 Obtain a copy of *The Manual of Learning Styles* by Peter Honey and Alan Mumford (3rd edition) from your library and make some photocopies of the questionnaire at the end – as well as the scoring sheets. (The questionnaire is freely photocopiable so you could ask your adviser to obtain these for you if you have a problem.) Then work out your own learning style and study the type of learning activities which are likely to suit you best. You may find it helpful at this point to obtain the second booklet in the series – *Using Your Learning Styles*.

2 Ask the staff for whom you are responsible for identifying learning activities to undertake the questionnaire and work with them to analyse their scores and styles of learning.

3 If you have time, read through both books. They are only short and very interesting. Section 9 of *Using Your Learning Styles* even gives you advice on keeping a learning log – which is an ideal method of producing evidence towards this unit.

4 In your section, Andy is the Activist. Keen to get on with the job, he is renowned for ignoring computer manuals and learning by doing. Ralph is the reflector – he often surprises you by saying little at a meeting until the end, when he comes up with some extremely good ideas. Trudy is a theorist. She loves reading and is usually found poring over a book or journal. Phillipa is a pragmatist. She has little time for discussions but wants to get on with action planning at the very beginning.

Using the range of development opportunities in Figure 1.1.5, which would you recommend for each person and why?

Repertory grid

Individual views on development activities are often coloured by previous experiences. Whilst there is a limit to how much you may decide to take past views (and/or prejudices!) into account, it is at least useful to know the opinions of your staff. If your organisation has been in the habit of employing an external consultant to give health and safety training and he/she is loathed by everyone, it is as well to be aware of this fact. Otherwise you should not be surprised if the absence statistics show a sharp increase on the days such training events are scheduled to take place!

A technique for finding out how people think is called a *repertory grid*. This can be usefully employed to discover people's perceptions about a range of subjects and is used to inform market research, product design, interviewing and selection methods. It can also be used to evaluate people's views on different types of training or development activities. A study undertaken by Provident Mutual Life Assurance Association linked this to people's preferred learning styles.

The first stage in constructing a repertory grid is to define the *elements* you want to investigate. In this case your elements would be different types of training or development activities such as a selection from the list in Figure 1.1.6. In the study by the Provident Mutual, employees were asked to write down nine different learning events on pieces of card. These had to include events they had both enjoyed and had not enjoyed, had benefited from and not benefited from. The activities identified ranged from driving lessons and cookery courses to reading a book, taking a correspondence course and learning new computer programs. Each participant selected his or her own nine events or elements, though these could have been selected by an administrator, trainer or tutor. Equally, either fewer or more than nine activities could have been selected, though nine is quite high for a repertory grid construction.

At this stage the cards are shuffled and the learner must select three. Two of these have to be 'paired' by deciding what they have in common that the third did not – in relation to how the person *felt* or feels about this type of event. In repertory grid terms this pair of words is called a *construct*, and it is usual to repeat the activity a few times with different groups of cards to generate several constructs.

A grid is then constructed which links the constructs to the elements. The easiest way to draw this is shown in Figure 1.1.7. Ratings are then entered for all the elements on a scale from 1 to 7 across the grid: 1 indicates the description is most like the word given on the left, 7 shows it is most like the description given on the right.

Non-participative/limited interaction
Lecturing
Distance learning
Correspondence courses
Computer-based training

Participative
Instructing
In-tray exercises
Structured activities (e.g. work-based projects and assignments)
CCTV and feedback
Coaching
Mentoring

Group activities
Case studies
Role plays
Seminar groups
Problem-solving groups
Brainstorming
Fishbowl technique
Games and simulations
Self-development groups

Figure 1.1.6 Ways of delivering training

	ELEMENTS				
Constructs	Coaching	Work-based project	Short course	Distance learning	Computer-based learning
On the job/off the job	1	3	5	6	4
Workplace assessed/independently assessed	1	3	6	6	5
Company-centred/self-oriented	1	2	4	7	4
With others/alone	6	7	1	5	3
Supervised/unsupervised	1	5	1	6	3

Figure 1.1.7 Repertory grid example (scores 1–7)

The findings for each individual can then be linked with the Honey and Mumford learning style questionnaire results to see if there is a correlation between learning styles and types of learning experience. They can also form the basis for discussions about learning activities from which the learners feel they could benefit, and ways in which each person could develop his or her less preferred styles.

1 Use the descriptions on page 54 of the *Manual of Learning Styles* to make a list of general activities from which you think you learn the most and the least. Add to these any other types of learning opportunities you have experienced that are not on these lists.

2 Make out between six and nine cards, covering learning experiences and activities you have undertaken, and compile a repertory grid for yourself, using the example in Figure 1.1.7 as a model. If possible, repeat this exercise with the two individuals with whom you carried out the learning skills questionnaire.

3 In each case, and in consultation with these individuals where appropriate, use the information to select learning activities which would be most appropriate for each person.

4 Check to see if you can find any correlation between the learning activities each person has selected and his or her most preferred learning styles.

Ways of delivering training

Although there may be a wide range of training opportunities in your area or even in your organisation, the ways in which *you* are expected to be involved in your colleagues' training is likely to be restricted to those where you can actively help to improve their performance – often on a day-to-day basis. The aim of this course is not to turn you into a professional trainer! Indeed the buzzword today is *facilitator* – a person who makes it possible for others to achieve their potential by helping them identify opportunities for self-development and removing obstacles to their progress.

Action learning is the name given to development activities where a number of people operating at the same level in different organisations meet to share their experiences. *Networks* are formed out of groups of people operating in different business sectors – normally with no two direct competitors involved in the same network as this would prevent free exchange and dialogue. *Action learning sets*, as these networks are called, can decide the skills they need, and some use a facilitator in the early stages to help the group to form relationships and to focus upon the needs of the members.

Key development activities

Five development activities are specifically covered in the range for the NVQ scheme you are following. Given that you need to prove your involvement in these areas, more specific information is given below for each one.

Identifying training needs

This has already been covered on pages 12–25.

Specific work assignments

The aim of a work assignment or project is that both the individual and the organisation benefit from the learning activity. A particular assignment – usually of an investigative nature – is allocated to a person who is then expected to research the information, collate and evaluate it and then submit his/her conclusions and recommendations. At senior level such a task can be very useful as it enables the individual to find out more about the organisation and the way in which it operates, usually outside the confines of his/her normal work role. At the same time, the results can be extremely informative for management. It goes without saying, however, that if the whole assignment is then shelved without another word, the process may be actively demotivational for the person concerned. The same applies if the assignment is beyond the person's capabilities or if internal factors mean that valuable information is withheld or the conclusions are politically unacceptable. For this reason any potential assignment or project needs to be carefully considered and structured so that the person undertaking it is not placed in an untenable position.

At first sight, it may be felt that work assignments or projects will be unsuitable for more junior staff. However, with a little foresight and imagination this is not true. Indeed, if you are the person who is responsible for setting, monitoring and evaluating the assignment then you may be able to benefit from the investigation yourself! For instance, even a junior member of staff should be capable of carrying out an assignment to investigate wastage of paper and other consumables and to recommend ways in which this can be reduced. It is also nearly always true that the person who does a particular job is the one most capable of making recommendations to improve it! You are therefore a foolhardy administrator if you do not take advantage of this resource. You then have the benefit of improving productivity and quality in your own area as well as improving staff effectiveness and motivation – all at the same time. Do bear in mind one golden rule however – *never* claim the credit for a new working practice which results from the investigation if this rightfully belongs to your staff. Otherwise future suggestions may be few and far between!

Direct training activities

Direct training refers to those activities which are specifically designed to assist the development of particular skills and abilities – often for several people simultaneously.

If money is no object, then there are literally hundreds of direct training activities in which either you or your staff can participate. These can range from a team-building session at an outdoor pursuits centre, to a fire-training event at your workplace, to a part-time MBA course! The selection in Figure 1.1.8 is by no means exhaustive but shows some of the wide range of courses available.

Short courses

Assertiveness training
Customer service skills
Public speaking
Interpersonal skills (working with others)
Minute-taking
Health and safety training
Team-building
Employment law
Stress awareness/management
Telephone selling
Sign language
Understanding equal opportunities
Managing change
Problem-solving
Quality management
Reception management
Counselling skills
Running induction programmes
IT training and the Internet

Time management
Making oral presentations
Project management
Managing your boss
Confidence building
Managing the office team
First aid
Negotiating skills
Creative thinking
Personal safety training
Leadership skills
Coping with change
Business writing skills
Telephone skills
Appraising staff
Organising the office
Windows 95
Word for Windows 6.0

Professional development/vocational skills

IT qualifications (WP, DTP, CLAIT, IBT 2/3, NVQ 2/3 IT)
NVQs – Customer Service, Administration, Accounting
IPD Certificate of Personnel Practice
Association of Accounting Technicians courses
Institute of Purchasing and Supply courses
Certificate/Diploma in Marketing
Language courses
Supervisory management (NEBSM)

Academic development

GCSEs and A levels
HND/HNC in Business with Finance, Marketing or Personnel
Certificate in Management Studies (CMS)
BA degree in Business Administration or Business Studies – or Open University degree in relevant subjects (BA/BSc)
Diploma in Management Studies (DMS)
Master in Business Administration (MBA)

Figure 1.1.8 Training activities and courses

Direct training can take place on-the-job or off-the-job, at a private institution or in an FE or HE college or Business School. An activity or course can last anything from a few hours to a few years. It may be practical or theoretical – and at this point you may consider whether the *style* and *content* of different training activities would suit people's individual learning styles (including your own!).

The type of training activities you could suggest for yourself or for your staff will vary depending upon:

- the opportunities available within your organisation
- the amount of support (both financial and otherwise) you could obtain for external or specialist activities
- the needs of both yourself and your staff in relation to your existing work roles, planned changes and organisational objectives.

A few points should be borne in mind at this stage.

- Don't be overly impressed because of the cost of an activity. Some organisations deliberately inflate the cost of their courses and activities to foster an atmosphere of exclusivity. Whilst you might have an enjoyable day or two you may not learn very much that is usable in practice.
- Consider the length and commitment required carefully. Sometimes it is better to become involved in a short intensive activity where you can see definite progress.
- Think about whether the activity is more suited to being carried out on-the-job or off-the-job. Generally, the latter is more reflective and allows for an exchange of opinions from beyond the workplace. The skills of an expert can be sought. On-the-job training is more appropriate for practical activities – particularly where specialist equipment or techniques are involved which may be unique to your organisation.
- Be aware of the fact that some people are more reticent or wary of participating in activities than others. Some of your staff may need considerable encouragement to undertake an activity which would have obvious benefits for themselves and the organisation. Others have to be almost forcibly restrained from participating in everything in sight!
- British organisations and managers have long been criticised for their reluctance to train and develop staff – in case these same staff promptly move on to another company and take their new-found expertise with them. Try to restrain yourself from thinking in this way. If *everyone* took that view, no-one would do anything! Conversely, if everyone positively encouraged staff to participate in training activities then all organisations would benefit.
- Finally, if your staff have an obvious need and external activities are too expensive, investigate the possibility of either holding a session in-house or one person (you?) attending and then cascading the information to everyone else.

Advising

Taking the role of adviser is never easy – even experts may be concerned that they are giving too much advice, or the wrong type of advice or should be helping a person to find his/her own way rather than prompting too often.

You will have been assigned an adviser as part of your NVQ scheme. This person is responsible for giving you information in relation to specific aspects of the scheme and the jargon used, to help you to link your own work role and duties to the performance criteria and range statements, to encourage and motivate you if you become disheartened, and to provide practical assistance in overcoming difficulties and problems – whether these are concerned with your work role or your personal circumstances. Undertaken properly, this is no mean feat. You should therefore think carefully, yourself, before offering to become someone's adviser. You will need thorough knowledge of the path he or she has chosen to take and a working knowledge of his/her job responsibilities and the way in which the chosen method of development can help the person and the team or organisation as a whole.

Occasionally, the most important skill an adviser can learn is how to say 'no' without causing offence! The employee who wants to take an NVQ award which bears little relation to his/her actual work role, the trainee whose ambitions far exceed any practical ability or potential he/she has shown to date, and the person who wants to take up every opportunity, no matter how obscure, each has to be advised appropriately. It is always easy to give praise, to encourage, to commend. It is far less easy to counsel, to criticise constructively, to point out that a particular course of action is inappropriate or even far too expensive! As an adviser you have a duty to the employee to be compassionate yet honest, to your organisation to link staff development with the needs of your department and your team, and to yourself – to know that, so far as is possible, you have made the best decision you could with the facts you currently have to hand.

A different term for adviser, often used in relation to new staff, is that of *mentor*. A mentor is someone who gives advice, often over practical, political and even esoterical aspects of the organisation. This can assist a new employee to become familiar with the culture of the establishment more quickly, to appreciate who does what, who has the power, who has influence and who, therefore, to keep happy! A mentor can also be an invaluable asset when major decisions have to be made, difficulties overcome and conflicts handled constructively. In this case, both an adviser and mentor are more likely to be responsible for ongoing development and personal growth – rather than for the imparting of specific information in a particular context.

Coaching

Coaching is an extension of a very fundamental method of training – desk training – more often known as 'sitting with Nellie'. This method usually involves a new or inexperienced worker watching an experienced person who, ideally, not only demonstrates the correct way to do a job but imparts useful and appropriate information at the same time. After an initial period of basic instruction, the learner is encouraged to try for him/herself whilst the experienced worker watches and encourages. The aim is to familiarise a new recruit into the correct way to do a job within the working environment as quickly as possible. It works only if the older worker is skilled and competent (as mistakes will otherwise be replicated), if he/she is committed and loyal (otherwise the new recruit is given information on how to cut corners and bend the rules), and if there is a fairly open agenda. Otherwise the experienced worker will deliberately withhold important information to sustain his/her own power and position.

In the same way, coaching someone also takes place in a working environment and uses naturally occurring working practices as the way in which development can be achieved. Coaching usually takes place on a 'one-to-one' basis and is undertaken by an expert practitioner. It is used:

- to improve a skill beyond a basic level – where more advanced techniques need to be learned
- to include new skills or duties beyond those originally covered
- to identify and remedy faults and problems which are still being experienced after the usual period of instruction
- to revise, recapitulate or consolidate earlier skills which may have been allowed to lapse
- to groom someone for promotion or career development
- to train someone where the facilities are available at the workplace and this would be a more cost-effective method than sending him/her on a specific course.

Coaching may be undertaken by an individual's line manager or supervisor if this would be appropriate. However, if there is an extremely hierarchical structure or formal culture, this may be counter-productive if the learner feels that his or her performance will be noted and remembered forever more and used in evidence at a later date! Coaching also takes a great deal of skill, tact and patience – as anyone who has watched a driving instructor at work will realise! Getting the best out of someone who may be nervous, confused or under stress is never easy. The job of the coach is to set the scene and organise an environment where learning can take place, give counselling, advice and encouragement, and constantly review progress against planned objectives. Professionally trained coaches often use the Socratic method, where structured questions are asked to stimulate the learner's thinking – as well as his/her awareness and commitment to the process.

In 1996 the Institute of Personnel and Development launched a pilot scheme to study on-the-job training activities to find out the extent to which trainers receive guidance on how to train others in the workplace. The study is particularly concerned with the wide range of informal training which occurs when existing employees are asked to show other workers – or new recruits – what to do. The study commenced by examining how training is carried out and evaluated in the manufacturing sector and the type and degree of guidance given to both trainers and trainees. The research was then to be continued into other sectors.

1 You should note that the five ways of delivering training above are by no means exclusive. Dozens of other ways exist – from role playing to discussion groups, from watching a video to using a manual with a new computer package. Look back to Figures 1.1.5 and 1.1.6 to check on other methods of training – as well as the learning opportunities given in Honey and Mumford's *Manual of Learning Styles*.

2 Assume you have a new employee who has the task of entering important data into a pre-formatted spreadsheet. No matter how much you counsel her, she rushes through the job in order to impress you and regularly makes critical mistakes. Her checking skills appear non-existent. The spreadsheet is long and complex and it is taking you hours to check all her entries. What methods would you use to improve her performance, and why?

Monitoring progress and performance against planned development objectives

No training or development activity is complete simply because it has taken place. In itself, the holding of the actual event is just one stage in a process which encompasses a series of steps from planning and consultation to assessment and evaluation. Unless you have some way of monitoring performance against the original objectives then you have no way of knowing whether the activity is appropriate, effective or producing the required results.

Various mechanisms can be used to monitor progress and performance – some formal and some informal. You may:

● obtain feedback from the person concerned or from others affected by his/her performance
● observe performance yourself – in terms of both output and quality
● hold formal discussions (or appraisals) with your staff or chat to them informally about their progress
● note the planned schedule and plot achievements against this.

There are also other variables to consider. You may be responsible for assessing the progress of all your team at regular intervals or just that of nominated individuals. You may be considering overall performance, specific skill levels or the range of skills achieved. The speed at which achievement is required may vary – depending upon the urgency of the situation and whether new or additional skills must be learned quickly or may be acquired over a period of time. You may be looking to evaluate the progress and performance of people or the success of particular developmental activities.

The important point to note is that you should obtain information regularly and promptly. Monitoring should be an *ongoing process* – not something which takes place only at formal, pre-specified intervals. The last thing you want to find is that a particular activity was practically useless, months after everyone was forced to participate! Neither do you want to be the last one to hear that the newest recruit has been skipping her day-release class for the last four months and is now too far behind to catch up. It is also unlikely that you want to be the one to break the news to your own line manager that a new system can't be up and running by the deadline because the staff haven't yet learned how to operate it successfully. Prompt remedial action can only be taken if you have a constant stream of accurate information and evaluate this properly.

> Human resources software now exists which can take much of the hard work out of the monitoring process. Training and development plans can be agreed and then held on computer and regularly updated. This enables the manager to have constant access to the plans and gives him/her the advantage of being able to check which staff have undertaken which type of activity at a glance.

Assessing and evaluating performance and progress

To help you to assess and evaluate performance and progress you need to set up a suitable system for obtaining feedback and information both on particular activities and on individual performance. Obviously, the methods you devise or implement will depend upon the systems operating in your organisation and the aims of your investigation.

Assessing individual performance

To do this accurately you need to collect information on:

- the range of activities you are assessing (these are usually the objectives set as part of the last performance or appraisal review)
- standards of performance which can be generally determined to be satisfactory, less than satisfactory and better than satisfactory
- the level of performance at the outset and the degree of improvement identified.

Information can be obtained from a variety of sources including the individual concerned, his/her peers and colleagues and by observation yourself.

Performance review sessions should be held *regularly* and designed to improve learner motivation and commitment. Informal feedback should be constant and should capitalise on naturally occurring learning opportunities in the workplace (see below).

Assessing development activities

The most common method of assessing development activities is by obtaining feedback from participants. This may be undertaken formally or informally. However, most organisations do this by asking participants to complete a questionnaire to evaluate the activity. The basic problem with this approach is that such an evaluation examines the activity itself, rather than the learning that was achieved. It may therefore be the case that everyone enjoyed the activity (which involved a pleasant lunch, a day away from work and a friendly chat over drinks afterwards) but no-one learned very much. However, staff will be reluctant to admit this in case external activities are immediately curtailed!

Even in the case of internal activities problems can occur. If everyone likes the leader of the event, or no-one wishes to appear disloyal to a colleague, then internal training activities will also receive predominantly favourable reports!

Finally, employees can easily become inured to post-developmental questionnaires and simply see these as a signal that the activity is at an end. They therefore give little thought to their completion. If this is compounded by all feedback questionnaires being consigned to a filing cabinet without further consideration, then the process is worse than useless.

A more productive method is to focus attention not on the activity itself but upon its results. Questions should be asked (either in a verbal feedback session or in written form) which require the participant to link the contents of the activity with his/her work role and job and the degree to which the activity has made or can make a *difference* to the participant. This difference may be identified not only in improved performance but also in increased motivation and commitment, for instance by the suggestion of new ideas or better methods of working which can be applied in the organisation.

It is true to say that in many cases organisations themselves are at fault for allowing people the opportunity to develop themselves and then neglecting to take advantage of any benefits which might accrue from this process. This may be because of personal prejudice or entrenched attitudes of managers, bureaucratic procedures or hierarchical structures which prevent bottom-up suggestions from taking hold or even being culturally acceptable.

The most difficult part of evaluation is trying to link development activities to hard-edged cost–benefit targets. How, for instance, do you quantify whether a training course costing £400 has been twice as beneficial as one which cost £200? How do you quantify the potential savings which could be made by your section if the training budget were increased by 50 per cent? The difficulty for administrators 'managing' staff development is that benefits are likely to be 'soft-edged' whereas the costs of development are 'hard-edged'. It is very difficult, if not impossible, to quantify the benefits of increased motivation and commitment, better customer service or even increased productivity unless you can clearly demonstrate that customer complaints have decreased, order processing has increased or routine wastage has been reduced.

Providing feedback on progress and performance

You should note that feedback may not be restricted to staff who have undertaken an activity, but also to your own line manager in relation to the success of the activity.

Feedback to your staff

Giving feedback honestly and constructively – whether as part of an appraisal interview or in an informal discussion – is a skill which is essential if you are to manage your staff effectively. Destroying their motivation and commitment to the department and the organisation will benefit no-one – least of all yourself – and using feedback sessions as an opportunity to give your staff increased confidence and renewed belief in their own abilities is the least that you owe to loyal, hard-working members of your team. Investigating carefully and thoroughly the reason for any lapses in performance is the duty you owe to all your staff. Deciding when such lapses are through deliberate neglect and/or sheer idleness – and taking immediate action to remedy this – is the obligation you owe both to your own staff and to your organisation.

Before you give any feedback – either positive or negative – there are several actions you should take.

- Obtain sufficient information to make an informed view on performance and/or achievement. Assemble your facts and evidence and decide which are the critical areas on which you should concentrate.
- Think about the way you will give feedback *bearing in mind the individual concerned*. Whereas tact is an essential requirement in all feedback interviews, with some people it is even more critical than others. Try to consider the individual attributes, traits and characteristics of the person concerned and how he/she will react to the situation. For instance, some may flatter to deceive – by telling you what they think you want to hear rather than the truth. Others will be brutally self-critical or even self-destructive. Others may appear supremely self-confident but, in reality, be very insecure. Be prepared to adapt your approach to take such considerations into account.
- Be prepared to be honest. People normally value what they perceive to be an honest evaluation of their performance – they *know* where they are doing well, and where they are not. You will lose credibility if you appear ignorant of their true performance.
- Note – and try to avoid – common pitfalls such as:
  - being too generalist. The more specific you can be when giving feedback by having actual examples of performance to back-up your arguments, the better.
  - using words carelessly. It is staggeringly easy to prejudice an entire session by the use of one critical term, such as untidy, silly, impulsive, etc.
  - being critical and negative and focusing on failures rather than successes. Your subordinate is then immediately placed in the position of having to defend his/her behaviour.
  - trying to evaluate too much in one session. Feedback should be frequent following coaching and mentoring sessions so that specific incidents can be discussed in full.

- talking too much. Feedback should be a two-way discussion, not a monologue or a dispute!
- being influenced by the power of an employee to cause problems or trouble (e.g. being tempted to pacify the informal leader).
- Always end on a positive note, *or* (if that is completely impossible) with an agreed plan of action and a date set for the next session.

Giving positive feedback

It is obviously easier to give feedback where you are giving praise and positive 'strokes' to a member of staff. When performance has been particularly good, however, it can be difficult to determine new areas for achievement or revised targets. There is a danger in continually expecting an already willing workhorse to achieve even more. A better approach is to focus on other areas where skills and abilities could be extended or developed. Avoid, too, the temptation of giving much shorter feedback sessions to those who have achieved positive results so that the length of the session is an immediate determinant of the success of the participant! This can also mean that some staff may feel 'cheated' that they did not have time to discuss their needs as fully as some of their colleagues.

A final point – do not be mean or stingy with your praise. If you are the type of manager who no-one can ever really please, eventually everyone will stop trying!

Giving negative feedback

No manager – apart from the natural sadist – enjoys these sessions. It is quite natural to feel drained and exhausted afterwards – but this is usually an indication that you have done a good job. Feeling triumphant should certainly not be one of the sensations you experience!

There are five basic points to bear in mind.

- It is very rare that a person has *no* positive attributes! Try to focus on using these as a model for development across the areas where there is poor performance.
- There is a huge difference between constructive criticism, comment and advice, and negative nit-picking. It is easy to develop good practice if you think about how *you* react to criticism and the most 'palatable' way in which it can be given!
- It is important that you give the person concerned the opportunity to explain his/her actions (or lack of them) in full – and that you *listen* and take heed of the points being made. If the reasons given justify the results then you can jointly decide how problems can best be overcome. If they do not, then at the very least you need a note of what was agreed for the *next* session.
- Do be prepared to review the targets which were set originally in case these were unrealistic or inappropriate for the person concerned. Adhering to an unworkable policy or unrealistic standard will never result in success.

- In the case of substantial under-performance or repeated problems, it is your responsibility to ensure that your staff know the consequences of their actions (or lack of them) before facing formal disciplinary procedures.

See also Chapter 4, page 316.

Feedback to your own manager

You may have to report to your own manager about the performance and progress of your staff or about the success of particular development activities. The type of report you are asked to give will usually depend upon the reason your manager has asked for the information. This may be as informal feedback to keep 'in touch' with the activities of the department, to inform a budgetary process or to prepare a more formal report.

It can be difficult to walk the tightrope between being loyal to one's own staff and keeping your own manager informed of critical areas or potential problems for which you may need support at a later date. For instance, if you have just had a fearful row with one of your staff who is now theatening formal grievance procedures against both you and your own boss, you would be wise to give your manager prior warning! A normal rule of thumb for most managers is to keep the faith with their own staff unless a problem is likely to result about which their manager needs to be forewarned. If you have the advantage of having a manager yourself who is the epitome of wisdom and good advice, then you may find it useful to ask for guidance on difficult personnel problems. If, on the other hand, your own boss is task-focused and has little patience or interest in the human relations side of the job, then you would be wise to keep your own counsel unless it is imperative you pass on the information.

Normally, objective evaluation and feedback of the processes you have undertaken and their results is easier to give. You can assess the facts, identify strengths and weaknesses of any current systems in force and give your recommendations for improvement. You should note that the difficulties of calculating quantifiable benefits to staff development have already been mentioned on page 46.

Legal and regulatory requirements relating to the provision of training and development

We are an equal opportunities employer. All eligible applicants will be considered on the basis of merit irrespective of gender, ethnic origin, marital status, religious belief, sexual orientation, age or disability. Applications from women and people from ethnic minorities are particularly welcome as they are currently under-represented in this area of work. We will accommodate, wherever possible, work patterns involving other than full-time attendance. (Extract from HSE job advertisement)

Today almost everyone is familiar with the wording of equal opportunities policies – which normally identify more areas against which the organisation allegedly does not discriminate than are covered by current legislation. In the above extract, only three areas are currently covered by British legislation – gender, ethnic origin and disability. However, you may be less familiar with the fact that discrimination does not relate just to recruitment. It also relates to a variety of other areas – including opportunities for training and development. Therefore discrimination in the three areas of gender, ethnic origin and disability is unlawful. However, an organisation with a positive equal opportunities policy, such as the Health and Safety Executive, would also extend this remit to cover other areas such as age and marital status.

The difficulty for line managers and others involved in promoting training and staff development is not usually in avoiding direct discrimination – which is relatively easy to identify – but in refraining from any form of indirect discrimination, particularly where this may stem from misguided preconceptions or relate to especially difficult areas. As an example, in late 1996 the Disability Discrimination Act took its place on the statute books. For the first time, it became unlawful to discriminate directly or indirectly against a disabled person. This has left many questions unanswered – and many may only be solved after several test cases. For instance, would you be guilty of discrimination if you arranged for a specially extended training programme to be given to an employee who has learning difficulties? How would you fare if you genuinely considered it would be more equitable to set lower standards of performance for a disabled worker?

Basically, the law protects minority groups from actions which would disadvantage them, whether these stem from prejudice, misconceptions or sheer ignorance.

- *Direct discrimination* occurs when a person is treated less favourably then another person – for instance, if a safety course were offered only to male workers it would obviously be discriminatory as female employees have the same need for safety training as male employees.
- *Indirect discrimination* occurs when a practice or condition results in unfair outcomes for different groups of people. An example would be an organisation which devised a written test for all production workers, many of whom were from ethnic minorities and some of whom were known to have learning difficulties, as a criterion for promotion to line supervisor. This could discriminate against those whose English was not their mother tongue, against those whose ethnic backgrounds meant they were less familiar with formal tests, and against those who had learning difficulties or dyslexia. This would be discriminatory – and indefensible if written English was not a necessary skill for the job. The likely outcome would be the promotion of fewer ethnic minority and disabled workers, despite the fact they may be equally capable of undertaking the work of line supervisor.

The major Acts which relate to discrimination are the Sex Discrimination Act 1975, as amended by the Sex Discrimination Act 1980, the Race Relations Act 1976, as amended by the Race Relations (Remedies) Act 1994, and the Disability Discrimination Act 1995.

Many organisations undertake monitoring activities to check the results of their actions and to ensure that unfair or disproportionate outcomes do not result. As an example, monitoring the take-up of training activities could determine whether there was equal interest by all sectors of the workforce. If this was not the case then investigations would be needed to find out why. It may be, for instance, that the wording or promotion of the activity has been undertaken in such a way that it only attracts certain types of employees.

You should note that none of the Acts mentioned above forbids positive action to encourage take-up from minority groups. In addition, this means that specific training courses can be held for particular parts of the workforce, such as personal safety for women or English as a second language. However, positive discrimination during a selection process (whether for recruitment, training opportunities or promotion) is not allowed.

> In April 1996 the Adventure Activities Licensing Regulations came into force. These cover all outdoor activity centres that offer training and development programmes. In addition, those providing adventure activities for under-18s must be licensed. The aim of the Regulations is to improve safety awareness and risk assessment, and make compulsory the production of written emergency procedures.

The content of staff development programmes

It is not only in the area of discrimination that line managers should be aware of legal influences on training. The content of training and staff development programmes is also influenced by legislative changes and cases brought in tribunals. Most newspapers covered the case of *John Walker v Northumberland Country Council* where the plaintiff won damages of £175 000 after proving that his 'impossible workload' had resulted in two nervous breakdowns. This was followed by a case where a Scottish social worker was awarded £66 000 damages from South Lanarkshire Council after being forced to take early retirement through stress-related illnesses caused by the behaviour of her manager. The cost of stress to organisations may now, therefore, be two-fold and encompass both absenteeism costs and the potential risk of damages through the courts.

This has resulted in training programmes to ensure managers are aware of their responsibilities in this area, in addition to stress management training, counselling and the development of employee assistance programmes.

In addition the requirement for health and safety training has been long-standing since the implementation of the Health and Safety at Work Act 1974 and the various regulations which have followed (see Chapter 2).

A new European data protection directive, introduced in 1995 but enforceable from 24 October 1998, will mean that employees will have the legal right to access all their files – both on computer and on paper. This will mean that all personnel and training records will be accessible by employees. Currently, under the 1984 Data Protection Act, employees only have the right to inspect any computerised records on them held by their employers. You may also be aware that since the 1990 Access to Health Records Act, it has been possible for all employees to access any health records held by their employer – both manual and computerised.

All amendments to existing legislation mean that training is required for those staff directly affected in working with the organisation in its efforts to comply with the various Acts and regulations. Many organisations develop policies and procedures to give ongoing responsibility for staff training in these areas to designated managers or officers – such as the Health and Safety Officer or the Human Resources Manager. In smaller companies, however, the responsibility may rest with the individual line manager. The aim of such procedures is to provide guidance to both managers and employees on the policies which operate in this area and the way in which such issues are addressed.

Ageism is predicted to be the next area where there will be legal protection against discriminatory practice. In many recent studies, organisations have become vulnerable through delayering and selecting older employees for redundancy and through policies of downsizing by offering early retirement. This has left an 'experience gap' which is resulting in organisations mistakenly following strategic and tactical paths which were rejected as counter-productive in earlier years – simply because no-one is around to give the warnings any more! Older workers, with their in-depth knowledge and experience of market conditions, have enormous potential if they are retrained to cope with modern conditions and methods of working.

A private member's bill to outlaw age discrimination in recruitment advertising failed to find sufficient support in 1996. A further bill is scheduled to be put before Parliament during 1997–8. Media activity and pressure is relatively absent on the subject. It remains to be seen whether market forces can become a spur to good practice if further attempts at legislation are equally abortive.

THEORY INTO PRACTICE

1 Obtain a copy of your organisation's procedures on training and development and draft a brief commentary to identify how this encompasses the legal requirements relating to this area. Check this with your adviser.
2 Identify the areas in which your organisation's policies and procedures for training and development go beyond the letter of the law to include non-statutory requirements aimed at promoting fairness and equality of treatment for all employees.

Element 1.2

Contribute to the coordination and achievement of team activities

How often have you seen one of the following phrases in a job advertisement?

'... must have the ability to work to tight deadlines and remain a team player'

'... self-motivated individuals required who can work as part of a team'

'... only committed team players need apply.'

The accent today in most organisations is on teamwork – the factor which links together groups as diverse as the Red Arrows, a serious crime squad, the Hallé Orchestra and a board of directors. This section examines the difference between working groups and teams, the importance of teams and the methods used to improve team performance. Above all, it considers your role as a team member and coordinator. The more you understand the interactions and psychology of teamwork, the better equipped you are to improve team performance and enhance job satisfaction of the members. In addition to examining various aspects of teamwork this section guides you in strategies for getting the best out of any team with which you are involved, over a wide variety of activities.

Your own role and responsibilities

Unless you work in a very small organisation or a 'one-man band', you are likely to work as a member of a group or as part of a team of people. In fact, if you are undertaking a level 4 award, then you may be the leader or facilitator of that team – with responsibility for coordination, productivity and quality of output. If this is your role, then you have several responsibilities – both as a group member and as a group or team leader. Before you can appreciate your role and responsibilities, however, it is important to understand how groups and teams function and the role of the leader in facilitating their activities and improving their motivation and productivity.

What distinguishes a team from a group? Why have teams suddenly become so fashionable? And how can this change affect your own role and responsibilities?

If you have worked for an organisation for some years then you are likely to belong to several working groups. In some cases, you may have been able to select the members of some groups or teams yourself and have the knowledge and skill to select those who possess complementary skills and talents to give the best possible mix of ability. However, this is a rare occurrence. It is more likely that you have inherited a team of people of varying skills, abilities and temperaments, all with unique personal and professional experiences and different perceptions of the organisation, each other – and you! Getting the best out of the individual members, keeping harmony, providing inspiration and focus is all part of the job of a leader or facilitator, but is also a responsibility of all the other members – given that an effective team consists of members who are mutually supportive.

Working groups

What factors differentiate a group of people from random sets of people who happen to be in the same place at the same time? Basically, in a group, all the people involved have a common characteristic and a collective identity. The characteristic could be attending the same course, having a common hobby or interest or working in the same office. Normally, to form a recognised group, the members need to meet and communicate regularly and have shared or common goals. Therefore, you may interact with a group of people at a social gathering but you wouldn't describe this as belonging to a group in the same way as you might describe your affiliation with people in the same work group as yourself or on the same committee. Normally each person knows to which groups he or she belongs and acknowledges association with it. This then results in the formation of a *psychological group* in which each person has a particular role and there are common group norms or standards of behaviour.

The first group to which anyone belongs is usually their family. It is no coincidence that all families have names – to differentiate themselves from other family groupings. In the same way, other groups also give themselves a name – to differentiate themselves from other groups and to give the members a sense of identity. In business, working groups are identified by departmental names, committee names, section and unit titles. If no-one is interested in naming a new group, it is likely that no-one is interested in becoming a member!

Working groups have some common characteristics in that:

- members are usually dependent on each other in some way
- they have a reason for being together
- each member knows he/she is part of the group
- different members of the group will undertake different roles or take on different responsibilities
- they will work together, communicate and interact regularly
- there is usually an assigned group leader.

Groups will differ, however, in the following ways.

- *Size and strength.* Small groups (especially those which have been in existence for some time) are usually closer with the same ideals. Strong groups may impose sanctions against members who do not conform with the norms of the group as a whole (see page 97).
- *Structure.* Some are tightly structured and everyone has specific tasks to undertake, in others roles and relationships vary and the structure is far more flexible. Meetings may be more infrequent or sporadic.

- *Cohesiveness*. Groups which are small and have been together a long time are more likely to 'stick together' if there is a challenge from outside the group (see page 96).
- *Style*. In some groups all members are equal in rank and status, in others one leader predominates. Likewise, in some the atmosphere is informal and 'laid-back', in others it is aggressive and confrontational.
- *Power*. Some groups have considerable influence on other people because of the type of decisions they make or their ability to enforce these. Other groups are less powerful. However, it is doubtful whether, in a working situation, anyone would want to be the member of a group which was recognised by everyone to have absolutely no power at all.

There are basically two types of working groups – those which are formal and those which operate informally. *Formal groups* are designated by the organisation itself and are often shown on an organisation chart. They are task-oriented with goals linked to organisational objectives. They may be permanent – such as a unit, section, department or committee – or temporary, such as a task group, project group, working party or *ad hoc* committee. They may be charged with carrying out investigations and making recommendations, undertaking specific activities or making decisions and problem-solving. They can range from those comprising base level employees to the top command group of senior executives.

Membership of a group may be selected by senior or middle management with members of the group itself having little, if any, say in the composition of the group. The groups are formed for a specific purpose and are seen as beneficial for the organisation as they allow specialisation to take place as well as encouraging creativity and breadth of vision. Studies have shown that judgements and decisions made by groups are improved through the pooling of experience and the existence of a broader knowledge base. In addition, people working in groups are more creative and prepared to take greater risks through the interaction and mutual support processes which exist.

Informal groups are formed through friendships or the mutual interests of the members. Membership is voluntary and may be temporary – to support a particular common cause, for example. This is often the case with action groups which may form to express disagreement with a management decision. Informal groups are usually formed because they help people to do their jobs more effectively (e.g. through the rapid exchange of information) and because they meet personal needs for affiliation which may not be otherwise satisfied within the organisation.

The ability of a group to make and enforce effective decisions can vary considerably depending upon its ethos, the views, skills and influence of the leader and the cohesiveness of the group. This can have advantages and disadvantages for organisations. If the group is mutually supportive and has a goal which links to organisational goals, then there are likely to be few problems. Members will support and assist each other and all will work towards the common goal. Difficulties arise when a group has objectives that conflict with those of the organisation – particularly if it also has the power to disrupt others or if it is in a key position – or if it is ineffective or if there is a poor leader. This can cause problems for other groups who are dependent upon it for information or inputs (see page 78) and be actively demotivational for committed or hard-working members of the group.

Obviously, at supervisory level, your aim should be to provide a positive role model to members of the group, to reinforce positive or desirable behaviour, and to encourage the group to adopt norms or standards which positively reinforce organisational objectives.

It is unlikely that any group of disparate individuals, even with a common goal or purpose, will get on well together all the time. Minor disagreements or difficulties may arise which should be aired, not suppressed, for a healthy group ethos to exist. Whilst open aggressive conflict is rarely helpful, and allowing group members to voice their opinions is a difficult tightrope to walk – especially for the inexperienced – such strategems are essential if resentment (and disgruntled subgroups) are to be avoided. Dealing with disagreements and conflict is covered on page 87.

Working teams

A team is different from a group and the two terms are not synonymous. Whilst, like a group, a team may have a common purpose, leader and identity, a team utilises complementary skills to achieve a common purpose for which the members are collectively accountable. There is therefore more mutual or joint participation in a team than in a group – with 'bystanders' or 'passengers' less easily tolerated. In this case the members of a team are *dependent upon each other* for success. The team goal then becomes the predominant factor and is more important than the needs of individuals. This is easy to see if you think of a sporting team. The efforts and skills of all the players are required for success to be achieved. If some members are playing badly then the performance of the team as a whole will be affected – as will the eventual outcome. To achieve success team members must be prepared to subjugate individual ambitions to achieve the team objective – and use the strengths of each person to the best effect.

The role of the leader or facilitator is to manage the collective assets to achieve specific objectives. However, the leader of a team – particularly a multifunctional, problem-solving team or a self-managed team (see page 58) – has a different remit from a traditional 'manager' or leader. Whereas the latter usually exists within a hierarchical or semi-hierarchical structure, with legitimate authority and power to give orders and instructions, a team leader technically operates in a 'flatter' environment with far greater emphasis on collectivism and joint participation. This requires different skills as the roles undertaken range from technical adviser, coach, resource acquirer, facilitator, counsellor and mediator to chief planner, organiser, evaluator, negotiator and devil's advocate. The team leader needs to be confident of his/her ability to influence team members through a process of rational argument and respect – and be prepared to concede on issues where he/she is outvoted. This requires courage, confidence and considerable 'people skills' but is likely to be the shape of things to come in the future, because of the significant advantages to be gained from the formation and operation of effective teams. You may like to note that both power and influence are dealt with in more detail later in this chapter, and leadership is covered in Chapter 4.

The growth of teams

Groups have been around for many years but currently it is more fashionable to refer to 'team working' and 'operating as a team player'. Teamworking has increased in popularity because of the benefits which can be gained, both by organisations and by individual members. Individual members gain through greater participation and personal involvement in decision-making and problem-solving processes, through increased interaction with other people and through the mutually supportive and 'open' atmosphere which exists in an effective team. The organisation benefits because of the increased productivity and enhanced performance which can be achieved as well as lower costs through flatter structures. Teamworking suits the modern trends of delayering and non-autocratic management styles which are typical of today's organisational cultures and the increased flexibility which is now virtually essential for organisations to survive in rapidly changing environments.

Basically, all the traditional benefits of working groups are increased and accentuated in a team. *Synergy* is a major benefit where 'the whole is greater than the sum of its parts'. This is particularly important for creative teams whose members can bounce ideas off one another and interact to enhance both the quality and quantity of their ideas. Multifunctional problem-solving teams have proved to be extremely effective in analysing difficulties and proposing improvements in a variety of work areas. Well-coordinated teams can be highly efficient in terms of productivity and highly effective in terms of operational competence and work standards. Teams have become important in business because productivity gains *and* high quality have become crucial to organisational success. An effective team works collectively to achieve the productivity and quality objectives set by the organisation and members will encourage and support each other to do so. They will collaborate with one another and take joint responsibility for the success of the team and for its achievements. They will be effective because they will bring together a 'mix' of different skills and abilities so that *between them* the members of the team can cope with a variety of tasks and problems often under tight deadlines. The focus in this case is on higher morale, better communications and increased motivation.

A more cynical view is that teams have become fashionable simply because of their cost-effectiveness – it is cheaper to hire team leaders and facilitators than middle managers. Unfortunately, it is the case that teams are often introduced unthinkingly into organisations without the structure, culture or support to sustain or develop them. Certainly, in America, where teamwork was all the rage in the 1980s, lately there has been greater consideration of the key factors which must be in place for teams to operate effectively and an acknowledgement that 'teams' *per se* are not the panacea for all organisational problems or evils.

Self-managed teams (SMTs) are those which combine the trend for empowerment with the popularity of teamwork. SMTs are small groups who are empowered to manage themselves and the tasks they do. They are responsible for planning, scheduling, maintaining quality, solving operational problems and meeting performance goals. In some cases SMTs decide their own work schedules, rewards and bonuses. They are charged with making decisions on how to allocate work and task activities, for training and developing each other, and for monitoring and evaluating team performance. In some cases they may even hire and fire their own members, which has repercussions in relation to their legal responsibilities (see page 104).

The potential is for increased motivation of the members as each person has a greater involvement in the operation and strategic direction of the team (see job enrichment, pages 73 and 221). However, again it must be noted that SMTs cannot simply be introduced as a 'cure-all'. Participation and empowerment must be perceived as genuine for the team members to be committed to team development, and there must be full, ongoing support and commitment from all top executives. Moreover, the values and culture of the organisation must be such that open communications, a positive atmosphere and a flatter structure all coexist to reinforce the team's role and purpose.

Empowerment is discussed in more detail in Chapter 3, page 221.

Work roles and responsibilities of other members

The definitive academic work on team roles and members was undertaken between 1969 and 1976 by Dr Meredith Belbin, a researcher from Cambridge. Belbin argued that an individual can never be perfect but a team can. He meant that, given the right mix of people, a team can collectively possess a variety of qualities which result in more collective 'strengths' than can ever be found in one person.

Belbin and his colleagues researched the interactions of teams participating in a business game at the Administrative Staff College at Henley in Oxfordshire over a period of seven years. From the mass of data produced, Belbin originally identified eight team roles. Each role was ascribed typical features, positive qualities and allowable weaknesses. Belbin then developed psychometric tests so that members of a team could identify their own 'team type' before participating in the business game. In addition, these tests enabled Belbin to measure psychological traits and relate these to particular roles. He then measured the performance of the team against the mix of team roles which constituted that particular team. Finally, Belbin could predict the outcome of the business game by the composition of different teams – although he commented that it was far easier to predict which teams would fail than which would be certain to succeed!

Four principal psychological traits were identified by the tests – intelligence; dominance; extroversion/introversion; stability/anxiety. At this point Belbin's research sounds a note of warning for managers who are prone to select all the cleverest and most talented people they can find for their team, as the most disaster-prone teams were those which were composed exclusively of very intelligent people (termed the 'Apollo effect').

Many people who first read about Belbin's research were concerned that the ideal size for teams must therefore be eight, given that each team role must be filled. In Belbin's view this is not necessary as a person can take on more than one role – therefore a team with fewer than eight members can work effectively. Moreover, people have a dominant and a subsidiary role and can be persuaded to focus on the subsidiary role if their dominant role is filled by someone else. Indeed, some executives displayed the ability to undertake up to five or six different roles. The key point is to avoid a replication of roles within a team with omissions in other areas as this will create an overall imbalance of skills and abilities.

Belbin's questionnaire and his original description of team roles are contained in his book *Management Teams: Why They Succeed and Fail*. Since then he has increased the number of team roles to nine and revised some of the names of the team roles following feedback and comment from practitioners who have used Belbin's analysis. His updated roles are given in Figure 1.2.1. Belbin has also continued his studies to analyse why those who may be considered suitable or eligible for particular positions through qualifications, experience or interview performance then fail to live up to expectations. He has also examined the different relationships which are formed between different team members according to their roles, and how each person can develop his or her own natural style both as a team member and potential team leader for personal benefit and the benefit of the team as a whole.

THEORY INTO PRACTICE

Visit your library and obtain Belbin's book *Management Teams: Why They Succeed and Fail* and use Belbin's questionnaire to find your own dominant style. The book gives more information on the research itself, the composition of different teams and their relative success. If you can obtain this book from a local library you are likely to find it invaluable in helping you to analyse and develop members of your own team.

If you have time you would also benefit from reading one of Belbin's later books, *Team Roles at Work* (Butterworth Heinemann, 1993), in which he develops and applies his study of team roles further.

Figure 1.2.1 Belbin's nine team roles

Role	Description and strengths	Acceptable weaknesses	Unacceptable weaknesses
Plant	Creative, imaginative and unorthodox; good at solving difficult problems	Ignores practical aspects and details; often preoccupied, so poor communicator	'Owns' own idea regardless of effect – even when cooperation with others would be more beneficial
Resource investigator	Extrovert, enthusiastic and communicative; explores opportunities and develops contacts	Overoptimistic; loses interest when novelty wears off	Letting people down by neglecting/ forgetting to follow up
Coordinator	Mature, confident and a good chairperson; clarifies goals and promotes decision-making; good delegator	May be seen as manipulative; pushing work onto someone else may be thinly disguised as delegation	Taking credit for team achievements
Shaper	Challenging, dynamic, thrives on pressure; has both drive and courage to overcome difficulties	Can provoke others and hurt feelings; easily irritated and frustrated	May be unable to recover situation by apologising or by good humour
Monitor evaluator	Sober, strategic and discerning; objectively evaluates all options, usually accurately	Lacks drive and ability to inspire others; critical and sceptical of proposals	May be illogically cynical
Teamworker	Cooperative, mild, perceptive and diplomatic; listens, builds, averts friction, calms the waters	Indecisive in difficult situations; can be easily influenced	May try to avoid pressurised situations
Implementer	Disciplined, reliable, efficient, conservative; converts ideas into practical actions.	Rather inflexible; slow to respond to opportunities, likes the orthodox and known	Obstructing change
Completer	Painstaking, conscientious and anxious; searches out errors and omissions; delivers on time	Apt to worry unduly; reluctant to delegate; may nit-pick; perfectionist	May display obsessive behaviour
Specialist	Single-minded, self-starting, dedicated; provides knowledge and skills in rare supply	Contributes only on narrow front; likes to acquire knowledge for its own sake	Ignores areas outside own sphere of expertise

Adapted from *Team Roles at Work* by Meredith Belbin, Butterworth Heinemann, 1993

If you are able to do so, ask the members of your own team to complete the self-perception inventory and analyse the composition of your own team. Write a brief report for your assessor indicating any major areas of strength or weakness in the team. State any strategies you could use to reassign roles if required. Finally, try to analyse how the composition of your team affects its performance and identify any insights into its operational effectiveness (or lack of it!) that the Belbin profile has given you.

If you are unable to undertake the exercise above, you may like to consider the following scenario. Assume you have been asked to form a task group by your line manager and can select members of the team from the group of staff with whom you work. Bearing in mind Belbin's team roles in Figure 1.2.1, who would you choose and why?

Coordinating work activities

Earlier in this chapter the Red Arrows, the Hallé Orchestra and a serious crime squad were given as classic examples of teams. This is because, in these cases, the coordination of team members is absolutely critical to the overall success – and, in one case, survival – of the team.

If skill relates to the attributes of the team, then *coordination* is the cement which integrates the efforts of the different individuals. Remember that within every team there is interdependence. Everyone depends upon someone else – there is therefore *reciprocation* between the members. Those who do not fulfil their responsibilities or fail to follow their remit let down not only themselves but also the other members of the team. If this occurs frequently it can lead to miscommunication, resentment and animosity and destroy team spirit. (You may like to note how many screen detectives are famous for following their own hunches, rather than coordinating their activities with their colleagues – despite desperate pleas and remonstrations from their superiors! This may work in fiction, in reality it would be disastrous.)

The role of the facilitator or team leader is to coordinate the efforts of the team so that everyone is pulling in the same direction and all the activities link together within the agreed time scale. This keeps the focus on the goals of the team and reduces the likelihood of individuals pursuing individual goals and objectives. For that reason, coordination does not happen on its own – it must be carefully planned.

Within every organisation there are both formal and informal mechanisms to ensure coordination takes place:

- Meetings are held at which objectives are discussed and operational tactics are decided. They may range from board meetings and departmental meetings to working parties, committees and subcommittees.

- Liaison roles may be held by specific individuals – frequently to coordinate the efforts of geographically separated individuals or teams.
- The formal organisation structure denotes functional areas, and job descriptions not only state job roles but also include reference to areas of responsibility and accountability. There are usually formal mechanisms for reporting from one level to another in the hierarchy.
- Some staff may be allocated official coordination roles and job titles or be asked to head task forces or coordination groups.
- Policies and procedures will be developed so that the activities and processes undertaken by different groups are harmonised and standardised.
- Formal and informal networks will be developed and encouraged between people.
- Communications will be facilitated through new technology – electronic mail and MIS (Management Information Systems) being obvious examples.

Coordination has been likened to throwing several balls in the air with a plan that they all land in the right place at the right time! It is doubtful if the team leader of the Red Arrows has such a haphazard approach to the subject. Seeing such a team fly in perfect formation makes it obvious that coordination incorporates planning, scheduling, practice, feedback, endless refinement and an excellent system of communications between members. Communications are covered on page 101.

The degree of coordination required by a team depends to an extent on the type of work being carried out and the degree of interdependency of team members. Generally, work which is complicated or unpredictable will require a high degree of coordination. This will also be the case in a fast-moving or rapidly changing environment or one where quality or production targets are very high. A supervisor or team leader faced with a higher need for coordination than can be supplied with the information available may need to examine the possibility of restructuring the work to manage the tasks with the degree of coordination possible. The other alternative is to redefine the degree of coordination required and put in place mechanisms and communication systems to enable this to occur.

The growth of IT networks and the increased need for group and team communications has resulted in two major developments. Novell, Lotus, Microsoft and Netscape are all developing versions of group working software – otherwise known as groupware – which enables staff to work in virtual teams no matter where they are located. The system facilitates communications between team members and the coordination of activities by enabling information to be shared from creation through development to completion from basic e-mail documents to shared databases.

A different system, devised for helping teams to complete business projects more quickly, is the Dynamic Systems Development Method (DSDM). A DSDM

Consortium has been established of organisations which want to participate in Rapid Application Development (RAD). This is a technique for developing business software applications more quickly through the ongoing interaction of customers and developers. Technical skills and communications expertise are major requirements of participants with teams being put in place to provide a mix of these abilities. British Airways and British Telecom are just two of over seventy companies who have committed themselves to achieving DSDM accreditation.

Motivating and influencing people

MOTIVATION – theory and practice

Motivation theory is used to predict behaviour by analysing the forces which make individuals act in the way they do – and persist with their attempts, even in the face of adversity. Motivation can be described as the willingness to act – but what causes this willingness, and why does it exist for one individual in one situation but not another? Writers, theorists and researchers have gone to considerable trouble over the years to find out what causes motivation, with the result that there are probably almost as many theories of motivation as there are days in the month! However, some are more well known than others and at this level your grasp of the theories should go a little beyond the basics!

It is possible to subdivide most theories of motivation and categorise them into various types:

- *traditional theories* – as propounded by early management writers
- *content theories* – which relate to the content of a job and how these relate to people's needs
- *process theories* – which examine the process of motivation and why people choose to act as they do
- *behavioural or reinforcement theories* – as propounded by behavioural psychologists and those concerned with human responses to situations
- *management/organisational theories* – which look at how the structure of organisations and the attitudes of managers can influence motivation. There is a strong overlap in this area between theories of motivation and studies of leadership.

Traditional theories

The forefathers of modern management had the problem, at the turn of the century, of motivating an uneducated, indisciplined and often unwilling workforce to produce goods in a relatively new environment – the factory. Much has been written about the social conditions of factory workers during the nineteenth century, far less about the problems of management!

For instance, did you know that children worked mainly because their families had no other option but to take them to work with them? And that previously, the family had usually worked at home, in a 'cottage' industry – but at times and at a pace of their own choosing. Little wonder that regulations, rules and even such routine aspects of working life as punctuality were alien to them.

It is unsurprising that early management theorists, such as Frederick Winslow Taylor, considered that, given the high levels of illiteracy, workers did not understand their jobs, nor the implications of work. Their indiscipline and seemingly disorganised methods of working led to allegations of laziness – at a time when the Protestant work ethic ruled supreme. Managers saw it as part of their role to educate workers and introduce a moral code to encourage hard work and commitment. Adages such as 'the devil makes work for idle hands', 'hard work never killed anyone' and 'early to bed, early to rise' were representative of this philosophy. To achieve their objectives, in addition to their aphorisms, managers needed to identify a way of motivating workers to undertake highly repetitive tasks quickly and accurately. They therefore appealed to man's basic (or base) need for monetary reward. Piecework rates were common, designed to reward high levels of productivity. Given the low standard of living of most workers at the time, it is unsurprising that good results were achieved.

It was not until the 1930s that these ideas were seriously challenged by Elton Mayo and his associates working at the Western Electric Company in America. In what are commonly referred to as the 'Hawthorne Studies' – because the experiment took place at the Hawthorne plant near Chicago – Elton Mayo and his associates discovered that regardless of whether they introduced better conditions or worse conditions to a test group of workers, productivity continued to rise when compared with a control group for whom no changes were introduced. The findings, termed *the Hawthorne effect*, were that the good results were due to the increased attention given to the members of the test group. The eventual conclusion was that the social needs of workers to interact with other members of a group are extremely important, as is recognition by management. However, of the two, peer group pressure was more important than that inflicted by management. This type of finding has obvious implications and relevance for team leaders and facilitators.

THEORY INTO PRACTICE

The research and findings at the Hawthorne plant are particularly significant in relation to teamwork, given that they focused upon the reactions and responses of groups of workers and the social needs of man. You would be well advised to read about the Hawthorne experiment in more detail by obtaining any management book which deals with this.

Content theories

Content theories relate to job content and individual needs. They examine which human needs are important and how these can be met in a working environment to improve/increase motivation. They were first introduced in the 1950s when researchers started to consider people more as individuals with complex needs and wants.

Maslow's hierarchy of needs

Abraham Maslow was one of the first writers to consider people's individual needs. He designated these as a pyramid or series of steps upwards (see Figure 1.2.2). At the base of the hierarchy are the basic animal needs required for self-preservation. Once this need is satisfied humankind moves upwards – the next need is for safety, then for other people, i.e. social needs, and so on. You can easily equate this to the needs of a Robinson Crusoe on a desert island. Water and food would be of paramount importance, followed by a safe place to sleep. Only then would our Crusoe start to look for Man (or Woman) Friday!

If we follow Maslow's thinking, Crusoe would next need to earn Friday's respect – because the next set of needs relate to self-esteem and status. The final set of needs is when Crusoe decides that he wants to improve his mind or skills and participate in activities which will result in his own personal development and fulfilment.

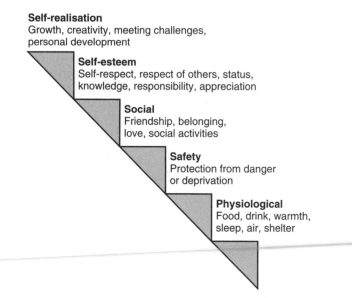

Self-realisation
Growth, creativity, meeting challenges, personal development

Self-esteem
Self-respect, respect of others, status, knowledge, responsibility, appreciation

Social
Friendship, belonging, love, social activities

Safety
Protection from danger or deprivation

Physiological
Food, drink, warmth, sleep, air, shelter

Figure 1.2.2 Maslow's hierarchy of needs

Generally Maslow's theory holds fairly true. It is unlikely, for instance, that we would be preoccupied with completing an urgent report if we suddenly discovered the building had caught fire. This links with Maslow's conclusion that safety needs are more critical than those for self-realisation or self-esteem. However, several critics have pointed out that people do not move systematically up and down the hierarchy. A person who has been bereaved, for instance, may join a language or wine-tasting course for friendship and companionship. However, it is unlikely that the person concerned would choose to attend a course in which they had no real interest. This indicates that self-esteem and realisation needs can challenge social needs on occasion. Apart from this, Maslow's theory is generally accepted as being a useful indication of the type of needs people have when they are at work and which managers can help them to meet.

Another writer, Clayton Alderfer, offered an alternative model of needs. He identified three categories of needs – *existence needs, relatedness needs* and *growth needs*. The first category relates to those items required to enable us to exist – i.e. Maslow's basic needs plus the hygiene factors identified by Herzberg (see below). The second category relates to social relations and interactions, and the final category to personal development, power and status.

In contrast to Maslow, Alderfer considered that if higher needs are frustrated the importance of lower needs will return, even though they were previously satisfied. He felt that needs varied over time, relating to current events and the situation in which people found themselves. Additionally, research has shown that many employees categorise their needs in a similar way to Alderfer, rather than Maslow.

Herzberg – motivation and hygiene

Frederick Herzberg was a management writer who undertook considerable research on job satisfaction. He concluded that some factors at work actively cause satisfaction. Herzberg termed these *satisfiers* or *motivators*. He also found that all these factors were closely related to the content of the job and the most important of these were achievement, recognition, the work itself, responsibility, advancement, and personal growth.

Some factors at work, whilst causing dissatisfaction if they were not present, did not lead to actual job satisfaction. Herzberg called these *dissatisfiers* or *hygiene factors*. The most important were company policy and administration, supervision and relationship with one's supervisor, working conditions, salary, relationship with other workers and subordinates, status, job security, and one's personal life.

The major finding is that whilst motivators can create job satisfaction, hygiene factors can only prevent dissatisfaction. Their importance is in their power to cause dissatisfaction if they are not of an adequate standard. Therefore, the organisation which concentrates on improving the decor, reviewing its procedures and offering an annual bonus is less likely to employ motivated staff than the one which concentrates on job content and recognising and rewarding achievement. All it will do is prevent staff becoming more dissatisfied and possibly retain them a little longer. Herzberg's theory led to several techniques to improve job content, such as job rotation (where people move around jobs), job enlargement (where more tasks are added – often synonymous in today's world with multiskilling) and job enrichment (where the work is made more challenging and stimulating). In Herzberg's view only job enrichment was of any use (see page 73).

An interesting facet of motivation is that individuals generally consider that different factors motivate other people. You can test this yourself by selecting from the following list, in order of importance, the top five factors which motivate you, your boss and the office junior. If you find you have three completely different lists you will be following the usual trend, *but* you should stop and consider *why* it is that you believe that the factors which affect you do not also apply to other people.

security, salary, self-fulfilment, power, status, advancement, job interest, recognition, companionship, achievement, advancement, responsibility

One argument to explain why you may have been correct to have three different lists is given in the next theory.

McClelland and Atkinson – acquired needs

A different theory of needs was put forward by David McClelland and Bernard Atkinson following original research undertaken by Henry Murray. This theory takes into account dominant personality traits and how these affect motivation. Murray identified more than 20 different needs which could be activated through particular situations. These were reduced to three basic needs by McClelland and Atkinson:

- *Achievement* (nAch). Those with a high need for achievement set difficult goals for themselves, take responsibility for solving problems and are prepared to take calculated risks to achieve their goals. They are motivated and respond well to a challenge or working in a competitive situation and enjoy work which is complex and stimulating. They welcome autonomy and variety and highly value feedback on and reward for their performance, such as bonus payments. They are usually high performers.
- *Affiliation* (nAff). Those with a high need for affiliation consider social contacts more important than personal achievement. They may rely on the workplace to satisfy their need for social satisfaction and interaction. They prefer conformity, stability and group work and value security and predictability. They look to their manager to show consideration of their personal needs rather than objective analysis of organisational needs.
- *Power* (nPow). Some have a strong need for power and are highly motivated by operating in a position where they can command, control and influence other people. This may not simply relate to controlling the physical environment or job content, but can extend to trying to control

behaviour. At its extreme, this may result in game playing to manipulate the behaviour of subordinates (see also page 70 and Chapter 4).

(see also page 70 and Chapter 4)

THEORY INTO PRACTICE

1 Which of the above acquired needs do you consider is the most active for you? What evidence can you offer to support this?

2 To what degree do you think the above needs are mutually exclusive, or do you consider that individuals may have high needs in more than one area?

3 Some needs are held to be predominate because of fears held by an individual, e.g. the fear of failure (and loss of face) or the fear of success (and the problems this may bring). To what degree do you think this theory may therefore explain why
   - adult learners are usually more concerned about their performance on a course of study than school leavers
   - a successful business person refuses the opportunity to expand the business
   - a good team player may refuse the opportunity to become team leader?

4 Which need(s) would you prefer to be predominant in your team, and why? As team leader, what actions could you take to encourage this?

Process theories

Whilst the basic views of motivation focus on the attitude of the manager and the content of the job, more contemporary theories have regarded motivation from the point of view of the perceptions people hold and how these influence actions. In other words, the *process of motivation* has been studied, rather than individual needs. You can apply this to yourself, for instance, if you think about *why* you are more willing to do some jobs than others or why you procrastinate or put off some tasks – perhaps almost until you are forced to do them! This is likely to be linked to your own views and perceptions of the situations and people involved.

For this reason, many contemporary writers have argued that motivation is too complex to be explained by any basic needs theory because needs change, behaviours are different and even cultural differences have been shown to affect which needs are paramount.

Expectancy theory

Expectancy theory was first propounded by Kurt Lewin. Later researchers who have refined the theory include Victor Vroom, Lyman Porter and Edward Lawler.

Expectancy theory states that motivation depends on the interaction of two components, *expectancy* and *valence*, i.e. $M = E \times V$.

- *Expectancy* relates to the expectations or perceptions people have that undertaking a certain action will have a particular outcome.

- *Valence* relates to the value placed on the outcome by the individual. Valence may be high or low.

The other variables which influence motivation are *effort* and *performance*. This results in the following sequence of thoughts and actions:

I am set a task. I will only do it if
- I feel the task is within my capabilities to perform
- I will be rewarded or gain satisfaction in some way for doing the task
- I value the reward or satisfaction I will receive
- the size of reward or degree of satisfaction will be commensurate, in my view, with the amount of effort I was prepared to expend.

You should note that rewards and satisfaction can be *intrinsic* or *extrinsic*. Intrinsic rewards relate to inner feelings such as achievement, accomplishment, exhilaration, self-satisfaction. Extrinsic rewards are those concerned with pay and bonuses, praise and promotions. However, motivation will only ensue if the individual puts a value on the reward being offered. If I place a high value on pleasing my boss then I will do almost anything to earn that praise. If, on the other hand, I do not value his opinion nor his praise then this reward will not be enough to encourage me to make the required effort to do the task.

Finally, experience either reinforces our views or makes us change our perceptions. If I always try to do a task to the best of my ability and receive constant criticism then I change my expectations in relation to my ability to perform the task satisfactorily. The next time I am asked to do a task I will expend less effort because my perception of the outcome will be different. Equally, if I am disappointed because I have been promised a reward which never materialises then I will again rethink my approach. This is a major reason why people who work hard for promotion are disenchanted with the organisation and their job if they are constantly passed over.

THEORY INTO PRACTICE

Expectancy theory contains several key lessons for team leaders and organisations, given that it demonstrates that people will adjust their behaviour in the light of past experience. Points you may like to bear in mind, therefore, include:

- considering which types of rewards are valued by different members of a team
- the importance of giving team members tasks which they can undertake successfully – this may mean additional training or resourcing to guarantee a positive outcome
- linking the level of rewards to the degree of difficulty of a task, the amount of effort expended and the level of performance
- not promising rewards which cannot be delivered

- specifying your requirements clearly, giving positive and encouraging feedback, and providing appropriate rewards
- structuring jobs and fostering personal development to increase intrinsic motivation – particularly if extrinsic rewards are outside your power or in short supply in your organisation.

Equity theory (J. Stacy Adams)

This theory is similar to expectancy theory except that it stresses the importance of fairness or justice as a motivating factor. Therefore, if you offer rewards to your team members but are perceived to offer better or higher rewards to your favourites then you can expect a dissatisfied and disenchanted team. It is a naive leader who considers that staff will not compare their rewards and draw their own conclusions as to whether these have been allocated fairly or not.

Behavioural or reinforcement theories

At first sight, one theory of reinforcement appears to contradict equity theory by stating that managers should *not* reward all individuals equally. W. Clay Hammer considered that averaging rewards is likely to result in average performance – there is no incentive to strive if the rewards are the same for everyone.

All behavioural theories examine how people respond to different situations. They use previous behaviour and reactions to predict future reactions and examine ways in which behaviour can be changed or modified if it is considered inappropriate. Early behavioural scientists such as Pavlov and Skinner worked with animals to predict responses to different stimuli. They examined the way in which behaviours are repeated if the consequence is favourable and rejected if the consequence is unfavourable. If you had bought a puppy and were giving obedience training then you would be very involved with *positive reinforcement* of good behaviour. You would also be involved in *avoidance* (negative reinforcement) of undesirable behaviour (e.g. using a stern voice), *punishment* (introducing negative consequences) to stop bad behaviour, and *extinction* (the ignoring of certain behaviour to suppress it).

Many supervisors and group leaders almost subconsciously adopt these techniques to control behaviour. They will praise good work, criticise bad work, introduce sanctions or punishments (e.g. demotion) if performance continues to be poor, and may deliberately choose to ignore inappropriate behaviour (someone making ribald comments) so that there is no reinforcement whatsoever and the behaviour will then cease.

This theory links with motivation if we assume that workers are motivated by positive reinforcement – such as the payment of a bonus, a high regard by management, promotion opportunities. The theory is criticised for its association with manipulation. According to this view, unethical or unscrupulous managers will identify a person's needs and deliberately withhold/give rewards to control their behaviour.

On a more positive note, this does not deny that most of us react favourably to praise and recognition provided we perceive it to be genuine. Hammer's rules for improving behaviour through the use of behaviour modification are basically common-sense rules for all leaders and supervisors.

1 Reward according to performance. This reinforces high performance.
2 Remember that failure to respond also modifies behaviour. Therefore forgetting to praise or reward will also have its own effect – the subordinate will be less motivated to perform next time.
3 Make sure people know how to get reinforcement. This means setting clear performance standards.
4 Tell people what they are doing wrong. It is unfair to withhold rewards if the subordinate or team member is confused about what behaviour is appropriate. This also links to manipulation and causes stress and anxiety.
5 Never punish in front of others. Reprimands should be in private or there is the danger of the group uniting to defend the group member.
6 Be fair. In Hammer's view this means that behaviour should be rewarded appropriately, otherwise reinforcement loses its effect. To motivate *teams* to perform, many organisations are now offering team incentives and team performance bonuses. This aspect is dealt with on page 82.

Management and organisational theories

Although not predominantly motivation theories, there have been various studies which link the type, size, structure and culture of the organisation and the style of management operating within the organisation to staff motivation and morale.

- Organisations may have hierarchical or flat structures, may be predominantly bureaucratic or 'free thinking'. The degree of bureaucracy will influence the division of labour, the number of rules and regulations and policies over a wide range of areas – from recruitment and promotion to salary scales and grades. The ability of individual managers to take risks and reward according to innovation or style is likely to be limited in a bureaucratic organisation.
- The culture of the organisation relates to many areas of operation – from communication methods and systems to dress code. Handy identified four disparate cultures as shown in Figure 1.2.3. A person with a disposition more suited to a culture which encourages free thinking and autonomy may struggle to remain motivated in a role culture.
- Management styles range from authoritative to participative. In some cases and situations an authoritarian approach may be preferred (e.g. in a war zone) although in the majority of circumstances it is disliked, particularly by individuals who feel they have the ability to make a positive contribution to the enterprise.

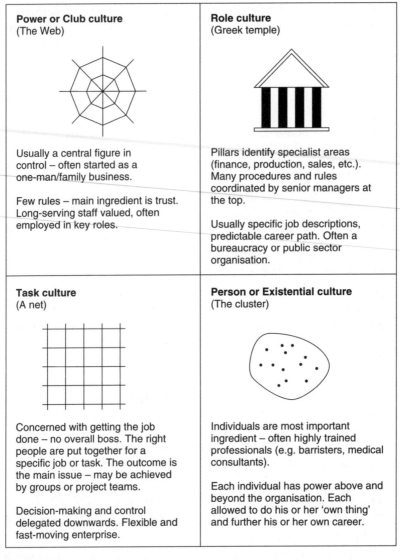

Power or Club culture (The Web)	Role culture (Greek temple)
Usually a central figure in control – often started as a one-man/family business. Few rules – main ingredient is trust. Long-serving staff valued, often employed in key roles.	Pillars identify specialist areas (finance, production, sales, etc.). Many procedures and rules coordinated by senior managers at the top. Usually specific job descriptions, predictable career path. Often a bureaucracy or public sector organisation.
Task culture (A net)	Person or Existential culture (The cluster)
Concerned with getting the job done – no overall boss. The right people are put together for a specific job or task. The outcome is the main issue – may be achieved by groups or project teams. Decision-making and control delegated downwards. Flexible and fast-moving enterprise.	Individuals are most important ingredient – often highly trained professionals (e.g. barristers, medical consultants). Each individual has power above and beyond the organisation. Each allowed to do his or her 'own thing' and further his or her own career.

Figure 1.2.3 Organisational cultures
(Adapted from *Understanding Organisations* and *Gods of Management* by Charles Handy)

THEORY INTO PRACTICE

It is simple to sit back and announce loftily that you would always allow your team members total freedom to make a decision! In theory, so would most of us. However, there are occasions when:

● time is short
● the issue is complex and not understood by all members
● key members of the team are not available.

On such occasions not only would you be hard-pressed to adopt a team approach but it may even be inappropriate and unsuitable – particularly if it resulted in a late but wrong decision!

However, empirical studies prove, time and again, that as individuals we consider we deserve to be consulted about important issues by our line managers. We *like* important problems and decisions to be delegated to us, particularly when they critically affect our own working area. However, when we are asked how we would act if we were passing on an idea (or problem) to our own subordinates we frequently opt for a different style. This is discussed more fully on page 103.

Job satisfaction

Overall, motivation is enhanced through an organisational structure and culture which is keen to foster job satisfaction. Given that individuals are more interested when they are undertaking challenging work which actively involves them in the planning and organising of their own job, this has led to various techniques designed to make jobs more interesting, such as:

- *job rotation* – initially a basic system of rotating jobs or duties undertaken by people at the same level to give variety
- *job enlargement* – additional duties are included into a job, often with progressively more difficult duties or varied activities being added (*multiskilling* is a modern version of this type of technique).

According to many management writers, including Herzberg, there are dangers in considering either technique particularly effective in increasing job satisfaction. In his view, no-one becomes more motivated simply by undertaking a greater number or greater variety of meaningless tasks. In his view the only worthwhile technique is job enrichment:

- *job enrichment* – in this instance people are given more responsibility for their work and encouraged to contribute in activities such as planning, organising, problem-solving and decision-making. They are given more autonomy and more responsibility for achieving negotiated outcomes.

Teams which are effectively organised and allowed to function creatively, by their very nature contribute to the job enrichment process in that members can gain security from the support of their peers whilst they are learning to make decisions and take responsibility for their own performance. Self-managed teams (see page 58) are the epitome of this process. Note that job design is covered in more detail in Chapter 3, page 219.

In summary

Behaviour and motivation are affected by the relationship between the team members and the team as a whole and the degree to which this satisfies personal needs at that particular time. Within a group or team situation an individual will value membership if his/her social needs, task needs and status needs are met by the group as a whole and if its values accord with his/her own.

Knowledge of the expectations and standards of the leader is crucial to success. Feedback should be frequent, honest yet tactful. Negative feedback should take place in private. The rewards should accord to the effort required and be seen to be fair by all members of the group.

The greater the motivation of individual members the less the need for rules and regulations to control behaviour. The leader who ranks group ethos, team dynamics and team spirit as highly as task performance is the one most likely to lead a successful group.

Teams, particularly self-managed teams, offer considerable opportunities for job enrichment through increased autonomy and responsibility which enhances job satisfaction.

INFLUENCE – theory and practice

Influence is the ability to affect a person's behaviour. Therefore, whereas motivation relates to 'getting people going', influence relates to steering people in a particular direction – or getting them to do what you want them to do (preferably without complaint!). One person's ability to influence another basically depends upon two main factors:

- the power relationship between the two
- the type of request being made.

Influence and power

Individuals have power either because of their position or because of their personal attributes.

Position power

Position power relates to the degree to which people can control or influence others through their official status and position and the resources which this gives them.

- *Legitimate power* is given to official team leaders to control the activities of a team. In other words, legitimate power relates to the formal authority vested in official leaders by the organisation. This gives the leader the right (and the responsibility) to make certain decisions, and related to this is the status and respect accorded to 'the boss'. The fact that the boss also usually has prestige and is privy to greater information than subordinates also accords position power.
- *Reward power* derives from the ability of the official leader to give rewards to subordinates who conform or comply with requests. These can include recommending people for promotion, salary increases and bonuses, or the granting of particular privileges.
- *Dependence power* relates to the fact that one person wants what another is offering. Under certain conditions this can give considerable power to subordinates whose willing cooperation is essential. It also links with *coercive power* which implies sanctions, punishments or the withdrawal of favours by the official leader if compliance is not granted.

Personal power

Personal power, on the other hand, is not dependent upon an official position. It therefore accords more accurately with our everyday interpretation of the word 'influence'. It is broadly accepted that many people have influence who do not have an official position (e.g. the chairman's PA, the cabinet minister's spouse, the MD's golfing partner!). It is often referred to as *invisible power* and equated with 'the power behind the throne'.

The two main types of personal power are described below.

- *Expert power* is given to those perceived as experts in a given area, e.g. the finance director, IT manager or health and safety officer. This can cause conflict with those in other positions of authority. An obvious example is a ruling by finance that particular procedures must be followed even if these cause considerable inconvenience for marketing and production. Another example of expert power is the influence a doctor can wield over a patient through his/her expertise. Expert power can give people greater influence than is normally expected and this may be resented by others. The team member who has a wide network of contacts or specialist knowledge can gain power from his/her expertise in this area.
- *Personal power* refers to the ability and qualities which enable some people to make the most of other power resources. Charm, intelligence, sensitivity and empathy are all positive attributes in this situation. Whilst these may appear to be personal qualities, they may also be learned behaviours and used to get people to agree to a certain course of action.

The type of request

Whilst a team leader may have considerable power or influence over individual members to undertake routine tasks, he or she would need even more if the request being made were outside the person's normal frame of reference. According to Chester Barnard, normal requests fall into a person's *zone of indifference* – in other words, the individual is indifferent towards meeting these and will comply without question. However, if the request falls outside this zone then it is far less likely to be met with agreement. This is because it offends the core beliefs of the individual and falls outside the *psychological contract* which exists between the two people – or the normal expectations held by the individual. Therefore, whereas you will agree to undertake a basic activity in your job description without question, you may be more hesitant to work late without payment or make the coffee every day without some type of inducement or incentive. However, no matter what the inducement you would be unlikely to agree to participate in serious crime such as fraud or embezzlement or to become involved with unethical practices – such as deliberately misleading potential customers.

The degree to which a request falls outside your zone of indifference will directly affect the incentives which you will need to be offered to undertake the activity. The boss who believes that 'every person has his/her price' is likely to consider that, provided the reward is great enough, a person can be persuaded to do almost anything – although others would refute this view.

Ethical and moral issues are rarely clear-cut and unambiguous and can often create quandaries as each person's zone of indifference is slightly different from the next. Therefore, whereas some team members may consider that cutting corners on quality or fudging an expense account is quite acceptable, others may disagree. The degree of difference which exists can affect team performance and the degree of cohesiveness (see page 96). Moreover, the power of some groups to make individuals conform to group norms and values can cause dilemmas for those who hold different opinions.

Persuasion or manipulation?

People have different needs, standards and expectations from their interaction with a group or team, which will affect how they will respond to rewards, sanctions and how amenable they will be to other instruments of power and influence.

Whereas a group or team has the ability to provide social interaction and satisfy virtually the full range of interpersonal needs, including security and emotional support, identification and ego involvement by membership, each member's individual characteristics and needs must be considered by anyone wanting to influence individual members of the group. William Schutz argued that team members may have a high need for inclusion, control or affection. All of these identify needs which can be utilised (or exploited) by a leader who wishes to influence the person concerned. Those with a high need for inclusion want to be involved in informal activities, to be invited to events, to be involved in decisions. The biggest sanction would be to be ignored or left out. Those who have a high need for control are not easily led and would need higher rewards to be persuaded to do something outside their zone of indifference. They want to be dominant – keeping them down would be seen as punishment. Those who have a high need for affection aim to have close personal relationships with other team members. They will offer favours and friendship in order to become close to others. Again this can be utilised or manipulated by the leader to achieve prescribed ends.

Some leaders – particularly with a high need for power themselves – will deliberately exclude those who don't 'play ball' to bring individuals back into line. Generally this indicates an insecure leader who struggles to identify with the ethos of managing a team. In addition, it is important to realise that manipulation through playing upon people's weaknesses and inner fears results in negative power which does not result in effective teamwork or positive working relationships. In this situation, only the leader has power – and only through his or her position. In contrast, in an effective team, power and influence is diffused and distributed amongst the members equitably to the mutual benefit of all and the leader or facilitator has *earned* the respect of the members through technical skill and personal attributes, but has neither the wish nor the inclination to impose unpopular decisions on the group.

A true story relates to the frustrated Computer Services Manager of a mail-order company trying to get improvements to a recently installed IBM computer system. Despite constant attempts to register complaints at senior management level, the manager found his attempts blocked by gatekeepers to IBM's MD or Chairman. Eventually he wrote a letter and drove to IBM's headquarters and spoke to the car park attendant. He checked that the attendant parked the Chairman's car each day and often engaged in social pleasantries for a few moments. Agreement was reached that the attendant would pass on the letter to the Chairman the next day. This he duly did. The result? Instant action on the computer system.

The manager had been successful by using those who had influence to help in the attempt to lobby those who had power!

Monitoring team performance

As we approach the millennium, effective and, preferably, self-managed teams are alleged to be the best way to enhance organisational effectiveness and increase job satisfaction. If this is true, then monitoring team performance displaces monitoring individual performance as the most appropriate way of measuring results and outcomes. This is particularly so if we accept Belbin's argument that whereas an individual cannot be perfect a team can be – in which case there is every reason to believe that a well-structured, well-motivated team can achieve greater heights than any single person operating alone.

However, before team performance can be monitored effectively several other criteria need to be met. It is not enough to simply set up a team, give it instructions, walk away and then hope it does a good job! Whilst this may seem blindingly obvious, research suggests that British industry frequently fails to produce high-performing teams mainly because of its failure to maintain and develop teamworking over time.

Unlike individuals, teams have two areas to maintain:

- *task performance* – meeting goals of output and quality
- *meeting human needs* – the maintenance of good interpersonal relations between team members, between the team and external groups and the continuous growth and development of team members.

Therefore, if team effectiveness is considered from the point of view of *a control system*, then this must be a system which has two areas of output – one relating to task accomplishment and the other relating to meeting human needs.

Identifying effectiveness

Before you start monitoring team performance it is useful to be able to identify the hallmarks of an effective team – otherwise you will never know what you are aiming for or when you have succeeded! Generally, a high-performing team displays most or all of the following characteristics:

- Members have a high level of identification with the team, its aims and objectives.
- There is strong support for each other and the leader.
- Members have a high degree of trust and confidence in each other.
- Members share information and openly communicate with each other. Open, frank debate is encouraged.
- Members support each other and assist each other's development.
- There is effective decision-making with full and frank participation by all members.
- A supportive group atmosphere exists with team members actively working together to achieve the task.
- The team learns from experience.
- Disagreements and personality clashes are dealt with positively and conflicts resolved.
- Relationships with other groups and teams are positive and cooperative.

A control system for teamwork

Whereas systems and procedures will be discussed in more detail in Chapters 6 and 7, the basic principles of open systems can usefully be applied to create a model for monitoring and control (see Figure 1.2.4).

An open system is one which uses a process to translate or transform inputs into outputs. It is 'open' in that it interacts with the external environment. In the case of a group or team, the inputs will be received from the environment (possibly some from other teams) and its outputs will also be used by the environment (again, in some cases by other teams).

Inputs ⟶	Process ⟶	Outputs
Organisational support Organisational resources Team characteristics Task complexity	Team dynamics (required and emergent behaviours)	Task achievement Meeting human needs

Figure 1.2.4 Control diagram for monitoring teamwork

Inputs

Unless the inputs are of the right standard and quantity the team cannot function effectively. Broadly the inputs relate to all aspects which affect the resourcing of the team.

- *Organisational support and resourcing.* In this category key elements include
  - the rewards and incentives offered
  - the achievability of the goal
  - the culture and climate of the organisation as a whole
  - the leadership/management style
  - the space and technology and physical resources provided
  - the policies and procedures in place.

- *The characteristics of the team*, such as
  - the compatability of the members
  - the degree of training/staff development on teamwork
  - the skills possessed by members
  - the composition of the team
  - the size of the team (usually 5–7 is considered the ideal number).
- *The complexity of the task*, such as
  - the degree of technical ability required
  - time constraints
  - the degree of interaction required by team members to achieve the task
  - the degree of coordination required
  - the frequency/amount of changes to task parameters.

THEORY INTO PRACTICE

It is held that creative teams should comprise an odd number of members. This is because a majority vote is likely and therefore more disagreements and a higher level of conflict are probable which, if managed effectively, result in greater creativity. In contrast, a team which needs to consider its views rationally, methodically and objectively is better formed from an even number. This may be one reason why juries comprise twelve people.

The process

The process relates to the ability of the team to utilise its inputs. In team terms this is usually known as *group dynamics* – a phrase often used to describe the workings or interactions of the group. Group dynamics will be influenced by the members themselves and their individual personality traits. A strong, forceful character is likely to inhibit weaker members who may be reluctant to make a contribution to the group if they will be derided or ignored. However, if the group comprises a number of forceful individuals the situation is likely to be rather different.

George Homans developed a model for analysing group dynamics which differentiates between the *required* and *emergent behaviours* of group members. Required behaviours relate to the formal, specified behaviours or responsibilities of individual members. Emergent behaviours relate to 'additional' behaviours which group members expect of each other. Homans then applied this theory to group *activities*, *interactions* and *sentiments*.

- Required activities relate to job roles or responsibilities. Emergent activities relate to additional activities, such as assisting and helping each other or cleaning up one's own area, which are expected of members.
- Required interactions relate to essential communications between group members. Emergent interactions are additional communications, such as a detailed explanation of a difficult instruction, a supportive discussion with another member of the team, or phoning an absent member to keep him or her up-to-date with progress.

- Required sentiments relate to standards of behaviour expected of the group, such as common courtesies and social etiquette. However, it is beyond the manager to control the emergent sentiments of the group – the personal attitudes, beliefs and feelings of members. These may be different from the required sentiments and also differ from one group member to another.

The importance of group dynamics is its influence on group behaviour. The manager who considers only required behaviours is looking only at the surface or 'public face' of the group. It is therefore important to look beyond this to identify and, preferably, guide emergent behaviours in the way which best accords with group performance targets and organisational objectives. In addition, it is impossible to specify fully the behaviours required of members in a high-performing team. Therefore emergent behaviours are essential to effectiveness and, provided they complement the required behaviours, should be encouraged.

Monitoring task performance

In this case the team is concerned with the suitability of its resources and the effectiveness of the process. The measures for success relate to task achievement – both productivity and quality and meeting human needs. It is usual for monitoring to be part of an ongoing control system which concentrates on setting standards, monitoring and evaluating results and continuous development, as illustrated in Figure 1.2.5.

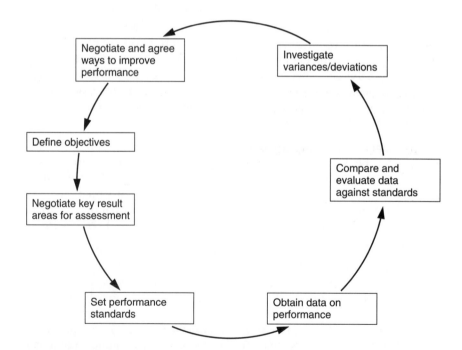

Figure 1.2.5 The monitoring process

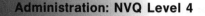

Defining objectives and key result areas

The key requirements for all *objectives* – that they should be specific, measurable, agreed, realistic and time-related – was discussed on page 19. However, for team performance to enhance organisational effectiveness there must be a clear link between organisational strategy and corporate objectives and the performance objectives of individual teams. In addition, the team should be fully aware of these objectives and, preferably, have participated in negotiating the *key result areas*. These are the areas which most accurately reflect the main purpose of the job and where performance will have the most significant effect on outcome achievement.

Objectives and key result areas were originally formulated as components of the management technique known as *Management by Objectives* (MBO). This was introduced by Peter Drucker to translate organisational goals into management objectives which can be measured, and feedback and evaluation can inform both succession planning and financial rewards. It aims to provide control over outcomes which specifically affect overall organisational performance through ongoing monitoring and feedback of individually negotiated performance targets. The aim is to enhance motivation by involving managers in identifying and setting their own objectives.

Today MBO techniques have been developed, refined and, often, customised to suit individual organisations. The system is no longer confined to management staff but used for all employees at different levels. There is an obvious link with an appraisal system which links feedback on performance to staff development and the review of current targets.

The technique is considered beneficial as it actively involves employees in setting their own objectives and encourages staff to take on greater responsibility for both their own achievements and their own development. However, there are some disadvantages which are even more pronounced if the system is adapted for group or team targets rather than individual targets. These are discussed more fully below. MBO is also discussed in Chapter 3, page 196.

Setting performance standards

It is always easier to measure quantitative standards as the outcome then gives clear, unambiguous feedback on performance to the team. This means identifying quantitative measures which accurately represent realistic targets relating to productivity, quality and behaviour.

Setting *performance standards* or *performance indicators* (PIs) has always been fraught with difficulty, apart from for routine duties and basic production tasks. Therefore, in an area such as administration or customer service, various anomalies can occur. Some of the major problems are summarised below.

- Standards are easier to set for output or routine aspects of the job (e.g. number of enquiries handled in a given period) rather than for behavioural aspects or intrinsically desirable characteristics (e.g. quality of customer service). In addition, personal qualities and abilities such as 'commitment', 'initiative', 'cooperation' or 'creativity' are extremely difficult to assess or measure in a *definitive* or comparable way.

- Some jobs have a higher component of behavioural aspects than others – nursing is a prime example. Being an effective member of a team in itself means that certain traits are necessary (sharing ideas, giving assistance, communicating). A high performer in terms of measurable targets may be a poor team player, and vice versa.

- For some jobs, targets can skew performance with individuals or teams concentrating only (or mainly) on measurable aspects of the job. This may lead to unethical practices or the neglect of other areas to achieve targets.

- 'Bargaining' power can influence target setting – a good negotiator or a strong or cohesive team may be able to argue targets down whereas others may not.

- Constant achievement of targets always creates problems if the highest achievers constantly have to meet increased targets.

- Targets focus on the short-term. Teams involved, for instance, with a long-term research and development project may have great difficulty setting or achieving short-term 'staging-post' targets.

- There may be a high dependency upon other factors for targets to be achievable, factors which are outside the team's control because they are concerned with inputs rather than process. These may range from external factors relating to the political or economic environment, to internal cooperation from other teams or departments. With a team, of course, there is also high dependency on *other members* for team goals and targets to be achieved. This can be a source of comfort or frustration – depending upon the ability, motivation and attitude of the other members of each particular team.

Some organisations have decided to focus on team rewards and bonuses for performance rather than individual rewards. Rank Xerox has introduced team bonuses for about 2000 staff, management and engineering staff, linking team performance to company goals of customer satisfaction, sales revenue and market share. Bonuses range from 15 per cent on basic pay for managers, to £1600 for engineers and £2000 for sales people. A salesperson in a good team can earn an extra £160 a month.

Sun Life pays its brokers team pay, based on a customer service index. This shows how efficiently teams deal with their customer requirements in terms of speed, time and quality. The 1400 employed covered by the scheme can earn up to 10 per cent of their basic pay if they operate in a successful team.

Those who advocate team pay schemes claim it encourages teamworking, persuades people to share ideas, enhances flexibility and motivates ineffective workers to improve. However, the problem for good staff comes when they are locked into a non-performing or poorly-performing team and do not have the authority to change the way it operates. Whilst this may be irritating and demotivational at any time, the situation becomes even more critical when it affects an individual's pay packet.

Assume your organisation decided to pay its successful teams a bonus.

1 What advantages and disadvantages can you think there might be for you as a team member?
2 What would you do if you were placed in a team which didn't perform well?
3 How might this initiative affect your role as the leader of a team?
4 How do you think the members of a team might react if the team was continually successful and management increased its targets for performance every year?

Home Office attempts to introduce performance targets and performance-related pay (PRP) in both the probation service and the police in 1996 were strongly rejected as being inapplicable, insulting and in grave danger of leading to unethical practices. In the US, false-arrest complaints soared when the police were given PRP based on arrest rates. In the UK sergeants found they were spending more time assessing police constables than doing their own work. John Hicks, Vice-Chairman of the Chief Probation Officers, expressed serious reservations about PRP, given that it would act as a disincentive for any probation officer to deal with perpetual reoffenders. He likened the approach to paying doctors for their success rates and then wondering why they refused to treat the old or incurable.

Nor is such scepticism confined to the public sector. The 1996 Ashridge Management Index, which gives an indication of management attitudes every year, highlighted the fact that organisations often overestimate the ability of incentive schemes to improve performance and underestimate intrinsic aspects such as job satisfaction and freedom to operate – the basic components which have been instrumental in motivating employees for decades.

Obtaining, comparing and evaluating data

These aspects are at the crux of all monitoring systems. For data to be valuable they have to be current, accurate and valid for the purpose for which they are being used. Far too frequently one set of data is used for a myriad of purposes or 'adjusted' to suit one purpose when it was originally designed to provide information for another.

Data on output performance is available through a variety of computer-generated reports and statistics. These are supplemented by quality checks and other automated recording systems which quantify what is happening or has happened, when and how on a regular basis – but beware the information overload syndrome! Too many reports giving too much detail simply swamp everyone. The trick is to define exactly what data you need and obtain just that.

However, data alone rarely show the true picture. You will always find that those involved can provide dozens of explanations for trends, variances and deviations – and only some of these will be genuine factual reasons for any differences. Therefore, so far as is possible, it is always easier to identify and agree the data which can be used unequivocally to justify performance beforehand. If this is difficult with an individual, it is even more difficult with a team – particularly one which is highly cohesive and may even have its own interests and agenda to pursue.

The following are examples of team performance standards and objectives used by organisations.

- Standards relating to defined criteria such as sales, customer satisfaction, speed of information or enquiry processing (i.e. productivity), or accuracy of processing (i.e. quality). These are used by financial organisations including Norwich Union, Lloyds Bank and Pearl Assurance. A new trend is measuring *internal* customer service and satisfaction as well as external.
- Standards relating to an overall criterion – such as 'valuable contribution to performance'.
- Achievement of specified organisational or team objectives or productivity targets. Dartford Borough Council pays teams according to targets set for three types of tasks: those that are suitable for the team to undertake together, those that will benefit the directorate most if undertaken successfully, and those which are distinct from the normal duties of individual team members.

Investigating variances and deviations

All variations need to be investigated – even those which give a positive result. If a target or performance indicator is shattered completely, rather than achieved comfortably, then it is likely that the forecasting and planning process – and the base data on which the target was identified – were flawed in some way. Either key information was missing or the person setting or agreeing the target was misinformed or misled as to its applicability. The danger, of course, is that someone experienced at handling targets *continuously* muddies the water or misinforms to keep targets at a comfortable level. Potential managers should note that this is only possible if the data being used are ambiguous, out-of-date or capable of being manipulated in some way.

Basically, there has to be an attempt to define the reason for the variance so that corrective action can be taken. The best type of corrective action will depend upon the reason for the variance. In some cases no action is possible. Organisations which lost (or gained) sales and revenue with the outbreak of the Gulf War can hardly prevent or precipitate another similar crisis in the future. However, it is usually the case that if targets have been compiled with due regard for any external sensitivity factors, then these issues should not overly affect variance investigation (apart from confirming or denying their existence).

Finally, it is often sensible to take steps to confirm any unexpected or dramatic trends or findings to check that these are accurate before making drastic changes to methods of operation or measurement. Redesigning the entire customer service operation in response to negative survey findings would be unpopular and unnecessary if it were later found that the data input clerk had keyed in the responses against the wrong codes!

Modern telesales teams are given specific performance targets and are highly charged towards reaching them. 'Hits' are displayed on large electronic screens, staff can express their delight verbally with shouts of joy when a sale is made. The system is fast-moving and highly pressurised and rapid burnout is common. All trainees undergo an intensive programme of practising scripted techniques to persuade potential customers to 'buy' the product – and a large part of their pay is made up of incentive payments.

One of the 'products' sold by this means by the big banks are personal loans – at high APR rates. You can make your own judgement about the ethics of high-powered sales people persuading the gullible and uninformed to borrow as much as possible by this means.

Monitoring the human aspect

It is unusual, though not impossible, to find a high-performing team where its members are actively unhappy or dissatisfied. However, it is the case that individual members may feel their needs are being neglected or that they are being dominated by their more forceful colleagues. It is, of course, quite possible that one of the reasons why high performance levels are not being met is because the team is not functioning properly as they are more concerned with in-fighting, back-biting or constant disagreements than doing their jobs! Methods of addressing and dealing with conflict are dealt with below.

However, as a basic point it is quite obvious that the amount of team spirit which exists is unlikely to be measurable through staring at a computer printout! This has to be observed or feedback has to be obtained from other sources which can record and document impressions or views. Methods include the following:

- 'walking the job' – the modern practice of managers observing at first hand what takes place rather than supervising activities from an isolated ivory tower
- talking and listening – to a variety of stakeholders from employees to customers to suppliers
- surveys and questionnaires to find out opinions and views of stakeholders
- holding review meetings to identify attitudes to performance trends and 'where the team is coming from', particularly if problems are being experienced
- identifying key aspects which illustrate good team spirit and effective team interaction – some of these are quantifiable and others are not.

A basic checklist for assessing the degree to which a team meets the human needs of its members is given in Figure 1.2.6. One of the main points to bear in mind is that new teams take time to settle down and to operate as a unit, rather than as a disparate set of individuals. Strategies to develop teamwork are discussed on page 93.

Quantifiable targets to check		
	Effective	*Ineffective*
Turnover of team members	Low	High
Absenteeism	Low	High
Punctuality	Good	Poor
Output	High	Low
Quality of work	High	Low
Achievement of team goals	Good	Poor
Achievement of individual targets	Good	Poor
Qualitative factors to observe		
Communications between members	Open/honest	Closed/secretive
Commitment to goals	High	Low
Understanding of team needs	Clear	Confused
Trust factor between members	High	Low
Reaction to individual difficulties	Supportive	Critical/hostile
Reaction to team problems	Investigative	Passive
Response to new ideas	Accommodating	Negative
Team decision-making	Consensus	Conflict or domination
'Buzz'/creativity factor	High	Low
Need for external guidance	High	Minimal

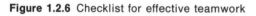

Figure 1.2.6 Checklist for effective teamwork

Methods of improving performance

It is one thing to identify ways in which performance can be improved, it is quite another to negotiate and agree these with the people involved. The way in which changes are put forward will depend very much on the nature of the team, the degree to which it is supposed to be 'self-managed', and its current levels of effectiveness.

The best way to improve performance will depend upon:

- the variance or problem that occurred
- the reason for its occurrence
- the people (or team) involved.

Generally, there are several options, including:

- modifying or changing the process or procedure being followed
- modifying or changing the objectives or standards to be achieved
- reassigning work duties amongst the team
- restructuring the team completely (though this is drastic action and usually very unpopular and unsettling)
- changing the team leader
- re-evaluating the resources available to the team
- instigating individual or team development or training to improve specific weaknesses.

In the unlikely event of a team scoring dismally on every count listed on Figure 1.2.6, radical action would be required – popular or not. However, in most situations a range of options is available. The pragmatic leader is unlikely to think that success will be achieved by 'dictating terms', however tempting and time-saving this may appear to be. Usually, the main choice is the degree to which the team members should be consulted over any proposals or whether these should be outlined in advance and then 'sold' to the team. This decision will depend upon several factors, including team size and cohesiveness, the experience of the team, its role and tasks, the strength of individual personalities, the influence of the leader, the style of the individual manager, and the particular area(s) under consideration. It would, for instance, be futile for a highly experienced and creative team to have radical changes forced upon them when they may be much better at finding appropriate solutions themselves. Equally, an inexperienced team operating on basic tasks and duties may appreciate experienced guidance and help. However, it is unusual for practitioners in any area not to be able to make informed comments on possible improvements and it is a foolhardy leader or manager who ignores such inputs. A team (or an individual) which is given the freedom to make and implement proposals is far more committed to their success than a team which has new methods of working forced upon it. On occasion, a team may actively work to discredit suggestions and methods with which it does not agree!

Dealing with disagreements and conflict

Disagreements and conflict can occur both within the team and between the team and other groups.

People vary in their reactions to disagreements and conflict. At one extreme is the passive, 'peace at any price' individual, who will conform, compromise his/her beliefs or do almost anything to prevent conflict. At the other extreme are those individuals who thrive on conflict, enjoy the cut and thrust of an argument and almost actively seek an issue on which to be abrasive if life becomes at all routine.

Most of us fall between the two extremes but show certain tendencies. These include:

- feeling more passionate about issues which are clearly unfair or discriminatory than those which are neutral
- reacting more strongly when the issue affects us personally
- having an unfavourable reaction to criticism (though some people are more prickly and defensive than others)
- having an adverse reaction if our reputation, honour or integrity is challenged.

By and large it is essential that we all have an in-built defence mechanism. The completely passive person would have to be prepared to accommodate other people's wishes unendingly for peace to be sustained. This is untenable for any length of time – therefore we all have to act to defend our own personal space and beliefs from time to time. However, *how* we do this – and the degree of animosity, aggression or defensiveness we display – can vary tremendously. And if we lose the argument our reactions can range from acceptance to anger and from shrugging it off to bearing a grudge forever more.

It is fortunate that in a working environment most people confine their behaviour to what they perceive as professional limits. This means they are more guarded and more controlled than they may be at home. Additionally, given that the workplace usually comprises a number of mature adults, temper tantrums and sulking *should* have been left behind years ago (though this is not always the case!). In some organisational cultures, open conflict may actually be encouraged in the mistaken belief that this will improve and enhance performance. In reality, unless this is handled very cleverly it is more likely to demotivate and discourage all but the toughest adversaries – the type who thrive on disagreements, but who may in fact be poor performers themselves.

What normally goes wrong in such situations is that no-one can distinguish between *positive* or *constructive conflict* and *negative* or *destructive conflict*.

Constructive conflict

Constructive conflict is essential in order for teams and individuals to be effective and creative producers – basically because it emanates from an open communication system where people speak their minds (although tact should not be discouraged!). Given that no group of people will always agree on everything, by definition there are going to be disagreements if people are allowed to have an opinion – and it is the 'being allowed to have an opinion' which is so critical to healthy working relationships and positive teamworking. A team leader who is so fearful of a challenge that he or she will steamroller through ideas and opinions will, quite rapidly, end up with a team which is disenchanted, demoralised and will ultimately passively accept anything it is given to do, for better or for worse.

However, if ideas, suggestions, opinions and critical analysis are to be encouraged then, as in other forms of conflict, there must be some clear rules of engagement. Breaking these rules is tantamount to a 'foul' and must be penalised. The rules include:

- no blame allocation or apportionment of blame to other people – a team is *collectively* responsible for its activities and blame allocation simply shifts the emphasis, it never solves the problem
- no personal or destructive criticism of a negative nature which will demean another person (see below)
- no deliberate withholding of important information to prevent an informed opinion being reached
- no hidden agendas or game-playing to skew the result beforehand, such as lobbying other members of the team for support, or to outflank another member
- acknowledging that each individual has a slightly different perception of reality or is operating from a different frame of reference and therefore has every right to hold a particular view
- understanding that assertiveness gives one the right to put forward a view, but it does not give anyone the right to put it forward aggressively or to expect everyone to agree with it
- realising that only if individuals have mutual respect for each other can a 'win/win' situation be achieved.

If there is open hostility and disagreement then the aim of the team leader is to move towards a 'win/win' situation (where, theoretically, there are no losers), rather than a compromise (where no-one wins) or a 'win/lose' situation. This is discussed in more detail in Chapter 4. However, a practical point for team leaders is that harmony is not always achievable and neither is a 'win/win' situation. At times, trade-offs are inevitable. As long as these are perceived to be *fair* and in the best interests of the team as a whole, there is generally consensus and acceptance by the majority of individuals.

Destructive conflict

Destructive conflict is identified by personality clashes, outright hostility, aggressive behaviour, blame allocation and deep divisions or rifts between particular individuals or teams. It occurs when a conflict situation gets out of control and generally makes life worse for everyone. Even those not directly involved can be affected if they are working in a difficult, politically charged atmosphere every day and having to choose between different factions. Needless to say, such an environment usually has a negative effect on productivity.

Before discussing how to deal with this, it is first important to identify why it occurs. Although arguments and disagreements can occur about almost anything (and the triviality of the issue has little to do with the potential scale of the disagreement!) these can range from basic misunderstandings or short-lived differences or arguments to full-blooded vendettas and feuds against people or opposing groups.

Organisational issues

Examples of conflict 'triggers' include:

- competition over scarcity of resources, such as space, equipment, time, assistance
- disagreement over allocation of duties or responsibilities
- disagreement over ends and means – this can relate to inputs expected from another department or the method by which work should be done
- disagreement over individual interests (status, rewards, freedom of action).

Personal issues

In this case examples include:

- scapegoating and blame allocation – blaming another person or department (rightly or wrongly) for an outcome
- role conflict – where the individual is not clear about the role he/she has been given or is given conflicting instructions/directives or subject to conflicting loyalties (this causes stress as well as conflict – see also Chapter 4)
- blocking behaviour – preventing someone else from taking action
- attacking the passengers – where members of a team turn on the obvious 'weak link' or most laid-back person in the chain
- destructive personal criticism against an individual
- miscommunications and misunderstandings
- basic personality clash where there appears to be no mutual area of interest between two competing members of a group or team.

The fundamental difference between constructive and destructive conflict is in the way it is managed and the behaviour of the protagonists. Basically, the only way in which conflict can be resolved is through some form of negotiation between the parties concerned – although in some cases the intervention of a third person may be useful. It is naive to consider that any person will totally concede an issue – given that each of us always considers our own view to be right! It is more realistic to expect that 'give and take' – and a recognition of a different perspective – is essential for any form of agreement to be reached. Generally, this is also linked with strategies to assist each person to move more readily towards a 'win/win' or a centralist position. D. G. Pruitt, a management writer concerned with bargaining strategies, described a variety of techniques for resolving conflict which could be useful team leaders, including:

- broadening the pie – in other words adjusting resources so that both can share in the rewards
- logrolling – conceding a low pay-off issue in order to obtain a reward of higher value later
- nonspecific compensation – one person is the winner, the other is compensated for losing (the compensation may relate to a different issue entirely)

- bridging – basically a compromise where neither achieves their original objective but a different option is put forward or developed of interest to them both
- cost-cutting – whilst one person is the winner, the 'cost' to the other is minimised so far as possible.

Basically, the key point to bear in mind is that it is impossible to neutralise, manage or negotiate through conflict unless there is some form of recognition for the other point of view and *neutral* – rather than antagonistic – communication. Teamwork involves learning negotiation rather than combative or game-playing skills. The team leader or facilitator must be prepared to act as mediator or negotiator in conflicts which may result in either side becoming entrenched or a 'stand-off' position. If those involved are genuinely committed to achieving a 'win/win' outcome – rather than overpowering the other side – then harmony can usually be achieved without loss of status on either side. (Note that further information on managing conflict and game-playing strategies is contained in Chapter 4.)

Groupthink

Groupthink is a phenomenon that occurs when the group develops an attitude in which it overestimates its own importance *vis à vis* other groups or teams. The group begins to consider it is always right and starts to stereotype all competitors as inferior. In this case it will more readily adopt aggressive or non-cooperative strategies in relation to other groups and be less amenable to reconsidering its own position. This reduces innovation as the group becomes focused upon defending itself to the detriment of other activities. Objective analysis and rational thought are subjugated and group consensus is valued above all.

Irving Janis identified eight symptoms of groupthink:

- An illusion of invulnerability. The group considers it is above criticism or attack.
- Rationalising unwelcome information. The group refuses to accept unwelcome findings or alternatives.
- Group morality. Members feel they are morally right and above reproach.
- Stereotyping competitors. Other groups are considered as weak, stupid, evil and 'the enemy', leading to a 'them and us' approach.
- Conformative pressure. Dissenters are forced to conform to group wishes or leave.
- Self-censorship. Members are forbidden to voice personal concerns, and group loyalty is paramount.
- Illusion of unanimity. Unanimity is accepted prematurely and without due consideration of its appropriateness or completeness.
- Mind guarding. Group members protect each other from other ideas or viewpoints expressed by outsiders.

The role of the group manager is to prevent or minimise the effects of groupthink. Janis suggested this could be done by:

- assigning each group member the role of critical evaluator to encourage a diversity of opinions
- encouraging open communications, shared discussions and not – as leader – prematurely favouring one course of action rather than another
- creating subgroups to work on the same problems to obtain a variety of proposed solutions
- obtaining outside opinions where appropriate
- assigning the role of devil's advocate to at least one member during discussions
- holding a 'second-chance' meeting to review the decision and test consensus again.

Another strategy would be to implement a decision for a pilot phase and then hold a review meeting at which modifications can be made based on experience.

Internal conflict can be minimised if particular groups or teams are not unduly favoured or held as 'good examples' for others to follow (which usually annoys everyone and irritates even the 'good' teams!). Cooperation, interaction and consensus should be seen as attributes which deserve reward, whereas insular viewpoints, game-playing tactics and win/lose strategies should be discouraged. Rotating members between teams also minimises groupthink and the possibility of a team becoming so strong and cohesive that it becomes a serious force to be reckoned with. However, this strategy has disadvantages also – as teams become more mature in their development both the motivation of individuals and overall productivity are likely to suffer if team membership is too fluid. Basically, a good leader recognises that in times when resources are scarce and there is increased pressure to solve problems quickly, all team members will be under stress, tension will rise, commitment and motivation will fall and internal squabbles are more likely to occur. Keeping the team focused on its objectives and motivated to achieve its goals, as well as confident of its ability to succeed, is crucial in reducing potential disagreements and conflict.

Creating Top Flight Teams by Hilarie Owen (Kogan Page) is a book which concludes that the success of the Red Arrows is not due to the exceptional leadership or superlative skills of the members but the 'synergy chain process' which virtually guarantees successful teamwork. It includes elements such as objectives and goals, clear procedures, openness and confrontation and inter-group relations. According to Owen, the key to the process is to acknowledge that total support and trust is required by every team member, each of whom is assured of the importance of his or her role. Developing this type of relationship requires complete honesty and self-criticism – from the top downwards – so that time is never wasted apportioning blame when it can be used positively to prevent a repetition of a problem. In today's corporate culture this would, without doubt, be a considerable challenge for many managers and facilitators.

Establishing constructive relationships

In one sense, this is the basis upon which good team relations are built. Done well, it minimises the likelihood of destructive conflict at a later stage. A wise team leader – or team member – appreciates that it takes time for any group or team to learn to work together. A 'mature' team is never achieved overnight.

The process of group development was analysed by Tuckman, who identified five stages, each with recognisable behaviour patterns.

- *Forming*. At this stage the group is new and membership is unknown, therefore dependence upon the leader is high. At this stage members may be anxious or apprehensive – there may be considerable informal banter or 'ice-breaking'. They need information on the reason for the group, the rules which will apply and the methods and behaviours which will be considered appropriate.
- *Storming*. This is when differences between members, between expectation and reality, and between goals and needs begin to surface. Opinions may be polarised and there are likely to be arguments and conflict as members resist the right of the leader to control the group and specify group norms. The task of the leader is to facilitate the allocation of roles and responsibility of individual members and the place of each person within the group. In voluntary groups, the group may be disbanded if agreement is not reached or if the degree of conflict and difference is too great to solve.
- *Norming*. At this stage there is some group cohesion and members accept their individual roles and give mutual support. This leads to closer relationships as mutually agreeable solutions to problems are sought and found. There is an open exchange of opinions, cooperation between members and more camaraderie. Group consensus leads to a shared responsibility for group activities. Harmony is valued and group identification is high.
- *Performing*. The group has now developed to the stage when its energies can be focused on task performance. Group members are secure in their identities and feel valued. They feel free to express their opinions and offer solutions to problems. There is role flexibility as the needs of the group are paramount. This is the major productive period of group formation.
- *Mourning*. This is the final stage for temporary groups when they disband and members go their separate ways. Formally, it may be characterised by evaluation or a plenary session at which members review their performance and effectiveness. Mourning is a descriptive term because members usually feel some sadness, and there may be

ritual endings (e.g. an end-of-year dinner for students finishing a course of study) and promises of reunions in the future.

THEORY INTO PRACTICE

Tuckman's stages of group development can be applied to groups as diverse as committees, residential courses and working groups.

For instance, an effective committee will be steered by a chairperson who allows for the group to go through all five stages in the course of a single meeting. This includes coffee at the outset as members arrive and then an outline of the content (forming), the introduction of a controversial topic or difficult task (storming), agreement over how it should be attempted (norming), a decision as to what will be done (performing) and a review and adjournment (mourning).

Any participant on a residential course will tell you about feelings of apprehension on arrival, identification with the group and how this becomes stronger during the week, and the mixed feelings at the end of the week as the group breaks up (probably forever) and members return home.

Stages in team formation and team building

J. R. Hackman identified four discrete stages of team formation and development.

- The first stage is the *prework stage* at which those responsible for allocating teams should be identifying
  - whether a team is necessary
  - the work which it would carry out
  - the degree of authority or 'self-management' it should possess
  - the probable goals, objectives and targets.
- At stage two, the conditions are provided for effective performance. At this stage
  - the personnel need to be recruited according to their complementary strengths and combined abilities
  - the team needs an appropriate level of resources (see page 78).
- Stage three, team formation and team building, commences:
  - the limitations and boundaries of the team are identified
  - agreement is reached on the tasks to be performed
  - the values and norms of the team are established and also the range of acceptable behaviours and strategies for operation.
- Stage four is the stage at which the leader
  - intervenes when and as required to reduce or eliminate conflict – this may mean changing the team members
  - monitors, reviews and replenishes resources and/or upgrades these as required
  - replaces members who leave the group.

It could also be argued, of course, that an essential part of group maintenance is the development of team spirit and team dynamics to improve the way in which it operates and functions. This is normally undertaken by involving the team in team building activities (see page 99).

Woodcock and Francis, both experts in team development, identified similar phases in team development to Tuckman.

- *Ritual sniffing.* This is similar to the 'forming' stage – new team members have to test out their new compatriots. At this stage they have little regard for other members, are concerned that their own feelings, apprehensions and weaknesses are kept hidden and will concentrate on 'following the leader' and keeping to a neutral, established line.
- *Infighting.* This can be equated to 'storming' in that the role of the team leader is now evaluated, alliances start to form and differences are expressed more openly. At this stage there is more expression of individual commitment, strength and weaknesses and the needs of the team become more important.
- *Experimentation.* By now the team is operating in a more dynamic way. More members start to contribute and the agenda is broadened so that more contentious issues can be debated. There is a willingness to try new things and conflict can be addressed more positively. Different methods of working may be tried and reviewed. However, although by now members will act to protect the team as a unit, there is still little unity and no systematic way of attempting to solve problems or undertake activities.
- *Effectiveness.* At this stage the team has become more skilled at solving problems creatively and has identified clear objectives which it is prepared to review at regular intervals. There is pride in team achievements and accomplishments and an urge to improve its skills and utilisation of resources.
- *Maturity.* A mature team works effectively, achieves high performance standards and has concern for the human relationships which exist between team members. Team members show mutual respect and concern, interact effectively with other groups and obtain satisfaction and motivation from their participation in team activities.

Edgar Schein identified 10 separate criteria which indicated a mature group; these are outlined in Figure 1.2.7. He argued that at this stage *distributed leadership* is identified – all team members possess the skills to step in and meet the task or human relationship maintenance needs.

- *Degeneration.* Whilst this is not a feature of all teams, it is the case that some teams cease to function effectively after a time. They may become stale or overly complacent or victims of groupthink. For this reason team facilitators or leaders need to be aware that they cannot become complacent once a team reaches maturity – otherwise the team may degenerate and cease to function effectively.

Adequate mechanisms for obtaining feedback
Adequate decision-making procedures
Optimal cohesion
Flexible organisation and procedures
Maximum use of resources
Clear communication systems
Clear goals accepted by all members
Feelings of interdependence with those in authority
Shared participation in leadership functions
Acceptance (and tolerance) of minority views and persons
Adapted from *Process Consultation* by Edgar H. Schein, Addison-Wesley

Figure 1.2.7 Ten key features of a mature group

THEORY INTO PRACTICE

1 Identify a group with which you have been involved, either on a temporary or a permanent basis, and apply one of the above theories of development to ascertain its degree of maturity.
2 If you regularly attend meetings, assess the ability of your chairperson to allow for the appropriate stages of group development to take place. Assess, also, the reaction of group members if a stage is curtailed for any reason, such as:
   – the chairperson starts the meeting when only half the members have arrived
   – insecurity means the chairperson cannot cope with the 'storming' phase and prematurely insists on consensus.

Note that meetings are discussed in detail in Chapter 5.

Other aspects of team development

Over time, some groups and teams exert a powerful influence on their members to conform to group norms and beliefs whereas others do not. It is important to understand how and why this power occurs so that peer pressure can be taken into account when analysing the behaviour of individual members of a group or team. The relevant factors include

- the degree of cohesiveness of the group
- the norms of the group
- the roles of individual group members.

Cohesiveness

Cohesiveness has many positive features. It is likely to produce better social relations within the team as members are mutually supportive. This commonly leads to greater commitment and productivity – but not always. On the down side, cohesiveness means that the team is more likely to display common forms of behaviour which is only appropriate if this behaviour conforms to that required by the organisation. A strongly cohesive group or team is more difficult to control if, for instance, it is antagonistic to the aims of the organisation.

Cohesiveness is likely to be greater in the following circumstances:

- The group is small in size – normally below 10 members. Subgroups or splinter groups are likely to occur above this number.
- The group has been in existence for some time and membership is relatively unchanging.
- The group is relatively homogeneous in terms of the backgrounds, interests, values and attitudes of its members.
- Membership of the group is restricted and 'closed' rather than open to anyone.
- The group is involved in similar tasks.
- Members are located physically close to one another. Any physical barriers (stairs, corridors etc.) are likely to reduce cohesiveness quite substantially.
- Members can communicate frequently and freely.
- Membership of the group strongly meets the needs of the members (e.g. for affiliation needs – see page 67 – and recognition)
- The leader is a charismatic figure with a strong personality, who is respected, admired or feared by group members because of his/her contacts and the type of sanctions he/she can enforce. This will encourage members to conform with the norms espoused by the leader.
- The group is successful as a unit.
- The group is threatened from outside by a competitive group or external enemy.
- The group can be classed as a 'mature unit' in relation to its development.

Group norms

Group norms colour the ethos and culture of the group as well as influencing members' behaviour. Norms are accepted or approved ways of behaving to accomplish specified goals according to the ideas and views held by existing members. For example, in a particular group the norms may include the following.

- No member ever criticises another group member to a senior member of staff (this may be termed as 'ratting', 'tale-telling', 'snitching' or 'squealing').
- No member ever works so hard as to show up other members or threaten existing targets (often known as 'rate-busting').
- No member ever volunteers him/herself, or the group, for additional work or responsibility.
- Older, senior members of the group receive the perks, such as coming in later, leaving earlier.

Norms usually result in conformity to group standards of dress and language. In one case documented by Miller and Forms, a man who changed his flat cap for a hat was rejected by his work group. Newcomers may be subjected to initiation rites – often being expected to run errands or to be the butt of practical jokes. The group may require attendance at social events to celebrate birthdays, weddings or retirements of group members. Moreover, group norms will tend to reinforce stereotypes about other groups – such as beliefs about management – and will use these stereotypes to rationalise events and situations.

The degree to which norms are enforced is usually dependent upon four factors:

- the degree to which the norms aid group survival or provide group benefits
- the degree to which they simplify group roles and responsibilities
- the degree to which they solve group problems
- the degree to which they reflect the core values and identity held by the group.

THEORY INTO PRACTICE

A group of (honest) employees are responsible, between them, for running an entertainment event at a leisure complex. In haste, one evening, the member who carries out the calculations makes a mistake, with the result that the surplus at the end of the evening is higher than it should be. Only group members know and, after much agonising, they decide the best route would be to split the surplus between them. Three months later the same problem occurs. This time there is little agonising over the difficulty and the surplus is again distributed amongst them.

1 What forces were at work to make perfectly honest group members reach the decision they did?
2 What would happen if the problem continues to occur, and why?
3 Why is the decision progressively easier to make on each subsequent occasion?
4 What actions, if any, can managers take to avoid this problem?

Group roles

Group roles are different from the team roles identified by Belbin, although there is obviously a degree of overlap. Research into group roles undertaken by R. F. Bales, and later by K. D. Benne and P. Sheats, has divided group roles into three categories:

- *Task roles or supportive activities* – concerned with accomplishing tasks and achieving group goals. These include initiating ideas and activities, giving information or opinions, seeking information or opinions, giving explanations or elaborating on basic facts, suggesting solutions, coordinating activities, summarising and critically evaluating progress, motivating others, making notes, testing for consensus.

- *Maintenance roles* – concerned with supporting and maintaining the group as a whole. Roles here include encouraging others, representing the group, keeping, making or suggesting compromises, protecting or defending the group, diagnosing problems, setting standards, making observations, giving information, mediating, accepting group decisions, relieving tension or anxiety.
- *Individual roles or negative behaviour* – which relate to the personal agenda of individual members. These include aggressive behaviour, blocking ideas of others, recognition-seeking, domination of others, needing support or help from others, acting the 'fool' or 'comedian', seeking sympathy, special pleading, competing with others within the group, withdrawing from the group, introducing 'red herrings' or other distractions.

Group members are capable of undertaking a variety of roles simultaneously, although some may be mutually exclusive. For instance, aggression and 'blocking' roles are not in the interests of group maintenance. It is the leader's job to ensure that all the key roles are played and there is the right balance of roles. The leader should be particularly vigilant in relation to:

- ensuring that maintenance roles are met, if the group is going to survive
- ensuring that task roles are performed in the most effective way, at the most effective time and in the most effective order (for instance, there is little point in suggesting solutions before everyone has received and analysed the information).

Positive roles should obviously be encouraged and negativism discouraged – not least because of its effect on other group members. A variety of techniques have been used to record and analyse the behaviour of groups and the effect of individual members upon others. Interaction analysis can be undertaken whereby a group activity or meeting is observed and analysed with feedback given to members on their performance and reactions at different stages. Members who persistently reject the ideas of others, are constantly critical, deflate other people or 'withdraw' when they do not receive immediate support may be considered 'unsociable' in group terms and threatening to those who are trying to build motivation through positive behaviour.

Effective team building

Successful teams have a clearly defined purpose and an effective leader. Team building techniques are used to turn a group into a team – to bring together people with a common interest and to help them to identify the most effective way in which their strengths and abilities can be combined to achieve a common objective.

There are three basic ways in which this is usually achieved:

- *Retreats* or 'away days' when the team can concentrate on planning strategy, problem-solving and decision-making, rather than operational issues.

- *Continuous improvement* through review meetings and regular feedback cycles.
- *Outdoor experiences* where the whole team is given a range of problems to solve, usually concerned with problem-solving, coordination, teamwork and communications skills. Team building experts are not as much interested in whether the team achieves the particular objective – of, say, a survival game – but the way in which individual members interact with each other. Some members may be the most vocal – and shout down others who may have better suggestions. Others may have high-level thinking and analytical skills but be wary of putting their views forward for fear of rejection or criticism. Another group may think of good ideas but want to hoard information or resources rather than share them – preferring to have personal success and security rather than put the aims of the team first. The role of the facilitator is to help each member of the team to identify the roles they should play, the roles they can play and the best way to link together – and to encourage a mutually supportive, rather than competitive, ethos. For that reason, one of the most important parts of team building is feedback and analysis of performance.

Many people argue that it is the calibre of leadership that makes a successful team. The team leader should be responsible for removing barriers that prevent people operating effectively and give them ideas for contributing positively and imaginatively. This is not easily achieved. It implies providing practical support, sharing responsibility for performance with the team, and having a clear idea of where the team should be headed. Many teams feel they are not performing adequately when the reality is that no-one ever praises their achievements. In other cases, people rush to put a team together without thinking of the implications. Many people struggle to put team values first if they are used to being rewarded for individual achievement. (Note that leadership skills are discussed in more detail in Chapter 4.)

A study by Dr Adrian Ibbetson of the University of Birmingham and Dr Sue Newell of Warwick Business School found that only participants on the *winning* team are motivated by adventure-based learning experiences. In a study of 160 people they found that the negative feelings experienced by those on a losing team outweighed the positive feelings of those who won. In their view, when teams or departments were sent on courses to compete against one another, this demotivated the losers and destabilised working relationships.

One recommendation was that participants should not be given marks or scores, but feedback on how their individual efforts had contributed to the team's performance. In this case there are no winners and losers and the focus is on the value of improving individual contributions to enhance the team as a whole.

Seeking and exchanging information

The role of communications in developing and maintaining a team cannot be overestimated. Open, clear and frequent communications between members enable:

- information to be distributed, disseminated and evaluated on a regular basis
- team discussions to be carried out positively because team members have developed the skills of
  - listening to others
  - responding constructively
  - supporting others through encouragement, positive 'strokes' and praise
- minor difficulties and differences of opinion to be aired and talked through (to avoid repressed anger which later erupts destructively)
- errors and problems, which could occur through miscommunications or misinformation, to be minimised
- team decisions to be made as rationally as possible based on adequate information.

Communication networks

Teams may operate on a *centralised* basis, where the leader is the hub at the centre of a wheel, or as a *decentralised* unit where members function independently. In this case the network can be drawn as a star where information flows around the group (see Figure 1.2.8).

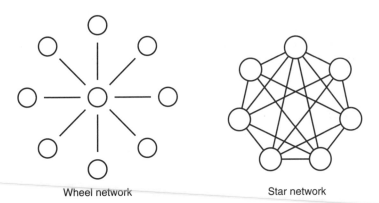

Wheel network   Star network

Figure 1.2.8 Communications networks

Both can be useful in particular circumstances. The wheel is particularly suitable for basic tasks that are easily broken down into small units which can be controlled by the leader, who is responsible for central coordination. Given that the leader is responsible for controlling all the information given to members of the group, this would obviously be unsuitable if the task were complex and there were huge amounts of information to be sifted and considered, as the leader would become overloaded. In this case the star network is more appropriate. Because there is far greater delegation of duties, complicated tasks, difficult problems and complex information flows can be dealt with. The system works because, although no single member knows enough to make a decision alone, *together* the team can operate extremely effectively. This network also results in the greatest satisfaction for members as everyone is involved in the decision-making process.

However, there are problems when a leader tries to manage a team undertaking complex tasks through a wheel network. This can occur when the leader has a strong personal need to control the actions of the members and 'have a finger in every pie'. In this case the flow of information will be slowed down and, when it becomes too great for the leader to cope with, communications are in danger of breaking down completely.

A different type of problem is encountered when a large group divides into subgroups, each of which develops a culture of limiting information to the 'other side'. In this case each subgroup is operating on limited information, which will result in biased discussions. The tendency to compete with the other group fosters antagonism and negative dynamics.

Communications and decision-making

An effective team will obtain information and make decisions through active participation and contribution by all members. An ineffective team will not. However, there are many ways in which decisions can be made, quite apart from a straightforward positive/negative approach. Decisions may be made:

- apathetically or by default or disinterest in a demotivated or non-performing team
- through domination by the leader – this is time-efficient but obviously the leader cannot always be right
- by domination by a subgroup which steamrollers its views past other, less strident or assertive members
- by majority vote (which implies there must be losers)
- by consensus
- through unanimity.

Unanimity, of course, presents the ideal as this means that all agree. However, in reality this is rarely achievable and there will normally be some differences of opinion, even if these are minor. Consensus means that discussion and dissent have been allowed, that the issue has been debated, and that those who dissented have been allowed to make their points and have an opinion. Achieving consensus regularly requires skilled leadership and direction and open communications between team members. A useful strategy for achieving this ideal is given in Figure 1.2.9.

Outline the issue under consideration as fully as possible. Detailed information should be given for study beforehand and be in writing.

- Suggestions and alternatives, amendments and variations should be aired and considered by all.
- Key issues should be debated.
- The strengths and weaknesses of each suggestion should be identified and summarised.
- Disagreements should be allowed, with each person encouraged to respect other people's views and opinions.
- A 'win/win' outcome should be encouraged. Alternatives should be considered if a suggested outcome would result in clear losers.
- The team should be discouraged from trying to curtail any debate artificially (e.g. by bargaining, tossing a coin or by adopting any other shortcuts).
- The leader should encourage participation from everyone, with each suggestion given consideration.
- Perceptions, reasons and assumptions underlying different ideas should be brought out into the open.
- When a final decision is being made, the team should be encouraged to support the issue, not the person.

Figure 1.2.9 Strategies for building consensus

Teams take some time to develop decision-making and consensus-building skills and, even then, if time is at a premium it may not be possible for every single issue to be debated at length. In this case, a pragmatic leader will make routine decisions bearing in mind the overall values and norms of the team, leaving the team itself to debate those which affect its operation more intimately. A range of development exercises have been devised for teams to learn to communicate more effectively and make collective decisions. When undertaking these exercises, it is not so much the final decision that is evaluated for applicability, but the team dynamics and the strategies used to exchange information between team members.

There is obviously a major difference between *giving information* and *consulting* a person for his/her opinion. In fact a range of strategies for giving information or recommendations to a team exist, which range from

a   telling someone to do something
b   'selling' your idea to someone
c   asking someone to comment on your idea (but not expecting radical alterations!)
d   consulting someone, openly, about an issue and asking him or her to comment on your ideas
e   asking someone to come up with the idea him/herself.

It is an interesting fact that, when people are tested on which strategy they would adopt as a leader to a team, they nearly always select either 'tell' (a) or 'sell' (b). However, when they are asked which technique they would prefer their own leader to use they select either consultation (d) or delegation (e). Perhaps we should all ask ourselves why it is that we expect our own bosses to give us more responsibility than we are prepared to give those below us!

Legal and regulatory requirements

The ways in which the law, prescribed regulations and recommended procedures impact upon teamwork obviously vary depending upon the particular team and the area of work in which it is involved. However, some broad generalisations can be made which apply to all teams.

The degree of responsibility and authority enjoyed by self-managed teams puts a clear onus on all members and, particularly, the team leader to ensure that decisions taken are in accordance with the law, particularly in relation to equal opportunities and health and safety.

Teams operate as a unit, with all members directly affected by each other's actions. Unsafe working practices, misuse of equipment or substances, recklessness or simple ignorance of standard procedures will therefore create hazardous working conditions for other members.

Teams involved in hiring and firing their own members may be in grave danger of contravening employment law in relation to issues such as contractual rights, terms and conditions of employment, variation of contracts and termination of contract if they have no means of obtaining specialist advice. Variation of contract may be an issue if greater flexibility is required – for instance through the hire of freelance workers or the issue of short-term or flexible-hours contracts. Termination of contract may be an issue if there is redundancy or dismissal. The factors underlying whether dismissal is justified, summary, unfair or constructive are critical and should be understood by all team leaders. For further discussion see Chapter 2, page 183.

Employment contracts can create problems in relation to areas such as express and implied terms, performance-related pay and team bonuses, appraisal procedures, confidentiality and restraint clauses and disciplinary procedures. Decisions relating to all these areas should be taken only after due consideration of the legal implications.

The inclusion of female team members in traditionally male areas (engineering, chemicals, quantity surveying and construction) may be welcomed by management. However, team leaders and facilitators need to be aware that more traditional views may be held by grassroots team members or on the shopfloor (or its equivalent). All team members should be aware of the legal penalties relating to sex discrimination, victimisation and sexual harassment as well as having an appreciation of the aims and objectives of equal opportunities legislation (see also Element 2.2, page 187 and Element 4.1, page 333).

Multicultural teams are a common feature of many workplaces. Team members may have different methods of working, different attitudes towards sharing and cooperation, and different ways of reacting to conflict purely because they bring different norms and standards to the team. American studies, for instance, found that employees from the Pacific basin had a greater need for peace and harmony and valued consensus more highly than competition. Asian, Indian and Jewish cultures place a high value on networking and family support units. Japanese companies, on the other hand, have an ethos whereby difficulties are not made public (and so they dislike appraisals), coupled with greater deference to 'the boss' (e.g. no-one leaves until after the boss has gone).

Difficulties with multicultural teams can range from simple lack of understanding, through to language barriers and difficulties forming working relationships, and even to full-blown racial harassment and discrimination. Team leaders should be in the business of promoting harmony and understanding through open communications, clear policies on multicultural relations and an appreciation of the values and benefits of promoting multicultural understanding and alliances.

Teams responsible for dealing with customers, making contracts with suppliers and buying and selling goods in general should be aware of consumer legislation which affects their negotiations (Trades Descriptions Act, Sale of Goods Act, Supply of Goods and Services Act, Consumer Protection Act) as well as any legal regulations relating to their specific area of work, such as the Financial Services Act, Property Misdescriptions Act, plus general regulations that constrain other related activities – from advertising codes of practice to environmental considerations. See also Element 4.2 and optional Unit 8.

Other legislation that could further affect the issues team leaders must consider includes the Disability Discrimination Act 1995, which means that appropriate action has to be taken if disabled employees have difficulty carrying out any duties or coping with particular working arrangements. Reasonable adjustments are called for – such as assigning the employee to other duties – before dismissal can be considered. The 1995 Data Protection Directive means that information on employees (including team members) which is kept in structured paper files will be subject to the same constraints and conditions as that kept on computer.

In addition to the legal and regulatory restrictions and requirements, there are obviously standard organisation procedures designed to regulate the work activities carried out by the team. In a large organisation it is likely that these are officially documented for reference and to prevent accidental breach of legal requirements. This may not be the case in smaller organisations and it is then important that outside expertise be sought in relation to areas where disputes may arise. Further information relevant to these areas is given in Chapter 10 of this book.

- Team leaders planning adventure activities for young team members should be aware that the Adventure Activities Licensing Regulations 1996 require that all centres offering training and development activities for under-18s must be licensed.
- Employees at British Nuclear Fuels are involved in monitoring and improving safety through focusing on cross-functional teams reviewing and agreeing the recommended behaviour which should be taking place. Individuals, selected by their team members, are trained to observe their own colleagues and report on unsafe practices.

- Japanese companies in Britain are reviewing their employment and equal opportunities procedures following a series of legal actions taken by British employees. To help, the Commission for Racial Equality is producing a guidance pack for Japanese employers which will include a Japanese translation of the 1984 code of practice for race relations in the workplace and a translation of the EOC's working document on gender.
- City of London regulators are recommending financial penalties for companies whose performance-related bonuses tempt high-flying financial teams to take unacceptable risks and become involved in unethical practices to meet or beat targets. This follows scandals such as the Nick Leeson affair and the discovery of a £50 million black hole by NatWest in its derivatives business.

THEORY INTO PRACTICE

New laws, European directives, regulations and recommendations by watchdogs, consumer bodies and other organisations all mean that legal and regulatory requirements in the workplace are constantly changing.

What changes are taking place in your area of work? Check that you know what these are, how they will affect your role as a team member and/or leader, and whether corresponding changes are being made to working practices and organisational procedures to accommodate them. If not, perhaps you should find out why – and suggest a few amendments yourself!

2 Organise and maintain conditions for productive work

Element 2.1

Maintain productive working conditions

Your own work roles and responsibilities

One leading health and safety writer makes the point that although most managers are employed because of their professional expertise and not their knowledge of health and safety, they still run the risk of *personal* liability, should they contravene any one of the growing number of health and safety regulations in the workplace. Now there's a cheering thought for you!

Health and safety is not a field in which you should choose to practise the art of hands-off management. Even though you may subscribe to the theory of the empowerment of staff in other areas, it is not a theory that works well in this arena. You may find that in your job you not only have a personal responsibility as regards health and safety but also the even more onerous responsibility of ensuring that your staff comply with all the necessary requirements.

It is important, therefore, that you *do* have some knowledge not only of health and safety legislation but also the part you are expected to play in implementing it.

Although your most obvious source of reference as to your responsibilities should be your job description, you may find that any reference to health and safety matters is an indirect one and included in a catch-all phrase such as 'any other duties as may be reasonably required of you'. Moreover, in many organisations there is a two-tiered management system, the first comprising specialist management staff such as the safety officer and other safety-related specialists, and the second, line management staff, all of whose primary responsibilities relate to areas other than health and safety and whose job descriptions reflect this.

Another useful starting point, therefore, may be to examine your organisation's safety policy. Section 2(3) of the Health and Safety at Work Act 1974 (HASAWA) states that except in such cases as may be prescribed (i.e. if an organisation has fewer than five employees) every employer *has a duty* to prepare and, as often as may be appropriate, revise a written statement of his or her general policy with respect to the health and safety at work of his or her employees. In addition, employers must outline the organisation and arrangements in force for carrying out that policy and for bringing it to the attention of all employees.

Ideally the safety policy should be reviewed once a year – two years at the most – unless certain changes make it essential that it be revised more frequently.

Examples include:

- a change in the organisational structure and a consequent change in the responsibilities for health and safety
- changes in processes or operating systems
- changes in the law or regulations relating to health and safety.

Format of the safety policy

The recommended format for a safety policy is:

- the policy statement or statement of intent by the organisation with regard to health and safety
- the responsibilities of various members of the organisation to see that the policy is implemented
- the rules and procedures covering areas such as health and safety training, identification of risk areas, rules for safe systems of work, emergency procedures, accident reporting and investigating, first aid, etc.

The policy statement need only be short, covering the attitude and ethos of the board of directors or equivalent towards health and safety. The second section, however, should be more detailed – and should be the section of which you are fully aware since it is highly likely to have a considerable impact on your own responsibilities. Indeed it should indicate the responsibilities of everyone in the organisation from Managing Director or Chief Executive downwards and especially those of the safety officer or manager. It should also distinguish between the *common* and the *specific* responsibilities of all managers.

Even so you may find that you still do not have a complete description of what you are expected to do and you may have to research further. The most obvious step to take is to consult your senior manager who should be able to give you some practical advice – preferably in written form – as to what he or she expects to be your responsibilities in the field of health and safety. Alternatively you can examine the job description of the safety officer or manager which should contain reference to his or her relationship with line management and what is expected of both parties.

Employers' responsibilities under the HASAWA 1974

Whatever else you do, however, you *must* familiarise yourself with the relevant sections of the HASAWA in respect of the responsibilities of employers.

Section 2(1) outlines the *general duty* of the employer to ensure, 'so far as is reasonably practicable', the health, safety and welfare at work of all his or her employees. Section 2(2) extends this to cover five specific requirements:

● the provision and maintenance of a safe plant and systems of work (s.2(2)(a))
● arrangements for ensuring safety and absence of risks to health in connection with the use, handling, storage and transport of articles and substances (s.2(2)(b))
● the provision of such information, instruction, training and supervision as is necessary to ensure the health and safety at work of the employees (s.2(2)(c))
● as regards any place of work under the employer's control, the maintenance of it in a condition that is safe and without risks to health, and the provision and maintenance of means of access to and egress from it that are safe and without such risks (s.2(2)(d))
● the provision and maintenance of a working environment for employees that is safe, without risk to health and adequate as regards facilities and arrangements for their welfare at work (s.2(2)(e)).

'Practicable' means something more than physically possible. It must be *feasible* – i.e. possible in the light of current knowledge. The word 'reasonably' requires that a comparison be made between the risk of injury (including the severity of any injury which might occur) and the time, trouble and expense of preventative action. If there is a gross disproportion between them, the defence that an employer has done what was reasonably practicable will succeed.

THEORY INTO PRACTICE

Proving that an action was not 'reasonably practicable' involves the production of certain evidence about the risks and costs involved. Suppose, for instance, your employer had not arranged for the provision of notices in all washrooms reminding staff that the water from the taps was extremely hot and one member of staff was scalded. Discuss with your adviser all the additional information you would need before you could try to determine whether or not your employer was in breach of the 'reasonably practicable' requirement.

Employees' responsibilities

Tempting though it may be for you to read the above information and to comfort yourself with the thought that you are not the employer – merely an employee, albeit of managerial or administrative status – it would be potentially dangerous for you to do so. Apart from the obvious fact that as a manager you may be responsible for a group of employees and may therefore be expected to ensure that they comply with health and safety requirements, you also have, as already mentioned, a *personal* responsibility as regards health and safety. This point is emphasised by section 7 of the HASAWA, which states that *every* person in a business is an employee, whatever his or her status, and therefore must comply with the duties set out in the section:

s. 7(a) requires all employees to take reasonable care for their own health and safety at work *and* that of others who may be affected by their acts or omissions

s. 7(b) requires all employees to cooperate with their employer in all the things which he or she does in order to discharge his or her health and safety responsibilities.

In addition section 8 requires all employees not to interfere intentionally or recklessly with or misuse anything provided in the interests of health, safety and welfare.

Section 37 of the HASAWA states that where a breach of the Act is committed with the consent or connivance of, or due to the neglect of any director, manager, secretary or other similar officer, the individual as well as the organisation is to be held guilty. Thus in one case, *Armour v Sheen* [1977] IRLR 105, an HSE inspector prosecuted a senior employee because he had been given the responsibility for drawing up the health and safety policy, but had not done it! It could also, for example, affect a finance director who does not release funding for any necessary safety work.

It is clear, therefore, that if a company commits a health and safety offence and the blame for the breach is found to be that of a director or manager, the individual concerned may be indicted, whether or not proceedings are taken against the company.

Responsibilities towards non-employees

If you work in a managerial capacity in an area in which not only employees but also other types of worker are employed, or one to which there are a number of visitors, you cannot exclude these people from your ambit of responsibility. Section 3 of the Act requires employers to ensure that persons *not* in their employment (including the self-employed) are not adversely affected by their operations.

Non-employees normally fall into one of the following categories:

- business callers such as sales representatives, prospective customers
- members of the general public such as people seeking work at job centres, making enquiries at the town hall, waiting for a job interview, etc.
- contractors carrying out work on the premises (including people engaged in such areas as window cleaning, photocopier repair, maintenance of washroom facilities, etc.)

- people living in the proximity of the premises who might be affected by noise, atmospheric pollution, smell, etc.

Again, the guide is what could be considered to be reasonably practicable action for an employer to take in such circumstances.

> Recently one supermarket was fined £4000 over an accident which occurred in one of its car parks. The person injured was not an employee or a customer but a two-year-old boy who was thrown out of his mother's trolley when a wheel caught in a rut in the car park's surface. Section 3 of the HASAWA was held to apply.

THEORY INTO PRACTICE

There is a distinct legal difference between an 'employee' and a 'worker' (normally, but not always a self-employed person), the first being considered to be employed under a 'contract of service' and the second under a 'contract for services'. Although both the self-employed and employees have certain legal rights, health and safety being one of them, in general employees enjoy greater protection. Determining the nature of your employment status can therefore assume some importance.

(At this point you may want to refer to the THEORY INTO PRACTICE exercise on page 755 of Chapter 10, *Facilitate compliance with legal and regulatory requirements*, if you want to research this item more fully.)

> When temporary staff are required to cover for holidays, staff absences, etc., the temporary nature of the arrangements often means that they are overlooked when it comes to health and safety requirements. However, Regulation 13 of the *Management of Health and Safety at Work Regulations* 1992 (MHSW) now requires that all temporary staff, whether engaged directly by the employer or through an agency, must also receive all the necessary information about the health and safety arrangements, the risks associated with the work and the measures taken to ameliorate them in the premises where they will be working.

THEORY INTO PRACTICE

You are in charge of the public relations section of the Marketing department and are becoming increasingly concerned about your health and safety responsibilities towards certain groups of non-employees. There are

- groups of visitors who arrive each week to tour the factory. This is of particular concern to you in that last week, one visitor wandered off on his own, lost contact with the main party, and was not accounted for when the fire alarm went off and the building had to be evacuated (fortunately it was a false alarm on this occasion)
- ex-employees who call in occasionally for a chat with their former colleagues.

Bearing in mind that you do not necessarily want (nor are you able) to exclude entirely all these people from entering the premises, consider in each case what corrective action should be taken to ensure that the requirements of the HASAWA are met.

Contractors

Notwithstanding the problems which can occur with the types of visitor described in the last THEORY INTO PRACTICE section, by far the greatest problems tend to be created by the employment of contractors.

It has been clearly established by case law that an employer cannot discharge his or her health and safety responsibility to a contractor simply by informing that contractor of the organisation's health and safety rules and arrangements. He or she must ensure that the contractor is complying with the safety policy and that any subcontractors brought on to the site by the main contractor are similarly trained and briefed.

> The only circumstance where the above principle does not apply is where the contractor is carrying out his or her contract in a separate, secured and delineated area to which only his or her employees have automatic right of access and egress and where the staff of the client (i.e. the organisation) may enter only by appointment and by 'signing in' as visitors. Even then, access to and from the defined site by the contractor and those delivering goods must be over roads which have been assigned exclusively to the contractor for the duration of the contract and are not shared with the client, his or her employees or carriers delivering goods to the client.

Significant problem areas

If, therefore, your work role includes responsibility for the work of contractors, you should be particularly aware of the additional problems they may cause you.

- The contractor's workforce may be inadequately supervised and not therefore confined to one area of the building.
- The contractor's workforce may not feel the same commitment (or fear of being found out!) as do the rest of the staff. This may partially be caused by the fact that they feel they are treated as 'second class citizens'.
- Although you have briefed the contractor, he or she may fail to brief subcontractors on the health and safety requirements of the organisation.

Different organisations take different approaches to these problems. However, it is common practice – particularly in cases where contractors are used frequently – for an organisation to produce a handbook for contractors which covers all relevant health and safety matters about which the contractor should be aware while working on the premises. Some organisations go a step further and require every contractor's employee or subcontractor to be given a copy. In organisations where the use of contractors is less frequent, an abbreviated form of the handbook (possibly comprising a pocket-sized card or booklet) is often used.

What is equally important is that if you are the administrator responsible for overseeing the work of the contractor you should avoid the temptation to distance yourself from the work being carried out. It is difficult and obviously unwise, of course, for you as a non-specialist to give detailed instructions to the contractor about the way in which the work should be done, but you should be prepared to institute certain checks.

- If the contractor has been asked to provide a 'method statement' at the tender qualification stage, you should check it regularly to see that what was promised is, in fact, being implemented.
- You might either wish to assume the role of 'contract coordinator' through which all information relating to the contract is channelled, or delegate the job to someone else who will report back regularly to you on any problems.
- Most contracts make provision for the contractor to provide all the necessary tools and materials. However, in the event of a request to borrow any items of equipment, you should ensure that the loan is accompanied by a clear statement from an appropriate member of your organisation that at the time of the loan the item was safe, properly maintained and suitable for the purposes for which it was going to be used.

Legal and regulatory requirements relating to working conditions

The law relating to health and safety is extensive. The major statutes are supplemented by a larger number of statutory instruments or regulations, each of which tends to concentrate on a particular area of health and safety. In addition, the common law imposes a duty of care upon employers and employees. (For further general information about common law, statutes and statutory instruments – and also how to find relevant case law information – see Chapter 10, *Facilitate compliance with legal and regulatory requirements*).

Legal requirements – non-statutory (or common law)

Most common law cases relating to health and safety are to be found in the area of civil law known as the tort of negligence, under which an employer has a duty of care arising out of his or her position as employer and as owner or controller of premises. The elements which have to be present are:

- a legal duty of care owed by one person to another
- a breach of that duty by the person owing it resulting in damage to the person to whom the duty is owed.

Duty of care

The meaning of the duty of care is well illustrated in a long-established case, *Donoghue v Stevenson* [1932] AER 159 (HL), in which a company manufactured ginger beer, in one bottle of which a snail was discovered by the eventual consumer. The ginger beer was sold to a retailer who in turn sold it to a person who gave the ginger beer to a friend. As the bottle was opaque it was impossible for anyone other than the eventual consumer to discover the partly decomposed snail. The friend discovered the snail on drinking the beer and was made seriously ill. The House of Lords held that the manufacturer owed a duty of care to anyone he could *reasonably foresee* would be likely to be injured by drinking the ginger beer, if he failed to take sufficient precautions against harmful matter entering the bottle; i.e.

'persons who are so closely and directly affected by my act that I ought reasonably to have them in contemplation as being so affected'.

He, therefore, owed a duty of care to the friend.

THEORY INTO PRACTICE

The following cases both dealt with the question of the existence of the duty of care. Try to determine in each case whether or not you think a duty of care existed. Check your answers by looking up the judgements in the actual cases (or if you are short of time, check the answers on page 190).

- A crane manufacturer sold a crane to certain builders whose expert was under the obligation of assembling the crane. The expert, finding that a cogwheel was inaccurate, marked it to show the inaccuracy but proceeded to use the crane. As a result of the discovered fault he was killed. His widow brought an action alleging negligence by the manufacturers of the crane. (*Farr v Butters Bros* [1932] 2 KB 606)
- A taxi driver carelessly reversed his taxi in the road and ran over a little boy's tricycle whereupon the little boy screamed. His mother, who was in an upstairs room of a nearby house, heard him scream, ran to the window and saw the tricycle under the taxi. The sight caused her shock and made her ill. She sued the taxi driver. (*King v Phillips* [1952] 2 AER 459)

Interesting to note is that the concept that a person owes a duty of care only where it could be 'reasonably foreseen' that a negligent act would cause damage to a certain person, mirrors the statutory concept that employers are responsible for ensuring the health, safety and welfare of their employees only 'so far as is reasonably practicable'. In neither case is an absolute liability imposed.

Breach of duty

Once the duty of care has been established, the injured party (the plaintiff) must show that the other party (the defendant) has broken his duty of care, the test normally used being to balance the magnitude of the risk of injury against the importance of the object to be achieved and the measures taken to prevent injury. In one case, for instance, a garage hand, who, to the knowledge of his employers, had only one good eye, injured this eye at work underneath a vehicle. No protective goggles had been supplied to him nor was it usual in the trade at that time to supply them. The likelihood of the eye being injured was not great but the consequences of the injury were very great, and therefore the magnitude of the risk was considerable. Unsurprisingly, therefore, it was held that the employers were liable – particularly since the measures necessary to prevent injury were slight (the provision of goggles).

THEORY INTO PRACTICE

How do you think the decision may have differed if the employer had *not* been aware of the incapacity of the worker (and he had taken steps to conceal that fact from them)?

More modern cases extend the duty still further. In *Crouch v British Rail Engineering Ltd* [1988] IRLR 404, for instance, it was held that the duty of care was not fulfilled by making safety goggles available for collection from a point about five minutes away, as it was considered that this lack of immediate availability encouraged risks to be taken. In *Pape v Cumbria County Council* [1991] IRLR 463, even though the employers provided gloves for cleaners handling chemical cleaning materials, it was held that the duty of care went beyond this and extended to warning the cleaners about handling such materials with unprotected hands.

Statutory legal requirements

Chapter 10, entitled *Facilitate compliance with legal and regulatory requirements*, outlines the difficulties of total reliance upon common or case law as a legal source and the consequent necessity for more responsive and adaptable statutory legislation.

One major Act, the Health and Safety at Work Act, has already been referred to in some detail (see page 109). This was promulgated partly as the result of some difficulties which were being experienced with existing health and safety statutes such as the now repealed Offices, Shops and Railway Premises Act 1963 (OSRPA). Although the provisions of OSRPA were extremely specific, it nevertheless indirectly allowed the unscrupulous or careless employer to fulfil the letter rather than the spirit of the law. For instance, it provided that floors and steps had to be washed at least once a week. In reality a workplace which is cleaned only once a week is not likely to provide too healthy an environment, but there could be little legal comeback on an employer who insisted on doing just that. What also caused some concern was the fact that if a health, safety or welfare problem had *not* been specifically mentioned in the Act, again there was some difficulty in proving that there had been a breach of the law.

The HASAWA therefore tried to avoid both these problems by setting out the duties of employers in broad terms only (look back to page 109 to remind yourself of the contents of s.2). If, therefore, an employee now complains that the workplace is so dirty that it is becoming a health hazard, the employer can no longer rely for a defence on the fact that the floors are cleaned once a week, but must instead try to prove that he or she has not contravened s.2(2)(a) (the provision and maintenance of plant and systems that are safe and without risks to health) *or* s.2(2)(e) (the provision and maintenance of a working environment for employees that is without risk to health and adequate as regards facilities and arrangements for their welfare at work).

THEORY INTO PRACTICE

Most of the statutory legislation is monitored by the HSE. What is the HSE? Practise your research skills by finding out as much as you can about this organisation and its responsibilities.

Regulatory requirements

Workplace (Health, Safety and Welfare) Regulations 1992

The health and safety regulations brought in to comply with EU directives give additional protection. The Workplace (Health, Safety and Welfare) Regulations, for instance, attempt to give the employees the best of both worlds! They supplement the HASAW, which allows employees a very wide discretion as to what health, safety and welfare issues they can raise, but they also encompass some of the best features of the two previous Acts by laying down specific regulations in certain instances – normally in areas in which, traditionally, problems have arisen. Figure 2.1.1 gives a summary of the main provisions as supplemented by their associated approved codes of practice.

Figure 2.1.1 Extracts from the Workplace (Health, Safety and Welfare) Regulations 1992 (HSW)

Regulation 5: Maintenance of workplace, and of equipment, devices and systems
Workplace and equipment must be properly maintained and kept in efficient working order, in good repair and properly cleaned. A suitable system of maintenance should include – regular maintenance; isolation and prompt attention to defective equipment; confirmation that regular maintenance routines are carried out properly.

Regulation 6: Ventilation
Although concerned with the provision of sufficient fresh or purified air to every enclosed workplace, this regulation recognises that for some industries or processes such provision may not be possible without affecting the process or product. In these cases, workers involved should have adequate breaks in a well-ventilated area.

Regulation 7: Temperature in indoor workplaces
The regulation calls for reasonable temperatures inside buildings, during working hours, demands that no heating system shall cause fumes, gas or vapour to enter workplaces where this might be injurious or cause offence, and requires sufficient thermometers to be available to enable staff to check the temperature. Workroom temperatures should be at least 16°C, or 13°C where the work being done demands severe physical effort.

Figure 2.1.1 Extracts from the Workplace (HSW) Regulations – *continued*

Regulation 8: Lighting

Every workplace shall have suitable and sufficient lighting which should, whenever reasonably practicable, be natural light. Suitable and sufficient emergency lighting must be provided in every workroom where its absence would give rise to dangers to those working there in the event that the artificial light failed.

Regulation 9: Cleanliness and waste materials

Every workplace and its furniture and fittings must be kept 'sufficiently' clean, and, as far as is reasonably practicable, waste material must not be allowed to accumulate, except in suitable receptacles. Where it is not possible to provide suitable receptacles, waste materials must be removed from workplaces at least once a day. There should be a procedure to deal promptly with spillages of all kinds and the method of cleaning should not create health and safety risks – e.g. the misuse of substances as cleaning materials.

Regulation 10: Room dimensions and space

There must be sufficient floor area, height and circulation space to allow work procedures to take place without compromising health, safety and welfare.

Regulation 11: Workstation and seating

The proper ergonomic arrangement of the workstation is required, together with protection from adverse weather when reasonably practicable, the facility to leave the workstation quickly in an emergency and elimination of the danger of slipping and falling. Where work can be done in a seated position a suitable seat must be provided. Such seating is not acceptable unless it is suitable for the person for whom it is provided as well as for the operations performed and a suitable footrest is provided where needed. Note: ergonomics in relation to work with display screen equipment is covered by the Health and Safety (Display Screen Equipment) Regulations 1992. See further page 133.

Regulation 12: Floors and traffic routes

Ideally all floors and traffic routes should be non-slip, without holes or slopes and have sufficient drainage where necessary. They must be kept free from obstructions and from anything which might cause persons to slip, trip or fall.

Regulation 13: Falls or falling objects

Wherever possible, tanks, pits or structures containing dangerous substances, where there is a risk that persons might fall into them, must be securely covered or fenced as must any traffic route over, across or in them. Note that the measures must be taken in addition to the provision of personal protective equipment (PPE) and information, instruction, training and supervision. See further page 133.

Regulation 14: Windows and transparent or translucent doors, gates and walls

Every window or other transparent or translucent surface in a wall or partition or door or gate must, where necessary for reasons of health or safety, be of safety material to protect it from breakage and be appropriately marked so as to make its presence apparent.

Regulation 15: Windows, skylights and ventilators

No window, skylight or ventilator should be capable of opening, closing or adjusting in such a way as to risk the health and safety of the person performing these operations, or when it is open.

Figure 2.1.1 Extracts from the Workplace (HSW) Regulations – *continued*

Regulation 16: Ability to clean windows safely

All windows and skylights must be of a design or construction capable of safe cleaning. 'Suitable provision' should be made for windows and skylights to be cleaned if this cannot be done from the ground or another suitable surface.

Regulation 17: Organisation of traffic routes

Every workplace must be organised so that pedestrians and vehicles can circulate safely. The routes must be suitable for the persons or vehicles using them, be sufficient in number and of adequate size. Pedestrian or vehicle routes must be capable of being used without causing danger to persons at work near them and must be suitably indicated.

Regulation 18: Doors and gates

Doors and gates must be suitably constructed, including being fitted with any necessary safety devices.

Regulation 19: Escalators and moving walkways

These must function safely and be equipped with the necessary safety devices; they must also be fitted with one or more emergency stop controls which are easily identifiable and readily accessible.

Regulation 20: Sanitary conveniences

Suitable and sufficient sanitary conveniences must be provided at readily accessible places. They will not be suitable unless the rooms containing them are adequately lit and ventilated, they are kept in a clean and orderly condition and separate rooms are provided for men and women except where it is possible to lock the conveniences from inside.

Regulation 21: Washing facilities

The basic requirements are running hot and cold or warm water and washing stations large enough to facilitate effective washing of the face, hands and forearms. Showers or baths should also be provided where the work is particularly strenuous, dirty or results in contamination of the skin by harmful or offensive materials.

Regulation 22: Drinking water

An adequate supply of wholesome drinking water must be made available for all employees. It must be readily accessible at suitable places and be clearly marked by an appropriate sign where necessary. A sufficient supply of suitable cups or other drinking vessels must be provided, unless the supply is from a jet or fountain which people can use easily. Where the type used are non-disposable, a facility for washing them should be located nearby.

Regulation 23: Accommodation for clothing

Suitable and sufficient accommodation for clothing must be provided for any workers' clothing which is not worn during working hours and for special clothing which is worn by a person at work but which is not taken home.

Regulation 24: Facilities for changing clothing

Suitable and sufficient facilities must be provided for any employee who has to wear special clothing for work, and cannot, for reasons of propriety, be expected to change in another room. There must also be separate changing facilities for men and women if this is required.

Figure 2.1.1 Extracts from the Workplace (HSW) Regulations – *continued*

Regulation 25: Facilities for rest and to eat meals
Suitable and sufficient rest facilities should be provided at readily accessible places. The rest facilities must include suitable facilities to eat meals where food eaten in the workplace would otherwise be likely to become contaminated and where meals are regularly eaten in the workplace. They must include suitable arrangements in rest rooms and areas to protect non-smokers from the discomfort caused by tobacco smoke. They must include suitable rest facilities for pregnant women.

THEORY INTO PRACTICE

1 Ascertain whether there is a copy of the Workplace (HSW) Regulations together with the associated code of practice in use in your organisation and, if so, who is responsible for overseeing their implementation. Try to determine what your responsibility is as regards their implementation in your own work area. (If, for some reason, your organisation does not have a copy, write to HSE Books, PO Box 199, Sudbury, Suffolk CO10 6FS for a list of their priced publications and free leaflets).

2 Check also to see whether any adjustments have been made (and if so, what they are) to your working environment to comply with the regulations.

Use the information you have obtained to assist you to complete the following THEORY INTO PRACTICE exercise.

THEORY INTO PRACTICE

1 One of the criticisms of the Factories Act and the Offices, Shops and Railway Premises Act is that they were too detailed. Consider whether or not the same criticism could be levelled at the Workplace (HSW) Regulations.

2 One management writer points out that two factors militate against safe cleaning of windows and glass in many buildings:
   – finding a safe way to do the job particularly where the building is modern and incorporates many more windows than perhaps an older building may
   – the attitude of some window cleaners who, owing to tight schedules, may be under pressure to get the job done quickly regardless of safety requirements.

   Consider:

   a what, if any, action your organisation takes to try to solve these problems and how far, in your opinion, it is successful, or

   b if (a) is inapplicable, what action *you* would suggest should be taken in such circumstances.

3 Regulation 17 requires that every workplace should be organised so that pedestrians and vehicles can circulate safely. The car park at your workplace is rather small and your senior manager is concerned that the organisation's lorries are being reversed in and out of it rather carelessly. Consider the suggestions you might make for improving the situation. Note: you may wish to refer to *Road Transport in Factories and Similar Workplaces* (HSE).

Organise and maintain conditions for productive work   119

Management of Health and Safety at Work Regulations 1992

At least of equal if not greater importance to both employers and workers are the Management of Health and Safety at Work Regulations 1992. Whereas the other regulations (including the Workplace (HSW) Regulations) deal with *specific* aspects of health and safety, the MHSW spans a range of requirements which relate to the management and organisation for health and safety in the workforce. Not only does it complement the HASAWA, it also contains additional – new – requirements. Figure 2.1.2 contains a brief outline of them.

Figure 2.1.2 Extract from the Management of Health and Safety at Work Regulations 1992

Regulation 3: Risk assessment

This regulation requires that a 'risk assessment' be carried out by every employer and self-employed person if the enterprise employs five or more people. The risk assessment should address significant risks inherent in the enterprise which might affect employees or other people, the objective being, of course, to ensure that suitable measures are taken to protect those likely to be exposed to risk. (This regulation will be discussed in more detail in the section on ways of maintaining compliance with requirements for working conditions on page 121.)

Regulation 4: Health and safety arrangements

This is largely a repeat of s.2(3) of the HASAWA; i.e. a duty to produce a health and safety policy.

Regulation 5: Health surveillance

The employer must ensure that employees are provided with health surveillance appropriate to the risks to their health and safety (as identified by risk assessment).

Regulation 6: Health and safety assistance

This calls for the appointment of one or more 'competent' persons to assist the employer in the discharge of his or her statutory health duties. They may either be employees or consultants. Until this regulation was enacted there was no statutory duty to appoint safety officers (or advisers as they are now normally called) except for some aspects of construction.

Regulation 7: Procedures for serious and imminent danger

This calls for a reappraisal of an employer's existing emergency arrangements which must, of course, take account of the conclusions of the risk assessment exercise carried out to comply with Regulation 3. (Again, this regulation will be discussed in more detail on page 121.)

Regulation 8: Information for employees

Employees (including trainees and those on fixed-term contracts) must be given clear and comprehensible information on all health and safety risks and mitigating measures adopted by the employer.

Regulation 9: Cooperation and coordination

The objective here is to ensure that where two or more employers share a workplace, either permanently or on a temporary basis, there is cooperation and coordination on all health and safety related matters. These will include emergency evacuation and the disclosure by each employer to the other of any aspects of their operations which could give rise to danger.

Figure 2.1.2 Extract from MHSW Regulations – *continued*

Regulation 10: Persons working in host employers' or self-employed persons' undertakings

Employers and the self-employed must provide the employer of any person who may come to work in their premises with complete and comprehensible information about any risks that may exist in the premises and of the measures that they have taken to deal with these risks.

Regulation 11: Capabilities and training

This is a permutation of the existing law which requires employers to provide sufficient information, instruction, training and supervision as is necessary to ensure, so far as is reasonably practicable, the health and safety at work of their employees.

Regulation 12: Employees' duties

These equate to but also amplify ss.7 and 8 of HASAWA.

Regulation 13: Temporary workers

Refer back to page 111 for further details.

THEORY INTO PRACTICE

1 Research the *precise* wording of ss.7 and 8 of the HASAWA (which is quite concise) which outline the health and safety responsibilities of employees and also of Regulation 12 of the MHSW (which is far longer), and consider the version you prefer. Consider also any difficulties you think there may be in interpreting Regulation 12.

2 Regulation 11 requires employers to take account of the *capabilities* of their employees as regards health and safety when entrusting tasks to them. Assuming that you are asked to allocate such tasks to a group of your staff, think about how you would match up the task with the individual to ensure a successful result.

Monitoring compliance with requirements for working conditions

Risk assessment

The deputy director general of the Health and Safety Executive recently made the point that

'Assessing risks is an everyday activity. In the workplace, it is a common sense check of what could harm people and whether enough safeguards are in place. Many businesses see risk assessment as an end in itself rather than as a tool for managing health and safety better and controlling losses.'

This comment came as part of a response to concerns expressed by many employers about the additional work (and consequent expense) caused by the introduction of the EU-originated health and safety regulations, and in particular by Regulation 3 of the MHSW which required a risk assessment of the workplace to be carried out by employers.

In reality, many employers had already carried out many of the measures required in order to comply with other health and safety legislation such as the Control of Substances Hazardous to Health Regulations 1994 (COSHH) or the Manual Handling Operations Regulations 1992 (MHO). (For further details see pages 135 and 141.) Moreover, those employers who had an effective health and safety policy in operation would also have carried out such assessments automatically.

Even so the emphasis placed on risk assessment has meant that many employers have had to re-examine the methods they use or, somewhat belatedly, set up systems to begin such an exercise.

Identification of risks

The focus of the exercise should not necessarily be on every possible contingency but rather on risks that could reasonably be expected to arise given that every business has different types of risk to consider. Some organisations rank possible risks in terms of (a) probability and (b) seriousness and attach a 'low', 'medium' or 'high' risk factor to each of them. They then use the information to determine what measures should be taken to mitigate the effects of accidents and emergencies.

Other methods of calculating risk include giving numeric values to seriousness and probability and multiplying the two in order to determine where the most effort is needed to reduce the risks. More simply, an examination of past accident records, whether of the organisation or relating to the industry as a whole, can give some indication of the types, frequency and seriousness of certain risks within the workplace or over a wider area.

> Some industry groups and trade or professional associations might be of assistance in producing risk tables for their members.

THEORY INTO PRACTICE

The Health and Safety (Young Persons) Regulations 1997 now require employers to assess particular risks to young persons they employ. Obtain a copy of the HSE publication *Young People at Work: A Guide for Employers* to check how, if at all, these regulations will affect your own workplace. Consider also what additional steps you might have to take when dealing with the risks associated with particular worker groups such as lone workers or new starters.

Health and safety monitoring

It is relatively easy to *introduce* procedures to ensure compliance with legal regulations. It is less easy to ensure that those procedures are followed.

Monitoring health and safety is as much part of an employer's legal duties as is any initial compliance with the law. Indeed it has been argued that the principle of assigning tasks to named individuals followed by appropriate checks at regular intervals on those individuals is the *key* factor in ensuring that there has been compliance with health and safety legislation. In many organisations, for instance, there is a named representative on the Board of Directors or in the senior management team, whose responsibility it is to ensure that the safety policy is being implemented and to report back regularly to the group. He or she in turn normally has the power to name particular staff within the organisation to carry out certain tasks and report progress at regular intervals.

> Regulation 4(1) of MHSW requires every employer to make and give effect to such arrangements as are appropriate, having regard to the nature of his or her activities and size of business, for the effective planning, organisation, monitoring and review of the various health and safety measures which are in place.

Self-certification

One method of keeping health and safety an ongoing issue, and to ensure that there is regular feedback up the chain of command, is to adopt a self-certification approach which is carried out at regular intervals and which normally involves requiring individual managers to complete a questionnaire affirming that certain action has been taken and checks carried out. It has the effect of keeping the manager's mind focused on health and safety and consequently that of his or her staff. However, it can cause certain problems.

THEORY INTO PRACTICE

Consider how you might try to solve the following problems if you were the safety adviser in charge of the self-certification audit.

1 Managers who tend to be evasive, such as one who, in answer to the question 'is every member of your staff aware of the new Health and Safety (Display Screen Equipment) Regulations?' replies 'a copy of the regulations is displayed prominently on each departmental noticeboard'.
2 Managers who use the questionnaire as a vehicle for expressing their own personal grievances or hobby-horses.
3 Managers who leave certain parts of the questionnaire uncompleted on the grounds that 'it doesn't apply to them'.
4 Managers who affirm that certain actions are being carried out by their staff when your personal knowledge (from overhearing a conversation between their staff in the lift) tells you that this is not the case.

Methods of monitoring

A quick dash round the department the day before you have to complete a questionnaire or write a report about health and safety, accompanied by sporadic outbursts of temper each time you see a safety rule being disregarded, is not the best example of management expertise in this area, even though it might solve the immediate problem. It is far better to adopt a more systematic approach.

- Make certain that your staff have been equipped with sufficient information to enable them to carry out their work in accordance with health, safety and welfare requirements.

Organise and maintain conditions for productive work

- Alert them to the fact that periodic checks will be carried out and a written report sent to a senior manager. Interesting to note at this point is two schools of thought – one in favour of giving staff forewarning of any checks to be made, and the other in favour of unexpected random checks. Both have obvious advantages and disadvantages.
- Ensure that any reports you have to prepare for senior managers are planned in advance and forwarded at the correct time.
- Ensure that any reports you expect to receive from any of your staff are similarly planned and forwarded. In many cases a team approach is useful whereby each member of staff is allocated a particular monitoring task according to his or her expertise and the feedback report then becomes a group exercise.
- Take time at the end of each process to brief staff on the results of the report and to involve them in preparing an action plan in response to its findings.

The safety adviser

Health and safety now assumes such considerable significance that internal checks alone are insufficient to meet current legislative requirements. Section 2 of the HASAW put emphasis on the inclusion in the safety policy of the organisational arrangements for carrying out the policy, but did not extend that requirement to encompass the need for a safety officer or adviser. However, Regulation 6 of the MHSW makes it clear that such a person must be appointed, paragraph 3 stating that 'the employer shall ensure that the number of persons appointed ... and the time available to them to fulfil their functions and the means at their disposal are adequate having regard to the size of his undertaking, the risks to which his employees are exposed and the distribution of those risks throughout his undertaking.'

No other guidance is given and it is therefore up to the employer to decide more specifically who to appoint and the type of duties and responsibilities to be allocated to him or her. Obviously, however, it is essential that the monitoring of compliance with safety requirements forms a significant part of his or her role. See Figure 2.1.3 for a sample job description.

- To be the company adviser on all matters relating to health and safety
- To give advance warning to senior management of any impending changes to health and safety legislation
- To advise on health and safety training
- To carry out safety inspections
- To ensure compliance with statutory reporting requirements
- To investigate accidents/incidents
- To act as the company liaison officer with all external safety bodies
- To maintain and update the company safety policy and to ensure the dissemination of its contents to all staff
- To organise and act as secretary to the company safety committee

---

Figure 2.1.3 Duties of the safety adviser

Given that safety advisers often have to make critical reports to the board of directors or Chief Executive – sometimes about the activity or non-activity of a senior manager – their position may become untenable particularly if that senior manager has some influence over their career prospects or could prove awkward when asked for resources, etc. Consider how the board or Chief Executive might try to overcome this problem.

The safety committee and safety representatives

In large organisations, even a full-time safety adviser will have difficulty in fulfilling all his or her functions without any assistance. Much depends on company policy as to the numbers of administrative staff made available to assist the adviser, but what may also assist him or her is the establishment of a safety committee and the appointment of a number of safety representatives.

Article 11 of the EC Framework Directive (89/391/EEC) places emphasis on worker consultation and collaboration over health and safety requirements by establishing the principle of consultation with workers together with their right (and/or the right of their representatives) to make health and safety proposals.

The Safety Representatives and Safety Committees Regulations 1977 (SRSC); and the Health and Safety (Consultation with Employees) Regulations 1996

In this context the requirements of both the above sets of regulations assume some importance. The 1977 regulations are binding upon companies having recognised trade unions and allow trade unions to appoint safety representatives from among the employer's workforce where one or more of their members are employed. Normally the appointed representative must have been in the employ of the company for two years or must have had two years' experience of similar work. Exceptions include a newly established employer or workplace, where the work is of short duration or where there is a high labour turnover.

Useful though these regulations are, they do not cover the considerable number of organisations with no recognised trade unions. The 1996 Regulations remedy the situation to a certain extent, however, by requiring employers to consult all employees not already represented by trades-union safety representatives. In this case every size of organisation is covered irrespective of activity or status.

Functions of safety representatives

The major function of the safety representative is to represent employees in consultations with the employer and to ensure the health, safety and welfare of those employees in such consultations. See Figure 2.1.4 for further details.

- To investigate potential hazards and dangerous occurrences at the workplace whether or not these are drawn to their attention by the workers they represent
- To examine the causes of accidents at the workplace
- To investigate complaints by any employee represented relating to that employee's health, safety or welfare at work
- To make representations to the employer about matters arising from the above or in respect of any other health, safety and welfare matters relating to the workplace
- To carry out inspections at the workplace
- To represent employees when consulting HSE inspectors or any other enforcing authority and to receive information from such inspectors
- To attend meetings of safety committees

Figure 2.1.4 (above) Functions of safety representatives

The *liability* of safety representatives in respect of any health and safety requirement is no greater than that of any other employee. Although they are allowed to undertake a number of functions which their employers must permit, they are not legally obliged to carry out any of them, nor are they criminally liable in respect of the performance of any of them.

Safety inspections

Of prime importance is the safety representatives' role in taking part in inspection of the premises. They must do this:

- at least once every three months after having informed the employer in writing
- where there has been a substantial change in working conditions
- where there has been a notifiable accident or dangerous occurrence.

- Safety representatives are entitled to inspect and take copies of any documents relevant to their enquiries subject to the following limitations:
    - where national security or a statutory prohibition is involved
    - where an individual would be identified (unless the individual agrees)
    - where the information is not relevant to health, safety or welfare or would cause substantial injury to the employer's undertaking
    - where the information was obtained for the purpose of any legal proceedings.
- The *Code of Practice on Time Off for Training of Safety Representatives* requires that safety representatives should undertake basic training provided by the union as soon as possible after appointment. The training should be approved by the TUC or the independent trade union to which the safety representative belongs, and there should be further training for any special responsibilities or changes in legislation or work circumstances. A safety representative may complain to an industrial tribunal if refused reasonable time off or refused pay for such time off.

Safety committees

One of the usual responsibilities of the safety adviser is to act as secretary to the safety committee (although he or she does not automatically qualify for membership of the committee). The safety committee itself must be established by an employer within three months of being requested to do so in writing by at least two recognised safety representatives. Its terms of reference should also be agreed through joint negotiation and, once agreed, should be included as an appendix to the company's safety policy.

To be at their most effective safety committees should

- be as compact as possible provided the interests of both management and employees are adequately represented
- not allow management numbers to exceed those of employees
- include all relevant areas
- allow certain specialists to be *ex officio* members and others to be co-opted as the need arises.

Its functions are again a matter for negotiation, although Figure 2.1.5 gives a broad outline of the type of functions most commonly included in the terms of reference.

- To investigate and report on accidents/incidents
- To study health and safety reports/statistics/trends on a wider basis than merely the workplace so that relevant comparisons can be made
- To review health and safety audit reports
- To draw up works rules and instructions on safe systems of work
- To oversee health and safety training
- To promote and advise on publicity measures in relation to health and safety
- To maintain links with external health and safety bodies
- To recommend updates to the company safety policy
- To consider and advise on impending legislation

Figure 2.1.5 Functions of the safety committee

Safety inspectors

Monitoring compliance with health and safety requirements is not only an internal process. External monitoring is also carried out by HSE-appointed safety inspectors whose powers are outlined in Figure 2.1.6. As a consequence, any employer who makes either no or only minimal health and safety arrangements runs the risk of incurring certain penalties should an inspector visit the premises and find that health and safety legislation has been breached.

- To enter premises at reasonable times or at any time where there is danger
- To make examinations and inspections
- To take samples
- To take possession of articles and substances
- To take measurements and photographs
- To make recordings
- To have something tested, removed or dismantled
- To require that certain areas be left undisturbed
- To obtain information and receive answers to questions
- To inspect and copy any entry in documents required to be kept by statute

Figure 2.1.6 Powers of HSE Inspectors

In terms of local authority enforcement, the principal role is performed by district councils and usually by the department which has an environmental health function. In addition, enforcement in relation to such activities as petroleum licensing, certain explosives including fireworks, and the packaging and labelling of dangerous substances in consumer premises, is normally carried out by trading standards officers or fire authorities as appropriate. If, however, there is any doubt about whether enforcement is in the hands of the HSE or a local authority (or which local authority) employers can check with the enforcement liaison officer for the appropriate HSE area.

Prior to the promulgation of the HASAWA, certain employers might have been tempted to take a chance that the then members of the inspectorate would be so overstretched that they would never happen to visit their premises. Given the establishment of safety committees and the role of the safety representatives, which includes that of liaison with external health and safety bodies, any negligence on the part of the employer can now be reported direct to the inspector who will then invariably visit the premises.

Consequences of non-compliance with requirements

There is never an action without a consequence! Modern business managers are used to taking calculated risks in most areas of their work – otherwise they lose the competitive edge. However, admirable though that attitude may be in most activities which they undertake, it is positively dangerous to adopt the same approach towards health and safety. The penalties which attach to non-compliance with health and safety legislation are becoming increasingly draconian and can lead to sanctions imposed by not only civil but also criminal law. The prospect of a spell in even the best-run open prison should be sufficient to deter most managers from flouting health and safety rules.

Offences attracting sanctions

The HASAWA sets out clearly what are considered to be breaches of its requirements:

- failure to comply with the general duties of the Act (ss 2–7) (if necessary, look back to pages 109–110 to remind yourself of what they are)
- contravention of ss 8 and 9, i.e. duties not to interfere with safety equipment or to charge for safety clothing and equipment or a necessary medical examination
- contravention of health and safety regulations
- making false statements
- obstructing an inspector
- preventing anyone from talking to an inspector
- pretending to be an inspector
- contravention of the terms of a licence
- contravention of an enforcement or prohibition notice (see further page 130)
- improper use or disclosure of information.

The role of the manager

In many organisations the initial identification of risks is carried out by individual departmental managers or administrators. The information is then collated centrally and an overall plan is prepared.

You may, for instance, be expected to analyse which work activities within your span of control could entail a certain risk and then carry out an assessment of each of them, giving details of

- the activity
- the possible hazard
- what control measures are already in place, such as any personal protective or other type of specialist equipment
- the level of risk
- possible remedial actions.

Two of the difficulties of such an exercise, however, are that (a) you require a certain expertise to carry it out successfully; and (b) your interpretation of what is a low, medium or high risk may not be the same as that of other managers. Many organisations, therefore, do not expect their managers to undertake the initial assessment entirely independently but either in conjunction with the health and safety adviser or with the assistance of a very detailed questionnaire prepared by the adviser on which they can indicate any uncertainty they may have over a specific point and which guides them as to the type of information they should provide.

> Many businesses with outlets in various areas prepare 'model' assessments for everyone to follow on the assumption that all the operations and risks will be the same no matter what the geographical area. Some companies also adopt this strategy and develop a company-wide assessment procedure so that the individual manager is required only to delete those items which are not relevant to the particular area.

Statutory sanctions

Although the HASAWA has invested its inspectors with considerable authority (as Figure 2.1.6 outlines), it is apparent that most of them make great efforts to persuade employers to comply with the relevant legal requirements before resorting to using that authority. If their powers of persuasion do fail, however, they are able to take certain specific action. *Enforcement orders* allow the inspectors to issue the employer with two types of notice.

Improvement notices are issued where an inspector is of the opinion that someone is contravening one or more of the relevant statutory provisions. The order directs an employer to carry out prescribed actions or improvements within a specified period – generally about 28 days. The employer can appeal to an industrial tribunal within a period of 14 days.

Prohibition notices are a more serious affair. Obviously the issue of this type of notice can have major and harmful consequences. The operation or machine *must stop* until the required improvements have been made. It is possible to appeal against a prohibition notice, but the notice must be complied with pending the hearing, which is before an industrial tribunal.

THEORY INTO PRACTICE

Because an improvement notice is the less serious of the two orders, there is sometimes a tendency to treat it as non-urgent. Indeed, in your own organisation it has been discovered on a couple of occasions that an enforcement notice issued by an inspector on the factory floor has been ignored by the Production Manager, which has caused considerable difficulties for the company when the inspector has returned to check that action has been taken. Consider what systems you would put into place to ensure that every enforcement order issued is logged and then monitored until the action demanded has been taken within the required timescale.

Powers of the courts

Maximum penalties for different types of offence are laid down in the HASAWA. They are dealt with either by the magistrates' courts (or sheriff courts in Scotland) which can impose fines up to a maximum of £20 000 or a sentence of imprisonment of up to 6 months, or by the Higher Courts which can impose unlimited fines and up to two years' imprisonment. In addition, the courts can order specific forms of action in order to ensure safety.

Employer defences

An employer can, of course, claim that there is no breach of statutory duty because, for instance, he or she has done all that it was 'reasonably practicable' to do to reduce the risk. If he or she argues that financial difficulties facing the firm mean that safety improvements cannot be afforded, the claim is unlikely to be successful. However, the courts may weigh the costs of such improvements against the overall size and resources of the company to decide what action could reasonably have been taken.

In one case, *Piggott Bros & Co. Ltd v Jackson and others* [1991] IRLR 309, an employer's failure to get a definitive explanation of the cause of the employees' symptoms (experienced as a result of exposure to fumes) was held to amount to unreasonableness. This was so even though ventilation had been improved and the problem had been investigated by HSE inspectors who thought it was a 'one off' situation which had now been remedied. The Court of Appeal upheld the decision.

THEORY INTO PRACTICE

The fact that the most frequently used sanction for non-compliance with health and safety requirements is that specified under statutory legislation does not preclude individual employees from bringing a claim for damages under the common law on the grounds of negligence. For full details of what constitutes grounds for a claim for damages in the civil courts, see Chapter 10 entitled *Facilitate compliance with legal and regulatory requirements*.

Internal sanctions

Even if a breach of health and safety legislation does not come to the attention of the inspector, it is common for such a breach to result in disciplinary sanctions against the employee who has committed it (and/or the manager who has failed to prevent it from happening).

- A proper disciplinary procedure, including the carrying out of a reasonable investigation, must take place.
- The application of the sanction must be consistent and the sanction must be of the appropriate level of severity depending on the nature of the offence.
- Any mitigating circumstances must be taken into account such as long service, exemplary previous record, provocation, domestic or personal problems.
- The employee must know the nature of the charges, be allowed to be accompanied by a union representative or a friend, and should be given a right of appeal.
- Except for gross misconduct there should be no dismissal for a first offence. Instead a system of oral and written warnings should be used. The reasons for the choice of disciplinary penalty should be explained to the employee.

THEORY INTO PRACTICE

Check the *ACAS Code on Disciplinary Practice and Procedures* for detailed guidelines on the disciplinary procedures which would normally be acceptable to an industrial tribunal.

If an employer changes existing safety rules or introduces new rules as a direct result of new legislation, the change automatically becomes an implied term of each employee's contract of employment. Where, however, the change is effected because of a change in company policy, the employer needs to consider the existing terms of employment and whether or not the change could represent a breach of contract.

THEORY INTO PRACTICE

Your organisation wants to introduce a policy of no smoking despite opposition from parts of the workforce. Consider what steps you would recommend senior management should take in order to avoid the possibility of their being in breach of contract. Note: if you want to research further into the law relating to the terms and conditions of employment, refer to Chapter 10 for a list of standard texts.

Refusal to work on grounds of lack of safety

One rather damaging consequence of any failure to comply with health and safety requirements might be the refusal of employees to continue working under what they consider to be unsafe or unhealthy conditions. Although employees are contractually obliged to obey the 'reasonable' instructions of their employer, employers are equally obliged to manage reasonably and in particular to provide their employees with a safe place of work. The problem, of course, is the interpretation of what is meant by the word 'reasonable'. In the case of a group of employees who refuse to carry out a certain task or work in a certain area because they feel it to be unsafe, recourse to the law for a legal ruling may be a far too long and costly process. In such circumstances, it is wise for senior managers to follow certain procedures.

- They should seek the advice of specialists, such as the safety manager, the union representatives, the HSE inspectors.
- They should investigate all bona fide complaints brought to their attention.
- They should try to apply the test of 'reasonableness' by examining factors such as the attitude of other employees in the same position and by treating certain categories of employees (such as pregnant women) as sympathetically as possible.

Monitoring conformity with requirements in the replacement, maintenance and use of equipment

Although the ethos behind the statutory health and safety legislation is the imposition of a general duty of care, modern business and industrial processes have become too sophisticated for that principle to be applied without further elaboration. Consequently a number of regulations have been instituted which cover certain specific areas of health and safety, many of which apply to the increasingly complex range of equipment now in use in both office and factory. Four of the most important are:

- Health and Safety (Display Screen Equipment) Regulations 1992 (DSE)
- Personal Protective Equipment at Work Regulations 1992 (PPE)

- Provision and Use of Work Equipment Regulations 1992 (PUWER)
- Manual Handling Operations Regulations 1992 (MHO).

See Figures 2.1.7–2.1.10, which outline the employer's duties in respect of each regulation.

Employers' duties:

- To explain the regulations and risks from using DSE/VDUs to all employees, even those who, although occasional users of DSE, are not 'users' within the meaning of these regulations
- To determine who the 'users' are
- To allow any user who requests it, an eyesight test at the employer's expense
- To pay for a prescription for basic standard glasses or contact lenses recommended as a result of the eyesight test
- To assess the workstation equipment*
- To arrange to have the necessary improvements carried out should an assessment highlight the need for them*

* NOTE: Appendix 1 of the Regulations gives very detailed information about minimum requirements for workstations. See page 299 for further discussion.

Figure 2.1.7 Health and Safety (Display Screen Equipment) Regulations 1992 (DSE)

Employers' duties:

- *Not* to use PPE as the first means of protection but only as a last resort
- To provide all equipment (including clothing affording protection against the weather) which is intended to be worn or held by a person at work and which protects him or her against one or more risks to his or her health or safety*
- To provide any addition or accessory also designed to meet that objective

* NOTE: PPE will not be suitable unless (a) it is appropriate for the risk or risks involved, (b) it takes account of ergonomic requirements and the state of health of the person who may wear it, (c) it is capable of fitting the wearer correctly, and (d) so far as practicable it is effective to prevent or adequately control the risk involved.

Figure 2.1.8 Personal Protective Equipment at Work Regulations 1992 (PPE)

Employers' duties:

- To ensure the suitability of work equipment
- To ensure that dangerous parts of machinery are safeguarded
- To comply with specific 'hardware' requirements for equipment, e.g. controls, isolation, stability
- To provide training in respect of the use of equipment

NOTE: PUWER replaces 17 previous regulations or the parts of them which related to machinery and equipment.

Figure 2.1.9 Provision and Use of Work Equipment Regulations 1992 (PUWER)

Employers' duties:

- To avoid hazardous manual handling operations so far as is reasonably practicable
- To assess any hazardous manual handling operations that cannot be avoided
- To reduce the risk of injury as far as is reasonably practicable
- To liaise with third parties to ensure that all reasonable measures are taken where employees carry out manual handling away from the employer's premises

Figure 2.1.10 Manual Handling Operations Regulations 1992 (MHO)

Two relevant 'back-up' regulations relating very closely to the use of equipment are:

- Electricity at Work Regulations 1989 (see Figure 2.1.11)
- Noise at Work Regulations 1989 (see Figure 2.1.12).

The Regulations cover:

1 Fixed electrical systems
2 Portable electrical tools and appliances
3 Systems of work involving electricity

An appropriate checklist might therefore involve ensuring that:

- there are written and understood procedures for undertaking work on electrical systems and equipment
- these procedures specify the requirements for the necessary safe systems of work
- there is a clear management policy setting down the justified circumstances when live working is permitted
- the procedures for live work specify the procedures to prevent injury and the requirements for the necessary safe systems of work including the provision and use of specialist equipment
- the staff are appropriately trained (and retrained where necessary)
- records are kept of all training and assessments
- the staff are adequately supervised and the manager understands his or her duties

NOTE: although the work itself might be undertaken and supervised by others, the local manager must be kept thoroughly informed and must also have a basic knowledge of the reason for the work and what dangers there may be created by it.

Figure 2.1.11 Electricity at Work Regulations 1989

Although there is a general duty for all employers to reduce the risk of hearing damage to the lowest level reasonably practicable, there are definitive requirements where workplace noise reaches certain 'action levels'.

Employers' duties:

- To reduce the risk of hearing damage to the lowest level reasonably practicable
- To initiate a noise assessment when there is a likelihood that noise is approaching or has reached the first action level
- To ensure assessment is carried out by a competent person
- To keep a record of assessment
- To carry out noise reduction by means other than hearing protectors if noise reaches second or third action levels
- To provide information, instruction and training about risks
- To mark 'ear protection zones' with notices if the noise levels reach the second action level
- To provide ear protectors to employees who ask for them when noise reaches the first action level and automatically when it reaches the second action level
- To maintain and repair ear protectors and to ensure that these meet the relevant requirements of the task

Employees' duties

- To use ear protectors for second action levels
- To use any other equipment provided by the employer and report any defect to their employer at all action levels

Figure 2.1.12   Noise at Work Regulations 1989

THEORY INTO PRACTICE

You will probably need copies of the above Regulations before attempting this exercise.

You are a trainee manager and, as part of your training schedule, you have to work in a number of different departments. During your spell in the Production department you are made aware of the existence of certain problems.

1 The Production Manager asks you to check what is covered by the word 'equipment'. Read the appropriate regulations and identify any potential problems you feel may be caused by the definition.
2 The manager is also concerned about the use of hand tools by some employees and wonders whether they are covered by PUWER. He is particularly anxious to know the position about the hand tools which traditionally have been the personal property of each employee. Research the problem and consider how you might advise him.
3 The manager finds your comments helpful and asks you to check whether there are any exceptions to the PPE regulations. Carry out the necessary research.
4 An employee complains about the noise of certain equipment which runs on average about an hour a day. No-one else seems to mind. Research the legal position.

Monitoring compliance with the requirements

Monitoring compliance with these regulations initially takes the same format as monitoring compliance with the more general health and safety legislation, an area which has already been discussed (see page 109).

However, regulations concerning the use of equipment are very detailed in nature and it is more difficult for employers to assure themselves that they are not in breach of any of them by using only the above means of monitoring. They are helped, however, in that many of the statutory regulations contain specific instructions as to what monitoring should take place.

The Health and Safety (Display Screen Equipment) Regulations, for instance, state that all workstation equipment must be assessed against generally accepted criteria. Such an assessment should normally be carried out when there is:

- a significant change to the software or hardware in use
- a major change to workstation furniture
- a substantial increase in the time to be spent using the VDU
- a fundamental change in the task requirements – more speed, greater accuracy, etc.
- a relocation of a workstation
- a significant modification of the lighting
- a report received which indicates significant new risks or that a recognised hazard should be re-evaluated.

Similarly, the Manual Handling Operations Regulations include information on operating an assessment system which involves:

- the appointment of an assessment team all equipped with differing skills
- an indication of what type of questions should be asked when carrying out any assessment; i.e.
  - is the lifting really necessary?
  - if it is unavoidable, need it be carried out so frequently?
  - can it be mechanised or automated?
  - is there a risk to the health of the employees?
  - if so, has an assessment been carried out to determine the safest way of carrying out the work?
  - has sufficient information, instruction, training and supervision been provided to all involved?

Equally important instructions are contained in PUWER which obliges employers to select the correct equipment for the task. As a consequence, all organisations must now ensure that:

- the instructions and guidance of the manufacturers of the equipment are followed in detail
- factors such as weather and atmospheric conditions are taken into consideration
- the capacities of the equipment are noted
- the special problems of equipment in confined areas are recognised.

Given that list of requirements, it is apparent that even if no other monitoring takes place, the situation will be reviewed sufficiently frequently to prevent any major problems from developing. Indeed, PUWER *requires* employers to ensure that their work equipment is maintained properly and that appropriate records are kept, including the completion of a machinery maintenance log if this is provided.

Even so, there remains the problem that although specific systems can be introduced to monitor the purchasing, the use and the maintenance of the equipment, it is the managers responsible for that particular piece of equipment who must ensure that their forward planning systems encompass both periodic reviews and also a report-back system, both from their deputies to them and from them to their senior managers. If a company-wide system is not in operation, the individual manager would be wise to devise one for his or her specific use.

Establishing and monitoring procedures for dealing with emergencies

The word 'emergency' should strike dread into the heart of any manager. Managers are paid to take responsibility for either an area of work or a group of workers (sometimes both). Part of that responsibility includes forward planning which involves planning for any emergency. If those plans fail when such an emergency does occur, the manager concerned will find it difficult to disclaim responsibility. This again is *not* an area which can be safely delegated to others.

In most cases, however, managers are not left to operate totally independently. The senior management team in the organisation should have formulated a policy in respect of any major foreseen emergencies such as:

- illness
- accidents
- fire
- evacuation
- breaches of security (including the possibility of terrorist activity)

Illness

When someone becomes ill at work the natural first step is to send them home either on their own or accompanied by another member of staff. Common sense normally prevails in such circumstances and the decision made is usually the correct one. However, problems can arise if, for instance, an employee who has been allowed to set off for home alone collapses in the street or reaches home and collapses there. Similar problems can occur for the person asked to accompany them, if the illness increases in severity and that person does not feel equipped to deal with it. Both legally and morally, therefore, it is incumbent upon employers to have in place some form of workplace-based first aid facilities.

Regulation 3(1) of the Health and Safety (First Aid) Regulations 1981 states:

'An employer shall provide, or ensure there are provided, such equipment and facilities as are adequate and appropriate in the circumstances for enabling first-aid to be rendered to his employees if they are injured or become ill at work.'

In addition every employer must provide one 'appointed person' as a minimum and not less than one first aider for every 50 employees.

Although the words 'adequate and appropriate' are open to several interpretations, the revised edition of the *HSE Approved Code of Practice* indicates that any calculations on the amount of resources required based purely on the *number* of staff is not the best approach. Other factors which should be considered include:

- the type of workplace and the nature of the work – in high-risk areas there should be a higher proportion of first aiders
- the size and location of the establishment and the distribution of employees within it
- whether or not there is shift working
- proximity to medical services.

The agency responsible for providing advice and guidance to businesses on first aid and all other occupational health matters is the Employment Medical Advisory Service (EMAS) which is part of the Health and Safety Executive.

First aiders

First aiders, although volunteers, are required to train, to take and pass an examination and to be available at all the times specified. They must also be considered to be temperamentally suitable for the work. They must not carry out any treatment other than that for which they are trained and no medicines may be prescribed by them. If a business has particular hazards which the recognised training does not cover, the employer must arrange special training.

Where it is not considered necessary to provide a trained first aider because the premises are small and the risks are very low, or where in exceptional circumstances the first aider is not present, the employer may nominate an 'appointed person' whose duties are to provide emergency first aid, summon professional medical assistance or arrange transport to a hospital, etc. There are short one-day courses specifically designed for such people.

First aid facilities

At one time it was necessary to provide a first aid room only if there were 400 or more employees. Now the type of facilities provided are subject to employer decision, the test again being what is practicable in the circumstances.

Quite often the first aid room is the room which, because of its infrequent occupancy, is cleaned less thoroughly than the other rooms. Either a weekly inspection by you or a named representative is normally the best method of ensuring the same (or an even higher) standard of cleanliness in the first aid room as in the rest of the accommodation.

THEORY INTO PRACTICE

1 Check the first aid facilities available at your workplace – including first aiders, first aid facilities and/or first aid rooms. Check also what arrangements, if any, you make to cover the following eventualities:

 a when the appointed first aider is on holiday
 b when he or she is absent unexpectedly
 c where there is a substantial amount of night shift work
 d where there is more than one employer on a site or in a building
 e provision of first aid to non-employees.

2 Obtain a copy of *Revised 1990 First-Aid Needs in your Workplace: Your Questions Answered* and *HSE Approved Code of Practice: Health and Safety (First Aid) Regulations 1981 (rev. ed. 1990)* and compare the recommendations contained in those documents with your workplace facilities.

3 Try to determine whether or not (a) you have any possible cause for concern and, if so, (b) what recommendations you would make for improvements.

Monitoring the first aid provision

Just as every accident should be formally recorded, so too should every incident where first aid is required. Although the inspection of such records should be an integral part of your normal planning and monitoring procedures, in this instance you should also be able to rely upon the safety manager, part of whose remit will be to present that information to the safety committee at regular intervals.

However, you should also be aware of the need for the regular retraining of the first aiders who come within your ambit of responsibility and devise some means of reminding yourself of that necessity.

Accidents

Even a cursory glance at the potential consequences a serious accident can have for an organisation, whether or not it is held legally responsible for it, is sufficient to influence most managers to regard accident prevention of prime importance. There can be:

● loss of production
● reduced productivity because of absence of skilled or experienced staff
● expense of recruiting temporary staff
● unfavourable press attention
● visits from HSE inspectors
● loss of customer confidence
● possible criminal prosecution or claims for damages in a civil action.

Obviously employers must try to ensure that every precaution is taken to prevent accidents from occurring by complying with the health and safety legislation already outlined. Where, however, despite their best efforts an accident occurs, they are obliged to follow additional procedures. In particular, they must comply with the Reporting of Injuries, Diseases and Dangerous Occurrences Regulations 1995 (RIDDOR), a brief summary of which is contained in Figure 2.1.13.

- All fatal injuries and a number of listed major injuries should be reported to the enforcing authority immediately – normally by telephone.
- A written report of the accident should also be sent within 10 days.
- Any other workplace injury to an employee which results in his or her absence for more than three days or an inability to perform normal work for the same period must also be reported.
- There is a requirement to telephone immediately and follow up in writing one of a number of stated dangerous occurrences.
- If a general practitioner notifies an employer that one of his or her employees has a notifiable disease, the employer must notify the enforcing authority in writing.

Figure 2.1.13 The Reporting of Injuries, Diseases and Dangerous Occurrences Regulations 1995 (RIDDOR)

Although the regulations give detailed information about the type of occurrences which must be reported, it is up to the individual employer to make the necessary back-up administrative arrangements. The safety manager and safety representatives normally have a major role to play in this respect (look back to page 126 to remind yourself of their duties and responsibilities) but so too has the individual manager (particularly if the organisation is not large enough to warrant the employment of a safety manager).

Ideally there should be both an external and an internal system of accident reporting – the first to satisfy the requirements of RIDDOR, the second to satisfy what should be the even more stringent requirements of the organisation itself.

This can be partially achieved by requiring *all* accidents, however minor, to be recorded on a company-designed accident report form or in an accident book. What then has to be decided as a matter of company policy is:

- to whom the report should be sent
- who is expected to take immediate action
- what periodic review must take place.

Obviously the safety committee and representatives are ideally suited to act in an advisory or monitoring capacity, as is the safety manager who may be empowered by senior management to take any action required. Where problems can occur, of course, is where there is no such group of people either because the organisation is too small or it is non-unionised.

A relevant set of regulations in this respect is the Control of Substances Hazardous to Health Regulations 1994 (COSHH) the purposes of which are:

- to keep to a minimum situations where workers are exposed to hazardous substances
- to warn employees of the dangers and the measures taken to minimise their exposure to them
- to provide suitable protective clothing and equipment where exposure to hazardous substances is unavoidable
- to ensure medical review and feedback on the results for those employees exposed to hazardous substances.

Employers must therefore maintain an inventory of all substances whether deemed hazardous or not and equally are under a statutory duty to provide certain key information. They must also ensure that all employees are aware of and understand the importance of the regulations.

Fire

The disastrous consequences which can ensue from a fire in the workplace are such that it could perhaps be reasonably assumed that fire precautions are regarded as a high priority by everyone in an organisation. Unfortunately that is not an assumption which is always borne out by the facts, as a glance at an extract from the notes made by one safety manager indicate – see Figure 2.1.14.

FREEMANTLE CO. LTD

Area: B Floor Main Building

Date: 5 June 1997

Room B101	Fire emergency instructions missing
B corridor (midway down)	Fire door propped open
Room B104	Fire emergency instructions out of date and defaced
B corridor	Filing cabinets blocking emergency exit
Room B107	Fire extinguisher propping open door
Room B110	Two black bin bags full of waste paper left in the corner of the room
Room B112	Fire extinguisher damaged and unusable
Room B113/114	Dividing wall erected and fire extinguisher/ notices only in one half
Reception	Cigarette stub found – in a no-smoking area

General comments:
1 General lack of staff awareness about fire precautions.
2 New member of staff apparently unaware of fire emergency arrangements, i.e. nearest escape route/evacuation assembly point.
3 It was in this area last month that two members of staff were found setting off fire extinguishers 'as a joke'.

Figure 2.1.14 Accommodation safety inspection report

You are the manager of a department, part of whose duties is to liaise with the company safety manager and to ensure that her instructions are carried out. Given the report outlined in Figure 2.1.14, you are not proving too successful in doing so. Consider:

a the steps you would take to solve the immediate problems
b the long-term measures you would institute to prevent the same problems recurring.

Fire certificates

A fire certificate is required for all business premises in which more than 20 people work or where more than 10 work above or below ground level, although the issuing authority can grant exemption where it considers that the risk to occupants is insufficient to warrant certification. Two classes of business premises require a fire certificate even though they may not reach the above-mentioned occupancy levels:

- hotels and boarding houses which provide sleeping accommodation for more than six people or which provide sleeping accommodation above or below ground level
- where explosive or highly flammable materials are used.

The certificate is normally issued by the Fire Authority and it is an offence to occupy the above type of business premises without either possessing a certificate or an official receipt for having applied for one. The fire certificate itself will show:

- an endorsement of the plans of the building which indicate fire exits, fire fighting equipment and exit direction signs
- any special consent for areas such as the storage of highly flammable materials
- requirements for tests of fire fighting equipment, fire alarms, fire training and evacuation – for each individual requirement there will be a stated frequency of test and for each test there must be an entry made in a 'fire log'.

The fire certificate must be kept on the premises and be available for inspection by the fire officer. Note that it is an offence to carry out any material alteration to a building for which a fire certificate has been issued without obtaining prior approval to do so from the fire officer.

Evacuation

Regulation 7 of the MHSW Regulations now requires employers to appraise their arrangements for dealing with emergencies, to encompass:

- the establishment of proper emergency procedures with adequate staffing to implement those procedures – particularly in the case of an emergency evacuation
- the nomination/appointment of sufficient competent staff to implement the evacuation procedure

- the prevention of employees from entering any area where there are health and safety risks until they have been properly trained and given instruction on the hazards present
- where practicable, informing those exposed to serious imminent danger of the nature of the hazard and the steps being taken to protect them from it
- allowing those people to stop work immediately and to proceed to a place of safety if they are exposed to serious, imminent and unavoidable danger.

Some organisations have introduced a two-stage alarm system to avoid the large amount of lost time which can occur by false alarms. The normal procedure is for the evacuation signal to sound only in the area in which the alarm bell has been activated. Elsewhere an intermittent alarm sounds warning everyone that they *may* have to evacuate. One major problem, however, is that there can be difficulties in informing staff that the emergency is over. In most cases, staff are asked to assume that it is all clear after a specific period of time has elapsed.

THEORY INTO PRACTICE

1 In order to test the effectiveness of your fire and other hazard emergency procedures at your workplace, check:
  - the extent of your own responsibilities
  - the contents of any fire certificate issued by the fire authority and whether or not the information is up to date (i.e. whether any alterations to use have been notified, etc.)
  - who is responsible for the fire log and for overseeing the fire precautions in the company
  - whether or not the fire log is up to date
  - the appropriateness of the fire emergency notices
  - whether there are sufficiently good directional signs so that both staff and visitors know how to vacate the building quickly
  - whether the instructions in relation to the calling of the fire brigade are understood by everyone
  - the effectiveness or otherwise of the arrangements for evacuating the building
  - whether the fire marshals have received appropriate training
  - the positioning of fire extinguishers and the training of those likely to use them
  - whether or not the fire brigade have to attend, supervise or be informed of a fire drill
  - whether those permitted to stay in the building for the sake of business continuity (e.g. college lecturers in charge of examinations, switchboard operators in hospitals, etc.) know that they can do so – and can distinguish between a drill and a real alarm
  - whether alternative arrangements are made should a drill be scheduled during really bad weather – and if so, what they are
  - how often a 'walk about' takes place to check items such as the obstruction of fire exits, etc.

Organise and maintain conditions for productive work

- what different procedures exist (if any) if the evacuation is because of a bomb threat rather than a fire
- what arrangements are made for feedback.

2 If applicable, consider any possible improvements.

Breaches of security

If you work in an organisation which has its share of older managers, you may find it difficult to convince them that times have changed to such an extent that an office can no longer be considered to be a 'safe' place in which to work, particularly since, until comparatively recently, the perception has always been that it is on the shopfloor where danger occurs. Nowadays, however, risk management is becoming an essential part of almost any manager's role. Although the risk of personal injury caused by an accident at work may be higher in some areas of the workplace than others, the risk of commercial loss or damage or of attacks on staff by outsiders is not so easy to compartmentalise.

As always your starting point should be to assess what risks are involved, and it might therefore be advisable for you – or a designated individual – to address the issues outlined in Figure 2.1.15.

- Are the existing systems capable of identifying the total cost of vandalism, theft, bomb damage, arson, etc.?
- Has a risk evaluation survey of the premises been undertaken and its recommendations acted upon? Has that evaluation taken account of possible terrorist attack?
- Is it possible to allow distinctions to be made between the cost of criminal damage and damage caused accidentally?
- Is a specific budget set aside for crime, vandal and terrorist prevention measures?
- How much money has been spent on such measures? Should more be allocated?
- Have any particularly vulnerable areas been identified?
- Has guidance been sought on security and damage control from the police Crime Prevention Officer and/or the security industry?
- Are staff warned to note suspicious activities and to inform management when they see strangers on the premises? Are they trained in security awareness?
- Do the police know how to contact keyholders promptly in the event of any damage occurring?
- How are acts of vandalism reported and recorded? Are all staff aware of the procedures to follow? Are the police always notified?
- How quickly is damage made good to discourage further similar damage?
- Is there a contingency plan to minimise disruption after an incident?
- Do you exchange relevant information with other organisations in the area?

Figure 2.1.15 Risk analysis

Security measures

A useful checklist for senior management wishing to carrying out a risk assessment of their security arrangements is to concentrate first on three major areas:

- the external environment
- the physical environment
- the interior areas of the building(s).

Within those areas an assessment can then be made of certain specific items.

With regard to the *external environment*, consider: perimeter protection and site control; earth banking; ditches or moats; crash barriers; mobile passive infrared systems; external lighting; measures to deal with trespassers; motor vehicle security.

With regard to the *physical environment*, consider: target hardening (i.e. preventing walls, etc. from being knocked down by vehicles); mobile barriers; anti-scaling roof devices; solid doors; use of window locks, laminated glass, externally fitted roller shutters, privacy film (to prevent anyone from surveying the interior prior to forced entry); closed-circuit TV.

With regard to the *interior areas of the building*, consider: internal security stores (which will resist physical attack); catering security; physical presence (e.g. security guards/store detectives); security marking and inventory of valuable equipment; security of valuable documents, computer disks, etc.; key security; security procedures in respect of the movement of cash, receipt of packages, etc.; alarm systems; security for staff working alone or late at night; security measures in respect of visitors.

THEORY INTO PRACTICE

Check what action is taken at your workplace to protect computer software and other valuable documents from being copied or stolen. Research in the library or from any other relevant source how those measures compare with those recommended by security experts.

Security measures in case of a terrorist attack

Most organisations nowadays are only too well aware of the vulnerability of their premises to terrorist attack. Many of the measures previously described are designed not only to prevent theft and vandalism but also, as far as possible, to prevent the planting of bombs or other incendiary devices. In addition, the establishment of any procedures to evacuate the premises in case of an emergency almost invariably now include additional measures to be taken should the emergency be a bomb threat. Interestingly, some employees are now given guidance on what personal documentation they should have pre-prepared for identification purposes should they have to evacuate a building because of a suspected bomb.

After the bomb blast in Manchester which damaged the Co-operative Bank's head office, the company issued a guide to emergency *personal* planning. The guide advises staff to:

- draw up a list of key telephone and reference numbers such as credit card and bank account details
- photocopy savings and investment documents and birth, death and marriage certificates

– and then give them to a relative, a friend or a bank in case of emergency!

An organisation's procedures for recommending improvements to working conditions

The constant monitoring which is an integral part of any organisation's health and safety procedures presupposes that some action will be taken should the results of such monitoring reveal the need for improvement. The most formal method of recommending any such improvements is through the safety committee, part of whose remit is to review health and safety audit reports, to foster health and safety awareness throughout the company, and to ensure that its recommendations are acted upon (see page 127 for fuller details of its role).

However, the effectiveness of such a committee very much depends on its membership and on the real – as opposed to the nominal – commitment given to it by senior management. The guidance on safety policies suggests that a director at board level or a manager of equivalent senior status should be assigned responsibility for promoting health and safety throughout the organisation, and it is the norm for such a person to chair the safety committee. Because of the accountability which accompanies such a role, it is probable that he or she will be committed to developing procedures for ensuring that any recommendations made are effected. The safety manager might be similarly motivated. However, the same enthusiasm may not be as evident in other members of the committee. This is significant given that their cooperation is essential in checking that the health and safety measures recommended and implemented at board or senior management level are actually adhered to in their own areas and – equally importantly – that the concerns of the people they represent or any suggestions made for improvements are reported back to the relevant decision-makers.

The two normal methods for trying to ensure that the safety committee operates effectively are:

- to pay considerable attention to the appointment of safety representatives to the committee – although finding and recruiting the most able staff can sometimes be difficult given their other work commitments
- to ensure that the committee itself operates smoothly:
  - regular meetings are held at the most convenient times

- the documentation is clear, understandable and not too extensive
- the physical environment is comfortable
- the chairperson is able to encourage contributions from all members
- the minutes are concise and accurate and can be circulated to all members of staff in a readable form
- there is some tangible outcome from the recommendations made by the committee and this outcome is communicated to all staff.

However effective the safety committee may be, it cannot operate in isolation. As a manager, it will be an important part of your role to ensure that communication channels between you and your staff, and conversely those between you and your senior managers, are as effective as you can make them. Any recommendations for improvements suggested to you by your staff can therefore be communicated to the relevant authority, and vice versa, in the expectation that they will be considered and possibly implemented. It is important, of course, that even if a recommendation is not acted upon, a reason is given and a report is given to the person making that recommendation.

Organising the workplace to promote safe and productive work

As already discussed, s.2(1) of HASAWA imposes a general duty upon the employer to ensure that his or her workforce is kept as safe, healthy and comfortable as far as is reasonably practicable, whereas s.2(2) outlines the more specific requirements with which he or she has to comply.

If, therefore, you have the responsibility for an area of work or for a group of staff, it might be useful for you:

- to carry out an audit of your surroundings to check whether or not they comply with the requirements of the Act and its supplementary regulations
- to repeat the process each time, for instance, you want to alter the physical layout of the area, to introduce a new working practice or to use a new piece of equipment.

All work areas within your own limits of responsibility

It is sometimes easy to ignore the fact that there are *three* main thrusts in modern health and safety policies – health, safety and *welfare*. Although the law tends to concentrate on the first two – possibly because of the greater risks involved – the employer is equally obliged to pay attention to employees' welfare, which in general terms means not only ensuring that the workplace is safe and free from any obvious health hazards but also that it is as comfortable as possible given all the circumstances of the job. In addition, managers are well aware that employees who are working in an area which is well planned, light, airy and pleasant are likely to be more productive than those whose working environment, although meeting all legal requirements, is poorly organised, drab, dark and generally uninviting.

Office layout

You may have little control over the general layout of your work area – particularly as regards whether it is laid out in open plan or traditional style. You can, nevertheless, try to minimise any problems that may be caused as a result of such a layout.

Read the following comment made by a safety representative on behalf of a group of workers.

'Sure, the open plan office is nice to look at. Yes, it makes a clear statement about the organisation and – OK – it saves money. Why is it then, that our workers have given it the thumbs down? It's yet another example of management imposing an unwanted – and less effective – system on the workforce.'

Consider whether you agree with the above statement, giving reasons for your answers. Discuss also:

a the possible causes of employee dissatisfaction
b possible solutions (other than abandoning the open plan idea entirely).

Workflow

What you may be able to control or at least influence is the way in which the furniture and equipment in your area is positioned and used. Factors you should bear in mind – in addition to any legal requirements – include:

- organisational policy
- the size of the area at your disposal
- the number of people working there
- the number of people visiting the area for whatever purpose
- links with other work areas and the possible need for a similar approach to layout
- the type, number and size of furniture, fittings and equipment to be accommodated in the area
- the intended workflow
- your workspace
- aesthetic issues – colour schemes, use of plants, pictures, screens, etc.

If you work with a group of people, assess (a) the extent and layout of your work area; (b) the number of staff it accommodates and their specific job roles; (c) the type of office furniture and equipment it contains; and (d) the decor, the state of cleanliness, the lighting and heating facilities and the noise level.

Consider (i) the reasons for the layout chosen; (ii) what you think works well; (iii) what you think could be improved; and (iv) possible costs of any improvements.

If you work on your own, select another appropriate area in your organisation and carry out the same exercise.

Factors influencing safety and productivity in the workplace

Stress

When organising your work area it is unwise to ignore the possibility that emotional factors can affect both the safety and the productivity of your workforce. Personal problems, for instance, can make even the most effective members of your workforce less accurate, less skilful or less motivated. They can also affect powers of concentration and hence increase the possibility of accidents occurring. So too, it has been argued, can stress.

It is commonplace nowadays to maintain that an unacceptable level of stress at work can lead to loss of productivity. Note, however, the emphasis on the word 'unacceptable'. Many employers still regard a certain amount of stress as not only inevitable but also, to an extent, an aid to productivity. Managers who are required to achieve a set of targets within a certain period of time will probably need to put themselves under a certain amount of stress to achieve them. So too will a worker required to complete a job to a certain level of accuracy and speed. Conversely, if the targets are unreasonably high, the pressure to achieve them is too great or if the work is to be carried out under a set of conditions which are above an acceptable limit of tolerance, then stress can cease to be a motivator and become a hazard.

Up until 10 years ago, however, stress at work was not a recognised issue. Absence through physical illness was acceptable, whereas absence through stress tended to cause more concern. A number of surveys were then published which sought to prove the existence of stress as an illness and most of them came to the same conclusion – that many workers were indeed suffering from work-related stress. The causes of the stress varied but included:

- pressure of work arising from 'downsizing'
- increased pressure to achieve constantly increasing targets
- fear of redundancy or major changes in working conditions
- repetitive and monotonous tasks
- loss of decision-making powers
- isolation from other workers
- deteriorating physical conditions.

A number of claims of constructive dismissal were then made by employees on the grounds that their working conditions had led to a stress-related illness.

Response from the judiciary, however, has been mixed. One employee did win his case but in somewhat extreme circumstances – despite two bouts of nervous illness and many requests for assistance, his workload had continued to increase. In other cases, judges refused to recognise stress as an illness possibly in response to a suspicion that the relatively recent upsurge in such claims was leading to the situation whereby people who may not otherwise have considered such a possibility were encouraged to make 'copycat' claims. Both sides of the argument are still being hotly disputed.

Physical illness or injury

Equally damaging to productivity is staff absence caused by a work-related physical illness or injury such as RSI or work-related upper limb disorder.

THEORY INTO PRACTICE

The following comment was made in an office equipment journal:

'The term "repetitive strain injury" covers a range of conditions including tennis elbow and tenosynovitis, the condition usually suffered by keyboard operators. All occur when certain movements are repeated so frequently that the tendons or muscles in the arms become inflamed and painful. It is close to becoming established as a recognised industrial injury.'

Research further into the legal developments that have occurred recently in this area. Consider whether you think the problem is sufficiently serious to warrant further legislative action.

Sick building syndrome

The so-called sick building syndrome is difficult to diagnose even though the World Health Organisation has stated that it could affect up to 30 per cent of buildings.

Interestingly, some supposed hazards have still not been clearly identified as such. For instance, it has been claimed that electromagnetic radiation is emitted by many electronic products including computers, carphones and TVs, but no conclusion has been reached as to whether that level of radiation is unacceptably high.

Other hazards are more clearly identifiable. Many photocopiers, for instance, give out ozone, an undesirable addition to the air breathed in by the operators. Some chemicals in cleaning products have a similar effect and faulty air conditioning and poor ventilation only add to the problem. Dust build-up in carpets, particularly those made with artificial fibres, tends to go unnoticed despite its potentially harmful effects on health.

The HSE has made the point that many workers most at risk from the 'sick building syndrome' are too concerned with loss of job security to run the risk of reporting any potential hazards. They have to rely instead on legislative assistance – which may or may not be forthcoming.

Ergonomics

Because of the growing emphasis on work-related injuries there has been a corresponding increase in interest in the science of ergonomics – the study of the working environment to ascertain how best to minimise discomfort to the workforce. Most manufacturers' equipment or furniture manuals now contain assurances that their products have been 'ergonomically designed and tested', and some of the more recent legislation also requires that employers should ensure that the principles of ergonomics are taken into account when, for instance, they install VDU equipment into an office.

Despite all the recent publicity, some employers are still accused of purchasing office furniture for aesthetic rather than ergonomic reasons.

From your study of the Health and Safety (Display Screen Equipment) Regulations (in particular Appendix 1), check that you know the legal requirements in respect of display screens, keyboards, work surfaces and work chairs. Consider how far you think the workstations in your workplace comply with these requirements.

Element 2.2

Acquire, allocate and control resources to enable productive work to be maintained

The scope and limit of your authority

One dictionary definition of the word 'resource' is 'the means of supplying what is needed'. Although your first response to the idea of managing resources in a certain area may be to think of money, equipment or other materials, you might also have to include in your calculations any human resources for which you are responsible. Indeed it is customary nowadays to refer to a Human Resources Manager rather than a Personnel Manager.

Your job description should define your duties and responsibilities. However, you may also need to refer to other sources of reference for more detailed guidelines. Your normal first approach would be to your senior manager to discover company policy on this issue or, failing that (if, for instance, your organisation is relatively small), to a colleague who occupies the same position as you or has done so in the past.

Generally, however, most managers are given fairly specific criteria to which they must adhere, whether the resources in question are physical or human.

In the case of physical resources, for instance, it is normal for an employer to specify:

- who has the overall responsibility for the budget
- who has the authority to purchase or agree to the purchase of materials and equipment and to what limit of expenditure
- whether or not that authority can be delegated
- the means of checking and controlling the expenditure.

In the case of human resources, the employer will usually decide:

- who has the power to determine whether or not staff should be recruited, at what level of salary and on what terms and conditions of employment
- who has the responsibility for organising and directing the work of those staff

- by whom the staff must be trained
- who has the power to appraise, reward or discipline the staff
- who has the ultimate power of dismissal.

Specifications of resources in the operational plan

In most operational plans, no matter what their format, the objectives outlined are accompanied by a statement of the probable resource implications. Thus the stated objective of a Jobcentre Manager to increase the number of clients entering some form of employment would probably be linked with the need for more staff, more money and possibly larger premises. The objective of a departmental manager to increase staff computer literacy may be dependent on funding being available for training and on there being adequate equipment. Even a general objective such as an intention to increase overall efficiency could have some resourcing implications.

Ideally, when the plan is discussed at senior management level, the resources will be made available at the time the objective is approved. In reality this might not prove to be the case and the manager in question may have to accept the fact that he or she is committed to achieving the objective without necessarily being given all or any of the resources requested.

Nevertheless, establishing what is required at the outset does give you a bargaining point either immediately or at a future date, and it is wise, therefore, to take some time to consider exactly what the financial implications would be each time you commit yourself to achieving an objective. What you should also attempt to do is to match your objectives to the stated priorities of the organisation's strategic plan. If, for instance, your senior management have a stated objective of downsizing the workforce, it is pointless your suggesting that your staffing budget be doubled. If, however, customer care or the promotion of a corporate image is a high priority, you may be more successful in requesting resources for new office furniture or staff uniforms if you made either of those your objective.

A useful starting point is to consider your resource requirements under the three headings of equipment, materials, and people.

Equipment

Most modern offices need much more equipment than was the case even five years ago. It is wise to make sure, therefore, that you concentrate not only on updating and replacing existing equipment but also on scanning the horizon for any new developments in the field. Beware, however, of giving in to the temptation of requesting a piece of equipment just because it is new. Prioritise your essential requirements (e.g. the replacement of a much-used computer) and then – as a speculative bid – ask for a 'luxury' such as an interactive video for training purposes.

> Remember to include maintenance and repair costs in your calculations unless you are sure that these will be dealt with centrally.

Materials

When assessing your resource requirements it is relatively easy to determine what items of equipment you require. It is almost as easy to *forget* to determine your requirements for smaller items and for any back-up materials such as computer consumables, printer toner, etc. If you are kept to a tight budget, running out of any such items before the end of the financial year is as much of a problem as attempting to operate without an essential piece of equipment. When drawing up your specifications, always include an extra column headed 'materials required' simply to remind you to include an appropriate sum in your bid. Avoid the temptation, however, of stockpiling. Not only does it take up valuable office space, you may also find that if, for instance, you have ordered a huge amount of a particular type of printer cartridge, the printers are then changed and you are left with a costly, yet obsolete, number of goods – whose existence may be difficult to justify should there be a stocktaking exercise.

People

In your negotiations with senior management, you will probably have to be at your most persuasive when requesting additional or even replacement staff. Staffing is normally the most costly resource of any organisation, and consequently your employers will need to be convinced of the necessity for adding to the wages bill. Points to assist you in your argument may be:

- an historical analysis of the work of your area – indicating, where possible, any increase in the workload that has not resulted in a corresponding increase in staffing
- possible future developments which could lead to an increase in profits, productivity, etc. if the additional staffing were agreed
- the consequences of not agreeing to the request, such as a reduction in the service offered, an increase in the number of customer complaints, etc. (although it may be politic here not to sound too threatening!)
- the need for a specific skill or qualification which none of the existing staff possesses (although in this case you may have to be prepared to compromise if staff development funding is made available to you rather than an additional member of staff).

THEORY INTO PRACTICE

You work as the Telephone Orders Manager of a large organisation, and, as requested, have prepared a departmental operational plan based on the organisation's strategic plan. As one of the principal objectives of the organisation is stated to be researching into customer needs, you have included in your plan the following objectives.

Departmental strategic objective
To research into customer satisfaction with the present telephone ordering system

Departmental operational objective

- *To carry out a survey of a 20 per cent sample of those customers placing telephone orders with the department in the last three month period*
- *To analyse the results*
- *To prepare a report outlining the findings and recommending any necessary improvements*

a Think of the factors you would consider when completing the resourcing sections of the plan and how you would calculate the exact amount of money you would need.

b Determine what further action you might take to try to ensure that you obtain the necessary resources to achieve your objective – particularly if you are aware that resources are limited.

c Consider what you would do if no resources were available and yet you were still expected to achieve your objective. Address in particular the question of whether you *would* still try to achieve it.

For further information on strategic and operational plans see Chapter 3, *Plan and control activities to meet objectives*.

> When making any bids, you should take into account the quantity and quality, when you require them and the cost. For further discussion see pages 159 and 160.

Dealing with resources that do not conform to specification

Even if you are part of an organisation which prides itself on its planning procedures, there will be times when you have an unexpected need for certain resources, or some resources become available unexpectedly, or some resources are allocated which are not entirely what you wanted.

THEORY INTO PRACTICE

You are the manager of one of a chain of hotels. Consider how you would deal with the following eventualities.

You are expected to meet a target of catering for a certain number of wedding parties each year. Mid-way through the year the main banqueting suite is damaged through fire and needs urgent repairs. The money from the insurance company is not immediately forthcoming and you realise that if some action is not taken, a number of wedding bookings may have to be cancelled.

After a reorganisation of certain parts of the chain, a memorandum is sent out to all managers informing them that a number of qualified bar personnel are available for redeployment. You are up to your agreed level of staffing in your hotel, but you always have a large turnover of staff each year and you do not want to miss the opportunity of acquiring any experienced personnel.

You have argued for some time that the hotel reception area needs a CCTV security system. Your senior manager agrees to fund this but only to a level which will preclude you from purchasing the system you feel is tailor-made for your needs.

Methods of allocating resources

Action taken by others

Allocation of resources is initially a task for the senior management team and the primary approach to it in most organisations is by means of the budgeting system.

In most organisations this process involves planning at various levels in a 'back and forth' fashion over a period of time, involving managers at both departmental (or strategic business unit, SBU) level and board or corporate level.

After the objectives of each department or unit have been discussed and approved at a senior level, the next stage is the compilation of the organisational budget.

To a new manager the budgeting process may seem complicated. In most organisations, however, it is simply a matter of carrying out a series of consecutive actions within an established timescale.

Step 1

Top management begins the budgeting process by attempting to correlate the objectives of the organisation with the financial resources available to it. In trying to forecast possible income it has to take into account projected product demand; and in trying to forecast possible expenditure it has to take into account projected production requirements – materials, capital expenditure, cash flow, personnel, etc. It then has to decide what it can afford in the way of operating expenses for the purpose of determining a profit level.

Step 2

The Financial Director or equivalent then communicates the contents of the budget to the management team responsible for preparing individual budgets.

Step 3

The department or SBU prepares a preliminary budget for the next period. It is normally good practice for the manager to begin with the previous period's budget and to adjust the new budget on the basis of the amount of money still available plus or minus expected changes. The budget should, of course, link with the objectives in the unit's strategic plan.

Your organisation may be satisfied to receive from you a broad outline of your resourcing needs – such as another member of staff, an increased budget for travel expenses, an item of equipment, etc. – provided that you can write a sufficiently convincing narrative to accompany your request. In some cases, however, you may have to substantiate your claim with more specific information. If, for instance, you want to request an increase in your overall consumables budget, you may be wise to spend some time checking on your present level of spending and the reasons for any projected increase. One method is to prepare a statement in which you outline on a line-by-line basis your current level of spending, emphasising the ways in which you currently practise cost control through:

- the use of standard purchasing procedures
- the maintenance of effective stock control systems (see further page 163)
- the employment of fewer staff at lower levels of pay than other departments of comparable size.

You are then in a strong position to justify asking for an increase in your budget either on the grounds of a general increase in prices or because, for instance, the number of people you manage or the overall workload has risen, both of which require additional resourcing.

Brian Knight, a financial management expert, outlines the following possible strategies for managers to adopt when preparing their bids:

- *Personal charisma.* If a manager knows that senior management respond to a 'wheeler dealer' attitude, he or she may be able to obtain the required resources simply by preparing a flamboyant presentation covering far-reaching and impressive sounding goals. Little detail is included.
- *Open market or zero basing.* Here estimates and justifications are submitted for every item comprising the request. Although this method is searching as it takes no account of the previous year's budget, modest estimates can be ignored at the expense of the more carefully crafted bids unless each item is examined in detail.
- *'Creeping' incrementalisation.* An easy method of preparing a bid is simply to repeat last year's request adding a certain percentage to cover inflation. However, this takes no account of any changing needs or new developments, and could indicate to senior management that the department or unit concerned is less than dynamic.
- *The formula approach.* This method is normally dictated by senior management as budget estimates and allocations are all based on certain factors to some of which a certain weighting is applied. Each department or unit, therefore, receives a centrally predetermined amount.

Step 4

These budgets are then approved or amended by senior management, who are likely to analyse each unit's past performance and determine whether the projections are realistic.

This is the stage at which the resource allocation choice will be made – who is going to be allowed to recruit more staff, buy new furniture, equipment or machinery, etc.

Step 5

At this point the overall budget is usually prepared. Projected income and expenditure are amalgamated and subsidiary budgets are developed into, for example, the operating budget, the financial budget, the capital budget and the expense budget.

- The *operating budget* specifies materials, labour, overheads and other costs.
- The *financial budget* projects cash receipts and disbursements.
- The *capital budget* projects major additions or new construction.
- The *expense budget* projects expenses not covered in other budgets such as marketing costs.

Finally, the *summary budget* (profit and loss or income statement) outlines the total obtained by combining the subsidiary budgets subtracted from the projected income. The remainder is a profit or loss.

Two types of budget deal with long-term rather than short-term issues.

- The *life-cycle budget* is used where it is unreasonable to expect financial commitment to last for a short period only – capital projects, research and development, etc. The financial estimates are therefore prepared over the whole life-cycle of the activity.
- The *flexible budget* requires a series of different budget plans to be prepared depending on a particular event – rise or fall in rates of inflation, costs of raw materials, etc. It is therefore often used as a controlling and monitoring device.

Note that budgeting is covered in more detail in Chapter 9.

THEORY INTO PRACTICE

The question of who gets the most money from the budget can have a major effect on the work of a department and on the role of its manager. If, as a manager, you are perceived by your staff as having 'lost the budget battle' you may find that you have lost some credibility in the eyes of your staff. Consider how you would attempt to address that situation.

Centralisation versus departmental allocation

Some organisations prefer not to take the final step of delegating resources direct to each department or unit. Instead they hold all resources centrally and allocate them on a perceived need basis. There are advantages to this approach:

- the economies to be obtained by consolidating like requirements of all areas, thus giving the purchasing and/or human resources departments a far better negotiating position
- the avoidance of anomalies whereby some areas are less skilful than others at negotiating and thus obtain the resources at less economic prices or of an inferior quality
- a better overall stock management and material utilisation
- economies of staffing, particularly in the clerical and accounts area, together with a uniform approach towards the relevant documentation.

Profit and cost centres

The converse approach is to allocate almost total responsibility for resource management to the individual sections. In some instances *cost centres* are established whereby costs are assigned to the section using the cost incurring items. Alternatively, *profit centres* can be set up in which both revenue (such as income from sales or the provision of services) and costs are made the responsibility of the relevant manager. In such a case the profit centre will probably have its own profit and loss account to use in future planning activities. Another approach is the introduction of the *investment centre* in which not only expenses and income are made the responsibility of the manager but also the management of the assets of the department. Such a centre would have its own balance sheet, showing the total resources invested in the section.

Obviously the use of these centres is intended to be a means of providing the manager with a certain amount of autonomy. In practice, however, there are normally some limitations. It is unlikely, for instance, that the individual manager will be able to negotiate his or her own wage rates with staff. Servicing from other areas can also cause certain problems, and it is equally unlikely that if a manager is unhappy about the service from the Human Resources or Computing departments, he or she will be able to contract with external providers.

> An essential feature of most cost or profit centres is the determination of the prices at which goods and services are transferred from one section to another. Although one option is to use the open market price, it is more common for a lower price to be determined – simply to prevent the internal customers from wanting to use external services.

Action taken by yourself

If centralisation of resources is not a feature of your organisation, allocation of resources then becomes more of a two-way process. You argue your case with your senior management; in turn your staff may be required to persuade you of the validity of their claims for additional resources.

If your span of control is considerable you can, of course, follow the same procedure with your staff as senior management have followed with you and require them to prepare draft budgets for your approval. If the structure of your workplace or your own job role makes that undesirable or unworkable, you may want to take a more arbitrary stance and allocate resources on the basis of your own judgement. What is normally more conducive to staff cooperation, however, is a more democratic approach in which their opinions are sought, even though you reserve the right of final decision. Sometimes, however, that final decision can be rather difficult to make.

THEORY INTO PRACTICE

Some organisations distinguish between items of capital expenditure and consumables and allow managers to spend the money allocated to them only on consumables. Consider the advantages and disadvantages of such a procedure.

Monitoring and evaluating the use of resources

Nowadays most managers work to a set of targets. If the targets are mutually agreed, they are normally achievable provided the manager has taken into account certain risk factors. A Production Manager, for instance, may have to build into his or her estimates the possibility that raw materials may arrive late or not at all. A Human Resources Manager may have to take into account the fact that an increase in the general level of employment may result in a more limited field of candidates for certain less-well-paid jobs, and so on. Some risk factors are not easy to predict or guard against, in which case the manager concerned may have a genuine reason for failing to meet the required targets. Others, however, can be predicted and action taken to minimise their effect should they occur. Consequently, failure to meet targets because of a shortage of or poor quality resources caused by bad planning or ineffective usage is not likely to be regarded too sympathetically.

An effective manager therefore monitors closely the way in which resources are used.

Physical resources

Stock (or inventory) control does not sound the liveliest of topics. Nor is it. Even so, it may be to your advantage to take some time to familiarise yourself with its basic principles. In some organisations, there will be a standardised system of stock control. In others – normally the smaller organisations – you may have to introduce your own system.

Quantity of physical resources

The reasons for keeping certain amounts of physical resources in stock are varied. They include:

- the convenience of having items available as and when required without having to make any special arrangements
- reduction in cost if the items can be purchased in bulk
- protection against the effects of forecast error, inaccurate records or mistakes in planning
- a hedge against fluctuations in sales or production.

You could therefore argue that the more stock you carry the better placed you will be to meet your targets. It is evident, however, that holding too much stock is expensive and carries an increased security risk. Consequently it is becoming common practice to try to reduce the stock carried without reducing the service provided by instituting certain procedures, such as:

- arranging for items to be delivered just in time instead of stockpiling just in case a need arises
- devising ways to reduce ordering costs and lead times so that the optimum quantities are smaller
- making forecasts more accurate, ensuring that records are correct, and better planning.

For further information on timing of orders see page 164.

Most managers operate some form of stock control system for the consumables allocated to them. Consider the system you use and the reasons for your choice.

Quality of physical resources

Obviously any goods ordered must be of acceptable quality. If you order goods and find them unsatisfactory for some reason, you are unlikely to use that supplier again. However, that will not solve your current problem, and even if the supplier replaces the goods or returns your money, your overall effectiveness is likely to have been damaged. One method of minimising this possibility when selecting a supplier is to evaluate his or her worth not only on the price of the goods but also on certain other factors.

Two approaches can be taken when making such an appraisal:

- desk research involving any written data obtainable about the relevant supplier, such as company reports, balance sheets, references, strike record, etc.
- field research, best undertaken on a team basis, by which each member of the team evaluates the supplier from a different viewpoint and shares responsibility for the decision to approve or reject.

Although it is not always possible, it is highly desirable that a visit be made to every potential supplier. Resist the temptation, however, to arrive without a clear brief. Otherwise you may find that you will be given a nice lunch, a quick tour round the premises and a flattering farewell from the Sales Manager – without your having been given the chance to ask even a remotely searching question. The Chartered Institute of Purchasing and Supply recommends the use of a checklist, a summary of which is given in Figure 2.2.1.

Figure 2.2.1 Checklist for visits to suppliers

Personal attitudes. Note any evidence of employee morale by checking on:

- the atmosphere of harmony or dissatisfaction among the production workers
- the degree of interest in customer service on the part of the supervisory staff
- the degree of energy displayed and the interest in getting things done
- the use of the workforce and whether it is economical or costly with a number of people apparently doing very little.

Adequacy and care of production equipment. Note:

- whether the equipment is modern or antiquated
- whether it is accurately maintained or obviously worn
- whether it is well cared for or dirty and neglected
- whether it is of proper size or type to produce the buyer's requirements
- whether it is of sufficient capacity to produce the quantities desired.

Figure 2.2.1 Checklist for visits to suppliers – *continued*

Technological expertise. Note:

● whether conversations with supervisors and members of the workforce indicate that they have the necessary technical knowledge
● whether they have the ability to control and improve the operations or processes under their supervision.

Means of controlling quality. Note:

● whether materials are chemically analysed and physically checked
● the frequency of inspection during the production cycle
● the employment of techniques such as statistical quality control
● the availability of statistical quality control data.

Housekeeping. Note:

● whether the plant is orderly and clean in its general appearance
● whether the dangers of breakdown, fire or other disasters are minimised.

Competence of staff. Note:

● whether the technical staff indicate a knowledge of the latest relevant materials, tools and processes
● whether the management seem competent and knowledgeable
● whether the organisation has been awarded the IIP award and the BS5750, ISO9000 or equivalent.

THEORY INTO PRACTICE

If you are a not a purchasing specialist, you may experience difficulty in coming to a firm conclusion in some of the areas outlined in the checklist. Consider which areas may cause you some concern and how you would try to resolve the problem, and/or check with the information given in Chapter 8.

Rating suppliers of physical resources

Once a supplier survey has been undertaken it should obviously then be assessed. *Subjective assessment*, although time-saving, can have certain disadvantages.

● It will be based on the impression gained by the existing manager, which may be difficult to substantiate should he or she leave – or difficult to justify should it be monitored by someone of a different personality or from a different background.
● It often has a 'halo' effect – a tendency to be biased in favour of one supplier simply because of possibly irrelevant impressions – the inspector could, for instance, have been in a good mood when inspecting the premises, or could have a relative working in that area, there could be a particularly close relationship between the inspector and the sales manager of the firm inspected, etc.

What is normally more acceptable, therefore, is an assessment based on *quantitative* methods which can be carried out in a number of ways. Two of the most frequently used are the following:

- weighted ratings by means of a checklist – the matching of a checklist with factors weighted according to the importance attached to them by the buyer
- index numbers – these are ratios based on a comparison of the present period with a base period, the value of which is defined as 100.

Index numbers are useful (a) in comparing the performance of a supplier with reference to given factors from one year to another; and (b) when orders are divided between two or more suppliers and the buyer wishes to monitor the performance of each vendor for purposes of comparison.

THEORY INTO PRACTICE

Consider what you would do if your experience told you that a particular firm was and always had been a reliable supplier of high-quality goods but the quantitative assessment had resulted in its being given a lower rating than that of another – untried – firm.

What would be the advantages and disadvantages of entering into agreements with local as distinct from nationwide or even international suppliers?

Evaluation by staff

No matter how carefully you select a supplier, in some cases a situation may arise in which although the goods themselves are of an acceptable standard, they are not as useful as you hoped they would be. A word-processor, for instance, which allows the operator to carry out a number of elaborate functions but which requires a series of complicated manoeuvres to produce even the simplest of documents may be of less use to you than one which is more basic but which is easier to operate – and yet there is nothing intrinsically wrong with the equipment.

User-evaluation, therefore, should be an important part of the overall monitoring system. In a small organisation you will be able to get informal feedback from your staff because you are working closely with them on a day-to-day basis and will be able to hear the muttered expletives as things go wrong or witness staff frustration at a piece of equipment which is too slow or otherwise inadequate. In larger areas, however, it is preferable to operate a more formal system by which goods are monitored under headings such as:

- *Frequency of use.* Is an item of equipment never or rarely used?
- *Quality of output.* For instance, is the quality of the photocopied material consistently poor, or are there complaints about the quality of the audio cassettes by the audio keyboard operators?
- *Frequency of breakdown.* Do the maintenance records or log books indicate that a machine is constantly breaking down because of overuse?

Consider what system of record-keeping you would introduce to ensure that you were kept informed of the type of problems just outlined. What action would you take should you find the complaints justified?

Timeliness of availability of physical resources

Goods must be available at the right time. Many organisations – particularly those with Purchasing departments – take some trouble to analyse all the different costs involved in stockpiling in order to reach an 'economic order quantity' (EOQ) which, ultimately, is the quantity that results in the lowest total of variable costs. If, for example, the annual usage value is low in relation to the cost of ordering and processing deliveries, the formula indicates that orders should be placed infrequently. On the other hand, if it costs appreciably more to hold a month's supply in stock than it does to order it, the formula indicates that frequent orders should be placed. Properly applied, the formula results in lower stocks, fewer orders and no reduction in service. However, it is a fairly complicated procedure and if it is applied inappropriately, its advantages are lost.

As a consequence, other methods of stock control have gained in popularity (see Figures 2.2.2 and 2.2.3).

Order-point order-quantity methods (also known as fixed order)

When the stock level of any stock item falls to a predetermined quantity called the order point (or reorder level), an order is placed for a predetermined order quantity which may be the EOQ or may be determined in some other way. The order point is the average quantity required in the normal lead time, plus buffer stock, which is a reserve to take care of requirements running at above the average rate, or delivery periods which exceed the normal lead time.

Fixed order

- On average stocks are lower than with the periodic review system.
- EOQs are applicable.
- There is enhanced responsiveness to demand fluctuations.
- Replenishment orders are automatically generated at the appropriate time by comparison of actual stock levels against reorder levels.
- It is an appropriate system for widely differing inventory categories.

Periodic review

- There is a greater chance of elimination of obsolete items owing to periodic review of stock.
- The purchasing load may be spread more evenly with possible economies in placing of orders.
- Larger quantity discounts may be negotiated when a range of stock items is ordered from the same supplier at the same time.
- Production economies due to more efficient production planning and lower set-up costs may result from orders always being in the same sequence.

Figure 2.2.2 Advantages of fixed-order and periodic-review systems

Fixed order

- The reordering system may become overloaded if many items of inventory reach reorder level simultaneously.
- There could be a random reordering pattern owing to items coming up for replenishment at different times.
- Under conditions of varying demand or ordering costs, EOQ calculations may be inaccurate.

Periodic review

- On average, larger stocks are required than with fixed order point systems, since reorder quantities must provide for the period between reviews as well as between lead times.
- Re-order quantities are not based on EOQs.
- If the usage rate changes shortly after a review period, a stockout may occur before the next review date.
- There may be difficulties in determining appropriate review periods unless demands are reasonably consistent.

Figure 2.2.3   Disadvantages of fixed-order and periodic-review systems

Periodic review methods

Order-point order-quantity methods are also known as continuous methods since they produce a continuous stream of orders – there is always some stock item which has come to the order point. Periodic review methods, on the other hand, allow for large batches of stock items to be reviewed periodically. Stock on hand is compared with a target stock figure and enough is ordered to bring the stock up to target. Typically, target stock is sufficient to last until the next review – plus the quantity likely to be used in the lead time – plus the buffer stock to cover variations.

Retailers often use a form of periodic review known as open to buy (OTB) – normally carried out on a month by month basis. If, for instance, the sales budget for a class of merchandise is £20 000 and the stock is £10 000, then the difference between the two is the OTB figure and the buyer can spend £10 000 on stocking up.

A specialised form of stock control in manufacturing industries is called Materials Requirements Planning (MRP), which is a standard computerised system for calculating the quantities of components, subassemblies and material required to carry out a production programme.

Just-in-time systems

Just-in-time (JIT) systems for production planning, stock control and purchasing were developed mainly by Japanese manufacturers. The basic idea is simple. If made-in parts are produced in just the quantity required for the next stage in the process, just in time for the next operation to be carried out, the work-in-progress stocks are almost eliminated. If bought-out parts are delivered direct to the production line without delays in stores or inspection, just in time for the needs of production and in just the quantity needed, then material stocks are also largely eliminated.

Perhaps the best known of the just-in-time systems is the *kanban* system developed by Toyota to meet customer demand for various vehicle models with minimum delivery delays. *Kanban* in Japanese means 'ticket' and refers to an information system in which instructions relating to the type and quality of items to be withdrawn from the preceding manufacturing process is conveyed by a card. It is a 'demand pull' system in which manufacturing planning begins with the final assembly line and works backwards, not only through the various manufacturing processes but also to the vendors and subcontractors supplying materials and components. The exact quantity to replace the items withdrawn to meet the requirements of one manufacturing stage are provided by the preceding process.

Cost of physical resources

Ensuring that any stock you require is delivered in the right quantity and at the right time is important. Equally important, however, is that it is at an acceptable price. If you work for an organisation in which a Purchasing department operates, this is a task which will fall to them. If, however, you are expected to purchase your own supplies within the budget allocated to you, you have to rely upon your own skill and knowledge.

One of your first steps (which should also be a continuing process) is to find out what the 'asking' prices are for each item. To do so you can consult various sources.

Catalogues

Many manufacturers and suppliers produce annual catalogues giving descriptions and prices of their goods – and also, in most instances, information about trade, cash or quantity discounts. Note also the growing practice of information being supplied 'on spec' by prospective suppliers, containing details of the organisation itself as well as of the goods it supplies and the prices it charges. One disadvantage, however, is that unless the catalogue is revised and reissued frequently, the information, particularly as regards price, can become outdated and can lead to your making false assumptions about the amount of money you have to commit to the purchase of a certain item.

Trade journals and/or trade directories

If you are planning to make regular purchases of the same item, trade journals are a useful source of reference. They contain information about general prices applicable to that type of commodity, and you are therefore able to judge whether or not your usual supplier is giving you a good deal. In some cases the information can be obtained from on-line databases such as Kompass Online, Pergamon Infoline, Data-Star Databases, Dialog Databases, Profile Information, etc. These, of course, can provide an almost instantaneous update. Trade directories such as Kompass, Rylands, Buyers Guides, etc. are also useful for new product requirements, unusual or occasional special requirements or emergency items.

Salespeople

Salespeople should be a very useful source of reference given that they are (or should be) equipped with up-to-the-minute information about the prices of the goods they are trying to sell. However, the dangers of relying solely on what they may tell you are obvious.

Individual quotations

One of the most usual ways of checking comparative prices is to send an enquiry to a number of selected suppliers. On receipt, the quotations are compared and evaluated.

For details of types of tender, see Chapter 8, page 626.

THEORY INTO PRACTICE

Assume that you have chosen one supplier and have entered into an agreement whereby he or she will supply you with a certain number of goods over a six-month period. After two months, your supplier writes to you and says that unfortunately the prices of the goods will now have to be increased because there has been a sharp and unexpected increase in the cost of certain raw materials. You are in a quandary because you cannot operate without the goods in question. Consider the action you would take in those circumstances. Consider also any future action you would take to prevent the situation from recurring.

Note: you may want to research the difference between *fixed* and *cost type* pricing agreements, both of which have certain advantages and disadvantages.

Human resources

The previous subsection concentrated on the four headings quality, quantity, timing and cost. The monitoring of human resources should also be considered under these headings, although it is likely that in this area the priority is nearly always that of quality.

The present subsection is intended to be an outline only of the different ways in which human as distinct from physical resources can be monitored and evaluated. For additional details of staff appraisal systems, see Chapter 1.

Staff appraisals

It is extremely important that your human resources function effectively. To this end, the way in which you monitor and evaluate the performance of your staff is of crucial importance to your effectiveness as a manager.

The most formal method of staff evaluation is by means of staff appraisals. Although the overriding purpose is the improvement of performance, this broad purpose has been interpreted in several ways:

- to enable the organisation to share out the money, promotions and other benefits as fairly as possible
- to discover the work potential, both present and future, of individuals and departments

- to aid manpower, departmental and corporate planning
- to discover learning needs
- to ensure that employees reach organisational standards and objectives
- to develop individuals
- to add to employee job satisfaction through understanding their needs, by recognising and measuring their achievements, preparing them for advancement, discovering opportunities for personal growth and resolving their problems
- to check the effectiveness of human resource procedures and practice.

THEORY INTO PRACTICE

Check on the system of staff appraisal in your own organisation and consider:

a how well it enables staff to measure their progress
b what strategies are used to recognise their achievements
c how any desire for career advancement is supported
d how staff are encouraged to air problems and grievances.

Appraisal methods differ slightly according to the needs of an organisation. One of the more common methods, however, is the following:

- the draft completion of the appraisal form by the employee
- a discussion between manager and employee based on the appraisal form
- a written summary of the discussion and finalisation of the form.

Most appraisal forms make reference to certain standard items, as illustrated by the example in Figure 2.2.4.

THEORY INTO PRACTICE

Consider how you would attempt to verify the answers given to the questions in the appraisal form outlined in Figure 2.2.4. Consider also what action you would take if you suspected that the member of staff concerned was merely trying to tell you what he or she thought you wanted to hear (or was giving an answer he or she hoped could lead to performance-related pay or to promotion).

The purposes of an appraisal discussion between you and your staff should be:

- to obtain a joint understanding of the duties and responsibilities attached to the job to ensure that efforts are appropriately directed and realistic job expectations are developed
- to try to improve working practices
- to summarise the regular informal feedback which has taken place on a day-to-day basis
- to identify training and development needs
- to plan progress, set targets and ways of achieving them and to implement actions
- to compliment and praise where merited.

Review of past performance

Outline your work progress (i.e. main assignments and accomplishments) during the past year.

What do you consider to be your strengths – i.e. skills, abilities and knowledge?

Have you encountered any difficulties – i.e. problems which have prevented the achievement of any targets?

What attempts did you make to overcome them?

Can you suggest any improvements?

List any development activities you have undertaken and their consequent benefits.

Future progress

What do you think are your future needs – i.e. skills, abilities and knowledge which, if developed, could lead to increased effectiveness?

What do you suggest should be
- your future training needs?
- your future work plans?
- the tasks or responsibilities which could be included into your present job which would promote your personal or career development?

Give an indication of your hoped-for future career or job development over a stated period (e.g. three years).

Figure 2.2.4 Sample staff appraisal form

Before the discussion

The member of staff concerned should try to establish what he or she thinks about the job, the career prospects, the reasons for good or poor performance, and any training or development needs.

In turn you must try to establish the ways in which the employee has carried out the job, his or her existing skills, the level of motivation, and whether the job environment helped or hindered progress.

During the discussion

Even though there are two parties to the discussion, it is you who normally has to take the lead and 'guide' it in the right direction. Some managers are more naturally confident than others in this area, but even the most gifted should bear in mind certain key concepts as outlined in Figure 2.2.5.

THEORY INTO PRACTICE

1 Consider which of the recommended actions outlined in Figure 2.2.5 you feel may be your particular strengths and which your weaknesses. Think also about what you intend to do to overcome those weaknesses.
2 Read the following extract from a discussion between Lara, a manager, and Shabbir, one of her staff, as part of the appraisal process.

LARA	Sorry I'm late – if it's not one meeting it's another. Can we curtail this session slightly – we can pick up any major issues later if needs be.
SHABBIR	Fine.
LARA	(reading from the completed form) Are you working to any specific targets? You didn't make them last year did you? That's a black mark to you.
SHABBIR	Well, we did agree at the last meeting that I should try to improve my team leading skills.
LARA	And have you?
SHABBIR	I think so – but I'm not very sure. Perhaps you should ask my team.
LARA	That's for you to do surely but, as it's you, I'll put down 'marked improvement' against that item.
SHABBIR	Fine – oh, another target I think I've met is an improvement in my IT skills. I've got an NVQ2 now.
LARA	That's pretty basic isn't it? I would have expected a higher level. Hand on heart now – can you really say you're computer literate?
SHABBIR	(hesitantly) Well, perhaps not – on second thoughts, that's a target I probably haven't reached. I told you I was a Luddite.
LARA	Any problems? I note you haven't put anything in that box.
SHABBIR	Well, I've been advised not to in case it's held against me if I apply for a promotion. But that can't be true, surely.
LARA	I shouldn't think so – but admitting to a weakness is a weakness in itself, don't you think? Anyway I've enough to go on now – you haven't much to worry about you know. I'll give you a good enough report.

Comment critically on the manager's handling of the interview.

- Allocate sufficient time for the discussion.
- Avoid having too formal an environment.
- Ensure that there are no interruptions.
- Attempt to put the member of staff at ease.
- Ask open questions.
- Make specific comments rather than mere generalisations.
- Find something positive to say early in the discussion.
- Encourage the member of staff to raise any of his or her concerns.
- Face up to difficult issues which are relevant such as weakness in a certain aspect of performance.
- Make constructive criticism if appropriate but link it to development plans.
- Accept criticism in return.
- Attempt to let the member of staff assess his or her own progress rather than making the assessment yourself.
- Try to match career aspirations with realism where necessary.
- Think ahead where an important or complicated issue is to be discussed.
- Avoid interrupting.
- Summarise what has been agreed.
- Put agreed actions in writing.
- Finish on a positive note.

Figure 2.2.5 Recommendations for appraisal interviews

Very few people admit to being poor listeners. However, one firm of management consultants who conducted a survey into the listening skills of a group of managers found that only 40 per cent of them recognised that certain listening techniques were useful. The techniques included:

- looking directly at the interviewee when he or she is talking
- summarising important issues the interviewee has raised to indicate an understanding of what has been said
- clearing up any possible misunderstandings immediately
- showing interest in what the interviewee is saying
- concentrating even when what is being said is not of the slightest interest!
- avoiding thinking of a reply before the interviewee has stopped speaking.

Note that listening skills are covered in more detail in Chapter 4.

After the discussion

In most cases, you as the interviewer will be expected to complete, with the interviewee, a joint development appraisal form comprising:

- a summary of the interviewee's strengths and achievements
- agreed areas for improvement, development and personal growth
- recommended development activities

together with a recommended timescale and follow-up procedures.

THEORY INTO PRACTICE

Many management writers suggest that you can judge your own personal effectiveness as an interviewer by analysing whether or not:

a the self-esteem of the interviewee has been increased as a result of the discussion
b he or she feels you have listened carefully to what has been said (see above and Chapter 4, page 289 to remind yourself about effective listening techniques)
c you have answered the questions asked
d the interview has been seen as a joint effort
e there is a clear idea of future direction.

Consider what quantifiable evidence you feel you would need to reassure yourself that you have indeed been personally effective in this area.

Identifying opportunities for improving the effective use of resources

If you implement good control mechanisms, these should allow you not only to check that the resources are being used effectively, but also to identify ways in which their use can be improved. The staff appraisal interview is an obvious example of a procedure which not only identifies staff strengths and weaknesses but also attempts to address them. A good stock control system can identify areas of over-expenditure or under-use which can assist you to adjust your requests for any future resources and to reorganise procedures in your own work area to overcome these difficulties. Your quality assurance procedures should also identify areas where either quantity or quality are below par, and should enable you to attempt to adjust or alter procedures, including the correct use of resources, to improve performance.

Some organisations make use of quality circles, an approach to the improvement not only of product quality but also of other aspects of company performance. In some cases they are called participation groups, in others they are known as small group improvement activities.

The normal procedure is for a group of the workforce to meet at least weekly to discuss better ways of doing things, including improving quality and increasing output. At these sessions any resource problems together with suggestions for their possible improvements are almost invariably discussed.

For further information on quality management, see Chapter 3.

What you should also be prepared to do, however, is to talk to the staff who are actually using the resources in question. The word-processing staff, for instance, will probably have a far better idea than you of how to improve their output simply because they are using the equipment every day and are accustomed to dealing with its shortcomings. The same is likely to be the case with any other frequent users of a particular resource.

One difficulty here, however, is to determine whether or not the suggested improvements are really likely to result in an increase in productivity. Some staff may try to conceal their inefficiency by claiming that it is all the fault of the equipment. Others may recommend the purchase of some additional resource simply because they have read about it in a supplier's handbook or because someone working in another area has one. In such circumstances you should try to make an independent judgement after listening to what your staff have to say. You can do this by:

- talking to other colleagues
- keeping yourself updated on new developments
- having regular contact with sales personnel of various office suppliers to enable you to compare what is on offer with regard to both quality and price.

Your presence in the workplace can also assist you to identify possible improvements. If you regularly observe your staff in action and the way in which they carry out certain tasks, you should be able to spot at least some areas in which resources are not being fully or effectively utilised.

An organisation's procedures for recommending improvements in the use of resources

Your organisation may operate a system whereby you, along with other managers, bid for a share of resources each year. (Look back to pages 155 and 156 to remind yourself of such a system.) If it does not, you may have to submit requests at your own discretion.

Whatever the procedure, the more convincing your rationale the better your chances of success are likely to be. It is normally to your advantage, therefore, to spend some time researching what you want so that your bid will consist of hard facts backed up with quantifiable evidence – rather than a nebulous statement of the advantages to be gained from agreeing to your request. If, for instance, you want to upgrade your switchboard system, you would be advised to:

- make yourself fully conversant with the existing system including its advantages and disadvantages
- obtain detailed statements from the operators of the system
- check what is on offer from various firms of suppliers or manufacturers
- compile a comparative analysis of the costs of each system together with the advantages and disadvantages of each
- check also the possibility of leasing as opposed to buying outright
- outline the benefits to the organisation of the purchase of an updated system (based on the analysis).

What you may also have to consider, however, is organisational procedures for improving rather than replacing resources. Some organisations, for instance, operate regular internal audits concentrating on specific areas such as:

- staffing
- staff training and development
- communication systems
- use of equipment
- storage and retrieval systems
- office environment

and audit each department or unit in turn. Others pick on one specific area (e.g. use of equipment) and use a standard checklist throughout the whole organisation. The results of such an audit normally reveal the need for certain improvements including whether or not they require any additional financing.

Even if your organisation does not operate such a procedure, however, it may be beneficial for you to operate a similar audit in your own work area. Not only should it allow you to effect certain improvements, it is also useful evidence for you to produce to senior management.

For further information on internal and external audits, see Chapter 3, *Plan and control activities to meet objectives.*

Legal and regulatory requirements relating to the acquisition and use of resources

Note that Chapter 8, entitled *Contract for the supply of resources and services*, deals in far greater detail with the law relating to the making and terminating of commercial contracts and the corresponding statutory and case law. Note also that Chapter 10, entitled *Facilitate compliance with legal and regulatory requirements*, covers general legal principles and terminology which may assist you with this particular element.

Physical resources

Sales people are paid to be convincing. The best of them will have a belief in the product they are selling and will quite genuinely argue that you are being given a good deal. The rest of them may not be so scrupulous, particularly if their commission depends upon your being persuaded to buy what they are selling. In your position and with your experience, you are not likely to be vulnerable to a blatant hard sell. However, you may be unaware of some of the more complex parts of an agreement you have entered into until a problem arises, when you then find that your legal rights are more limited than you anticipated.

Even though for many centuries the law has imposed duties on the sellers of goods and services – such as inn keepers and carriers – it is only in the second half of the twentieth century that there has been any concerted attempt for the law to protect the rights of the buyer. A combination of new business methods and changing social attitudes has produced changes.

The need for consumer protection has become greater because the consumer is no longer able to rely on his or her judgement, given the complexity of modern buying and selling transactions. Indeed the Molony Committee on Consumer Protection in 1961 made the point that there was a growing tendency for manufacturers to appeal directly to the public by means of 'forceful' national advertising and other promotional methods which was accompanied by a similar growth in the development of a mass market for complex technologically manufactured goods whose performance could not be accurately established by inspection or even short-term use.

Statutory requirements

The law itself now favours collectivism rather than individualism in its approach to the protection of the consumer. Consequently, modern legislation attempts to predict what problems may occur in this respect and to provide the buyer with some protection against abuse. The major relevant Acts include:

- Trades Description Act 1968
- Unsolicited Goods and Services Act 1971
- Fair Trading Act 1973
- Supply of Goods (Implied Terms) Act 1973
- Consumer Credit Act 1974

- Unfair Contract Terms Act 1977
- Consumer Safety Act 1978
- Sale of Goods Act 1979 (SOGA79)
- Supply of Goods and Services Act 1982
- Consumer Protection Act 1987
- Sale and Supply of Goods Act 1994 (SSGA94)
- Sale of Goods (Amendments) Act 1994 (SOGA94)

If your job description encompasses the right to purchase equipment or materials, a basic knowledge of the appropriate legislation is obviously advisable. Take the following scenario as an example.

You need a new photocopier. You select the one you want at what you think is a competitive price from a company which promises a good back-up service and you enter into a written agreement for its purchase. In most cases you need have no further concern. However, in the following scenarios you could face considerable problems:

- The sales person has no authority to agree to the sale.
- There is a fire at the warehouse in which the photocopier is stored and it is destroyed. The contract had been agreed and signed but no date had been agreed for actually delivering the copier.
- The total price (including VAT, delivery charges, etc.) was never agreed and when the invoice arrives it is for a much larger amount than was anticipated.
- The photocopier arrives and it is not the one you thought you had ordered.
- It arrives damaged.
- It does not perform all the functions the sales person promised it would.
- It doesn't look anything like the illustration in the sales brochure.
- Although the sales person promised that he would provide an instruction manual and that he would train one of the staff in the use of the photocopier, he has not done so despite repeated requests.
- The police arrive to say that the photocopier has been stolen from the company by the sales person who has now disappeared, and that therefore it should be returned.

Before you even begin to protest or seek recompense, you should be aware of your legal position.

THEORY INTO PRACTICE

Chapter 8 outlines some of the most relevant provisions of the Sale of Goods Act 1994 (as amended by the Sale and Supply of Goods Act 1994). Using that summary as a basic research tool, consider any possible legal claims the buyer may have under the Act in respect of each of the instances just listed.

Non-statutory requirements – consumer protection agencies

Consumer law is complex and it is unlikely that you will be expected to have a very detailed knowledge of it unless you are working in a Legal department. Even general managers, however, should be aware of the various consumer protection agencies which exist and which are able to offer useful advice and assistance.

The Department of Trade and Industry and the OFT

The Department of Trade and Industry (DTI) now has an Under Secretary of State for Industry and Consumer Affairs amongst whose duties is the making of regulations under the Consumer Credit Act and the Consumer Protection Act.

Closely linked with the DTI is the Office of Fair Trading (OFT) which was set up as a result of the Fair Trading Act 1973. The duties of the Director General of Fair Trading include:

- keeping under review the commercial supply of goods and services to consumers in the UK
- taking action against individual traders who have persisted in a course of conduct which is unfair to consumers
- providing information to the public
- encouraging trade associations to prepare codes of practice for their members
- supervising and controlling the consumer credit industry as a result of the Consumer Credit Act 1974.

The National Consumer Council

The NCC is an independent but publicly funded body which acts as a watchdog and pressure group to protect consumer interests. Recent activities have included investigations into the price of electricity and water and the problem of disconnection, the secrecy of drugs testing, the effect of competition between schools, and the proposals to change the joint liability of creditor and supplier under the Consumer Credit Act.

The British Standards Institution

The DTI makes a grant to the British Standards Institution (BSI) which is a voluntary body, one of whose functions is to lay down uniform specifications for certain products.

Local authorities

The county councils and London boroughs make a major contribution to consumer protection by employing trading standards inspectors who have extensive responsibilities in the enforcement of the Trade Descriptions, the Consumer Credit and the Fair Trading Acts. Local authority involvement also extends to the field of consumer advice, and Consumer Advice Centres have been set up in many parts of the country under the Local Government Act 1972. They give pre-purchase advice and advice on complaints.

The Consumers Association

The results of the Consumers Association's investigations are published in its monthly magazine *Which?*, and can be of great value to prospective consumers. The Association is also active in promoting legislation dealing with consumer affairs.

Local consumer groups

These groups carry out research into the quality of local services and publish the results to their members. There is a central coordinating body known as the National Federation of Consumer Groups, whose total membership is in the region of 2000.

Trade and professional associations

These associations (e.g. the Retail Motor Industry Federation and the Association of British Travel Agents) operate voluntary conciliation and arbitration procedures. A consumer with a complaint may well find that an approach to the relevant association produces a more satisfactory outcome than taking legal proceedings. In some industries (e.g. insurance) there is an 'ombudsman' to whom to make a complaint.

THEORY INTO PRACTICE

As part of your security network you have purchased a CCTV system which is faulty in some respect. Find out about the agencies – both nationally and in your locality – which you feel could give you some assistance in obtaining redress.

Human resources

When you recruit a member of staff you are immediately bound by certain legal obligations arising from the contract of employment. Although many of these obligations originated from the common law, nowadays most of the relevant law is contained in a number of interrelated statutes.

There are four principal types of contract. A *permanent contract* is still the most usual type, being open-ended with no fixed date of expiry. Unilateral ending of the contract by the employer is regarded as dismissal and may result in a claim for unfair dismissal.

A *fixed-term* contract has both a definite starting date and a definite end date. Although its ending is deemed to be dismissal, it is rare that this dismissal would be considered to be unfair.

A *performance contract* is discharged by the performance of a specific task. When it ends there is no question of a dismissal.

A *temporary contract* is for a limited period but is not fixed-term nor terminated by performance. Its premature ending would constitute a dismissal in the same way as the ending of a permanent contract.

The contract of employment

When a new member of staff appears in your work area, you are probably right in assuming that he or she is an employee of the organisation rather than a self-employed contractor. However, if you are at all doubtful, you should check the exact nature of his or her employment status as each status carries with it different rights and obligations under the law. (Chapter 10 requires you to research the different tests for determining employment status.)

If that member of staff is an employee, however, then he or she will be regarded as having entered a contract of employment (rather than a contract for services). The contract comes into existence once the employer makes an offer and the candidate accepts. If the offer is conditional, it will expire if the condition is not met, as in *Wishart v National Association of Advice Bureaux Ltd* [1990] IRLR 393, where satisfactory references were not provided. More generally an offer terminates after a fixed period, if specified, or otherwise after a reasonable length of time has elapsed. What should be noted, however, is that the concept of a contract of employment emanates from the common law and has as its basis the idea of exchange – i.e. consideration for services rendered. Consequently, although statutory legislation has introduced some refinements to the agreement between employer and employee, in essence it tends to have a number of sources all of which combine to form the eventual contract. The main sources include the following.

- *Express terms.* These are directly agreed between the employee and employer either in writing or orally (a promise made at the interview, for instance, will become part of the contract if there is sufficient evidence of its existence).

- *Terms incorporated from collective agreements.* These are terms which are collectively negotiated by an employer (or employers) and one or more trades unions. They are agreed by the union on behalf of the employee and have become expressly or impliedly incorporated into the individual contract of employment (for further discussion see page 180).

- *Works rules.* Many works rules are likely to be contractual, especially if they relate to discipline.

- *Custom and practice.* Where there are no express terms or other evidence of a particular point, custom or practice may be used to imply a term. However, such terms must be widely known, reasonable and precisely defined.

- *Implied terms.* Such terms are considered to be so essential to the operation of the contract that they need not be expressed. See Figures 2.2.6 and 2.2.7 for an outline of the most important of these.

Obedience to lawful orders

All employees must obey the lawful orders of the employer. Not only must the orders be lawful, they must not place the employee in a position of potential harm or danger, other than in those special occupations that are in themselves intrinsically dangerous.

Personal service

Employees, unlike self-employed contractors, are bound to give personal service. Should they refuse to work, the employer will have the common law power, though not necessarily the statutory power, to summarily dismiss them for breach of contract. Obviously a strike is a breach of contract but, although an employer may dismiss all strikers, in practice he or she rarely does.

Competence and skill

Employees are under a duty to demonstrate a certain level of skill. This duty also implies that the employee should be prepared to adapt to any 'reasonable' changes such as a willingness to learn new skills. In *MacPherson v London Borough of Lambeth* [1988] IRLR 470, for instance, the court upheld the right of an employer to withhold pay because the employees would not operate a new computer.

An employer has the common law power to dismiss an incompetent employee. However, statutory law has now introduced some safeguards for the employee and normally the employer has to follow a number of procedures before he or she can safely dismiss.

Duty of fidelity

During the course of employment, an employee must not use any secret knowledge for his or her own gain outside the workplace. Nor must he or she 'poach' customers for private work or 'foreigners'. Equally employees must not use information gained in the course of their employment to start up a rival business. However, employees may use any skills (such as computer programming skills) or information they learn in employment when they leave an employment and, unless there is a valid restraint of trade clause in the contract, they may probably also take any information they are able to retain mentally.

Provided there is no express term in the contract of employment forbidding an employee to work at any other job at the same time as his or her full-time employment, then an employee may do so – *unless* it is for a competitor or affects the employee's performance in the full-time job.

Figure 2.2.6 The contract of employment – implied obligations of the employee

Payment of wages

The Wages Act 1986 defines wages as 'any sums payable to the worker by his employer in connection with his employment'. It is a fundamental duty of an employer to pay wages and in most cases the amount will be an express term of the contract. If, for some reason, no mention is made of the amount, then a 'reasonable' amount will be implied (although at the moment there is no *right* to a minimum wage). However, the position as regards deductions is different. The Wages Act restricts the deductions that can be made from wages and allows complaints to be made to an industrial tribunal about unauthorised deductions. Even so, the Act does not specify *what* type of deduction is unreasonable. It simply aims to prevent deductions being made which have not previously been agreed.

Provision of work
If an employer chooses to pay an employee yet give him or her nothing to do, the law will not interfere except in certain specific circumstances. If, for instance, an employee is paid solely on results or is dependent upon being able to work in order to publicise what he or she can do (such as an actor or journalist), then failure to provide that work could be a breach. In more recent years, the courts have also listened sympathetically to claims that highly skilled workers need to be able to practise their skills and the fact that they are still being paid even though no work is being provided is irrelevant.

Duty to manage reasonably
It is the word 'reasonable' that has caused many problems for the courts and has led to a proliferation of unfair dismissal cases covered by the Employment Protection (Consolidation) Act 1978. Both employer and employee are under a duty to behave properly towards each other. Obviously that duty covers a variety of issues, not all of them quantifiable. Interestingly, one case has extended the duty of the manager to manage reasonably to providing information to an employee about contract terms which have not been agreed with the employee individually and about which the employee could not reasonably be expected to know. In *Scally and others v Southern Health and Social Services Board* [1991] IRLR 552, a group of doctors successfully sued their employers for loss sustained by them by reason of their employer's failure to bring to their notice their right to purchase added years of pension entitlement before that right lapsed.

Duty to maintain a safe system of work
Under common law the employer was under a duty of care to ensure that the workplace was safe. That duty of care together with the corresponding duty of an employee towards the employer and other employees is now contained in s.12(1) of the Management of Health and Safety at Work Regulations 1992.

Figure 2.2.7   The contract of employment – implied obligations of the employer

THEORY INTO PRACTICE

You are expected not only to familiarise yourself with the implied obligations in a contract of employment, but also to make sure that your staff are fully aware of them. Consider how you might try to convey that information to them in a short presentation.

Written particulars of employment

In addition to common law implied obligations, statutory law in the shape of the Employment Protection (Consolidation) Act 1978 (EPCA) as amended by the Trade Union Reform and Employment Rights Act 1995 (TURER), now requires an employer to give all employees, no matter the number of hours they work, *evidence* of their contract of employment by providing them with certain written particulars within one month of their starting work. Items which must be included are:

- the names of the employer and employee, the date when the employment began and the date on which the employee's period of continuous employment began (taking into account any employment with a previous employer which counts toward the period)
- the amount of pay and the method by which it is calculated
- when wages or salary will be paid and how many hours will be worked per week
- if relevant, terms and conditions relating to holidays and holiday pay, sick pay and procedures, pensions and pension schemes
- the minimum period of notice
- the title of the job or a brief description of it
- whether it is a permanent or a fixed-term contract
- the place of employment – where an employee is required to work at a number of different places, that fact should be noted together with the address of the employer
- whether there are collective agreements that affect the terms and conditions of employment, such as an agreement with a trade union
- any rules and regulations attaching to the work of an employee required to work outside the UK, including the method and currency of payment, the period to be spent abroad, and any additional benefits, terms and conditions relating to the return to the UK.

THEORY INTO PRACTICE

Research what is meant by a collective agreement entered into by union and management and to what extent it is legally binding on individual employees. Consider the possible reasons for the requirement that the existence of any collective agreement should be indicated in the written particulars given to employees.

In any dispute about the terms of a contract, the courts may *imply* a term. Sometimes evidence can be found in the terms of collective agreements or in custom and practice. In other cases the court may simply imply a reasonable term. In *Coslett Contractors Ltd v Quinn* [1990] 425 IDS, for example, it implied a term that expenses reasonably incurred in the course of employment would be reimbursed.

However, courts will generally enforce contract terms without reference to their fairness to the respective parties provided that the contract itself is not illegal, it is not contrary to public policy, it is not void by statute, and it has been entered into willingly. They may, however, restrict the operation of terms if they consider them too wide, especially if they are in restraint of trade or thought to have been imposed under duress. In *United Bank Ltd v Akhtar* [1989] IRLR 507, where an employee's contract contained a very wide-ranging mobility clause, the court implied a further term requiring the employer to handle any relocation reasonably.

Because a contract can consist of a number of documents ranging from the job advertisement and the job description to the letter of appointment, managers are advised to take particular care when preparing such documents, particularly in the three main areas which traditionally cause problems – location, hours of work and duties. In all three cases an employer has much to gain by drawing the contract terms widely because he or she is then able to alter them legitimately. Check your own letter of appointment and job description to see how far you think your employer has adopted this practice. Think also about the disadvantages such a practice may have.

Variation of contract

What you should also bear in mind – particularly if you are responsible for a group of staff – is that contracts are fluid and should be capable of being varied to meet changing circumstances. Obviously it is preferable to have a mutually agreed change to a contract. This can occur in one of several ways.

Express agreement

In law the contract is an agreement entered into voluntarily by both parties who, in theory, have equal power. Any agreed changes, therefore, do not offend the principle of mutuality and will be regarded as a consensual variation of the contract.

Variation by conduct

Situations can arise in which changes are made unilaterally (normally by the employer) but are accepted by the other party by implication. If, for example, the employer changes the agreed hours of work and the employees do no protest but merely continue working, after a period of time they will be considered to have accepted that change *even though they may not have expressly agreed to it.*

Incorporation of terms

Employers may be able to negotiate contractual changes with a union. Such a change will alter the contracts of individual employees only if the terms of the collective agreement become incorporated into those contracts, which agreement may either be express or implied. Refer to your answers for the THEORY INTO PRACTICE exercise on page 180 for further information.

Not all changes to terms and conditions of employment involve *contractual* changes. In this respect a distinction needs to be drawn between terms and conditions, the former referring, for example, to items such as the amount of holiday entitlement and the latter to the time when they can be taken; i.e. terms are based on contractual agreement whereas conditions are laid down by the employer unilaterally. In addition some employee benefits may be the result solely of employer goodwill – such as the employees' Christmas bonus.

In many job descriptions, a general clause such as 'and any other duties as may be required' is inserted at the end of a list of specific duties. Based on what you have already read about implied employer and employee obligations, consider whether you think the law will allow an employer to use that clause to ask an employee to do anything at all.

Unilateral changes

If an agreed variation is not possible the employer can, if he or she wishes, unilaterally change the conditions by:

- giving notice to the employees and offering new contracts containing new terms
- informing the employees that if they do not accept the change they will be dismissed
- imposing the change and waiting to see employee reaction.

Generally speaking any unilateral change which is not accepted can be regarded as a breach of contract. If the breach is substantial and the term is one which goes to the root of the contract (as in *Western Excavating (ECC) v Sharp* [1978] IRLR 27) then the contract will be held to have been repudiated and the employee may be able to claim compensation. Examples include a cut in pay, an (unpaid) increase in hours, or a substantial demotion.

When such a breach occurs, employees have the choice of electing to affirm the contract. If they do not, however, they have a number of options. In *Ferodo v Rigby* [1987] IRLR 516, where a wage cut was imposed on employees against their will, the resulting breach allowed them to sue for damages for the amount of the reduction. Similarly, in *Miller v Hamworthy Engineering Ltd* [1986] IRLR 461 an employee was entitled to claim lost pay caused by a shorter working week being introduced unilaterally by the employer.

What an employee may also do, however, is to treat the breach as grounds for terminating the contract and to claim unfair actual dismissal (if the employer chooses to dismiss) or unfair constructive dismissal on the grounds of fundamental breach of contract (see pages 183–4 for further discussion).

An employee may also have recourse to what are known as 'equitable remedies' – injunctions and orders for specific performance in which the court either stops an employer from performing *or* compels him or her to carry out a certain action. For further discussion see Chapter 10.

If an employee challenges the unilateral variation, an employer may defend the action by, for instance, claiming that the business required such a change because of financial difficulties or a need to improve productivity in the light of increased competition. If this is provable, industrial tribunals tend to regard such a defence sympathetically.

> To overcome some of the difficulties caused by unilateral variation of contract, some employers now insert a 'flexibility' clause into the contract which gives them the right to alter certain terms and conditions. The existence of such a clause means, in effect, that the employee has agreed in advance to that alteration.
>
> Alternatively, an employer may initially restrict any contractual changes to new employees who would be offered terms different from those of existing staff and would thus partially at least achieve his or her desired end. In firms with a high turnover of staff, the problem would resolve itself quite quickly. In other firms, the employer would have to be prepared to face the difficulties of staff working under different sets of terms and conditions. Frequently, however, existing employees (or their unions) tend to become more responsive to the suggested changes when they perceive the balance of those working under the new and those working under the existing conditions beginning to alter.

Termination of employment

The employment relationship can be terminated in one of several ways. The least contentious is where the employee either retires or finds another job. The most contentious is where he or she is dismissed or made redundant. Statutory legislation now allows employees to claim that they have been unfairly dismissed or made redundant, but to do so they have first of all to prove dismissal.

In most cases the fact of dismissal is easy to prove. It occurs when an employer dispenses with the services of an employee either by letter or face to face at the workplace. However, in some cases although an actual dismissal does not take place, the conduct of the employer is such that it amounts to a breach of contract enabling the employee to leave and claim 'constructive' dismissal. In order to prove such a dismissal, the employee often claims that the employer has breached his or her common law implied obligation to behave reasonably, which can cause considerable problems for the courts.

THEORY INTO PRACTICE

Consider why the courts should choose to interpret the term 'constructive dismissal' quite widely when it is within their power to lay down more definitive guidelines.

> In certain circumstances an employee can claim that his or her dismissal is *automatically* unfair, so that no defence by the employer is allowable. The circumstances include:

- dismissal on health and safety grounds (e.g. an employee who has been designated as having responsibility for health and safety and is dismissed for taking some action in relation to those duties)
- dismissal for being or proposing to become a member of a trade union
- failure to reinstate after pregnancy.

THEORY INTO PRACTICE

On occasions, an employee may claim he or she has been summarily dismissed, wrongfully dismissed or that the contract has been frustrated. Research the difference between these forms of termination of contract.

Sale of business

At one time the more unscrupulous employers tended to try to circumvent employment protection legislation by closing down their businesses if problems occurred, only to reopen them a short time later, sometimes under a different name. Alternatively they would transfer the business to someone else – often a colleague or a relative. The Trade Union and Labour Relations Act 1983 now brings UK legislation into line with the EU Directive on Acquired Rights (implemented in part by the Transfer of Undertaking (Protection of Employment) Regulations 1981) and protects the rights of employees when a business is sold or transferred. It states that:

- the terms and conditions of the employees must be maintained by the new owner of a business or enterprise that has been bought or transferred
- the dismissal of any employee for a reason relating to the transfer of the business is automatically unfair unless there is an economic, technical or organisational reason for the dismissal
- where there is to be a transfer or sale of a business, any recognised trade union in existence at the enterprise must be informed and advised as to how the transfer will affect the employees.

Employer defences

An employer can use one of the following defences to claim that the dismissal was fair.

Capability or qualifications

In one case, *Davison v Kent Meters Ltd* [1975] IRLR 145, an employee assembled around 500 parts in the wrong order. She claimed that the charge hand had shown her how to complete the tasks and that she had completed them in the way he required. He denied showing the employee how to do the work and said that she should have known how to do it without being told.

The employer lost the case. Nowadays it is a very poor defence to a claim for unfair dismissal merely to say that the employee was incompetent. In most cases, the court will require some evidence that the employer has tried to assist the employee unless it is perfectly obvious that no amount of assistance will effect an improvement. Obviously the more senior or the more qualified an employee is, the less likely it will be that such help should be expected.

Conduct

Misconduct comes in many forms and recorded cases include violence, theft, drunkenness, dangerous behaviour, refusal to obey a lawful order, failure to comply with safety regulations, abusive behaviour, sleeping at work, failure to follow a prescribed dress code, etc.

Unless the offence is so serious as to warrant summary or instant dismissal, it is normal practice to follow the *ACAS Code of Practice on Disciplinary Practice and Procedures in Employment* which outlines the disciplinary procedures that should be invoked in the case of a breach of company rules. The tribunals will invariably refuse to continue with a case if they find the *Code of Practice* has been ignored.

The tribunals will also expect the employer to be able to answer the following questions.

- Did he or she have 'a reasonable suspicion amounting to a belief' that the employee had committed the misconduct at the time the dismissal took place?
- Did he or she have reasonable grounds for that belief?
- Did he or she carry out a reasonable investigation?

It has now been established that even if the employer has a very strong defence to any claim for unfair dismissal, if the correct procedures have not been followed, he or she will lose the case. In *Polkey v Dayton Services Ltd* [1988] AC 344, the company employed four van drivers. It was decided to replace the four van drivers with two salespeople. Only one of the drivers was thought capable of carrying out the selling as well as the driving function, so the other three were made redundant. The first the drivers knew of this was when they were called into the office, told they were redundant and sent home. Even though there was a genuine redundancy case, the fact that the correct redundancy procedures had not been followed made the dismissal unfair.

THEORY INTO PRACTICE

Prima facie, it seems somewhat unfair that an employee who is guilty of some offence warranting dismissal should escape punishment merely because an employer has forgotten to carry out a certain procedure. Consider what may be the reason for the court's attitude in this respect.

Redundancy

An employee may justifiably be made redundant unless he or she is treated less fairly than other employees. The five basic principles for an employer to follow are:

- the employer should give employees and trade unions as much notice as possible
- he or she should consult with the trade unions to arrive at the best method of effecting the redundancies and the criteria for selection should be agreed

- the criteria for selecting employees for redundancy should be objective and therefore capable of being checked
- the selection for redundancy should be made in accordance with the selection criteria
- an employer should attempt to find alternative employment for a redundant employee.

THEORY INTO PRACTICE

The usual selection criteria for redundancy purposes include:

- length of service
- capability and skill
- qualifications
- experience
- flexibility/adaptability
- attendance or disciplinary record.

Consider the difficulties there may be in applying an objective approach to certain of these criteria.

A small enterprise may still be able to make a person redundant on economic grounds. In one case, a woman serving behind a bar was made redundant by the new owners of the pub who claimed they could not afford to employ her. They won the case.

Contravention of a duty imposed by a statute

Examples of this very limited defence include an employee who has been banned from driving but whose job requires him or her to use a car, or employees who have been dismissed because the firm has been closed down because of breach of statutory health and safety requirements.

Some other substantial reason

As is obvious, this last section is a 'catch-all' section designed to allow employers to claim that a dismissal is fair even though it does not naturally fall within one of the previous categories. In one case, for example, a school caretaker worked a 39-hour week of which 25 hours were cleaning duties and 14 caretaking. Following a successful inhouse tender for the provision of cleaning services, she was required to spend 34 hours a week cleaning and only 5 hours caretaking. The change, which did not affect her pay, was as a result of the removal of the post of cleaning assistant. She refused to accept the new duties even though if the Council had not undertaken some reorganisation it would have been unable to put in a competitive bid. She was dismissed and the dismissal was held fair under the SOSR defence – given that the other available defences were inappropriate.

The test of 'reasonableness'

If an employer cannot establish one of the above reasons for dismissal, his or her claim will fail. However, there is a second stage to the process. Even if the dismissal has been established as 'fair', the tribunal must then impose upon it a test of 'reasonableness'; i.e. it must take into account 'the size and administrative resources of the employer's undertaking' and decide the issue 'in accordance with equity and the substantial merits of the case'. In practice tribunals look at the procedures which have been followed (see page 185 for a discussion about the Polkey case) and the consistency and the appropriateness of the dismissal as a disciplinary measure.

Note, however, that they must not put themselves in the place of the employer and say what they would have done if they had been that employer. What they must do first is to recognise that for any disciplinary offence, there will be a range of reasonable responses. They should then ask whether or not the employer's response falls within that range.

Equal opportunities legislation

In general, employment legislation applies to all employees. However, equal opportunities legislation offers additional protection to certain categories of employee. In this respect UK legislation is strongly influenced by European Court of Justice decisions, many of which are equal-opportunities related and carry considerable financial consequences for those organisations found to be in breach of them. You should, therefore, make sure that even if you do not know the law in detail, you are aware of the general principles and know where to access any specific information when necessary.

Equal pay

The Equal Pay Act 1970 was intended to increase women's hourly earnings to the same level as those of men. If, therefore, a woman believes that she is not being paid on the same level she must find a male comparator who is employed on either:

- like work
- work rated as equivalent, or
- work of equal value.

Like work

If a woman decides to claim like work, she must make sure that the employer cannot claim that there are differences of 'practical importance' between her duties and those of her male comparator entitling the male to a higher rate of pay. Such differences have been held to include working antisocial hours, extra responsibility, additional duties, or working in less pleasant conditions.

The tribunal will not accept two apparently different job descriptions as evidence that the man has to undertake different duties from those of the woman. It will investigate what *in reality* the man and woman are expected to do.

Work rated as equivalent

If a job evaluation scheme exists that ranks equally the two jobs concerned, then the woman should be paid at the same rate.

Work of equal value

By acceding to the European Community, the UK accepted the Treaty of Rome, Article 119 of which states that 'men and women should receive equal pay for work of equal value'. As a consequence the Equal Pay (Amendment) Regulations 1983 (SI 1983/1794) inserted a new paragraph to this effect into the 1970 Act.

Obviously this new provision has proved very helpful to those women in occupationally segregated areas – such as assembly work, cleaning, canteen work – for whom finding a male comparator doing exactly the same work is very difficult. One woman, for instance, was able to claim that her work as a cook was of equal value to that of men working as painters, joiners and thermal heating engineers – when prior to 1983 she would have had no legal grounds for doing so.

Despite the obvious advantages, there have been some criticisms of the new right. The major problem is that of the complex procedure to be followed which involves:

- the claimant making the application
- an independent expert investigating the claim and making a report (a process which can take up to two years)
- the industrial tribunal considering the report and reaching a decision.

Employer defences

One defence – that of a difference of practical importance between the jobs in question – has already been discussed. Another defence open to an employer, however, is that there is a 'material difference' between the man himself and the woman herself. Examples include longer service, higher qualifications and more relevant experience.

THEORY INTO PRACTICE

Most employers, if called upon to defend a difference in pay between male and female employees, prefer to use the defence of a difference of practical importance between the two jobs, rather than that of a material difference between the two people concerned. Consider why that should be the case.

Other measures against discrimination

Sex discrimination

Equal-pay legislation, as its name implies, is concerned only with pay and relates only to terms of employment. It does not therefore apply to pre-employment situations such as interviews. Nor does it apply in situations where women are treated less fairly than men as regards promotion or training opportunities, etc. That 'gap' is filled by the Sex Discrimination Act 1975 (updated by the Sex Discrimination Act 1986) which prohibits unequal treatment in many areas, including that of employment. Discrimination can be direct or indirect.

Direct sex discrimination

Direct discrimination occurs where a woman is treated less favourably than a man. Examples include:

- a married woman who is not offered a job because the employer thinks she will be more likely to have time off to look after her children if they become ill
- a single young woman who is similarly treated because the employer in this case thinks that she will soon be married and will move to whichever area of the country her partner finds employment.
- a woman who is not offered promotion because it is felt that the company's customers prefer to deal with a male sales manager.

Equal opportunity legislation attempts to reduce the effect of stereotyping. In one case, for instance, it was held that discrimination had occurred when a Welsh County Council refused to send a woman on a training course in the London area because her husband worked there and it was 'assumed' that she would want to stay in London after the completion of her course.

Indirect sex discrimination

Indirect discrimination occurs where the employer applies to a woman a requirement or condition which applies also to a man but which:

- is such that the proportion of women who can comply with it is considerably smaller than the proportion of men who can comply with it
- cannot be shown to be justifiable irrespective of the sex to whom it is applied
- is to the woman's detriment because she cannot comply with it.

THEORY INTO PRACTICE

In one case, a 37-year-old woman was refused a post because she did not meet the age criteria laid down: candidates – whether male or female – had to be between 17 and 28. Consider why the tribunal held that to be indirect discrimination.

THEORY INTO PRACTICE

An employer may still be able to justify a decision which results in discrimination against a woman on grounds of what in the US is called 'business necessity', but in the UK entails balancing the discriminatory requirement against the *reasonable* needs of the employer. An employer is entitled, moreover, to claim a 'genuine occupational qualification' in certain – very limited – cases. Check Section 7 of the Sex Discrimination Act to find out what these are. Check also the exemptions applying to:

- national security
- private households
- charitable trusts
- sports and sporting facilities.

Race discrimination

The Race Relations Act 1976 is phrased in very similar terms to the Sex Discrimination Acts and operates in much the same way. It prohibits both direct and indirect discrimination against ethnic minorities.

Disability discrimination

The relatively new concept of discrimination against the disabled has been encapsulated in the Disability Discrimination Act 1995. Again, its basic principles mirror those of the Sex Discrimination and Race Relations Acts, and it is now unlawful to discriminate either directly or indirectly against anyone with a physical or mental impairment which has a substantial and long-term adverse effect on his or her ability to carry out normal, day-to-day activities. Employers are therefore now faced with having to consider certain adjustments, such as

- reallocation of duties to another person
- alteration of working hours
- transfer to a different place of work
- acquisition or modification of equipment
- provision of supervision
- arrangement of leave for rehabilitation or treatment.

At present there is no Disability Commission to carry out work similar to that carried out by the Equal Opportunities Commission and the Commission for Racial Equality – which have the power to undertake investigations into possible breaches of the Acts. Instead, the legislation is monitored by the National Disability Council under the DSS, which has the job of advising ministers and preparing the relevant codes of practice.

ANSWER TO 'THEORY INTO PRACTICE' EXERCISE ON PAGE 114

In both cases it was held that the damage was too remote for a duty of care to exist.

Plan and control activities to meet objectives

Element 3.1

Prepare and update an operational plan

An organisation's objectives and priorities

The priorities and objectives of your organisation are probably set by your senior managers, whose role it is to:

- decide upon appropriate strategies
- prepare a mission statement
- prepare a strategic plan
- determine appropriate policies
- establish organisational objectives.

It is likely that they then delegate the associated operational issues to you.

Development of strategies

After your senior managers have debated an issue, the next logical step for them to take is to develop a *strategy* designed to enable them to achieve the agreed course of action. At this point, much depends on the type of management culture in your organisation. You may find, for instance, that your senior management team operates a strategy whereby risks are minimised by ensuring that all possible consequences of any action have been fully explored. Particularly valuable in this context, therefore, are their analytical and decision-making powers.

You may work in an organisation where the managing director makes every important decision (and sometimes the less important ones as well). He or she may use intuition when reaching a decision and be inclined to take risks when doing so. Because only one person is making the decisions, the strategy tends to be relatively uncomplicated.

Alternatively, you may work for a management team which is much more cautious and whose strategy is to carry out a series of measures designed to protect the organisation from competitors. Their aim is not the achievement of resounding success but rather avoidance of total defeat.

Difficult though it may be for you if you work in an environment in which senior management is constantly changing, resulting in an equally constant change of strategy, it might be heartening to note that there appears to be no general agreement on the most effective approach to strategic thinking. Even the most influential management writers tend to differ in their views about the type of strategies they feel should be implemented by organisations.

Select one of the writers mentioned below – preferably the one whose views either most interest you or are very similar to the views of your senior management team – and research further into his or her works.

Richard Beckhard advocates that:

- the total organisation should manage its work against goals and plans for the achievement of those goals
- decisions should be made by or near the sources of information
- internal competition should be kept to a minimum.

Charles Handy suggests that an effective organisation is a 'learning' organisation which has a *formal* way of asking questions and seeking out, testing and reflecting on various theories. He also advocates the growth of the federal organisation which takes the process of decentralisation a stage further by establishing each key operational, manufacturing or service provision activity as a distinct unit each running its own affairs, although linked together by the overall strategy of the organisation.

Sir John Harvey-Jones maintains that the whole of business is about taking an 'acceptable' risk and that the process of deciding on a particular strategy is an opportunity to seek and obtain the involvement of others.

Rosabeth Moss Kanter emphasises the importance of managing change, with managers and administrators acting as 'change masters'. She also advocates an organisational structure that produces synergies not conflict, creates more cooperative alliances with suppliers and customers, and allows for the maintenance of a flow of new ideas towards new products and new ventures.

J. Katzenbach and D. Smith suggest that high-performing organisations should have a top management whose primary purpose is that of focusing on performance and the teams that will deliver it.

Richard Pascale proposes a new paradigm for organisations in which they:

- operate as networks rather than hierarchies
- focus less on content and more on 'process'
- change from a military to a commitment model.

Tom Peters and Robert Waterman identify the following attributes which characterise good organisational strategy:

- a bias for action
- a willingness to keep close to the customer
- the fostering of leaders and innovators
- sticking close to the business they know, i.e. 'sticking to their knitting'
- a simple organisation structure.

In addition Tom Peters suggests that organisations be broken down into the smallest possible independent units, with flexibility being achieved by the empowerment of all staff.

Preparation of the mission statement

Once a strategy has been established, it is customary for a mission statement to be prepared which encapsulates that strategy. There are two schools of thought about such statements. Some management writers suggest that the mission statement should be broad to allow for:

- greater scope and flexibility to develop alternative strategies, objectives and growth opportunities
- the satisfaction of the needs of all the groups of people in the organisation.

Others suggest that the mission statement should encompass:

- a definition of the basic product or service
- a definition of its customers and markets
- aspirations for growth and profitability
- organisational philosophy
- social responsibility and public image (e.g. product reliability, efficiency of operations, general relationships with society)

and that such criteria should be influenced by:

- the organisation's history
- its distinctive features
- any opportunities and threats affecting it
- the availability of sufficient resources.

Whatever the approach, however, what most mission statements do is attempt to address the following:

- the nature of the business
- the customer
- the benefits offered
- how the demands and expectations of the customer are to be met.

> The modern trend of printing the organisation's mission statement on miniature 'culture' cards – designed to act as a constant reminder to employees and to be carried around by them – was introduced by a chairman of General Motors when he first took over the management of the company.

Preparation of the strategic plan

Although a mission statement containing the broad aims of an organisation can be instrumental in enabling it to establish its *raison d'être* in the eyes of the outside world, it is of only limited use in either strategic or operational planning. Hence the necessity for an organisational strategic plan. Most strategic plans do the following.

- They define the organisation's mission or overall purpose.
- They set objectives in the light of what the organisation must achieve to fulfil its mission.
- They encompass an internal appraisal of the strengths and weaknesses of the organisation and an external appraisal of the opportunities and threats which face it (i.e. a SWOT analysis).

- They analyse existing strategies which may include *gap analysis* to establish the extent to which certain factors might lead to gaps between what is being achieved and what could be achieved if changes in existing strategies were made. In a corporation with a number of distinct businesses, an analysis of the viability of each strategic business unit (SBU), known as a *portfolio analysis*, should also take place to establish strategies for the future of each unit.
- They define strategic issues in the light of the above analyses.
- They develop new or revised strategies and amend objectives where relevant.
- They decide on the critical success factors related to the achievement of objectives and the implementation of strategy.
- They require the preparation and implementation of operational and other plans designed to achieve the strategies and meet the critical success factor criteria.
- They encompass the monitoring of results against the plans and feed back information which can be used to modify strategies and plans.

> When preparing their strategic plan, some organisations make use of the services of the Strategic Planning Society, an organisation set up in the early 1960s, the majority of whose 4000 members are corporate strategists in the private sector.

Determination of policies

Again, even though a strategy may be inspirational, it will not normally provide a sufficient basis for a realistic business plan. In most cases, therefore, once your senior management have formulated a strategy, they will devise a *policy*:

- to establish the longer-term objectives of the organisation and the basic strategies for their attainment
- to define the relevant areas – finance, human resources, marketing, etc. – involved in implementing the organisation's strategies
- to decide the organisational structure
- to develop management planning, information and control systems appropriate to the organisational structure.

THEORY INTO PRACTICE

Your staff are practical individuals who tend to lose interest if you mention the word 'policy'. They argue that policy is a deterrent rather than an aid to good management and are consequently indifferent to the proposed introduction of any new policy. Consider how you would try to persuade your staff of the benefits of the introduction of a new staff appraisal policy, bearing in mind that *you* know that the advantages of policies are that:

- they can effect a change of thinking as well as of practice particularly in areas which are hidebound by custom and practice or by a *de facto* system

- they make a manager's position clear
- they make *management's* position clear
- they can produce *consistent* management behaviour
- they can reduce dependence on individuals.

Establishment of organisational objectives

Traditionally, organisational objectives have been concerned with the maximisation of profits, with managers acting as the decision-makers in the process. In reality, however, they tend to be much more varied. Traditionally too they have been regarded as the prerogative of larger organisations. Nowadays, smaller organisations benefit equally well from the setting of objectives, although the scale of the operation will be different.

Categorisation of objectives

The type of objectives selected by the decision-makers as organisational objectives obviously depends on the type of organisation. However, in general they can be categorised into directional, performance, internal or external types.

Directional objectives are concerned with the direction the organisation must take with regard to its competitive standing – commonly measured by market share:

- *market leadership* measured by competitive position, degree of innovation and technological advances
- *market spread* measured by the number of markets, the number of customer groups, the number of industries and the number of countries
- *consumer service* measured by product utility, product quality and product reliability.

Performance objectives relate to the outcomes expected to be achieved by the organisation:

- *growth* measured by sales revenue, volume output and profit margin
- *profitability* measured by return on capital employed, return on assets, profit margin on sales revenue and return on shareholders' funds.

Internal objectives are concerned with the general efficiency, effectiveness and economy of the organisation:

- *efficiency* measured by sales on total assets, stock turnover, credit period, liquidity and department costs on sales
- *human resources* measured by employee relations and morale, personal development, average employee remuneration and sales revenue per employee.

External objectives relate to the standing of the organisation in the eyes of the outside world. For example it has a *social responsibility* measured by corporate image, price–profit relationship, resource utilisation, public activity, and community welfare.

In order to encourage more organisations to become socially responsible, several research studies have been undertaken to try to equate social responsibility with higher profits. Unfortunately they have proved inconclusive. The more socially responsible organisations are not necessarily more productive than their less caring competitors!

Management by objectives (MBO)

Few organisations now operate without a set of objectives. However, certain organisations make that set of objectives the very core of their management strategy. This concept, first made popular by Peter Drucker in the 1940s and 1950s, was referred to in Chapter 1, page 81. Its rationale assumes that objectives:

- enable the organisation to explain the whole range of business phenomena in a small number of general statements
- allow the testing of these statements
- enable behaviour to be predicted
- facilitate the examination of the soundness of decisions while they are still being made rather than after they fail
- provide for performance in the future to be improved as a result of the analysis of past experience.

Other writers have expanded the concept further by suggesting that the basics of MBO are:

- ensuring the commitment of *all* managers at *all* levels to *all* the objectives within the area of their responsibility
- starting the system with the initial setting of organisational goals
- outlining clearly managers' goals and obtaining their agreement
- allowing varying degrees of individual manager participation in the setting of objectives
- once agreed, giving autonomy to the managers to achieve the objectives
- including in any review of performance, the teamwork that went into establishing the objectives and amending the objectives accordingly.

Your own role and responsibilities in achieving agreed objectives

Preparation of business objectives by yourself

A major part of your responsibilities is to be aware of the overall strategic plan prepared by senior management and to ensure that your own objectives and those of your department or unit reflect the objectives contained in that plan. Although *organisational objectives* relate to the organisation as a whole and are based on the total performance of all parts of that organisation, it is the *business objectives* that tend to affect individuals more directly. These objectives should form the major part of any *operational plan* prepared by departments, strategic business units (SBUs) or individuals (for further discussion, see page 198). However, although essential, they are obviously subservient to organisational objectives, representing as they do the planned contribution of each unit to the total performance of the organisation.

You may, for instance, work in the Human Resources department. One of the objectives of the organisation as stated in the strategic plan may be to encourage staff development. Consequently one of the objectives in your operational plan should relate to the way in which you intend to implement that overall objective – by means of staff training, an audit of staff skills, etc. Similarly, if you work in the area of Sales, one of your business objectives is almost certain to reflect the organisational objective of increasing sales revenue, and so on.

> One commonly used method of assessing the usefulness of objectives is to ask whether they pass the SMART test; i.e. are they **S**pecific, **M**easurable, **A**greed between manager and members of staff, **R**ealistic, and **T**ime-related?

Shelf life of objectives

Objectives are not always fixed for all time. For example, there may be changes in the expectations or aspirations of management. There may be a change in individual managers, necessitating a change of objectives. The onset of a crisis may precipitate a change, or powerful individuals – the Board of Directors, the shareholders, etc. – may request such a change.

Consequently you should link objectives with a period of time in which they are to be achieved – the higher the level of objective, the longer the timescale normally allocated to it.

THEORY INTO PRACTICE

Timescales should also be reviewed periodically, and the most common approach is to examine them annually to measure actual against planned performance. However, it is argued by some management writers that a year is too short a period for such a review as it may lead to measures being taken to meet objectives which, although expedient, may not necessarily be helpful in the long term. Select a specific objective which may (or does) apply to your own work situation and consider whether you feel it would be better achieved over a longer rather than a shorter timescale.

Acceptance of objectives by others with work-related activities

No matter how skilfully prepared a set of objectives may be, it is destined to fail if your staff either try to ignore its existence or feel resentful at being committed to it. A major role of a manager or administrator, therefore, is to ensure that the staff not only know about the objectives but also appreciate the need for them (see also Chapter 1).

It is easy to make the statement that the organisation's objectives must be 'owned' by everyone working in that organisation. It is less easy to ensure that that statement is translated into reality. In order to be effective, therefore, objectives should possess certain qualities.

- *Acceptability*. Even in very hierarchical organisations, it is preferable to try to gain the cooperation of the workforce in achieving a particular objective rather than merely to impose it on them.
- *Flexibility*. Effective objectives maintain a balance between flexibility and rigidity. They should be sufficiently precise to avoid any confusion as to their purpose, but sufficiently flexible to adapt to any unexpected change in circumstances.
- *Measurability*. This is particularly important in the case of quantitative objectives, but even qualitative objectives should be framed in such a way that their outcome is measurable. For instance, a qualitative objective such as 'increase staff morale' could be measured by reference to staff absence or staff turnover.
- *Suitability*. Each level of objective should reflect and be consistent with the higher levels.
- *Comprehensibility*. Over-complicated objectives tend to be ignored and allow those who ignore them to argue that they did not understand what was expected of them.
- *Achievability*. This is probably the most important quality of a good objective. An impossible-to-achieve objective is again an objective that tends to be ignored – or results in staff frustration and demotivation.

The scope of the operational plan

Of necessity, strategic plans have to be broad in outlook. However, as a manager or administrator, you should have a more tangible tool with which to work. Hence the need for an operational plan – which is a working rather than merely a reference document.

Ideally, individual department or unit plans should 'interlock' with each other to become a complete plan for the whole organisation. Indirectly, therefore, they can assist communication both inside and outside the department or unit, given that they will highlight the areas in which a common approach can be taken or where common goals need to be achieved.

Construction of operational plans

Different organisations favour different types of plan. At their simplest, such plans are merely lists of actions to be carried out by managers, administrators or individuals in order to achieve the requirements of the particular unit in which they work, even though these may be accompanied by budgets which act as a control mechanism. Specific examples of such plans include:

- the *functional plan* – which is produced to guide decisions and actions in the various functional areas of an organisation
- the *project plan* – which is produced on a one-off basis in order to control a specific programme of work.

A more sophisticated and possibly longer-term operational plan of a large organisation may, however, comprise:

- a financial plan against which income and expenditure can be measured
- planned capital expenditure with accompanying justification

- targets for quality improvements against which performance can be measured
- plans for improving efficiency in the use of resources (see further page 225).
- plans to improve management systems.

A purely sales-oriented organisation, on the other hand, may prefer to use an operational plan which outlines:

- the nature of the business
- the competition
- potential customers
- potential suppliers
- staffing
- accommodation issues
- financial costings
- periodic financial and activity targets for the forthcoming year.

Performance indicators

One major purpose of both the strategic and operational plans is to act as a controlling device by providing criteria for the judgement of individual or group performance. Included in many operational plans, therefore, are a set of *performance indicators* (PIs) which are designed to measure the extent to which the objectives contained in the plan have been achieved. Indeed, as already indicated by the SMART test, one of the criteria for a successful objective is that it should be capable of being measured.

Most organisations have an overall set of performance indicators, their content depending on the nature of their business. Refer to Figures 3.1.1 and 3.1.2 for examples of the differing PIs of a manufacturing company and an educational establishment.

- Return on capital employed
- Earnings per share
- Price–earnings ratio
- Profits
- Asset turnover (ratio of overheads or expenses to sales or income)
- Cost per unit of output
- Liquidity
- Gearing (ratio of term loans to shareholders' funds)
- Debtors (ratio of sales to debtors)
- Inventory (ratio of sales to stock)
- Productivity
- Market share
- Quality (e.g. percentage deficits)
- Customer service
- External reputation
- Employee satisfaction

Figure 3.1.1 Performance indicators set by a manufacturing company

- Student enrolments
- Student attendance records
- Student retention rates
- Student achievements
- Student progression
- Student perception
- Inspection reports
- Ethnic minority participation
- Participation of students with learning difficulties and disadvantages
- Staff development
- Staff satisfaction
- Employer satisfaction
- Cost-effectiveness

Figure 3.1.2 Performance indicators of an educational establishment

Once established centrally, PIs should then be delegated to various departments or SBUs, according to their particular specialisms. Some PIs (such as quality) will be common to all, while others will be very user-specific (e.g. inventory control). Whatever the subdivision, however, the end result has to be based on the performance as a whole. Hence the importance of the efforts of individual managers and administrators to ensure that their contribution is no less than those of their peers.

Although some organisations prefer to monitor the current year's performance against that of the previous year, it has been suggested that such comparisons are less valid than a comparison of actual against planned performance, the rationale being that the former can perpetuate the inefficiencies of the past and ignore any significant intervening changes – whether for better or worse.

THEORY INTO PRACTICE

Consider the department or unit in which you work at present in relation to *either*:

a   the extent to which you think the PIs in operation within that area are effective
   or
b   the PIs which you would like to introduce if you were given the authority to do so (give reasons for your choice).

Identifying, prioritising and agreeing operational outcomes

Your responsibility does not end with the preparation of the operational plan. Possibly the more difficult part of the process is yet to come in that you have to identify and agree *targets* with your staff, and to prioritise their activities.

Identifying and agreeing targets

The three most commonly used methods of identifying operational outcomes and agreeing targets with staff are:

- a top-down process in which managers or administrators are given targets to achieve which they pass on down the line
- a bottom-up process in which functional and line managers or administrators, in conjunction with their staff, submit plans, targets and budgets for approval by senior management
- an iterative process which involves both the top-down and bottom-up setting of targets: there is a two way process between the different levels until agreement is reached – provided the eventual agreement is consistent with the organisation's overall mission, objectives and priorities.

If you are given a choice as to which method you can adopt, you may be tempted to try to speed up the process by drafting out a set of targets for each of your staff based on those set for last year or on what you think may please senior management. However, try to resist that temptation. If *you* set the targets, you leave the way open for your staff to claim that they were not consulted, that they did not agree to them and that they were therefore bound to fail right from the start!

What you should try to do is to make sure that targets:

- are precise, unambiguous and, if possible, quantitative
- relate to the most significant elements of their jobs
- are consistent
- are accompanied by a statement of how they are to be achieved, in what timescale, with what resources and how and where these resources will be acquired.

Ideally, therefore, you should treat the setting of targets as a staged process.

Stage 1

You and the member of staff concerned should work separately on possible targets. Remember, however, to make sure even at this stage that the targets proposed match the overall organisational and unit objectives – and also, of course, that they are within the ambit of the job description of the individual concerned. Your specification will obviously be concerned with the unit's targets, while those of the member of staff will be concerned with his or her own area of work.

Stage 2

The next stage is to compare the two and to see how far, if at all, they agree. If the terms of reference under which they have been prepared have been sufficiently precise, any discrepancies should be minor. If, however, there are major differences of opinion, you, as the manager or administrator, have to use your negotiating skills to try to obtain some consensus.

Stage 3

Once agreement has been reached as to *what* the targets are – often referred to as the *key result areas* – it is advisable to allow the member of staff concerned to concentrate on *how* to achieve them. You should be available to give advice, support and encouragement but he or she should be in charge of their implementation. Otherwise any principle of accountability becomes almost meaningless.

Stage 4

Obviously, however, you want to see the target achieved as much as does the individual concerned, and it is therefore to your mutual advantage to check any slippage. Consequently, rather than leaving the review of progress until the yearly appraisal meeting – when it may be too late to repair any damage – you would be wise to institute a series of reviews throughout the relevant period.

Stage 5

The last stage in the process is the formal review or appraisal which comes at the time when the target should have been achieved. Given that the target is realistic and progress towards it has been monitored periodically, the outcome should have been successful – and the employee should be congratulated – or even rewarded. If, for some reason, the target has not been achieved, then the reason for the failure must be analysed. If the employee has been wilfully at fault the possibility of some sanction cannot be ruled out. However, the more likely scenario is that a number of factors have contributed towards the failure to achieve, in which case the discussion should centre around how to make the necessary adjustments to the following set of targets to prevent the situation recurring.

Compiling a target statement can be quite difficult unless you follow certain guidelines.

- Always use an 'action' word such as *will* – not *may* – otherwise you will introduce an element of unwanted flexibility.
- Name the person responsible for the achievement of that target.
- Specify any costs involved – time, money, human and/or physical resources.
- Give a date for completion.
- Specify a measurable end-result.

THEORY INTO PRACTICE

You have to persuade your senior manager to sanction the targets you propose to set for members of your staff. Although your manager seems to have only a vague idea of what comprises a realistic target, unfortunately he still thinks he has a valuable contribution to make in the process. Consequently, you find on your desk one morning the following comments:

'Make sure that the targets of your two VDU operators pin them to producing a certain amount of work each day – and make sure too it's a target they're not likely to meet unless they half kill themselves. I don't think they're exactly overworked at the moment.'

'Can you give that new receptionist of yours the target of smartening herself up a bit? I know it's politically incorrect to want a pretty girl meeting visitors, but I don't want them all scared off by someone who looks as if she's been dragged through a hedge backwards.'

'I know the computer services assistant makes a lot of mistakes but she is young and inexperienced – and incidentally is the daughter of a good friend of mine so I can vouch for her – and I'd take it as a personal favour if you went easy on her when setting targets.'

'That new technician of yours is hopeless. I thought he was supposed to be fully qualified to operate all the desktop publishing packages. He obviously doesn't know what he's doing. Tell him that his target is to improve 100 per cent or he'll be looking for another job.'

'I think all your group should be given a target of cutting costs – the lights are always left on at the end of the day, the heating is at full blast no matter what the weather and I suspect half of them go home each night with their bags crammed full of office stationery.'

Consider (a) what targets you would set for each member of staff, and (b) how you would respond to your senior manager. Note that despite his obvious prejudices, your manager has given a truthful summary of staff strengths and weaknesses.

Prioritising outcomes

If the target is reasonable it is equally reasonable to expect that it will be completed on time. If, therefore, it is not achieved within that period, you may be faced with having to explain why progress towards its achievement has not been monitored more closely – particularly since the periodic monitoring exercise you have carried out should have alerted you to any problems.

On some occasions, however, it becomes an impossibility to achieve all the targets set within the specified period. You may, for instance, be faced with long-term absence, a change of job role, a redundancy situation – all of which can affect any planning system you operate. In such circumstances, it would be useful for you to have a set of priorities as to which targets *must* be completed and those that ideally *should* be completed. The effective manager or administrator, of course, prioritises objectives and the corresponding targets in anticipation of an intervening event, rather than waiting for that event to happen.

Prioritising objectives is no different an exercise from prioritising any other activity. Several management writers have suggested that only 20 per cent of a manager's time creates actual results, the remaining 80 per cent being spent on unstructured trivia. Consequently it is advisable for you to ensure that you ascertain first of all which of the objectives are (a) the most important, and (b) the most urgent. You should then determine which of them are:

- very important *and* very urgent
- very important but not urgent
- very urgent but not important
- neither important nor urgent

and deal with them accordingly. It has also been suggested that a follow-up procedure to such an exercise should be to decide whether the priority is:

- *feasible* – how likely is it that you will be able to achieve it?
- *suitable* – will it assist in improving productivity?
- *acceptable* – is it too risky to pursue?

Methods of operational planning

Vital though it is to plan strategically, it is equally important that any long-term planning is supported by short-term operational plans covering day-to-day activities. In direct contrast to long-term plans which can afford to be far-reaching in scope, short-term plans should be highly specific and should relate directly to the objectives of the department or SBU concerned. It is advisable, therefore, for any manager or administrator involved in operational planning to carry out a fairly detailed planning process.

Establish the mission

The first step you should take is to define precisely the basic task; i.e. establish clear terms of reference. At this point, it is important that you clarify the *purpose* of the task – particularly if you want to delegate part of it to others and to convince them of its value. It is equally important to examine any constraints that could have an adverse effect on the hoped-for outcome.

Analyse what it entails

This phase involves gathering all the available information and analysing:

- the timescale involved
- the resources necessary to complete the task – staff, materials, equipment, services, finance
- the existing skills of the people involved in carrying out the plan, to ensure that their individual expertise is used to the full
- any staff development needs.

Set objectives

By this stage you should be in a position to establish priorities for the completion of the task, either individually or with the assistance of your team. Even if *you* think you have a clear picture of what these should be, unless you are working totally in isolation it is good practice to seek the views of your team. A commonly used method is that of *option evaluation* in which the team considers the consequences of different courses of action and then determines which are the most viable.

Develop working strategies

You should then decide on the strategies necessary for completing the task. One option, if the task is sufficiently complex and requires the efforts of several people, is to segment it into various sections which can be delegated to the relevant individuals. Another option is to divide up the task so that the team can deal with one section at a time. In such a case the sections need to be both manageable and logically sequential.

Integrate all strategies into a working plan

Whatever the division of labour, the tasks should be assigned to a named person (or, if more than one person is assigned to it, the person who is the lead officer) together with a timescale for completion. A thorough briefing process is also advisable at this stage to ensure that all members of the team are aware not only of their own responsibilities but also those of the rest of the team. At this point, too, it may be necessary to set both group and individual performance indicators.

Provide appropriate controls

Monitoring progress is, of course, an essential activity in any planning process – but it should be monitoring with a purpose:

- regular meetings of a steering group
- individual meetings with members of the team
- judicious use of planning aids (see page 206 for more detailed information).

If your control systems indicate that work is not being completed within the anticipated period, you must then consider how to deal with the discrepancy between planned and actual performance. If the discrepancy is minor, you may decide to do nothing and to allow the situation to resolve itself. It is more likely, however, that you will want to make some necessary adjustments involving allowing more time, drafting in additional staff or allocating more resources. In very extreme circumstances – and normally only where it will be financial suicide to continue – you may decide that you have little option but to abandon the project and admit that the objective has not been achieved.

Evaluate the results

Whatever the outcome of the plan – whether successful or not – you should always institute an evaluation exercise. A valuable tool in this exercise is the set of performance indicators. If they have been met, it is reasonable to assume that the objectives of the plan have also been achieved. What is also important, however, is that there be adequate feedback – both positive and negative – to all involved in carrying out the plan. Ideally the feedback should be a two-way process and you should seek the views of your staff as well as relaying your views to them. Ideally also, you should be prepared to accept their views about your performance. The final stage is the storage of all the information gathered throughout the process together with a summary of the outcome – which prevents a reinvention-of-the-wheel exercise should a similar plan of action be needed at some future date.

Whatever planning process you use, you should be aware that at certain stages in that process you may encounter certain barriers. Consider how, in each of the following instances, you would try to maintain your own motivation in the preparation and implementation of an operational plan.

- *Individual barriers.* Many members of your staff might feel that they are so busy, any forward planning is a luxury they cannot afford. They may also be somewhat reluctant to commit themselves to a plan which makes them accountable and which puts them at risk of failing.
- *Organisational barriers.* You may find that your senior manager is reluctant to work to a clear plan – or that he or she produces a plan which is too abstract, complicated or technical for you to implement successfully.
- *Environmental barriers.* A volatile economic situation can discourage too much forward planning, particularly if those plans depend on a stable economy and exchange rates, a guaranteed supply of materials, etc.

In addition to planning the work of others, you also have to plan your own work. In this respect, a useful first step for you to take is a *goal-planning* exercise. In essence it requires you to:

- decide on a specific objective
- list the criteria needed to achieve that objective
- draw up a planner, listing on one side the requirements you think you already have and on the other what additional requirements you must have
- analyse any problem you feel you may have with a particular requirement and break it down into a series of smaller objectives through which you intend to solve the problem.

Types and uses of planning aids

The term 'planning aids' can have a variety of meanings. At its most sophisticated level it encompasses a variety of both quantitative and qualitative planning techniques, most of which involve some sort of forecasting in an attempt to predict what will happen in the future (see further page 253). However, as a manager or administrator, you also need your own personal planning aids – the diary, the spreadsheet, the wall planner, etc. You should also ensure that any storage and retrieval system you operate is organised in a way that best suits your requirements.

Diaries and planners

You will be a very unusual administrator if you do not make daily use of your diary, not only to note down your appointments but also to act as an *aide mémoire* to remind you of certain tasks you want to carry out at a particular time or people you wish to contact. In addition, skilful use of a diary allows you to forward plan very effectively. If, for instance, you have to organise a particularly important meeting, it is good practice to put the date of the meeting in your diary as far ahead as is possible and to work backwards by then pencilling in what action you must take during the weeks and days before the meeting actually happens. To assist and supplement that process there are now on the market a wide variety of personal planners and wallcharts which allow you to plan your work over virtually any period of time. Remember, however, that the simpler the system you use, the easier it is for you to maintain it – even though in the first flush of enthusiasm you may feel that you want to use a variety of aids involving elaborate tags, signs, updating mechanisms, etc. Much, of course, depends on the administrative assistance available to you. If you are fortunate enough to have a personal assistant, he or she may be able to afford the time to operate any system you require no matter how complicated. Even so, you would still be wise to consider whether what you are asking your assistant to do is the most effective way of using that person's time.

THEORY INTO PRACTICE

1 The use of electronic diaries has increased considerably over the past few years and there is a constant stream of updated versions coming on to the market. If you use one already, check to see whether a more recent version has any additional facilities. If the idea of an electronic diary is new to you, check in an office equipment publication to see the full range available and try to determine the extent to which one would assist you in your present role.

2 Planners can be used on a weekly, monthly or yearly basis.

   a Review the ways in which you plan your work to determine how such planners might be of use to you.

   b If you already operate such a system, review how effective you think it is and whether you can institute any improvements. Most modern office equipment catalogues normally contain a section on planning aids which should assist you in your research.

THEORY INTO PRACTICE

Using your present job as a model, assess the way in which you make use of your office diary, particularly in relation to:

- the type of diary
- access to the diary
- coordination of personal and office diaries
- average length of appointments and preferred spacing throughout the day and/or week
- amount of information to be included in each entry
- dealing with regular appointments
- dealing with appointments which overrun
- unexpected callers
- other crises
- any other specific criteria.

Consider any improvements you might make.

Carry-forward systems

An equally simple and well-tried planning aid is that of a carry-forward system. Most administrators know only too well that no matter how persuasive a memo or e-mail may be, there is always the danger that no response will be made to it – unless a reminder is given. Indeed, it is only too true that if your staff or colleagues realise that you seldom or never follow up any request you make, they cease to rush to respond to you at all. Again, the diary or the wall planner can be of use. All you need to do is to pencil in a note that you require a reply from someone by a certain date. On that date you can then check whether a reply has been received and, if it has, not send a reminder. Again, it is surprising how quickly word will get round that you don't give up easily!

One slight difficulty, however, is that if you are coordinating a large number of activities or are corresponding with a large number of people, the diary and/or the wall planner will not provide you with sufficient space. A more modern method, of course, is the use of the electronic diary, which allows you to key in any information you require and which has a much greater capacity for storing that information than the normal paper-based reminder systems. Failing that, you might have to resort to the traditional card index system, which comprises a series of index cards for each day of the month and behind which notes can be kept of responses requested for that particular day.

Lists

Few administrators operate without the use of lists. The most usual and normally the most effective way of maximising the advantages of a list is to prepare one at the beginning of each day and to check at the end of the day on progress made. In some cases, of course, this can be a depressing experience – particularly if you haven't progressed very far. However, once it becomes as much an integral part of your planning system as the regular checking of your diary, it is self-perpetuating – as one job is completed another moves up or on to the list. The electronic diary can again assist this process by allowing you not only to enter lists of 'jobs to do' but also to prioritise them. If, for instance, you have an existing list but wish to enter another item and need to be reminded that it is urgent, the system will re-sort your list into priority order.

> Some administrators have refined the use of the list to include other people and each week note down not only what they but also what each member of their staff must do during that period. At the end of the week, in addition to checking the list, they expect a checked and initialled list from everyone else.

THEORY INTO PRACTICE

Although the whole idea of planning aids is to prevent you from relying solely on your memory, they should not prevent you from placing any reliance on it at all. An accepted theory is that you have both long-term and short-term memory and that you are capable of improving both. One noted management theorist, Tony Buzan, outlines what can be done to improve recall in his book, *How to Make the Most of Your Mind*. Try to obtain a copy of it (or any other publication covering the same topic) to see whether you can gain any useful tips.

Filing systems

A good filing system is invaluable, given that a misplaced file is often a lost file. Moreover a desk piled high with papers which have never reached the filing cabinet is not normally a sign – either to you or to your senior manager – that you are planning your work in the most efficient way. At this stage in your career you have probably organised your filing system at some time in the past to suit your own particular needs, but it is useful to review that system periodically to check whether it remains the best system to meet your *current* needs.

THEORY INTO PRACTICE

1 Figure 3.1.3 lists the standard systems of storage and classification. Check that:
   – you are aware of the advantages and disadvantages of each of them, and
   – your system is still the most suitable for your needs.
   If you do not make use of electronic filing, consult an appropriate business journal for more details to enable you to determine the extent to which introduction of such a system would benefit you.
2 Consider the procedures you have in place for ensuring that:
   – records, once borrowed, are returned
   – unwanted or obsolete records are weeded out on a periodic basis
   – documents are adequately cross-referenced
   – confidentiality is maintained.
   Assess whether or not you can effect any improvements.

Methods of storage

Vertical filing cabinet
Lateral filing cabinet
Horizontal filing cabinet
Mobile filing trolleys
Automated filing systems
Microfiche/microfilm
Electronic filing systems; e.g.
– word-processing directories
– computer databases
– total document management – normally a centralised system and possibly incorporating such features as document scanning, the ability to fax material directly from the computer to its destination, the ability to reproduce material directly onto optical disks.

Document holders (for use inside the file storage systems above)
Document wallets (which can be used as part of the system or as independent document containers)
Individual suspension folders (in which wallets or filing folders can be placed)
Continuous suspension folders
Lateral suspension folders

Methods of classification
Alphabetical
Numerical
Subject
Geographical
Other (e.g. terminal digit, chronological)

Methods of indexing (for non-electronic systems)
Vertical card
Strip index
Visible edge card index

Figure 3.1.3 A filing checklist

Identifying and defining resource requirements

In Chapter 2, page 152, reference was made to the specification of resources in the operational plan. It is obviously unwise to agree to an objective without ensuring that sufficient resources are to be made available. What can also be difficult, however, is the identification and definition of the exact nature of the resource required. Much, of course, depends upon the nature of your objective, but it is likely that at some stage you will be requesting additional finance, people, equipment, materials, and time.

Suppose, for instance, one of your stated objectives is to make certain that every member of your staff undergoes annual fire training. The resources you require would probably include:

- *finance* to cover the total cost of the exercise
- the use of certain *people*, such as an outside training agency or a suitably qualified employee to conduct the session, cover for key staff involved in the exercise, etc.
- the hire or purchase of certain *equipment* – a large scale TV screen, multimedia presentation equipment, etc.
- the provision of *materials* such as handouts, videos, etc. – or even the booking of suitable accommodation
- the *time* you will need both for the training itself and for planning and organising it.

Avoid couching such requests in terms that are too general. It is of little use, for instance, merely to state in the operational plan that 'funds must be available' or that 'additional accommodation and staffing are required'. In order for senior management to be able to prepare a workable budget, the operational plan must contain very specific information.

When you are at the stage of submitting your operational plan for agreement by senior management, you should spend at least as much if not more time in analysing the exact costs of the required resource as you do in formulating the objective.

Consequently, at this stage it may be useful for you to have at least a broad knowledge of the general principles of costing out a product or service (referred to in costing terms as a 'cost object') given that such knowledge may assist you in putting forward the best possible case for adequate resourcing. Obviously, if you do not have a financial or accounting background, it would be unwise of you to act independently without the benefit of the advice from financial experts in your organisation.

For further details of costing see Chapter 9.

Producing and presenting operational plans

Most organisations have their own methods of producing and presenting their strategic and operational plans. Generally speaking, the strategic plan has a two-fold purpose in that it not only acts as a reference point in respect of organisational strategy but also forms part of an overall public relations exercise. Many strategic plans are therefore produced in an elaborate glossy format to be circulated not only to senior management, shareholders or important clients but also to potential clients, visitors to the organisation and even prospective employees.

Conversely, operational plans tend to be working documents used by senior management in their budgeting efforts and by the staff concerned in their day-to-day activities. Consequently, they should be comprehensive, easy to read and clearly set out. One of the most effective ways of presenting the information is in tabular form. See Figure 3.1.4 for one such example.

The completion of this format depends upon a number of factors. It presupposes, for instance, that attached to it as an appendix are:

- the organisational objectives – which may be more extensive than those which are relevant to the SBU concerned
- the performance indicators on which the success or otherwise of the SBU will be assessed.

It also presupposes that it is readily accessible by staff and regularly monitored by the person (or lead officer) responsible for the achievement of the various objectives.

Name of Department/SBU ....

Date ....

Organisation strategic objective	Departmental/SBU strategic objective	Departmental/SBU operational objective	Timescale	Performance indicator(s)	Lead officer(s)	Resources required (items and amounts)

Figure 3.1.4 An example of an operational plan pro forma

Element 3.2

Implement the operational plan

Your own role and responsibilities

The very fact that you are called upon to implement an operational plan assumes that you are in an administrative or managerial post and that your level is likely to be that of *middle management*. Senior management is more concerned with the strategic plan: junior managers and other staff will probably be working under your direction. The immediate difficulty you face is that your level is not sufficiently senior to allow you any significant autonomy or decision-making powers. Conversely it is not sufficiently near 'the shop floor' to allow you to carry out each task personally.

> In 1956, W. H. Whyte used the term 'organisation man' to describe those managers who become over-preoccupied with, and dependent on, the organisations of which they are a part. He suggested that the role of the middle manager has a life of its own, quite independent of the actual purposes of the organisation itself. He also argued that the job prospects of middle managers (other than within the organisation itself) are likely to be poor given that their expertise tends to relate solely to one particular organisation.

Middle managers or administrators have a wide variety of roles. Some are responsible for a large number of staff, while others are responsible for a particular task or project. Some have only one layer of management above and below them, some have several. However, research has revealed certain common elements, one such example being the survey carried out by J. H. Horne and T. Lupton in which the most common activities (in order of frequency) were discovered to be:

- giving and seeking information
- seeking and preparing explanations
- coordinating and reviewing plans
- giving, receiving and confirming instructions
- giving, confirming and reviewing decisions
- giving and seeking advice.

THEORY INTO PRACTICE

It is interesting to note that the least time spent by managers or administrators is on making decisions and giving or seeking advice. Given the information already outlined it is easy to determine the reason for the small amount of time they devote to actual decision-making. However, it is perhaps less easy to understand why the giving and seeking of advice should occupy so little time. Consider the possible reasons for this.

The middle manager *does* have a distinct role to play in relation to the operational plan. This is to ensure that the objectives agreed in the plan are, in fact, achieved. What he or she has to be careful not to do is to assume the entire workload. A 'hands on' manager or administrator is generally speaking a popular and effective manager. However, this is a concept which can be taken too far and managers who do not delegate or who spend every waking moment at work, are likely to suffer excessive levels of stress. The skills of allocating work to others are not easily acquired but they are essential!

Middle managers and administrators are supposedly one of the groups of workers most at risk from work-related stress. Researchers at the University of Manchester Institute of Science and Technology have discovered that people 'who have very little control over their destinies' such as the middle manager or administrator are more likely to suffer from stress than their senior managers who have greater freedom of action. Adding to their stress levels is the fact that the introduction and increased use of computerised information systems has put them at risk of redundancy. Those systems enable senior management to bypass middle managers and administrators and thus reduce a traditional part of their power – and hence their usefulness in the control of information.

Establishing and defining individual responsibilities and limits of authority

If an organisation is well structured then staff will be able to recognise and establish their own responsibilities with the minimum of difficulty. Ideally such a structure should be:

- *logical* – where related activities are grouped together; where flows of information, decision-making and processing activities are consistent; and where there is a framework for operations which avoids duplication of activities and facilitates the allocation of accountability for results
- *coherent* – where roles and relationships are clearly defined and understood
- *cohesive* – where, although individual roles and responsibilities have been differentiated, attention has also been given to the integration of such roles with others
- *flexible* – where teams and individuals are given scope to respond to new or unexpected demands.

THEORY INTO PRACTICE

As part of their induction programme, you are asked to outline the structure of your organisation to a group of new employees. At the end of the session, a number of them ask you some questions. Think about how you would answer them.

'How can a very large structure be flexible? Surely the bigger it gets, the less flexible it can be.'

'I didn't understand what you meant about cohesion. Could you clarify that part please?'

'Surely too structured an organisation stifles individual initiative. If we all have to do the same thing in the same way, we'll turn into robots.'

Organisation charts

Whether or not an organisation is effectively structured, almost invariably one of the first documents brought to the attention of a new member of staff is an organisation chart, which normally indicates:

- how the work is allocated
- how activities are grouped together
- levels of authority and responsibility.

The entrepreneurial structure

Such a structure tends either to be small or to represent an early stage in the organisation's development. It is normally headed by a very strong leader around whom all other activities centre. There are few rules or procedures and control is exercised by one or a very small number of key individuals. Consequently the chart is circular in structure. For one example see Figure 3.2.1.

Figure 3.2.1 An entrepreneurial organisation

The bureaucratic structure

This type of structure (see Figure 3.2.2) is perhaps the most common. It is based round the principle that jobs should be grouped according to some common feature and be ranked in a hierarchy of responsibility. Grouping can either be by *function* (e.g. marketing, sales, human resources, etc.), less frequently by *geography* (e.g. factory, head office, warehousing, etc.), by *product*, *process*, or *customer*.

Such a structure tends to perpetuate status distinctions and any system of delegation is limited to strictly delineated functions. It can therefore stifle individual initiative and flair. However, it allows a considerable amount of specialisation, provides a predictable working routine, and allows a rational allocation of work and responsibility.

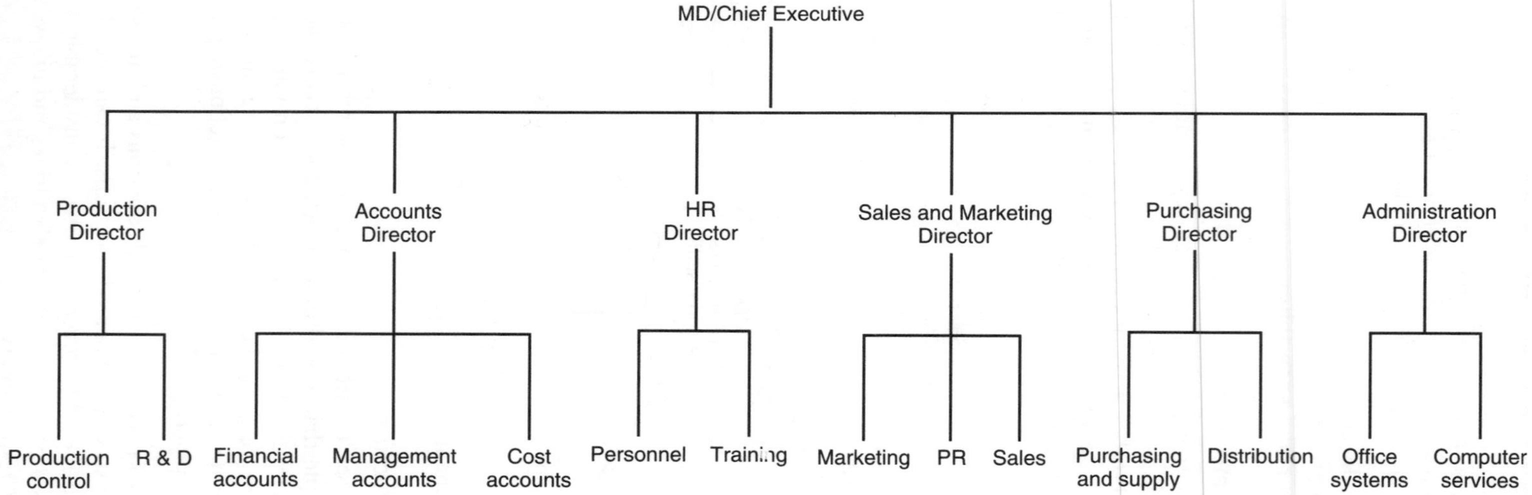

Figure 3.2.2 A bureaucratic organisation

The matrix structure

A third structure has evolved which was developed as a result of an American government demand that contracts allocated to the aerospace industry should each be dealt with by an individual manager to whom all inquiries could be addressed (see Figure 3.2.3). The structure requires one manager to be responsible for all aspects of a particular project – the production, the personnel, the financing, etc. – and therefore to be able to call upon the services of the staff in each of those areas even though these employees would also report to their own superiors (i.e. their functional managers).

Obviously this is in direct contrast to the concept of unity of command as postulated by Henri Fayol – that business organisations should have a clear chain of relationships, with all members knowing precisely to whom and for whom they are responsible. Equally obviously, for the structure to work there has to be a major investment in skilled staff to allow people to be allocated full time to a specific project. Otherwise the project manager and the functional manager may be in dispute over the release of a particular member of staff to a particular project. Consequently, it is advisable that the introduction of a matrix system should be phased in over a period of time.

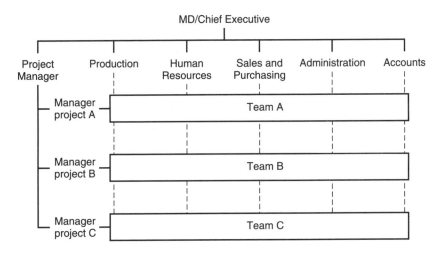

Figure 3.2.3 A matrix organisation

Useful though organisation charts may be, if they are taken in isolation they can paint a slightly misleading picture of the organisation itself. Not only do they become outdated very quickly, more importantly they give little indication of the informal structures that exist within the formal framework. They can also harden divisions between members of staff and thus make the organisation too hierarchy conscious. Indeed, on the subject of organisation charts, one management writer, Robert Townsend, comments 'Never formalise, print and circulate them. Good organisations are living bodies that grow new muscles to meet challenges.'

Job descriptions

Even though the same criticism can be levelled against a job description as against some organisational charts – it does not give a complete picture of the responsibilities to be assumed by the member of staff concerned; nor does it give an up-to-date picture of them – it is normally the individual job description to which reference is first made when determining the responsibilities of members of staff (see Chapter 1, page 2). All members of an organisation need some definition of their role and tasks especially where their activities interlink with those of others. To this end, some organisations prefer to use the term 'role definition' rather than job description, and to concentrate on the required performance and delivery rather than any specific tasks. The definition generally outlines:

- the job title
- reporting relationships
- purpose of the role – the reason for its existence
- the main areas of responsibility defined in terms of the results expected rather than a detailed list of duties
- the context – how the job interlinks with others, the level of flexibility required, decision-making powers, any specific requirements, etc.

Some human resource management writers suggest that there should be different job descriptions for different purposes.

- *Job descriptions for organisational, recruitment and contractual purposes* – which define the place of the job in the organisation, inform job applicants about the job and act as the basis of the contract of employment. The main requirement of such a job description is flexibility and it should therefore concentrate on results rather than stating in detail what tasks have to be carried out.
- *Job descriptions for job evaluation purposes* – which not only contain the information included in an organisational job description but also attach to each task, certain job evaluation factors such as knowledge and skills, responsibility, decision-making and complexity.
- *Job descriptions for training purposes* – which again are based on the organisational job description but which also include an analysis of the knowledge and skills required in the job.

Methods of allocating work activities

When allocating work activities to staff, your first point of reference should be your own job description as you have to establish the limit of your responsibilities in this respect and also your *span of control*. Your next step is to assess the area of work for which you are responsible and to analyse the work that needs to be done.

The division of work by breaking down tasks into component parts so that individuals are responsible for an activity rather than a whole task was advocated by Adam Smith in *The Wealth of Nations* in 1776 and supported by other management writers such as Frederick Taylor. The advantages of this method are that:

- less skilled workers can be used because each task has been broken down into a small number of simplified operations
- relatively little training is necessary
- proficiency can be achieved in a short period of time
- no time is wasted by workers moving from task to task
- workers can be assigned to the task for which they are most suited.

However, the corresponding disadvantages are that:

- constant repetition of a single task is monotonous and therefore demotivating
- teamwork is not encouraged
- an unskilled and untrained workforce is ill-equipped to deal with any changes forced on the organisation by increased competition, new technological developments, etc.

Consequently, many organisations now encourage a team approach to even the most mechanical of operations. Saab Motors, for instance, developed a system of producing its cars by teams of workers and abandoned the assembly line process. (See further comments on job enrichment and empowerment on page 221 and Chapter 1.)

Job design

What you have to try to determine is the degree of specialisation you require for all jobs within your span of control. In this respect you may find it useful to list the characteristics of each job:

- *The skill involved.* Is the work operational and repetitive? Does it require the use of a more skilled approach? Is initiative required? Are certain qualifications necessary?
- *Autonomy.* To what extent does the individual asked to carry out this task have the freedom to plan and schedule his or her own work?
- *Dimension.* What, if any, job satisfaction is involved?
- *Significance.* To what extent does the job affect other people? Does it involve health and safety? Does it interlink with other jobs? Is it regarded as of low, medium or high importance?

Having completed that exercise, you should then be in a position to match each task against the various abilities of your staff. To do this you need to:

- persuade particular individuals that they are sufficiently skilled to be able to carry out the task successfully
- maximise, where possible, their responsibility for performance and quality
- allow the highest possible degree of staff control over the setting of goals and defining of performance indicators
- give meaningful feedback to them about their performance.

At this point you may also need to consider the advantage you gain from having a staff which is multiskilled or a group of activities which are constructed in such a way that more than one member of staff can perform them.

Multiskilling

Multiskilling is based on two premises:

- competency within the workplace; i.e. the ability of an individual to deal with problems as they occur regardless of what they are or when they might be likely to occur
- full utilisation of capabilities; i.e. the only limitations on the allocation of work are the skills an individual possesses or could be trained to possess.

It allows staff to undertake a diverse range of tasks or to assume greater responsibility than before. As a consequence accounts clerks could be expected to become computer literate in order to deal with modern accounts packages; a supervisor may take the responsibility for the health and safety of his or her staff in addition to the responsibility for the work they produce; and so on.

However, there can be difficulties in achieving true multiskilling. Initially there was some union opposition particularly among those unions who had previously negotiated demarcation agreements. However, such opposition has decreased as more and more unions have conceded the need for flexibility in working arrangements. More significant is the amount of investment required in training staff in the different skills they will be expected to use. It is therefore important that any organisation wishing to maximise the benefits of multiskilling should set itself clear objectives as to exactly what it perceives these benefits should be – better use of resources, focusing attention on critical success factors, increased productivity, etc. – and to monitor progress towards their achievement.

Being multiskilled can have an effect on possible redundancies. In one recent case, *Johnson v Peabody Trust* [1996] IRLR 387, Mr Johnson was initially employed as a labourer. During the course of his employment he developed skills as a roofer and was promoted and paid accordingly. In 1988 he was offered a new employment contract which stated that he was employed as a roofer but which also contained the following provision:

'Where possible, trades persons will be expected to carry out multi-trade operations'.

Two years later the firm decided to make a number of workers redundant, including Mr Johnson who, in addition to undertaking his roofing work, had carried out many other manual activities. He appealed to the courts. Although in this instance the Employment Appeal Tribunal held his redundancy valid, employers have now been warned to take care when inserting a flexible working clause in a contract to ensure that it does not preclude them from making an employee redundant in circumstances where, although the main responsibility of that employee has diminished or ceased to exist, other duties remain in existence.

Job enrichment

Many forward-thinking organisations extend the philosophy of multiskilling to embrace job enrichment by providing the employee with a job which:

- has a definite outcome
- affords the employee as much variety, decision-making responsibility and control as possible
- provides direct feedback through the work itself on how successful it has been.

Consequently, when allocating work, you may want to consider:

- increasing the responsibility of individuals for their own work
- giving them scope to carry out the work in the way they want to do it, rather than imposing upon them prescribed methods
- reducing task specialisation by ensuring that more than one person is capable of carrying out a particular task
- allowing staff more say in setting targets and standards of performance
- making sure that employees have all the information they need to help them to carry out their work
- asking for their assistance when planning the work, considering new ideas and evaluating their effectiveness
- gradually increasing the difficulty of the task as the individual progresses.

THEORY INTO PRACTICE

Aspiring to job enrichment and succeeding in implementing it can be two quite different things! Consider how you would proceed in the face of the following difficulties.

Jennifer is irritatingly slow. It took her weeks longer than anyone else to master the new telephone system. Your heart sinks at the thought of training her to do anything else – or giving her any responsibility!

Dieter is always coming up with ideas. The only problem is that he doesn't follow them through – and he gets very upset if you reject them in favour of someone else's.

Imran wants to be left alone to carry out his work in his own way. His results are very good but he refuses to let anyone else participate on the grounds that it slows him down and that therefore his overall productivity will be affected. He is not at all keen on the idea of training anyone else.

Empowerment

Job enrichment is given its most prominent support in the form of empowerment, which entails giving scope or 'power' to employees to exercise control over and take responsibility for their work. Charles Handy suggests that the rationale for empowerment is the belief that individual employees can be expected to perform to the limit of their competence with the minimum of supervision. People should be trusted to get on with a job. Consequently empowerment can:

- speed up decision-making processes
- release the innovative capacities of employees
- provide greater job satisfaction
- enable employees to gain a greater sense of achievement
- reduce operational costs by eliminating unnecessary layers of management, quality control and checking systems.

It has been suggested that such empowerment could be achieved in the following ways:

- organising work around basic operations to form 'whole tasks'
- making the primary workgroup (of between 4 and 20 people) the basic organisational unit
- designating a leader for each workgroup
- allowing the leader and workgroup to plan and organise their own work as far as possible
- expecting the group to evaluate their performance against agreed standards
- structuring jobs so that group members can complete at least one process fully from start to finish
- expecting all group members to participate in the processes of planning, problem-solving and evaluation.

From the concept of empowerment has evolved two types of work group.

The *autonomous work group* enlarges individual jobs to include a wider range of operative skills and allows the group to decide on the methods, planning, scheduling and control of the work. The group itself distributes the tasks among its members and decides on the work pace.

The *high-performance work group* extends the concept further by placing greater emphasis on higher levels of performance in new technology environments. After management has defined what it needs in the form of new technology and the results expected from its introduction, autonomous working groups are then established with full responsibility for the task. Managers and administrators adopt a supportive rather than a strict supervisory stance.

Delegation

When allocating work activities you must be prepared to delegate work to others. Your success or otherwise in doing so depends to a large extent on your attitude towards delegation. In principle, delegation should bring nothing but benefits to the hard-pressed manager or administrator. In practice, however, it is sometimes not perceived as being totally advantageous.

Helena is in charge of a small group of staff in a busy computer services unit. Because a number of her experienced senior staff have left and have been replaced by less-experienced junior staff, she finds herself working longer and longer hours and taking on an increasing number of duties. Her senior manager notices this and, during her staff appraisal interview, asks her why she does not delegate more. After some thought Helena gives the following reasons.

a Some of my staff are very new and are just not capable of doing anything else at the moment.

b Steve is quite able but he isn't at all keen on taking on anything new – he daren't say it to my face but I know he thinks that I'm being paid more than he is and that therefore I should have to do more. I suppose to some extent I agree with him.

c Our targets are so demanding that I'm afraid to take the chance of delegating to others. After all, if those targets aren't met, I'm the one who has to take the blame.

d I've been doing this job for some years now – I'm bound to be better at it than everyone else – and quicker too.

e I suppose in my heart of hearts – I *want* to be indispensable – and I suppose also I would be worried if someone else in the unit was seen as being as good – if not better than I am.

Consider which of the above comments you think may apply to you in your workplace. How could you overcome such anxieties? (You may wish to read further on in this unit for some possible solutions.) Finally, consider whether the fact that Helena is a female administrator could make a difference in her attitude towards delegation.

Definition of delegation

Delegation is not simply the allocation of work. It is the method by which a manager or supervisor gives a subordinate the authority to act and make decisions on his or her behalf. Poor delegators tend to make one of two mistakes. They either merely allocate the work but expect the employee to refer all decisions to them, or they allocate the work *and* all the responsibility without providing any backup support.

M. Inman suggests the following guidelines for effective delegation.

- Enough authority should be delegated to ensure that the task can be completed successfully.
- The person to whom the task is delegated should be allowed to make decisions within the parameters set without having to ask permission.
- Preferably there should be only one delegator.
- The person to whom the task is delegated is responsible to the delegator for the completion of the task. The delegator is still responsible to the organisation for the activities of that person.
- The responsibility of the person to whom the task has been delegated cannot be greater than the authority he or she has been granted.

- The clearer the brief of the department or unit concerned, the more effective delegation within it is likely to be.
- Again, the clearer the lines of authority in an organisation, the more effective will its lines of communication be and hence the more effective its delegation.

Planning delegation

Selection of the tasks

What you should do first of all is to identify the tasks within your span of control which you want to delegate. Ensure that they are not tasks that you should be carrying out personally. Ascertain whether the tasks will provide a challenge and/or a development opportunity.

Preparation of a brief

Having selected a particular task for delegation, you should then decide on the objectives for that task and the criteria by which success will be judged. If relevant, allocate a reasonable timescale for its completion. Consider the resources needed to complete the task – money, personnel, etc. Determine what type of monitoring will take place. Determine also the level of support you think you will need to provide.

Selection of staff

Where the task to be delegated is of the utmost importance, select the person who always does a good job. Where it is of less significance, you can select someone who may not be quite so capable at the moment but who could be developed into being so. Consider those members of staff you feel should be given greater responsibility or challenged in some way. You may want to test them out to see if they are ready for promotion. You may wish to assess their ability in a very specific role or their ability to work with other employees. You may even wish to boost someone's confidence or to remedy a perceived weakness by delegating a certain task.

Discussion with the selected staff

The basis for your discussion should be your perception of the task and its desired outcome. However, the staff member should be allowed to help in its ultimate structure. During the discussion, therefore, you should:

- make certain that both of you understand the task
- explain why that particular member of staff has been chosen
- explain the objectives and the potential usefulness and benefits of the task – both to the organisation and to the member of staff
- give authority for the whole task
- provide any material which may be useful
- encourage questions and suggestions
- agree a timescale.

Following that discussion (which may take place over a number of occasions) you should then be in a position to agree the nature and scope of the task, its expected outcomes, how it will be monitored and how much time will be allowed.

Monitoring progress

Given the emphasis that has been placed on the need for delegation of authority as well as of task, any monitoring exercise should be done with care. Monitor only at agreed points. Ensure that you are available to give support, advice and assistance when needed. Provide adequate resources to assist in the completion of the task.

Reviewing progress

There are three elements to be considered in the review process:

- Was the task completed successfully and were the desired outcomes achieved?
- How successful was the member of staff to whom the task was delegated?
- How successful were you in delegating the task?

THEORY INTO PRACTICE

You have delegated a series of tasks to several different people over the past few months. When you review the various outcomes at the end of the year you find that the following difficulties have arisen.

a One member of staff achieved what was required well within the agreed timescale; another completed about 60 per cent of the task within the time limit but failed to complete the rest until well past the agreed deadline. In her defence she claimed that her colleague had been given an easier task and a more lenient deadline.

b On one occasion you promised that some resources would be available but failed to keep that promise because at the very last moment your senior manager would not release the necessary funding.

c You saw that one member of staff was struggling with a particular task and therefore transferred him to a task which was better suited to his abilities. In the case of another member of staff who was having difficulty, you deemed it better to allow him to struggle on to see whether or not he could meet the challenge. He could not and was very resentful that you apparently had not given him the same assistance as his colleague.

d You delegated an important job to a relatively senior – and trusted – member of staff. You realised almost immediately that she was having some difficulties but when you tried to intervene she refused to admit there was a problem and accused you of trying to undermine her authority with the rest of the staff. You eventually became desperate enough to insist on completing the job yourself.

Consider where (if at all) you think you may have failed in the delegation process and what steps you would take to improve the process in the coming year.

Optimising the use of available resources

Human resources are always limited, no matter how profitable the organisation. Consequently the successful manager or administrator must develop various stratagems for maximising their use.

Flexible employment strategies

The idea that a job can be carried out other than on a permanent, full-time basis is relatively new. Indeed, prior to the 1970s it was generally assumed that the only alternative to full-time employment was total unemployment. However, with the advent of factors such as recession, increased overseas competition and important technological changes, new working methods have begun to proliferate. They include a growth in part-time employment, an increased use of subcontracting (or 'outsourcing') and new shift working patterns, and the introduction of a number of new working arrangements such as job sharing. Consequently the new 'flexible' firm is one that has a variety of types of worker.

- *Core workers* are responsible for key activities. These workers are normally expected to retrain and learn new skills where necessary and are to be found mainly in the managerial, professional and skilled technical positions.
- *Peripheral workers* do the less-skilled jobs requiring minimal training. Such workers tend to have a lower level of job security and fewer career prospects. In some organisations there is a second group of peripheral workers employed under fixed-term or temporary contracts as the occasion demands.
- *External workers* are the contractors, agencies and self-employed workers who can undertake both routine and specialist jobs. They are not employees of the organisation and therefore rarely accrue any employment protection rights.

Charles Handy illustrates the same concept in a different way. He likens it to a shamrock which has three interlocking leaves composed of the three different groups of workers. However he also adds a fourth leaf – that of 'the customer' – which, he suggests, represents another form of 'subcontracting' in that more and more frequently situations are being created whereby the customer carries out some of the work for which he or she is paying the organisation. Examples include self-service in a restaurant, self-service petrol stations, self-assembly furniture, and bank cashpoints.

THEORY INTO PRACTICE

1 Depending upon the size of the organisation for which you work, categorise the nature of the staffing – either in the whole or a certain section of it – into core workers, peripheral workers and external workers.
2 Check also to see whether or not your organisation employs part-time staff, job sharers, term-time only workers, or homeworkers.
3 If possible, talk to a member of staff who has worked for the organisation for a number of years to obtain his or her views of changes that have taken place in the staff profile over that period.
4 Having obtained such information, try to assess how the staff profile may change in the next five years. You may find it helpful to examine both current and past

issues of *Human Resources Management Journal* for relevant articles on projected changes in employment strategies. The journal, *Labour Market Trends* (incorporating the *Employment Gazette*) contains articles on similar issues.

THEORY INTO PRACTICE

'Nowadays only the most paternalistic – or hidebound – employers would refuse to acknowledge that it is more efficient and effective to offer work to an outside contractor on a fixed-term, temporary basis as opposed to a full-time employee on a permanent basis.' Consider how far you agree with that comment.

Flexible working patterns

The best way of optimising the use of time is to ensure that none of it is 'dead' time. A twenty-four hour shift system is the most obvious example since it maximises the use of both workforce and equipment and either avoids or at least minimises time spent on setting up or closing down a particular process. The shift system also allows a continuous service to be provided in those areas – such as nursing, the police force, the fire brigade – where any close down, however brief, would be unacceptable.

Flexible working hours

In some cases, it is good practice to organise the available time around the employee. Many employees with domestic responsibilities find it difficult to work a 9 am to 5 pm day. Other employees with different responsibilities find evening or weekend work a problem. In large cities where the travel-to-work area is extensive, a standard working day increases the time spent in getting to and from the workplace given that the travel is taking place at the busiest times of the day. Organisations take different approaches towards this problem. Some smaller organisations tend to allow departments or units to adopt informal mutually agreeable arrangements so that, for instance, the 'larks' cover for the 'owls' and vice versa, or lunch-time opening is covered by those who arrive late or depart early. However, even though the desire to be flexible is admirable, the inherent difficulties of such arrangements are obvious. Consequently the majority of organisations wanting to adopt a flexible hours arrangement for their employees do so on a formal basis.

Although there are many different versions, the most widely used system appears to be the flexitime system which contains a 'core' number of hours – generally from between 10 am to 4 pm – to be worked by everyone and a 'flexitime' period on either side of the core time. Employees can choose when they work the remainder of their hours, provided that they achieve the agreed overall total. Most organisations quantify the number of hours to be worked over a weekly period, some allow them to be averaged out over a month, and a few allocate each member of staff a yearly number of hours. In many cases employees may be able to build up credit hours in order to take time off during core time. They may, for instance, want to work longer hours over a 6- or 7-day period and then have the following day off.

An alternative form of flexitime is that of compressed hours, which enables employees to work for four and a half or even fewer days a week by extending the time spent on each day. It is a work method which tends to be favoured by many employees, but unions have expressed their concerns about workplace fatigue and possible health and safety risks.

THEORY INTO PRACTICE

Flexitime is about to be implemented into your organisation by your senior management. You are not totally overjoyed by this decision, although you realise you must attempt to implement it as successfully as possible.

a   You have a belief that it is peer pressure in your department which makes everyone arrive on time – an empty desk at 9.10 am is very noticeable. You feel that there may not be the same peer pressure with a more flexible working arrangement.

b   You have a concern that you will be more restricted in holding meetings, discussion groups, etc. given that all members of your staff will be present together within a more limited time period.

c   You are anxious that your peak time of the day tends to be late in the afternoon when half of your staff may have gone home.

d   You doubt that you will ever be able to achieve agreement amongst the staff as to who takes advantage of the late start and who the early finish. You suspect that most of them will want to finish early, which will add to the problem outlined above.

e   You have a feeling that the *esprit de corps* of your group might diminish if they no longer feel a cohesive whole but rather a collection of individual workers coming and going at different times.

f   There is a question of how your part-time staff can be integrated into the new system.

Consider possible solutions to these problems.

Time management
Frequently the scarcest resource of managers and administrators is that of time – one management writer argues that to improve *effective* time usage they should decide personally what they ought to be doing, whereas to improve *efficient* time usage they should learn to organise their time better. Consequently, maximising the use of time is likely to be one of your most important stratagems.

Recognition of the problem
You should first of all analyse your key result areas, both personal and professional, so that you can establish a basis for all your ensuing actions. In the same way you should analyse yourself – your strengths and weaknesses, your character and personality – and also your job particularly in relation to the mission statement of the organisation and your role in carrying it out. You should also examine the goals or priorities you have set yourself – or which have been set for you.

An analysis of the present situation

Your next step should be to analyse how you are spending your time at present – you may be quite surprised at the results. Not many people can afford the luxury of asking someone to record their every movement over a specified period and summarise their findings, although that method tends to produce the most effective data. However, on a more limited scale you could independently record your activities over, say, one full day. If you do so you should first of all prepare a suitable record sheet outlining the activity, the time it took and the people involved – and for the purpose of this exercise it is self-defeating to say that you haven't got the time to do so! Ideally you should repeat the exercise two or three times on different days over a period of a couple of months so that the sample, although still random, should begin to take on some sort of a pattern.

The next stage is to analyse your findings. Sometimes a glance down the list is sufficient to alert you to activities which are time-wasting or irrelevant. However, it is normally more helpful if you use some form of checklist. You could, for instance, analyse your findings under the headings 'essential', 'desirable', 'irrelevant'. In a very high-pressure situation, you might merely distinguish between 'crisis' and 'non-crisis' activities! Alternatively you might follow the advice of one management writer and divide your activities into 'constructive' and 'non-constructive'.

Possible courses of action

Before you can take any corrective action in situations where you can see that you are spending too much time on unimportant or irrelevant activities, you have to bear in mind certain possible constraints.

- *Control.* There are likely to be some activities over which you have no control. You are required to carry them out and must therefore tailor your other activities to fit in with them. If your senior manager requires your attendance at a meeting, no matter how time-consuming, badly run or irrelevant it may be, you will have to organise your other work around that requirement.
- *Urgency.* Again, if you work in an environment in which you may frequently be required to carry out certain activities at the last moment, then your freedom of action is somewhat curtailed. It may be, for instance, that you are expected to stand in for a senior manager in his or her absence, which absences are sporadic but relatively frequent.

Given those constraints, however, you should be able to follow two distinct courses of action. The first is to eliminate, as far as possible, activities which are of little value. The second is to *prioritise* those which you have to carry out.

THEORY INTO PRACTICE

The following situations involve time-wasting activities. Consider what action you would take in each situation to try to improve matters.

a You have recently been promoted to be in charge of the sales team and want to be thought of as helpful – and also as one of them. Consequently whenever anyone asks you to do something or to lend them a hand, you do so even though your own work is suffering as a result.

b You have a job which requires a lot of concentration. However, you also have a friendly but talkative boss who, whenever she has nothing else to do, tends to wander into your office for a chat.

c A major part of your job is spent on the telephone. However, you find that some of your most frequent – although not-to-be-offended – callers
  - talk for far too long
  - find it difficult to end a conversation
  - telephone you several times because they have not given you the whole story the first time
  - should really be speaking to your colleagues.

d You have established an 'open door' policy and although you now get to know much more about what is going on, you find that you have little time for anything else.

e You have never subscribed to the '80%–20%' accuracy rule in relation to the finished result of your activities. You always aim for 100 per cent but it takes you a very long time.

Prioritisation

In an ideal world you should prioritise your work on a long-term, medium-term and short-term basis. In other words you should analyse what is expected of you during the year as outlined in the operational plan and then subdivide it into work to be carried out on a monthly, weekly and daily basis. That tends to work only in the most settled of situations. Although you should obviously always be working towards the objectives as stated in the plan, it is likely that the most pressing need for prioritisation is at the beginning of each week and, subsequently, each day.

Use a variety of planning aids (rather than relying totally on your memory – normally a rather poor time management tool). Refer back to page 206 to remind yourself of the type of planning aids you might wish to use.

Avoid too much paperwork. All management writers recommend this: the fact that they have done so over the past 30 years is an indication that it is easier to recommend it than actually do it. Indeed it has been suggested that too much paperwork is the result of managers' or administrators' desire to cover themselves in case something goes wrong, increase their visibility, impress senior management, or merely justify their existence.

It is good practice to try to follow certain basic rules when dealing with paperwork. You may find, for instance, that a mass of paperwork accumulates on your desk. Ideally what you should do is to set aside a time each day to look at it and then immediately either to throw it away, delegate it, respond to it or file it. Placing it neatly in the pending tray makes your desk look a bit tidier and you feel a bit happier – but it doesn't really solve the long-term problem.

Avoid over-filing. Either you or your assistant should have a filing system which allows you easy access and also the opportunity of dispensing with unwanted documents at the earliest possible moment.

Use other forms of communication where possible. A telephone call, a face-to-face discussion or even an e-mail are all less permanent methods of communication but they are quick and convenient methods of both imparting and receiving communication.

Research has shown that many managers and administrators waste time either by selecting the wrong method of communication or because their skills of communication are ineffective. The researchers found, for instance, that amongst the most common faults were:

- a tendency to write an over-elaborate memo when a simpler one would have sufficed
- the use of too complex or technical language
- poor grammar, punctuation and spelling – which tends to downgrade the content of the document in the eyes of the reader and which therefore does not produce the required response.

See Chapter 4 for further information on communication.

Flexible use of physical resources

Managers or administrators who jealously guard their 'territory' may be causing considerable damage to the overall efficiency of the organisation. It is important, therefore, that you recognise that flexibility in the way in which physical resources are utilised is as valuable as flexibility in staffing or time management. The pooling of resources – whether as a result of their being offered as a centralised provision or being made freely available through a computerised management information system – should be an advantage rather than a disadvantage, provided of course the service offered is at least equal to the one previously provided on a decentralised basis!

Centralisation of resources

One method of optimising the use of your physical resources is to place them under a central control. This has several advantages.

- The best possible price can be negotiated both in relation to the initial purchase and also to any maintenance deals.
- Properly trained staff are always available to operate any specialist equipment.
- The working environment can be adapted to maximise the efficient use of the resources and to accommodate any health and safety requirements.
- The possibility of theft or damage is reduced.

Opponents of centralised services, however, argue that the system is not totally beneficial, for the following reasons.

- The system is time-wasting as the requirement that all requests be placed centrally rather than locally creates a greater time lag.

- Specialist requests are harder to deal with centrally as the requisite resource is less likely to be available. In addition the operating staff have of necessity to be generalists rather than specialists.
- It creates a certain rigidity of procedure and is less able to cope with emergency demands.

The use of information technology

Another method of optimising the use of many physical resources is through the introduction of information technology (IT). Among the many reasons for introducing new technology are the following.

A reduction in operating costs and an improvement in efficiency

New technology can effect a reduction in the workforce and therefore a reduction in expenditure, either by providing a technological substitute for existing workers or by facilitating a more economical allocation of work. Examples include automated processing, robotics, computer-controlled machine tools, fully computerised production systems, and information processing systems such as electronic point-of-sale systems in retailing.

Costs can be reduced by computerising and therefore improving stock control, and by using computerised scheduling to reduce waste and improve plant utilisation.

An increase in flexibility and speed of response

If an organisation is unable to respond quickly to an opportunity, it will lose the competitive advantage. Consequently, if a manufacturing company wants to be able to offer custom-built products produced in small batches rather than a limited number of mass-produced, off-the-shelf products, it will need the assistance of computer-controlled technology which can produce a range of items through a single facility with the minimum of cost and delay. In addition, many organisations such as mail-order firms or finance houses are dependent on computer technology for instant information when dealing with their customers.

An improvement in quality

Manual quality-control systems can be effective. However, in order to ensure a level of consistency in both the manufacture of a product and the monitoring of its progress, most manufacturing organisations are dependent on computer technologies such as robotics, computerised process control or electronic monitoring systems.

An improvement in control

Nowadays many managers and administrators would feel helpless without some form of on-line information system to assist them to make decisions or to control the work of their staff. In the retail area, for instance, the electronic point-of-sale systems allow data to be captured through the scanning of bar-coded items. These data can be used by store managers to ascertain how many and what type of goods are being sold and the effect of those sales on stocks. It is equally useful for central buying and distribution departments.

Read the following verbatim extract from a set of notes taken at a meeting of a Board of Directors of a small family-run organisation, who are debating whether or not to replace the existing manual payroll system with a computerised system.

JEAN   I can't see anything but advantages in introducing the computerised payroll system. Look, we all watched the presentation given by that computer boffin last week – and we were all impressed. Fewer mistakes, quicker turnaround, a database that can be constantly updated – and all for a relatively reasonable initial outlay. Why are we hesitating?

CONNOR   What about the present staff? Some of them have worked for us for years and have been very loyal to us. Are we just going to tell them to go without any further ado? And if we do, what will it cost us?

JEAN   We can keep four of them – the rest are superfluous to requirements. I'm sorry, but that's the harsh reality of modern business. The days of looking after old retainers are long gone.

CONNOR   Most of them are anything but old retainers – they've come to us because of our good reputation for treating staff well and we've been only too pleased to have them, given their expertise. If we do let them go, I bet they'll be re-employed pretty quickly by one of our competitors. Do we want to risk that? Our staff are still our major asset no matter what sort of sophisticated IT systems we introduce.

Consider a possible compromise that could be reached combining the advantage of new technology with that of being able to recruit and keep a motivated and capable staff.

Legal and regulatory requirements relating to work methods and activities

Many of the legal and regulatory requirements relating to work methods and activities have already been covered in Chapter 2:

- health and safety requirements (see page 109)
- employment law (see page 177)
- equal opportunities legislation (see page 187).

What managers and administrators may also be expected to know, however, is the way in which the structure of their organisation is affected by the law, particularly since the strategic and operational plans they have to try to implement will almost certainly have been influenced by that structure.

Sole traders

Normally the smallest type of organisation is that operated by a sole trader, and because it is the simplest form of business organisation there are few legal implications. However, one requirement universally applied is that imposed by the Business Names Act 1985. The intention of the Act is to prevent people from giving names to their businesses that falsely suggest they:

- are part of another company
- have the same name as another company
- are by 'royal appointment'
- are a society, institute or charity, have some type of international connection or are some type of financial organisation
- have some connection with a government department.

Under the provisions of the Act a person trading under a business name must declare his or her real name and an address at which he or she can be contacted in the UK. This is to enable the serving of writs or summonses against him or her. The required details must be included upon all the business documentation used by the business and must also be supplied if requested by anyone dealing with the sole trader. Failure to comply with the provisions is a criminal offence.

> If you decide to trade using a name which is not permissible under the Act, you will run the risk of being unable to sue anyone against whom you may have a legitimate legal claim as the court will refuse to enforce any obligation in your favour.
>
> A trader may also be liable under the tort of 'passing off'; i.e. trading under a business name that is liable to be confused with that of another existing business. If, for example, you decide to use the name Virginia Records, you may find that you become the subject of an application for an injunction issued by the management of Virgin Records. Note, however, that if you are actually called F. W. Woolworth, you would be able to trade under that name, provided you did not claim a false connection with the famous store bearing the same name.

Partnerships

Although sole traders need not work alone – a plumber may employ a workforce to assist him or her and yet still retain sole trading status – if a business increases in size it eventually becomes advisable for the sole trader to consider either setting up a partnership or becoming a limited-liability company.

It is almost as simple to establish a partnership as it is to set up business as a sole trader. However, because of the potential difficulties in such an arrangement, partnerships are normally governed by a partnership deed which will specify the basis upon which the partners have agreed to work. In addition, the Partnership Act 1890 governs the relationship between that partnership and any third parties.

> Although the Companies Act 1985 provides that a partnership may not contain more than 20 partners, solicitors and certain other professions are exempted from this provision and may have more partners.

Law of agency

One legal implication arising from the existence of a partnership is that a partner will be an agent of the firm and will have the power to bind the firm by his or her *actual* authority; i.e. the authority that the partners have agreed, either expressly or impliedly. In addition, however, he or she will also be able to bind the firm by any act carried out under his or her *apparent* authority. In one case, for instance, even though a partnership agreement of a firm of car repairers forbade the buying and selling of cars, one of the partners, without the knowledge of the others, bought a car and resold it. The sale turned out to be void and the original owner repossessed the car. The person to whom the car had been sold sued the partnership. He succeeded. It was held that the buying and selling of cars could be considered by the general public as a normal transaction for a firm of car repairers and that therefore the partner concerned had been cloaked with 'apparent' authority to do so.

Although partnerships are supposedly based on trust, section 24 of the Partnership Act 1890 provides a series of rules relating to the interests and duties of partners.

- All partners are entitled to an equal share in the profits and must bear an equal share of the losses.
- The firm must indemnify a partner against any payment he or she makes and any liability incurred in the course of the business.
- Where a partner makes a payment into the firm above his or her prescribed amount, he or she will be entitled to 5 per cent interest per annum.
- A partner will not be entitled, before the ascertainment of profits, to interest on the capital subscribed by him or her.
- Every partner may take part in the management of the business.
- No partner shall be entitled to remuneration for his or her part in the business.
- All existing partners must agree to the introduction of a new partner.
- Ordinary matters may be determined by a majority of the partners.
- The partnership books should be kept at the place of business and all partners should have access to them.

In addition, partners have a duty to render true accounts, account for private profits, and not compete with the firm. Where any of these terms are broken the other partners will have a right of action for damages or an injunction to prevent the breach from recurring.

Companies

Although it is possible that if you work for a sole trader or a partnership, you will be actively involved in preparing strategic and operational plans, it is probably far more likely that you will be so involved if you work for a company – given the extensive regulations under which most companies operate.

Corporations aggregate

There are three main types of corporations.

- *Registered companies* are the most common type of company and are governed by the Companies Act 1985 (as amended by the Companies

Act 1989). Once the promoters of a company have complied with the stated formalities, the company's details will be available for public inspection. Such companies may be limited by shares or by guarantee or may have unlimited liability.

- *Chartered companies* (e.g. non-commercial organisations such as the British Broadcasting Corporation) may be created by Royal Charter, a method of creation which is now no longer used.
- *Statutory companies* are created by Act of Parliament and in the past have been used to create nationalised industries. Since the present trend is towards de-nationalisation, this method of creation has also fallen into disuse.

THEORY INTO PRACTICE

A company may be registered as being either public or private under the Companies Act 1985. Research the differences between the two entities and compile a table indicating what they are. Make reference to the following items: name, certificate of incorporation, certificate to trade, initial capital, accounts, shares, membership.

An incorporated company is a *juristic person*; i.e. it is recognised as having a legal personality and being capable of enjoying and being subject to legal rights and duties. It can therefore have a legal identity separate from its members. This concept was firmly established in the early case of *Salomon v Salomon Ltd* [1897] AC 22, in which Aron Salomon was a sole trader who turned his business into a limited company. The purchase price of the business was set at £38 782. Aron took 20 000 shares valued at £1 each, while six other members of his family took one share each. The balance of the purchase price was lent to the company by Aron as a secured loan. The company then experienced difficulty and was wound up. The question arose as to whether the secured loan could be paid to Aron. Although the creditors claimed that Aron had merely lent money to himself, the House of Lords held that as the company was a distinct and separate entity, the secured loan was valid and had to be repaid before any other debts. Consequently, apart from Aron, all the other creditors got nothing!

The principle of a company having a separate identity from its members is known as the *veil of incorporation*. However, in certain circumstances the veil may be lifted to enable any person – normally a company director – to be prosecuted where he or she has acted fraudulently or failed to comply with any of the regulations.

Registration of a company

Both public and private companies must register with the Registrar of Companies by giving details of their memorandum of association and their articles of association.

Memorandum of association

The memorandum must be constructed in the form prescribed in the Act. Apart from the name and registered address of the company, the objectives must be stated. These should be related to and reflected by the company's strategic plan and subsequently the SBUs' operational plans. The company must, for instance, state its general trading objectives. Interestingly, this is the section of the Act which has caused major problems when a company has attempted to change its objectives. In *Ashbury Railway Carriage Co. Ltd v Riche* [1875] LR 7, for instance, a company's objectives stated that its business was mechanical engineering and general contracting. It then entered into a contract to build a railway in Belgium but later withdrew from it. The subcontractor, who lost a lot of money because of the repudiation, sued the company. He was unsuccessful because the court held that the company was acting *ultra vires*; i.e. beyond the limit of its powers.

> Because of the potential unfairness of such a rule, section 9(1) of the European Communities Act 1972 (later incorporated into section 35 of the Companies Act 1985) allows a company to make a very general statement as to its objectives so that nowadays a claim of *ultra vires* in such circumstances will be very rare.

Articles of association

The articles – a model set of which are outlined in the Companies Act 1985 – govern the internal administration of the company, such as meetings, categories of shares, and the appointment of directors.

> In addition to the memorandum and articles of association, the Registrar of Companies also requires the completion of:
>
> - Form G10, on which should be outlined the details of the directors, the company secretary and the location of the registered office
> - Form G12, which should contain a declaration as to compliance with all the necessary requirements by one of the named directors, the company secretary or a solicitor who has been involved in the formation of the company.

Element 3.3

Monitor and evaluate work activities

Types and sources of information required for your own use

Managers and administrators are inevitably information gatherers. Otherwise they would be unable to operate. In this context, however, their success or failure lies in the accuracy of the information they collect, the speed at which they obtain it, and the extent of their knowledge of available sources.

Internal information

Obviously this depends to a large extent on the nature of the organisation and the nature of the job itself.

What every manager or administrator should have, however, is a detailed knowledge of his or her own organisation.

THEORY INTO PRACTICE

Information about the organisation

1 Look at the questions in Figure 3.3.1 to determine the extent of your knowledge of your own organisation. If necessary, research those items about which you feel you have an incomplete knowledge.
2 Consider which of the items of information are of most use to you as a source of reference and which the least. If relevant, think also of other types of internal information (not mentioned the list) which you frequently use and for what purpose.
3 A new member of staff arrives in your workplace. Try to assess what information you think that member of staff *must* have immediately and what could be delayed until later.

Personal information

Of personal importance to you as a source of reference are the terms and conditions under which you work. Your job description will indicate to you what is expected from you as a manager or administrator. However, you should be equally aware of your *contractual* obligations. Current employment legislation requires that you be given a written statement of the terms and conditions of your employment (see further page 177) but you may find that your contract contains additional information on your rights and duties in your current employment. It is, of course, vital that you are aware of them.

Figure 3.3.1 How well do you know your organisation?

1. When was the organisation first established and for what purpose? Is it part of a larger organisation?

2. What type of legal entity does it possess?

3. How is it financed? Does it publish an annual report? What did its balance sheet indicate at the end of last year?

4. What are its major products/services? Have they changed at all in the past five years?

5. Who are its major clients, customers or users of the service?

6. What are the names, titles, qualifications and experience of the present senior management team? Are there any external members? To whom, if anyone, is the team responsible?

7. How many departments/strategic business units are there? How long has it been since the last restructuring of the organisation?

8. How many people does the organisation employ?

9. What proportion are women? What proportion are from ethnic diversity backgrounds? How many are registered disabled?

10. How many work part-time or term-time only? Are there any seasonal workers? Is job sharing allowed? Are there any homeworkers?

11. Is there a standard working day? Is there a shift system in operation?

12. What are the pay scales? Are they incremental? Do they differ from job to job and/or between shopfloor and office? Is there a system of performance-related pay? What is the procedure for claiming expenses? Is overtime paid and if so, to whom and on what basis? Are there any unsocial hours payments?

13. Does the organisation participate in Modern Apprenticeship or graduate traineeship schemes?

14. Does it favour internal promotion? If so, how many people were promoted last year and in what areas?

15. What methods does it use to recruit staff? What interviewing/assessment methods does it use?

16. Does it have a policy on staff development? Does it operate any in-house training? Does it have a policy of funding or subsidising external courses?

17. Is there an early retirement scheme and/or a redundancy policy?

Plan and control activities to meet objectives

18 Is there a system of centralised purchasing?

19 Are contracts for goods and materials etc. put out to tender? If not, how is a supplier chosen? Is there a favoured list of suppliers?

20 Does each department or unit have its own budget? If so, on what criteria are funds allocated? If not, how do managers obtain funds?

21 What is the policy on the replacement of equipment? is there a system of rolling replacement?

22 What storage and retrieval systems are in operation? Are they common throughout the organisation?

23 What is the policy on photocopying? Is it centralised or departmentalised? Is there free access or does the photocopying have to be carried out by certain members of staff?

24 What are the major means of internal communication? Is there a house policy on the preparation of reports, memoranda, minutes of meetings, etc.? Do all departments or SBUs operate the same system of meetings?

25 How many computers are in operation throughout the organisation? Are they stand-alone or networked? What software is available? What are the various levels of access?

26 Is the organisation unionised? If so, what facilities are available to trade union representatives? If not, how are negotiations carried out with the staff? What disciplinary and grievance procedures are in operation? Where can the relevant information be obtained?

27 How is quality measured and controlled? Who is ultimately responsible for it? Is there a complaints procedure? Does the organisation have a customer care policy?

28 Is there a health and safety officer? If so, what are his or her terms of reference? If not, who is responsible for the implementation of health and safety legislation?

29 How does the organisation sell its products or services? Does it have a marketing department or officer? Who handles publicity? Who researches local market intelligence?

30 Are any services – such as cleaning, security or catering – contracted out to private contractors? If so, on what terms?

Given below are extracts from a widely used contract of employment.

'You will be employed as ... in which capacity you will be required to perform such duties consistent with your position as may from time to time be assigned to you.'

'You are expected to work flexibly and efficiently and to maintain the highest professional standards.'

'You will be expected to work such hours as are reasonably necessary for the proper performance of your duties and responsibilities with a normal working week of 40 hours.'

'Your principal place of work will normally be the company's headquarters. However, you may be required to work on a temporary basis at any of the branch offices.'

'You are required to devote your full time, attention and abilities to your duties during your working hours. Accordingly, you must not, without the written consent of the Board, undertake any employment or engagement which might interfere with the performance of your duties or conflict with the interests of the organisation.'

'You shall not, either during your employment nor at any time after its termination, use for your own purposes any confidential information belonging to the organisation.'

a Check your own contract to see whether it contains any of these (or similar) terms.

b Assess the possibly restrictive effects some of these terms may have on you.

External information

Obviously not all your queries can be answered from within the organisation, and you may find that you need to refer to certain specialised external sources for the information you require. Even though these sources will differ depending on the nature of the work, many managers and administrators need on occasion to seek information from:

- local or regional reference libraries
- local chambers of commerce and industry or chambers of trade
- professional and trade associations
- employment agencies
- local authority departments
- government departments
- the Registrar of Companies
- local Training and Enterprise Councils.

Read the following extract from a newspaper article and consider to what extent you agree with what it says.

'Chambers of Commerce are strong in delivering practical services to businesses at a local level but are very much less effective nationally. In part this is because local chambers guard their position too jealously to let a national organisation have any real influence. Some trade associations are competent and content with their traditional roles. Others, now deprived of the opportunity to be involved in national pay bargaining, are less happy. Many professional associations have an effective functional role but tend not to have a broader business agenda.'

Although unions have a national focus in the Trades Union Congress (TUC), there are at least 230 different employer bodies, most of whom operate as independent entities.

Reference books are expensive and tend to become outdated. Unless you have a particular need for one – or you can obtain it in loose-leaf form which is regularly updated – you are better advised to obtain any information you need from relevant magazines or journals. If, for instance, you or your senior manager are a member of a professional association – such as IPD – you may subscribe to their official publication in which you should find up-to-the-minute information. In addition, most libraries subscribe to a wide variety of business journals and keep as many back issues as they can accommodate. See Figure 3.3.2 for some of the most widely stocked journals.

Accountancy
Accountancy Age
Accounting and Business Research
Accounting Review
Accounting Technician
Administrator
Bulletin of Comparative Labour Relations
British Economy Survey
British Journal of Industrial Relations
Business Equipment Digest
Business Law Handbook
Buying Business Equipment and Services
Buying and Selling Law
Chartered Secretary
Consumer Law Journal
Consumer Law Today
Croner's   Business Information Briefing
*   Health and Safety Briefing*
*   Exporter's Briefing*
*   Importer's Briefing*
*   Employer's Briefing*
*   Europe Briefing*

Employment Law
Employment Law and Practice Update
Encyclopaedia of European Community Law
Equal Opportunities
Europe
European Business Information Sources
European Industrial Relations Review
European Journal of Industrial Relations
European Law Review
European Management Journal
Executive Companion
Export Digest
Harvard Business Review
Health and Safety at Work
Human Resource Management Journal
Incomes Data Service: Brief/Report/Study
Incomes Data Service: Pensions Manual/Pensions Service Bulletin
Industrial Relations Journal
Journal of General Management
Journal of Management Studies
Journal of the Market Research Society
Journal of Marketing
Labour Market Trends
Labour Market Quarterly Report
Local Authority Law
Management Service
Marketing
New Law Review
Occupational Pensions
People Management
Personnel Managers' Factbook
Purchasing and Supply Management
Supply Management
The Economist
What to Buy for Business

Figure 3.3.2 Business journals with a wide circulation

An invaluable initial source of information is Croner's *A-Z of Business Information Sources*, which offers:

● a list of sources of business information alphabetically by subject area and then alphabetically by source
● a telephone number for each entry
● a loose-leaf format so that sources can be kept permanently up-to-date through a regular quarterly amendment service.

Choose *one* of the following areas – preferably one which has some relevance to your present job – and research the journals published on that area. Consider how effective you find the different layouts and styles, and the breadth and depth of content:

- accounts and finance
- management
- human resources management
- business equipment
- health and safety.

Computer-based information

Internal database systems

By no means all information is paper-based. Nowadays the electronic office is almost commonplace, even though the completely 'paperless' office still remains more of a dream than a reality.

Various types of system can be incorporated into a total Management Information System (MIS) and can – potentially – provide an organisation with a completely centralised information system.

- *Office support systems* such as electronic mail, word-processing and computer networks provide assistance with routine office functions.
- *Data-processing systems* such as accounts, payroll, production control and stock control record, process and report on daily activities within the organisation.
- *Decision support systems* such as spreadsheets, forecasting techniques, decision models, linear programming and statistical analyses are intended to provide management with assistance in planning and decision-making. See page 253 for further discussion on this point.

External database systems

In addition to any internal computer-based information systems you have, you may also be able to access other external information retrieval systems. It is almost certain, for instance, that any major reference library will have such a system. In addition, many information retrieval systems are available which enable subscribers to them to recall from databases a wide variety of information displayed either on the screen of a computer terminal or on an adapted television set. Two established forms were Teletext and Viewdata, but these have been largely superseded by the Internet.

The Internet

The Internet has been described as the 'network of networks'. It allows users around the world to connect to the network no matter what type of computer or operating system is used, and provides a simple standard way for them to log into the network. It allows not just one-to-one communications but also communications between groups of individuals. The means of obtaining information are varied.

- There are a large number of 'mailing lists' which allow people to carry on discussions and exchange ideas and information on topics of common interest.
- Many universities are building 'Campus Wide Information Systems' as a way of consolidating campus information and computing services in one place. Users around the world can therefore access their library catalogues.
- Individual scientists and scientific institutes are making available large collections of papers and databases.
- Excerpts from certain books and magazines are being put on open access on the Internet so that subscribers can read them and decide whether or not to subscribe to the paper copy.
- Current weather forecasts and maps are available.
- Not only the written word is available – with the necessary equipment, subscribers can listen to audio documents over the Internet.

The Internet is not the only large data network of multinational scope. As well as the commercial public data networks and specialised commercial data vendors which offer specialised data services (to which reference has already been made), there are also private corporate networks operated by large corporations to support their national and international data communications.

There are also mass-market information services which sell access to online discussion groups, up-to-the-minute news summaries, airline reservations and travel information, etc. Note, however, that although millions of subscribers belong to such services as Compuserve, America Online, Prodigy, Genie and Delphi, a Boston-based firm of researchers has predicted that these are likely to be outnumbered by the *World Wide Web* users on the Internet by the year 2000.

Among the hundreds of additional information services it offers are:

- banking services
- news releases, minutes of meetings, speeches and economic data from the Treasury
- Jobserve – a job-seeking service
- property purchases.

Note too the recently launched *Virgin Net*, which advertises itself as affording easy access to 'the best textbooks in the world' together with the ability to ask questions of every teacher, classmate or expert on the Net, all for the price of a local call.

Major users of the Internet include:

- lecturers, researchers and students at colleges and universities
- an increasing number of business organisations – not only for the information the Internet contains but also to advertise their products or services – particularly if they know that their competitors are doing the same
- members of the general public – in recent times, for instance, a number of cyber cafés have been established to allow access to the Internet by members of the public alongside the provision of refreshment and entertainment facilities!

Claims made for the Internet are that its 'navigation tools' make it easy for individuals to 'cruise' the network for the information it contains, and that its index allows users to scan large databases quickly to locate documents of interest. Either from your own personal experience or through personal research, consider how far you agree with that statement.

> The Internet operates without any central agency or authority in charge. This can cause problems in relation to some of the material displayed on the network – it could be pornographic, misleading or even fraudulent. The various constituent networks that make up the Internet have therefore adopted their own *Acceptable Use Policies* governing their portion of the Internet. Common prohibitions include harassing behaviour towards others, fraudulent use of others' identities, unauthorised access to systems or services, and unsolicited advertisements. (For an interesting extract from a newspaper article on this subject, see Chapter 10, *Facilitate compliance with legal and regulatory requirements.*)

Obtaining and validating information

Ways of obtaining information differ depending on:

- the nature of the information
- its source
- its level of complexity
- the urgency with which it is required.

At the most basic level, information can be obtained simply by asking the person sitting at the next desk or telephoning someone in an adjacent office. At its most complex level it requires detailed and time-consuming research using a variety of sources. In the latter case, a knowledge of research methodology is obviously useful.

Your first step should be to clarify the terms of reference and, if necessary, break down the information required into a series of smaller elements. Suppose, for instance, your senior manager wants to find out exactly what is meant by total quality management. Your first step may be to agree with him or her a more precise definition of what is required. Is a list of book and/or journal references sufficient? Has your manager a particular organisation in mind which already operates such a system? If so, should you provide a summary of the way in which it operates in that organisation, or should you go further and make some useful comparisons with other organisations? Is information required about the cost of implementing such a system, etc.?

Consultation with internal sources

You need to identify the appropriate sources of information. Internal sources are important – and you may be guaranteed a more sympathetic hearing to your requests for information than if you contact an external source. You may also feel less hesitant about asking for further information should the need arise. In many cases the internal source is obvious – you would automatically discuss a human resources issue with a member of the Human Resources department and a financial issue with a member of the Accounts staff, and so on. However, you should also be aware that there are often a number of internal sources of information in an organisation which are untapped simply because few people are aware of their existence.

If you are researching into total quality management, for instance, you are unlikely to be able merely to telephone the quality assurance officer for the information you require – if the organisation did employ such a person the query would have been addressed to him or her in the first place. However there may be a someone employed in the organisation who is undertaking a senior management course involving a study of total quality management techniques or who, although now in charge of a different area, has in a previous role some knowledge of the topic. The problem here, of course, is discovering whether, and if so where, that type of expertise exists.

> Many organisations now carry out staff audits on a regular basis in which they record staff expertise in a number of areas including qualifications, experience, an update on the training they have received or are undergoing, and any preferences they may have expressed in relation to areas of work. It is then relatively easy for anyone who is authorised to do so, to interrogate the information contained in the database to see which members of staff might be able to answer a particular query.

Consultation with external sources

The type of external source to be used depends, of course, on the nature of the research. Again, do not underestimate the importance of involving people in your queries. If, for instance, you want to obtain some information about false trade descriptions, you may decide to visit your library and obtain a copy of the Fair Trading Act 1973. Alternatively you may decide to obtain a copy of the *Code of Practice* issued by the Director General of Fair Trading. In both cases, you will eventually find the information you want. A quicker method, however, may simply be to obtain the telephone number of the Office of Fair Trading and to speak to an official there. At the very least you will be directed more specifically to the information you require.

Where such assistance is not available, you have to develop further research skills. If you require more information than even a specialist librarian can provide, you may have to perfect your knowledge of the basic library indexing systems *and* learn how to manipulate them to your advantage. The index will, for instance, direct you towards specific subject areas. It may also – particularly if it is a computerised index – list all books and journals on a certain topic. In many cases your queries will then be answered.

However, some information is not as easily obtained. Suppose, for instance, you have been asked to find some information on exporting agricultural equipment to the EU. If you are fortunate, you may immediately find the section in the library which contains the relevant books and bound copies of journals. It may be, however, that you will have to work on a trial-and-error basis by using different keywords to scan the library catalogue and databases to see whether you can discover any relevant material. In such circumstances, you also have to have sufficient perseverance to follow up any cross-references!

Research methodology

Methodology is important. The most experienced researchers never begin any research without certain preparations.

Provide yourself with the appropriate means of recording information – a notepad and pen/pencil. Some researchers prefer to use a small lined notebook which is easy to prop against a shelf or on the edge of a desk as notes are taken; others prefer A4 lined paper which can be filed in an A4 binder for future reference. For obvious reasons, the use of the laptop computer is also growing in popularity.

Prepare a definite plan of action. Rather than waste time by simply wandering from shelf to shelf or searching at random through an index, have a prepared list of topic headings and possible sources which you will use as a starting point for your research. See Figure 3.3.3 for an example.

The topic:

> Part-time employment

The parameters:

- Language (English, French, German, etc.)

  > English

- Time period (1 year, 5 years, infinite, etc.)

  > No later than 5 years

- Type of material (books, journals, databases, etc.)

  > Library catalogue: British National Bibliography: Employment law textbooks (classification ?): IDS Briefs: LEXIS CD Rom (for latest cases): New Law Review: HR Management Journal

Possible search terms:

> Part-timers; low-paid workers; sex discrimination; equal opportunities; European legislation; Social Chapter

---

Figure 3.3.3 Information search

Adopt a methodical approach. Some researchers consult one source of reference at a time to make the necessary notes and take any relevant photocopies. Other researchers prefer to skim through a number of possible sources before making a selection and then extracting the relevant information. In both cases, however, they will have devised a format for noting down the information they require. They will, for instance, always note down the source of their information – title, author, publisher, date of publication, country of origin, etc. They will also have made a note of the names, addresses and telephone numbers of anyone listed as being able to provide further information.

Ensure that the information you record is legible and complete so that you do not have to return to a source of reference.

THEORY INTO PRACTICE

Assume you want some information on performance-related pay.

a   Using the example in Figure 3.3.3 as a guide, prepare an information search sheet outlining the initial sources of reference you think you may use together with any relevant search terms.

b   Consider the ease with which you obtained the information you required as a result of that information search. Think about what, if anything, you would change in your approach should you be required to research any further information.

Validity of information

Believing all you hear and all you read is high risk! You have only to compare the same story reported in the different newspapers and tabloids to realise that facts can sometimes be distorted out of all recognition. It is important, therefore, that once you have obtained your information you then pause for a moment to reflect on it, to make sure that you are not going to base any assumptions on what may prove to be an inaccurate source.

What you should be looking for initially is *reliability*. To a certain extent you can make a subjective assessment, particularly if the source is one you have consulted previously and which has always proved reliable. In some very limited cases, however, you can use more objective methods.

- *Test and retest*. If you are unsure of some information you have been given by a colleague, you can allow a certain period of time to elapse and then re-make the same request (possibly in a different format) to see if the two answers coincide.
- *Alternative forms*. If you are doubtful from the start that the reply to any request you make will be reliable, you can again ask for the information in two alternative forms to see whether there are any discrepancies.

You should also be trying to check the *validity* of the information. If an item of information is unreliable, it must be invalid. However, just because it comes from a reliable source does not necessarily mean that it is valid. For instance, when you were researching information about performance-related pay, you may have found that some standard, and therefore supposedly reliable, sources of reference contained conflicting information – hence the need for a means of validation, which could include:

- looking at the date of publication to see whether the older version contains out-of-date information
- if both your sources are current, consulting a third source
- ignoring both sets of information as being potentially invalid and starting afresh (in such circumstances, however, be careful to check that you are comparing facts and not opinions – obviously opinions will differ).

Another problem of validation arises where the source of reference is a person, not a book or a journal. If you consult two people and receive two different answers it is not easy to determine who is correct other than by relying on what traditionally has been the most reliable source. Again, however, you might be advised either to cross-check with a third source or to ask someone else to pose the same questions – surprisingly a different approach can sometimes produce different results!

> Incorrect information or information that has not been validated can cause more than just mere embarrassment. Shareholders of one investment company were told that they would not after all be paid an end-of-year dividend because the company accountant had left out the minus sign on a net capital loss of $1.3 billion and had incorrectly treated it as a net capital gain. This meant that the dividend estimate spreadsheet was wrong by $2.6 billion. The Managing Director said that although many of the processes were computerised, the requirements of the tax code were so complex that it required some steps to be handled manually by tax managers and accountants. The lack of cross-checking of the manually input information had caused the error.

Integrating, analysing and evaluating information

Integration of information

Even if you are the most methodical researcher, you may find that at the end of the initial research period the information you have collected is so vast that it seems impossible to sort out into a coherent form. In such cases you might find it helpful to follow this guidance:

- Determine in what format you want to put the information you have collected – a report, a summary, a list, a handbook, etc.
- Begin to re-sort the information you have collected into relevant areas. At this stage you need make only general categorisations – don't agonise for hours deciding on the most suitable area for a particular reference – you can fine tune at a later stage.

- If there is some information which can genuinely belong to one of several areas, either make out a cross-reference index card or take the relevant number of photocopies.
- Work systematically through the information you have collected under each heading. Sometimes you can suffer from a surfeit of relevant information. If, for instance, you have been asked for some information on occupational pensions, you may find that you are overwhelmed by the information available to you, all of which looks relevant and much of which overlaps. At this stage you *have* to be decisive and select one or two documents only as your primary source of information. Criteria which you may wish to use to assist your choice include:
  - knowledge of the author of the document or originator of the information
  - the length and apparent substance of the document
  - the age of the information
  - the way in which the information is written and presented
  - whether or not you have successfully used the same source on a different occasion.

  It is then a good idea to draft some notes from this major source and to treat them as a basic framework.

Remember that it is a poor researcher who thinks that he or she has then done enough and who completely neglects to look at the rest of the documentation to see whether it includes any different information which can be incorporated into the basic framework. Remember too that some management writers make the point that no-one, however skilful, can produce a perfect first draft. Rewriting is always necessary – and that includes adding to and amending the material through the integration of additional information.

> If you are sufficiently computer literate you should be able to make use of advanced word-processor facilities to enable you to input all your original information and then to add to, delete or change it at various stages in the process.

Analysis and evaluation of information

Information is there for a purpose. When it is presented to the reader, it is intended that it should create a response. An adequate response can be given only if sufficient time is devoted to analysing its content. Obviously much depends on the complexity of the information. A simple memorandum takes very little time to digest; a 20-page report on the other hand needs both time and careful attention. Indeed, in some cases it is a good idea to prepare a short précis of the information under a series of headings to make it easier for you to ensure that you have extracted all the relevant points. See Chapter 5, *Influence and facilitate decision making*, for further discussion on this topic.

> If you work in certain areas, you may be required to use more specific analytical procedures, particularly if your work requires you to forecast what is likely to occur in a given situation or if a certain action is taken. See page 253 for further discussion on this point.

Identifying changes in circumstances which affect planned activities

Risk factors

Most senior managers recognise that an operational plan can be affected by both internal and external changes.

- It could, for instance, be affected by a change in thinking by senior management. It may be that they feel that the plan is too conservative and that more can be achieved in the allocated period of time. They may be alerted to a new challenge by one of their competitors. They may be affected by the arrival of a new member or members of the senior management team, who want a different approach to be taken. They may be equally affected if a key member of staff leaves suddenly, and so on.
- There might be an economic crisis. If the market for a particular product or service disappears or its major customer changes to another supplier or goes out of business, the original operational plan becomes almost meaningless.
- There might be a change in government, bringing with it new policies or restrictions.

They therefore include in the plan certain *risk factors* – possible occurrences which may affect the plan's stated objectives – together with proposed procedures to be taken should there be such an occurrence.

Suppose, for example, your organisation plans to launch a new product and you are involved in promoting it. You therefore include as one of your objectives in your operational plan a 6-month direct mail campaign aimed at all retail stores of a certain size and within a certain area. You have included as a resource requirement in the plan a sum to cover the costs of such a campaign and the timescale within which you intend to complete it. However, what you should also do if at all possible is to include in the plan (or add to it as a rider) any factors you feel may prevent you from achieving your target. You may, for instance, want to make the point that you will need a certain complement of staff, which if not provided will affect the progress of the campaign. You may also want to include the proviso that full details of the product itself must be provided to you by a certain time so that you can be assured of meeting the required deadline, and so on. As you become more senior, you may also have to include what action you intend to take should any of those problems arise.

THEORY INTO PRACTICE

Useful though it may be to attach risk factors to particular objectives, there is a danger that some managers or administrators may use these factors as an excuse for failing to fulfil their objectives – or a safeguard in the event of possible failure. Consider what steps you think senior management could take to retain the accountability of individual members of staff in such circumstances.

Scheduling techniques

Some operational plans are so detailed that it is difficult for managers or administrators to identify all possible changes. What they can do in some circumstances, however, is to make use of certain established scheduling techniques to assist them to coordinate the activities of people and business units, and maximise the use of resources in order to achieve the completion of a specific task.

For instance, when a new product is being introduced, the Marketing Manager needs to know exactly what customers want and the Production Manager needs to translate these wants into the production of the required product. Consequently a schedule of a logical sequence of actions together with the coordination of the people and resources required is necessary to ensure the production of a successful product. The basis of the technique is not only to plan activities to achieve a desired end but also to check on discrepancies between planned and actual achievement as the project progresses. If a gap does appear, then managers and administrators are alerted to the fact and can provide extra people or resources to fill the gap.

Two other techniques commonly used are Gantt charts and network analysis. These are discussed in Chapter 7.

Measures which can minimise adverse effects on planned outcomes

The use of the scheduling techniques just outlined is intended to minimise the possibility of any adverse effects on a plan arising from lack of coordination of activities or failure to recognise that the work is not progressing according to plan. However, in some circumstances, no matter how efficient the scheduling, the resultant action which may have to be taken to redress any problems can resemble 'fire fighting' – something that all managers and administrators have to be prepared to do at times, but which is obviously best kept to a minimum!

Forecasting techniques

Where possible it is preferable to put in place measures that can minimise any adverse effects *before* any action at all is taken. The skill of forecasting what may happen, therefore, takes on some significance.

The simplest form of forecasting is based on quantitative data; e.g. the number of people who have taken advantage of the service offered or bought the goods produced during the previous year. Such data are obviously more reliable than the use of any subjective methods, particularly since many statistics – on sales, turnover, marketing expenditure, etc. – are already available to most organisations and can be analysed to produce ratios and trends. Various systems of analysis can be used.

Time series analysis

This involves charting a variable, such as sales, over a period of time. The assumption is that the past is a good predictor of the future. For example, if sales figures have risen over the last few months, then it may be assumed that this rise will continue. A similar exercise can be carried out in respect of trends such as seasonal variations in sales and the rate of growth, which can then be analysed in order to plan production and marketing as well as cashflow for the company.

One difficulty in relying upon past performance is that managers may fail to allow for the possibility that past trends will not always be a good guide to the future. Consequently time series analysis should allow for a sufficiently long period for any fluctuations to be perceived and included in any future calculations. For example, if it can be deduced that a product has a cycle of success which dips every few years and then revives, the managers concerned can build that dip into their calculations and start, for instance, either to develop new products to militate against an inevitable fall in sales or to 're-market' the existing product to prevent the dip from occurring.

Correlation and regression modelling

This may be used to consider the effects of different variables on each other. If, for example, an organisation wants to know the results of a marketing campaign on sales, *regression analysis* will estimate one variable (such as the sales volume) on the basis of one or more other variables (such as marketing expenditure) which are assumed to have some causal link with it. *Correlation analysis* compares two associated variables where a change in one will be assumed to effect a change in the other (such as an increase in advertising being assumed to effect an increase in sales). While correlation shows whether *there is* an association between the two variables – and if so the strength and direction of the association – regression indicates the *rate* of change in one variable against the other; e.g. an indication of the amount of change in sales caused by a particular increase in advertising expenditure. See also Chapter 7.

Linear programming

This is a more advanced statistical process used to determine the best combination of those resources and activities which are necessary to achieve an objective. If, for example, the objective is to reduce costs, the constraints in doing this have to be identified – which may be resource constraints, lack of capacity or shortage of available time. Both the costs and constraints then need to be expressed in linear terms either algebraically or in a graphical form, in order to provide a means for the manager or administrator to come to a decision.

The spreadsheet

This is one of the computer industry's most successful creations given that it is capable of handling ever-more sophisticated accounting and budgeting tasks. Modern spreadsheets now have analytical abilities that far exceed those of even the most sophisticated calculator. They can use 'what if?' calculations to determine how a set of figures – such as sales figures – will be altered by changes in individual elements, and they can also use their built-in mathematical functions to highlight levels of diminishing returns or to maximise the overall profitability of a complex product line. However, despite its success, the spreadsheet remains burdened with the image of a financial tool rather than a managerial one, the blame often lying with the complexity of the software itself.

- Where established data are not available or are unreliable, qualitative forecasting may have to be used (e.g. where potential customers' opinions are sought about a new product). This could involve surveys, questionnaires and interviews combined with the use of rating scales requiring consumers to rate a particular service or product on a scale of 1–10. Alternatively it could involve the use of the Delphi technique by which a panel of experts are asked their opinions on a new product or service. An average of these opinions is then used as a base for arriving at a decision about a new product.
- Not all potentially adverse effects on an operational plan can be resolved by even the most powerful of forecasting techniques. Of equal importance is the ability of the manager or administrator to build as much flexibility as possible into the plan to allow him or her to make adjustments to the plan in order to achieve the required end result. Look back to page 220 if necessary to remind yourself of the ways in which job, hours and skill-based flexibility can assist you when any changes need to be made.

Planning and implementing adjustments to allocated work activities

Suppose you are a senior administrator in a Public Relations department of a large local authority. One of the objectives contained in the authority's strategic plan is to promote public awareness of the services offered by the authority; a corresponding objective in the department's operational plan is to organise a series of information sessions open to the general public. At the management team meeting held to discuss the department's operational plan, you are given the responsibility for organising those sessions. You therefore decide to draw up your own action plan to cover those areas for which you have been made specifically responsible. See Figure 3.3.4 for your first draft.

ACTION PLAN

PUBLIC AWARENESS SESSIONS, W/E 1.6. – –

Number of sessions: A series of six in total, held in two separate venues.
Action: Book two suitable venues on the relevant dates.

Timescale: First session to take place 10 weeks from today. Final session to be held within a six-week period from then.
Action: Establish exact dates and times.

Format: Establish whether the session will be static (e.g. a literature display with a member of staff on hand to answer queries) or whether it will be in the form of a presentation held at certain times of the day. Establish what form the material is going to take – posters, leaflets, information booklets, etc. and whether presentation material will be required – OHTs, multimedia material, etc.
Action: Discuss with senior management what format is preferred – outline the necessary consequences of either choice.

Venues: In the past similar sessions have been held at (a) the exhibition area at the local library, (b) the foyer of the Town Hall.
Action: Contact the various venues to check availability, facilities available, cost, etc.

Staffing: Who is to be involved? What are their specific duties?
Action: Make the necessary decisions in relation to own staff. Seek permission of senior management for involvement of staff from other areas.

Resourcing: Establish what resourcing there is available to (a) book the venues, (b) prepare and produce the material, (c) cover staff costs if necessary.
Action: Draw up an estimate of possible costs and submit to senior management.

Procedures: Select and brief team. Monitor progress
Action: Arrange an initial meeting. Draw up a series of subsequent progress meetings.

Figure 3.3.4 Example of a draft action plan

You will be extremely lucky if everything goes according to plan! The more likely possibility is that at some stage in the implementation of the plan, you will want (or need) to adjust some of those activities to ensure that the overall objective is met. You may have forecast the need for such adjustments by including certain risk factors in your plan. However, not all problems can be forecast, and even if they are you are still faced with the fact that the potential problem has now become a reality and you have to take practical steps to resolve it.

THEORY INTO PRACTICE

During the course of the arrangements, various incidents occur which make the original plan difficult to implement in its entirety.

- Neither of the suggested venues is available at the times and dates you request.
- Two weeks before the first session, you receive word that there may be a one-day strike of staff in your organisation.
- The reprographics staff say that they are without a key member of staff through long-term sickness and are so inundated with work that they cannot guarantee that all the literature will be produced on time. You have budgeted on being able to avail yourself of their services at a lower rate than any commercial organisation would charge.

- A decision has been made that there will be a series of presentations held throughout the day. However, the staff who have been selected as presenters have not received any relevant training and you are concerned that they will be under-rehearsed.
- During the first session, a local councillor queries some information in one of the information leaflets – he says it is out of date and therefore misleading.
- When the staff arrive to set up the exhibition at one of the venues, they find the electrical system is totally unsuited for the equipment to be used.
- On the day of one session, you receive a phone call from the presenter to say that she is unwell.
- Half way through the programme, you receive an initial costing sheet and discover that you are very near to your budget limit – because, as you belatedly realise, you have failed to include staff expenses in the original plan.

Try to determine:

a which of the above possibilities you should have foreseen and therefore treated as a 'risk factor'
b what you should have included in the plan to cover such eventualities
c what adjustments you would now make to the plan to ensure that it reaches a successful conclusion and the objective is achieved.

Monitoring and evaluating adjustments to plan

Some of the problems just outlined would be relatively easy to solve, others less so. No matter what the problem the sooner it is identified (or better still, anticipated) the more likely it is that it can be resolved successfully. Consequently, an effective monitoring and evaluation system is a necessity.

However good your memory is, it is obviously unwise for you to rely upon it entirely and to check on the progress of the plan only when it occurs to you. A systematic use of planning aids is essential – normally combined with a series of meetings of all the relevant personnel. The most useful planning aid in this respect is normally the wall chart on which the progress of a plan can be charted. Remember the Gantt chart and PERT – the programme evaluation review technique which allows you to check at which stage a project should be at any given time and the possible consequences of any delay.

Nevertheless, no planning aid, however sophisticated, can operate in isolation. It is the human element that is all-important in ensuring that adjustments are made and the results evaluated. However, this is not as easy as it sounds. Setting up an initial planning meeting is relatively simple – the project is in its infancy, it sounds interesting and/or worthwhile, it is normally well publicised throughout the organisation, you are motivated and usually so are your staff. Difficulties can arise as the project progresses when initial enthusiasm wanes, where other work commitments start to intervene and when problems start to be encountered. In such circumstances you must ensure that not only are you monitoring the progress of the plan, but so too are the rest of the people involved.

The usual way to monitor and evaluate progress is to hold a series of regular and frequent steering meetings. The dates should be established in advance at the first meeting of the group and adhered to until the plan is completed. During the course of those meetings any required adjustments can not only be identified but also implemented and monitored by the same group.

What you, as the implementer of the project, should avoid, is that after the first couple of meetings you find that you are the only one present!

THEORY INTO PRACTICE

Areas of possible difficulty for you include key members of the meeting who are:

- very overworked and who genuinely have to juggle with conflicting priorities, all of which are important
- disorganised and forgetful – even if they do remember that there is a meeting, they arrive late and leave early
- 'borrowed' from another department and who do not really want to be involved in the project
- easily deterred if there is a problem and who tend to miss a meeting where they think anything difficult is going to be discussed.

Consider how you would try to resolve these problems.

Legal and regulatory requirements relating to work methods and activities

Confidentiality

By their very nature, strategic and operational plans are likely to contain some confidential material. Anyone who is involved in their preparation, therefore, should be aware of their legal position if they reveal that information to an unauthorised person or even allow such a person access to it.

As already discussed, when you start work you are bound not only by the express terms of your contract but also by those which are so obvious a part of the contract that they do not need to be stated. One of these duties is to 'act in good faith'. Consequently, if you disclose confidential information to someone else without authority to do so, you could very well be held to be in breach of the good faith obligation, as the courts tend to regard information as a property right which cannot be taken from the employer without his or her consent.

However, determining what exactly constitutes 'confidential' information can prove somewhat difficult. In *Coco v A. N. Clarke (Engineers) Ltd* [1969] RPC 4 it was established that in order for a breach of confidentiality to occur:

- the information itself must have the 'necessary quality of confidence about it'

- it must have been imparted in circumstances importing an obligation of confidence
- there must be an unauthorised use of that information.

However, that definition was not sufficiently precise for the majority of employers or employees! Fortunately, therefore, in *Thomas Marshall (Exports) Ltd v Guinle* [1978] ICR 905, a number of additional relevant factors were identified.

- The information must be information the owner believes that, if released, would be injurious to him or her or advantageous to his or her rivals.
- The owner must believe that the information is confidential or secret; i.e. not already public knowledge.
- The owner's beliefs must be reasonable.
- The information must be assessed in the light of the custom and practice of the particular trade or industry concerned.

THEORY INTO PRACTICE

In the Marshall case the Managing Director of a company (which was in business purchasing clothing from manufacturers in the Far East and Eastern Europe for resale to large mail-order and multiple stores) secretly set up a rival company. He was prevented by injunction from using any confidential information relating to that company. Try to assess the type of information to which he was likely to have had access which would be regarded as confidential. To check your answer either refer to the case itself or see page 261.

The nature of confidential information

A distinction has to be made between confidential information and the general 'know-how' each employee possesses in relation to the method and manner of performing his or her work. In *Faccenda Chicken Ltd v Fowler* [1986] ICR 290, a company sought an injunction to restrain Mr Faccenda and other former employees who had formed a rival company from using 'confidential' information which they had acquired whilst working for the company. The information included the purchasing requirements of the customers and the pricing and marketing strategies. The Court of Appeal laid down certain criteria to distinguish between confidential information (which the employer can protect) and general knowledge (which he or she cannot).

- *The nature of the employment and the nature of the information itself.* If secret information is habitually handled, an employee will be aware of the sensitivity of the information.
- *The emphasis laid upon the confidential nature of the information by the employer.* It is essential to establish whether the employer impressed on the employee that the information was confidential.
- *The 'detached' nature of the information.* For information to be classified as confidential it would need to be shown whether it could

be easily isolated from other information which the employee is free to disclose.

In the Faccenda case, the court refused to grant an injunction on the grounds that:

- some of the information – such as van routes – was clearly not secret
- the information about prices could not be severed from the rest of the information
- the information had been acquired in order to allow the employees to do their work and could have been memorised anyway
- the information available was not restricted to senior staff.

THEORY INTO PRACTICE

Based on the above criteria, consider whether or not the information contained in (a) the strategic plan of your organisation, and (b) the operational plan of the individual department or unit in which you work, is likely to be regarded as so confidential that revealing it to anyone would be deemed a breach of confidentiality. If you work in an organisation that does not have a strategic or operational plan, base your assumptions on your knowledge of the information such plans generally contain.

One German materials firm has developed an anti-copying film for masking documents that prevents them from being photocopied. The recently patented invention uses a transparent film that is fixed to the document with adhesive. The film makes the content of the document disappear when viewed from an oblique direction, thus protecting it against photocopying machines.

Duty of disclosure

Although the greater part of the law in this area centres round the duty of an employee *not* to disclose certain information, in certain circumstances he or she may also have a duty to reveal information which may harm the employer's interests – such as an illness which may have health and safety implications.

Possibly more controversial is the case of *Swain v West (Butchers) Ltd* [1936] 3 AER 261, in which it was held that an employee had a duty to inform an employer of the misconduct or deficiencies of *another* employee. What tends to be important in such cases is the position of the employee in the hierarchy so that those with managerial responsibilities may find that they have a duty to report the misdeeds of their subordinates.

Despite the fact that the law may require employees to inform employers about the misdeeds of their colleagues or junior staff, there can be grave problems for those employees who actually do so. The University of East London, which carried out a recent survey amongst hospital staff, found that many doctors and nurses who did report poor standards of care by others had either been transferred or put under pressure to resign. Another Australian survey carried out by the New South Wales 'Whistle Blowers' Unit found that 34 out of the 35 people interviewed had been victimised as a result of exposing misconduct. They had been ostracised by the rest of the staff, made to work unsocial hours or put on to rotas which isolated them from the main workforce.

Express confidentiality clauses

Even though the law recognises an implied duty of good faith on the part of the employee, many organisations prefer to ensure that their employees do not reveal any confidential information by inserting an express confidentiality clause in their contract of employment. It is then far more difficult for employees to claim that they were unaware that what they were doing was in breach of contract. Consequently a former housekeeper of the Prince of Wales was prevented by injunction from publishing a book about her life in the royal household because such a confidentiality clause had been included in her contract. Similarly, in the US a leading tobacco company managed to stop the televising of an anti-smoking documentary in which a former Vice President of the company allegedly claimed that the company had abandoned plans to develop a safe cigarette and had suppressed information about the addictiveness of the tobacco. It also sued him for breach of an express confidentiality agreement.

For further discussion on the way in which computerised confidential information must be dealt with under the Data Protection Act 1984, see Chapter 4, page 336 and Chapter 5, page 449.

THEORY INTO PRACTICE

The duty not to disclose confidential information applies both during employment *and* afterwards. Consider the difficulties you think may be caused by extending the duty outside the period of employment.

ANSWER TO 'THEORY INTO PRACTICE' EXERCISE ON PAGE 259

The Managing Director was prevented from using confidential information relating to (a) the names and addresses of manufacturers and suppliers, (b) prices paid by his employers for goods, (c) details of the employer's new ranges of products, and (d) prices paid by customers to the employer.

4 Establish and maintain productive working relationships

Element 4.1

Establish and maintain productive working relationships with colleagues

It is an old saying that, whilst we cannot choose the members of our family, we can at least select our friends! The implication, of course, is that the process of selection means we can avoid developing relationships with those people we don't like. Unfortunately, when we are at work, we have almost as little choice as we do with our family! With luck, some people with whom we work will have attitudes, personalities and values we find pleasing, attractive and compatible with our own. Others will not. However, to function effectively as a professional – particularly at a relatively high level – you need not only to 'get on' with these people but also to develop relationships which will enable you to communicate, negotiate and relate to them in such a way as to enable you to accomplish your objectives – preferably in a spirit of cooperation and harmony.

The subject of human behaviour has long been studied by behavioural scientists and their findings have often been applied to the workplace to try to analyse people's responses to situations. However, before you start to try to analyse other people, a useful starting point is yourself! This is essential, given that each 'transaction' with another person has two distinct components – you and them. You need to know what attitudes, values, expectations and traits *you* are bringing to the transaction – and the effect these can have on the outcome – before you start to look at other people in more detail. In addition, you need to stand back to examine your own actions and motives objectively to determine those which, if modified, would produce a more effective outcome.

Developing your understanding of this complex area is the topic of this element. It involves examining yourself as a person, analysing your relationships at work and the interactions that take place in the workplace. The aim is to help you to identify skills and strategies to develop and maintain productive working relationships so that you are better able to achieve your aims. This is not manipulation, but sound common sense. Forcing people to do what you want them to do is the remit of a dictator. Even if you had such power at work you would often find your victories pyrrhic and short-lived. In contrast, encouraging people to put forward their views to contribute towards solving a difficult problem and to negotiate a mutually beneficial course of action is the skill of an accomplished 'people person', which all administrators should strive to become.

Your own work role and responsibilities

What is a 'role' – and how does your work role differ from your job? All jobs comprise two aspects – the *prescribed elements* and the *discretionary elements*. The prescribed elements are those that relate to the tasks conferred upon the job holder together with his/her responsibilities. In most organisations these are the elements of the job which are outlined in the job description. The discretionary elements relate more to the way in which the job should be carried out – in other words the judgements the job holder will have to make in accordance with his/ her conferred rights, duties and the status of the position. These, in turn, are linked to the norms and values of the organisation. The discretionary elements are the aspect of the job upon which you may need most guidance when you start work and which may change if you move to another organisation with a different culture and management style.

The discretionary elements of your job – or your *work role* – go a long way towards determining the way in which you can behave and the range of actions you can take; i.e. how you can and will *perform* your job. There will be a range of permitted behaviours which you are expected or allowed to use and these are both culturally and socially determined. For instance, because the state and society wishes to reduce crime, the police have the remit to stop and search a suspect. For obvious reasons, this action is not allowed for civilians. Permitted behaviour as part of a work role can change over time – twenty years ago it was acceptable for teachers to use corporal punishment on pupils who misbehaved. Today that behaviour is no longer allowed.

Every one of us performs several roles in our everyday lives. All these roles have a range of acceptable and unacceptable behaviours but the roles change as the social context changes. Therefore at home you may be partner, husband, wife or parent. At work you may be colleague, subordinate and boss. With your parents, friends and siblings you take on different roles again. However, none of these roles is performed in isolation. In each case the person brings his or her own personality, attitudes and values to bear on the individual roles, performing *each one* according to his or her own 'definition' of the role. This can cause problems, as we each consider our own definition to be superior to anyone else's. Therefore, although the broad remit of the role is socially and culturally constructed, the finer points are individually determined – which is why people differ in their perception of *exactly* how a role should be performed.

The whole idea of 'roles' and 'performances' has been borrowed from the world of the stage. Erving Goffman, a sociologist, took this even further by examining the way in which people play their roles to manage their performances in life, even to the extent of using stagecraft and stage management to influence their 'audience'.

The analogy is also used in relation to *life scripts* which we learn to use in certain situations. For instance, there is a recognised script for a meeting, another for a social gathering, a third for an appraisal interview and so on. Experienced actors use the right script on the right occasions and are aware of the repercussions of not doing so. This is discussed in more detail on page 273.

1 Together, the whole construct of a person's roles resembles a large jigsaw with each of the roles linking together and forming the larger picture of the complete person. Figure 4.1.1 shows Sally Mason's role jigsaw (simplified). Sketch out a similar one for yourself, identifying the main roles you undertake in your life.

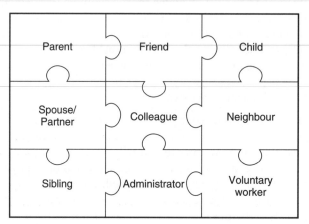

Figure 4.1.1 Simplified role 'jigsaw' for Sally Mason

2 Identify *socially* and *culturally* permitted and unacceptable behaviours for at least three of your own roles.

3 Our own personality, values and attitudes influence the way we consider a role should be performed – and this can often cause problems in our relationships. As an example, identify the ways in which you and a partner may hold different views on either (a) the role of a husband/wife, or (b) the role of a parent.

All roles help to give us a social identity. Indeed, we often describe ourselves in relation to our roles: 'My name is Jack, I've two sons and I work as an accountant' or 'My name is Jill, I work part-time as a nurse and enjoy amateur dramatics.' This is a major reason why people who are unemployed often struggle to keep their sense of self-worth as they are deprived of a key role in their lives and, in effect, lose an important part of their identity.

Generally, our own ideas of the accepted and expected behaviours of a role are held so deeply that we adopt this behaviour almost unconsciously. A useful example is a group of mature students who start a course together. Whilst they may hold responsible positions at work and be parents or even grandparents, on days when they attend the course they will become 'students' again – and their behaviour may change accordingly. They may dress more casually, arrive late (or at the last minute) and immediately seek a desk at the back of the room (as far away from the 'teacher' as possible) – all behaviours they learned in this role many years ago!

You and your role set

R. K. Merton described a role set as the 'complement of role relationships' which exists for a person. At work, this relates to the range of people with whom you have to interact on a regular basis. Members of your role set will include:

- your line manager, immediate colleagues and subordinates
- other senior managers and other members of your peer group with whom you regularly interact
- stakeholders of the organisation with whom you have regular dealings, such as customers, suppliers, shareholders, etc.

These people are sometimes termed *significant others* who influence the way in which you perceive your role because of their expectations of your performance. Given that these expectations may not be consistent with your own beliefs, or may even contradict each other, this can cause problems and stress in your own job. As you are probably aware, some people are apt to be more significant than others – either because they have more power over you or because you accord them more personal and professional respect, in which case they become a *role model* for your own performance.

Problems with roles

Role conflict can occur when you hold two roles which are mutually conflicting. A typical example is the middle manager who is a member of a union which then calls a strike. The manager experiences conflict in deciding where his/her loyalties lie. This is exacerbated if going on strike will damage promotion prospects after years of hard work and, at the same time, the manager feels a strong obligation to display loyalty to colleagues and support the union's aims and objectives.

Role conflict can also occur when you are faced with conflicting expectations relating to one particular role set. At work this could be:

- conflicting expectations from one significant member of your role set; e.g. your line manager asks you to make an excellent job of a complex task in a time scale you believe to be impossible
- conflicting expectations from different people in your role set; e.g. your staff or peer group want the freedom to make their own decisions about work layout, but your boss wishes to impose a specific design upon them
- the expectations of your role set differ from your own beliefs and values; e.g. your colleagues expect you to turn a blind eye to their inflated expense claims – even though this is against your principles.

Merton considered that several strategies can help an individual faced with role conflict. These include:

- initiating or lobbying for organisational procedures which formalise or separate potentially conflicting relationships – this, of course, assumes that the individual has the power to influence organisational procedures to this degree

- identifying which particular individuals in a role set have the most power and influence, and satisfying them
- minimising the influence of conflicting interests by making protagonists negotiate directly (to avoid being the 'jam in the sandwich')
- joining with others who are experiencing similar difficulties against a particular individual or source of pressure
- going on the offensive.

Further strategies include role negotiation (see below), information-seeking (to inform a more rational choice), and advocating a cooling-off period to see if other factors come to light to help to solve the problem. Other strategies are more usually associated with game-playing, such as playing for time or covering one's back, and often simply defer the issue rather than solve the problem (see page 292).

A different problem associated with roles is that of *role overload*. This can mean you are trying to carry out too many disparate roles in your life or, more commonly, that there are too many expectations of you in one particular role. Your own manager, for instance, may only perceive his/her expectations of you and ignore those of others in your role set. If everyone wants everything doing yesterday you will experience both role overload and role conflict in deciding whom to please first and whom to disappoint.

All these problems may occur because of *role ambiguity*. That is, no-one has ever made it clear exactly what is expected in a particular role – or if they have, the person concerned either hasn't listened or felt the issue was still open for negotiation.

Role negotiation

Role negotiation, first described by Roger Harrison, is a technique which can be used to isolate and identify the discretionary elements and interactions between role set members more precisely, to the benefit of both. In this case you both specify:

- what actions you can do to increase the effectiveness of each other; e.g. send copies of particular documents, pass on certain information more promptly, etc.
- what actions you should *stop* doing to increase the effectiveness of each other; e.g. querying the reasons for actions taken, asking for reports too often, criticising in front of other people, etc.
- what actions you should continue to do because you both benefit from them, e.g. meeting weekly, sending monthly progress reports, communicating daily by e-mail.

At this stage you meet and discuss your individual lists and negotiate an action contract which you both sign. The contract is monitored and updated at regular intervals.

Do bear in mind that it can be very difficult to negotiate an action contract with a boss who is particularly status conscious, or with any individual who prefers to operate with a largely hidden agenda – as in this case, the action contract isn't worth the paper it is written on. However, in an open and trusting relationship, role negotiation can be a valuable way of removing ambiguities and assisting each other to operate more easily and more effectively. (Note that conflict and conflict resolution are dealt with in more detail on pages 301–310.)

THEORY INTO PRACTICE

1 A friend of yours is very ambitious and hoping for further promotion at work. However, you know her husband is a traditionalist who may have problems coming to terms with a high-flying wife, particularly if she earns more than he does. If she gains promotion but there is no negotiation between them, what problems are likely to arise (a) for her – in both her work role and her wife role, and (b) for him?

2 A trainee administrator has recently been appointed to work in your office after working in a family business for several years. Although she performed well at interview, upon her arrival you quickly note that her informal way of talking to people and casual appearance is not going down well with older members of staff. To what degree is this a 'role' problem? What would you do to solve it?

3 Figure 4.1.2 is the role set of Graham Young, the sales administrator of a medium-sized company making machine tools. The expectations of Graham among the main players involved are as follows:

Players	Their expectations of Graham Young
MD	To run the office smoothly
	Constantly to improve performance and reduce costs
	To know the answer immediately to any question fired at random
Sales Director	To run the office smoothly
	To deal with man-management problems without assistance
	To meet targets (currently focused on cost savings and improved customer support)
	To display loyalty to himself and to the department when there are delays or difficulties
Staff	To treat them fairly
	To find time to listen when they have problems
	To obtain the resources for them to work effectively
	To manage the workload effectively
	To defend them against attack from above

From these, what potential problems can you identify and how do you think Graham could minimise them?

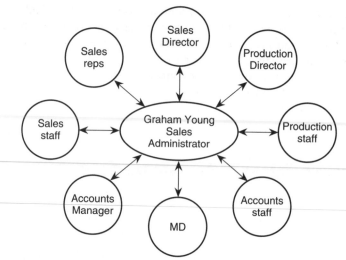

Figure 4.1.2 The role set of Graham Young

4 Draw your own role set and see how accurately you can chart the expectations of the major players in your working life. If possible, do this by drawing up *your* ideas of their expectations and asking each person if he/she agrees. You may be surprised at some of your findings.

Your responsibilities

Your responsibilities in relation to your working relationships are likely to be rather different from those in your job description! Interestingly, although working with people harmoniously is an important facet of building a positive and productive atmosphere, few (if any) job descriptions highlight 'being a cooperative person' or 'having a positive attitude' as essential requirements.

It is too simplistic to argue that all individuals are capable of building productive relationships if they simply put their minds to it. To do this effectively implies considerable knowledge of how people interact and the factors that influence this. Understanding this is all part of your responsibility if you are to become an effective 'people person'.

- Understand what *you* bring to any relationships in terms of the way you think and feel. These, in turn, are determined by your own past experiences, your own ideas of your personal identity and your own expectations.
- Consider how your perception (see page 271) has been coloured by people who have been influential in your life – parents, teachers, friends, even fictional characters who have impressed you – and how distortions in this area can influence the way you analyse people's behaviour.
- Try to see yourself more through the eyes of other people by extending your self-knowledge. Do you see yourself as tolerant whilst they perceive impatience? Do you consider yourself as frank and open when they discern tactlessness and a capacity to hurt?

- Review how you communicate with people – both verbally and non-verbally – not just in terms of the messages you transmit but also in terms of your ability to listen and empathise with the messages they are sending to you.
- Identify the barriers you can erect which get in the way of building a relationship – such as insecurity, anxiety and even prejudice.
- Recognise the strategies you use to protect yourself and how these can often be self-defeating.
- Understand how to develop a relationship steadily and openly.
- Identify the way in which your thoughts and perceptions can influence your emotions and affect your behaviour.

It is only by understanding yourself, and your colleagues, that you are better equipped to deal appropriately with the multitude of different personalities and attitudes which you meet every day in a range of different situations. Samuel Butler said, 'Life is the art of drawing sufficient conclusions from insufficient premises.' The rest of this element has the aim of helping you to increase the range of premises on which you base your conclusions!

Colleagues' work roles and responsibilities

The importance of awareness

In this context, your colleagues are your line manager(s), your immediate work colleagues (predominantly your peer group, members of your working group or team), and other colleagues with related work activities (e.g. colleagues in a different department, subordinates and junior staff). Your own understanding of their roles and responsibilities affects your ability to manage your relationships with your colleagues.

At a fundamental level, you must be aware of the areas of work for which each person is responsible and the areas where performance is critical, accuracy is vital or there is pressure to complete work to tight deadlines. At a more enlightened level you should be able to identify as accurately as possible each person's role set, to identify the expectations other people will have of them and the ways in which your colleagues may encounter role conflict. If nothing else, you should make sure that you do not add to their problems!

You should also be aware that each person you deal with has other roles as well as his or her work role. For that reason, people may have additional pressures from their personal lives which will vary over time but affect performance in the short run.

You should also appreciate that each person will undertake his/her role in a slightly different way, so how you perceive a job should be carried out and how a colleague may perceive it will be rather different!

Finally, you should be aware of the way in which the organisation's structure, culture and politics will affect your relationship with various people.

- In a formal or bureaucratic culture there may be more written communications, official meetings and coordination or liaison roles allocated to certain individuals. Communications are likely to be more formal and guarded. (See also page 297.)
- In an informal culture or a flat structure there are likely to be a greater number of face-to-face encounters and probably greater freedom for frank exchanges and negotiation between individuals.
- In an open culture, where risk-taking is encouraged and failure classed as a learning experience, people will generally be more creative and enterprising. Conversely, where a blame culture operates, people will try to avoid responsibility and be more tempted to tell the boss what he/she wants to hear.

In most organisations there is some division between line and staff functions and traditional competitiveness between production and sales! *Line functions* are those which are directly involved in the profit line (i.e. production and sales), whereas *staff functions* are those which exist in a specialist or support capacity (i.e. accounts, personnel, purchasing).

Friction can occur because of inherent conflicts in the different types of role and a basic lack of understanding of the objectives of the two. Line managers often resent interference from staff managers whom they may accuse of being out of touch with reality or having a 'softer' remit because they are not responsible for achieving 'the bottom line'. Staff managers may accuse line managers of ignoring or dismissing their requests for information or not taking their warnings or advice seriously enough. Some authorities argue that the difference in perceptions is caused by one concentrating on the reality (line) and the other on the ideal (staff).

Similarly there may be considerable antipathy between production and sales staff who fail to appreciate or understand each other's problems. Sales staff are under pressure to meet targets and, to do this, may be tempted to promise the customer almost anything to make a deal. Production staff, on the other hand, are faced with the problem of making and delivering the product, to the specifications agreed by sales. In this situation, if there is a failure to deliver, there is great temptation for each to point the finger at the other – sales alleging lack of flexibility and foot-dragging, production alleging that sales have little comprehension of the actual mechanics of carrying out the request.

THEORY INTO PRACTICE

If all is sweet harmony in your place of employment you can skip this section! Otherwise, spend a few minutes thinking about the culture, ethos, politics and attitudes which are prevalent in your own organisation. Consider:

- where traditional disaffections lie and the degree to which these are openly expressed
- the reasons why they exist

- the degree to which they are problems of situation (and therefore relatively unsolvable) and the degree to which they are problems of personality or perception
- the degree to which senior management might actually encourage competitiveness or disharmony (and even insecurity and fear) in the mistaken belief that this will make people work hard.

The importance of perception

It is a fact of life that no two people view the world in exactly the same way. For that reason, experiences, events and the behaviour of other people are all interpreted rather differently by different individuals. For instance:

- We go to a presentation by the Chief Executive and I think he is pompous and arrogant, you say how impressed you were with his style, whereas Harry was bored stiff and almost fell asleep half-way through.
- When I deal with Mary I get the impression that she is efficient and helpful, you think she is manipulative and devious and Harry thinks she is rather vulnerable and needs a lot of support.
- When we are busy John offers to work late. I think he is being helpful, Harry thinks he is only agreeing because it suits him (and he'll probably ask for a day off next week or be angling for the next promotion) and you think he is naive as the boss will now expect him to do it every week.

Why do we differ in our views and what can be the results of this?

The perception process

We all receive huge quantities of information every day which we have to process. Unless we were selective about this we would go insane through information overload. For that reason each person's brain is very selective about the information it stores, organises and retrieves.

Our ability to notice and pay attention depends upon several factors.

- As the *perceiver* we are affected by our current mood, our motives, attitude, past experiences and personality.
- We are attracted and take an interest if the event or person perceived is unusual, large or novel in some way. You would notice a receptionist with green hair, a man who was particularly small or a flashing warning sign. You would also notice behaviour that was out of place in a particular setting, such as the new junior greeting a status-conscious director by his first name.

At this stage we try to process the information we have received. When we see people behave in a particular way we want to know why – and analysing the reasons for their behaviour may be the subject of various conversations with our colleagues. There is a sensible reason for doing this. The more we understand about why they operate in the way they do, the more likely we are to approach them in a way conducive to achieving our objectives.

Causal attribution and *attribution theory* are related to determining what caused a person to act in a certain way. Basically, attribution theory involves the following.

- Assessing whether the behaviour was caused by internal or external factors. Internal causes relate to factors such as personality traits, whereas external causes relate to events that have occurred or particular situations that have affected the individual.
- Analysing the degree to which their behaviour:
  - occurs across different situations (*distinctiveness*)
  - is consistent over time for that person (*consistency*)
  - is matched by the behaviour of others (*consensus*).
- The greater the amount of information we receive for one person, the more we are able to predict his or her future behaviour – which is why you can 'second-guess' your best friend much more accurately than a comparative stranger.

The way this works is quite simple. Imagine your line manager attends a senior management meeting each Thursday. He always returns in a bad mood. As a new employee you try to work out whether the pressure of the meeting causes the problem or whether he is generally bad-tempered.

The distinctiveness test may tell you that he is normally quite good-natured. The consistency test may tell you that he is always in a bad mood on Thursdays, and the consensus test may show that several of the others involved in the meeting are also badly affected. In this case your logical conclusion would be that the meeting causes the problem.

However, if your boss is often bad-tempered in other situations, is bad-tempered over a long period and if the other members of the management group are not so affected by the meeting, then you would logically conclude that you have a genuinely bad-tempered boss and the Thursday meetings don't make much difference!

- In the absence of clear information, we are apt to assign internal causes to behaviour, rather than external causes.
- We tend only to analyse unusual or noticeable behaviour, not normal responses.
- We will have more patience with temporary causes of behaviour (whether internal or external) than those we consider are permanent. Therefore, if Bill is late every day this week because of family problems (which are temporary) we will be tolerant. If he is late because he is lazy (rather more permanent!) we will be far less understanding.
- We are apt to remember recent behaviour and use this to form ongoing conclusions. Therefore if Mary has been difficult lately (but was cooperative last year) you may find that if you are appraising her you will focus on what has happened most recently instead of analysing her behaviour objectively over a period of time.

Over time, the information we receive is converted into *schemata* or frameworks for ease of reference. *Person schemas* are the 'internal pen portraits' we hold for each person we know containing known information on their personality traits, appearance and behaviour. This is the description you would give if you were asked for confidential feedback on a person.

An *event* or *script schema* is the framework you hold for particular events which tells you how to behave and what to say. You would not, for instance, do or say the same things in a formal meeting as you would on a night out with your closest colleagues – or at least, we would hope not!

You are also capable of putting the two schemas together so that, for instance, you may predict that Shireen would be good at running a meeting or Mario would be great during an evening out – but not vice versa.

THEORY INTO PRACTICE

We all hold a *self-schema*, which is our own portrait of ourselves – and how you would describe yourself in terms of your appearance, personality and behaviour. Your self-schema will be different from the person schema even your best friend or your partner holds of you. An interesting – but brave – experiment is to compare these with someone you know very well. Basically, the better you know someone (and he or she knows you) the closer the match you should get.

Problems with perception

Unfortunately, there are several factors at work which can act to distort the perceptual process so that we only see what we want to see.

Fundamental attribution error is the tendency to ascribe behaviour to internal rather than external factors (basically because it is easier than analysing the complex external pressures which may be affecting a person). The danger is that we then expect people to be more predictable than they really are and are surprised when, in our view, they act 'out of character'.

Self-serving bias is our tendency to ascribe our own success to internal factors ('wasn't I good!') and blame our failures on external factors ('but it was his fault I couldn't complete it in time'). Research shows that men are more prone to this than women, but that this has a positive aspect in that it helps to protect self-esteem. Personalising failure is not only difficult but also depressing and leads to lack of confidence.

Stereotyping is the tendency to assign attributes to groups of people to save having to process and analyse individual sets of information. In this case the person schema has become generalised and becomes a labelling process, as it assumes that all members of a certain group will have common characteristics. The problem is that until or unless we know someone well there is a tendency for a stereotype to predominate. In addition, if we have problems understanding someone, life becomes easier if we rely on the stereotype. If, therefore, a male manager considers that women are more unreliable than men and one of his female staff has to take personal leave, he will attribute this more easily to the stereotypical image than to the actual event that is causing the problem.

The halo and horns effects are opposite ends of the same problem. These effects occur when we are overly impressed or unimpressed with one aspect of an individual, and this influences our judgement of other attributes. Research has shown that interviewers often display bias to candidates based upon initial impressions of appearance and voice. Thereafter they are prone to ask questions in a way that will substantiate their initial views.

Self-fulfilling prophecy is our ability to create the situation we think will occur, in that our beliefs affect our behaviour and this has a reinforcing effect upon the expected result. Myriads of tests have been done in education to prove that a pupil's performance is directly affected by the attitude of the teacher. If the teacher believes the pupil will do well then he/she acts with positive expectations, which result in good performance. If the teacher believes the pupil is lazy or is lacking in ability, this provokes negative stimuli which in turn reinforce poor performance.

Selective perception is the term given to our tendency to remember or focus on only those aspects of a situation that suit us! If, therefore, we consider someone is 'bad-tempered and moody' we will unconsciously look for evidence to prove our opinion right. If, however, we think someone has a sunny disposition, then we will make excuses for her behaviour (and ascribe external factors) if she has a bad day. It is worth noting that selective perception is often the cause of long-standing disagreements between people in an organisation who fail to see each other's point of view. Each is only concerned with viewing the problem from their own perspective (e.g. the line/staff and sales/production problems discussed earlier).

The similarity factor predisposes us to be more sympathetic or empathetic to those who we think are most like us. Our first 'matching point' is in terms of background – similarity of experience, age, home circumstances, ethnicity, and so on. Our second is in terms of outlook and values – political viewpoint, moral and ethical code, etc. In a work situation, we then relate more closely to people who hold the same views and opinions as us on organisational operations and actions, different staff, attributes in staff that should be rewarded, methods of undertaking work, etc.

Projection is a dangerous trait. It predisposes us to imagine that the similarity factor occurs when it does not! This causes us to project our own needs and feelings on to other people and to think that the solution which would please us would please them also. Therefore, if I will do almost anything for money I will believe that you will react in the same way – and this will affect the way in which I deal with you and the suggestions I make. Counsellors are regularly warned against giving their clients ready-made solutions on the basis that each individual is different and what works for one person might be an anathema for another.

Impression management is a technique adopted by some people to influence the perception of others (usually someone in an influential position) in a positive way. Common tactics include

- nodding in agreement or adopting 'reflecting' or 'sympathetic' body posture – even dressing to please
- giving undeserved praise or outright flattery
- doing favours and being always in agreement
- requesting advice or feedback on minor aspects of performance
- telling the person what he/she wants to hear, always agreeing with his/her opinions.

Frequently, the only person who fails to see through such strategies is the person who is being targeted for such attentions! However, before you become too complacent about never being the target, you may like to know that research shows it is *extremely rare* for the person targeted to realise what is happening!

THEORY INTO PRACTICE

Apply what you have just read about perception to each of the following situations. In each case determine (a) what perceptual problem occurred, and (b) what, if anything, you could do about it.

1 You were impressed with Tony, who is always helpful and cooperative – until you heard that he is arrogant and discourteous with the junior staff.
2 You are surprised to find that one of your staff has reacted negatively to a proposal for job enrichment. You have always thought everyone would be more keen to do work which is complex and challenging than work which is routine and boring.
3 Your boss has had a 'down' on Wendy since he saw her crying last week. He refuses to listen to reason and simply labels her as an 'emotional woman'.
4 You cannot get Hamid to see that his poor performance is caused by his lack of attention to detail. He always blames someone or something else for the problem.
5 You find yourself irritated when you have to approach Sarah to give her a job. You know she won't listen and then she'll make a mess of it.
6 Computer services have introduced a complex and laborious procedure for logging computer faults which all of the sales staff in your department say they are too busy to follow – though they still expect computer problems to be rectified immediately. Your job involves ensuring the forms are completed and liaising with computer services. Your boss has made it quite clear she wants nothing to do with it and it is up to you to sort it out.

Establishing constructive relationships

Relationships with people take time to develop, basically because a relationship deepens the more we know someone and the more we allow that person to know us. This process, known as *self-disclosure*, takes time and cannot be hurried. It is also risky and can go wrong – causing problems and difficulties between the two people involved. Frequently those who have had several disappointments in relationships can become guarded and defensive, protecting themselves from further potential hurtful situations by disclosing very little indeed. They are the people with whom you will find it most difficult to build up a relationship.

The fundamental process involves three stages. In *stage 1* you reveal information about how you feel about events which are occurring/have occurred. In the early stages you will normally stick to 'safe' social interchanges and general comments while you test the reactions of the other person (e.g. the weather, the cricket score, a television programme). Also in stage 1 you encourage the other party to disclose his/her views on general topics. In this way you start to gain an indication of how the person thinks and feels. The best way to encourage this is to take an interest in the person's viewpoint and reactions and not to be judgemental or dismissive.

On the assumption that you are not immediately rebuffed, when stage 1 would begin again, and that the exchanges become more frequent, then you will proceed to *stage 2*. Now you disclose your views about a wider range of topics and events. At this point you may move towards more personal exchanges which are less 'safe'. It is at this point that trust starts to build up in a relationship. It is normal for disclosure to be reciprocated. Therefore, in an 'open' relationship the other party will become more frank and open with you, and a mutually supportive and cooperative atmosphere develops.

If trust and the exchange of confidences remain unviolated and if neither party misinterprets or over-reacts to the situation, then the relationship moves to *stage 3*. Now, information of an intimate or highly personal nature can be disclosed in the knowledge that it will remain confidential. Trust and support is reciprocated. Each party can agree to differ but still remain mutually supportive and accepting of the other's point of view.

Basic points you should note which also affect the development of the relationship are as follows:

- It is our views and reactions to events (i.e. our feelings) which help people to get to know us better – not facts about ourselves or diatribes on our personal history.
- Generally, the more open we are with other people, the more open they will be with us.
- Some people find it difficult to trust people they know well yet will disclose to a stranger (hence the success of the Samaritans). They feel safe because a stranger cannot use the information against them later.
- It is quite possible to accept a person and his/her view of reality whilst still disagreeing with his/her views or behaviour.
- The more open we are the more likely it is the other person will like us. It is difficult not to like someone who is supportive and empathetic!

- To get to know someone we have to be prepared to *listen* and find out their views, interests and values (see also page 289).
- Refusing to disclose increases our isolation and creates stress in our relationships. To build a relationship means occasionally taking risks.
- There is a sensible pace for disclosure. Too much too fast alarms people. We all become alarmed when faced with someone who 'comes on' too strongly.

The Johari Window

A technique for examining how people change in a relationship through disclosure and feedback is seen in the *Johari Window* – named after its originators Joe Luft and Harry Ingham. You have just read about disclosure. Feedback can be defined as the responses we receive from other people which tell us how our behaviour is affecting them. Progressive self-disclosure builds a relationship where we regularly get feedback from other people and give it in return. In a caring relationship feedback is sensitive and designed not to cause anxiety or distress.

The standard Johari Window is shown in Figure 4.1.3. The four squares (or window panes) can best be described in terms of two rows and two columns. The rows represent other people whilst the columns represent yourself.

- The Arena represents things you know about yourself and others also see.
- The Blind Spot represents things you don't know about yourself but which are clear to others.
- The Facade represents the part you know about but keep hidden from other people. This includes your feelings and opinions about yourself and other people which you prefer to keep to yourself, possibly because you feel you will be more vulnerable if you reveal it.
- The Unknown links to your unconscious in that it is the area that no-one sees. It includes early childhood memories and latent potential of which you are not aware.

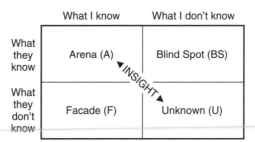

Figure 4.1.3 The Johari Window

The key point about the Johari Window is that it is never static. The panes can move up, down, backwards and forwards through disclosure and feedback. For instance, at the beginning of a relationship disclosure is at a basic level and there is no feedback. The shape of the window is shown as in Figure 4.1.4. If this shape is retained, Luft and Ingham term this 'the turtle', symbolising one who stays in a shell and finds it difficult to form relationships.

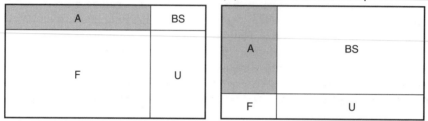

(i) The 'closed' windows of the turtle

A	BS
F	U

(ii) The 'open' or ideal window

A	BS
F	U

(iii) The 'interviewer'

A	BS
F	U

(iv) The 'bull-in-a-china-shop'

A	BS
F	U

Figure 4.1.4 Movements of the Johari Window

In an open relationship with a high degree of trust the window changes considerably. At this stage 'what you see is what you get'. Feedback has resulted in a reduction of the blind spot and trust has resulted in the reduction of the facade. If the person is also 'self-aware' then the unknown is also much smaller (though it is debatable whether this can ever totally disappear). This situation is described as the 'open' window.

Two other contrasting styles are identified by Luft and Ingham. The 'interviewer' wants to know what others think before making any commitment at all. If this continues for long in a social context it usually provokes irritation, distrust and even anger. The 'bull-in-a-china-shop' feels it quite permissible to tell people what he/she thinks and feels. This person is usually insensitive, mistaking destructive criticism for being 'open' whilst either being personally immune to feedback or over-reacting and walking out. This means feedback is never internalised so there is never any change in his/her behaviour.

Quite obviously, the way in which feedback is given affects the recipient, and this is dealt with in the next section.

THEORY INTO PRACTICE

Sketch your own Johari Windows, (a) for a close relationship you have which is mutually trusting and supportive, and (b) for a more formal, distant or 'newer' relationship with a work colleague (or your boss!). Try to identify the specific differences in your behaviour with each person (e.g. what you would choose to disclose/not disclose), and what types of behaviour on their part could affect the shape of each 'window'.

It is more difficult for trust to exist in large organisations than in small firms – regardless of the style or type of management. Think of it this way. A small firm may have a very informal arrangement whereby staff who do extra work can take time off in lieu. As the firm increases in size this becomes unworkable, simply because no-one knows where anyone is and – before too long – there will be fears that someone will take advantage of the arrangement. At this point a more formal system will be implemented with set procedures to follow. This is sensible but, to the workforce, implies a lack of trust as a reporting/monitoring system is now in place. As the organisation grows still further, even more systems and procedures are initiated – all for good reason – until a wide variety of behaviours are 'controlled'. This can cause resentment, particularly in staff who consider they have earned the right to some degree of professional autonomy and responsibility.

Providing, seeking and exchanging information

Information is the blood which flows through the organisational veins. Without it the organisation would die. With the wrong type or quality of information the organisation becomes sick – unable to react and respond as it should to inside and outside forces and events.

In a similar way, the people who work in the organisation need information to be able to undertake their own roles and fulfil their responsibilities, both to the organisation and to each other. Information causes us to think and respond in different ways. Without accurate or complete information we fail to respond appropriately because we make the wrong decisions. This could relate to a basic task, such as failing to cancel an appointment because we don't know someone is absent, or a more important issue, such as giving inaccurate feedback in an appraisal interview.

There is a fundamental difference between *raw data* and *information* – and both the amount of data and its transfer into information have cost implications. Collecting data, such as basic facts and figures, takes time – and there may even be an additional external cost (such as buying-in a database). To be of use, a data set must then be transformed, by merging it with other data, analysing it, assessing it and reorganising it so that it is useful and appropriate for the purpose for which it is required. The more experienced you become at your job, usually the better you become at undertaking these tasks because knowledge, familiarity and experience all interact to enable you to react in the most appropriate way.

Cost-effective data collection concentrates on collecting only necessary data and identifying the most effective sources of supply. Cost-effective information processing requires the most appropriate people handling it in the most efficient and effective way. Therefore the way in which information is transmitted, processed and stored, as well as its availability, can have fundamental cost implications.

Information variables

Several variables in the information we need or process affect both its value and the methods we use to obtain it, provide it or exchange it. These include factors such as:

- form of transmission
- source
- sensitivity
- quality and completeness
- timeliness

- complexity
- quantity and relevance
- accuracy
- validity
- legality.

Although you may not think about it consciously, you actually undertake quite a complex analytical and monitoring role in relation to information you receive, expect to receive or require which incorporates all the above factors!

- A complex verbal message needs to be written down immediately, whereas a 22-page report can be put aside for later scrutiny. Wherever possible the method of communication should be appropriate to the content and situation (see also pages 288 and 310).
- Some sources (e.g. the grapevine or the office gossip) can be noted in passing or semi-discounted (although several authorities now consider 'gossip' to play a key role in providing employees with relevant information). However, you are not advised to treat this information in the same way that you would deal with an urgent directive from your line manager!
- Highly sensitive or confidential information is handled differently at every stage of its life (or certainly should be) to restrict access. Generally, information about people is more sensitive than that relating to tasks and work-in-progress.
- The quality and completeness of the information affects the amount of credibility we are apt to accord both the information itself and the sender. In many cases irritation is caused if we have to seek out additional information to complete the gaps or insist on a rewrite because of poor quality.
- Timeliness is essential. Information received or transmitted at the last minute can create panic and can lead to costly errors and omissions.
- Complex information needs higher-level skills to analyse and more time in which to do it. On some occasions expert skills may be required if the information is highly technical.
- Too much information can seriously detract from someone's ability to process it accurately. *Information overload* is a known cause of stress as people have to work much harder to find what is relevant and important. The error (and cost) factor in handling a plethora of disparate information also increases considerably.
- The degree of required accuracy may vary depending upon the information type. It may be permissible to guess when a telephone call was received, far less so to estimate the sales figures for last month! However, it is not cost-effective to insist on higher degrees of accuracy than are actually required as this simply wastes time and effort.

- Information is only valid if it represents reality – it is therefore important to be able to recognise when people are making assumptions or jumping to conclusions rather than transmitting valid information. From what you have read about perception, you should realise that people can give invalid information unconsciously, simply because they are giving you their own version of events. One obvious method of checking validity is *triangulation* – where you check that version with someone/something else.
- Legal issues affecting information are those which relate to slander, libel, copyright and data protection. When in doubt, check! See also pages 335 and 336, 430 and 478.

Needless to say, the above provides important pointers for you when you are providing information yourself – in that your image and reputation depend upon it being timely, accurate, valid, and of high quality.

It is easier to validate and check the accuracy of *hard information* than *soft information*. Hard information is that which is quantitative and refers to facts and figures. Basically, it is either correct or it isn't! Soft information is qualitative and involves opinions, views, feelings and attitudes. Your own knowledge of the provider of the information and the situation can usually help you to judge its probable accuracy, validity and usefulness because you will be aware of their sources (role set), perception and usual behaviour.

Information processing

During the average day you will deal with a large amount of information: written reports, statistical reports, oral information, proposals and submissions, letters, memos, minutes, messages, e-mails, faxes, and so on. Computers are significantly increasing the flow of information – and the dangers of information overload. Therefore whilst you need information to make decisions, it is not the case that the more information you have the better the decision will be (see also Chapter 5). What you need is high-quality, relevant and timely information – the standard aims of most Management Information Systems.

The exact type of information you receive will depend very much upon your job role. However, broadly speaking, you will need information to help you to

- make and progress current plans and activities
- monitor progress.

Some of this will cross your desk as a matter of course if your organisation or department has appropriate monitoring and control systems in place. Some of it will not and will have to be sought. That which you receive will vary in its usefulness, whether it must be disseminated to others in its raw form or whether it will need modifying in some way before it is passed on. You are therefore constantly in a situation where you provide, seek and exchange information – both to obtain information and then to revise or adjust it. However, when and how you interact with others to do this can have important implications for your working relationships.

A Management Information System (MIS) is usually only one of the subsystems provided through an Organisational Information System (OIS). Kroenke and Hatch have identified up to six distinct systems within an OIS which, whilst interlocking, also undertake different operations.

- OAS is the Office Automation System based on a local area network functioning within an organisation.
- TPS is the Transaction Processes System. This records data on basic operations (sales, stock movements, financial transactions, etc.) and therefore becomes the key source of management information – whether it is sales in a supermarket or holiday bookings in a travel agency.
- MIS is the Management Information System which processes data captured through the TPS and converts this into information for use by operational managers.
- DSS refers to a Decision Support System which can be installed – at considerable cost – to test decision-making based on information held in the MIS and ESS.
- ESS is again expensive. It refers to an Executive Support System which directs information, often daily, to senior executives. It is able to process and summarise data to produce key figures, ratios and analyses in easy-to-read formats.
- PIS is a Personal Information System which individuals can customise for their own use, such as a combination of personal software and files plus networked information and programs.

Providing information

People who handle information in organisations can be classified into three different types: bottlenecks, conductors and filters! A bottleneck stores, hoards, ignores or forgets to transmit information. A conductor passes on everything, as quickly as possible to keep a clear desk. The filter analyses information for its potential, identifies which is the most important, modifies or extends it where necessary, and converts it to the most appropriate format for the recipient, without delay. Put another way, the bottleneck can be accused of dereliction of duty, the conductor of devolution of duty and only the filter truly accepts or delegates his or her remit for handling information in a responsible manner.

When you are providing information, do bear in mind the basics. Pick your time and your approach – particularly if the information will be unwelcome or create extra work. The reaction will vary from one recipient to another. Some people react very poorly to being given additional work to do – though beware the 'willing workhorse' who appears to shoulder it all and then goes absent with a genuine (or convenient) illness. You are more likely to be successful if the person concerned will achieve personal growth and can be convinced of the benefits and be motivated to achieve (see also page 318).

If the information is worrying or distressing (e.g. threats of cutbacks or redundancy) then *how* you give it will be remembered long after the details have been forgotten. Don't create undue alarm, and do allow people 'space' to lick their wounds if they are distressed. Don't try to empathise or sympathise if the news affects them more than it does you, as this will be seen as spurious and patronising (after all, it isn't you who is suffering). When people receive bad news they go through four stages – disbelief, denial, anger and acceptance – and none of these can be rushed.

Do not make 'providing information' a guessing game. Get to the point, focus on the main issues/key data and specify clearly what you want and by when. Make it clear which aspects are negotiable and which are not.

Tailor-make your information for the recipient – his/her job, status, knowledge and style. A boss who likes information in bite-sized chunks should not be sent a three-page report on a topic which could have been summarised in a paragraph. A new junior member of staff who started last week should not be overwhelmed with organisational details or jargonistic phraseology – and so on.

Do not give misleading signals. Saying you would value someone's input is rather different from saying they have got to get on with it. Make it clear when you are giving an order, an instruction or a request by synchronising your body language, tone and vocabulary. Do, however, bear in mind that a request is always more graciously received!

Check understanding – particularly if the information is complex or technical (or if the recipient is distracted for some reason). If you have any doubts, follow up later to check everything is satisfactory.

Finally, never discuss personal information or give criticism in public. You, of all people, should be the soul of discretion and the epitome of tact.

> The more you are respected and liked by your colleagues the more welcome your input will be – people will know that you are trying to help, not to undermine them. A person who brings solutions and suggestions rather than problems, who keeps a cool head in a crisis, who makes helpful comments, fills in the details and then lets people get on with it is always great to have around!

THEORY INTO PRACTICE

Think about the last time you received bad news or had a shock (from losing your keys, to having your car stolen, to the loss of a close friend or relative). Now identify the stages you went through (disbelief, denial, anger and acceptance) and the time it took you to work your way through the process. You should see that the worse the shock or the news, the longer it took you to 'work through' the process.

Seeking information

At the level at which you are operating, it is assumed that the majority of routine items of information arrive on your desk automatically (or are easily accessed). Otherwise you need to set up systems and procedures to deal with this and to read Chapters 6 and 7 as a matter of urgency! This means, for instance, that you don't spend the better part of every week asking people for routine items or chasing up information they should have given you several days ago. The very basics include a good filing system, a reliable and up-to-date computerised information system (see page 282), clearly labelled folders on your own desk for work-in-progress, visual planners and scheduled meetings with those you need to consult regularly. However, there will always be information colleagues will not give you (e.g. who is working hard, who is slacking; who is overloaded, who has nothing to do) so observation should never be discounted as a useful tool.

Information from your own section is normally easier to obtain than that from far-flung outposts – or from another department if there is an atmosphere of suspicion and mistrust in the organisation. This can lead to political game-playing, given that information is a major source of power. In this situation, strategies include:

- deliberately withholding information (particularly if the information would be to your benefit but not to theirs)
- being consistently 'unavailable' to provide it (until it is too late)
- selectively disclosing certain facts – but withholding the rest
- overwhelming you with irrelevant details.

This puts you at a disadvantage because you are having to make decisions based on a greater degree of uncertainty – and this increases the risk of making the wrong choice. On occasion, it can also freeze you into inaction.

In this case, if charm cannot help you then your only recourse is to appeal to higher authority – then at least you are not to blame if anything goes wrong. Sharing the problem with your line manager and asking for assistance is better than shouldering the burden alone, and – if you have an effective boss – may often get results. A point to note, of course, is that in a highly political organisation your boss may then want you to join the game by deliberately withholding information from the other party in the future! More on game-playing is given on page 292.

You should note that, yet again, hard information is easier to deal with than soft information. To obtain the latter, you are effectively canvassing opinions and finding out the views of other people. On a basic level you may find that informal chats, quiet discussions, lunchtime sessions and a fundamentally 'open' communication system work wonders. However, this will operate effectively only if your colleagues know that, far from being judgemental or condemning, it will actually be to their benefit to share confidences with you. It also implies, of course, that you can keep a secret and are sensitive to other people's feelings. On a more formal basis, many organisations operate employer/employee surveys (such as exit questionnaires for leavers), suggestion schemes, corporate hotlines and management information sessions to seek employee views. Their value is normally determined by two factors: the degree to which people feel they can contribute freely without later retribution, and the degree to which they feel their views are *genuinely* required. Spurious attempts at participation and consultation usually fail quite quickly (see exchanging information, below).

The UK Association of Suggestion Schemes operates an annual UKASS Best Suggestion Competition – in 1966 won by a British Airways employee who designed a new computer booking programme which is estimated to save BA £18 000 a year. Other contenders represented the Co-operative Bank (which had paid a member of the workforce £20 000 for an idea that saved the bank at least £1 million), HM Prison Service and the Telford office of the Inland Revenue.

UKASS has been in existence only for the past ten years but its popularity has grown and it has now moved to larger premises. If you're interested in knowing more, contact the Association at 9 Rosethorne Close, Middleton, Manchester M24 6TP (tel: 0161 653 4728).

No matter how high you rise, remembering the basics will mean that people are far more prone to give you information. Golden rules include:

- always ask, never demand (unless essential)
- repay favours
- repay trust with trust
- never 'drop someone in it' – they will never forgive you
- never think you are too important to say 'thank you' or 'sorry'.

---

1 You have thought of a good idea over the weekend which, if your colleagues adopt it, will save you hours of work on a new project. Would you:

   a tell them your idea and ask them to get on with it?

   b tell them your idea, spell out the benefits and then ask them to get on with it?

   c tell them your idea, ask them for comments, refine it a little if absolutely necessary and then let them get on with it?

   d tell them your idea, ask them for their comments, work out a mutually acceptable solution and then let them get on with it?

   e tell them the problem, ask them for suggestions, mention your idea if appropriate, and then select the best route forward?

2 The critical question now follows. Assume it is *your boss* who has had the idea but you are the one who has to steer the project. Which of the above options would you prefer?

Exchanging information

If you have answered the two questions above *honestly* then substantial research shows that you are likely to have chosen a different option for each question! This is because we tend to impose our own views downwards or horizontally but prefer to be an active participant upwards! The five options (a)–(e) match the five different approaches you may have to imparting or exchanging information. These are shown in Figure 4.1.5. It is likely that you chose options (b) or (c) for question 1 and (d) or (e) for question 2.

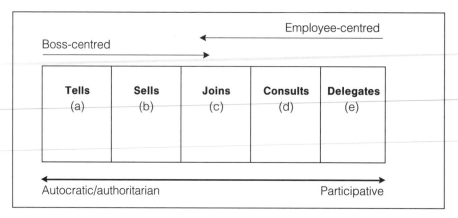

Figure 4.1.5   Approaches to giving and exchanging information

However, it is not always the case that a participative approach is suitable. There are occasions when even option (a) would be the most appropriate – much depends upon the particular issue and its sensitivity, time constraints, the political situation, and the degree of complexity/technicality of the information. One of the major problems of the 'worker director' initiative was that workers put into this situation often felt out of their depth handling certain types of information and ill-equipped to comment upon it knowledgeably. Ask for your colleagues' opinions only if you are willing to accept their views and big enough to adopt them when appropriate!

Exchanging information normally implies that both sides have information that can usefully be traded. Depending upon the person involved, and the issue, you may wish to be more reticent on some occasions than others. You will manage this only if you are a good listener. In this case, through skilful open questioning and a sympathetic stance, you can often tempt your opposite number into telling you all you wish to know. However, if you are to keep the relationship on an even footing you should also make a contribution – to add, suggest or amend the finer points. Alternatively, of course, you may be dealing with someone who wishes to steamroller through their own views – in which case you will have to be more assertive and decisive to cope (see page 290). Regardless of the lack of communication or 'people' skills of your opposite number, your objective should be an open and friendly exchange with the aim of retaining a positive and productive working relationship.

Information and teams

If you are dealing with a team, rather than individuals, then you must be aware of the different members of the team and their particular personality traits. If you can deal with only one person (preferably the leader) do not be surprised if that person needs to refer your information to the rest of the team for comments. Allow for this in your scheduling – but, if the situation is critical, you would be advised to make certain that *you* are the one who puts the issue to the team to assure it is your perception of the facts they receive and no-one else's.

The way in which a team or group information session operates will depend very much on the nature of the team and your relationship with them. A strongly cohesive team coupled with a contentious piece of information is not a good mix and you would need to prepare carefully for such an encounter (and possibly enlist support from your boss). Useful strategies include:

- getting the leader on your side beforehand (so at least you have some support)
- quietly lobbying some of the more amenable members for their views beforehand
- leaking the information on the grapevine beforehand, assessing the response and reacting accordingly
- breaking the news, letting everyone have their say and, only when they have run out of steam, putting your views
- adopting conflict resolution and negotiation tactics (see pages 307–310).

It is essential before you enter such a meeting that you decide upon which issues you can accept a compromise. It is a foolish person who attempts a no-compromise situation – you often need to be prepared to lose a battle or two to win the war! In addition, this enables everyone to save face.

If the issue is far less contentious and/or the team far more amenable, then your basic considerations include trying to ensure that all aspects have been covered and the views of each person have been heard. Knowing who will speak much (and needs to be controlled a little) and who will not (and will need to be encouraged) will help you to obtain a broad consensus from the team.

The advantages of consulting a team are that a greater range of views is expressed, some may have specialist knowledge and all will be more willing to implement a negotiated decision than one which is imposed. The drawbacks include potential conflict, intimidation by strong members, and time. It is usually much more time-consuming if you genuinely want to obtain views and exchange information with a variety of people.

THEORY INTO PRACTICE

The layout of your office and the layout of the workplace in general can facilitate or hamper the flow of information between people. From the sketches in Figure 4.1.6, identify which one says:

a 'Let's talk. I really value your opinion.'
b 'I'm your boss but I really want your views.'
c 'I'm the boss and I've something to say to you. I'll only listen if I must.'

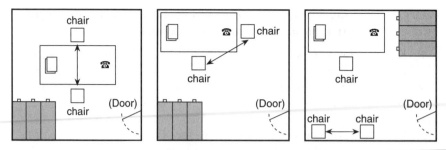

Figure 4.1.6 Office design and non-verbal communication

Issues that can affect working relationships

The issues that affect working relationships can be divided into two categories, *behavioural factors* and *environmental factors*. Unless you run the company, those in the first category are usually more in your control than those in the second. Behavioural factors can be further sub-divided into communication skills, breaking the relationship cycle, and game-playing.

Communication skills

Your working relationships will be adversely affected if you regularly miscommunicate or forget to communicate, thereby causing chaos, confusion and annoyance wherever you go. You will also cause irritation (and make mistakes) if you never listen. Therefore your communication skills must encompass both transmitting and receiving information.

Transmission skills

Communication is effective when the message is received and the recipient confirms the same understanding as the sender originally intended:

- The message sent is clear in the mind of the sender and encoded into words or symbols which the recipient will understand.
- The message is communicated accurately with no distortion (commonly known as 'noise'). This can relate to something as basic as an interrupted fax transmission or a lack of transmission skills (such as speaking to someone when they are on the 'phone or in the middle of a critical piece of work).
- The sender decodes the message – applying his/her understanding *and perception* to the words received. This is where misunderstandings can arise!
- Ideally, there is feedback from the sender to the recipient to confirm the message means the same to both.

Problems can arise if either the sender or the receiver are unskilled at communicating, if their perception and attitude are at variance, if the form of the message is poor (too long, complex, technical, full of jargon) or if the transmission chain is too long (when Chinese whispers can come into play!). In fact, you will be fighting an uphill battle when you communicate with other staff if the structure and culture of the organisation actually impedes rather than enhances, a free flow of information and communication (see below). Golden rules to follow include the following:

- Keep your messages as simple as possible (this isn't patronising, it's just good sense). Remember the KISS principle – keep it short and simple!
- Select the most appropriate medium (see Figure 4.1.9 on page 312 and also Chapter 5).
- *Always* check the message has been received by obtaining feedback. Use questioning of critical points, if necessary.

In the same way as you communicate in words, your body language also says much to other people! Abercrombie wrote an article on Paralanguage in 1988 in which he said 'We speak with our vocal organs, but we converse with the whole body.' The science of body movements in social interactions is known as *kinesics* and was pioneered by Ray Birdwhistell. He analysed body movements (posture, stance, etc.), facial expressions and gestures by breaking these down into component parts. For instance, we signal our desire to speak next by making eye contact. Having started to speak we break the gaze until we are about to hand over the floor to the other person. As a listener we watch the speaker, making head movements or giving brief verbal expressions of interest ('Really', 'I see', 'Oh'). If we give the right signals then we encourage our speaker to continue talking – for instance, a relaxed and 'open' body posture. This indicates you are receptive to information and suggestions. In contrast, a rigid or defensive body posture, frowning or grimacing and turning away from the speaker all indicate that you really don't want to know!

Listening skills

You will never receive messages accurately if you never learn to listen! Listening is an active process which gives affirmation to someone else that what they are saying has some importance. If you have any doubt about its importance, imagine living in a world where no-one could hear you or took any notice of you. You would be virtually isolated – the equivalent of a psychological death penalty, according to many experts.

Most people have difficulty listening because of interference from other aspects of their life or because of protective barriers. Here are some examples:

- If people stray on to a topic about which we have strong feelings, we may have an overpowering need to 'put them straight'.
- If we are angry with someone we can't wait until they have finished before giving our opinion.
- People often mention 'trigger' words and phrases which create a reaction because they imply blame and therefore put us on the defensive – so we either tell them or 'switch off'. In addition, some people make us feel insecure and defensive, as do some situations. In this case we are prone to be defensive and want to concentrate on our own agenda.
- Other 'trigger' words will spark our creativity and give us an idea, or remind us of something we should have said. Just in case we forget, we feel we have to interrupt.

- If we are distracted because of something else which has happened recently or which is bothering us then we find it more difficult to be attentive.
- Some topics are 'undiscussable' with certain people. For instance, a couple having problems with their sex life or children may cope by avoiding the issue completely. If a television programme on the subject is shown they will switch over or switch off – because it is too close for comfort. In this case when the topic is raised the person hedges or dodges to change the conversation – or starts to game-play. If one of your undiscussable topics is raised by someone else you will 'shut down' and refuse to listen and/or try to distract them.
- If people tell us something that does not easily fit into our frame of reference we are unlikely to continue listening. Examples include unwelcome, surprising or critical feedback. Because this triggers denial, displeasure and discomfort we prefer to deny the validity of the statement rather than listen and take it on board – which is more painful or involves a greater 'shift' in our thinking patterns.
- If we are physically uncomfortable then we are distracted – being overtired, having toothache, being too hot or cold all contribute to reducing our listening ability.

THEORY INTO PRACTICE

Carl Rogers, a psychotherapist and counsellor, developed a method for improving listening skills which is used to train many counsellors today. He considered that to *really* listen means making sense of what the other person is saying *without* first encoding it as part of our own belief system. He argued that you can practise this by a technique known as *reflective responding*. This means that you don't give *your* interpretation after a statement, but reiterate and rephrase that of the speaker. Therefore, if a member of your staff said to you 'I really can't cope with everything I have to do at the moment', your response would not be 'Why not?' or 'I'm not surprised' or even 'Tell me about it'. Instead you would open with a reiteration of his or her statement to confirm you have understood, such as 'I understand that you can't cope with all the work you have to do at present. Let's talk about it.'

You may think this sounds very 'false' but there is considerable research to prove it works. Why don't you try it and see? Just expect the conversation to last a little bit longer than normal!

Assertiveness skills

Assertiveness has sometimes had something of a bad press – mainly because of over-enthusiastic 'converts' who preach assertiveness at all times and start every sentence with 'I hear what you say but ...'. Like everything, assertiveness has a time and place and can be over-used or even abused. Assertiveness skills are invaluable when:

- you need to make a point, but struggle because you are normally placid and prefer to take a passive, 'easy-life' stance
- you are causing major upsets with your natural 'tell it how it is' aggressive style.

Whereas both approaches may sometimes be pragmatic or necessary, as a general rule they leave much to be desired. If you are normally passive you will often struggle to say 'no' and regret it later, if you are regularly aggressive then you are likely to upset your colleagues regularly – particularly the more sensitive ones.

Assertiveness theory holds that every person has certain fundamental human rights:

- the right to refuse without feeling guilty or selfish
- the right to consider that one's own needs are as important as the needs of others
- the right to make mistakes
- the right to express ourselves provided this doesn't mean violating the rights of others.

Therefore, assertiveness involves facing up to a difficult situation in an independent manner. The emotional aspects include being prepared to acknowledge your own feelings in a frank and honest way, and verbal language is non-threatening but cooperative and empathetic. Qualifiers such as 'I wonder if' and 'If you don't mind', fillers such as 'You know' and 'um', and negaters such as 'It's not important' or 'It doesn't matter' should *not* form part of the exchange. Body language includes eye contact, head held high, hands unclenched and a steady (but not raised) tone of voice. The aim is to neutralise any unequal power balance and to be prepared to give respect and expect it in return.

Do note that it is quite acceptable to opt *not* to be assertive, provided you are happy with this choice. This may be because you are talking to the company Chairman who is a capable and courteous person himself. Not only are you happy to live with the power difference, he does not play power games, there are no negative consequence from any encounters, and you would envisage no useful purpose in being assertive. The situation is rather different if you work for a temperamental bully who treats acquiescent staff disdainfully and takes pleasure in making people look small. *Then* is the time to practise your skills – politely but ever so firmly!

Breaking the relationship cycle

You have already read how relationships are developed, on pages 275–277. Any activity which interferes with the 'building' process will affect your relationship, such as:

- rebuffing someone or 'putting them down'
- betraying a trust or a confidence
- being too shy to interact
- being insecure so that you practise disclosure one minute and withdrawal the next
- being dishonest (and being found out!).

To this list two more should be added:

- not learning from mistakes
- being too proud to apologise.

The first point to note is that *everyone* is suspicious and wary of new relationships, although the degree to which this affects their ability to form any relationships at all will vary. The second point is that, although someone would have to be hypersensitive to react unfavourably to every slight misunderstanding or tactless remark, if you are continually insensitive to the reactions of other people you will obviously cause offence and find people avoid you rather than seek you out. The golden rule is to try, wherever possible, to ensure that people always leave you feeling better for the encounter, rather than worse. This is easy if you are giving them praise or good news. Far more skill is required if you are giving constructive criticism or bad news. This requires 'getting into the head' of the other person, viewing the situation from his or her point of view, and focusing on the positive aspects of the situation rather than the negative. It also implies good timing, privacy and sensitivity.

THEORY INTO PRACTICE

One of the crucial roles for administrators and managers is giving feedback on performance. Do this in the wrong way and you can kill a positive working relationship stone dead. Information on how to do this to retain motivation is given on page 316.

> Research from the Industrial Society gives cause for concern over the ethics of managers in relation to their staff. When executives were asked to identify what they considered to be the essential aspects of ethical management and to say whether these were followed in their own businesses, this was rarely found to be the case. Most managers agreed it was important to respect people's dignity, to consult people on decisions which affected them, to give fair rewards and to be honest and open when communicating with employees. However, in practice most did not consult people and fewer than 60 per cent considered their communications were open, honest and habitual. Most said staff were paid unfairly and 25 per cent agreed staff dignity was not respected in their organisations.
>
> Since then there has been a resurgence of interest in social and ethical audits to identify how staff perceive the activities of management. One, concerned with exit interviews, found that *staff* frequently misled their organisations about reasons for leaving, and some later claimed unfair dismissal or harassment. Others were concerned that honesty would lead to a problem with references.
>
> Given the fact that trust and honesty seem to be at a premium in both areas, how much faith should we put in the findings?

Game-playing

Game-playing has been mentioned at several points in this chapter already. The original work on game-playing was produced by Eric Berne, and his *Games People Play* is well worth reading. The first point to note is that whilst everyone plays games to some degree, others make a career out of them! If this applies to you then you will regularly give people around you a headache, as they will always be looking for the hidden meaning in your actions and behaviour. In addition, if you are an inveterate game player you will also assume other people have hidden motives and hidden agendas (often when they have not) and will waste a considerable amount of time wondering what these are!

Common features of games

Games consist of a series of *transactions* (i.e. initiative and response) which are usually complementary, followed by at least one ulterior transaction. The game commences when the initiator adopts a role, and the responder adopts a complementary role. Play commences but at the right point the initiator switches into a different role which requires a change of behaviour by the responder.

All games are also played for a '*pay-off*'. This can be anything from outright winning, to the pleasure of playing well, to the satisfaction of ensnaring the 'victim'. In an organisation people play games:

- to preserve or extend their freedom of action
- for specific stakes, such as budget share, reputation, territory or an easy life
- to change or prevent the change of certain organisational policies.

All games have *rules* which indicate the moves that can be played. For instance, in a 'power struggle' or an argument over resources there may be an unspoken agreement that neither party will resort to outright coercion (though there may be implied threats) and neither will have recourse to higher authority.

All games involve *strategies* – such as planning, forming alliances, anticipation, taking chances and manoeuvring. For instance:

- Power struggles usually concern the cultivation of certain resources (people, equipment, territory) which can be used in open conflict (e.g. 'I will withdraw my active cooperation in an area that is important to you unless I get [at least some of] what I want').
- Token gestures may be made ('Rather than refuse you outright, I will have "good reasons" for not being able to comply') which are more difficult to argue against than outright refusal.
- A redefinition of the issue may be put forward (arguing that this is the most important perspective). You can see this one coming at meetings when someone interjects with 'Ah, but the *real* issue here is...'.

All games have an *outcome*. There are four possible positions:

- we both win
- I win and you lose
- you win and I lose
- we both lose.

Figure 4.1.7 shows the different results if you and your opponent are cooperative or uncooperative or assertive or unassertive. In the middle is the compromise solution which neither of us really likes. The optimum outcome is win/win (top right-hand corner). Moving to this position means either changing the game, calling the game, refusing to be hooked, or – best of all – trying to replace game-playing with open negotiation.

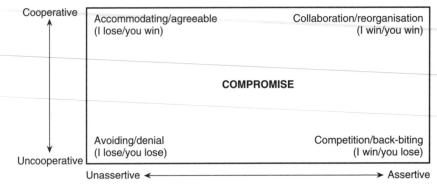

Figure 4.1.7 Possible outcomes to games, depending upon attitudes

THEORY INTO PRACTICE

Below are just a few of the games Eric Berne identified. Before you read on, in *each* case consider how you could end the game.

Yes, but – a very common game where a person insists on maintaining a negative position throughout whilst appearing to ask for advice. If 'hooked' the other player continues to advise but finds all suggestions countered with 'yes, but' (and the reason). Eventually the advice-giver gives up – probably in some frustration. This is the pay-off. A typical example is shown below.

'I can't possibly finish this report in time.'

'Could we draft in someone to help you?'

'Yes, but there's only Natalie with any free time and she knows nothing about this.'

'What about me, could I help?'

'Yes, but it'd take me so long to explain it I'd lose more time than I'd save.'

'Could we take some other work off you?'

'Yes, but no-one else knows how to do the statistics Bill wants tomorrow.'

Harried – is also very common. The member of staff who plays harried is always busy, says 'yes' to everything, volunteers to come early, always tells you when he/she has stayed late, walks around with a harassed expression. The aim of the player is to achieve a constant air of being depressed and put upon – the pay-off being that no more jobs or responsibility will be given to him/her yet he/she will always be regarded as a very hard and willing worker.

See how hard I tried – here the basic strategy is to avoid blame. No matter how poor the outcome I really tried my best, I worked all hours, I had problems with the time-scale/people/documents – but I really tried so hard you can't blame me for what went wrong.

Now I've caught you – the aim here is to set someone up to make a mistake and then make them suffer. A superior who plays this game will be looking for a weakness – and will try to find one by piling on the work, giving complicated tasks without sufficient guidance, and deliberately putting the victim in difficult situations. The pay-off is when the person targeted makes a mistake.

Let you and him fight – this is basically setting someone up to fire your bullets, e.g. 'I don't know why you put up with it, I'd tell him straight if I were you.'

Dealing with games

A skilled games-player can be difficult to deal with. Basic tactics include the following:

- Recognise the game is being played. This is crucial.
- Refuse to be hooked or to give the pay-off (e.g. in 'Yes, but' you immediately admit defeat and refuse to make any further suggestions).
- Call the game (e.g. in 'Yes, but' you say 'Let's stop a moment and try to analyse why you block all my suggestions'). Needless to say, you would have to be brave or foolhardy to try this strategy with your boss!
- Recognise who plays what game with you.
- Recognise the games you play with others.
- Change the game and substitute negotiation tactics instead. Changing the game is easier if you have some awareness of transactional analysis (see page 315). Conflict resolution is discussed on pages 307–310.

The games played are often linked to the style of organisation and the motivation of the individuals who work there. Guy Beneviste, in *Bureaucracy* (1977) observed specific games played in large or bureaucratic organisations – from government offices to large private-sector companies. He attributed these to the fact that many individuals – particularly those at the top of their salary scales – may have no inclination to move further up the ladder or move out of the organisation but need to protect their position. For that reason they might indulge in one of the following games:

- *Risk avoidance.* In such organisations success is threatening as it implies criticism of past judgements and procedures. Equally, failure equates to poor judgement and making mistakes. The answer is to avoid change by using a variety of strategies to delay or defeat new initiatives.
- *Sending risks upstairs.* This means that anything even faintly risky is referred upwards. Those at the top cannot cope with the plethora of information and requests, so they panic and make minor amendments rather than major reforms.
- *Excessive coordination.* A way of avoiding personal risk is to operate in a committee or as part of a coalition. In this way there is no personal responsibility for decisions, though a disproportionate amount of additional

time is required for all the meetings and documentation needed to prove collective responsibility.

- *Documented histories.* This also avoids risk by providing proof. In this case every conversation, request or proposed action is documented and sent to everyone who may have an interest in the matter. Instructions are always requested in writing. Files are meticulously updated. There is then documentary proof that blame should be shared if any mishaps occur. Those who receive requests for permission to act in turn defend themselves by asking for additional information – or setting up a committee to include all interested parties, who then squabble over details with neither wanting to take responsibility for the initiative. Any move forward is only through informal 'tradings' with long-serving and trusted confidants.
- *Doing nothing.* This is the safest route but difficult to achieve given that the organisation is constantly calling for action. Strategies include
  - making procedures for new initiatives so complicated that they take an inordinate time to be approved, by which time the proposal is outdated so has to be begun again
  - starting pilot projects to dissipate the energy of those who do want to do something; once one is completed it is effectively shelved and another takes over
  - introducing proposals from competing departments or even from outside experts; energy is then spent arguing the pros and cons between diverse interests
  - restructuring and reorganising so that everyone is distracted by a major period of internal insecurity; during this time all new proposals are delayed or deferred.

Environmental factors

The attitude of individuals towards taking risks, and their subsequent behaviour as identified by Beneviste, identifies a clear example of where an environmental factor affects the relationships of individuals within an organisation. It is worth noting that whilst the game-playing strategies above may appear to have more in common with *Yes, Minister* than a modern organisation, variations of this type of protective, non-risk-taking behaviour will always be in evidence if there is a culture or management style which encourages fear or insecurity, or fosters a blame culture and/or a highly competitive internal environment.

Environmental factors which can affect working relationships include:

- the organisational structure
- the organisational culture and management style
- job roles and their content (and the degree to which role conflict or any conflicts of loyalty may exist)
- the degree of change
- the layout, resourcing and organisation of the workplace
- the stress factor
- the contractual terms under which people are employed.

The organisation's structure

A small organisation with a relatively flat structure is likely to have more open relationships and freer (and franker) communications. There is less overt status and power and it is likely that communications are more informal. It also means that you are likely to get to know a small number of people relatively well. This has benefits and drawbacks. If you interact well together then there is likely to be a positive, lively and supportive team atmosphere. If you do not get on well with someone, it is more difficult to avoid them in this structure. As the chain of communication will be shorter, messages are less likely to become distorted.

As an organisation grows in size relationships are likely to become more formalised and distant and there are a greater number of official procedures (see the discussion of trust on page 292). A hierarchical structure, with a large number of coordination roles, will be more apt to suffer from communication problems, an inability to respond quickly, and the disenchantment and demotivation of individuals.

Organisational culture and management style

In Element 1.2, the different cultures of an organisation were shown (Figure 1.2.3 on page 72) together with a brief discussion on their suitability for different people, depending upon their own internal values and preferred methods of working. Obviously, the style of the management can also impact upon the organisation and its staff, in addition to the type of culture which predominates.

Michael Maccoby in *The Gamesman: The New Corporate Leaders* identified four organisational types.

- *The jungle fighter* – who may be a lion or a fox – is in pursuit of power. The world is viewed as a jungle where winners destroy losers – at home, at leisure, when networking and at work.
- *The company man* is mainly concerned with the feelings of other people although this leader is also concerned with maintaining the company image and its integrity. Working for a protective and powerful company provides a sense of identity and self-esteem.
- *The gamesman* is a team player who values the cooperation and input of others. He/she is extremely responsive to a challenge – new ideas, initiatives and techniques are meat and drink for this leader.
- *The craftsman* obtains pleasure through being involved with the *process of creation*. The overriding focus is on innovation and quality with little interest in the mechanics of commercialisation or the intricacies of finance.

THEORY INTO PRACTICE

1 Which of the four people below would you put into each of Maccoby's categories?
   - Sir Clive Sinclair (remember the Spectrum computer and the C5?)
   - Richard Branson
   - John Major
   - Margaret Thatcher

2   Identify the way in which their styles would be most likely to affect the
     working relationships of their staff.

3   Charles Handy developed this cultural theme in his book, *Gods of
     Management*, in which he likened managerial styles in such cultures to four
     Greek gods – Zeus, Apollo, Athena and Dionysus. His book gives
     considerable insight into the effect of culture, structure and management
     style on the organisations themselves, their performance and the staff who
     work in them. It is well worth obtaining for further insights into this area.

Ministers calling to see former prime minister Margaret Thatcher during a
cabinet reshuffle were understandably very often fearful of the consequences of
the encounter. To give them warning, a chief aide used to whisper 'Good news'
or 'Bad news' before they entered the room. This, at least, gave them a brief
chance to compose themselves rather than give an unprepared response which
might be remembered for a very long time!

Job roles and conflict

This aspect has already been fully discussed on pages 265–268.

The degree of change

Change creates problems in that, unless it is handled extremely carefully, it
causes worry, stress and anxiety. Even positive changes have been proved to
do this, if they arrive too thick and fast for the individual to cope with
them. Basic changes, such as a change in working practices, can cause
irritation if not introduced properly. Changes in job role or technology can
be frightening for some people if there are no developmental activities
included. Far-reaching changes such as reorganisation and delayering can
cause severe anxiety for everyone.

The net result of this may easily be a workforce which is more preoccupied
with personal worries and concerns than getting the job done. Conflict can
rule as competing interests vie to block, renegotiate and influence the
change process. This is exacerbated if the management of change is poor
and leadership is weak. Often management give too little consideration to
the impact of change and how it will affect the people involved. For
instance, it has long been documented that people rapidly acquire territorial
rights to their own workspace in an organisation and react very
unfavourably to being moved or to having to work with new colleagues.
Despite this, many managers will plan a restructuring or reorganisation
without taking account of people's basic feelings in this respect.

People are often wary of change because they fear it will affect their self-
interests. The status quo is preferred if they consider they may lose power,
respect, status, prestige and/or security. They may also be uncertain of their
ability to cope. Kurt Lewin was the originator of the well-known three-step
model for introducing change, which involves:

- *unfreezing* current behaviour patterns by developing good relationships
  and trust, giving reassurance and minimising resistance to change

- *changing* behaviour into new patterns – and giving leadership, support and direction during this period
- *refreezing* by creating an atmosphere where there is acceptance for the new behaviours, additional resource support where required, and positive reinforcement to stabilise the process.

However, the way change is introduced in the first place is crucial to the type of reactions that are likely to be received.

- *Imposition* has the highest resistance rate. In this instance the boss imposes change without discussion.
- *Adaptation* is a 'tell and sell' method which can be seen as necessary by all involved or perceived as a veiled threat. This is likely to result in uncertainty and rumour.
- *Growth* is a consultative method where people are given the opportunity to develop themselves within the change arena. This is likely to be viewed in a much more positive light.
- *Creativity* is the participative method whereby individuals are encouraged to instigate change and be in control of the process as it affects them. This is positively motivational as it treats people as mature and responsible adults with a stake in their own future.

Obtaining the commitment of individuals whilst coping with the change process is essential to retain harmonious and cooperative working relationships. Understanding how to do this is a key requisite of all managers and administrators at a time when change is a continuous process given the plethora of external and internal forces which compel organisations to react and respond. People and their feelings, behaviours and emotions create the biggest problems for change managers – and the biggest opportunities. Ignoring this is not only foolhardy, it is downright dangerous.

Many organisations who are planning large-scale redundancy programmes employ experts to help to give support to employees. It has been proved that keeping people's self-esteem intact helps them to readjust and to find another job more quickly. Outplacement consultants help by counselling, fine-tuning rusty job application skills, providing interview coaching and helping clients by networking to find alternative employment. It is argued that their popularity has been increased by employers wishing to appear caring and concerned about employees, even when they are having to close down large sections of their operations.

Layout, resourcing and organisation of the workplace

Although Health and Safety legislation (see Element 2.1) provides guidance on certain minimum requirements, it is likely that the organisation which provides only the basic necessities as and when required by law will oversee a basically discontented workforce. To operate effectively and harmoniously, employees need

- sufficient working space with adequate furnishings, equipment and other essential resources nearby

- a layout which assists people to work effectively, rather than impedes movement or workflow
- appropriate lighting, heating and ventilation (whereas, in Britain, most organisations provide suitable heating, it is amazing how many offices are little short of greenhouses in a heatwave!).

Without these requirements people become fractious and irritable. Minor difficulties assume greater importance when they are encountered on a regular basis, and the general atmosphere is one of dissatisfaction and frustration rather than mutual harmony and cooperation.

The stress factor

In a similar way, high levels of stress also affect working relationships. Stress is caused when individuals perceive that they have little or no control over significant aspects of their lives. Employees who have no control over the amount of work received, the method of processing it or important decisions that personally affect them will suffer stress. They may work both harder and longer in an attempt to cope, take reduced holidays and cut corners. The result is extremely likely to be poor-quality output and an over-fatigued employee.

Enlightened organisations avoid this by encouraging employees to enjoy rest breaks, holidays and leisure time to return refreshed. They approve of (and even organise) occasions for staff get-togethers, out of hours, as this both fosters and reinforces team spirit and camaraderie.

Enlightened managers realise that people react very differently to identical pressures. They watch for signs of increased stress in their staff – heightened irritability, poor concentration, mood swings, loss of sense of humour – even heavy drinking or eccentric behaviour. They encourage other staff to tell them if they notice such a problem with a colleague. First-stage tactics include a discussion with the person concerned and some reorganisation of his or her job or work routine if this is the problem. Serious problems should be referred to the professionals. Many large organisations will arrange stress counselling; otherwise the person concerned should be encouraged to discuss the matter fully with a doctor.

In addition to causing problems with working relationships, stress results in poor-quality work, absenteeism and the loss of experienced and valuable members of staff. It is therefore expensive. If it results in litigation then it can cost the company very dearly indeed (see page 51). For this reason, if no other, cost-conscious organisations need to be actively seeking to reduce the problem.

Contractual terms

There are more patterns of working in and for an organisation today than ever before. Short-term contracts, flexible working, job sharing, freelancing, part-time employment, contracting out, the increased use of temporary staff, homeworking and teleworking are all part of the trend to 'free up' the labour force, reduce costs and improve flexibility and response times. The result can be a pool of different individuals who operate rather like 'ships which pass in the night' or who communicate more on an electronic than a face-to-face basis. All these patterns of work have implications for modern working relationships.

As a starting point, a group of staff with an almost constantly fluctuating membership will find it more difficult to relate to each other than one that is together every day (see also Element 1.2). In addition, unless there is excellent leadership to unite the staff, there is likely to be a 'them' and 'us' atmosphere between different groups, such as permanent and temporary workers, full-time and part-time employees, office staff and homeworkers. Competitive game-playing may occur between two people in a job-share, with the most amenable ending up with all the worst jobs. Communications become more difficult if they have to be coordinated amongst a larger group of staff – some of whom are not always around. Managing this is a considerable challenge. Success involves a mix of good systems and procedures to ensure that all staff feel they have a role to play and are able to make their voices heard, and good leadership to encourage, support and further the links between a greater diversity of staff.

Cultural diversity is a feature of most workplaces today. This can bring both benefits and problems for an administrator keen on fostering good working relationships. The beneficial aspect is a wider range of viewpoints, styles and methods of operation. This can all be wasted, however, if the differences in values and attitudes cannot be accommodated by the individuals concerned. Whilst overt racism and racial harassment should obviously be a cause for disciplinary action, more covert forms can create problems – such as fundamental intolerance of different beliefs, prejudice and unconscious 'conditioning', perhaps from childhood. Interestingly, many of the latter are created through fears about the unknown. Therefore, when people work together every day there are useful opportunities for learning and understanding more about individuals from different cultures and ethnic backgrounds. As each person becomes an 'individual', fear lessens and stereotyping decreases. At this point diversity starts to produce positive advantages.

Dealing with disagreement and conflict

The difference between constructive and destructive conflict and different forms of conflict were covered fully in Element 1.2 (pages 87–93). This section examines the problem in relation to the type of conflict individuals may encounter in the organisation, the range of possible responses, and the managing of conflict situations.

The first point to note is that there is always conflict or the potential for conflict in organisations. Anyone who claims to work in an organisation where there is no conflict is either wearing blinkers or being extremely economical with the truth! Conflict can occur:

- between the organisation and its external contacts (see Element 4.2, page 370)

- between departments, divisions or units
- between an individual and the organisation
- between individuals and their managers
- between working groups
- between individuals
- within an individual.

It may operate both vertically and laterally at the same time, with some individuals involved in different conflicts simultaneously – with their antagonists in one battle being their champions in another. Conflicts can be short or protracted – with some resulting in bitterness which fuels later conflicts. For that reason conflict is not a clear-cut, hard-edged problem that can be solved with a few simple rules and regulations but an ongoing fact of life which must be managed effectively for positive outcomes to ensue. As you have already seen in Chapter 1, properly managed constructive conflict can result in tangible benefits for all concerned – and is essential for both ongoing organisational efficiency and productive working relationships.

Many studies have been carried out to identify the sources of *organisational conflicts* and to separate these from *interpersonal conflicts* which exist between individuals. However, both types of conflict have the same features:

- There is disagreement about the goals or issues involved.
- This is compounded by a difference in perception on the part of the those involved resulting in *perceived conflict*.
- The situation results in increased tension and/or a sense of loss. There is now a situation of *felt conflict*.
- When conflict manifests itself it is either suppressed or expressed by the parties involved. The danger with suppression is that this can also fuel future conflict situations.

You will be subject to internal conflict and stress if you have to make incompatible choices from a limited range of options. These include:

- two competing positive options (e.g. promotion or a better job elsewhere)
- two competing negative options (e.g. increase your workload or take a pay cut)
- a mixed bag of options which comprises both positive and negative qualities.

Your decision will also be affected by the amount and quality of information on each possible choice, your perception of the long-term benefits and disadvantages of each course of action, and your own personal characteristics, style and needs.

Organisational conflict

Organisational conflict can occur for any of the following reasons.

- *Scarce resources* lead to arguments and disagreements about allocation.
- *Work flow interdependence* means that the work activities are structured in such a way that individuals are reliant upon

contributions from others to do their jobs. If contributions are not of the right quality and delivered on time this breeds resentment and annoyance.

- *Group orientation* results in a loyalty to a particular department, section, unit or work group above and beyond the goals of the whole organisation. This has been referred to earlier in relation to marketing and production disputes and line/staff misunderstandings.
- *Territorial possessiveness* results in individuals being prepared to fight to retain ownership over what they consider they 'own'. This may relate to their working space or physical resources but more often to their working activities and current role. A suggestion to split up a job can lead to severe disputes with the existing post holder over which 'bits' can be hived off.
- *Perceived injustice* can occur if a situation occurs which is considered discriminatory and therefore unfair. This can relate to working hours, working conditions, reward systems, time allocation or a myriad of other reasons where one person or group feels they have been unfairly treated.
- *Role ambiguity* and *role conflict* have already been discussed on pages 265–267.

The degree and extent to which conflict is perceived, felt and manifested will also be affected by the ethos and management style of the organisation, the scope for the divergence of interests within it, the degree of change and competition that exists, and the extent to which people feel they will receive a fair hearing – based upon historic evidence.

If the ethos is open and trusting, with a history of positive outcomes to conflict, then people will be more likely to enter into discussions openly and non-aggressively to clear the air and seek *integrative agreements* (see below) where both sides benefit. If, on the other hand, there is a distinct 'them and us' tradition, a history of deceit and game-playing and a management style which inflames potential conflict through contentious tactics such as threats and coercion, then this will encourage suspicion and resentment as well as promoting secrecy, mistrust and the lowering of self-esteem in individuals.

Change or escalating external competition contribute to this inflammatory situation by increasing anxiety and lowering tolerance. Management introduce new procedures, more regulations and increased targets for efficiency and may introduce cost-cutting programmes which run counter to the objectives of individuals for fair pay, independence and individual freedoms. If this is coupled with a culture that actively encourages a high degree of internal competition which rewards the 'winners' and penalises the 'losers', then the fear and insecurity this causes is likely to create an organisation more focused on its internal strife and problems than on its external relationships. Not only is such a situation potentially very damaging to future organisational performance, the stress levels of those who work within this witches' brew are likely to be very high indeed.

Interpersonal conflicts

Employees may be involved also in interpersonal conflicts, given that every workplace comprises a mix of individuals with different personal styles, values, beliefs, expectations (of each other and the workplace), attitudes and perceptions.

Interpersonal conflicts arise basically caused because every individual views the world slightly differently. That is, you have your perception of reality and I have mine. Disagreements occur when we cannot match the two *and* we deny each other the right to have our own version. If we then consider each other's behaviour to be deliberately hostile and aimed at preventing the achievement of our own objectives, this will harden our stance. If the outcome results in one of us being thwarted, losing face or feeling the victim of injustice *and* having to repress these feelings, then this creates bitterness which can harden into a long-term grudge. Poor communications, which are initially created by our emotional reactions to the disagreement and compounded by misunderstandings of motive and intent, fuel the dispute as they encourage us to look for hidden (negative) meanings behind each further exchange. The danger is that what started as a minor difference of opinion can spiral into an almost uncontrollable sequence of events – depending upon the personal characteristics of those involved.

Other factors which will affect the situation include our relative power positions, our individual self-esteem, our ability to cope with stress and our ability to negotiate. The power difference may be one of status, one of ability in managing the situation, or one of tactical advantage – for instance, if the status quo or if overall opinion favours my preference but not yours. If I am also able to play a waiting game, hide my feelings and cope better with a stressful situation, then I am armed with several implicit advantages. You may be frustrated, angry, confused or depressed but may struggle to redress the situation – particularly if your own self-esteem is low, you find assertion or negotiation difficult and feel isolated in your current situation. Needless to say, it is unlikely that you will be motivated to do your job properly either. Ongoing disputes and repressed conflict are counterproductive both for the people involved and for the organisation as a whole. Therefore *conflict management* techniques are vital.

In a working situation, it is likely that individuals will mask their personal interests by each claiming that his or her view is the one which is the 'best option' for the organisation as a whole. However, to do this, it is necessary for an individual to convince himself or herself first! For that reason it can be argued that we are all 'victims of our own propaganda'. That is why we never see ourselves as being unreasonable – only other people!

Managing conflict

Suppressed conflict leads to resentment, whereas expressed conflict leads to resolution. However, this is not as simple as it sounds – particularly in relation to interpersonal conflicts which involve protagonists of unequal status. Studies have shown that there are five main reactions to conflict depending upon the characteristics of those involved and the importance of the outcome versus the risk involved. These are shown in Figure 4.1.8 and link closely to the stances depicted in Figure 4.1.7.

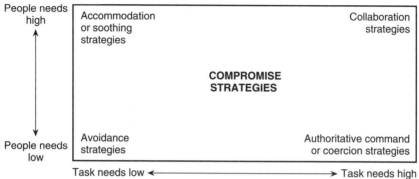

Figure 4.1.8 Conflict management options

Avoidance strategies

Avoidance strategies are adopted by those who prefer to pretend that the conflict does not exist or, if left alone, will go away. At corporate level this can manifest itself in a structure which denies individuals any channel to express their discontent (e.g. no personnel specialists or recognised trade unions); a culture which insists on artificial unity with low-key issues only being aired and major differences being suppressed in polite meeting forums; or if there is a tradition of 'kicking the problem upstairs', to be dealt with at a more senior level.

At individual level, avoidance strategies are practised by those who have either little regard for people or little concern for the outcome of the issue. Such a person is a loner, preferring to distance himself or herself from any contentious issues or close personal relationships.

The danger with this approach is that, at corporate level, it can ignore legal requirements for employee representation and, at all levels, rarely solves the problem but simply results in repressed anger and resentment which later erupts in a major conflict.

Accommodation or soothing strategies

Accommodation or soothing strategies appeal to the 'anything for a peaceful life' cohort. At the organisation level there will be an emphasis on team-playing, conformity, the benefits of mutual agreement and peaceful coexistence through the adoption of agreed policies and procedures. Managers will appeal to others to put aside individual differences and achieve common goals for the greater good, in an attempt to minimise disputes and disagreements as petty and individualistic.

In interpersonal disputes, an individual with a high regard for personal relationships and low concern for the outcome will act in this way and will prefer to be accommodating rather than risk personal unpopularity.

The problem with this strategy is its fundamental failure to examine the root cause of the problem, given that the focus has been on prevention rather than cure.

Authoritative command or coercion

Authoritative command or coercion is a 'forced medicine' situation. In this case one protagonist is determined to win, regardless of the effect on the other. At the corporate level there are many instances of organisations attempting to smother industrial conflict by threats. A typical strategy is to present the opposing side with a series of progressively worse 'no-win' options until they concede defeat – often severely bruised from the encounter.

At individual level this type of tactic is employed by the ruthless achiever who has power or resources on his/her side and who will adopt any method to win the fight.

Given that this type of win/lose approach suppresses the needs of one party at the expense of the other, nothing is resolved. Therefore the same battles may be fought again and again.

Compromise strategies

Compromise strategies imply finding a solution acceptable to both parties. In this case each party is persuaded to relinquish part of their planned benefit so that both save face. Often a 'split the difference' strategy is adopted at corporate level over issues such as resource allocation and reward payments.

At individual level, a compromise solution can often be found where neither party totally gains, but neither totally loses. The problem lies in the fact that neither has won, so neither feels totally satisfied by the outcome. One party may then later try to renegotiate to make up perceived lost ground.

Collaboration

Collaboration is considered by all authorities to be the most beneficial strategy. This involves:

- expressing or confronting the problem, with all concerned recognising that there is a difficulty which needs attention
- exploring its nature and separating the 'people' issues from the problem itself
- identifying possible alternatives
- negotiating a *mutually beneficial* outcome – often referred to as an integrative agreement.

Individuals who prefer this route have a high concern for people as well as a high concern for performance goals. Conflict is perceived as a problem and a mutually satisfactory outcome is negotiated to resolve any tensions and negative feelings caused by the conflict. The obvious method for this to be achieved – whether at organisational or individual level – is through bargaining, negotiation, mediation and, if necessary, arbitration.

Choice of best strategy

It is worth noting that *any* of the strategies listed above can be used appropriately on occasion – although there are obvious dangers in some approaches, most of which have already been mentioned. For instance, a manager would be justified in using avoidance strategies if time was pressing, a dispute could be costly or if other issues were more important. Accommodating strategies are appropriate if the issue is more important to one individual than another (or the loss would be greater) but would be inappropriate if they interfered with the overall objectives of the organisation. Even authoritative command can be justified if the situation is critical, *provided* that there is due concern for individuals and no exploitation or manipulation based on power. Compromise may be the only sensible choice if there are absolutely no mutual benefits to be gained by collaboration.

THEORY INTO PRACTICE

1 Identify at least one conflict that occurred in your own organisation and identify the overall strategy which was used to resolve it. To what degree do you consider this strategy was both appropriate and effective?

2 Try to identify the preferred styles of conflict resolution that are practised by (a) your line manager, (b) a close colleague, (c) yourself. What evidence do you have to support your views and to what degree do you consider the preferred styles are both appropriate and effective?

A revolutionary way of resolving conflict has been suggested by E. Van de Vliert. In this, the intensity of the conflict is deliberately increased through a system of *escalative intervention*. Tactics include:

● increasing contact between protagonists
● increasing the range of issues on which the conflict is based
● refusing to accept accommodating, avoidance or compromise strategies
● encouraging openly hostile confrontations.

The theory is that all these tactics 'up the stakes' by increasing pressure for a settlement, given that the situation rapidly becomes intolerable. At this point it becomes essential for the protagonists to work out a solution – to be able to survive! Despite scepticism by many, studies have shown this strategy to work on several occasions *provided* that the conflict resolution sessions are managed very skilfully.

Conflict resolution

Conflict can be resolved only if it is brought out into the open and confronted by all the parties concerned. This usually requires a five-step approach.

1 Prepare for the encounter.
2 Listen to the debate.
3 Contribute additional relevant information and summarise the issues.
4 Negotiate the optimum agreement for both parties.
5 Monitor its implementation.

Whilst this list may seem very straightforward, it is evident that life isn't quite so simple or all conflicts would be solved almost as soon as they started! For that reason, it is worth examining each stage in rather more detail.

Prepare for the encounter

This does not just mean planning what must be discussed but also taking account of factors which may, accidentally or deliberately, disadvantage one party to the dispute.

- Consider the *timing* of the meeting. Is one party more 'ready' to reach agreement than the other, are some special circumstances mitigating against one party?
- Consider the *power balance* of those involved (and the degree to which this may be redressed).
- Consider the *skills*, *abilities* and *personalities* of those involved and their ability to influence the debate (fairly or unfairly).
- Consider the *number of people* involved and their representatives. An additional factor is whether spokespeople, observers or others need to be present.
- Consider the *issues* involved and the *history* of the dispute so far (which may explain the attitudes of the parties).
- Consider the *style* and *order* of the proceedings. There is much more likelihood of success if both parties can be persuaded to have a *positive attitude* and to focus on possible benefits, rather than a *negative attitude* where they concentrate on perceived losses. In addition, an integrative agreement is far more likely to be achieved if there is trust, openness and a high degree of shared information. It is therefore better to obtain all the information from both parties (preferably juxtaposed, so that one does not have to declare all their intentions before the other starts to respond) before any comments are made.

Listen to the debate

It is obviously helpful if both protagonists in any conflict understand the fundamental rules to facing up to an issue. These include:

- focusing on positive outcomes (ranging from 'best possible' to 'one I can live with')
- expressing feelings assertively and honestly
- backing up opinions with information and evidence
- having a united front within their own group (if the confrontation is between two separate groups)
- admitting to misconceptions and false perceptions and genuinely trying to see 'the other point of view'
- avoiding unfair or coercive tactics
- identifying hidden agendas which cloud the main issue
- being prepared to change position.

Of course, this is the ideal and it is unlikely – for very many reasons – that you will encounter this situation. However, two weaknesses that people often display which can actually be used to help to solve the problem relate to *fixed-sum error* and *incompatibility error* – and both of these relate to perception. Fixed-sum error occurs when one party assumes that the other party puts the same degree of value on each issue as themselves, whereas in reality it is more likely to be different. This may often lead to the identification of an area where some shift in stance may be possible. Incompatibility error occurs when the parties have become so entrenched in the dispute they believe there is no common ground at all. Therefore finding any mutual area of agreement, however small initially, helps to break the deadlock.

Quite obviously, the better you know the parties involved the more likely you are to be able to 'second-guess' the stance they are likely to adopt – and why. If there are any hidden agendas or misconceptions you should then be more capable of identifying these accurately as you listen to the debate.

Contribute additional relevant information and summarise the issues

There may be relevant information which is unknown by the parties involved. Given that the proceedings are only likely to be perceived as productive if all relevant areas are fully discussed, then it might be your role to highlight this additional information. It is also your job, if you are mediating between two protagonists, to control the proceedings and to keep everyone's minds focused on positive aspects. This means summing up by:

● concentrating on key issues and facts
● separating factual issues from personality issues
● taking account of counter-arguments and claims
● summarising the differences.

Finally, you can help the situation by keeping the peace! You are unlikely to achieve your objectives if the atmosphere is hostile and bitter – a key aim is to keep the debate professional and objective.

Negotiate agreement

At this stage in the proceedings your protagonists should feel marginally more satisfied because they have had the opportunity to put forward their own arguments and reasons. The mood should change more towards problem-solving with the meeting now focused on:

● sounding out possibilities
● floating ideas and making suggestions
● asking for opinions
● clarifying any doubtful issues.

At the same time, *responses* to suggestions should be well considered and possible consequences debated. Do remember that no-one wants a conflict to last forever! People therefore have a vested interest in trying to negotiate the best agreement. If your role involves attempting to identify mutual areas of benefit, then you are likely to find both parties more than willing to make some adjustments to their original positions. If this still seems impossible there are two other options. Adjourn the meeting for each person to give further thought to the discussion and set up another meeting in a few days' time, *or* ask the parties to attempt a temporary solution and schedule a review after a trial period. Do make certain, however, that the agreement reached is completely understood by each party so that there can be no possibility of non-compliance through misunderstandings or confusion. Neither can this be used as an excuse for inaction. Sometimes it is helpful to summarise the discussion and agreement in writing afterwards, with any review period, to clarify the issue.

Monitor its implementation

'My word is my bond' may work on the Stock Exchange but it is doubtful whether it could always be taken as read with everyone you deal with. Some people agree to take a course of action and then renege on this later. You therefore need to ensure that those involved are carrying out the agreement in the manner *and spirit* in which it was intended. If the agreement was on a temporary basis then you will need to follow up your promise to review progress by setting a follow-up meeting in the not too distant future.

THEORY INTO PRACTICE

Whereas the section above was written to describe a mediation role, you may like to stop and consider how you behave if you are involved in conflict yourself and are therefore one of the protagonists. If you don't wish to put this in a work context, reflect on how you react if you have a conflict situation with your partner, parent, child or friend. Particularly with our own family, we are apt to neglect the 'niceties' of conflict resolution and therefore fail to achieve a win/win situation. We may then carry forward these strategies and behaviour patterns at work.

Unless you particularly want to discuss the issue further, you may prefer to keep your own counsel on your findings rather than share them with your adviser!

Methods of communication to suit individual needs

The role and importance of communication has already been discussed in the information section on pages 279–287, and many issues discussed in that section are equally applicable to this. Examples include methods of supplying information and the difference between consultation and participation. If it is some time since you covered that section it would be wise to reread the appropriate pages.

All communications are undertaken for one of three purposes – to instigate action, to give information or to ascertain feelings and/or possible reactions. D. Clutterbuck and D. Dearlove, in 1993, described these as *task communications, educational* or *context communications* and *motivational communications*. However, the ability of any communication to achieve its objective will depend upon a variety of factors linked crucially to the method by which it is transmitted and the style and tone within it.

An American survey found that managers who were *media sensitive* scored a much higher success rate with their communications than those who were not. Most successful managers preferred to use written media for basic, unambiguous information and verbal communications where there was a high degree of ambiguity and considerable clarification might be required. Because only verbal communications allow for immediate feedback it is not surprising that this type of manager was found to be the most effective.

Communications choices

When you communicate with another person you have a variety of decisions to make, such as:

● which *channel* would be better – formal or informal
● which *direction* the communication will take in relation to the organisation structure – upwards, downwards or horizontally
● which *form* it should take – verbal or written
● which *media* should be used – interview/discussion/group meeting; memo/letter/e-mail etc.

Your choice will determine:

● the tone of the communication
● the ability of your correspondent to respond
● the type of response you are likely to receive
● your ability to prove what you have done
● the likelihood of achieving your objective.

Your first question should be to ask yourself 'What do I wish to achieve by sending this communication?' If, for instance, you want to test opinion on a new idea without committing yourself, you would be foolish to select a formal channel and copy it to your own boss and most of the department. Equally, if you had received a serious allegation about your behaviour from a line manager with whom you had a personality clash, you may be equally foolhardy to think that suggesting an informal chat over a couple of drinks would be the best solution. Thinking through the implications of communicating in different ways is important – if you opt for safety then you may prefer to keep the majority of your 'sensitive' communications either as informal as possible or as restricted as possible so that at least you leave yourself an open door through which to retreat if necessary.

A skilled communicator will vary the channel, direction, form and media according to the content of the communication, the urgency of the situation, the culture of the organisation, the key recipient(s), and the objective of the exercise. This leads to an immense number of variables to be assessed – often very quickly. In today's world a wide variety of communication methods exists, the major forms of which are given in Figure 4.1.9.

Upwards

Written:
Reports, memos, e-mail
Copies of minutes
Results of surveys
Results of suggestion schemes

Verbal:
Telephone
Departmental meetings, management meetings
Briefing groups
Project groups
Working parties
Focus groups
Responding to 'open-door' policy
Responding to 'walking the job' managers

Lateral (horizontally)

Written:
Reports, memos, e-mail
Information documents and bulletins
Official paperwork and documentation
Manuals

Verbal:
Telephone and hotlines
Liaison team meetings
Interdepartmental meetings
Team rep meetings
Training sessions/conferences/seminars
Informal events and networking

Downwards

Written:
As lateral, *plus*
Newsletters/bulletins/house journals
Company newspapers
Company reports
Employee reports
Company noticeboards
Departmental minutes

Verbal:
Telephone
Mass meetings
Team briefings
Section or unit meetings
Formal presentations
Cascading sessions
Feedback sessions
'Open-door' policy
'Walking the job'
Informal day-to-day contacts

Figure 4.1.9 Methods and directions of communications

Modern methods for spreading and disseminating information and obtaining feedback quickly include hotlines, networking, team briefings, 'walking the job', and e-mail. Contrast these with more traditional methods such as memos, meetings and surveys, and those which are apt to be 'one-way' only, such as noticeboards, newsletters and departmental meetings.

1 Identify how many methods of communication – both modern and traditional – are available in your organisation.

2 For each of the forms of communication shown in Figure 4.1.9, ascertain:

    a   whether they operate in your organisation

    b   examples of when they may be utilised to good effect

    c   examples of when their individual use is *in*appropriate.

L. Festinger, an American researcher, found that people cope much more easily with information which conforms to their beliefs and expectations. They can almost unconsciously absorb, remember and action it appropriately. In contrast, information which does not accord with their beliefs causes immense difficulties of comprehension – let alone remembrance and action. This links to the four stages of disbelief, denial, anger and acceptance discussed on page 283. The 'denial' stage manifests itself in a distortion of the information as someone desperately tries to manipulate the input into a more acceptable form.

Methods of communicating

Your own personality, sensitivity and language skills all play a part in the way you actually 'frame' your communications. This chapter has covered perception fairly thoroughly. At this point you may wish to stop and think about the way your own perception of people 'colours' the way you communicate with them – quite apart from other aspects such as the time available, communication skills, your ability to empathise with the recipient and so on.

A golden rule when framing communications is to put yourself in the position of the recipient. This means that you are sensitive not only to the content but also to the situation in which *that particular person* will receive it – and their probable reaction(s). Of course, this consideration will mean that you are far more wary about sending 'group' communications – unless they contain only basic, unambiguous and uncontentious facts.

Your communication skills – both written and verbal – are a topic beyond the scope of this book. However, it is hoped that if they are amiss then you will try to rectify them before someone forces you to address the situation. Otherwise they are likely to cloud your effectiveness for ever more. However, you are more likely to formulate the right type of words and phrases if you are aware of the way in which your own attitude can affect how you communicate – regardless of the method you choose.

Attitudes and interpersonal communications

Probably the most comprehensive research in this area was carried out by Eric Berne. Quite apart from game-playing (see page 292), Berne was involved in examining the way in which people's attitudes affect their communications as well as the different ways in which communication transactions take place. He then used these findings to identify the factors which were involved when transactions were complementary (or effective) or crossed (and therefore ineffective).

Berne identified four possible positions – shown in Figure 4.1.10. He argued that everyone, as a child, starts life in the 'I'm not OK, you're OK' position, given that the child is powerless but the parent appears to have unlimited power. The 'not OK' part of the child 'reads things' into remarks which aren't there and struggles to accept praise or compliments, considering them undeserved. The focus is on 'self' – and in the case of the child the 'self' is always disadvantaged regardless of the situation. The ultimate learned behaviour of the adult should be that of 'I'm OK, you're OK'. This is a conscious development which needs thought, faith and action to surpass natural feelings and take ownership of the consequences of our own actions. It is a recognition that we have free will and do not blame others – or the situation – for the results of our action or inaction. In Berne's view, only in this mode can we communicate freely and openly without inherent feelings of innate disapproval from others or feeling threatened by our own actions.

I'M OK, YOU'RE NOT OK	I'M OK, YOU'RE OK
The 'I'm better than you are' position. Can result in patronising attitude, over-confidence, egotism, little concern for people – they don't deserve it.	The only deliberately learned position. Is based on deliberate thought and reflection rather than satisfying feelings. Accords with positive 'why not?' view of life.
Stance – 'get rid of the people'	Stance – 'get on with people and get on with life'
I'M NOT OK, YOU'RE NOT OK	I'M NOT OK, YOU'RE OK
'My life is a mess' coupled with 'life is a bastard' or 'the world is full of fools and idiots'. Cynical view of life.	Childhood position – reinforced by inaccurate picture of self and capabilities. Can be painful to be around 'OK' people. The most common position of game players.
Stance – 'get nowhere'	Stance – 'get away from the people'

I+ ↑   I− ↓   U− ←   → U+

Figure 4.1.10 Eric Berne's 'OK Corral'

These findings link to Berne's studies on transactional analysis. Berne identified three modes of communicating – Child, Parent and Adult – and subdivided these into different categories (see Figure 4.1.11). Only in Adult mode are we capable of handling and transmitting communications rationally and competently because we are prepared to accumulate data, estimate probabilities and then react in a logical, objective and rational way. In contrast, when in Child mode we yearn for certainty and when in Parent mode we insist on predictability. Communications between two people both in Child mode are unsustainable as each is interested only in the self. Communications between two people in Parent mode are likely to be sustainable but focus on fault-finding or criticism. Only communications between two people in Adult mode are likely to achieve results and be constantly complementary. Equally, if one party refuses to adopt Adult mode or to sustain it for very long, then the transaction is likely to be 'crossed' and will fail to achieve its desired outcome (see Figure 4.1.12).

Mode	Sector	Characteristics
Adult	Rational	Making a decision, collecting information, assertiveness
	Primitive	Intuitive – sensitive to 'vibes' and sixth sense
Parent	Critical	Judgemental, critical, domineering, paternalistic
	Nurturing	Protective, helpful, giver of advice (for your own benefit!)
Child	Free	Emotional, playful, curious, wanting own way, excitable
	Adapted	Wanting to please, clinging or attention-seeking
	Rebellious	Devious, jealous, revengeful

Figure 4.1.11 Berne's transactional analysis modes

Complementary	
Child to Parent	'I'm hurt' = 'Let me make it better'
Parent to Child	'I'll do this, I know more than you' = 'That's fine by me.'
Child to Adult	'I really don't know what to do' = 'Let's talk about the options'
Adult to Parent	'Stop me if I go wrong' = 'Don't worry, I'll tell you'
Crossed	
Adult to Parent	'Stop me if I go wrong' = 'You've no business doing it in the first place'
Parent to Parent	'Do what I say' = 'Who are you to tell me?'
Adult to Child	'What do you want to do?'= 'Don't know, don't care'
Child to Child	'I hate Mondays' = 'I hate every day'

Figure 4.1.12 Berne's complementary and crossed transactions

Those who operate in Berne's Adult mode are far more likely to have *sender creditability* and this enhances their chance of success. Adults are reliable, trustworthy, knowledgeable, assertive and thoughtful. They make their motives and meanings clear by specific statements which logically 'lead' the recipient onwards. In addition, they:

- take responsibility for their own actions and emotions and are assertive (i.e. use 'I' statements) rather than adopt an aggressive or accusatory stance (e.g. through the use of 'you' statements or generalisations, such as 'everyone' or 'most people')
- match their verbal and non-verbal signals to avoid confusion or 'mixed messages'
- select the most appropriate method of communication and reinforce the message through more than one channel or mode (e.g. confirming a discussion in writing).

THEORY INTO PRACTICE

1 You have been invited to attend a high-level meeting for the first time and it has been suggested that you accompany a more experienced member of staff on this occasion. Decide which 'mode' of transaction he/she would be using if you were greeted with:

a 'Sit next to me and I'll look after you.'

b 'They're all a waste of time, these meetings. I skip as many as I can.'

c 'Sit down and keep quiet. As you don't know what to do I'll expect you to do nothing this time except listen.'

d 'Always agree with Mr Burns – he's the most important person there.'

e 'There's a fairly straightforward agenda.' *Passes you a copy.* 'Perhaps we can discuss the proceedings afterwards when it'll make more sense.'

2 What would your reaction be in each case – *and why*?

You may like to note that even Eric Berne can offer few suggestions for getting the bane of your office life to operate in Adult mode more often, if at all! If nothing else, however, his theories do give you some insight into *why* people say the things they do – even if you can do little to influence other people apart from trying desperately hard to stay in Adult mode yourself!

The hardest skill of all?

One of the most difficult areas of communications relates to telling people what they do not want to hear. This is bad enough when it concerns factual information, but even more tricky when it relates to personal performance and therefore involves personal criticism. However, given that providing regular feedback is essential to achieving objectives of productivity and quality, it is important that your communication skills include being able to do this without destroying motivation, even with someone who is highly defensive. We all enjoy receiving praise for our own efforts ('positive strokes' in the language of behavioural scientists) but are often shocked, horrified and even aggressive when faced with criticism – even if it is meant to be constructive.

The rules which apply to giving effective feedback can usefully be translated to apply to any situation where excellent communication skills are highly desirable.

1 Prepare in advance. Both the time, the length of the session and the content are important. The meeting should be timely both in relation to the issue *and* the 'state of mind' of the other person. The session should be of appropriate length for the content *but* the latter should not contain so much it overwhelms the other person. Make sure you have uninterrupted privacy.

2 Get to the point quickly – never keep someone guessing what the session is about. Make it crystal clear your aim is to help and assist, not to judge or criticise.

3 Focus on the issue, not the person or his/her personal characteristics. Your aim should be to protect the self-esteem of both of you.

4 Be descriptive, rather than evaluative. This means giving good clear examples which can act as a 'mirror' of behaviour. Do not be judge and jury. Never threaten or resort to sarcasm.

5 Give specific and tangible examples, otherwise you will create frustration and misunderstandings. For instance, do not say 'You regularly make mistakes.' It is far better to say 'I was concerned about the error in ...'.

6 People are protective and sensitive about their own attitudes, emotions and needs – if you attack these 'hidden areas' you can expect the other party to become defensive. Therefore discuss actions rather than feelings, deeds rather than thoughts. Bear in mind you can only try to second-guess other people's thoughts, motives and feelings – and you may be very wrong!

7 Focus on the positive, not the negative. It is useless to spend most of the session analysing a past error. Instead focus on the action which should have been taken – and why.

8 Give the other person the right of reply – though if you handle the situation well there will be less need for defensive explanations. Practise your listening skills (see page 289).

9 Check that you mutually agree the scope of the problem, its effects and its solution.

10 Check that you both perceive the meeting the same way by asking the other party to sum up the discussion and the action to be taken.

THEORY INTO PRACTICE

Of course, it is quite possible that on occasion you may have to *receive* criticism – and from someone less skilled at giving feedback than you should now be! Bearing in mind your previous reading about Berne's communication modes, you may like to consider:

a which mode you should be in when giving feedback
b which mode you should be in when receiving feedback
c how you would react if you were faced with feedback from someone who was in Critical Parent mode!

Consider the 'golden rules' which you think should apply for receiving feedback and then check your answer with Figure 4.1.13 on page 320.

Ways of motivating people

Motivation theory was covered in detail in Chapter 1, pages 63–76. This section applies and develops that knowledge to examine the way in which working relationships can affect motivation and the action you can take to improve and sustain motivation in your colleagues. If it is some time since you read Chapter 1, or if you have not yet covered motivation theory, it is recommended that you read the relevant pages before you continue this section.

Motivation in the workplace

There are a variety of ways in which motivation theory can be applied to working relationships. Elton Mayo's studies showed the importance of *social relations* in the workplace. Those who are isolated from contact with others will miss out on a key aspect of motivation. Do bear in mind that it is not only physical proximity which is important. Emotional isolation can be even more psychologically damaging. This can be on a minor scale, such as a temporary disagreement between colleagues, or major league – when one employee is deliberately excluded from discussions or events, targeted for derision or even 'sent to Coventry'.

Many of Mayo's findings link with Maslow's theory that *social needs* are one of the more fundamental human needs. However, Maslow also identified 'self-esteem' as a higher-order need and the latter is reinforced through interaction and feedback from other human beings. Constant or thoughtless criticism will erode self-esteem and create a loss of confidence that actively impedes effective working and destroys motivation.

Equally, Mayo's higher-order skill of *self-realisation* is also affected by personal relationships – particularly where an immediate superior has a key role to play in facilitating (or frustrating) the personal development needs of subordinates (see page 325).

Alderfer's study of *relatedness needs* indicates that a person who displays a high degree of relatedness will be more dependent on his/her social relations at work and therefore more vulnerable to neglect in this area. This links with McClelland and Atkinson's finding that a person with a high need for affiliation is drastically affected if there are poor relations with his/her working group, colleagues or line manager.

Herzberg, in one respect, is the 'odd man out' in that, whereas recognition and personal growth (for which we need self-esteem) are to him important motivators, he argues that relationships with one's colleagues and supervisors are merely *hygiene factors*. Many who are subject to the whims and fancies of an unreasonable boss or irrational colleague may heartily disagree with this finding – and this topic is raised again on page 321. It is worth noting that several experts have criticised Herzberg's theory as being too simplistic and having no regard for either individual or situational differences. However, Herzberg's studies are valuable in relation to their findings on job content, which actively affects the motivational level of the vast majority of people.

Expectancy theory can be applied in this area given the importance of intrinsic motivation factors – many of which are dependent upon other people. If the most people can expect for working hard is to be given even more work, or to be told that they could have done better, they rapidly reach the conclusion that extreme efforts produce no intrinsic satisfaction. Initially, this is manifested by feelings of disappointment, later by being disheartened and ultimately by disenchantment and even cynicism. At this stage, efforts to please or impress will be abandoned.

Equity theory states that each person compares his or her own treatment with that meted out to other people – and that if you consider you are unfairly treated in relation to others you will become demotivated. Do bear in mind that unfair treatment can be either deliberate or accidental – given the halo and horns effect discussed on page 274 and our own individual perceptions. Therefore, although we may *intend* to treat everyone the same, if we find a person difficult to deal with it is likely that this will affect our style and manner of communicating. If people perceive this difference as unfair or biased against them then this is likely to result in demotivation, and to confirm their original perception of the relationship. This will reinforce their behaviour, which will signal to you that your original perception was correct. (Back to self-fulfilling propheciesy again!)

It is also worth noting that modern studies of motivation incorporate the *contingency* view that people change and situations change, and that the factors which apply at one time may not work at a different time. It is fairly obvious that people are motivated by different needs, given that each person is a unique individual. It is also apparent that needs change over time – there is little point appealing to the security needs of a footloose, highly qualified 25-year-old but such needs may be paramount for a person with a young family or someone nearing retirement. Edgar Schein, a management consultant and social psychologist, identified *career anchors* that affect people's attitudes. These are based on an individual's perception of his/her own talents, abilities, values, attitudes and needs, which are usually fairly well formed by the time a person reaches the early thirties.

- Those with *technical anchors* are interested in job content.
- Others display *managerial competence anchors* and wish to succeed in high-level management positions.
- Some prefer *creativity* or *entrepreneurial activities* – and prefer to innovate, build and develop products or ideas.
- A fourth group is mainly concerned with *security* and *stability*.
- Members of the final group aim for *autonomy* and *independence* and prefer to manage themselves.

In a separate study, Schein described people as complex beings, whose needs change over time because they are influenced by experience and changing situations. If we also consider the fact that people have critical life stages when they need to review their own circumstances and that their job itself may change (through technical development, promotion or transfer) then it is hardly surprising that no single motivational theory can be applied to any individual in any situation.

That said, motivational theory does identify some common denominators which affect the vast majority of people, although the degree to which they apply may differ.

Up to middle age, people consider their lives in terms of the years they have lived and, therefore, by their current age (e.g. 'I am 25'). During middle age people start to face their own mortality. At this point their focus changes as they now view their lives in terms of the number of years they have left to live. This can vastly change attitudes, perception and personal needs.

It is worth noting that 'middle age' in this context does not have a precise chronological age attached to it – some people undergo the process in their early forties, whilst others may not reach it until their early fifties.

1 Avoid being over-defensive. Don't refuse to give a brief reason but remember over-explanations are likely to be counterproductive.
2 Focus on the issue. Keep to facts – refuse to refocus the blame on other people or to enter into a personal war of words. If you are faced with a torrent of abuse, refuse to participate. Say you will return when your counterpart is prepared to discuss the issue objectively.
3 Positive criticism is helpful, negative criticism is destructive. Refocus a negative session by identifying positive solutions or by asking your accuser for suggestions.
4 Accept positive criticism with as much grace as you can muster – particularly if it is true. You are likely to be praised afterwards for your attitude! Try to work out the areas where you may be particularly touchy or sensitive – and whether this is justifiable.
5 If you dispute the allegation, ask for substantive evidence and don't accept generalisations or statements unsupported by facts. This is particularly important if the encounter could lead to disciplinary proceedings (see also page 320).
6 If you are enraged after the encounter, don't take action before you have slept on it, discussed the problem with your friends, and tried to analyse the situation from your boss's point of view.
7 If you have a constantly critical boss (who rarely gives praise), ask for a short meeting to point out how upset you are, how you would appreciate regular positive feedback and an improvement in communications. Highlight the benefits of this approach.
8 Remember – without feedback we cannot develop as people. Although a lesson may be painful to learn it is better than not learning at all.
9 Start the session in Adult mode – and remain in it. Or identify the mode your boss is in and try responding in the most complementary way.
10 Be charitable – perhaps your boss is not as good at giving feedback as you are.

Figure 4.1.13 Coping with critical feedback

From the information you have read so far, draw up a list of guidelines for motivating people at work. Check your list with your adviser. A useful starting point – as well as this text – is to think of the way in which your colleagues' behaviour and attitudes can affect your own motivation.

The role of leadership

It is interesting to note the 'role of the boss' in relation to motivation theories. Despite Herzberg's theory, many people consider the attitude and behaviour of their immediate line manager as critical in affecting their own motivation. If you work in a team then the same arguments will apply to your leader. In many cases, this factor is held to be more important than the culture of the organisation (which is more intangible), the attitude of other senior staff (who are more distant), and the content of the actual job (which it may be difficult to vary significantly). In this case it is leadership ability that is being measured, rather than managerial ability – and there is a significant difference. According to one writer, C. M. Watson, managers are concerned with strategy, structure and systems whereas leaders are concerned with style, staff, skills and shared goals. This has been developed by other writers who argue that whereas the function of managers is to get things done through other people and achieve organisational goals, the leader is more personally involved with people, can empathise with individuals and motivate staff to operate productively through personal influence and enthusiasm.

A particular facet of leadership which affects an individual's ability to lead effectively is the leader's influence with outside contacts. If the leader is influential and can usually obtain benefits for those who follow or negotiate better conditions, then he/she will have greater power and influence than if the perception is of a weak leader who may have useful opinions but has little chance of having these accepted at higher level.

Leadership theories

There have been many studies of leadership and theories as to the attributes which make a successful leader. Early in the 1900s, theorists considered that certain personality traits, including intelligence, self-assurance, dependability and originality, lead to successful leadership, particularly when combined with charisma. The problem with this approach is that although it is usually easy to identify charismatic leaders (e.g. Churchill, Hitler, Richard Branson) it is less easy to use this explanation exclusively. Many students wrestle with the problem of why Churchill was accepted as a leader during the war years and then rejected so forcibly immediately afterwards. In addition, any list of 'qualities' is prone to deter most people from putting their cap in the leadership ring because it is so comprehensive – and may be totally inapplicable to many successful leaders they know.

The next theory relates to situational leadership. In this case, it is argued, Churchill was chosen leader during the war because he was perceived to be the most likely person to lead the British people to success *at that particular time*. This is a sounder argument – although it still has its critics as it implies that leadership skills are irrelevant and that factors outside the situation are meaningless. In addition, in organisations it is impossible to change leader every time the situation changes – even if this might be considered beneficial by some!

In the 1940s, leadership studies started to focus upon behavioural studies, i.e. what leaders did, rather than who they were or the situation in which they were leading. Because behaviour can be learned this implies that leadership skills can be developed – people can be taught how to become good leaders in a variety of situations. Researchers Tannenbaum and Schmidt concentrated upon two aspects of behaviour.

- *Leadership functions.* The effective leader is the one who can best meet the three areas of need, i.e. for task functions, group maintenance functions and individual functions.
- *Leadership styles.* Two different styles were identified – task-based styles, where the focus is on task-completion, and people-based styles where the focus is on motivation and job satisfaction. In reality, an effective leader needs to operate both styles although one is usually predominant in any human being. Tannenbaum and Schmidt originally considered that the higher a leader was on one style, the lower he/she would be (correspondingly) on the other.

Studies undertaken by Ohio State University and the University of Michigan tested this premise and found that the most effective style of leadership depended upon the situation. In the armed services, task-based styles were preferred, because of the authoritarian environment and the critical aspect of the work undertaken in many areas (e.g. by air crews). The same preference was found in production environments. However, employee-centred environments were more successful with people-based leadership styles as this encouraged group interaction and supportive, open relationships. A key finding from the studies was that both task and people skills are important to effective leadership and the two are not mutually exclusive.

THEORY INTO PRACTICE

Robert Blake and Jane Mouton developed a managerial grid, which is summarised in Figure 4.1.14, to measure a manager's concern for each area.

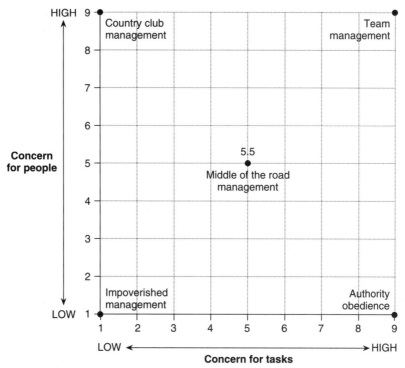

Figure 4.1.14 Blake and Mouton's managerial grid

Example scores

1.1 This is rated as *impoverished management* with little concern for either productivity or people. In some cases it is synonymous with *laissez faire* leadership where the leader abrogates his or her responsibilities.

1.9 Termed *country-club management* by Blake and Mouton, this is a belief that if people are happy they will do the job effectively. It is a naive, over-optimistic approach where the emphasis on care, concern and compromise is so highly valued that anything which will disrupt or upset group relations is rejected out of hand.

9.1 *Authority-obedience* relates to a high concern for production and virtually nil concern for people. It reflects autocratic management at its worse. Staff are regarded as a means of production and a resource – no more, no less.

5.5 Variously termed *organisation man management* and *middle of the road management*, this is the leader who prizes balance above all. This can result in 'stop–go' policies of leadership where policies are changed when pressure is exerted. Astute staff will quickly recognise this and use it to their advantage.

9.9 *Team management* is the ideal as this reflects a high concern for both production and people. The result is a committed staff who are trusted and respected by managers and a management who are prepared to consult staff openly and unambiguously, leading to a 'common stake' in the organisation. Blake and Mouton ascribed to this ranking improved performance, low absenteeism and turnover, and high employee satisfaction.

The grid allows for a total of 81 different 'mixes' with managers being encouraged to aim for a 9.9 ideal score. Blake and Mouton produced a self-assessment questionnaire which is widely used in leadership training to assess a leader's dominant concerns. You may like to consider where you would be likely to fall on the grid and the methods you could use to aim for 9.9 leadership! You may also like to note the grid's similarity to Figures 4.1.7 and 4.1.8.

Contingency theories

Contingency theories argue that no single facet of leadership can be held to result in effective leadership. Rather, leadership has a complex set of variables which interact at different times. This links with modern theories of motivation. The identified variables include:

- the individual leader and his/her personality, past experiences, expectations, values and abilities
- the style of management which predominates in the organisation and the leader's own 'most favoured' style
- the expectations and beliefs of senior managers and, in particular, the leader's own line manager
- the culture, ethos and structure of the organisation; e.g. whether it is bureaucratic, formal and hierarchical or task-based, informal or a professional group with a leader who is 'first among equals'
- the type of jobs being carried out and degree of skills, professionalism or autonomy of team members
- the skills, training, intelligence, needs, expectations and motivation of the subordinates
- the authority, influence and power of the leader
- the relationship between the leader and the group, past history and perceptions of the leader.

Different theories have concentrated on different variables but have generally determined that the most successful style of leadership is usually democratic, but that a different style may be more effective in another situation.

In many cases, individuals will be influenced by their perceptions of the leader and the degree to which he/she is considered capable of meeting their personal and group needs as well as furthering organisational objectives. Factors which will be considered, sometimes subconsciously, include reliability, honesty and commitment, the leader's need to please senior managers, and the leader's personal ambitions. You should remember that people often act in accordance with their own beliefs and perceptions rather than objectively analyse the situation. For that reason, assumptions may be made in haste or without conclusive evidence, yet a consensus is likely to emerge based upon these assumptions.

THEORY INTO PRACTICE

Details of several contingency theories can be found in a variety of management books. Research one or two of the following to improve your knowledge of leadership and your own potential abilities as a leader who can motivate his/her staff.

- Hersey and Blanchard's Situational Leadership/Responsible Follower Theory/Life Cycle Model (all different titles for the same theory!)
- Feidler's Contingency Theory (Least Preferred Co-Worker)
- Path–Goal Theory (Evans and House, and House and Dessler)
- The Vroom and Yetton or Vroom and Jago contingency model
- Attribution theory – Green and Mitchell.

The role of delegation

A final consideration for all those involved with scheduling and organising administrative work is the role of delegation and motivation. If a good leader is an important aspect of motivation, then so too is an interesting job and the ability to achieve our personal goals and ambitions. However, to achieve these we need the self-confidence to develop our abilities by continually moving into unknown territory. Goals and ambitions – as well as self-confidence – vary greatly amongst individuals. The majority need to be motivated by someone who believes in their ability to achieve greater heights, has the confidence to raise their awareness and support them in their efforts, and has the skill to reassure when the going is rough and offer constructive and useful advice. This calls for inner confidence and a considerable degree of self-worth on the part of the mentor or leader – as one who feels insecure will constantly feel threatened by the success of others.

Staff abilities can be stretched and developed through progressive and sensitive delegation. Delegation has already been discussed on pages 222–225 from the perspective of allocating work activities. This section considers its benefits for staff morale and to improve staff motivation and performance.

For delegation to succeed there must be a culture which encourages development and initiative through ongoing support and encouragement. Mistakes must be treated as 'learning experiences' rather than as a good opportunity for finding fault! However, mistakes can be minimised if delegation is properly planned. This means considering:

- the work available
- the time available for guidance/training
- the existing skills of the person who will receive the work
- your own job
- your own attitude!

Delegating effectively means adhering to some broad guidelines so that success is, as far as possible, built into the delegation process. Other key considerations include the following:

- The delegated tasks must be appropriate for the staff member selected, in terms of both scope and responsibility. Delegation is *not* a method of getting rid of tasks you do not want to do!
- The selected staff member should be carefully briefed on what, exactly, is involved. A check should be made that the instructions have

been clearly understood. (The more junior the member of staff, the more specific the directions must be.)

- Authority must also be delegated, so that everyone concerned knows that this particular person has the responsibility to carry out the task and the authority to make the necessary organisational arrangements.
- Control and monitoring of progress should be carried out. This should not be so tight the employee feels that he/she cannot make a move without permission, neither should all queries or feedback sessions be treated as a nuisance. A good balance is to use the *management by exception* principle of 'go with it as far as you can, let me know if you have any problems' – but this will depend upon the personal temperament of the person concerned and his or her 'risk-taking' tendencies. It is useful to specify boundaries clearly so that the person knows the degree to which freedom of action is approved and the areas which would be outside this remit.
- Training should be given where necessary so that the person can cope with the task.
- Do not overload a willing workhorse.
- Good communication is vital at all stages, so that
  - clear instructions are given and received
  - all other staff are also informed, so they know about the change in responsibility
  - monitoring is undertaken with tact and sensitivity
  - feedback is positive and the employee is encouraged to do his or her best.
- Leave the person to get on with the job. It is important for the employee's confidence that he/she is left alone to some degree. Those who believe in their staff can often achieve great things!

THEORY INTO PRACTICE

1 List the jobs you currently undertake.
2 Add any jobs you *should* do but currently don't because you are too busy.
3 Extract any you cannot delegate for *good reason*; e.g. confidentiality, knowledge required, authority essential.
4 Rearrange the remaining jobs in order of importance.
5 Check the time it takes (roughly) to complete each task *properly*.
6 Draw a line under the last task you would have time to do.
7 All remaining tasks are possible areas for delegation.

Now think of the best person to whom to delegate them, bearing in mind existing capabilities *and potential*. Then think of how to broach the topic with that particular person. Bear in mind that this should be different for the person who lacks confidence and the person who has been desperate for a challenge for the past six months. A different approach again is required for the over-confident, plus a far more watchful eye.

Consequences of inadequate consultation and interaction with colleagues

The consequences of neglecting to consult people or not interacting with colleagues will range from zero to catastrophic, depending upon the issue involved, the individual concerned, their position in relation to your own, and the situation.

The issue involved

Although consultation is usually beneficial, you should have noted already that spurious consultation is useless. There are also occasions when, because of speed, technical content or other important factors a decision has to be made and implemented without consultation. If this is perceived as reasonable in the circumstances and is communicated properly there are usually few problems. What people detest, however, is someone taking a high-handed approach on an issue upon which they could have made a valuable contribution or which will personally and profoundly affect them. If the issue falls within an individual's *zone of indifference*, therefore, you are on fairly safe ground. Even if it does not, provided there is a good, well-communicated reason for an exception to have been made in this case, the explanation may be accepted without argument. This is certainly the case if you are wise enough to sell the benefits rather than the problems! If, however, you have ridden roughshod over people's feelings and ignored their contributions, not only are you in danger of having made the wrong decision and therefore taken incorrect action, you are also likely to have upset a number of people.

The individual involved

Even if you frustrate and irritate someone to a considerable extent, the result can vary. One person may shout and rave, another may say nothing, another may ask to have a quiet word with you. In the same way, if you do not interact with your colleagues, one may shrug it off and ignore you in return, while another may be deeply hurt. You have already read enough about individual differences in this chapter to understand why.

On a practical note, you ignore at your peril the assistance and contributions which can be made by your colleagues at all levels. Quite apart from neglecting their (and your) social needs, you risk demotivating staff and making them hesitant to contribute even when you desperately need their help. You also ignore the possibility of receiving a variety of opinions and suggestions from a broader range of viewpoints and a wider range of experiences than your own.

Their position in relation to your own

At the start of this chapter you read about role sets and 'significant others'. Obviously, neglecting those who play a key role in your working life is far more hazardous than overlooking those who do not. Ignoring your immediate boss is foolhardy, discounting your immediate colleagues is both thoughtless and unwise, and disregarding your subordinates is cruel.

If you fail to consult and interact then eventually you will be the cause of your own errors or someone else's mistake – as they will not receive information they need to do their jobs properly. Whilst the reaction may depend upon the person and the degree of error involved, you are hardly likely to be popular if you cause this sort of problem!

The situation

There will be occasions when you reflect, with the wisdom of hindsight, that you could have done more to have consulted your colleagues or interacted with them. However, most people can understand and forgive such behaviour provided there is a history of good relations, a reason for the lapse and an acknowledgement or apology as well. Therefore, if you have personal problems, are fraught with overwork, had a critical deadline to meet or quite simply forgot – but admitted it – then it is unlikely working relations will be strained for long, if at all. Key factors here are respect and trust. If you treat all people – at all levels – with the degree of respect you wish them to give you, and if they know that they can trust you to consider their interests as well as the interests of the organisation as a whole, you are likely to foster good working relations with your colleagues throughout your working life.

THEORY INTO PRACTICE

In addition to the variables given above, other issues come into play if you neglect to consult or interact with a *team* of people. Given that your relations are likely to involve both individuals and teams, consider the *different* effects which may result from this situation.

Legal and regulatory requirements relating to working relationships

The law impacts on working relationships in several areas, with the result that most enlightened organisations have a variety of systems and procedures to ensure that the behaviour of individuals in these areas is kept within predetermined limits to avoid costly legal actions. The major areas relate to:

- grievance and disciplinary procedures and actions
- discrimination and harassment
- defamation
- record-keeping.

In addition, the European Social Chapter and European rights laws also relate to the working conditions of employees. Whereas Britain originally negotiated an opt-out from the Social Policy Agreement (Social Chapter) in 1991, this position has been reversed by the Labour government. The Chapter does not enforce legislation but does allow the participating member states to pass new laws by majority vote. Only two directives are currently in force.

- The first gives employees the right to 12 weeks of unpaid parental leave to look after children aged 8 years and under.
- The second establishes the right to works councils in multinational companies employing more than 1000 people and with more than 150 employees in two member states. A works council comprises a committee of employees which management must 'inform and consult' on issues of international significance. The minimum number of members is three (most comprise about 25) and the council must meet at least once a year. However, the councils have no right of veto on management action. Many companies have acted ahead of legislation and already set up works councils – including NatWest, Barclays, British Telecom, ICI, PepsiCo, Marks & Spencer, BP and McDonald's.

The Labour government also plans to give British judges the right to overrule government decisions if they breach fundamental human rights enshrined in the European Convention on Human Rights – rather than plaintiffs having to take their case to the European Court in Strasbourg.

> The working-time directive, which limits working hours to 48 per week, apart from in exceptional cases, is part of a Health and Safety Directive and *not* the Social Chapter. By the end of 1997, this directive will also give employees the right to three weeks' paid holiday. At the time of writing, the Labour government also plans to set up a Low Pay Commission to set a national minimum wage for all workers.

Grievance and disciplinary procedures

You have already read much about conflict. However effective individuals may be in handling such situations, standard procedures are required to control the way in which any escalation of conflict is handled. The aim is to ensure that, so far as is possible, a fair and equitable process exists for all employees and managers, with the ground rules known by all at the outset.

Grievance procedures – the facts

Grievance procedures are established to deal with formal employee complaints. Most are concerned with three broad areas – money (e.g. mistakes in the calculation of pay), work issues (e.g. a change in job content) and discriminatory or unfair treatment. There are usually three stages in a grievance procedure:

1 An interview at departmental level, usually with the line manager, with the individual accompanied by a person of his/her own choosing.
2 An interview at the next level of management, usually outside the department. This may involve a joint committee of both union and management representatives.
3 An interview with a third party such as ACAS (the Advisory, Arbitration and Conciliation Service) if the grievance procedure allows for this.

Individuals who feel they are unfairly dismissed or feel they were constructively dismissed (i.e. forced to resign) have the right to take the case to an industrial tribunal for a decision. Even then, this may not be the end of the matter if the issue is taken to the Courts of Appeal or even to the European Court of Justice.

Unless you are directly involved with a particular grievance, or work at managerial level, it is likely that the matter will be taken out of your hands once a formal complaint has been made. However, if you have been involved with the issue *at any point*, those dealing with the grievance will be reliant upon you for information relating to the problem. It will assist the process – and your own line manager – considerably if you have kept proper records and if you have acted with integrity throughout.

Grievance procedures – the reality

Employees who instigate grievance procedures are formally presenting a complaint relating to a particular issue or area where they perceive themselves to be dissatisfied. However, many employees with a genuine grievance never enter into formal proceedings and some who do so may have an underlying motive or hidden agenda for taking action. At the other end of the scale, some managers who attempt to behave with probity at all times may find, to their horror, that action has been taken against them whereas others, who appear to fly in the face of justice repeatedly, are never challenged or asked to account for their actions.

The reasons for this involve the complex make-up of individuals. A person who feels vulnerable and who has specialist (or few) skills will be unlikely to enter into formalised proceedings, particular if he/she values 'the quiet life' and has a high need for job security. People will be discouraged, too, if the manager appears to be all-powerful or seems to have covered his/her position very cleverly.

Managers, too, vary in their attitude towards grievances and therefore in their way of handling them. An autocratic, authoritarian manager who has little time for complaints or who escalates minor dissatisfactions into reasons for a major clampdown is likely to manage a section seething with repressed grievances. Individuals will seek to leave – even those whose expertise and skills will be sadly missed. The risk is that group dissatisfaction can easily escalate into industrial action.

Managers who view complaints and problems as an issue rather than as personal criticism are likely to investigate the cause more effectively and to identify the best solution more quickly. This is important as speed should be the essence when dealing with complaints and grievances. The longer a problem festers, the more each side is likely to become entrenched. Relationships will be strained, particularly between individual and manager – the individual becoming progressively more defensive and the manager often feeling personally vulnerable until the issue is formally clarified.

It is also worth noting that grievance procedures cannot, in themselves, provide fairness and justice if this does not exist in reality. If, for instance, there are different requirements of different sectors of the workforce, or if it is tacitly accepted that managers can operate with few controls upon their behaviour, then having a formal grievance procedure in place can do no more than ease the symptoms, rather than address the root cause of the problem.

There is a substantial difference between being worried about job security and having nothing to lose – as many organisations have found to their cost. Between 1989 and 1996 there was a threefold increase in unfair dismissal cases taken to industrial tribunal – from 29 304 applications to 91 568, with hearings rising by 176 per cent as fewer cases are settled privately or simply dropped. Reasons put forward for this increase include a greater awareness of legal rights and the existence of tribunals, greater freedom for lawyers to advertise their services, and more employees who, because of fundamental job insecurity, aim to get what they can, when they can.

Disciplinary procedures – the facts

In this case, it is the employer who is taking action because an employee has breached the terms of his or her contract of employment. Most organisations use the procedures recommended by ACAS in its code of practice, *Disciplinary Practice and Procedures in Employment*. This code of practice recommends that disciplinary procedures should be formal and in writing, and employers must ensure that everyone has access to a copy. The procedures must also specify:

- what disciplinary action may be taken
- the level of management that has the authority to take such action
- that the employee should have the opportunity to defend his/her position against any complaints
- that no disciplinary action should be taken without a full investigation
- that no employee is dismissed for a single incident unless it is gross (very serious) misconduct
- that the employee should be provided with a right of appeal against any disciplinary action.

It is usual for a disciplinary procedure to comprise three stages – a verbal warning (for a minor offence); a written or final warning (for a serious offence or repeated minor offence); suspension, demotion, transfer or dismissal for a gross offence. Summary or instant dismissal occurs when an employee's contract is terminated without notice for gross breach of expected behaviour. Normally, however, dismissal takes place only when all the other options have been exhausted – and there is still an appeals procedure to the top level of management. Usually, however, the first stage is a disciplinary interview, held promptly after the offence, to check on the validity of the claims and give the employee the opportunity to put forward his or her case.

Disciplinary procedures – the reality

Disciplinary procedures are the stick to encourage compliance, rather than the carrot. Whilst their use may be essential in extreme cases, where every other method has been tried and exhausted, the reality is that most people who are disciplined rarely recover from the experience and the majority bear a long-term grudge. Moreover, disciplinary procedures have been found to be notably unsuccessful in achieving their objective of changing or modifying behaviour. A survey by Huddersfield University, *The Disciplinary Experience and its Effects on Subsequent Behaviour*, found that, out of the 104 people surveyed, only 25 per cent were committed to changing their behaviour. Forty-five per cent thought they might break the rules again, and 30 per cent grudgingly felt that they would have to conform. This is likely to result in employees then being more concerned with performing to the letter of their contract rather than the spirit. In many cases, the Huddersfield study found that rules were broken because workers perceived that they existed for the benefit of management and that most people considered action had been taken against them because of personal motives by a supervisor.

The danger is that unethical organisations can use disciplinary procedures as a cheap alternative to redundancy. People can be disciplined, dismissed and then left to take their chances in a tribunal. Even though 38 per cent of claims were upheld in 1996, there are few ex-employees who would want to return to work for the organisation after such an experience – therefore the organisation can use this as a means to downsize its workforce.

In contrast, organisations that value the contributions of their employees will recommend a range of strategies to persuade employees to comply, such as immediate feedback, a mild rebuke (often termed 'there and then' authority), a restatement of the required behaviour *together with the reason*, full consideration of the problem, the individual situation and the alternatives before any warnings are issued. If the proceedings do become formalised then the style and length of the hearing are also important if the outcome is to be successful. The Huddersfield survey found that when hearings were 10 minutes in length the employee remained cynical. Only when hearings lasted an hour or more, the manager had acted with sensitivity, and the issue had been discussed fully with the person identifying his/her own future conduct and owning the problem, was it likely that the employee would leave feeling satisfied.

ACAS has published a small business series which includes information about disciplinary procedures. It is called *Getting it Right*. If you are interested, contact ACAS for a copy or obtain one from your library.

THEORY INTO PRACTICE

Not everyone reacts positively to even the mildest rebuke. Those classified as amongst the most difficult to deal with include:

- the uncommunicative, who refuse to say a word
- the tearful, who can turn on the tears as easily as the tap
- the aggressive, who believe that attack is the best form of defence.

Consider how you would cope with each one, assuming that you think you have a legitimate cause for complaint.

Discrimination and harassment

The law in relation to discrimination and equal pay has been discussed in earlier chapters. However, it is important to note that discrimination can occur as an ongoing condition in a workplace – either accidentally or deliberately – and that, in addition, workplace relations will be affected if any form of harassment is tolerated. This is quite apart from the expense of any legal settlements emanating from such situations.

Discrimination

The three areas in which legal action can be taken relate to sex, race and disabilities. However, despite the fact that, in the case of the first two, legislation has now been in place for several years, many organisations still have practices and procedures which can be classed as discriminatory. As an example, an EOC study in 1996 showed that women are still paid on average 20 per cent less than men – despite the fact that equal pay legislation has been in existence for 20 years. Other current issues include the following:

- Men are twice as likely to be offered a company perk as a woman (from share options to company cars to non-contributory pensions).
- Paternity leave requests are increasing with more than 50 per cent of British male white-collar workers now demanding more flexible working arrangements.
- The Commission for Racial Equality has launched a *Racial Equality Means Business* initiative, aimed at ending discriminatory employment policies by the year 2002. It is focusing on the advantages for business of managing diversity, using people's talents to the full, and identifying and valuing the different qualities ethnic minority employees can bring to their jobs.

However, whereas such issues relate to company policies, on a day-to-day basis relationships are more likely to be affected by individual attitudes and the culture of the workplace. If tolerance is lacking and diversity ignored, then relationships are likely to permeated with misunderstandings, prejudice and bias. This will not only lead to mistrust and bitterness but may also lead to cases of sexual or racial harassment.

The Disability Discrimination Act 1995 has been on the statute books for a far shorter time and many issues relating to this legislation still need clarification. However, it is important to note that the Act does not refer just to new employees but also to existing staff. Discrimination occurs when a disabled person is treated less favourably than other employees when this cannot be justified and when an employer fails to comply with a duty of 'reasonable adjustment' to a disabled person. This can include modifying job content or procedures for those who are already disabled or those who become disabled while they are employed, such as from diabetes, epilepsy, as the result of a stroke or an accident or because of physical impairment of their faculties. The tasks and duties they carry out may have to be reviewed, their working environment may need to be modified or their working hours changed. Moreover, the employer is legally bound to support the employee during a period of readjustment, including rehabilitation, training and by supplying specialist equipment or modifying existing facilities.

Legal changes have reduced discrimination against part-time workers, giving them the same statutory employment rights as full-timers. Therefore, since September 1994, excluding part-time staff from occupational pension schemes is classed as indirect discrimination. Although the UK originally opted out of EU plans to make equal treatment of part-timers mandatory, in some instances European law does allow part-timers to use Article 119 (i.e. equal pay for work of equal value) in order to claim equality of treatment.

However, a new European-wide agreement, destined eventually for inclusion in the Social Chapter, will guarantee equal rights on a pro-rata basis for all part-timers in areas such as pay, pensions and working conditions.

In the meantime, the Trades Union Congress is concerned that unscrupulous employers are deliberately paying staff below the National Insurance lower earnings limit (LEL) to avoid paying National Insurance, and are arbitrarily sacking workers just before they have two years' service and therefore qualify for protection against unfair dismissal. If you work part-time, or supervise part-time staff and are uncertain of the current situation, obtain a copy of the leaflet *Your Choice, Your Rights* by writing to the TUC at Congress House, Great Russell Street, London WC1B 3LS.

Harassment

The law does not define harassment on the basis of either sex or race, although both forms of harassment are an offence. The nearest definition is obtained by applying EC Recommendations which describe it as 'unwanted conduct of a sexual [or racial] nature'. It is therefore any *unwelcome* behaviour. This means that if someone perceives a remark or action to be unwanted or offensive this is sufficient – regardless of the opinion of other people. Furthermore, one act of harassment is sufficient to bring a legal action, as occurred in the case of *Insitu Cleaning Company Ltd v Heads*, where the son of the two directors (husband and wife) made an offensive sexual remark to a mature female secretary when she entered a meeting.

The tribunals have taken the view that it is the responsibility of the employer to take steps to prevent harassment provided it occurs in a situation in which the employer can be expected to have control. This also means that if an incident occurs, the employer is expected to take all reasonable steps to prevent its continuance.

Settlements have been increasing both in quantity and in value. In recent cases a policewoman was awarded £19 000 for racial taunts by a fellow police officer and a female firefighter was awarded £200 000 in an out-of-court settlement for sexual harassment and discrimination.

However, many experts are concerned that employers are still not putting the right procedures in place even after losing a harassment case at a tribunal. A 'zero tolerance' strategy should be adopted, with new employees informed of their rights at induction. Clear examples should be given of the type of behaviour that is unacceptable and a variety of alternative reporting routes made available to all staff. Managers who receive complaints should act promptly to investigate the substance of the complaint as well as having access to expert guidance. Steps should be taken to ensure that there can be no recurrence and, where necessary, company policies should be reviewed. Quite simply, it is both more cost-effective and more humane to spend money on preventing problems in this area than paying a lawyer to defend a claim or to settle a claim in court.

WASH (Women Against Sexual Harassment) exists to help victims (both male and female) who are concerned about harassment at work. The charity will train employers but mainly concentrates on giving advice or legal assistance to victims. It cannot, however, help with legal costs. Many victims, for instance, are unaware that they must apply to an industrial tribunal within three months of the last incident or dismissal or resignation arising from the incident. WASH operates a helpline on 0171 405 0430.

Defamation

Defamation relates to making statements about a person which could 'lower him or her in the eyes of right-thinking people'. If you write something defamatory you may therefore be accused of libel; if you communicate something verbally which is defamatory you may be accused of slander. There are, however, certain defences, which are discussed in more detail in Chapter 5, page 430. You should note that in cases of defamation it is the words, rather than the medium, which determine whether defamation has taken place. This was discovered the hard way by Asda after a store detective circulated details on its internal bulletin board in 1995, suggesting a particular person was a shoplifter. Whether the company is responsible again depends upon whether the wrong was done in the course of the employer's business or not. It is also worth noting that by law, e-mail is treated as the published word in libel cases. This is despite the fact that e-mail may be worded very informally or even sent as a joke.

The key point to note is that starting or spreading malicious gossip – by whatever means – could result in action against you or your employer.

A decision in the House of Lords in the case of *Spring v Guardian Assurance* changed the law on references, as it was held that an employer can be held liable for negligence in the preparation of a reference. As a result, most organisations have reviewed their procedures in this area – forbidding 'off-the-cuff' remarks made by telephone or fax and ensuring that all written references contain a disclaimer clause. If you are involved in writing references for staff, be certain you follow the guidelines or you may be held liable for proving the accuracy of anything you write or say.

Record-keeping

The Data Protection Act 1984 relates to information held on computer. The Data Protection Directive, which comes into effect on 24 October 1998, gives employees access to paper files held on them – at reasonable intervals and without excessive cost or delay. The Data Protection Registrar considers that there should be no charge for accessing the information and a reasonable time expectation may be 40 days – which is the current period in force under the Data Protection Act for computerised information. It is thought likely that employees will ask to see personal files that relate to areas such as their performance appraisals, any grievance they pursue, any disciplinary procedures with which they are involved. This means that all comments which have been written in the file will be open to perusal – and employers could be subject to legal action if negligence can be proved.

Employers will still be able to use certain defences to deny access to information, primarily under Article 13(g) of the Directive, such as details of wage and redundancy negotiations or plans for promotion or demotion. In addition, it is unlikely people will be able to see their own health records if the revelation will be harmful to their physical or mental health – similar to the precautions which currently apply under the Data Protection Act.

However, the message for organisations and senior administrators is clear. Paper records, as well as computerised records, will be open to scrutiny by employees from 1998. A careless word or phrase, written in haste, could be read at leisure, at best souring a productive working relationship forever, and at worst resulting in legal action. See also Chapter 5, page 449.

THEORY INTO PRACTICE

1 Your organisation has recently revised its policies on sexual and racial harassment and now has strict sanctions against any employee who is found guilty of either offence. You have an older – extremely effective – worker in your section with a relatively intransigent attitude whom you suspect to be prejudiced in both areas. What action would you take and why?

2 Obtain a copy of your organisation's disciplinary and grievance procedures and check you are familiar with each. If you can, compare this with your colleagues' perceptions of how grievances and disciplinary matters are handled within the organisation.

3 You have a colleague who has become hard of hearing as he has become older. Bearing in mind the Disability Discrimination Act, what action would you take to ensure that you make 'reasonable adjustments' for the disability?

Element 4.2

Establish and maintain productive working relationships with contacts external to the organisation

For a long time it has been held that the British appear to have a paradoxical attitude towards customer relations. This is demonstrated by the fact that, whilst they expect or demand high-quality service and high-quality products themselves, many people consider it rather undignified to offer such service to other people. Indeed, a recent study found that UK business is still rated highest on management skills and brand development but lowest on exceeding customer expectations. In other words, the average British organisation is often failing to provide even adequate customer service. If you find this argument offensive or object to its accuracy, then it is interesting to make some direct comparisons.

- On the Continent, being a waiter or a barperson is considered a skilled profession – particularly in a prestigious hotel or restaurant. One barperson in Switzerland *advertised* by stating how many cocktails he could make and how many customers he could simultaneously serve and keep happy. In America, barpeople *pride themselves* on remembering your 'regular order' so that, after the first time, you never have to repeat yourself!

- In the United States it is automatic to have someone offer to wipe your windscreen and check your tyres when you stop for fuel. In a café, bar or restaurant you pay for coffee and are offered as many free refills as you want. Scrupulous cleanliness and rapid removal of used dishes is considered absolutely essential. And whilst the phrase 'have a nice day' may grate on your nerves after a while, it is far better than a frown, a scowl, lack of interest or downright irritation at having to break off from some other task to serve you.

- At Disneyland in the States and in Paris the staff are trained to regard litter as a major cause of customer disaffection. They don't just take note of this philosophy but internalise it as part of the raison d'être of their jobs. There is no doubt in their view that 'keeping the park clean' is just as important as keeping the rides safe or introducing new ones. In addition, 'delighting' the customer or enhancing the customer experience is considered to be a vital component of *every* person's job – from Financial Director to car park attendant!

The point is not that there are more services on offer or that more services are free – even if this is sometimes the case. The point is that the *attitude* of *all* employees in relation to anticipating and satisfying customer needs is different. Until, and unless, you are prepared to view this attitude as an essential attribute rather than an unseemly chore, then you will never be able to take on board the real importance and value of developing and maintaining customer relations. This will affect your external contacts, your colleagues and your staff – as well as your own operational efficiency. All your contacts live in a competitive world and have every right to expect the best you can deliver – just as you, too, have the right to expect the best service in return. They can rightfully expect you to consider their needs, to consult them about their views and to take action to improve both products and service continuously. Bob Ayling, Chief Executive of British Airways, highlighted the importance of this philosophy when he was recently quoted as saying 'We're driven by customers, we're driven by the markets in which we do our business. If we don't understand what people want and don't, so far as we can, deliver what they want we'll lose our business. So we're always asking people what their reaction is to the service we offer.'

Relationship marketing is one of today's buzz phrases. Instead of adopting the traditional marketing approach of concentrating on attracting new customers, relationship marketing focuses on an *ongoing relationship* and *regular interaction* with customers which gives at least as much, if not more, prominence to retaining existing customers as it does to attracting new customers. Moreover it expands the framework of 'customers' to include suppliers, internal customers and even prospective employees – which links to the 'stakeholder' perspective of organisations. It unites the different disciplines of marketing, quality and customer service into an integrated whole which combines to affect the whole operation of the organisation – rather than seeing customer service as merely an adjunct to the marketing area. It places the focus on the customer as the key source of essential information and feedback on all aspects of the operation (see Figure 4.2.1). This is not only sensible but essential if companies are to survive and prosper in today's highly competitive world.

This approach is taken throughout this element to underline the importance of developing and sustaining productive working relationships with external contacts.

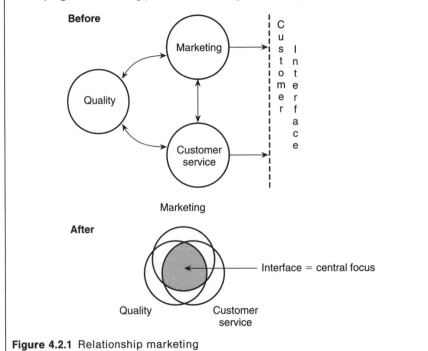

Figure 4.2.1 Relationship marketing

Contacts' work roles and responsibilities

Although you may deal with a variety of stakeholders, this section is concerned with those who supply you with goods and services and those to whom you provide goods and services – in other words, your suppliers and your customers. There is one simple brief for any staff who deal with suppliers and customers:

The more you know and understand the roles and responsibilities of your contacts, the philosophy, ethos and culture of their organisation, and the problems and difficulties they face, the more effective you will be in responding to their needs and the greater likelihood of consistently getting it 'right first time'.

This translates into:

- being able to form mutually beneficial and supportive relationships with all external contacts
- negotiating collaborative agreements with suppliers
- improving the retention rate of existing customers
- impressing and delighting new customers
- staying one step ahead of your competitors
- increasing profits and job security.

Knowing more about your contacts is nothing to do with being inquisitive or interfering in aspects of their work that don't concern you. It has everything to do with understanding more accurately the problems and constraints under which other people operate, knowing their strengths and weaknesses, identifying the issues *they* consider are important in the relationship, and being able to negotiate more flexible and mutually beneficial agreements.

One theory suggests that both staff and organisations can be classed as outward-facing or inward-facing. Outward-facing personnel are those who are mainly involved in dealing with stakeholders outside the company – particularly customers. Inward-facing personnel are those more concerned with the internal operations of the organisation, such as personnel, finance, computer services.

However, from the relationship marketing viewpoint, everyone in the organisation operates in a chain and supporting structure which involves both suppliers and customers (see Figure 4.2.2). The chain is supported by all the internal operations of the company. If *any part* of the chain or its support structure is weak, then the final result for the customer will not be in accordance with his/her expectations. If problems in the chain are exacerbated by bureaucratic management, ineffective systems and procedures and poorly trained staff, the eventual outcome is far short of the ideal and considerably removed from customer expectations.

Organisational culture/ethos					
Management philosophy/style					
Supplies	Goods inward	Operations	Logistics distribution	Sales and marketing	Customers
Customer service					
Finance and accounting					
Purchasing					
Human resources					
Computer services					

Figure 4.2.2 The relationship marketing chain and support structure

THEORY INTO PRACTICE

Take the daily routine test. Over the next day, estimate how many jobs you do, phone calls and e-mails you receive, and callers you deal with that are *externally focused* and how many are *internally focused*. Then see which way you – and your organisation – are currently facing.

Relationships with suppliers

Traditionally, the British approach to suppliers was *adversarial* – pitting the wits of one supplier against another to try to get the 'best deal'. This style of buying usually incorporated:

- a centralised purchasing facility
- 'shopping around' to get the best terms
- ordering through paper documentation in adequate time for stocks to be received
- storing stock until needed.

In most enlightened organisations this approach has changed dramatically over the past 20 years. Centralised purchasing is often seen as an unnecessary expense, so today the buying of most goods is undertaken by individual cost centres – or even contracted out for some items. In some cases there may be a list of recommended suppliers, in others a free choice is allowed provided the purchase is within budget. The merits of changing suppliers regularly have been contrasted with the benefits to be gained by developing a network of dependable suppliers, prepared to guarantee quality and delivery in return for some security of tenure; in other words, exchanging the previously adversarial style for a *collaborative* approach where the supplier feels he/she has a positive role to play. In many cases this has enabled organisations to introduce 'just-in-time' systems to reduce stocks held, and this in turn has been facilitated by the introduction of electronic data interchange (EDI) which allows goods to be ordered, invoiced and paid for electronically. Tesco, for instance, uses EDI to process the vast majority of its invoices and payments and expects goods to be delivered promptly, as and when they are needed. Using this approach, quality can be built in to the product and controlled at the design and supply stage. This is just as crucial for Marks & Spencer, who wish to retain their reputation in the marketplace, as it is for Philips, who are involved in assembling optical disk players from components which must be produced to very tight tolerance specifications.

This type of relationship can be defined as a collaborative arrangement between two organisations with the aim of securing mutual benefits through the reduction of unstable and unpredictable forces. Both organisations are formally independent although the power relationship between the two can vary. This varies according to the degree of *equality* between the two and the degree to which one organisation is *dependent* upon the other.

- There may be high dependency by a small supplier on a large organisation (e.g. vegetable producers supplying large supermarkets, clothing producers supplying large chain stores). In this case, if the supplier loses the contract it could well go out of business. This gives the buyer the ability to dictate precise terms for delivery, quality and price. Some buying organisations insist on full disclosure of the suppliers' accounts to check no excess profits are being made.
- There may be high dependency by a large organisation upon a small supplier that produces highly specialised goods or a technical service.
- There may be low dependency by a large supplier on a small company (e.g. Ford is less concerned about supplying company cars to a small trader than to one with 200 representatives and 50 executives).
- There may be equal status – between two large or two small organisations (e.g. Heinz supplying Sainsburys) or in joint ventures between two giants, such as British Aerospace and Airbus Industrie (BAe has a 20 per cent share in Airbus) or between several small organisations (e.g. Spar and Mace grocery outlets).

Wherever possible, organisations operate to reduce dependency as this increases their vulnerability. One method for suppliers is to diversify, as this will often improve their security by expanding their customer base. In Japan, however, many organisations with a power imbalance still operate highly positive and stable relationships mainly because of a different ethos and attitude towards the traditional supplier/buyer function. Rather than dependency being seen as a stick with which to beat the small supplier into submission, it is seen as a mutual benefit. Toyota, which originated the *kanban* system (see also page 165), the forerunner of JIT as we know it, integrated its supplier network to provide a continuous flow of components to their factory with a linked delivery system. Suppliers took it in turns to operate the delivery route through the entire network up to four times a day. Everyone gained from this arrangement.

- Toyota gained because it obtained regular supplies in small quantities up to four times a day from known and trusted suppliers.
- The suppliers could integrate their own production lines with those of Toyota and only had to undertake one drop a day each (though they had to call at other suppliers en route).

The system worked because there was a shared perception of the aims of the scheme, high levels of trust between the participants, and a focus on long-term benefits rather than short-term gains. It is worth noting that Japanese car manufacturers in Britain have attracted satellite suppliers in a very similar way.

If mutual trust helps both suppliers and buyers, then forming strong relationships with known suppliers has obvious benefits. Strategies used to develop such relationships include the following.

- Joint initiatives for the supply of particular goods. Many stationery suppliers, for instance, will undertake not only to supply goods but also to undertake stock control procedures for organisations and provide goods as and when needed (a variation of JIT combined with a contracted-out service).
- Staff exchanges – such as computer personnel who work at the client's premises or technical specialists who become 'partners' in developmental projects.
- Non-executive directorships for key suppliers (including 'supplies' such as finance or legal services).
- Nominated individuals to operate particular accounts and liaise directly with certain suppliers. This usually involves visiting the suppliers' premises at regular intervals – in some cases the individual is actually *located* with the supplier to negotiate on the spot. P. Selznick, in *TVA and the Grass Roots*, termed this *co-option*. Other experts have commented that this allows for *ideological penetration* in that it promotes a greater understanding of the culture and attitudes prevailing in both organisations.

Even if your relationship with your suppliers is far more fundamental than some of the variations described above, one concept is clear. The greater the level of understanding and the more open the communications between those undertaking specific transactions, the greater the likelihood of mutually beneficial undertakings. You should therefore be able to state, for every supplier with whom you are actively involved:

- the name, contact number and status of your opposite number
- his/her remit and extent of authority in negotiations
- the ethos, philosophy and culture of the organisation
- the dependency situation between the two organisations
- the degree of freedom you possess to negotiate key aspects of the contract (e.g. to increase or reduce dependency)
- the areas where you need to set precise specifications – mainly in relation to product type, quality, quantity, price and delivery date

- whether your remit includes the scope to offer financial incentives (or suggest financial penalties) to encourage cooperation
- company policy in relation to supplier relations in general (many or few, self-selected or pre-specified, long-term or short-term contracts), the degree to which collaboration is encouraged, and company policy in relation to issues such as contracting, express terms of contracts, penalty clauses and methods of dealing with poor service or substandard deliveries.

An imbalance of power in favour of the supplier is likely to lead to reduced profits for your own organisation. This is particularly the case if you work for a small organisation that buys essential goods from a large, monopoly supplier (known as a monopsonist) and if there is no direct substitute for the product they provide. This gives you little, if any, bargaining power to negotiate better terms or improved quality.

THEORY INTO PRACTICE

Adversarial relationships are the 'win/lose' outcome of game-playing illustrated in Figure 4.1.7 on page 294 and collaborative relationships equate to a 'win/win' strategy. Collaborative relationships also equate to the 'team management' approach advocated by Blake and Mouton in Figure 4.1.14 on page 323.

From what you read in the previous section, you should be able to identify the type of behaviour and outlook required to achieve this outcome – and the predicted effects of alternative strategies and behaviours by both parties.

Relationships with customers

Your customers are attracted to you because they think that you can provide something they want or need. This implies firstly that they have received information on your products or services (although the depth of their knowledge and interest will be variable) and that they have made some effort to contact you (or vice versa). They may have purchased from you in the past, been satisfied with the transaction and therefore want to repeat the experience. At this point you should note that the relationship will come to an end, at any point, if the customer finds that:

- you can no longer satisfy a need (i.e. you no longer provide the product or service he/she requires)
- someone else can better satisfy the need
- after contacting you (either to make an enquiry or to buy the item) the customer is disappointed with the encounter.

A key word is *perception*. Your perception of your customer's satisfaction with your product and your service is almost irrelevant. It is the customer's expectations and perception of satisfaction that affect future actions – not yours. This aspect of the relationship is developed further on pages 354–362.

A number of techniques can be used by organisations to determine their market, to plan to meet future market requirements, to target individual segments of the market, and to try to become more familiar with the individual needs and wants of their customers. There are many models of customer behaviour aimed at identifying the factors that interact to make customers want to purchase your product or service in the first place (see page 381). However, the bottom line is that whether your organisation sells to business organisations, private consumers or both, it is the *day-to-day* service and support that can make or break the relationship. W. E. Deming talked about 'delighting the customer', Tom Peters goes one step further and talks of 'loving the customer'. This does not mean just front-line staff who have day-to-day contact with customers, but also all those in the organisation support network who facilitate the work of outward-facing employees by giving them the information and assistance they need to satisfy the customer, when they need it and how they need it – see Figure 4.2.2 on page 340.

Learning to love the customer does not mean just being polite and helpful. It means 'getting inside his head' to the point where you can understand and empathise with his needs, identify his strengths and weaknesses, work out how you can *really* help him. This means operating on an individualist basis – the needs of customer A may be quite different from those of customer B. At its best, this means knowing each customer so well that you can build up an identikit for each individual you deal with and can make appropriate recommendations, give advice and assistance, helping each customer to be more effective and – in the case of business organisations – even more profitable. This is the route to indispensability – the more you help your customer to achieve his/her perceived objectives (and identify a few 'as yet to be perceived' as well) the more the customer will benefit from the alliance and the less likely he/she will consider that there are advantages to be gained from going elsewhere.

The role of private consumers

Consumers are not the only participants in buying decisions. The decisions we make as consumers often depend upon the role we adopt when we are buying.

- I may make one decision when I am on my own, buying for myself. In this case my role is buyer/user.
- I may make a different choice if my friend accompanies me and influences my decision.
- I may make a different decision again if I am buying on behalf of someone else (e.g. a present). In this case I am buyer/giver.
- I may buy something entirely different if I am buying on behalf of a group, such as my family or my work organisation.

This behaviour has even been linked with role theory to the extent that, in each situation, I am playing a part in a different 'play' and therefore behave differently. Knowing the role of a person in a particular transaction therefore helps you to give more targeted assistance.

Understanding the consumer has become big business thanks to the development of computerised databases. A huge range of information can be held about individual customers, including *demographic data* (age, sex, family structure, income, social class, occupation, ethnicity etc.) and *psychographic data* which relates to the customer's lifestyle and personality. As an example, supermarkets which operate loyalty schemes not only obtain a considerable amount of data when the customer first registers (and can buy-in other databases to expand the content) but can also track customer purchases to check levels of spending, patterns of spending and preferred products. This not only gives feedback on the success (or otherwise) of individual product lines but also enables targeted mailshots to be sent, for instance, advising customers of special offers relating to products of interest and linked to an individual's lifestyle.

However, concerns have been expressed about the legality of selling database information to other organisations. This is covered on page 389.

THEORY INTO PRACTICE

Consider the systems in place in your own organisation for identifying individual customers and predicting their needs. To what degree is modern technology used – or is the system informal and individual? How effective do you think it is in familiarising employees *at all levels* with the needs of particular customers?

The role of business customers

Business customers vary in their needs in just the same way as individual consumers. However, the buying behaviour of each contact will also be influenced by his/her individual responsibilities, job role and status, the systems in operation to control how purchasing decisions are made, and the influence of others involved in the process. This is why many selling organisations spend much time and money trying to contact the key decision-maker in each purchasing decision. However, often the decision-maker is influenced by others – or may even have to follow the remit of a central committee. In other cases, major buying decisions may have to be approved by a representative group or offers may be acceptable only if they conform to strict tender procedures.

The group of people with the responsibility for making a purchasing decision in an organisation is often known as a *buying centre* or the *decision-making unit* (DMU). The roles of the members, as identified by F. E. Webster and Y. Wind in *Organisational Buying Behaviour*, include the following.

- *Users* – those members of the organisation who will actually use the product or service (e.g. an administrator wanting a new computer). In many cases, the user will have a say in the type of product purchased and its specification. Depending upon his/her status, the user may even initiate the proposal to buy.

- *Influencers* – those employees who can influence the buying decision by defining the specification and providing information to enable a more informed decision to be made. Quite often influencers are technical specialists, such as the computer services person who advises the administrator on the most appropriate computer purchase for his/her needs.
- *Deciders* – the people who make the ultimate decision to buy. They may also have the power to decide which products are required and which suppliers should be used. In the case of our administrator, the decider may be the senior manager who has the authority to decide whether money from the departmental budget should be spent on a new computer.
- *Approvers* – this may be the same person as the decider but, for large amounts of expenditure, it is likely that higher level authority is required. Both buyers and deciders may be subject to authorisation by approvers.
- *Buyers* – the people who have the formal authority to choose the supplier and negotiate the terms of the purchase. For instance, the buying of computers in an organisation may be carried out centrally by a computer manager with in-depth knowledge of product specifications and suitable suppliers.
- *Gatekeepers* – the people who can prevent sales staff and sales information from reaching members of the DMU. They include receptionists and switchboard operators who may prevent sales representatives from contacting users or deciders and central buying staff and administrators, and secretaries who throw sales information into the wastebin unread.

In a small organisation it is likely that one person will have a multifunctional role, that there will be fewer gatekeepers and fewer formal procedures to follow. In a large organisation, it can take a prospective supplier a long time to bypass or overcome the gatekeepers. Even then, unless the person contacted is a decider or buyer, the proposed sale may fail at the last minute because the deal is blocked by an unknown approver. This is yet another reason why existing customers must be retained, fostered and even pampered.

THEORY INTO PRACTICE

1 Consider your external contacts. Identify the roles they play and the degree to which these are influenced or affected by other people.
2 As a basic strategy, what does this examination of roles tell you in relation to the success (or otherwise) of being helpful, pleasant and attentive to the needs of *every* external contact you meet?

Your own work role and responsibilities

A frequent cry from administrators who work in an inward-facing area is that their job is not concerned with external contacts. From the relationship marketing angle, *no-one* in an organisation functions in a job divorced from external contacts! The reason for this is simple and was illustrated in Figure 4.2.2 on page 340.

Another way to view this is to remember that all organisations are in business to process inputs in order to deliver a service or product to a customer. This is illustrated in a simple systems diagram in Figure 4.2.3.

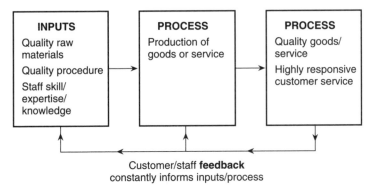

Figure 4.2.3 A simplified systems diagram

However, the processing of the inputs is not restricted to production and the delivering of the outputs is not unique to sales staff. The Finance department delivers a different type of output – that of the final account. Distribution has a key role to play in ensuring the output is in the right place, in the right condition and at the right time. Reception, switchboard and other 'front-line' staff deal with queries regarding the processing of outputs every day. Even those deeply embedded in areas initially presumed to be inward-facing, such as human resources or computer services, have a key responsibility to support those involved in delivering high-quality outputs as and when they are needed. Therefore the whole organisation is seen as being comprised of interdependent individuals, each of whom relies on inputs from other people to do the job properly. And, at the end of the line, the person who is affected (favourably or unfavourably) by the quality of these interrelationships is the customer.

This interdependence is often illustrated by means of a *value chain* which implies that, at each stage of the process, an operation will 'add value' for the customer (see Figure 4.2.4). Moreover, the primary activities in the value chain are highly dependent upon information and cooperation from the support activities of the organisation to achieve their objectives. In other words, inward-facing staff have *internal customers* who must be 'delighted' in order for them to do their job properly with external customers. One executive put this more picturesquely when he said that 'If you're not dealing with a customer, then you'd better be talking to someone who is.'

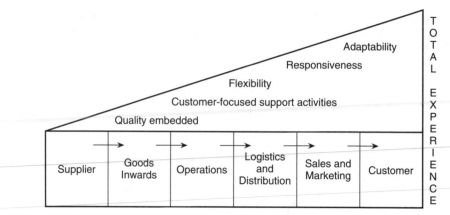

Figure 4.2.4 The concept of value-added

For competitive advantage to be achieved the organisation has two choices:

- It can organise itself to operate more efficiently and more promptly than its competitors, thereby achieving *cost advantage*.
- It can operate in a unique way, giving greater value to the customer, thereby offering *differentiation advantage*.

THEORY INTO PRACTICE

1 Cost advantages through efficient operation have been obvious benefits to supermarkets, which have been able to increase the variety of goods on offer whilst sustaining lower prices. However, as the potential for cost advantages has fallen there has been a race for differentiation advantage – particularly between Tesco and Sainsbury (e.g. loyalty schemes, faster checkouts, packers to assist shoppers, banking services, etc.). In your own organisation, identify the degree to which differentiation advantage has been implemented – or could be implemented.

2 Identify the internal customers who depend upon a rapid and positive response from your section or area to be able to delight their own customers.

3 What single thing, in your view, would enable you to increase the value you add for the customer – and why?

The role and responsibilities of administrators

Senior administrative staff have a particular role to play in the value chain. Firstly, they are involved in supporting their internal customers. Secondly, they may also be involved in handling queries and enquiries from external contacts on a range of issues. Finally, they may have the responsibility of supervising staff who both deal with the customer (or supplier) on a more direct basis and who are also involved in playing a supportive role to other internal customers. It is likely, therefore, that your role extends beyond your individual remit to encompass the behaviour, attitude and performance of other staff for whom you have responsibility which directly affects the quality of the service they provide.

Attitudes to quality have changed over the years, though too few people still 'own' quality as an essential part of their job. It is more likely to be considered 'part of production' or 'part of customer service' – or viewed as an operational technique such as total quality management (TQM). Yet, if high quality is essential to delighting the customer, quality must permeate every aspect of administrative life – from the manner (and speed) of those who answer the telephone, to the appearance of those who interact face-to-face with customers, to the calibre of photocopied or printed material, to the number of errors in a report or on a spreadsheet, to the accuracy of information passed on from one person to another, to the speed at which a file can be found. Many of these aspects concern routine jobs, but if they are mishandled, the consequences affect someone – and at the end of the line there is only the customer.

However, if a problem occurs it would be fallacious to pin most of the blame routinely on office staff or administrators. Studies have found that, in the majority of cases, problems for customers occur because of inadequate or over-elaborate procedures or processes in the organisation and not through negligent staff. If a procedure is faulty this affects the processing efficiency of the organisation – either on an assignable basis (the equipment malfunctions, a person is absent and no-one else can do the job, the information is missing) or on a random and less attributable basis across a whole range of processes (no-one can make a decision, the whole procedure is too lengthy or bureaucratic, the information required isn't anyone's job to collect). In each case, the problem affects *reliability* (of information and service), *speed of responsiveness, flexibility, staff confidence, staff attitudes* (including the ability to be empathetic to the customer's needs) and, inevitably, *customer attitudes*. It is rather like expecting a bus driver to operate effectively and provide good customer service when the bus is creaking along on three cylinders!

For the administrator struggling to cope with these problems it may be of some comfort to know that Deming estimated that 94 per cent of quality problems and opportunities are management's responsibility. On a more practical note, your own role and ability to influence those at managerial level may have dramatic effects. You need to identify the *source* of the difficulty before you try to improve the situation. Often the difficulty can be traced further back in the process than you originally think. It is also useful to be aware that most people have a tendency to blame people first, whereas it is more often the process that is to blame.

(You should note that there are clear links between this approach and the work you will be doing in Chapters 6 and 7 on designing and improving systems and procedures.)

Kaizen is a Japanese word which is used to signify the concept of *continuous improvement*. Its meaning is symbolic – 'from dust we make mountains' – in which case the 'dust' can be considered all types of basic input and resources. The rationale behind *kaizen* is that it is more expensive to make corrections after something has been produced than during creation – therefore it is beneficial to ensure that checks are carried out thoroughly during initial production. This approach is just as relevant to administrative work as it is to production work.

However, another aspect of *kaizen* refers to the importance of contributions from those actively involved in operating any process. Obtaining information from those who are using a system or procedure is the best way to gain new and relevant ideas for continuous improvements. This includes the staff who are involved as well as the customers. British companies are noted for being relatively good at asking the customer for feedback, much less good at asking staff for feedback and suggestions (particularly junior staff), and notoriously poor at doing something positive with the information once they have received it! (See also page 363.)

(See also page 363.)

THEORY INTO PRACTICE

You can identify the degree to which your own organisation provides effective internal support and efficient processing by identifying the degree to which any of the following problems – or similar difficulties – occur.

- At least one department, section, unit or person is considered 'a black hole'.
- Contradictory information is received from different sections or people.
- The ethos is focused more on colleagues and co-workers than on internal customers with important needs.
- The organisation *per se* is continually distracted with satisfying its own needs rather than those of its customers.
- There is no clear assignment of responsibility for certain tasks or duties.
- The effort involved in complying with internal procedures is disproportionate in relation to the outcome.
- To move speedily, you often have to refer the problem upwards
- Some staff operate from an isolationist perspective, far removed from the customer and his/her needs and wants.
- Rigid rules and procedures are in place which imaginative staff must circumvent to satisfy a customer.
- Customer or staff feedback is either unwelcome or ignored.

Now consider how you can effect any improvements, bearing in mind your own job role and your *individual* responsibility for providing value for both your internal and external contacts.

Scope and limit of your own authority relating to external contacts

In all job roles there are two main types of authority. The first is *prescribed authority* – those areas where you have clear, unambiguous authority as part of your job description. The second is *discretionary authority* where, because of the circumstances or situation – or even through 'custom and practice' – you are allowed to operate without obtaining specific approval. Often even these areas can be broadened by other variables relating either to yourself or to the environment. Examples include the amount of experience you have, the degree to which you have developed a trust relationship with your own line manager, the amount of influence or persuasion you have over deciders and approvers, and the degree to which the culture and ethos of the organisation and its procedures constrains (or encourages) individual initiative.

However, regardless of your own perception of your authority, it is always better to err on the side of caution when dealing with external contacts.

- By promising something you heighten customer expectations. The customer is then bound to feel disappointment if you cannot deliver.
- When you are a buyer you are part of your organisation's DMU. If you give the impression of being a decider when you are simply a user, then you will disappoint many people. This can be considered a callous disregard of their time and effort if it is done deliberately or without heed of the consequences.
- In both cases you establish a *credibility gap* between yourself and your contact. You are far less likely to be believed on subsequent occasions. In addition, the reputation of your organisation will have diminished, particularly in the eyes of the customer, who may even lodge a complaint and then take his/her business elsewhere.

If you are unclear on the scope and limit of your authority then it is always wise to check before taking action or making any promises. Depending upon the individual style of your boss, it is also better to assume that any previous freedoms do not constitute a precedent which can then be followed with impunity. When in doubt, check first and action later.

However, there is another side to the coin. If you are always focused on the importance of minimising personal risk and operating cautiously, then you will struggle when faced with an emergency or a sudden opportunity. You will always sorely try the patience of your contacts if you insist that due process must be followed in every transaction in order to cover your own back – and could well lose important business. If you have to make a key decision on your own, then experience and knowledge of your organisation and its processes will help enormously (e.g. how far is risk-taking or entrepreneurship encouraged or discouraged), as will the ability to 'second-guess' your boss. If your objective is always to operate in the best interests of your organisation, then it is unlikely you will go very far wrong.

Whilst the allocation of authority should be rational, progressive and easily justified, it is easy for anomalies to occur. This can happen because of over-prescriptive procedures in some areas but not others, computer systems which have been planned for the benefit of the designer not the user, unclear lines of authority or unclear roles and responsibilities. Over-prescriptiveness – which hampers or strangles flexibility, quick decision-making and instant action – is more likely to occur in large bureaucracies, but unclear lines of authority and roles often occur in small organisations that pride themselves on their *lack* of formalised procedures. This can also happen with rapidly growing organisations or during periods of change or restructuring. A major culprit is often a computer system that delights the designer but takes little account of user needs.

1 Identify your own role in your organisation's DMU for the purchase of
  – routine (low-cost) items
  – expensive capital items
  – office services and support.
  To what extent does the scope and limit of your authority vary in each case?
2 Identify *at least one* substantial commitment you could make to a customer which is within your authority and *at least one* commitment that is not. In the case of the latter, state whether you think this restriction has a justifiable and logical reason and give a reason for your opinion.

Establishing constructive relationships

Relationships take time to develop and trust is essential to more intimate levels of disclosure. This is as true of external contacts as internal contacts. However, external contacts may be more remote, both geographically and socially. In addition, there is the added complication of trying to build a *loyalty bond* in a competitive world. Communication with external contacts may only occasionally be face-to-face and both sides are more likely to exercise caution and a natural reluctance to disclose very much in early negotiations. There are sound reasons for acting in this way. As an example, if an inexperienced buyer were to be very easily impressed by a 'generous' supplier and more than willing to be given favours in return for orders, then he or she could be accused of unethical behaviour and even be subject to disciplinary action. Being too frank with a potential customer is also fraught with danger – given that he or she is under no obligation not to act on it purely in his or her own interests. For that reason, if no other, it is advisable to operate within the remits of a relatively formal and totally professional working relationship.

However, events can occur that result in strengthening of the bond between you and your contact. These can be *time-bound* or *situation-bound* – or a combination of both. Over a period of time, it is natural that with most contacts the level of intimacy and knowledge between the parties will deepen. This can even lead to a situation where the contact wants to deal with only one person in the organisation, because of the strong belief that only that person truly understands his/her position, problems and needs. However, this process can be accelerated if a situation occurs where the level of your relationship deepens through mutual need, as this fosters trust. This may happen, for instance, through a crisis where you help each other (or one helps the other), or where you meet face-to-face in informal surroundings and identify several areas of common interest. Indeed, it is on this type of basis that networks are created! Far from seeing this situation as the outcome of a relationship, Americans see it as a precursor to forming and developing several mutually beneficial relationships, given the value of personal recommendations.

From your own perspective it is important to identify the actions taken to establish and develop a constructive relationship with both suppliers and customers, be they individual consumers or business organisations.

Relationships with suppliers

Relationships with suppliers are built up through mutual trust and mutual benefit. In other words, there should be synergy in that, together, the mutual advantages are greater than the sum of each individual contribution. To a large degree, this means turning the traditional seller/buyer relationship on its head – as both parties benefit from the arrangement. This means not only knowing the supplier but letting the supplier know you! It means building a partnership with a supplier where he/she knows and understands the ethos and philosophy of your organisation, accepts your quality standards without question, will tackle problems with you and has as much interest in investigating damaged or late deliveries as you have. It means allowing your supplier access to your organisation to see how you operate and what makes you 'tick' and why certain needs are paramount. It means allowing the supplier to empathise with you. Such a relationship is not built overnight and is impossible if the organisation takes an adversarial approach. The attitudinal bias of both parties must be towards collaboration and be built on the sharing of mutual goals and the sharing of risks. To consistently play for 'win/win', you must be locked into a long-term commitment. As an example, Marks & Spencer, long renowned for developing good relationships with suppliers, encourages, advises and supports supplier investment in research and development. This has included collaborating to develop a new process to catch, clean and freeze Arctic fish in six hours, and linking with yarn extruders, fabric manufacturers and garment makers to create and use a new fabric for lingerie wear. Northern Foods, M&S's largest food supplier, has even been known to build a new factory on the basis of a handshake – clear evidence of a high-trust relationship.

If such a relationship would be considered laughable in your current organisation, it is worth noting that out of little acorns great oak trees grow! There may be nothing to stop you building up your own network of suppliers with whom you have an excellent working relationship. It is likely that you will be the last one in the organisation to be let down and the first to know if there is a problem with deliveries, and you may become a role model for others in the way you have fostered your supplier relationships.

There has been much press coverage of the battles between retailers and suppliers over 'copy-cat' practices, where the retailer packages own-label products to resemble branded ranges. In 1997 Asda was forced to rethink its Puffin biscuits pack after a successful legal challenge from United Biscuits, manufacturer of Penguin biscuits. Previously Sainsbury and Coca Cola had been involved in a dispute over the Sainsbury product Classic Cola and Tesco had changed its cereal packaging after complaints from Kellogg.

It goes without saying that it is extremely difficult to collaborate with suppliers if you are trying to compete with them at the same time. Yet a variety of companies attempt to do this – and not just major retailers. In an attempt to strengthen relationships with its suppliers, Tesco launched a review of all its own-label products and pledged to relaunch them with their own distinctive branding. It also offered to involve brand manufacturers by inviting them to provide a dedicated team to help develop Tesco products.

Tesco has also pledged to exchange immediate sales information with its suppliers to enable them to identify the best-selling ranges more easily and quickly. It considers that working alongside manufacturers will help it to find new ways of improving both cost efficiency and product ranges.

Relationships with customers

Organisations invest millions of pounds in attracting customers and building brand loyalty. In each case the organisation tries to understand its customers better than its competitors. It may work hard to foster an image of care and concern for the local community and the environment. It may hire market research agencies and advertising agencies to work out the motives, attitudes, expectations, needs and wants of individual customers, and spend billions of pounds on research and development programmes to try to meet these perceived needs. However, the aim may be thwarted if:

- the campaign or promotion fails to attract new customers
- there is a mismatch between customer needs, wants and expectations and the organisation's perceptions of these
- the organisation fails to satisfy its customers
- the organisation fails to give sufficient attention to building customer loyalty.

The importance of this is highlighted when you consider how and why consumers behave in the way they do.

Consumer behaviour

According to studies undertaken by Jagdish Sheth, consumers go through a four-stage process when they are considering whether or not to make a purchase. At each stage different factors interact to influence actions and behaviour.

Stage 1 – Problem-solving

At the problem-solving stage, the customer identifies a perceived need. This could be as basic as running out of an essential item, or identifying a new need (e.g. your dentist recommends you should start to floss your teeth or an expectant mother starts to find out about disposable nappies). In some cases marketers act to create a need – and then provide the solution – as in the case of microwave ovens, tumble driers and fabric conditioners.

However, the activities of the buyer will depend on the risk involved in making the decision about what to buy. In the case of a low-cost, routine purchase, where there are familiar products and brands, the buyer will be less motivated to spend much time making a decision. In this case choice is influenced by factors such as branding, product familiarity, recommendation, availability and in-store displays.

If, however, there is substantial risk involved in making the decision to buy, the customer will take a different approach. There will be much greater search for information and evaluation. Advice and assistance will be sought from friends, colleagues and experts. Comparative assessments of information will occur and there may be several visits to different outlets.

Stage 2 – Information search

Information search is the process of finding out about a product or service that will satisfy your need. If the central heating breaks down at Christmas and you already know a friendly heating engineer or plumber, then you will undoubtedly ring him first. Otherwise you might ring friends to see who they could suggest, or flick through *Yellow Pages* or the local paper to find someone who can help you cope with the emergency. In the first case you are resorting to *internal search*, in the second you are using *external search*. Because of the greater effort and higher degree of risk involved in external search you are more likely to use internal methods – another reason for the popularity of repeat business.

Search techniques also depend on the time available, the motives, skills and existing knowledge and personality of the individual, and the product or service being researched. For instance, some people may collect information and 'shop around' for enjoyment, others may be less keen (or have less time) and make a more rapid decision.

Stage 3 – Evaluation and decision

Evaluation and decision implies that customers make comparisons between features or characteristics after setting *evaluation criteria* to limit the range of choices. These will be the features or benefits which are important to that particular person. Both objective and subjective elements are involved in the evaluation process – objective relating to known data and information, subjective concerning the customer's personality and his/her attitudes, opinions and perceptions of the item or source of supply. Additional attributes associated with one product or source can influence the eventual decision, particularly between two similar choices.

Stage 4 – Post-purchase assessment

Post-purchase assessment occurs after the transaction is completed and is linked to consumer expectations of the product or service. If, at any point, there is a 'quality gap' between expectations and reality then the customer experiences disappointment or dissatisfaction, which creates *cognitive dissonance* – a condition described in more detail later in this chapter (page 383). Dissatisfaction is experienced either because the quality of the product or service – or the experience – was less than the customer expected (the item breaks down, delivery is delayed, a holiday is disappointing) *or* because later information proved the original decision to be flawed (e.g. the same product is found to be available more cheaply elsewhere, a friend buys a different model with more attributes for the same price).

Customer satisfaction

From this model it is easy to see that customers desire satisfaction and assurance at three stages of the buying process:

- pre-purchase
- at the point of purchase
- post-purchase.

The degree to which customers perceive they are satisfied at each stage, and the 'measures' they use, will depend upon the organisation and the type of product or service it offers. Expert advice, for instance, is crucial to purchasers of expensive technical equipment – from a video to a photocopier – but is unimportant to buyers of matches or soap. However, the key aspects of service that can be expected *as a minimum* to reassure all customers at each stage are shown in Figure 4.2.5. In the case of an organisational buyer the demands may be even more exacting.

Figure 4.2.5 Elements leading to customer satisfaction

Pre-purchase
- *Reputation* – Is the organisation known to be reliable and honourable with high standards of product quality, service and integrity? What is its record on consumer, social and environmental issues?
- *Policies* – Is there a written customer service policy which links to the mission statement? Do both put the customer first? Are there specific and quantifiable objectives which relate to fair and honest policies?
- *Accessibility* – Can the organisation be contacted easily, are there dedicated customer enquiry/service staff, is there a single point of contact, enough telephone lines, methods of handling out-of-hours enquiries?
- *Flexibility* – To what degree can individual needs be met? Is the organisation prepared to change delivery times, or packaging, adjust quantities or product specifications, offer training or provide detailed information, accept a range of payment methods or arrange an export package – all to meet the needs of individual customers?
- *Information* – Is sufficient information immediately available on the products/ services? Is it clear, unambiguous, easy to read and understand, eye-catching and available in different languages? Has it been written with the seller or the buyer in mind?

The point of purchase
- *Order processing* – How quickly does the organisation respond to enquiries? How soon can the order be filled and how rapidly can delivery be made? How reliable is the service? How are difficulties, problems or delays communicated to the customer? How often do they occur?
- *As advertised/expected* – How accurately does the product or service live up to advertising claims and customer expectations? Does close scrutiny result in disappointment? Are there 'hidden extras' in the pricing structure which the customer didn't expect? Is the price consistent with customer expectations for that product/service/seller?
- *Customer relations* – What is the attitude of customer service staff? Is friendliness, courtesy, excellent product knowledge, tact and diplomacy second nature? Do sales staff create the right image?

Figure 4.2.5 Elements leading to customer satisfaction – *continued*

- *Additional benefits* – What 'extras' can be offered to the customer to close the deal (customised extras, free service, clear instruction books, free training)? To what degree is the organisation committed to the 'augmented product' (see page 360)? Is the customer made aware of his/her rights if a fault occurs? What after-sales service is available?

Post-purchase

- *Product performance* – What is the likelihood of a fault occurring? How long would it take to fix? Are spare parts readily available? What arrangements are there for dealing with call-outs? What is the charging structure?
- *Guarantees/warranties* – How long does the guarantee last? Do all staff understand the statutory rights of buyers? Can warranty periods be extended at staff discretion for loyal customers/in special circumstances?
- *Follow-up* – What actions are taken to check customer satisfaction? What information on customers is retained in the company? To what degree is this confidential or 'sold-on'? How is customer feedback used?
- *Problems and complaints* – Is there a phone-in service for customers or an advice centre/desk? How are complaints acknowledged? What is the policy on giving compensation? What is the returns policy?

Basically, for a relationship to be developed between buyer and seller, the buyer must be assured that:

- the seller can provide all the information and all the services he/she considers essential at *each stage* of the transaction
- his/her particular needs will be identified and met (see also page 379)
- the seller will communicate with him/her in such a way as to provide understandable and honest information, good advice, expertise and reassurance
- the seller can be trusted to keep to his/her word, to give accurate information and to continue to provide good service post-transaction.

Relationship marketeers have likened the long-term and human side of customer/seller relationships to marriage, concentrating on the importance of developing long-lasting interactions and exchanges through the building of commitment and trust. Theodore Levitt in *The Marketing Imagination* went so far as to say that 'the sale merely consummates the courtship. Then the marriage begins. How good the marriage is depends on how well the relationship is managed by the seller.' Other experts have compared the relationship with a romantic involvement that goes through five stages:

- There is *awareness* of the product or brand.
- There is *exploration* of alternatives with a very small investment in the relationship. Norms and expectations begin to surface.
- There is *expansion* of the relationship as information is exchanged and the two parties become more interdependent.
- There is a *commitment* to continue or further the relationship.
- There is *dissolution* of the relationship unless the seller can take steps

to retain the buyer. Strategies to prevent dissolution include increasing loyalty and dependency (see below) and making exit more difficult. An example is the Air Miles incentive of Mastercard and the Profiles system for Visa cards. Both operate to 'anchor' the customer and dissuade him from choosing an alternative.

THEORY INTO PRACTICE

Customers usually react positively to efforts by the seller to develop the relationship – provided these are seen as genuine and sincere overtures. For instance, customers like to be greeted by name, to have their preferences known, to be accorded personal courtesies. In one organisation, a top administrator kept details of every important client on a record card. After each encounter she jotted down her observations and noted new developments. Each time a client appeared, she was able to greet him/her personally and refer to the previous information to make informed comments, such as 'Hello, John, how did you enjoy your holiday in Bermuda?' Her ability to 'get alongside' the client was respected by her boss and positively worshipped by the clients – who each felt they were individually important to her. Needless to say, none of them knew about the record cards!

Building customer loyalty

Branding is a deliberate strategy in building customer loyalty. Provided the product satisfies the customer, branding reduces the 'search time' in the future, so the customer will be tempted to repeat buy rather than shop around for alternatives. However, not all customers react in this way. Some may deliberately try alternatives at regular intervals, others may 'random buy', others will consider price more important. However, branding creates an association in the mind of the customer which is hard to deny. One taste test of Coke and Pepsi found that Pepsi was actually preferred when the volunteers were blindfolded. When they were not, the majority preferred Coke – suggesting that it is the Coke image that sells the drink more than the taste.

Image and reputation building is not the job just of advertising agents, marketing professionals and PR people. Today customers are more discerning and may have other stakeholding roles – from employees, to shareholders, to living within the same community. Shell found its livelihood and reputation deeply threatened and almost permanently scarred after the Brent Spar fiasco and controversy about its environmental stance in Nigeria. Other companies employ crisis management teams to help to restore customer confidence rapidly after a disaster (see also page 378). Organisations from Marks & Spencer to Whitbread involve themselves in local communities, from supporting local charities to helping the disabled, from supporting educational initiatives and community regeneration schemes to providing staff expertise and recycled equipment. In other words, they are keenly aware of their social and environmental responsibilities and are proactive in these areas, rather than reactive.

Creating a climate that actively encourages customer loyalty is not an easy task. Some of the factors that contribute towards this have been mentioned above. In summary, they can be identified as:

- producing a product which, whilst being profitable to the organisation and wanted by customers, is also socially and environmentally acceptable, legal and competitive
- communicating the advantages of the product accurately to the customer
- making the product as accessible as possible
- de-commoditising the product to meet special requests and special needs
- communicating with customers in a way which is honest, ethical and just (see also page 374)
- making the product as easy to recognise as possible
- treating the customer with respect by having all staff realise the importance of courtesy, responsiveness, politeness and friendliness.

The relationship marketing ladder of customer loyalty shows that customers move through five distinct stages in their relationship with suppliers:

- *Prospect* – Sam has heard that Vidal Sassoon is a great hairdresser, so she considers going there.
- *Customer* – Sam books a trial appointment.
- *Client* – Sam is very pleased with the result and books another appointment.
- *Supporter* – Sam goes regularly.
- *Advocate* – Sam can't believe her friends and colleagues don't go as well – she regularly tells them how good it is.

At the stage of advocate, you should note, Sam is doing Vidal Sassoon's marketing for him! If she becomes dissatisfied at a later date – or feels she is being taken for granted – Sassoon not only loses a customer, he also loses a lot of free referral marketing. The value of developing a constructive working relationship with her is obvious. Equally the dangers – of a careless or sharp word from a new receptionist, or a wrongly timed appointment or a delay for which no-one apologises – are also obvious.

Ironically, the human tendency to take long-term contacts for granted and to treat these people with less consideration than virtual strangers can be seen in the way regular customers can almost be disregarded in the mad rush to gain new business. Obviously, if you work in an industry where customers tend to make 'one-off' purchases (from estate agents to divorce lawyers, from luxury yachts to hydraulic lifts) then you may *have* to concentrate hard on fostering new business opportunities whenever you can. However, do remember that every previous and current customer is a potential advocate. Therefore, asking a known customer to wait because a new prospect has arrived unexpectedly, or answering queries from new prospects rather than established customers, or taking advantage of someone's good nature and reshuffling an appointment to fit in something else, are all dangerous strategies. At *any stage* of the customer relationship the customer is free to reflect and review on the benefits he/she is gaining – and conclude that these are considerably less than at the beginning of the encounter. The conclusion is inevitable.

Some pundits have argued that the Tories lost the 1997 General Election because they took their eyes off their past supporters or 'customers' even whilst they were trying to attract new ones. This is the equivalent of the leaking bucket effect where overall more is lost than is gained.

A model of *loyalty management* put forward by Peter Doyle, Professor of Marketing and Strategic Management at Warwick Business School, starts with the basic proposition that the principal task of an organisation is to create outstanding value for customers and to deliver this in such a way as to retain existing customers. In his view, all customers, suppliers and employees should be regarded as valuable long-term assets with whom a partnership should be developed so that each is given a shared interest in the value package. Controls and feedback systems should be in place to focus on monitoring the progress of the value chain. This strategy is not only essential for long-term success but is also cost-effective. Research shows that customers normally become more profitable the longer they stay with a company and repeat business opportunities generate much faster sales growth than new business opportunities.

The total product concept

Ted Levitt has suggested that customers buy a total offering, rather than an individual product. This offering can be viewed at several levels as shown in Figure 4.2.6.

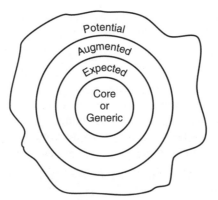

Figure 4.2.6 The total product concept

- The *core* or *generic* product comprises the basics. It is the minimum required to meet the need. For an airline, it may mean simply offering a basic, no-frills service which gets you from A to B.
- The *expected* product incorporates other minimal conditions that the customer expects to be met. On an airline you would expect the pilot to be qualified, the aeroplane to be safe and regularly serviced, baggage to arrive with you and cabin staff who are friendly and who will assist in an emergency.
- The *augmented* product differentiates one service from another. The product has added value above what the customer expects. In this case there may be good food, free newspapers, additional legroom, an up-

to-date video to watch, sociable departure and arrival times, a wide range of destinations.

- The *potential* product consists of all the possible features and benefits that could be included to give extra value to the customers. This will attract new users and retain existing customers. On our airline examples may include rapid check-in, shuttle services, self-ticketing, special lounges, free drinks, superb service in-flight, frequent flyer programmes and discounts.

Different customers will place a different value on each of the benefits, so it is the total offer that is important, not individual aspects of it.

Organisational perspectives of the 'best way' to offer an augmented product vary considerably – often depending upon the size of organisation, its ethos, aims and objectives and the *exact* business it is in. The three accounts below – all connected with aircraft – illustrate these differences and show clearly that consideration of the target market is a key requirement in deciding how the total product strategy should be applied.

Palmair Flightline has only one aeroplane and a very enthusiastic owner – who waves a giant red flag to welcome his plane as it approaches the runway at Bournemouth airport. Yet in March 1997 his airline was voted the world's fifth best by 60 000 members of the Consumers Association, who graded airlines according to food, cleanliness, legroom, in-flight entertainment and check-in staff. No negative comments were received from Palmair customers, all of whom said they would recommend it to their friends. Before departure, Peter Bath, the owner, personally checks that the aircraft is clean (including the toilets) and that the seat covers are ironed, and then personally greets every passenger.

At the other end of the scale, **British Airways**, which came thirteenth in the same survey, has announced it is now concentrating on repositioning itself in the travel market. Rather than being 'just an airline' it aims to expand into travel insurance and credit cards as well as to develop links with rail, sea and hotel partners across the world to offer a global route network with 'products and services to suit everyone throughout their entire journey'. BA already has partnership agreements with airlines in Australia, France and Germany and is currently attempting to forge an alliance with American Airlines, although this still has some way to go before being cleared. Further ideas include a similar arrangement with Japan Airlines and the establishment of a Far East base. BA is also changing the face of its workforce – contracting out many activities, reducing its staff by 5000 and recruiting more multilinguists and staff with up-to-date technological skills. BA aims to reduce its costs by £1 billion by the year 2000.

Providing customer satisfaction to business customers is a key aspect of **British Aerospace's** business philosophy. Obviously, it is hardly sensible to sell an aeroplane and then expect the customer to walk off with it. For that reason its customer support operations are seen as integral to its business success and over 1100 people are employed in this capacity supporting 28 international customers with a fleet of over 2200 aircraft.

The support package starts with involving customers in the design process and is aimed at reducing the lifecycle costs of an aircraft; i.e. the cost of servicing and maintaining it throughout its operation. This is vital given that lifecycle costs can amount to as much as five times the initial cost of the aircraft. Training ranges from mission simulations to maintenance instruction, and the support package includes BAe taking responsibility for spares and service to be available on an immediate basis for a monthly or annual charge – or face financial penalties.

The global nature of the customer base means that staff have to be trained to understand the culture and the history of their clients with a clear appreciation of the needs of individual customers, given their military circumstances and economic situation.

THEORY INTO PRACTICE

1 As a customer yourself, identify the number of organisations for whom you are a true advocate. How much business do you generate for them in a year? Now consider how much business they would lose if you became disillusioned with the relationship.

2 Compare the services listed in Figure 4.2.5 at each stage of the purchase transaction with the services offered by your organisation. At which services do you consider your organisation excels and at which is it weakest? What could you suggest to remedy any deficiencies?

3 How would you explain the 'buying experience' of your customers or the 'total product concept' offered by your organisation? What could be done, in your view, to develop further the potential product that could be offered?

Seeking and exchanging information

A vast amount of the information required and used by an organisation is concerned with its external contacts. This includes:

- data on the external environment which informs the strategic plan and organisational objectives relating to suppliers and customers
- data on the internal operations of the organisation which identify the degree to which previous sales and purchasing targets have been achieved
- information on the organisation itself and on the products or services offered – ranging from media reports and press releases to catalogues, brochures, leaflets and documents relating to contractual terms and finance
- information on competitors, their current products and their potential developments and innovations, such as press reports, company documentation and advertising literature, company accounts
- information on potential and actual customers, including market research surveys, government listings, sales reports, exception and variance reports, customer defections, repeat business reports, complaints documentation and data held in a customer database

- information on potential and actual suppliers, including approved supplier listings, trade association listings, supplier performance reports, supplier records, quality and inspection reports, complaints documentation and data held in a supplier database.

The need for good information

The reason for obtaining accurate information and for keeping it up-to-date is to inform the decision-making process relating to purchases and sales – from the point of view of both the organisation itself *and* the external contacts. For example, without accurate, appropriate, timely and comprehensive information the customer cannot make an informed decision. This might not be too important if you are selling a low-cost, fast-moving consumer item or if you are operating in a relatively non-competitive environment. It is critical if you are selling to a business organisation or selling expensive or technical consumer goods or operating in a highly competitive market.

The management must receive enough information of the right calibre to:

- assess accurately the success (or otherwise) of individual product lines or sales outlets
- identify accurately whether customer expectations are being met
- accurately assess, evaluate and compare supplier performance
- make appropriate decisions regarding future plans.

Suppliers must receive enough information to be able to collaborate effectively with your organisation as a customer. Lack of good information can result in incorrect specifications, late deliveries, poor quality goods or even the wrong goods arriving.

Customers and suppliers must receive enough *current* information to allay concerns, re-adjust their expectations and take appropriate actions. Examples include information on product changes and specification adjustments, problems with deliveries and details of product recalls. In a crisis, up-to-date information bulletins and help lines are vital for retaining customer confidence (see also page 378 for crisis management techniques).

Lack of clear information can result in misunderstandings about the terms of a contract, the delivery or payment details or the type of goods being required or provided. In a worst-case scenario this can lead to legal repercussions (see page 395 and Chapter 8).

Obtaining the information

The type of information with which you are specifically involved, your role in handling this information (e.g. to process, store, amend, update or evaluate) and the way in which it is used will depend upon the systems in operation in your organisation, the type of goods or services you offer, the markets you serve (e.g. domestic or international, specialised or diverse), the role of intermediaries (e.g. agents and wholesalers) and your particular job role. It is therefore impossible to give details of the specific ways in which you can seek and exchange information. However, in broad terms, you should consider the following.

Information may be gleaned through primary research or through secondary research. The first involves asking the customer or supplier (either yourself, or through using an agency), entering into direct negotiations. The second involves obtaining established data – even if you then use this for your own purposes. Examples include company reports and financial data, other information on suppliers and customers (including credit references), printed research reports and customer surveys.

Consider also the degree to which *in-depth* information on your suppliers and customers is required. If you are buying paperclips you will be less concerned about supplier references than if you were buying a jumbo jet! Similarly, if your customers are private individuals who pay cash for basic commodities, this is rather different from a private customer who buys an expensive service or a business customer who is entering into a long-term agreement and for whom credit references may be essential. Knowing the customer in this instance means being able to target your marketing, focus your conversations, reduce bad debts and more quickly identify ways to meet his/her needs.

Consider the style of communications between your organisation and its suppliers and customers. If the aim is to develop long-term relationships, or if expertise is a key factor, then it is likely that the process of buying and selling will involve lengthy negotiations starting with basic fact-finding and moving on through deeper levels of need analysis to include customising service or product provision. Once a relationship has been established a constant flow of updated information to external contacts retains and strengthens the link.

What is the degree of change in your particular industry? If this is high (e.g. in the financial services industry) then the organisation has an obligation to keep up-to-date with the products on the market and to keep its customers informed of developments that may be appropriate to their needs or legislative changes that may affect them.

Information can be obtained both formally and informally. A representative or adviser may be talking to the client – but a 'throw-away' remark on the telephone or in reception could indicate a fundamental customer need. For this reason the *listening skills* of those involved with the customer are crucial (see Element 4.1, page 289). Some organisations follow a policy of sending executives or sales staff on regular face-to-face service maintenance visits to suppliers and customers. These are relaxed, informal discussions to ascertain current levels of need and satisfaction. These meetings should be a two-way flow of information but, above all, it is essential to obtain up-to-date information on the perception of the other party. To quote Tom Peters, 'Perception is never neutral'. For that reason each customer and supplier has either positive or negative perceptions linked to every type of product and service your organisation offers. Establishing these on an on-going basis is critical to any process of continuous improvement.

Quite obviously, any changes in a consumer's buying habits should be investigated where possible. They may simply signify a difference in life-style or family requirements – or they may indicate that the customer is less than satisfied with the offerings of your organisation. Noting the differences and investigating these is a key part of customer management strategy.

Information can reach all staff in a variety of other ways. A leaflet through your door at home could give useful information on a competitor's latest product. A press report, read casually over Sunday breakfast, could provide crucial information relating to a supplier or business customer. Astute organisations are aware that all information – provided it is accurate – assists in evaluating and updating its customer and supplier information base and helps it to target its efforts more effectively to take decisive and appropriate action. It is therefore appropriate to encourage your colleagues to let you have any information they even *think* may be relevant to your current operations and customer base and to process and handle it appropriately. Certainly you should ensure that critical updates reach the ears of the decision-makers as speedily as possible.

Modern technology has increased the type and quantity of information available at the touch of a key and the methods by which information may be transmitted, as well as improving communications between organisations and their external contacts. Here are some examples.

A variety of *contact management software packages* are available which link sales and marketing support. These are used by telemarketers to hold all customer and prospect information on databases which store the address, phone number and contact information for each organisation. They also enable users to schedule, track, record and analyse all contact information, including phone and e-mail messages, appointments and outstanding tasks. Some packages enable appointments for a group of users, such as a sales team, to be viewed simultaneously. Most packages are compatible with laptops so they can be used by field sales people who can also hook into and exchange information with the central database. These systems also facilitate the creation and sending of targeted direct mailshots and faxes and follow-up letters.

The last few years have seen an enormous expansion in *telemarketing centres*, mainly in the regions. Today more than 1 per cent of Britain's working population are employed in what are euphemistically known as 'call centres'. The aim is not just to boost sales and to win new business but also to make regular phone contact with existing customers to improve and develop relationships. The boom in telemarketing has been made possible by the combination of new high-capacity telecom networks and advanced computer databases. This has enabled organisations to site their call centres away from major cities to process anything from complaints and enquiries to responses to advertisements or promotion campaigns.

Customer service is a contracted-out facility for some organisations who divert their enquiries and complaints lines to an outside call centre which handles the business, analyses the traffic and produces data on the enquiries and/or complaints received.

Other call centres focus on sales, customer care and technical support. Once a sale is completed the team at the centre manage every stage of the order until delivery. The aim is to provide a dedicated telephone number for ongoing after-sales service with a trained team of staff to answer and process enquiries quickly and effectively. Problems are handled proactively with customers being informed of any delays to re-adjust expectations.

Modern telephone systems and ISDN lines can provide a range of *automated customer service facilities* to promote rapid information search and retrieval whilst freeing other lines for direct customer contact. Examples include *interactive voice response* systems which play a recorded message followed by information to which callers respond by saying either 'yes' or 'no' or pressing appropriate numbers on their handsets and display screen handsets, on which incoming callers' names appear so that they can be greeted individually. In America, 'messages on hold' is the current trend – with companies trading music on hold for messages relating to the company's services, special offers or opening hours.

Intranets – secure internal computer networks – are revolutionising customer and supplier relationships with many organisations extending access to their external contacts. In addition to giving employees on the receiving end of calls all the information to deal with a customer's needs, BT has demonstrated that a successful Intranet can show a 1500 per cent return on investment with companies also saving money on travel costs to customers and suppliers.

From mid-1998, the British Interactive Broadcasting (BIB) joint £265 million venture between BSkyB, BT, Midland Bank and Matsushita Electric will provide more than 200 channels and a range of *interactive services to consumers* all through their television sets. In addition to booking holidays, buying tickets and playing computer games, customers with the ubiquitous digital box will be able to surf the Internet and send e-mails. Interactive services will be offered with participating companies ranging from Sainsbury and Thomas Cook to HMV and GUS, payment can be through credit card or Mondex – the electronic cash card. The full range of services will include armchair shopping, armchair banking, booking holidays and travel, downloading computer games, learning on-line, bookings services for sports and entertainments events, car buying facilities and public services such as training and job information.

THEORY INTO PRACTICE

1 Identify the items of information with which you are involved which relate to external contacts. In each case, try to identify the source and the relative importance of different types of information you handle. What action would you take if you knew that some information you had just received regarding a potential customer was substantially incorrect?

2 You read a press report which states that your main supplier of office consumables is experiencing financial difficulties. What would you do with this information, and why?

3 An established customer likes to call in personally and chat for several minutes to anyone who will listen. Your colleague takes the view that this is time-wasting and avoids the customer whenever possible. Identify the dangers of this approach.

4 Identify the degree to which your organisation has used state-of-the-art technology to improve information processing and handling for external contacts – and the extent to which you think opportunities may be being missed in this area.

Issues that can affect working relationships

Relationships with suppliers and customers can be affected by many events. At one end of the spectrum a serious unresolved issue can signal the end of the relationship; at the other the issue may have positive benefits for your future alliance – such as when a competitor ceases trading or when a customer is so impressed with your service he promptly gives you his account. You have already spent time studying how to establish a constructive relationship, so this section focuses on issues that can have a negative impact on your relationship with external contacts.

Firstly it is important to identify those issues which are unavoidable and about which the organisation can do very little – at least in the short term. Broadly these can be classified as *environmental* issues, which occur in the external environment. With other issues, however, responsibility for the eventual outcome can be laid fairly and squarely at the door of the organisation itself and/or its representatives. These are classified as *behavioural* issues.

Environmental issues

This category involves issues over which neither you nor your organisation has very much, if any, control. Examples are:

- a supplier or customer going out of business or moving away from the area
- your organisation no longer needing a particular item from a supplier or finding it can be obtained elsewhere more cheaply or on better terms
- discontinued product use by one of your customers, when this relates to life-style, age, fashion or any other factor unrelated to customer dissatisfaction
- a competitor inventing or modifying a product which is more attractive to some of your customers than your own offerings
- your organisation re-evaluating its product lines, dropping those that are unprofitable and losing a few marginal customers
- your international markets being affected by issues relating to either British or foreign economic and political situations
- a key component or item being unavailable owing to a dispute at your sole supplier or an international problem
- making a deliberate decision to make rather than buy a component or key requirement

- legislative changes that affect the composition or type of goods you are able to provide
- conflict-of-interest situations where a particular supplier or customer wants exclusivity of service which your organisation cannot profitably or ethically agree to.

Whilst all of these issues are unavoidable in the short term, long-term strategies should be targeted towards finding alternative products, sources, suppliers or markets to prevent a recurrence. No organisation can assume complacently that today's markets will be the same tomorrow – a fundamental survival strategy is therefore concerned with forecasting environmental issues that may affect the organisation and identifying methods of counteracting these, such as product innovation and the development of new markets.

Behavioural issues

Relationships can also deteriorate because of problems within the supplying or buying organisation. In each case it is the behaviour of a representative of the organisation – or the structures and processes within the organisation itself – which cause the problem.

Problems with suppliers

Problems can arise with a supplier if your organisation:

- regularly delays payment of accounts
- raises regular disputes over deliveries, specifications and quality of goods – at the extreme leading to non-payment of bills
- demands a service and/or personal attention which is out of proportion to the profit the supplier can make through doing business with you
- indulges in action perceived to be antagonistic or 'unfriendly' – such as starting up an operation in competition to a service offered by the supplier.

Problems can arise on the supplier's side if:

- there is non-fulfilment of the contract according to specification
- the supplier delivers sub-standard goods, or gives poor performance or service
- there are delays, inefficiencies, over-billing, errors of substance and of judgement, unethical behaviour, cheating or fraud.

Unless you are heavily dependent on a particular supplier for a specialist service or item – when the issue will have to be addressed in some detail at managerial level – it is likely that if you encounter continual difficulties with a supplier you will make an effort to switch sources. It is likely that suppliers will give you a rather larger margin for error, particularly if they are dependent upon your organisation for a substantial amount of business. However, this situation should never be abused.

As an example, several small suppliers in Britain are heavily dependent upon large organisations settling their bills relatively speedily to ensure they have a satisfactory cash flow. Large companies which deliberately make small suppliers wait inordinate lengths of time for payment will contribute to each supplier's individual downfall – and then complain because the market has become less competitive or they have to buy-in from a more distant or unknown source. Quite simply, retaining positive and productive working relationships implies mutual respect and concern for each party.

Problems with customers

Your organisation can suffer from any of the faults listed above for suppliers. In addition your organisation can suffer from:

- lack of positive marketing or promotion in contrast with your competitors
- better sales terms available from your competitors
- new 'improved' products or services which customers do not like as much as the old ones
- the existence of a 'quality gap' between what the customer expected and what he/she received (see below)
- unresolved complaints and disputes
- poor deliveries, poor-quality goods, inferior customer service leading to increasing customer frustration
- surly, unhelpful or impolite staff.

Note that you cannot force any customer to stay with your organisation for life! Everyone has the right to change their minds, try something new or shop around. This is particularly true if the item being bought is expensive. However, with cheaper items customers prefer their decisions to be simplified – particularly for regular purchases – which is why branding is so beneficial. Quite simply, it removes the need to make a decision. Retaining customer loyalty (see page 358) is therefore a key objective for most organisations and this may have as much to do with availability and quality as it does with service – particularly if your organisation supplies retailers rather than dealing directly with consumers.

The situation is different if customers negotiate with you directly or if you supply business organisations. For expensive items the customer is looking for individual service, specialist advice and attention to his/her needs. Business organisations are more concerned with the adequacy and accuracy of information, technical advice and the financial terms that can be agreed. Both will be concerned with post-transaction service, particularly if capital equipment is involved.

However, even if your organisation has put in place all the systems possible to monitor and support customer enquiries, offers a first-rate, top-quality product and provides a total offering which is second to none, this can count for nothing unless everyone in the organisation is committed to providing top-quality service on every occasion. This often means fundamentally changing attitudes to customers and attitudes to feedback (both positive and negative). Customer comments, views and criticism should be actively sought and immediately acted upon. Negative comments or criticism should be considered positively – as a warning – so that something can be done. In some cases you will receive no warning – the customer will simply go elsewhere. Some authorities put this as simply as arguing that there should be 'mutual respect'. This then encompasses a range of behaviours, such as the way outward-facing staff are dressed, the way they speak to customers and suppliers, even the fact that they wipe their feet when visiting a customer's premises! There is an argument that each external contact becomes an 'honoured guest' whose needs must be attended to – which dramatically alters the perception of many people who work in the organisation.

The contribution of individual staff members to building the customer base – and therefore long-term profitability – can easily be misjudged and is often ignored by organisations.

Imagine you move from your present job to open a pizza restaurant. You employ staff on a part-time basis, each person being responsible for six tables over a 4-hour shift. On a busy night each person therefore deals with approximately 48 people, on the assumption each table is occupied by up to four people for 2 hours. The average bill for each person is £10. Your staff are therefore *each* responsible for £480 of business each night. If they work five nights they generate over £2000 of business for you each week – over £100 000 of business for you each year. Now imagine the financial damage an untrained, unsociable staff member can inflict on you – and this is not allowing for the fact that disgruntled and dissatisfied customers are likely to tell each of their friends to stay away from your establishment! If you consider that everyone normally tells at least 10 other people, the financial value of good customer service becomes obvious.

THEORY INTO PRACTICE

1 Assess *honestly* the degree to which your colleagues are aware of the effort they must make to sustain and develop relationships with outside contacts. What do you think could be done to improve the situation?
2 Identify the problems that constrain your own effectiveness in sustaining positive relationships. These may be organisational, process-driven or related to other people. Have you any suggestions to offer for removing these obstacles?
3 Your new computer system has produced considerable difficulties in communicating accurately with several key suppliers. What action would you take to restore an effective relationship?

Dealing with disagreements and conflict

Disagreements and conflicts can be unpleasant and unproductive – and the strategies to deal with this were covered in full in Element 4.1. The aim, in every case, is to address the issues and move the problem to a 'win/win' situation wherever possible. In relation to external contacts, the following points are relevant.

Your suppliers are likely to be highly motivated to take a cooperative stance, given that they risk losing valuable business if they do not. However, if you are highly dependent on a particular supplier, this weakens your case. Imagine, for instance, that you have a sole supplier for a particular product and that there are no other feasible alternatives. In that case negotiation is essential as you cannot use power or any form of leverage (except good will) to control their output or quality.

Where customers are concerned, *you* are more motivated to be cooperative than they are – particularly in a highly competitive market. Your position is stronger, obviously, if you are a monopsonist, and the situation may be rather different when you are dealing with business organisations rather than private individuals.

- Individual consumers operating in a competitive market are often motivated to stay with a 'known' supplier because it takes time and effort to go elsewhere. This need is even more pronounced if the item you provide is expensive or includes expert service, rather than if it is a fast-moving consumer good, such as toothpaste. For instance, a consumer used to shopping at Sainsbury will be prone to stay a regular customer because their reasons for shopping there are several. It may be on the route home from work, they are familiar with the hours of opening, the layout of the store, the lines they sell, the range of additional services offered. Taking umbrage and transferring their business to Tesco or Safeway means they have to familiarise themselves with a new store and a new layout. Such organisations can use these factors to their benefit to retain customer loyalty provided they operate quickly enough to re-establish consumer confidence if there is a problem.
- Business organisations invest time and effort to vet suppliers, to establish contacts, to develop positive and productive relationships. They, too, will hesitate to disassociate themselves from known suppliers as this will mean reassessing alternatives from scratch, which incurs transactional costs. For that reason they, too, are more motivated to renegotiate to sustain an existing relationship rather than to shop around, particularly if they are committed to a joint collaborate relationship. However, do note that if you are working with a new customer, in a competitive market, then problems may have more disastrous consequences because the customer/client relationship is still in its infancy.

Disagreements and conflicts can range from basic issues to serious problems. As examples, consider the following:

- your organisation invoices a customer for a non-existent sale or overcharges
- you supply faulty goods or the incorrect goods or deliver them on the wrong date
- you promise to deliver goods which then do not arrive from *your* supplier

- you make a mistake which costs your customer money in rectifying the problem
- your company has a major disaster which has the press clamouring for blood on the first day the news hits the streets.

You know yourself, as a consumer, how you feel when a supplier does not deliver as promised. A holiday is a disappointment, your clothes are ruined at the dry cleaners, vegetables go rotten two days after they are purchased, your car hasn't run properly since the garage last serviced it. In each case you start from a position of disappointment and *expect* the supplier to make a reasonable offer to rectify the problem. Whereas ideas of 'reasonableness' can vary, they are based on the degree of inconvenience, difficulty and distress caused by the original problem. Therefore you can hardly expect a supermarket to give you a free run of its aisles because a chicken was out-of-date, but you can expect a rather different reaction from a tour operator that had expected you to spend your precious two weeks' holiday in a hotel which was still under construction. It is therefore fairly obvious that the expectations of the other party are usually directly related to the seriousness of the problem and the inconvenience which has been caused. Your first reaction in attempting to solve any conflict must be to recognise, rather than to deny, this situation. This means identifying and recognising exactly what the disagreement or complaint is about. If this is then dealt with effectively it is possible not only to restore but to improve the relationship as you have reassured the customer that he/she was wise to deal with you in the first place. This can be achieved by resolving the difficulty and/or acknowledging the complaint and giving the customer some form of positive 'stroke' in return – commensurate to the type of complaint and the inconvenience he/she has been caused.

However, you are bound to be constrained by the processes and procedures which exist in your organisation for dealing with supplier or customer difficulties. It is doubtful whether you will ever have completely free rein to make an offer or counter-offer without obtaining approval beforehand. The *real* problem occurs when you are instructed to make an offer or argue a case in which you have no confidence or do not believe, or where you work for an organisation which prefers to allocate blame internally rather than actively pursue the management of complaints as a positive strategy.

In the first case, if we assume that your organisation would not expect you, let alone instruct you, to operate unethically, then we have to assume that the person issuing the instructions is either not aware of the seriousness of the situation or is prepared to game-play for a while in an attempt to achieve an advantage. If this strategy is unsuccessful it may not be too critical if you lose only £100 of business next year. If, however, the customer is of key importance to your organisation's profitability then such a strategy is foolhardy. At this point, unless you are prepared to seek advice from higher echelons, your role may be as negotiator between the supplier or customer and your boss – rather than acting as your organisational representative.

In the second case, an organisation with the delusion that it is only successful if it receives no complaints, and any that do arise point to staff inadequacies that should be penalised immediately, operates on a very insecure basis. Such an ethos will drive complaints underground, and no lessons will be learned. Customers will still complain – but to their friends and relatives instead, with obvious results.

Basic strategies need to be in place if staff are to operate effectively. These include the following.

- There should be a clear chain of command so that everyone knows who to contact in a crisis.
- There must be open communications with the other party in order to recognise a problem and not deny it
- A complaints/recourse procedure is necessary which enables staff to negotiate relatively freely according to their position, status and experience.
- There should be good back-up from management if staff have tried their best.
- Good record-keeping systems are needed which at least can provide backing for each case and the decisions taken.
- Compensation should at least match the size of the problem – with an understanding that it is often cost-effective to go the extra mile to restore confidence and create an implicit obligation to continue trading.
- There should be a regular analysis of complaints to identify problem areas and to inform future planning.
- There should be proper customer service training for all front-line staff, which teaches staff to:
  - apologise on behalf of the organisation
  - identify the customer's perception of the problem (this may be an exaggeration of the actual difficulty but, if the customer is very annoyed or frustrated, such distortions are common and must be recognised)
  - respond quickly to rectify the problem
  - take action themselves wherever possible (there is nothing more annoying for an aggrieved customer than having to have to repeat the tale to more and more senior staff or to have to wait until the most appropriate executive can find time to make a decision)
  - follow through to check later that the customer is now satisfied
  - log all complaints for record-keeping and analysis.

However, even when the issue has been fully negotiated and agreed, it is a poor organisation which does not learn from the experience. The main point to note is that *all* organisations and *all* staff make mistakes. Making mistakes is therefore to err and to be human. Making the same mistake over again is far less forgivable.

Computer software is now on the market for handling and managing a complaints procedure. These systems allow for full details of a complaint to be entered together with action taken, and identify all personnel involved in the matter. All acknowledgements and replies are logged and the system will automatically produce replies as well as track correspondence. The key benefits are the tracking and monitoring of progress and the detailed reports that can be produced – customised to the user's requirements.

A financial adviser thought he ran a tight ship – until the day his staff undertook a probate valuation and his secretary typed the value of shares as £100 000 rather than £10 000 – and sent the valuation to the solicitors and executors. The estate was thus over-valued resulting in an over-assessment of inheritance tax which the executors had to borrow from their bank to pay the Inland Revenue. When the mistake was discovered the adviser had just submitted a bill for services for over £700. Because of the additional work for the solicitor in redrafting the documents and the inconvenience and interest charges which the executors had experienced, it was agreed the bill would be withdrawn.

Rather than reprimand his staff the adviser looked at ways to prevent any recurrence of the problem. From that day onwards *two* staff were involved in preparing any probate valuations and the adviser himself checked all valuations before mailing. He viewed it as a learning experience that cost £700 – but which could have cost far more. Interestingly, the secretary who made the mistake claimed she felt more responsible (and presumably more guilty) because her boss was so reasonable about the matter than if he had bawled her out. This is a prime example of positive attitudes showing positive benefits.

Methods of communication to suit individual needs

Communication with customers and suppliers is undertaken both formally and informally, through the printed and the spoken word. An organisation that aims to influence external contacts must have a communications strategy which enables it to interact and communicate regularly with its markets. This extends the basic marketing communications of advertising, public relations, selling, merchandising and packaging to incorporate a wide range of messages which include organisational philosophy on quality, external issues and customer care. Such a strategy must focus on managing the image and reputation of the company in the eyes of its customers and suppliers – and to do this it is essential first to identify the current views and beliefs of customers.

It is often forgotten that virtually every activity undertaken by every individual in the organisation communicates a message to the customer or to another group of stakeholders. Excellent product quality is one thing, but customers will soon forget this if they are annoyed because of constant mistakes made on their invoices. Another organisation may have a high reputation for honest and fair dealing but may irritate buyers because of bureaucratic procedures or because it fails to communicate which staff are responsible for which particular area of work. Suppliers may have a high respect for the ethics of the organisation but become annoyed because they are not notified when a major advertising campaign is going to affect their own order levels or delivery schedules or when a product specification is about to change. Finding out how customers and suppliers actually perceive the organisation, and how *they* perceive their needs could be met more readily, can come as a surprise even to many of the top executives in a company!

The company with a future is also aware of cultural and social issues which affect the perception of external contacts. Stakeholders are more critical than in the past; damaging press reports indicating that the company is prepared to sacrifice the needs of its employees and customers, environmental concerns and ethical standards in its pursuit of profit are likely to be critically assessed by consumers, suppliers, shareholders and other sectors of the community who will form their own judgements. The result is likely to be a downturn in trade, a reduction in talented staff applying to join the organisation, and a lack of respect for the organisation by many key decision-makers. It is for this reason that many organisations concentrate on promoting a positive public relations message through progressive campaigns to raise public awareness of the organisation, its philosophy and its strategies. This message must not only be convincing but must be actively demonstrated, time and time again, by the positive and practical actions taken by the organisation to underline its commitment to its published beliefs. It is no use a company having a mission statement which identifies customers as the key focus when press reports concentrate on client dissatisfaction and short-term profit-seeking strategies.

You may feel such strategies have little to do with your own job and your own dealings with suppliers and customers. It may help if you consider that all communications are a form of social interaction with another person – or other people. At this stage you can subdivide communications into those that are:

- specifically sent to one person or to a group of people
- verbal or written
- undertaken for a specific purpose – to inform, remind, reassure, persuade or thank.

Bear in mind that in each case you should also be sending a message that conveys the overall ethos of concern for other people.

The type, style and tone of your message will be received and decoded by the recipient according to his or her attitudes, beliefs and perceptions. When you communicate you have the power to convey positive and concerned messages – and therefore to confirm a positive perception of your organisation – or to destroy any previous perceptions, either positive or negative. Therefore each communication is an opportunity, or a potential problem. Further, because your communication may be personal and 'from the grass-roots' (rather than general marketing information) it has greater potential *source credibility*. The recipient will normally assume that you are competent at your job and are *accurately* reflecting organisational beliefs and attitudes. If, for instance, you respond carelessly or unconcernedly to a serious letter of complaint, you give the immediate impression that such an attitude is both sanctioned and endorsed by the organisation. Given the power of the complainant to communicate his/her feelings strongly to a variety of personal contacts you can do irreparable harm to your company and virtually nullify next year's advertising budget in a few terse phrases!

Golden rules for communicating

It is relatively easy to consider the best route to follow if you think about the type of communications that annoy you – as a consumer or supplier – and those that impress you. The following list is not comprehensive – you may easily be able to add several points yourself. However, the aim is to point you in the right direction when communicating externally.

- Consider your audience. Writing to a pensioner in the same words and phrases as a sophisticated business contact is obviously wrong. But don't patronise people!
- Keep the jargon to a minimum – both verbally and in writing – *even* when you are communicating to other business organisations. Your terms and acronyms may sound like a foreign language to anyone else.
- Tact and diplomacy are important skills and not easily learned. Junior colleagues should receive adequate training in these aspects of communication before you agree they can liaise or negotiate directly with a customer.
- Never 'rubbish' the competition. It sounds dreadful – highlight your organisation's strong points, not their weak ones.
- Double-check your facts *but* be prepared to own up when you make a mistake.
- Allow people to save face in a dispute – even if a customer is totally wrong, you cannot say so! Always acknowledge a person's right to another opinion even if you have to contradict him/her gently afterwards!
- Communicate relatively informally, preferably with personalised documents. However, don't forget to observe the niceties (such as not using first names without being invited to do so). Try to match your style to your audience – older customers, or those that give your organisation a lot of business, may prefer a rather more formal approach and a little deference.
- Be proactive in keeping customers and suppliers informed. Never withhold important information or forget to pass on essential updates – either to your external contacts *or* your colleagues.
- Keep your body language open and friendly during verbal exchanges and maintain eye contact.
- Be honest and genuine and never make promises you cannot keep.
- Clearly communicate that you recognise your contact's needs for confidentiality where this applies – and do not breach this without agreement.
- If you don't know the answer say so, but keep the person informed as to when you will find out and pass on the information.
- Refer upwards any situation which is becoming exceedingly difficult to handle – particularly if it will have repercussions on other individuals or departments. It is easier for your boss to solve a problem early rather than late, when attitudes and opinions have become more hardened.

- Many charities make a habit of writing to their regular supporters at regular intervals to thank them. Such letters are often gratefully appreciated. A friendly letter to regular customers can often work wonders for repeat business.
- Remember that the way the document is presented, the design of the letterhead, the spelling and punctuation and the speed at which a response is made are all advertisements for your organisation – quite apart from the phrases you write. Similarly, if the premises are clean and tidy and the staff are smartly dressed and attentive, this communicates a message that is only reinforced by the spoken word.

Negotiation skills

These were discussed in Element 4.1 under conflict resolution. Obviously, they can be a key asset if you are regularly involved in settling problems or finding acceptable terms for an irate customer – let alone if you are trying to finalise a sale or purchase with a customer or supplier.

It is impossible to negotiate with a customer or supplier if you do not understand or empathise with their frame of reference – as this affects the way they interpret your message. Henry Arthur, writing in the *Harvard Business Review*, argued that 'Bargaining is negotiating, comparing, making choices and arriving at an agreement with a partner – a supplier or a customer – who himself has been negotiating, comparing and making choices.' Everyone, in this situation, has a mindset that relates to their personal agenda, their own prejudices, attitudes and ambitions and which has been formed through previous associations either with your organisation or your competitors. The aim is to identify:

- some areas of common interest
- the points on which there is disagreement or conflict
- areas for compromise
- mutual benefits through collaboration
- agreed criteria for achievement.

To do this, not only are your own negotiating skills important but also your listening skills (see Element 4.1, page 289), particularly if you are communicating with someone who finds it difficult to express or communicate what he/she thinks or feels. Again, the better you know the person concerned, the better equipped you are to identify the points on which there is room for manoeuvre.

Quite often people will move position or change strategy if mutual advantages can be identified. A typical example was the move by Virgin Chairman, Richard Branson, to offer Railtrack a share of passenger revenues in return for an improved modernisation programme on the West Coast line. This would enable Branson to run his new trains at 140 mph much earlier than anticipated – but also increase the investment which must be made by Railtrack. This is an obvious example of a 'win/win' opportunity by both operators which forms the basis of a substantial deal with mutual benefits.

Today most forward-thinking companies have clearly thought-out strategies for dealing with crises, and crisis management techniques are considered essential for the organisation. In some cases crisis teams are on permanent stand-by to react immediately if a problem develops. According to Dr Stuart Smith, public affairs manager of 3M, 'having the proper skills to handle incidents or emergencies carries as much weight as financial control, product marketing or public affairs awareness'.

The importance of crisis management is obvious when you consider that every organisation has the potential to be hit by trouble – from a computer virus to pollution disasters, from mechanical failure to confrontation with environmental pressure groups, from product contamination to a bombing incident. All of these events can lead to immediate loss of profit and, more importantly, destroy a company's reputation with its external clients.

One approach to managing crises is to set up a crisis group that is familiar with every aspect of the company and has a tried and tested contingency plan. Responsibilities within the team should be clear and there should be recourse to experts in insurance, legal affairs, public relations and quality control. Studies have shown that companies who successfully manage crises – and even turn them from a problem to an opportunity – are those who acknowledge the difficulty, communicate quickly, honestly and promptly with all stakeholders (through hotlines and national advertising), and take immediate action to rectify the problem (e.g. halting production, recalling faulty goods). Perrier took just such an approach when its products were contaminated with benzine, Carlsberg Tetley acted equally promptly when a widget was found in a can of beer. British Midland turned a major commercial and human disaster around when the Chairman, Sir Michael Bishop, gave an exhausting round of interviews to the press after the flight in 1990 which crashed on the M1 killing 47 people. In each message he emphasised his determination to get to the bottom of the tragedy, immediately had staff contacting relatives and was perceived as totally caring and honest. The result was a 10 per cent increase in bookings for British Midland, rather than a fall because of reduced customer confidence.

Of vital importance is the way the problem is communicated. Not only is the attitude of each person critically assessed by an anxious public and a watchful media, their words need to be understood. Platitudes, bland reassurances and incomprehensible jargon all act against the organisation rather than in its favour.

THEORY INTO PRACTICE

1 What is your perception of your organisation's image? Now identify three other people who have heard of the organisation or have dealt with it in the past and try to find out (diplomatically) if their views agree with your own. If there are any differences in perception, how do you account for these and what could be done to bring them into line?
2 Identify the degree to which communication policies and training opportunities exist in your organisation to standardise, monitor and control the *quality* of communications – both verbal and written – of staff members.

3 Imagine the worst possible crisis that could affect your organisation. What strategies are in place to cope with the problem, and to what degree do you think it would be managed positively?

4 Obtain four random examples of communication from your organisation (brochure, leaflet, advertisement, letter, invoice, etc.) and assess each one for the overt and underlying message it gives the recipient. What improvements could you suggest, and why?

Ways of motivating people

In this section, motivation theory is used in an attempt to understand why external contacts behave in the way they do. This is particularly relevant to the behaviour of customers – both private individuals and organisations. Many studies have been undertaken to investigate the motives behind buyer behaviour – and an in-depth study of this topic is outside the remit of this book. However, a basic understanding of the relevance of motivation theory to the behaviour of external contacts is essential for all those involved in promoting and sustaining positive relationships.

Motivation can be defined as the force which drives a person to satisfy his or her needs. However, two criteria must exist for a person to act to satisfy a need:

- he/she must perceive that the need exists
- there must be the means available to satisfy the need.

To give a simple example, if you found one morning that your toaster had stopped functioning you would have a need to replace it *if* you used it regularly. If only your ex-partner liked toast you may decide to do without a toaster. Assume you like toast. You now have to know which shops sell toasters and the types of toasters available. You will visit the shop, examine different models, possibly ask the sales person for advice and make your decision.

In terms of marketing strategy this means that organisations must:

- be aware of the importance of needs
- act to make potential customers aware that they have a need for their product or service
- provide sufficient information for customers
- make the product or service available at the time the customer is making a decision.

The importance of needs

Although the terms 'needs' and 'wants' are used relatively interchangeably, it helps to start by defining the difference – as both motivate customers. We are all born with basic needs – these equate to those that Maslow identified. We start with biological, safety and affiliation needs for food, water, warmth, sleep and so on, then progress to needs for self-esteem and achievement. These needs can be divided into *biogenic* or innate needs, and *psychogenic* or learned needs.

Psychogenic needs are acquired through the assimilation of cultural norms and values and include the need for status, power and affiliation. In contrast, wants are learned through experience and knowledge of alternatives. Therefore a child may need to satisfy thirst but want a drink of Coke or lemonade, a teenager may need to occupy his leisure time but want to buy a computer – and so on. A third category of motivating force can be classified as desire – which can be described as 'a future want' which is not yet satisfied. Therefore you may need a car, want one which is reliable and cheap to run but really desire a red, drop-head sports car which is some way removed from your current budget!

Motivation is only *one* of several internal variables or basic determinants that affect buying behaviour. In addition, customers are influenced by external variables or environmental influences. The full range of factors that interact to influence buyer behaviour is shown below.

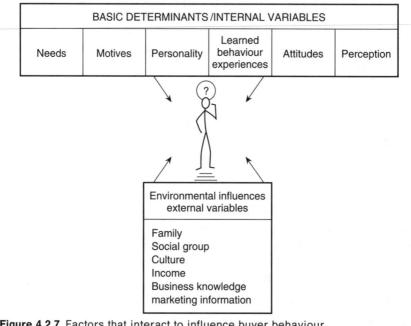

Figure 4.2.7 Factors that interact to influence buyer behaviour

The influence of external variables is fairly obvious. The relationship between internal variables is more complex but can easily be illustrated as follows:

Motive = thirst
Need = a drink
Personality = gregarious, likes company
Learning = pubs sell drinks, drinks satisfy thirst
Attitude = prefer long, cold drinks
Perception = beer is a 'good buy'.
Action = use thirst as an excuse to invite friend to a pub and order a beer!

Needs are insatiable – the moment one need is satisfied another appears to take its place. Moreover, wants are both interrelated and dynamic – as well as never-ending. They can therefore be influenced by additional knowledge and information, as well as by changing lifestyles. They can also be positive and negative. I may want to travel but my fear of flying may mean I have no 'want' or desire to use this form of transport. Conflict occurs when we cannot satisfy our desires or wants fully (because of fear, limited income, product scarcity, more pressing needs, etc.) and therefore we have to modify our behaviour. However, when dealing with customers a key point is that needs are perceived differently by individuals and the additional factors that influence buying behaviour are many and varied. Therefore, the 'triggers' which motivate one individual may be ineffective with another.

Theories of consumer buying behaviour

The stages of the customer buying process were described on pages 354–5. However, there have been many studies and theories which focus on the behaviour of buyers and consumers in the market.

Single-cause theories

Various alternative theories have been put forward, each identifying a single cause as the motivating factor:

- man (or woman) makes rational decisions based on income (i.e. economic man)
- man behaves instinctively through his inner nature (such as avoidance of pain and seeking pleasure)
- man is compelled to satisfy his most basic needs to maintain equilibrium (sometimes referred to as *homeostasis*).

These theories account for the human need to satisfy utilitarian needs through objective rational analysis (e.g. which car is the cheapest to run?) and yet also allow for hedonistic needs (e.g. which car is the fastest?). However, these theories do not explain many aspects of buyer behaviour and ignore key differences between individuals.

Partial-explanation theories

Humans make decisions based on:

- chance – by responding to sudden opportunities
- habit – which saves continual re-evaluation
- impulse – which provides a quick solution to a problem
- social orientation – based on the views of his/her peer group or influence group
- heredity – based on his/her inborn nature as a consumer.

All these theories are based on reaction or emotion. They assume humans to be simplistic and disregard their desire for information and the more complex and rational motives involved in making decisions.

Basic-explanation theories

In this case the consumer is either a risk-reducer or a problem-solver.

- People will minimise the risk of experiencing the consequences of making a bad decision (e.g. poor product performance, financial problems, social disapproval, etc.) by obtaining information and playing safe (e.g. buying a known brand).
- Desire creates a problem which is solved by obtaining information, examining alternatives and selecting the best option.

These theories assume a rational approach. They also assume that people always have time to invest considerable effort in a purchasing decision. However, they concede that there can be a trade-off between time and effort and imperfect product knowledge, and that the attitude to risk will vary depending upon the product. Therefore expensive 'high-risk' products will generate greater search for information to minimise risk than 'low-risk' ones.

Comprehensive theories

These theories consider that purchasing is a complex activity which is subject to both economic and psychological influences. Psychological factors include:

- human behaviour of consumers (related to perception, motivation, attitude formation, learned behaviour and personal/social aspirations)
- sociological factors (such as class, social mobility, social role, cultural background/beliefs/values, peer group pressure).

All these variables interact to influence and modify behaviour. Buying is undertaken for both irrational (hedonistic) and rational (utilitarian) reasons but customers often seek to justify irrational behaviour with rational explanations. The augmented product (see page 360) helps to satisfy this need as more 'reasons' for purchase are available to defend the decision.

These theories stress that over-simplification is dangerous – variables interact differently for different individuals.

Motivation and individuals

Although the influence of needs and motives is experienced differently by individuals, within common cultures and groupings there is a tendency for common needs to emerge. Maslow's original hierarchy of needs was discussed in Element 1.2 (page 65) and also in Element 4.1 (page 318) and this can usefully be applied to consumer needs. In addition, his 'smaller hierarchy' adds two additional needs which are also applicable in this context – the desire to know and understand and aesthetic needs. The relationship of Maslow's theories to consumer needs is shown in Figure 4.2.8.

Need	Satisfied by
Self-actualisation	travel, education, hobbies, leisure activities
Esteem	cars, furniture, credit cards, paintings, jewellery, larger house
Affiliation	club membership, fashion clothing, television, gifts, greeting cards
Safety	insurance, pensions, savings, burglar alarms
Physiological needs	food, medicines, basic clothing, glasses, soap
Maslow's smaller hierarchy of needs	
Need to know and understand	information, booklets, leaflets
Aesthetic needs	beauty, good design, visual appeal

Figure 4.2.8 Maslow's hierarchy and consumer needs

It is important to note that the types of products outlined alongside each individual need are not prescriptive. Marketers regularly link their product with a range of different needs to allow for differences in perception, attitude and values between different consumers. For that reason, Volvo emphasises safety whilst selling cars, the Royal Mail and British Telecom focus on affiliation in their television advertisements ('I saw this and I thought of you', 'Family and friends'), jewellery, perfume products and luxury goods focus on various needs from affiliation to esteem to self-fulfilment (think of Haagen-Dazs or advertisements for gold jewellery or diamonds).

Marketers and organisations have frequently been criticised for meeting the needs of male purchasers but ignoring the needs of women. At first it was car manufacturers and distributors who were under fire – many promoting car features and using sales patter which focused on engine size and performance rather than economy, storage space, safety or comfort. This not only ignored the fact that women made up a large proportion of the car-buying population, but also ignored the influence of women in relation to family car-buying decisions. The next industry under fire was the pubs trade. Large breweries consistently ignored the needs of women and families when designing pubs or offering services. Whitbread, which deliberately changed its policy to introduce 'family pubs', has benefited through making record profits in this area.

The latest bastion starting to crumble is that of the financial services industry. A survey carried out by the Goldfish credit card company found that women are more likely to pay bills, check financial statements and make major financial decisions than their partners. A further survey by Hill Samuel Asset Management showed that women exercise more prudence in investment decisions than men and are less likely to make a loss than men. They also make up 50 per cent of ethical investors, are less likely to go into debt and less impressed with flashy gold or platinum credit cards. The latest news is that the finance and investment industry – including banks and building societies – is now taking a new look at its marketing communications strategy given that this is still mainly targeted at men.

Cognitive dissonance and its importance

Cognitive dissonance is related to people's need for order and consistency. When beliefs, preferences or needs conflict then we experience tension. We are then motivated to reduce this inconsistency (or dissonance) to eliminate the tension. Three types of conflict can be experienced.

- *Need conflict*. In this case we have two competing needs both of which must be satisfied. We may want to treat ourselves but be concerned about the nutritional value of what we are eating ('full of vitamins and tastes good too'). If we are persuaded that one product can satisfy both (or several) needs simultaneously, then we have enough reasons to be convinced that buying it is a good idea. (It is interesting that we also try to convince ourselves that a rejected product has more flaws than the one we eventually choose!)

- *Need attraction/avoidance conflict.* Decisions to buy are complicated if we are torn between positive and negative wants or needs. We may want to take an additional qualification but be frightened of failing. We may want to drink lager or eat ice cream but be worried about putting on weight. We are persuaded if the focus is on the positive, attraction needs rather than on our negative fears. For that reason Weight Watchers focuses on affiliation and self-esteem needs rather than the fact its members are overweight; luxury goods are sold with exhortations to 'spoil yourself, you deserve it' to minimise guilt; health insurance is promoted with peace of mind as a bonus rather than a focus on illness.
- *Avoidance conflict.* In this situation the consumer is faced with a problem where alternative solutions all have disadvantages (e.g. the washing machine has broken down but I cannot afford a new one at the moment). In this case marketers play on minimising fear and making the decision more obvious. Examples include the fear of being socially ostracised through lack of attention to personal freshness (remember the Lifebuoy advertisements?), the fear of spending too much too soon (by advertising special credit terms), and the fear of mechanical breakdown (through advertising extended warranties and after-sales service).

Motivation and organisational buyers

It is tempting to believe that motivation plays less of a role if your customers are mainly, or wholly, organisational buyers and the organisation is motivated by profit. However, this would be neglecting the fact that organisations are comprised of human beings – who are driven by the same type of needs at work as in their private lives, even if these may manifest themselves in different ways.

Many of the items purchased by organisations are similar to those bought by consumers – such as cars, stationery, computers, insurance – although the reasons behind the purchases may be different. Firstly, they will be purchased because they help the organisation to achieve its objectives. Secondly they are bought for organisational use rather than for individual consumption. Thirdly, there may be high-level technical specifications linked to many expensive purchases with high need for specialist advice, expertise and ongoing service and support. However, a key requirement for any organisation is to satisfy its own consumers. Therefore, industrial buyers are involved in assessing their own markets and future demand for their own products. If this is likely to change, then the organisation will change its buying behaviour. For this reason, it is important that organisations understand the end uses of their own product and identify the best way to meet the changing needs of their own customers and those of *their* customers too!

The situation is further complicated by the fact that the process of organisational buying, as you saw on pages 345–6, is rarely the remit of one person and the repercussions of making a bad decision affect not only the organisation but also the reputation of the decision-maker. Given that individuals wish to maintain their self-esteem, reputation and personal prestige in an organisation – as well as conform to organisational objectives – this can create uncertainty and anxiety and a high concentration on risk reduction. The more the supplier helps to minimise risk the greater the chances of success. Risk reduction strategies include:

- *risk avoidance* – by reducing vulnerability or dependence on one supplier
- *risk minimising* – by evaluating different market opportunities, opting for the best package of benefits (e.g. including training, maintenance and servicing) – in other words, the augmented product (see page 360)
- *risk bearing* – dispersing risk through joint ventures, consortia operations, licensing agreements, etc.

Theories of organisational buying behaviour

In the same way that theorists, over the years, have put forward ever-more complex theories to explain the behaviour of consumers, other researchers have examined the behaviour of organisational buyers to identify common patterns and actions which can inform their suppliers.

Decision-process theories

These use a rational model which commences with identification of a need. The products and services that can satisfy the need are identified and specified and suitable sources of supply are contacted. Offers are evaluated and a supplier is then selected.

Quite obviously this behaviour is variable depending upon the risk involved in the decision. Low-risk items (e.g. stationery) may not be subjected to this procedure because purchase is routine and habitual. High-risk items, such as a new processing plant, may be subject to a long and rigorous process of selection. However, the model does not identify the complex variables that may influence choice, nor does it explain why some organisations may choose to remain with a known supplier rather than 'shop around' for each new requirement.

Behavioural theories

These theories attempt to identify the interactions between economic, social, cultural and emotional factors involved in organisational buying. Jagdish Sheth was interested in the following.

- The different expectations of those involved in organisational buying. In his view, users, buyers and engineers will have different criteria:
  - users desire prompt delivery, satisfactory installation and efficient servicing arrangements
  - buyers are interested in price and transport arrangements
  - engineers are concerned with quality, performance and product standardisation.
- The conditions under which joint decision-making takes place, rather than autonomous decisions by one person. According to Sheth, this depends on the ethos of the organisation, its size and the degree of centralisation.

- The inevitable conflict between decision-makers and the tactics which are used to resolve this. Conflict can occur for many reasons – lack of trust, poor communications, interdepartmental rivalry, different expectations/inputs from executives, lack of experience by executives, and so on. This creates an almost inevitable 'wheeling and dealing' scenario which works against rational decision-making.

An alternative theory was put forward by Frederick Webster and Yoram Wind, who considered that four different types of variables affect organisational buyers – individual, social, organisational and environmental – and each of these can be subdivided into task and non-task components. These link to the task needs and personal needs of those involved in making the decision. Therefore my individual task need may be to obtain a low price, my personal need may be to impress my boss. My social task need may mean meeting with others to decide exact specifications, my personal need may be to obtain advice from my opposite number in another department. Although the theory is useful to identify the variables that interact to influence the buyer, it does not explain how individual buyers actually operate within this framework, nor how they reach the decisions they do.

Interaction theories

These theories link with the relationship marketing model in that they examine the interaction between buyers and sellers as a two-way exchange and negotiation process. In this case the participants, the environment, the relationship between the buyer and seller and their past histories all interact to inform the process. Instead of the buyer simply reacting to a bid or offer from a seller, both parties contribute, formally and informally, to establishing and building a productive relationship. However, the theories do emphasise the key role of behaviour and stress the importance of understanding the needs and motives of buyers and the reason for their behaviour if sellers are to be successful in negotiations. Note that negotiating is also covered on page 377.

These theories incorporate a recognition that familiarity and knowledge lower the risks involved in decision-making.

THEORY INTO PRACTICE

Identify the degree to which organisational buying in your company is undertaken rationally and dispassionately, and the degree to which other variables interplay. Which theories of organisational buying do you consider most accurately represent the process your suppliers experience?

Consequences of inadequate consultation and interaction with contacts

No person – and no organisation – is an island. Therefore constant contact with others is not only inevitable but essential to promote productive relationships, and this involves both regular consultation and interaction.

Marketers and other experts have identified face-to-face encounter points with customers as opportunities for reinforcing motivation and giving reassurance – or occasions when problems and deficiencies can be recognised. J. Carlzson, the President of Scandinavian Airlines, described these as *moments of truth*. The aim for many proactive and confident companies is to increase the moments of truth by increasing customer contacts. A waiter who continually checks that diners are happy with the service and remains on hand to meet any request is managing moments of truth proactively. Obviously, if this becomes so frequent as to be intrusive it can act as a deterrent – but is still marginally better than irritating customers by disappearing from the scene when they have an urgent need for help.

Regular consultation with suppliers is essential over issues of mutual concern or interest – whether these relate to product specifications, new products and services or policy/procedure changes. Unless there is adequate consultation there is an assumption that the other person's opinion can be discounted – and this can be both dangerous and foolhardy. Successful organisations go to considerable lengths to involve suppliers in any discussions relating to product supply, specification, delivery or quality, given that their commitment and input is considered vital for plans to come to fruition promptly and profitably. No organisation can presume to know everything – consulting others (and listening their responses) acknowledges this fact and accepts that better decisions will be made if there is scope for wider input.

Consultation with customers is also essential if the company is not going to be misled by its own perceptions of customer opinion. What customers really think is often very different from what managers and executives think they think! Organisations that understand this actively welcome feedback – through customer panels, questionnaires or surveys and analysis of complaints received. Some even argue that every one complaint represents up to 400 dissatisfied customers – on that basis complaints should be welcomed, investigated, answered and considered carefully in relation to the information they provide on customer perceptions. Representatives who visit customers and telesales staff who make service or 'customer happy' calls should be able to report their findings freely and without prejudice. Managers should not 'shoot the messenger' as this will simply gag the informant rather than solve the problem. Organisations that do not actively invite input from customers are in grave danger of believing their own publicity; those who do not heed the information they are receiving are even more foolish.

A key way to improve and develop external relationships is by setting up procedures which almost guarantee regular interaction with external contacts. This can be done in a variety of ways and both formally and informally. To this end, many organisations operate a proactive communications programme. Rather than simply responding to enquiries, complaints and orders they try to make sure that the supplier or customer never has any need to make the first move – because he/she is always informed of the situation. This includes communicating through:

- personal visits by sales and purchasing staff
- calls by telesales staff

- calls by customer service staff
- direct mailings on new products and services
- actively advertising and promoting company policy and customer service
- providing customer service packs and information manuals
- holding customer and supplier workshops.

If your organisation deals mainly with industrial customers then it is worth noting that the value placed on visits by sales staff and the reliance placed on their expertise is considerable. The trust factor of the 'known' versus the 'unknown' plays a large part in gaining repeat business, and once this is lost it is usually gone forever.

Whilst you may actively promote additional 'moments of truth' or contact between your staff and their external contacts, what you may not realise is that according to a paper presented to the British Psychological Society you will be increasing the stress levels in their lives! Researchers at the University of Salford have discovered that constantly being friendly and pleasant is stressful because of the emotions and reactions that are being suppressed in an effort to be affable. Anger, disappointment and dismay have to be suppressed given the received wisdom that customers return only if they are pampered and cared for. The answer, according to Sandi Mann at Salford, is threefold. Firstly, acknowledge that the work done by customer service teams and front-line staff is stressful and difficult. Secondly, back them up and give them adequate support with particularly difficult customers. Thirdly, allow downtime away from the customer – to give staff a chance to recover and a rest from smiling for a while!

THEORY INTO PRACTICE

The Royal Mail service has produced a useful guide *Staying in Touch* which, whilst obviously promoting Royal Mail services, also gives useful information on keeping customers for life, ways and means of staying in touch, checking customer satisfaction and dealing with unhappy customers. Obtain a copy by phoning 0345 446633 or by writing to Royal Mail, Freepost, HR109, Ross-on-Wye, Herefordshire HR9 7ZX.

Legal and regulatory requirements relating to working relationships

A wide variety of legislation regulates the way in which transactions are undertaken and is applied in the case of any disputes. The basis of an agreement between a buyer and a seller is enshrined in the law of contract – which you have already encountered in relation to employment law in Chapter 3.

Over time, successive governments have acted to protect consumers from the power of large organisations, technological advances which the consumer may not be able to understand, unfair business practices, poor-quality goods and services, the unwise provision of credit, and high-pressure selling and advertising. Laws also exist which cover agency and franchising agreements and the use of trademarks or copyright issues. The health and safety of visitors is encompassed within health and safety legislation and rights to confidentiality of information are covered by the Data Protection Act (see Element 1.1, page 52, Element 4.1, page 336, and Element 5.2, page 449). The major areas of which you should be aware are those of

- anti-competition legislation
- the law of contract
- consumer legislation.

The Data Protection Registrar is currently clamping down on organisations that use the database information of their customers for the purpose of sending junk mail promoting other products. This is a breach of the 1984 Data Protection Act and, in the case of privatised companies, also contravenes the legislation that privatised them, which states that customer information can be used only for billing purposes. Companies being investigated at the time of writing include BG, Southern Electric, Thames Water and others – many of whom sent magazines to customers offering other services. The aim now is to clamp down on all companies wanting to make money by exploiting their databases without customer consent. According to the Registrar, customers must be fully aware of the way personal information may be used when it is first requested.

Data protection watchdogs were also involved after confidential details of Halifax building society customers were found outside a Plymouth branch, including names, addresses, account numbers and balances. The Halifax (now a bank) was warned that it had a duty of care in disposing of client information to protect individuals from the unauthorised disclosure of their computer records. The Data Protection Registrar has the right to serve an enforcement notice and to prosecute the offender if there are subsequent breaches.

Anti-competition legislation

There has been a variety of legislation aimed at curbing the ability of the strong to manipulate the weak, by ending restrictive practices and resale price agreements enforced by monopoly suppliers or large manufacturers. A variety of Acts have been passed to promote competition.

The Monopolies and Restrictive Practices Act 1948

This created the Monopolies Commission and gave the (then) Board of Trade the power to investigate and report on potential monopolies.

The Restrictive Trade Practices Acts 1956, 1968 and 1976

These Acts regulated agreements to restrict prices, limit supply, dictate the terms of a sale or the process of manufacture, persons or areas to be supplied. Basically, agreements are only allowable to protect the public from injury or if there will be substantial benefits to the consumer or if they are in the public interest. The 1968 Act held that all informal agreements between organisations to exchange information – particularly about prices – must be registered.

The Resale Prices Act 1964

This banned large manufacturers from dictating the retail price – although they could still 'recommend' a price. The only goods not covered were pharmaceutical goods, books and newspapers, on the grounds that, in the first case, lower prices may endanger public health and safety and, in the second, the quality and variety of goods offered may deteriorate and/or the number of retailers would be substantially reduced. The ending of the Net Book Agreement in 1995 means that books are no longer exempt and can now be discounted by supermarkets and chain stores.

The Competition Act 1980

This strengthened free competition and defined anti-competitive practices in relation to both the private and the public sector. These were held to be any conduct which intended to restrict, distort or prevent competition in relation to the production, supply or acquisition of goods or the supply or securing of services in the United Kingdom.

The Fair Trading Act 1987

This gives power to the Director General of Fair Trading to investigate anti-competitive practices and refer such conduct to the Monopolies and Mergers Commission, which then submits its report to the Secretary of State. Also covered are the services of statutory corporations who may abuse their monopoly position.

The Labour government has made a commitment to reforming competition policy, building on proposals put forward by the Conservatives in their Green Paper, *Tackling Cartels and the Abuse of Market Powers*. In addition to strengthening the powers of the Director General of Fair Trading, the government is also aiming to prevent dominant companies in a market from setting predatory prices to force smaller competitors out of business. Further details on the Competition Bill are given in Chapter 8.

The law of contract

You have already met the law of contract in relation to employees in Element 2.2 (page 177). Further, details relating to commercial contracts between buyers and sellers are included as part of optional Unit 8. However, at this stage it is important that you be aware of the basic facts relating to legal agreements between a buyer and a seller.

When an agreement is made for goods or services to be purchased, then those involved become 'parties to a contract.' However, for this to be legally binding certain conditions must be met:

- There must be an offer from one party – to provide goods, perform a service or pay a particular price for an item.
- There must be unconditional acceptance by the other party. This means that all the terms of the offer must be accepted – neither party can pick and choose certain elements.

- There must be consideration of some kind. In other words, something must be undertaken or given in return for the goods or service. Normally, of course, this is represented by payment, although it is perfectly legal to agree to exchange goods or services (as in house exchanges). The principle of consideration, however, does not apply in Scottish law.

When goods are advertised at a particular price this does not constitute an offer but rather an invitation to treat. This means that the supplier can accept or reject a purchaser's offer – so long as the refusal is not on grounds of race or sex. However, when organisations are invited to tender to provide a service and then do so, they make a legal offer to provide the goods or service at the specified price.

The terms of the contract can be *express* or *implied*. Express terms are those that are specifically stated – for instance, the date of delivery may be made an express condition of the contract. Implied terms refer to the clear but unexpressed intentions of the parties to the contract. Contractual terms can also be divided into conditions and warranties – the former being more important than the latter. A photocopier you have purchased may have a smaller paper tray than was described, which is technically a breach of contract, but is not very important – you may agree to live with the difference. However, if you had ordered a colour copier and a black and white one arrived you might be rather less satisfied. In this case the supplier has breached the contract more substantially and failed to honour a condition of the contract.

Both parties to the contract must be prepared to show they intend to create a binding agreement – otherwise the contract cannot be enforced. There is an assumption in business agreements that intent exists unless it is formally stated that the agreement is 'binding in honour only'.

Offers must be communicated to the person to whom the offer is being made. However, an offer does not last indefinitely. If either party dies, the offer is allowed to lapse. If the offer is subject to the fulfilment of a condition which is not met then the offer lapses. In addition, an offer can be revoked at any time before it has been accepted.

Acceptance must be unqualified (unless a counter offer is made and accepted) and certain. The acceptance can be verbal, written or by conduct (such as accepting a deposit on an item).

The law aims to protect those who may be restricted in their capacity to make a contract, such as minors (under 18 years of age), those who are mentally disabled (in accordance with the Mental Health Act 1983) and those who are drunk at the time of signing the contract.

A contract may be void, voidable or invalid in certain circumstances. These include:

- *Mistakes* – if a genuine error occurs (the most common being mistaken identity). However, carelessness is not covered – the mistake must be both genuine and significant.

- *Misrepresentation* – where false statements have been made to induce an agreement.
- *Lack of good faith* – refers to contracts (such as for insurance) where all relevant facts must be declared. If relevant information is withheld the contract could be void or voidable.
- *Unlawful intent* – contracts are not enforceable if they involve an unlawful act.
- *Undue influence* – a contract is not normally enforceable if it can be proved one party was forced to sign it under pressure from the other.

Additional protection is given by the following Acts of Parliament.

The Unfair Contract Terms Act 1977

Under the Unfair Contract Terms Act 1977, exclusion clauses or disclaimers are invalid unless an organisation can prove these terms are fair and reasonable. You could not, for instance, disclaim responsibility for loss or damage for customers' goods left on your premises if such loss or damage occurred because of negligence. Any exclusions are either considered void or subjected to a test of 'reasonableness'.

The Unfair Terms in Consumer Contracts Regulations 1995

Under these Regulations, customers are given the right to contest a contract they consider to be unfair through the courts or the Office of Fair Trading. This law also demands that plain English must be used and that all wording must be clearly readable.

The Consumer Credit Act 1974

Consumers buying on credit are further protected by the Consumer Credit Act 1974, which places strict controls upon organisations that provide credit facilities in the course of their business. All such organisations, with the exception of local authorities, must be licensed. The Act lays down strict rules governing the form and content of credit agreements and aims to protect the borrower by providing full information about his or her legal rights and obligations.

- Advertisements relating to the provision of credit or hiring of goods of less than £15 000 in value must contain specific and accurate information. Both the finance company and the publisher of the advertisement would be liable if the advertisement contained false or misleading claims.
- Door-to-door selling at the homes of private individuals is an offence unless a visit has been requested in writing.
- A credit agreement must be issued to the buyer in a specified format giving the names and addresses of the parties concerned; the APR (Annual Percentage Rate of interest); the cash price, deposit and total amount of credit, the total amount repayable, the repayment dates and amount of each payment, the sums payable on default, and other rights and protections under the Act.
- Consumers have the right to cancel the agreement over the next seven days if they change their minds provided the agreement was not

signed on the trader's business premises and the goods were bought in a face-to-face transaction. During this 'cooling-off period' the creditor cannot contact the other party unless specifically requested to do so. As yet, goods bought over the telephone are not covered by law although reputable organisations do offer up to 14 days cancellation rights for goods bought in this way.

- Copies of all signed agreements and signed contracts must be sent to the debtor within seven days of the agreement and must include rights of cancellation. If the agreement is signed at home then the prospective debtor must receive a copy of the agreement immediately which also includes details of cancellation rights. A further copy or separate notice must be sent by post a week later and from the day after the second copy is received the buyer has five further days in which to give the creditor written notice of cancellation.

- If an agreement is cancelled, any sum paid by the debtor is repayable and the goods must be returned.

- If the buyer defaults on the debt, the creditor must serve a formal default notice which gives details of the recovery action to be taken, and the action which can be taken to remedy the situation and the date by which this must be taken. If the defaulter complies with these terms then no breach of contract is deemed to have occurred.

- The creditor cannot reclaim goods sold under a hire-purchase agreement once the buyer has paid one-third or more of the price, unless entitled to do so by court order.

- No creditor can prevent a debtor from making an early payment to settle the debt and must respond to any request to give information as to how early payment may be made.

A scathing report on photocopier hire and lease agreements by the Office of Fair Trading in 1994 has now had some effect. A survey in 1997 has found that most dealers and leasing companies have improved their selling practices significantly. Whereas in the past a range of unethical practices had been uncovered, today most agreements are much clearer although there are still problems with incomprehensible jargon being used, often to mislead buyers. Terms to watch for include 're-manufactured' or 'newly-manufactured' and 'cost-per-copy' – which can distract attention from the overall cost of the package.

Some reputable manufacturers have now appointed authorised suppliers in an attempt to raise standards and accredit reputable dealers who subscribe to defined operating and ethical business standards. In some cases quality standards such as ISO 9002 and BS 7850 (Total Quality Management) and BS 7750 (an environmental control standard) are required. However, as yet consumer bodies remain unconvinced that approved suppliers and distributors are *always* checked rigorously by manufacturers, but acknowledge that at least this is a start to some form of quality control and a clear move towards more transparent, ethical practices.

Consumer law

The rights of consumers, in particular, have been a key force in the way in which consumerism and the laws governing business/consumer relations have developed over the past 30 years. Before the 1960s, there was little protection for any consumers in the UK, given the basic *caveat emptor* (let the buyer beware) principle. Today there are a variety of laws, in addition to statutory and voluntary bodies, which recognise the rights of consumers to safe products, accurate information and free choice in the marketplace. The five major Acts which relate to consumer protection are given below. All apply to items bought face-to-face, by mail order or electronically.

The Sale of Goods Act 1979

Whilst much of the content of this has been amended by the Sale and Supply of Goods Act 1994, this Act was the first to provide buyers with protection from being deceived into buying goods which were not fit to be sold. The Act stated that goods for sale had to be:

- *as described* – correspond with any description
- *of merchantable quality* – free from defects unless these are pointed out at the time of sale
- *fit for the purpose for which they are intended* – the verbal assurance of the seller could be held to be binding.

If the goods did not meet these criteria then the buyer had the right to a cash refund, although proof of purchase might be requested.

The user had no legal rights to return the goods if he/she had had a change of mind, had damaged the item, was aware of the fault at the time of purchase or did not enter into the contract him/herself (i.e. if the item was received as a gift).

The Trade Descriptions Act 1968

This Act includes as an offence any false descriptions whether these be inaccurate, deliberate or implied and regardless of whether they relate to the goods themselves, their composition or method of manufacture. Complaints under this Act are investigated by the local Trading Standards Officers.

> Product endorsements are covered by the Trade Descriptions Act and, where appropriate, by the Food Safety Act. This applies to endorsements on packaging and also in advertisements or leaflets. Advertised endorsements are also the responsibility of the Advertising Standards Authority and/or the Independent Television Commission or the Radio Authority. At present the law simply says that descriptions must not be false or misleading, although the ASA would prefer that advertisements make it clear when endorsing companies are paid for their approval.

The Supply of Goods and Services Act 1982

This Act extended protection previously provided by the 1979 Act to include goods supplied as part of a service, on hire or in part exchange, as well as the standard of services. The aim is to protect consumers against poor workmanship, delays or exorbitant charges. Under the Act, all services must be carried out for a reasonable charge, within a reasonable time and with reasonable care and skill.

The Consumer Protection Act 1987

This Act introduced two new areas to consumer protection, pricing and safety. Under the Act it is an offence to mislead consumers about the price at which goods, services, accommodation or facilities are available. In particular, there must be no false comparisons with recommended prices or previous prices, no 'hidden extras' which are not included in the advertised price and the method of determining the price must be clearly stated.

It is also an offence to sell or provide goods that are not reasonably safe, or to possess unsafe goods for supply or to offer or agree to supply such goods. Under the Act the buyer can claim against the manufacturer if the product is defective and causes either personal injury or more than £275 damage to property.

The Sale and Supply of Goods Act 1994

This legislation has replaced the term 'merchantable quality' found in the 1979 Act with a new term – *satisfactory quality*. This means that the goods have to be safe, durable and free from minor defects. The law also provides consumers with the right to inspect and examine the goods properly before losing the right to reject them and claim a refund. The time period for returning faulty goods is undefined but must be 'within a reasonable amount of time' after purchase. What is reasonable is likely to depend upon the particular type of goods purchased and the individual situation. As yet this law is in its infancy and it will be some time until precedents exist to define this term more precisely.

Faulty components that affect the reputation and sales of the industrial buyer can lead to expensive settlements in the courts. In the 1980s, Amstrad purchased computer disk drives from Seagate, the world's largest supplier of drives. The drives were installed in the Amstrad PC2000 range but their constant failure was a source of embarrassment to Amstrad and substantially damaged its reputation as a supplier of business computers. In a settlement in spring 1997, Amstrad was awarded over £100 million in compensation – the amount representing lost profit on delayed sales, lost interest on profit, lost sales and the cost of managing the problem. Seagate is expected to appeal, so the matter has yet to be completely resolved. However, in the meantime Amstrad is taking another supplier, Western Digital, to court in Los Angeles over faulty components.

Law enforcement

A variety of organisations are involved in monitoring organisational behaviour and protecting consumer interests – many of which were mentioned in Element 2.2 on pages 175–176. 'Watchdogs' such as Oftel, Ofgas, Ofwat and Oflot monitor the behaviour of privatised monopolies and have occasionally been known to show their teeth – as when British Gas was ordered to reduce prices between 20 per cent and 28 per cent in 1997 and then to peg price rises at 5 per cent below inflation between 1997 and 2001.

Consumer bodies such as the Office of Fair Trading, the British Standards Institution, the Trading Standards Office, the Environmental Health Office, the National Consumer Council and the Consumers Association oversee the interests of consumers. Trade associations such as the Cable Communications Association, the UK Association of Frozen Food Producers, the British Bankers' Association and the Association of British Travel Agents, and other organisations such as the Advertising Standards Authority, ITC and other regulatory bodies, operate voluntary codes of practice to which their members and/or other reputable organisations subscribe. These normally act as a guide in relation to the way customers should be treated and complaints should be handled. Trade associations will also deal with complaints about companies in their industry. Finally, there are Ombudsmen covering local government, insurance, legal services, the health service, investment, estate agents, banking, building societies and pensions, who will investigate complaints that remain unresolved.

On 1 July 1997 a new banking code of practice came into practice with the aim of improving the exchange of information and customer service standards. The code is purely voluntary, although all the main banks and building societies are signatories. All staff members should be able to give details of the code on request and an independent review panel has been set up to reprimand those banks that flout the agreement. Perhaps you should contact your bank to test whether they can give you the details on request!

One step in front – or behind?

Where consumers are concerned, most reputable companies do not just comply with the law or with codes of practice – they inform modern business practice. In other words, their policies and procedures are such that they allow scope for their staff to placate or recompense a customer far beyond their legal responsibilities. This is eminently sensible if it leads to repeat business or if the customer is known to be genuine and a 'regular'.

A typical example is the varying policies of organisations on returned goods where there is no fault – the buyer has simply changed his/her mind. A *Which?* report in 1996 surveyed 54 high street retailer organisations and discovered a range of policies in use. Only three organisations would refuse a refund if the customer had a receipt, and one of these would also refuse to exchange the goods or offer gift vouchers. Most establishments allowed an exchange or gave gift vouchers if there was no receipt, and in some cases a refund was at the discretion of the manager or customer service staff. This enables the store to be sensitive to the customer's feelings without being vulnerable to sharp practice or deceit. Finding the balance between protecting business interests and consumer responsiveness is not easy, but it pays dividends if it can be achieved.

You should note that contract law, consumer law and other issues covered in this section are discussed in more detail in Chapter 8.

THEORY INTO PRACTICE

In many cases particular sections of business and industry are further constrained in their operations through specific legislation. Examples include the Financial Services Act 1986, which regulates the operations of the investment industry; the Warsaw Convention of 1929, adopted into UK law in 1961, which operates as a regulatory framework for travel firms and tour operators; the Property Misdescriptions Act 1991, which relates to estate agents and lettings agents; and various banking and building society Acts, which affect the operations of banks and other financial institutions. Those in the food and drugs industry are, of course, subject to a variety of legislation in relation to food safety, labelling, hygiene and weights and measures, such as the Food Hygiene (General) Regulations 1970, the Food Hygiene (Amendment) Regulations 1990 and 1991 and the Food Safety Act 1990.

1 Find out the additional legislation relating to your particular industry and the way in which this affects your operations.
2 Identify the way in which your organisation 'adds value' to the customer experience by going beyond the letter of the law – and the degree to which procedures have been instigated to protect against false or exaggerated claims.
3 If you can, identify one serious complaint involving a supplier or customer that led to legal action, and assess the degree to which you consider your organisation acted fairly throughout.
4 What guidelines are given to your salesforce in relation to ethical practice, if any? To what degree do you consider business ethics to be an issue in your particular industry?

5 Influence and facilitate decision making

Element 5.1

Lead meetings to facilitate decision making

Your own role and responsibilities

Imagine that you have just joined a new organisation and you find that you are expected to attend a number of meetings. Your senior manager informs you that you will also be expected to chair at least two of these meetings – the weekly meeting of the staff for whom you are line manager and, on a rota basis, the cross-departmental meetings held periodically to discuss the role and effectiveness of the centralised services.

Some meetings will be specifically concerned with your own area of responsibility. If you are accustomed to chairing meetings of your own staff you will probably find that, before the first of the weekly meetings, you need only check:

- the terms of reference (i.e. the purpose) of the meeting
- its membership
- the rules and procedures
- the follow-up mechanisms.

If, on the other hand, it is your first experience in acting as chairperson, you may need to pay some attention to:

- the exact nature of your role and responsibilities
- the role and responsibilities of the other participants
- ways of establishing a meeting's objectives
- its rules and procedures
- the ways of organising, analysing and presenting information
- types and characteristics of non-verbal language
- methods of promoting and encouraging debate
- ways of summarising and clarifying discussions and decisions
- ways of dealing with disagreements and conflict
- the legal and regulatory requirements relating to the conduct of meetings
- ways of ensuring that key issues and decisions are recorded.

Other meetings may be broader in their remit and membership when they are connected with organisational issues. For instance, chairing the cross-departmental meetings on the role and effectiveness of the central services may cause you greater difficulty. Not only will you have to bear in mind the points just outlined, you will also have to be aware of:

- the different backgrounds of the participants
- their different objectives – you may find, for instance, that cross-

organisational meetings are far more competitive and less collaborative than departmental or SBU meetings

- the need to remain unbiased.

It is important, therefore, that you feel confident that you have both the personal and the technical skills to deal with all the potential problems and to ensure that each meeting you chair has a successful outcome.

THEORY INTO PRACTICE

Assume now that you have sat through one or two of the cross-organisational meetings – prior to taking over the chair – and have found them unproductive, inefficient and highly irritating. Indeed in your notebook you have jotted down your feelings:

'Why is this meeting taking so long? It should have been over at least half an hour ago.'

'Does anything ever start on time here? Why do we have to wait for all the latecomers before we start?'

'How much is the departmental manager being paid to sit here and listen to all this? What's it got to do with her anyway?'

'Why are we meeting at all? I don't understand what we're supposed to be talking about.'

'Has anyone actually read the papers circulated before the meeting? If they have, they're doing a good job of concealing it.'

'Talk about a one-man band! From 1 pm to 4.30 pm no-one but the Chair has got a word in.'

'All right, it wasn't a very good idea, but need she have been made to look such a fool? I bet she doesn't say anything again in a hurry.'

'Is this a set-up? Everything looks a bit cut and dried to me. That item should have been discussed in far more detail.'

'Is this really the only room available? We're all frozen and the acoustics are awful – and why have it on Monday morning when most of us are trying to schedule the week's activities?'

'I'll have to ring Jack to check what, if anything, we're supposed to do before the next meeting.'

'What a complete shambles!'

Consider (a) where you think the chairperson was at fault, and (b) what you would have done differently to ensure that those problems did not arise. If you are uncertain about what you should do in any of these instances, read through the element and then return to this exercise.

Skills needed to run a meeting

Personal skills

One management writer, John Adair, suggests that the leader of any group should satisfy three areas of need:

- the successful completion of the task
- the creation and maintenance of team spirit
- the harmonisation as far as possible of the needs of the individual with those of the group.

Technical skills

Even the most charismatic chairperson is destined to fail if he or she does not cultivate the technical skills necessary to run an effective meeting. Indeed, if he or she is ill-prepared for the meeting, there is probably little point in holding it at all.

Composition of the meeting

A good chairperson, if given the opportunity, should take care in choosing the members of the group. If you are expected to take over the chair of a meeting your first job should be to look at its composition and to ask in each case why that particular person is expected to attend. Your answer could be illuminating. It may be that some people are members of the meeting because they:

- have some knowledge which is related to the purpose of the meeting
- control certain funding
- have special skills which can be used

If so, they are likely to be useful contributors to the meeting.

Equally, if they just 'turn up' because traditionally someone from a particular department or area has been invited to attend, you may find that not only do they have little to contribute, they can hamper the contributions of other people simply because their presence makes the meeting too large to allow for meaningful discussion. In such circumstances, an informal chat with the head of that particular unit or department should result in a satisfactory conclusion. What should be remembered, however, is that someone who attends a meeting may not be a particularly effective contributor but his or her position or status in the organisation may be influential. In such a case, it is obviously advisable that you leave well alone – remember that one of the marks of a good chairperson is intelligence! More difficult to deal with is the person who does not make a particular contribution but whose hidden agenda or hurt feelings should he or she be asked to relinquish membership may cause you difficulties outside the meeting room.

THEORY INTO PRACTICE

Unfortunately not all chairpersons have the freedom to choose who should attend their meetings. Consider what action you would take should you find that you are expected to chair a cross-departmental meeting that is

- too large
- unrepresentative of all the departments
- highly political.

Preparation for the meeting

The checklist in Figure 5.1.1 indicates the actions a good chairperson should take when preparing for a meeting.

Informal meetings

- To decide whether a meeting is necessary. Would a better form of communication be a discussion with various individuals, a memo, an e-mail, etc.?
- To decide on the *purpose* of the meeting. Is it to give advice, to receive advice, to generate some ideas, to make a decision, etc.?
- To ensure that the members know the purpose of the meeting and what their particular role is to be (e.g. to read certain documents before the meeting, to talk to certain colleagues prior to the meeting, to come prepared to discuss their ideas on a particular topic or to make a final decision on a particular issue, etc.).
- To ensure that the meeting is scheduled at a convenient time and is of an acceptable length.
- To ensure that the meeting venue is acceptable.
- In consultation with the meetings secretary, to ensure that all the necessary documentation is prepared prior to and after the meeting (for further discussion on this point see page 402).
- To control the meeting and ensure that the required result is achieved (see further page 426).
- To ensure full – and effective – participation by all the members (see further page 403).

Additional duties of the chairperson in formal meetings

- To see that the meeting is properly convened in accordance with the rules and properly constituted; i.e. that a proper notice has been sent, that there is a quorum of members present and that his or her own appointment as chairperson is in order.
- To carry out the necessary formalities during the meeting; e.g.
  - to ensure that motions and amendments are dealt with correctly
  - to deal with points of order as they arise
  - to see that decisions are made in accordance with the rules and procedures; e.g. by a show of hands, by poll, etc.
  - where relevant, to make use of his or her second or casting vote
  - to sign the minutes.

For fuller details about the rules, procedures and terminology attached to formal meetings see further pages 410 and 436.

Figure 5.1.1 The chairperson's role

Roles and responsibilities of participants

The meetings secretary

Your most valuable aid in the running of a meeting should be your meetings secretary. He or she should work closely with you over the necessary administrative arrangements and should therefore be able to relieve you of much of the paperwork involved in the organisation of a meeting. Ideally he/she should undertake the following.

- Prepare and submit to you an estimate of the potential costs involved.
- Prepare all the necessary documentation:
  - the notice of the meeting
  - the agenda (together with an annotated agenda for you)
  - other relevant papers to be distributed before and tabled at the meeting
  - a summary of the proceedings.
- Arrange the accommodation. Ideally you would expect him or her to make sure that the meetings area is:
  - of an appropriate size
  - set out in the most effective manner
  - equipped with the relevant facilities.
- Arrange for the appropriate refreshments.

For further discussion on the preparation of meetings documentation, see page 410. See Figure 5.1.2 for a more detailed list of all the duties normally expected of a meetings secretary.

Figure 5.1.2 A secretary's role in preparing for a meeting

1 To liaise with the chairperson about the date of the meeting to prevent over-booking in his or her diary. To ensure also that he or she is reminded about the meeting – either directly or through his or her personal assistant.
2 To check that the chairperson has received any relevant documents in time to consider them before the meeting.
3 To discuss the items to be included in the chairperson's agenda (see further page 412).
4 To anticipate the implications of any relevant current developments and, in consultation with the chairperson, to keep a special file for potential agenda items.
5 To draw the chairperson's attention to new members and to prepare relevant notes about them.
6 To prepare all other relevant documentation (see further page 410).
7 To check the venue and to ensure that nothing is overlooked that may cause a problem; e.g.
  - the room has been booked for an adequate time so that meetings do not overlap
  - refreshments are booked and appear on time
  - any relevant seating plans are implemented
  - early arrivals are catered for
  - car parking arrangements have been made
  - if required, another secretary or administrator has been asked to take a note of the proceedings
  - the receptionist is informed of the event and those who are expected to attend
  - the switchboard staff are informed that certain people will be present at the meeting and therefore unavailable to take calls other than in an emergency

Figure 5.1.2 A secretary's role in preparing for a meeting – *continued*

> – all relevant items are available in the meeting room; e.g. OHP or other visual aids, means of recording attendance, spare packs of relevant documentation, etc.
> **8** To carry out the relevant follow up action; e.g.
> – notifying all relevant personnel when the meeting has ended
> – collecting and refiling immediately any confidential or important information
> – drafting the notes of the meeting for the attention of the chairperson
> – attending to any relevant correspondence
> – noting any action to be taken by any member of the meeting and devising an aide mémoire to act as a follow-up reminder.
> – if necessary, ensuring that the date for the next meeting has been entered into all relevant diaries.

THEORY INTO PRACTICE

Even though you may feel that you can leave all the administrative arrangements to your meetings secretary, you retain the ultimate responsibility for the success or otherwise of the meeting. Consequently, you should be prepared to give him or her support when the occasion arises. Consider how you would advise your secretary when he or she raises the following issues.

'Are you going to allow smoking during the meeting? If so, I'll have to provide ashtrays.'

'I'm not absolutely sure how many people will turn up – it may be as many as 45 or as few as 15. The main meetings room is ideal for up to 30 – otherwise it will have to be the main hall – which seats up to 80! What should I do?'

'Do you want me to circulate these papers beforehand – or table them at the meeting?'

'The canteen manager has just telephoned to say that he can't provide coffee and sandwiches at the meeting today – three of his staff are off with flu and he can only just manage to staff the main canteen.'

'I've had no replies from anyone confirming their attendance at the meeting.'

'I can't cope with this job – I'm dealing with too many people – and because they are senior to me, they all feel they can push me about!'

Other members of the meeting

Even though roles and responsibilities of the members of various meetings may differ, all have the responsibility for acting as responsible *team members.*

The most effective meetings team is the one that demonstrates maturity both during the debate and at the decision stage. Unfortunately, meetings have a tendency to bring out the most immature instincts in what are normally the most mature of people! Ideally the group should exhibit the following features:

- Participants should *demonstrate involvement* by working together to achieve a successful outcome.
- Participants should *assume responsibility* for their own behaviour and the impact that it has on others.
- They should *maximise individual abilities* by both allowing and expecting diversity of viewpoints.
- They should *listen* to other ideas without feeling the need to interrupt.
- They should *carry out a self-examination* and display a minimum of defensiveness if there are problems with the task, with the group or with interpersonal relations.
- The group should be *experimental* by trying different ways of discussion, decision-making and problem-solving.
- The members should *recognise the need for 'flight behaviour'* by allowing a breathing space after a decision has been taken, a problem solved, a task completed – but *not* allowing difficult problems to be shelved, awkward members to dominate the group or decisions to be taken too rapidly.

In many meetings the roles and responsibilities of some of the members are affected by the nature of their membership. For instance, the rules of some meetings allow a member to be invited

- on an *ex officio* basis – someone invited to attend 'by virtue of office' but who has no voting rights (e.g. the official secretary of a committee or the chairperson of an organisation)
- to be 'in attendance' – someone present on invitation to give expert help, advice or information, but again with no voting rights
- as a co-opted member – someone invited to serve on a committee as a result of a majority vote of that committee, usually because of some specialist knowledge or expertise he or she can provide.

Establishing objectives of meetings

Calling a meeting can be an expensive exercise. Consequently unless there is a sound reason for having a meeting, a good administrator finds another, more appropriate and almost certainly cheaper, method of communication. However, in some cases a meeting is essential. It may be essential simply because your senior manager tells you to have one – and no argument! In less draconian circumstances, it may be up to you to decide.

If you are a relatively new chairperson, it is a good idea to write down what you feel is the purpose of the meeting you wish to hold and then to outline the ideal outcome. You can then consider other options, such as:

- individual meetings with a number of relevant personnel
- a memorandum or group e-mail requesting or imparting information
- a draft report or list of suggestions about a particular topic which you compile and circulate together with a request for comments
- a completely individual approach in which you consider the problem or issue and take the necessary decision or action.

Look at Figure 5.1.3, which summarises the results of a debate on the usefulness or otherwise of meetings, and consider:

a those arguments with which you agree and those with which you do not

b any additional arguments you would have made either for or against

c how you would have voted in the debate.

Debate held on 22nd January 199-

Topic: 'Meetings – they're simply a waste of time!'

Speaker for the motion: Danny Khan

Speaker against the motion: Cameron Beattie

Summary of main points:

DANNY KHAN:

- Only individuals can make a decision requiring subtlety of reasoning – there will always be someone at a meeting who cannot or will not examine all the angles.
- In a meeting the quality of the final decision is always determined by its most able member – so why have a meeting?
- An individual can make a decision faster – and cheaper.
- One experiment which involved asking four individuals to work separately and then as part of a group found that they showed far more creativity when working individually.

CAMERON BEATTIE:

- Meetings get the best out of people. They generate ideas and any decisions that are made are likely to be more logical, better thought through and less prone to error than any comparable decision made by an individual. In addition, peer pressure compels all members of the meeting to make some form of effective contribution.
- If a decision has been made by a group of people they will be more enthusiastic about implementing it and also in encouraging others to do the same.
- If a meetings structure did not exist, all the decision-making power would be in the hands of a small group of individuals at top management level.

Figure 5.1.3 Notes from Lanchester College Debating Society

Once you are convinced that a meeting is the most appropriate form of communication you then have to decide what it is that you want to achieve. Indeed experienced chairpersons invariably spend a considerable time prior to the meeting:

- discussing possible objectives with senior colleagues or with one or two of the key members of the meeting
- having informal chats with everyone involved to gauge the prevailing climate of opinion.

Suppose, for instance, that you are in the process of preparing your annual departmental or unit operational plan. You may hold a series of meetings with your staff to achieve various things.

- *Gain agreement for a course of action*. You realise that the success of the plan depends upon the cooperation of your staff.
- *Impart information*. Both the draft and final versions should be known to all your staff and explained in more detail where necessary.
- *Generate ideas*. You could prepare the plan in isolation. It is far preferable, however, to seek the ideas of your staff who are then more likely to adopt ownership of the plan.
- *Solve a problem*. If you are undecided on a particular course of action or individual members of staff are offering you two or three potentially different solutions to a problem, a meeting of all members of staff could resolve the problem or at least help you to reach a decision.
- *Settle an argument*. Some individual members of staff may be determined that different courses of action should be pursued. In a meeting, the different arguments could be aired and a consensus opinion reached.

Remember that the way in which you conduct the meeting – including the way you prepare the relevant documentation – can affect the extent to which you achieve your objectives.

Rules and procedures relating to meetings

Meetings can be classified in many different ways. For example, a *large* meeting called either to give bad news such as a takeover bid or proposed redundancies – or alternatively to give good news such as success in receiving a major contract. It might be called to announce a change of direction such as a reorganisation or proposed diversification. In such cases, the people attending will comprise virtually the full workforce. Smaller meetings can take various forms:

- the *vertical slice* meeting which involves people at different levels of the hierarchy meeting to discuss issues of general concern such as health and safety, equal opportunities policies, etc.
- the *horizontal slice* meeting comprising people with similar levels of responsibility across the organisation, again meeting for the purpose of discussing topics of common interest
- the meeting of *'experts'* – sometimes known as a task group – where people are asked to attend because of a common expertise
- the *interface* meeting which involves members of the organisation discussing relevant matters with people from outside the organisation
- the *hierarchical* meetings of the senior management team, the departmental or subunit team, the works team, etc.

Some of these meetings can be conducted relatively informally. Others, however, will be much more formal and will be bound by a set of rules and procedures.

It is interesting to note that in general the formal meetings are primarily concerned with *strategic* issues and the informal meetings with *operational* issues (although some meetings – such as the board meeting – concern themselves with both types of issue). If necessary, look back to Unit 3 to remind yourself of the difference between the strategic and the operational plan of an organisation.

Informal meetings

As a chairperson of an informal meeting you will probably be expected to ensure that all members are aware of the date, day, time and place of the meeting. Provided they are given the information they need, it is irrelevant whether it is given verbally or in written form.

You will have to ensure that an agenda is prepared. No matter how informal the meeting, you would be well advised to spend time on preparing this agenda. Indeed, even though an agenda may seem rather stylised when compared with other forms of communication, the fact that there is almost always a standard format to be used does have certain advantages. This means that routine and yet essential matters will not be overlooked. You can, moreover, construct the non-standard items in such a way and in such an order that they assist you to achieve your objective. There are various points to remember:

- Be realistic about the number of items that can be covered in the time available. Many meeting objectives fail to be achieved simply because the members are required to make too many decisions too quickly. The rule is that if a long list of topics *must* be discussed then they should be the subject of individual meetings or subcommittees – each having its own precise objective and each with a small and selective membership.
- Make sure that the items are in a logical order. It is the norm to put the most important item first so that if time does run out, at least the main objective of the meeting has been achieved. If you are genuinely undecided as to which may be the most important issue, a second parameter may be the length of time you think will be taken to discuss each one and to prioritise the one likely to take the longest.
- Ensure that the topics on the agenda concern the entire membership. Otherwise the above point applies.
- Distribute copies of the agenda prior to the meeting to allow members time to consider each topic scheduled for discussion.
- Make certain that you, as the chairperson, are thoroughly briefed on each item so that you can answer queries and control the discussion. Relevant questions you should ask yourself include:
  - Am I clear about the objectives of the meeting?
  - Am I sure that the other members are equally clear?
  - With whom do I need to discuss any of the proposed topics before the meeting?

The meeting should be conducted in such a way that everyone understands what is being said and has a chance to be heard, no-one is allowed to monopolise the proceedings, a sensible decision is taken and/or action plan compiled, and a summary is made of the main points discussed and action agreed. See Figure 5.1.4 for an example of an agenda for a marketing team meeting.

```
JOCASTA PRODUCTS LTD
16 Park Avenue,
LONDON W1

The next meeting of the Marketing team will be held in the
Marketing Manager's office at 9 am on Friday 11 June 199-

AGENDA
1   Apologies for absence
2   Minutes of previous meeting
3   Matters arising
4   Report back from senior management team meeting of
    Wednesday 9 June 199-
5   Staff appraisal issues
6   Any other business
```

Figure 5.1.4 A typical agenda for a marketing team meeting

THEORY INTO PRACTICE

In some meetings, it has become a growing practice for the chairperson not to issue an agenda prior to the meeting but, at the beginning of each meeting, to invite all the members to suggest items for discussion which are then summarised on a flip chart. When the list is completed the chairperson then invites the group to prioritise the items and then finally to allocate a period of time for the discussion of each of those items. Consider the advantages and disadvantages of such an approach.

Formal meetings – types and features

This subsection introduces and describes features of the most common formal meetings. The next subsection will go into the practical details and define some of the terms used here.

Board meetings

- *Business*. A body such as a limited company must act through its Board of Directors, which is responsible for managing the company's business. The conduct and business of such meetings is stipulated in the *Articles of Association*.
- *Frequency*. Table A of Regulation 88 of the Companies Act 1985 gives the directors the authority to meet as they think fit. In private companies meetings will be held as and when considered necessary. In public companies they will be held more frequently and usually on fixed dates. The frequency of the meetings depends upon the nature of the business and the composition of the board. Where there are both executive and

non-executive directors, meetings will normally be held at monthly intervals, with intervening meetings of the executive directors. Note that other organisations may follow a similar procedure. A college or health authority, for instance, may have regular fixed meetings of its board members and intervening meetings of its senior management team.

- *Notice*. No length of notice is laid down but it should be reasonable. It is normal practice to give at least seven days' notice.
- *Quorum*. A resolution of the directors may fix the quorum (this is defined in the next subsection).
- *Chairperson*. The power to appoint a chairperson is permissive. However, the Articles of Association of many companies make the appointment of a chairperson mandatory.

General meetings

Unlike meetings of directors, general meetings of a company are not conducted exclusively in accordance with the company's Articles of Association but also in compliance with statutory obligations and procedures. They are categorised into annual general meetings, extraordinary general meetings, and class meetings

Annual general meetings (AGMs)

- *Business*. The meeting receives the report and accounts as required by the Companies Act 1985; declares a dividend; elects directors; and then reappoints and fixes the remuneration of the auditors.
- *Frequency*. In accordance with section 366 of the Companies Act 1985 every company (except certain private companies) must hold an annual general meeting each calendar year and not more than 15 months may elapse between the date of one AGM and the next.

Extraordinary general meetings (EGMs)

- *Business*. Subject to Articles, such a meeting may be convened at any time for the transaction of business which requires attention before the next AGM.
- *Frequency*. See above.

Class meetings

- *Business*. The holders of a class of a company's shares can meet in accordance with the Articles or conditions attaching to the shares whenever their rights are to be varied as a result of some action proposed to be taken by the company.
- *Frequency*. As required.

For all three types of general meeting there are stipulations laid down as to notice, quorum and the appointment of a chairperson:

- *Notice*. A minimum period of notice is stipulated by section 369 of the Companies Act 1985. It must be a certain number of 'clear days' notice'; i.e. exclusive of the day on which the notice is served. The norm is 21 days (although in certain circumstances section 369(3) and (4) of the Companies Act 1985 does allow for the calling of a meeting at shorter notice than the minimum period allowed by statute or by Articles).

- *Quorum.* The quorum is stipulated in the Articles. Table A of the Companies Act 1985 provides for two members present in person or by proxy to be a minimum quorum. The Articles will also usually provide for the procedure to be adopted in the event of a quorum not being present.
- *Chairperson.* Most articles follow Table A by providing that the chairperson of the board shall preside at general meetings. Failing him or her, some other director (the vice-chairperson if there is one) or member can officiate.

Formal meetings in action

If you have to chair a formal meeting, you will probably find that you are expected to conduct the business in accordance with its *standing orders*. Such orders are a focal point of reference for all preparations for and proceedings at the meeting.

The notice

In order for a meeting to be validly convened, proper notice must be given to each member entitled to attend in accordance with the standing orders or rules of the body or organisation. Most organisations state the length of notice required, which is normally 21 days in the case of an annual general meeting, 7 days for unlimited companies and 14 days for other than unlimited companies. If no time limit is specified then a reasonable time must be given. Figure 5.1.5 shows two examples of the more formal types of notice.

JOCASTA PRODUCTS LTD.
16 Park Avenue,
LONDON W1

Date:

The next meeting of the Board of Directors will be held in the boardroom at 11 am on Tuesday 25 May 199-

Signed: (Secretary)

JOCASTA PRODUCTS LTD.

Notice is hereby given that the 15th Annual General Meeting of the Company will be held in the main meeting room of the Dunkenchurch Hotel on Wednesday, 14 November 199- at 10 am to transact the ordinary business of the Company.

A member entitled to attend and vote at the meeting is entitled to appoint a proxy to attend and vote instead of him or her. A proxy need not also be a member.

By order of the board,

.... (Secretary)
16 Park Avenue,
LONDON W1

Figure 5.1.5 Two types of formal notice

The requirement for notice does not arise in some cases. Certain bodies, for instance, hold their meetings on specified days and at specified times and places. Committees of local councils usually fix their meetings for the year shortly after the annual elections. Some companies have board meetings fixed in advance, and so on. Consequently, provided notice has been given at the beginning of that year or session no further notice is generally required (unless the regulations specifically stipulate otherwise).

In other cases, the failure to send a notice does not invalidate a meeting if:

● all the members entitled to attend actually do attend
● those members who did not receive a valid notice are 'beyond reasonable summoning distance' (e.g. seriously ill or abroad).

Interesting to note, however, is that you cannot simply rely on the word of a member of a meeting. In one case, a director of a company said that he would not be attending a meeting to be held the following week. It was held that this could not be relied on as a waiver of his right of notice, and as no notice had been sent to him the meeting was declared invalid.

The agenda

The same agenda *format* applies to both formal and informal meetings, as the example of a board meeting agenda given in Figure 5.1.6 indicates.

JOCASTA PRODUCTS LTD
16 Park Avenue,
LONDON W1

Meeting of the Board of Directors to be held in the boardroom at 11 am on Tuesday 25 May 199-

AGENDA

1 Apologies for absence
2 Minutes of the previous meeting
3 Matters arising
4 Correspondence
5 Presentation of first draft of the organisational strategic plan
6 Proposed new outlets for merchandise
7 Arrangements for presentation of gifts to long serving members of staff
8 Any other business
9 Date and time of next meeting
- -
Papers required for the meeting
Agenda item
2 Minutes of 13 April 199-
5 Copy of strategic development plan
6 Copy of Sales Director's report

Figure 5.1.6 A typical agenda

However, in the case of very formal meetings the language used may differ. For instance, item 5 in the agenda in Figure 5.1.6 would be reframed to read:

Item 5   Organisational Strategic Plan
      To receive the first draft of the organisational strategic plan.

What may also differ is the use of a second or *chairperson's agenda*. Such an agenda, if well prepared, is an invaluable tool if you are expected to chair a long and formal meeting. It reminds you of not only what *you* want to say about a particular topic and what contributions you can expect from other members, but also what *others* may say about it. See Figure 5.1.7 which gives an example of a chairperson's agenda drawn up by the meetings secretary to assist him or her in chairing the meeting.

Figure 5.1.7 A typical chairperson's annotated agenda

JOCASTA PRODUCTS LTD
16 Park Avenue,
LONDON W1

Meeting of the Board of Directors to be held in the boardroom at 11 am on Tuesday 25 May 199-

CHAIRPERSON'S AGENDA

Opening remarks	Meeting should be quorate. Welcome Menzies Ratcliffe to meeting.
Apologies	No apologies received as yet. NB Chianga may not be back from Portugal - I'll confirm with her PA whether or not she'll be able to attend.
Minutes	Unlikely to be any argument as to whether or not they are a true and correct record.
Matters arising	Questions may be asked on ● presentations to long-serving members of staff (Item 7 on the agenda) ● progress on the implementation of the recently approved staff appraisal policy (discussed at senior management team level and now in the process of being discussed at departmental level). NB ask Menzies for any additional information - I have already warned him he might be expected to report back.
Correspondence	None this month

Figure 5.1.7 A typical chairperson's annotated agenda – *continued*

Organisation SDP	● Questions likely to be asked. ● Kevan is bound to want to stay with the tried and tested range – he won't be keen on looking at new markets. ● I've heard on the grapevine that Chianga thinks we are underpricing. If she's arrived back, she might suggest some changes there.
New outlets	You should be able to rely on Jason – he has a list of options and is desperate to lead the discussion.
Presentations	Ask Menzies for details – he has the whole thing organised. There might be a bit of a problem over the cheques – Chianga might be unhappy about £250 a head.
AOB	None at the moment.
Date/time next meeting	Try to avoid the week beginning 21 June – you will be away in Brussels most of that week.

The quorum

Any meeting with any degree of formality will specify the minimum number of members who must be present to enable it to transact its business. In most cases the actual number is contained in the Articles of Association.

> The importance of having a valid quorum is illustrated by a quote from a newly elected President of the Society of Practitioners of Insolvency, that he had been appointed 'by the skin of his teeth'. Seven members were needed for a quorum but only six had arrived when the meeting was due to start, because of a rail strike that day. Two more arrived seconds before the meeting was preparing to adjourn.

Appointment of the chairperson

Most meetings will have set procedures for the appointment of officials – particularly the chairperson. Depending on those procedures, a chairperson can be elected for a particular meeting, annually, for a fixed period or even, in very rare cases, for life. Again in most cases a person nominated to take the chair must be proposed by one member and seconded by another. If there is more than one candidate, the decision of the meeting should be taken either by a show of hands or, if the relevant rules so provide, by a poll. Any objection to the appointment of a chairperson should be made there and then as later objections will not be accepted.

Preparation of relevant motions and amendments, and procedures for adjournments

Look at the following scenario. A meeting of the Board of Directors of Jocasta Products Ltd is under way and discussion is centring around the proposals contained in the draft strategic plan presented by the MD, who is chairing the meeting, to the rest of the Board for final approval.

MANAGING DIRECTOR	Are we all agreed that we should diversify into male cosmetics for a trial two year period? If so we can agree the first objective in the plan.
SALES DIRECTOR	I agree in principle but I don't like the term 'male cosmetics' – can't we use 'men's toiletries'?
PURCHASING DIRECTOR	I don't agree at all. I think we're better sticking to what we know – and what our customers expect from us. What we should be concentrating on is expanding our range of goods for women.

In an informal meeting the chairperson would at this point have to:

- direct the members' attention to the first issue – the proposed diversification
- allow discussion
- receive views on any suggested amendments – the difference in terminology
- ask for a vote
- reach a decision.

In a more formal situation, however – particularly if the meeting was an AGM or other type of shareholders' meeting – a correspondingly more formal procedure would have to be followed.

Stage 1

A proposal or *motion* should be put forward by its proposer. Traditionally it must start with the word 'that' and should consist of a single and concise sentence about which there can be no subsequent misunderstanding. It should also be positive, state an opinion and call for some action. In the Jocasta Products meeting, therefore, the motion might read:

'It is proposed that the organisation diversify into male cosmetics for a two-year period.'

Stage 2

If required by the rules, the motion may need to be seconded; i.e. it may need to be supported by at least one other member of the meeting. If it is not, then the motion cannot go any further (it 'falls').

In the House of Commons a motion does not need to be seconded. The Speaker habitually acts on the mover's proposal of a motion without calling for a seconder.

Stage 3

An *amendment* is an alteration or proposed alteration to the terms of the motion which is designed to improve it by inserting, omitting or replacing words. What it must *not* do is merely negate the motion. If, for instance, the Managing Director proposes that staff should be awarded a 2 per cent pay rise, however strongly the Financial Director may feel about it, it is not open to him or her to propose that the word 'not' should be inserted after the word 'should'! Nor should it be put without proper notice, if it is likely to substantially alter the motion.

Consequently any proposed amendment to the motion about diversifying into other markets would have to be treated equally formally:

'It is proposed that the motion be amended to delete the words "male cosmetics" and insert the words "men's toiletries".'

Note that the second amendment – that the organisation does *not* diversify into male cosmetics – would not be allowable as it merely negates the original motion.

Stage 4

The chairperson then takes over. He or she must then ensure that:

- only one amendment is discussed at one time
- each amendment is discussed in the order in which it affects the original motion – not in the order in which it has been proposed
- once voted on and agreed, the amendment is incorporated into the original motion which is then re-termed the *substantive* motion.

At Jocasta Products, therefore, the members would have voted first of all on the change of terminology. If agreed, the amendment would be incorporated into the original motion:

'It is proposed that the organisation diversify into men's toiletries for a two-year period.'

It is then re-termed the substantive motion and is voted on in the usual way. If approved it then becomes a *resolution*. (For an example of the way in which such resolutions are recorded, see further page 436.)

THEORY INTO PRACTICE

Sometimes a meeting can start losing its way. A motion has been proposed, some amendments have been dealt with but little progress seems to have been made. A good chairperson should be able to deal with this situation, but if he or she fails to do so there are some formal 'procedural motions' which can be followed to bring a discussion to an end, such as:

- closure
- previous question
- next business
- reference motion
- adjournment.

Unless you are already experienced in this area, research the difference between the terms for possible future use.

Read the following second extract from the discussions at the Jocasta Products board meeting.

SALES DIRECTOR   Our sales figures are falling – we don't have the same market share as we had even five years ago. We've got to do something.

FINANCE DIRECTOR Why don't we look at our existing range and see if we can adjust the prices? We may be able to recoup some money if we increase the prices at the higher level. A woman who is prepared to pay £45 for one of our products probably won't be put off if she finds it's now £50.

SALES DIRECTOR   I think all prices should be adjusted upwards – not just those at the top of the range. The increase could always be proportionate.

1 a Rephrase the Sales Director's proposal into a formal motion.
   b Assuming the amendment is carried, draft out the substantive motion.
2 Research and ensure that you know the difference between an *amendment* to a motion and a *rider* to it.

Methods of voting

In some meetings, the chairperson, at the end of the discussion or debate, merely asks who is in favour and who is against the motion. The volume of response is an indication of the majority opinion. It is, however, a somewhat inexact method of reaching a decision.

A more usual method of voting is by a *show of hands*. Normally the chairperson's word as to the number of people who have voted for or against a motion is accepted, but if his or her declaration is challenged, a second show of hands can be demanded.

In certain cases, however, voting is by *secret ballot*. This allows every member, whether present or not, to cast his or her vote. If a person is not present but still wishes to vote on a particular issue, the normal method of doing so is by proxy – the member completes a proxy paper giving his or her vote which is included in the count at the appropriate time. It is usual, however, to provide in the Articles of Association that a proxy should be lodged a specified time before the meeting.

Voting may also be by *poll*; i.e. by the marking of a voting paper in cases where a member may have more than one vote – if, for instance, he or she has a vote for each share held.

Although most decisions are made by majority vote, this method does have some disadvantages.

● Certain groups may reach private deals with one another – 'if you vote with us on this issue, we'll vote for you later on', etc.
● There is less room for compromise in a yes/no outcome.
● Some members may vote for the likely 'winning' side particularly if it includes senior members of staff.
● If a quick decision is forced by vote, the defeated minority (particularly if that is a sizeable group) may feel resentful and consequently less likely to cooperate in its implementation.

The appointment and powers of committees

In many standing orders provision is made for committees to be appointed for specific purposes, on either a temporary or a permanent basis.

- A *standing committee* can deal with continuing issues such as the approval of share transfers or other regular company business. This type of committee structure is also used in other areas. Within a local council, for instance, much of the work is carried out by standing committees such as for housing, education and social services. Such a committee will ultimately report back to the *executive* committee (see below).
- An *ad hoc committee* can deal with a single project. An example is a selection committee convened to consider the appointment of a senior member of staff.

In addition many organisations make use of the following:

- The *executive committee* is a committee with plenary power – and therefore normally quite powerful. Note that the Board of Directors of a limited company will itself be an executive committee.
- The *advisory committee* is a less powerful committee which does not have decision-making powers. It may be expected to advise the executive committee and may therefore form its own subcommittees which will report back directly to it to enable it to make the necessary recommendations to the executive committee.
- The *joint consultative committee* is normally aimed at improving communications with the workforce and often used to negotiate with trade unions.

Formal versus informal procedures

The modern tendency is to allow as much informality as possible when conducting a meeting, in order to encourage participation by all members, speed up the proceedings, and cut down on expense. However, in some circumstances a certain amount of formality can be very positive:

- One management writer found that groups with more than 30 members welcomed strong centralised control and a set of fixed procedures simply because they realised that the alternative would be unmanageable.
- Gatherings such as political or trade union conventions would again find difficulty in functioning without elaborate procedural rules – often drawn up by specially convened subcommittees. If such rules did not exist, the basic principle that the majority opinion should be accepted, but minority views heard, would be unachievable.
- When a highly controversial topic is under discussion, or when there are two mutually hostile groups, compelling the members to recognise a structure and to follow a set of rules maintains order.

Research into over 50 committees in different organisations showed that most participants appreciated set procedures being carried out at meetings – mainly because they felt that the procedures ensured that everyone got the chance to participate.

Organising, analysing and presenting information to promote debate and decisions

'It's not what you say, it's the way that you say it!' Although this is a truism, you would be well to remember the saying when deciding on the way you will present any information to a group of people at a meeting. Indeed, quite often, even the most mediocre of arguments, if presented effectively, can succeed at the expense of other more telling arguments. Much depends on the type of meeting and the composition of its membership as to the lengths you should go, and the money you should spend, on a particular presentation. It is wise, therefore, to regard the presenting of information as a staged process.

- the minimum standards you would expect
- any additional embellishments you would introduce should funding be available and should the occasion warrant it.

Even for informal meetings there are house rules which apply to the preparation of the standard documentation (see pages 407 and 433). What remains for you to organise, however, is any supplementary information that may be required.

It should be *reproduced attractively* in as professional a manner as funding will allow. For small, internal and regularly held meetings, the documents can be photocopied to a sufficiently professional standard. For larger, more formal meetings, particularly where external members are attending, documents should be either professionally printed or desktop published. OHTs should be similarly prepared.

The information should be *consistent*. Meetings documentation is not an area that lends itself to experimentation with colour, different fonts, etc. although there is more license to experiment in the case of OHTs.

The information should be *concise*. At a meeting, only a certain amount of information can be assimilated at one time. Consequently, if you intend to speak to a certain paper, even if it has been circulated before the meeting, ideally the information it contains should be kept to a minimum. If you are speaking to a paper or using an OHT as a visual aid, then you may want to consider the use of key words or phrases rather than closely written paragraphs covering sheet after sheet of A4 paper.

The information should be *disclosed progressively*. A number of OHTs or handouts, each containing key points, can allow you to direct the discussion and to stimulate debate in a far more organised way than if you disclose all the information at once.

Use, where relevant, pictures or other artwork to stimulate interest, particularly at the beginning of a discussion. Make use of diagrams or graphs in preference to tables. Data can usually be absorbed more quickly in simple graphical, bar chart or pie chart forms.

Types and characteristics of non-verbal language

A chairperson has many ways of determining whether or not the members of a meeting are both listening to and participating in its proceedings. One of the main indicators is the noise level. If the only sound is that of the chairperson's voice, the resultant decision is unlikely to be representative of the group as a whole. On the other hand, no effective decision is likely to emerge from a meeting conducted in total chaos with all members speaking at once. Although a good chairperson has many methods of dealing with such situations (for further discussion see page 422) he or she should realise that not all messages are conveyed through speech. Most people either consciously or sub-consciously allow some of their emotions to be expressed non-verbally.

Facial expressions

Two researchers, Paul Eckman and Wallace Friesen, have suggested the following interpretation of six principal facial expressions.

- *Happiness* is indicated by a smile.
- *Sadness* is indicated by the turning down of the corners of the mouth, a downward look and a general sagging of the features. Obviously extremes of sadness are characterised by tears.
- *Disgust* is sometimes shown by a narrowing of the eyes with the head turned aside.
- *Anger* is frequently characterised by a steady gaze, a frown or scowl or an obvious gritting of the teeth. In some cases there will be a change of complexion – either paler or redder.
- *Fear* is shown by extreme pallor, perspiration or trembling.
- *Interest* is indicated by a tilt of the head and wider open eyes than normal.

> 1 The study of facial expression is not new. In 1872, Charles Darwin published the first serious scientific study about it entitled *Expression of the Emotions in Man and Animals*.
> 2 There is some research evidence to indicate that when a member of a meeting wears glasses, his or her IQ rating as perceived by other members of the meeting increases by about 13 points.

Gestures and body movements

Similarly, research has suggested that there are five different functions of gestures:

- movements substituting for words
- movements accompanying speech
- movements maintaining or signalling a change in a person's listening or speaking role
- unconscious movements or mannerisms
- movements revealing emotions – in the same way as facial expressions.

> Experiments have shown that such gestures occur even in situations where the other person cannot be seen as when making a telephone call or responding to a telephone answering machine.

Kinesics

You may remember from Element 4.1 that *kinesics* relates to body language. Ray Birdwhistell, the American researcher mentioned, began to study body motion techniques in the late 1940s and to define them in relation to a *kine*; i.e. the smallest observable unit of body movement. He discovered, for instance, that the most common shoulder movement is the shrug. If both shoulders are raised, the message conveyed is that of hopelessness or doubt. If one shoulder is raised, the message is more likely to be one of opting out or refusing to play further part.

The arms, hands and fingers are used for a great variety of gestures. For example, the 'steepling' of hands, in which the tips of the fingers are placed together in what resembles an attitude of prayer except that the palms are kept well apart, signifies confidence – or at least the desire to make any observer think that that is the case! The 'fingers crossed' gesture, although often used to invoke protection, can also mean that the person using it is telling a lie – and unconsciously trying to ward off any punishment for telling it.

The movement of feet can be telling, particularly if the person concerned wishes to conceal something. A tapping foot could mean that he or she has managed to control the upper half of the body but is unable to exercise control over the rest of the body.

> An interesting phenomenon is the 'gestural echo'. If one person in a group uses a particular gesture, it frequently happens that other members will then use the same gesture.

Posture or stance

Like other aspects of body language, postures have patterns which can be interpreted. For instance, it has been observed that when people stand in groups, those who are part of the group have quite different postural patterns from those who are not. Outsiders typically stand with the weight on one foot, whereas insiders will lean forward a little.

Posture can also signal *status*. At its simplest, high status is signalled by an upright posture and low status by a slouch. Equality of status, on the other hand, is often indicated by matching postures – if one person leans back in a chair the other one will also do so.

Posture may also indicate *aggression or threat* in the form, for instance, of a progressively exaggerated exhibition of high-status or dominant behaviour. Hands may be held by the side with the fists clenched in readiness and the forehead or jaw may jut out more obviously.

Proximity

The term *proxemics* is used to describe the study of the use of space when communicating. Various *zones* have been identified:

- the *intimate* zone in which people are actually touching or are easily able to touch each other
- the *personal* zone where people are able to shake hands or are, at most, no more than an arm's length from each other

- the *social–consultive* zone which is most commonly used in everyday encounters of a social or business nature, and normally runs from 1.2 to 3 metres.
- the *public* zone which extends from 3 metres outwards.

Robert Sommer has defined *personal space* as that area around each person which should not be entered other than by invitation. In preventing violations of such personal space, orientation can often be used as a territorial marker. Most people, for instance, are reluctant to pass between two other people or to disturb someone with his or her legs stretched out. Other indications of territorial marking, of particular interest to a chairperson, are the ways in which it can signal a conspiratorial relationship, with one member approaching another from the side, or two members who automatically turn away to prevent anyone else from joining them.

Proxemics and seating arrangements

A good chairperson can make use of proxemics to ensure that the seating arrangements at a meeting are conducive to the best possible outcome. He or she may choose a formal seating arrangement – a long oblong table with the chairperson seated at the top, if the meeting is formal and the members are expected to act accordingly. If the meeting is less formal and potentially more creative, the chairperson may choose to seat members around a table with no obvious form of hierarchy so that they will feel more at ease in making a contribution. One management writer suggests that a 'zig-zag' form of seating has certain advantages to allow people to talk to each other as well as to the chairperson.

The places in which members of a meeting *choose* to sit can give some indication of whether or not they relate well to each other or to being in the group as a whole. Allies may choose to sit opposite one another to give each other appropriate eye signals for support when relevant. The same, however, could be the case if two potential antagonists decide to make the meeting an opportunity for confrontation. Those seeking approval from the chairperson may either sit as near as possible to him or her or again try to position themselves so that they can give encouraging smiles and nods at the appropriate place. Newcomers or those for some reason excluded or ignored by the rest of the group tend to sit near the door and in the place where the least eye contact is necessary. An experienced chairperson should be able to pick up these signals quite quickly, although dealing with it depends on factors such as the size, the formality and venue of the meeting and the status of the people involved.

---

1 Status can also be conveyed and conferred by positioning at a meeting. Research has indicated that low-status individuals tend to stay nearer the door, those of higher status choose a seat near the middle of the table, and those of equal status go directly to the top.
2 An Australian communications specialist argues that touching people at work is acceptable and, if done in the right way, can pay dividends. He maintains that brushing a hand against the point of the other person's elbow for less than three seconds will win the other person's cooperation!

Chairperson's use of non-verbal communication

As already discussed, one of your duties as a chairperson is to ensure that everyone has a chance to contribute. What you should therefore be aware of is the way in which body language can affect the extent to which you allow those contributions. For instance, an experienced member can make use of direct eye contact, a raised index finger or a generally alert body posture to constantly get your attention. A shy or inexperienced member may never make eye contact and may indicate a wish to speak merely by an indrawn breath or slight shoulder movement which you have to be very experienced to notice.

Of equal importance is your awareness of how *your own* body language can affect the progress of the meeting. Indeed you have considerable power in this respect. You can, for instance, prevent someone from speaking simply by denying eye contact and looking at others to show it is their turn to speak. You can indicate facially very clearly whether or not you approve of what is being said. You can nod to show approval and thus encourage a member to continue. You can gesture to others to keep quiet when someone else is speaking and thus deter the timid from speaking at all. You can affect not to hear or see someone who is trying to attract your attention – and so on.

THEORY INTO PRACTICE

'A chairperson *must* be effective. Consequently any tactics used to further this end should be acceptable.' Consider to what extent you agree with this statement, particularly in relation to the way in which you may use non-verbal communication to control the outcome of a meeting.

Methods of promoting and encouraging debate

To be a successful chairperson you must be a good communicator, and conduct the meeting in such a way that all members take part and make their views heard. In some respects it is easier to do this in a formal meeting, given that the chairperson is expected to see that the following standard rules of debate are obeyed.

- Members who wish to speak on a motion must address their remarks through the chair. They can also, if the chairperson wishes, be allocated a time limit within which to speak.
- They should limit their remarks strictly to the motion under discussion and should not normally be allowed the right of 'second speech' – the right of reply, unless they happen to be the mover of the original motion.
- The order in which they speak must be decided by the chairperson. In very formal meetings the proposer of the motion speaks first, followed by the opposer and then by the two seconders. After discussion the proposer of the motion is then allowed to respond before a vote is taken. In less formal meetings, the chairperson has to decide on the order by announcing the name of the person who is to speak first. He or she also has to allow discussion of any proposed amendments or points of order as they arise.

However, probably most meetings you will be expected to chair will be informal and conducted in a more relaxed manner. In such circumstances you will have to make more use of your personal skills to ensure that all issues are fully discussed before a decision is taken. The remainder of this section deals with those skills.

Dealing with individual differences

No chairperson can assume that identical strategies can be used to promote and encourage debate at every meeting. Much depends on the various personalities sitting around the table! Consider the following types of personality:

- the compulsive talker
- the silent listener
- the reminiscent member
- the team bigot
- the timid member
- the overbearing member
- the blamer.

You have to let the overbearing person talk but know when – tactfully yet firmly – to bring his or her contribution to an end. You should take the same approach with the member who always remembers 'how things used to be'. You may have to be sharper with the team bigot – otherwise you run the risk of appearing to agree with what he or she says simply because you give no sign of disagreeing. Obviously you have to try to encourage the silent and the timid – but you should avoid embarrassing them by turning the spotlight too brightly on them.

Translating complicated information into an easily understandable format

Suppose that you are chairing a departmental safety meeting during which the safety representative reports back on a meeting he has recently attended, in which there was some discussion about a proposed Law Commission Enquiry into possible corporate responsibility for manslaughter and bodily harm. The representative has obviously studied the issue in some depth and is anxious to impart that information to the rest of the members. However, he cannot translate what he knows into sufficiently simple language. You should, of course, have anticipated that problem – particularly if you know the person involved – and have either asked for or prepared a simple written summary of the issue. Any subsequent discussion is then relatively easy to direct. Alternatively, you could ask for the item to be put on the next agenda so that all members have the opportunity to read and digest the information provided. What you should *not* do is allow the discussion to flounder because no-one other than the representative has fully understood the nature of the issue.

Handling questions

A major part of any discussion often consists of questions and answers and the chairperson may be expected to handle both. For instance, in the case of the issue just outlined, you might want to take the lead yourself and ask the representative to explain certain aspects of the issue which you feel might be puzzling not only you but the rest of the members. The usual rules relating to the art of asking questions apply:

- Use a series of short, simple questions rather than one long, complicated question. For example: 'What exactly is meant by corporate manslaughter?', 'When is the Law Commission going to report back on its findings?', 'Can you give us any examples of how it might affect us?', 'Is there any action we should be taking?', etc.
- Ask probing secondary questions, such as 'So the organisation might be responsible as a whole for an industrial injury or fatality. Does that mean that each of us individually, no matter at what level of management, must take a share of that responsibility?'
- Use a 'summary' question, such as 'So all we should be doing at the moment is to take a watching brief?'

The next stage is to encourage the rest of the members to ask their own questions. If you have constructed your questions sufficiently carefully, you should find that other people will automatically add their questions to yours as the discussion continues and the individual issues become clearer. Your usual chairperson's role obliges you to step in if you see that one person is asking too many questions and dominating the discussion, or alternatively if some members appear to be taking no part in the discussion.

Listening

Listening skills have already been discussed in Element 4.1, page 289, and are equally important when you are running a meeting, given that there is a big difference between taking the lead or initiating a discussion and monopolising it. You must know when to keep silent and encourage others to speak, so that you have the opportunity not only to listen to what is being said but also to summarise all viewpoints at the close of the discussion. As with all personal skills, effective listening is an art that can be developed – even though, according to some researchers, it is one that not many people possess. One researcher, for instance, found that even at the purely informational level, 75 per cent of oral communication is ignored, misunderstood or quickly forgotten. In addition, much of it can be 'passive' listening – merely a matter of waiting for the other person to finish before responding. Ideally what you should be doing when someone else is speaking – as well as noting the content of what is being said – is the following.

- Try to identify what the tone of the voice is expressing – boredom, depression, enthusiasm, astonishment, defensiveness, anger, disbelief, etc.
- Where possible – or relevant – determine the motivation of the speaker. If you are chairing an internal departmental meeting, you may be well aware that one member is supporting a particular course of action because he or she (a) wants to be seen to be agreeing with the boss, (b) sees an opportunity to score a point over a colleague, or (c) genuinely wants to make an effective contribution, etc.
- Make sure that the speaker is aware of your undivided attention. Non-verbal communication is important in this respect. Make effective eye contact – avoiding, of course, the tendency to stare unblinkingly and unnervingly at the speaker – and also avoid distracting him or her by

fiddling with a pen, doodling on a piece of paper, examining your fingernails, etc.

● Determine the length of silence you will allow to fall when either you or another member of the meeting has finished speaking. A common fault of many chairpersons is to feel obliged to talk when there is any lull in a discussion, when in reality the ensuing silence might encourage someone else to speak. Again a knowledge of the people with whom you are dealing helps. You might be aware, for instance, that one member can make a positive contribution to a discussion but will only do so if allowed time to think and to digest what is being said. Too hurried a pace would effectively blot out any such participation.

Summarising the results

When you think that a discussion has run its useful course it is then up to you to bring it to a close and to summarise what has been said. That is the topic of the next section.

One mistake a new chairperson can make is to be so anxious to control the meeting and to summarise its proceedings that he or she stifles any discussion that does not look immediately relevant or which seems likely to be prolonged. In some cases this is welcomed by the members; in others it can be both irritating and counterproductive, particularly if the meeting is one where the members want to be creative.

THEORY INTO PRACTICE

Read the following extract from a discussion at a departmental meeting about the way in which a company handbook is to be compiled.

ZOFAR	Why don't we get hold of a number of other company handbooks and see what they look like?
CHAIR	Mark, you can't be serious about wanting to include staff profiles in the handbook?
MARK	As a matter of fact, I am. What's so funny about that?
CHAIR	Whether I think it funny or not, the boss isn't likely to approve the idea so we might as well forget about it right now.
DAWN	Could we describe an average day in this department?
CHAIR	We tried that a couple of years ago. It didn't work.
SHABANA	As a starting point why don't we summarise all the job descriptions?
CHAIR	Good idea. Can I leave that to you?
CONRAD	We could get some really good colour photographs and flow charts to brighten up the book.
CHAIR	No money available. Besides it's always risky trying anything too new – if it goes wrong, we get the blame.
CHRIS	Can you give us some guidance then? We're struggling a bit.
CHAIR	We're out of time now. We'll have to defer this item to the next meeting – even though the timescale is pretty tight.

1 Consider the ways in which the chair did his or her best to stifle any creative thoughts on the part of the members.
2 Consider also the responses you might have given to the suggestions made by each member, and what you would have said at the end of the meeting.

Summarising and clarifying discussions and decisions

At the end of each meeting, however informal, you should ensure that a note is made of the proceedings and in particular of any decisions made or actions to be taken. However, you may also have to:

- clarify verbally certain issues throughout the course of the meeting
- summarise each point made in relation to a particularly complicated issue before allowing the discussion to continue
- summarise the main arguments before any decision is made.

Summarising in written form can be difficult (see further page 465). Summarising verbally – particularly in front of a group of people – can be quite daunting.

Be prepared for – and positively encourage – members to assist you. They will be pleased to have their contributions welcomed and you will not run the risk of overlooking a relevant point or of labouring under some misconception which may be difficult to correct at a later stage.

It is helpful to draw up a checklist in which you:

- remind yourself of the purpose of the meeting
- check that you know everyone's name – so that you can talk to each person directly if necessary.

Practise the art of speedwriting. Everyone expects the chairperson to make notes. If you can master the art of listening to what is being said whilst at the same time making notes of the relevant points, you can then relay that information to the group whenever relevant.

Realise that you are in control of the situation. If you cannot understand what is being said it is more than likely that you are not the only one in that position. It is far better to stop someone in the midst of a complex argument and to ask for clarification than to reach the end of the discussion and then have either to pretend that you understand the issue and to ask for a decision based on unclear facts, or to risk irritating the whole group by asking the speaker to repeat everything. Obviously, however, you should avoid constant interruptions. If you are genuinely confused and suspect that most of the other members are in a similar state, you might be well advised to ask the speaker to put a few basic points in writing for consideration at the following meeting.

Always impose a time limit – either formally or informally – on the discussion of each item. There is then a structure in which to work and you have at least some idea of the volume of information you must summarise.

Ways of dealing with disagreement and conflict

Although there are many advantages in working as a group rather than individually, the corresponding disadvantage is that no group is ever going to agree on every single point. The extent of the disagreement can differ, of course – ranging from polite reservation about a proposed action to downright hostility towards it! The general principles relating to dealing with conflict have already been discussed in Chapters 1 and 4 (page 87 and pages 301 and 370), and it is essential that you be aware of them if you are asked to chair a meeting. In addition, however, it is advisable that you also cultivate specific skills to deal with any conflict that may arise. You may, for instance, be faced with conflicts caused by:

- members of the meeting having separate – and sometimes concealed – objectives
- a personality clash between two members
- the general ethos of the meeting being combative rather than collaborative
- competition for a limited pool of resources
- poor meeting skills.

Conflict is easier to define than it is to solve. The following scenarios outline some possible solutions to the problems just outlined.

Divergent objectives

Suppose that you have two deputies, both of whom you value. During the course of a meeting with them, you realise that one is totally in favour of one course of action while the other is totally opposed to it. You have a number of options open to you.

- You can overrule both of them (a 'lose/lose' situation in that neither of them has won). You have lessened the potential antagonism likely to arise between them but you may have created a joint antagonism towards you.
- You can choose to reject the proposal put forward by the more accommodating of your deputies. He or she may accept the situation and the other deputy may be delighted (a 'lose/win' situation), but you may have to decide whether appeasing the stronger personality of the two is always going to be the wise choice.
- Where possible, you can try to reach a compromise between the two suggestions – preferably so that both deputies feel that they have at least partially won the day (a 'win/win' situation). This is probably the most pragmatic solution but you must beware of agreeing to a 'second best' course of action simply to avoid having to deal with the basic problem.

Personality clashes

Suppose now that two members of a meeting you chair tend almost automatically to disagree with one another. Their conflict could be a genuine disagreement over facts, goals, methods, or values. If so, a separate meeting with you and both individuals concerned should at least highlight the reasons for the conflict and possibly effect some meeting of minds. It may be, for instance, that both of them have misunderstood the reason for the other's stance over a particular issue, or that one is of the opinion that the views of the other are always preferred.

More difficult to deal with is a difference in values. One member may favour a hard-line approach towards staff and be willing to accept redundancy as an unavoidable fact of commercial life; the other may regard the staff as the most important resource of the organisation, to be protected at all costs. In such circumstances your action depends to a certain extent upon your own personality and whether you are sufficiently powerful to impose a truce upon the two – at least during the course of a meeting – or whether you prefer to persist over a period of time in trying to reconcile both members to the fact that two different viewpoints are acceptable even though not necessarily compatible.

If you are unfortunate enough to have two members of a meeting who genuinely dislike each other and who try to use the meeting as a form of 'boxing ring', again you have the option of taking a hard line and stopping immediately any public disagreement, or of seeking to effect some reconciliation behind the scenes – at least so far as their conduct at the meeting is concerned.

A combative ethos

It may be you who has caused the members of the meeting to be combative rather than collaborative. You may, for instance, be such a 'hands off' chairperson that the more aggressive personalities at the meeting feel able to say what they like without hindrance. You yourself may enjoy a combative atmosphere and encourage it. You may be very new and inexperienced and unable to control your older and more streetwise colleagues. Your most important first step in such a situation, therefore, is to determine the reason for the prevailing ethos. If you feel that the reason is your lack of chairing skills, check on page 401 for some guidance on how to improve them. If you like a combative ethos, you have to be prepared to deal with the ensuing problems, such as:

- the imposition of decisions which may be unwelcome and therefore carried out with the utmost reluctance and lack of enthusiasm
- the pleasure that will be caused if such a decision proves to be the wrong one
- the consequent responsibility for always making the right decision.

THEORY INTO PRACTICE

Despite the obvious disadvantages just listed, some management writers argue that a conflict situation at a meeting is not totally non-productive. They maintain, for instance, that conflict can:

- increase involvement
- prevent a meeting from stagnating
- force a re-evaluation of outdated procedures

- allow a 'healthy' release of emotions
- produce more creative solutions.

Consider to what extent you agree with such views.

Competition for a limited pool of resources

Most people at work tend to be very territorial and, often for good reasons, try to amass as many as possible of the available resources for their own little empire. Given that the outcome of many meetings results in the allocation of various resources – money, staff, accommodation, fringe benefits, etc. - it is almost inevitable that conflict will occur. In such circumstances, a good chairperson has done his or her homework and comes to the meeting armed with as many facts as possible. When, therefore, a disagreement arises as to which area or person a particular resource should be allocated, the chairperson can speak from a position of strength and will be less likely to be browbeaten into a decision by the most persuasive member.

Poor meeting skills

Whatever the area of potential conflict, a good chairperson has to have the skills to deal with it. You may be naturally gifted in this respect, or you may feel daunted by the very possibility. If so, a knowledge of how to control a meeting – particularly during the course of a discussion or debate – should prove invaluable.

Remember, it is not always the most aggressive personality who is the best chairperson. Some research carried out on roles and relationships in playgroups indicated that the most dominant child acquired that authority simply by subjecting himself or herself to the will of the others! Even so, it may be that you will need to cultivate two different styles of control depending on the nature of the meeting itself – one autocratic and the other democratic.

Autocratic style

An autocratic style may help when you have to take the initiative if members are meeting for the first time. You have to explain the rules, outline the procedures and begin to develop the required ethos.

This style may also be appropriate if the meeting has to deal with a number of routine and relatively easy matters. There is no point in allowing conflict to develop in such situations.

If the problem that has arisen is highly technical, rather than let an argument develop with little hope of a successful conclusion you as the chairperson can suggest quite strongly that the item should be deferred, referred to a subgroup etc.

An autocratic style may help when there is a crisis. If senior management have decided that a number of staff have to be made redundant, and you are asked to chair a departmental meeting to decide which staff fit the laid-down redundancy criteria, it is of little use allowing the meeting to spend hours arguing about the decision itself or the criteria to be used.

Finally, the autocratic style can be used if the meeting is very large and demands that a number of formal procedures be carried out.

Democratic style

Most management writers recommend that in all but the limited circumstances just listed, a good chairperson should cultivate a more democratic style when dealing with (or trying to prevent) conflict at meetings. Such a style is preferred when decision by consensus is necessary or even advisable – as is the case with the majority of meetings. It is also preferred when an informal atmosphere is required. The more relaxed a meeting, the more likely it is that conflict will be kept to a minimum.

Finally, the democratic style is appropriate when the quality of the decision is less important than its acceptability. If you want a particular meeting to end amicably – as may be the case in the first meeting of a group of people whose departments have just been amalgamated – you may be less interested in making effective decisions than in promoting an atmosphere of cooperation and goodwill.

Legal and regulatory requirements relating to the conduct of meetings

Statutory requirements

Reference has already been made on several occasions to the Companies Act 1985 (as amended by the Companies Act 1989) which among other things lays down the law in relation to meetings held by companies regulated under the Acts. Other relevant information is contained in the Tables A to F of the Companies Regulations 1985. However, even if a meeting does not fall within that ambit, there are certain legal requirements about which its chairperson should at least be aware:

- the effects of the Data Protection and Copyright, Designs and Patents Acts (see page 449) on the production of documents
- the consequences of any defamatory remarks being made during the course of a meeting.

Non-statutory (or common law) requirements

Defamation

A defamatory statement is one that tends to lower a person in the estimation of 'right thinking' members of society or which tends to make them shun or avoid that person. It may be written (i.e. libel) or spoken (i.e. slander). However, defamatory statements made on radio or television are libel and not slander.

1 Defamation on the Internet is seen as the next growth area of litigation. So far the issue has not been tested in court in Britain, although a scientist who brought an action against another scientist about remarks on Usenet won an out-of-court settlement.

2 A company cannot sue for defamation on behalf of individual members – only when the defamation is about the company itself. It can, however, sue one of its own directors or members for defamation.

Defences

Even if a member of a meeting makes a statement which at first sight would seem defamatory, he or she may be able to offer certain defences.

It may be claimed that the statement was justified because it was substantially true. However, it is not enough to have an 'honest belief' that the statement was true and consequently this is rather a difficult defence upon which to rely.

It could be claimed that the statement was 'fair comment'. In such a case, the member would have to prove that:

- the subject matter was of public interest
- the statement was of an opinion not of a fact
- the comment was 'fair', and an honest expression of opinion.

The person making the statement might claim that he or she had 'qualified' privilege. Provided the statement was not published more widely than necessary, and provided it was not motivated by malice, a member may use this defence where he or she is under a legal, social or moral duty to make a statement to the meeting about a person, in whom the members of the meeting had an interest. In *Bryanston Finance Co. Ltd v de Vries* [1975] QB 703 it was held that the publication by a shareholder to other shareholders alleging irregularities in the company's management was the subject of qualified privilege. In another case, a company director, who had received allegations that an employee of the company was habitually drunk, dishonest and immoral, communicated those allegations both to the chairman of the company and to the employee's wife. The communication to the chairman was held to be subject to qualified privilege since there was both the duty to make the statement and an interest in receiving it. The same did not apply, however, to the communication to the employee's wife.

Qualified privilege can also be claimed if a member makes a statement about a person to the meeting in respect of an interest he or she has and the other members have a duty to protect.

Evidence of malice

If the defence to a claim for defamation is that of justification, the motive is irrelevant. However, evidence of *malice* will destroy any defence of fair comment. Malice may be shown in two ways.

- Remarks made carelessly, negligently or in anger will not be defamatory if the person making them honestly, albeit irrationally, believed them to be true. However, repetition of gossip without a belief in its truth is capable of being held to be malicious.
- Malice may be shown when the dominant motive of the person making the statement is an improper one such as private gain or spite. It is often difficult, however, for the person suing for defamation to prove that is the case.

In the case of qualified privilege, unnecessary publication may be evidence of malice or held to be wider than justified in the circumstances of the privilege. Thus where a report is circulated to and dealt with by members of a committee on a privileged occasion, its subsequent recirculation may not be so protected unless a good reason can be given for doing so.

Mitigation

Even if all defences fail, the person making a defamatory remark may mitigate the damages he or she may be expected to pay by

- offering an apology
- offering proof of provocation
- giving evidence of the plaintiff's bad reputation prior to the publication of the defamation.

The presence of the press

Public meetings are often attended by the press. In such circumstances, the defence of qualified privilege is not lost *unless* the press have been expressly invited by the person making the defamatory statement – on the grounds that an opportunity should not be actively sought for extending the audience in front of which such remarks are to be made.

The Defamation Act 1952 extended the defence of qualified privilege to fair and accurate reports in newspapers of matters of public concern in meetings of a number of bodies. The list includes meetings and reports of local authorities, commissions of inquiry, lawful public meetings and general meetings of public companies. General meetings of private companies are not included and newspapers must rely on the common law defences of justification or fair comment in respect of any defamatory reports at such meetings.

In addition the Defamation Act 1996 created a new defence where there has been innocent publication and republication of libel by distributors, publishers, printers, etc. if they can show that they neither knew nor had reason to believe that they had contributed to the publication of a defamatory statement. What they have to do, however, is to make suitable correction and sufficient apology.

Ensuring that key issues and decisions are recorded

There is always a certain volatility about a successful meeting. The atmosphere is charged, people become enthused about a particular issue and there is a general feeling that some progress has been made. If you have chaired such a meeting you have the right to feel satisfied about the part you played in that success. However, your good work will amount to nothing if all action stops at that point. Even the most self-motivated of your members will lose interest if you do not make certain that action promised or agreed at the meeting does take place. In fact, you can guarantee that if it does not, any subsequent meetings will not be nearly as successful.

If you have been skilful in chairing the meeting you will have summarised verbally the outcome of each discussion so that all members understood fully what was agreed. However, memories fade and it is imperative that a note is made of the key points of any meeting no matter how informal.

Although the validity of the minutes or notes is always your responsibility, their actual recording should not necessarily be a task you undertake personally. If you are chairing a meeting, ideally you should be able to delegate the recording of the proceedings to someone else. At formal meetings the meetings secretary may be expected to undertake this task. At more informal meetings you can ask the members to take notes on a rota basis.

All is well if you have someone who is experienced at taking notes. If you have not, bear in mind the following.

- Ensure that only one item is discussed at a time. In fact in the early stages you may wish to pause at the end of each item to summarise verbally – or even dictate the conclusions that have been reached.
- Avoid too many references to past meetings or events about which the notetaker cannot be expected to be familiar.
- The notetaker should not be expected to carry out any other duties as well as taking the notes – such as serving the coffee, etc.
- Try to take time immediately after the meeting to go through the main points with the notetaker.

THEORY INTO PRACTICE

Sometimes you may have no alternative but to take the notes yourself – if, for instance, the meetings secretary is absent from a formal meeting. If you are aware beforehand that you will have to undertake a dual role, consider what additional preparations you might make to assist you.

Recording informal meetings

Much depends on the nature of the meeting and the house rules, if any, as to the recording procedures used. In some instances, you may wish only to record actions promised or decisions taken; in others you may also wish to record, albeit briefly, the discussions that took place. Figure 5.1.8 shows an example of the notes made of a marketing meeting. Note:

- the 'house style' that is used (which will obviously differ from organisation to organisation)
- the use of an 'action taken', 'by whom' and 'when' approach
- the circulation of copies to senior members of staff not present at the meeting
- the relative informality of language.

JOCASTA PRODUCTS LTD
16 Park Avenue,
LONDON W1

MEETING NOTES **TEAM:** Marketing

Copies to: Team members; Managing Director; Sales Director

Date: 11 June 199-

- -

Present: **Apologies:**
Glynn Hammond Ahab Sardar
Claire Walker
Nasreen Hussain
Fiona Castela
Martin Fyles

- -

Minutes of the previous meeting
Agreed as true and correct record.

- -

Summarised action points	**Action**	**When**
1 Matters arising		
● All expense claims now submitted		
● Tenders for new advertising campaign now in hands of MD. Decision next week.		
2 Report back from SMT		
Glynn reported that the first draft of the strategic plan had been completed and approved by the Board. Important issues for marketing included		
● move into men's toiletries		
● changes in pricing.		
Initial marketing ideas to be discussed at the next meeting.	All	18/6
3 Staff appraisal issues		
Glynn had now interviewed all staff except Fiona. Meeting to be arranged asap.	GH/FC	18/6
4 AOB		
All staff required to have photographs retaken for new security passes. Photographer available in reception from 10 am to 12 on 21 June.	All	21/6

Figure 5.1.8 Notes of an informal meeting

Recording formal meetings

Figure 5.1.9 is an example of the way in which the proceedings of a board meeting may be recorded.

JOCASTA PRODUCTS LTD
16 Park Avenue,
LONDON W1

Minutes of a meeting of the Board of Directors held in the boardroom on Tuesday 25 May 199-

Those present: Bernadette Mafia (Chair); Chianga Ramirez (Finance Director); Kevan Storr (Purchasing Director); Jason Hardman (Sales Director); Menzies Ratcliffe (Human Resources Director); Robin Franciosa (Secretary)

The Chairperson welcomed Menzies Ratcliffe to his first Board meeting.

Apologies:	There were no apologies for absence.
Minutes of previous meeting	The minutes of the meeting held on 13 April were agreed as a true and correct record.
Matters arising	The HR Director reported on the progress made towards the implementation of the staff appraisal policy.
Draft SDP	It was agreed that the draft plan be accepted by the Board subject to the following amendments:
	That the term 'male cosmetics' be altered to read 'men's toiletries'.
	That the existing price ranges be examined to determine whether or not there should be a proportionate increase on all goods.
New outlets	The Sales Director presented a report outlining the research that had taken place into possible new outlets for the products. It was approved and the Sales Director was authorised to act upon it subject to a monthly progress report to the Board.
Presentations	It was agreed that all employees who had completed 25 years' service with the firm would be presented with a cheque for £250. The HR Director was instructed to implement the decision.
AOB	No other business was discussed.
Next meeting	It was agreed that the next meeting would be held at 11 am on Friday 18 June 199-.

Figure 5.1.9 Minutes of a formal meeting

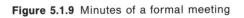

The minutes of most such meetings tend to follow a similar format and abide by similar rules.

- They normally include the name of the organisation, the type of meeting and the place and date of the meeting. At this stage, of course, the time the meeting was held may be irrelevant.
- Those present are listed with the chairperson's name being first and the secretary's name last.
- There is a brief note of what was discussed and decided. In formal meetings it is expected that sentence form rather than note form will be used and that the numbering of each item will, wherever possible, correspond to the numbering on the agenda. In some meetings – such as council or other local authority meetings – the numbering continues from meeting to meeting over a yearly period.
- The minutes show the date and time of the *next* meeting.

However, in some instances the formality required increases. In the case of annual general, extraordinary general, class or even some board meetings, for instance, the rules for recording the proceedings are very precise:

1   The names of all those present should be recorded unless the meeting is so large that it is impracticable to do so. For an annual general meeting, apart from the name of the chairperson and other officials, the number only may be recorded.

2   A record should be made only of any decisions taken. No note should be made of the discussions. The decisions are termed 'resolutions'.
- *Ordinary resolutions* are those through which the routine business of a company is transacted and agreed to by a simple majority of those present and voting.
- *Extraordinary resolutions* cover items such as the winding up of the company, the sanctioning of certain powers of the liquidator, and certain variation of class rights. The majority of three-quarters of those present and voting is required to pass such a resolution.
- *Special resolutions* are required to transact items of business such as the alteration of the Memorandum or Articles of Association, a change of name or a reduction of capital. The same rules apply as for an extraordinary resolution.

3   The wording of each decision must follow a standard format; i.e. 'It was resolved THAT the secretary be authorised to release to the Stock Exchange and the company's press agents, a preliminary announcement of the results for the year ended ...'
'It was resolved THAT the sum of £... be transferred from the profit and loss account to the general reserve account', etc.

4   In some meetings such as shareholders' meetings, it is customary to indicate the name of the proposer and seconder of the motion. In most other meetings, the names are unnecessary.

5   The minutes themselves must be dated and signed by the chairperson.

Every company *must* keep records of the minutes of all proceedings of general meetings. If it does not, the company and every official who is in default is liable on summary conviction to a fine.

THEORY INTO PRACTICE

Many chairpersons of formal meetings are reluctant to allow a shorthand notetaker, still less a cassette recorder, to be used to record the proceedings verbatim. They prefer instead to rely upon the longhand notes of the secretary. Consider the possible reasons for this reluctance.

Follow-up action

You can congratulate yourself on chairing a successful meeting only when the actions promised at that meeting have actually taken place. A common error, particularly for a new chairperson, is to check the minutes, approve their copying and circulation and then lean back with a sigh of relief. That relief lasts only until the next meeting, when the minutes are discussed and you discover that nothing has yet been done! Obviously a competent secretary is of great assistance in this respect. He or she should have taken the necessary follow-up action and reminded you or the relevant member of any action promised.

THEORY INTO PRACTICE

There may be occasions when you will have to take chairperson's action when, for instance:

a your secretary is having difficulty in cajoling or threatening a member into action

b your secretary is known to be forgetful and therefore cannot be totally relied upon.

c a member refuses point blank to do what has been asked and says that he or she never agreed to it in the first place.

Consider how you would deal with each of the above situations.

Element 5.2

Influence decision making through the exchange of information

Organising and presenting information to promote decision making

Consider the following scenario. You have been asked by your senior manager to provide some information on the advantages and disadvantages of recruiting part time staff through an outside agency rather than employing them directly. You have obtained as much information as you can, from your colleagues, from journal articles on the advantages and disadvantages of employing agency staff, and from the agencies themselves. You then have the task of organising that information in such a way that it assists your manager in making the final decision.

Organising information using standard techniques

First you need to decide on an appropriate format. It might be a series of numbered points, or a formal report with appendices, etc. You will then be in a better position to determine what material you need to include, and in what order.

Next, re-read your material to extricate the information you wish to use and, where relevant, summarise it. (See further page 461 for advice on summarising techniques.) On this particular occasion, for instance, you may decide to make reference to:

- the possible effects on present working practices; e.g. the present integration of part-time with full-time staff, the different legal responsibilities, the cost, etc.
- the other possible consequences; e.g. dissatisfaction of full-time staff, possible dismissal of existing part-time staff, possible effects on the achievements of targets, etc.
- the possible constraints; e.g. current immediate availability of staff, quality control procedures, etc.

Alternatively you might decide simply to divide the material into the advantages of employing agency staff as compared with the advantages of employing your own part-time staff.

You should then draft out the initial document, and photocopy certain sections of reports, journals, etc. to attach as appendices. If possible, allow some thinking time before you reach your final conclusion. You can then feel more confident that you have taken a measured rather than a hasty decision.

Although more limited in scope, in certain cases you may wish to use a diagrammatic technique of organising information, such as the *'fishbone' diagram*. Suppose, for instance, you are faced with making a decision about what to do with two receptionists who do not get on with each other and who consequently cause problems for the rest of the staff and for visitors or telephone callers. What may assist you in making that decision is to:

- sketch out your thoughts in terms of a fish skeleton and use the head of it as the focus of the main problem
- indicate on either side of the spine a number of possible causes.

At this stage you have completed your first analysis (see the square boxes in Figure 5.2.1 for an example). What you should then do is to delve more deeply into the causes or consequences as you obtain further information and, where relevant, add any refinements to the original analysis (the circular entries on Figure 5.2.1). You should then be in a position to develop a number of options upon which to base your final decision.

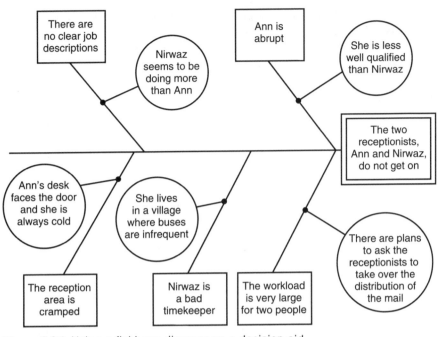

Figure 5.2.1 Using a fishbone diagram as a decision aid

Presenting the information

If you have to make the final decision, then the way in which you present the information need concern only you. Provided you can understand your set of rough notes even if no-one else can, there is no problem. However, when you have to justify that decision to your line manager, who possibly wants to present the information to others, then you have to be considerably more careful in your methods of presentation.

Written methods of presentation

The various types of written communication used for both internal and external purposes are discussed further on page 442. At this stage, however, you need to be aware of the ways in which they can best be compiled to assist any decision-maker. Use the following guidelines.

- Deal with *all* the points. Giving a half answer does not allow an effective decision to be made. Obviously accuracy is all-important, otherwise your credibility suffers.
- Even if the issue on which a decision is to be made is a complex one, your presentation need not reflect that complexity. Simple and straightforward language is easier to understand.
- Conform, where possible, to the conventions when drafting out your documentation – unless you have a particular reason for flouting them. Most managers have a lot of information to read and digest and it helps if they know their way around a document. (See further page 468.)

- Avoid irrelevancies or trivialities. Avoid the over-use of humour unless it is clear that the subject matter allows it.
- Try not to use emotive language – unless you are convinced that your reader will be suitably impressed.
- Distinguish clearly between facts and opinions – and try not to fall into the trap of making your opinion *look* like a fact. Even if your reader doesn't know much about the topic under discussion, you run the risk that someone else, to whom the document might be shown, does.
- Make your finished presentation look professional. (See page 468 for further discussion on this point.)

If the information you are asked to organise and present is to be distributed to members of a meeting, be careful to take account of the following.

- Provide *sufficient* information. Otherwise you run into the danger of members wasting time at the meeting familiarising themselves with a certain topic simply because they have not been properly briefed beforehand. You may also be the cause of decisions being made which are too wide-reaching and which are left to particular individuals to sort out – even where the decision is very important.
- Avoid providing *too much* information. If you provide an indigestible amount, then many of the members will leave it unread it or at best skim through it.

Oral presentations

There may be occasions when you are asked to give an oral presentation to assist in the decision-making process. Obviously the more skilful the presentation, the more successful the outcome. For further information on the way in which to prepare such a presentation see page 473.

Seeking and exchanging information

An uninformed decision runs the risk of being a wrong decision. Indeed, one management writer maintains that the best decisions are made incrementally – they are influenced each time some information is received.

Unless a decision has to be made in crisis conditions – and even then it will probably be influenced by factors such as your own personal knowledge or organisational constraints – you should ensure that you have obtained as much information as possible to assist you in making that decision.

Obviously you can obtain information in many different ways. You can read a memo or e-mail sent to you directly. You can sit through a meeting. More proactively you may obtain the information simply by telephoning a colleague, or accessing a relevant computer database. In most cases, however, such information searches will be relatively unstructured, particularly if they are not going to be used for any significant purpose. Where they are to be used for such a purpose, then your approach needs to differ as is indicated in Chapter 3, which outlines some of the major sources of reference available to you together with the methodology you might use in locating them (see also Element 5.3).

A less conventional method of obtaining and exchanging information, particularly in relation to decision making and problem solving, is the brainstorming technique. If you are tempted to use such an approach with your staff or colleagues you may find helpful the advice given by two researchers, Sashkin and Morris:

- Make sure that *everyone* contributes an idea.
- Make a list of *all* ideas.
- Record all ideas so that everyone can see what they are.
- Encourage more ideas.
- Don't discourage even the most ridiculous suggestions.
- Contribute your own ideas.
- Avoid any evaluation of ideas during the session – that comes later.

Exchanging information

Having obtained the information you require, you can then either use it for your own purposes or communicate it to others.

If you are initiating the communication, you will be able to choose the method you find the most appropriate. Make sure, however, that it *is* the most appropriate method. You may, for instance, prefer always to send information by memo or e-mail. What you may overlook, however, are the advantages of the personal approach – particularly if you want to persuade someone to do something for you or convince him or her that your proposal should be adopted. Again, a personal approach may be essential if you want to convey some sensitive information. If you have the unpleasant job of telling members of staff their contracts are coming to an end or that they have not been given the promotion they expected, you should be prepared to talk to them personally in the first instance even if you later follow up what you have said with a written communication.

On the other hand there are certain occasions when a telephone call or chat may be insufficient. If, for instance, you want to communicate some detailed information which needs careful consideration, it may be better to write a report or summarise a document so that the person to whom it is sent has the opportunity to study it in depth.

If you are responding to rather than initiating information, you may not have the luxury of choosing what means of communication you will use. Traditionally, if a memo is sent to you, you respond accordingly. If someone faxes you, you fax back – and so on. Indeed modern technology makes it very easy for you to reply in the same mode. If, for instance, you receive an e-mail, there is normally a facility available for you to press a reply key and create a new screen for your response.

In addition, you may be requested to write a report, compile a summary, prepare a set of statistics, etc. in which case you have no alternative but to display the information in the required format unless you are able to 'break the circle' – by, for instance, responding to a memo with a telephone call or putting in writing information you have been asked for verbally by a senior manager.

Channels of communication

Conventional channels

One method of communicating information – that of the meeting – has already been discussed in Element 5.1. Other methods abound, and several suggestions were given in Chapter 4, page 312. One management writer, for instance, suggests that there are at least 20 methods of *internal* communication, some more effective than others. In the following list the first nine methods are written and the final three oral:

- organisational strategic and operational plans
- organisational/departmental/SBU reports
- organisation charts, policies, procedures, etc.
- job descriptions, contracts of employment, disciplinary/grievance procedures, etc.
- direct communication with individuals – memoranda, e-mails, notes, etc.
- noticeboard material
- staff handbooks, bulletins or newsletters
- minutes/notes of meetings
- publicity and marketing material
- one-to-one contact
- one-to-one contact over the telephone
- group meetings.

Note also the use of the Intranet, which is a more sophisticated form of internal communication than e-mail.

Where the communication is *external* there are, of course, other options available, both written and oral:

- faxes
- letters – which may be standard, circular, 'blitz', quick-reply or form letters
- advertisements, journal articles, etc.
- press releases – or other publicity and marketing material
- shareholders' or other external reports
- minutes of certain meetings
- financial information – balance sheet, financial forecasts, budgets, etc.
- commercial information – orders, invoices, accounts, etc.
- one-to-one contact
- one-to-one contact over the telephone
- external meetings – occasionally videoconferenced.

Note also the use of Internet (see Chapter 3, page 244 for further details).

The Intranet

One disadvantage of the Internet is that it is so vast that finding relevant information can be difficult for all but the expert. It can be equally difficult to access – particularly after 11 am when US users begin to access it. Consequently the ability to download certain areas – such as the Web pages – on to an organisation's Intranet can be very useful. Access times can then be guaranteed and only relevant information downloaded. It can also be used for organisation-specific information.

Teleconferencing

Increasing in use and therefore in importance is teleconferencing. The term covers three different activities, each serving different purposes.

Audioconferencing

Individuals and small groups of people at two or more locations are linked into what effectively becomes the same telephone line. You can either hire BT's Conference Call bureau service on an 'as required' basis or, if you intend to make regular use of it, you can purchase the equipment.

Videoconferencing

This enables individuals and small groups at two or more locations to see and hear each other, face to face, over live video links. Again if you only want to hold videoconferences on an occasional basis, you can hire one of BT's UK public videoconferencing centres which in turn can be connected to a large number of international videoconferencing centres. If, however, you are a regular user you may prefer to invest in your own in-house centre.

> One of the largest single users of videoconferencing is the civil service. However, the use of teleconferencing is growing in the larger companies such as Ford, BP, BG, STC, the Royal Bank of Scotland, Barclays Bank and IBM.

Business television

This can be used to broadcast live or prerecorded material from a central location to audiences of any size and at any location. Unlike videoconferencing, it is a one-way video link and is ideal for one-off events such as sales conferences, product launches or annual general meetings where you want to transmit either live or prerecorded material from a central location to dispersed venues. It can also be used in permanent private networks for staff training or selling to customers, etc.

THEORY INTO PRACTICE

1   The advantages of using such methods of exchanging information are obvious:

   ● saving in time and money
   ● quick response to important issues
   ● ease of arranging meetings
   ● effective use of people
   ● reduction in stress and fatigue caused by travel.

   There are, however, certain disadvantages. Consider what you think they are, particularly in relation to your own organisation.

2   Internet conferencing is the latest method of group communication. Surf the Net yourself to find out about it!

Methods of problem solving

If you are asked or decide to become involved in a problem-solving situation, you should take care at the outset to establish the exact nature of your role.

You may, for instance, merely have to give your *opinion*. What you need to do in this case is to carry out the relevant research, form an opinion and then make certain that you state that opinion clearly, unambiguously and diplomatically. What you should also be prepared for is a response to that statement of opinion, such as a request:

- to supply more information to substantiate or clarify a particular point
- to consider and reply to an alternative or opposing opinion.

Note at this point that although it is unwise to vacillate too much – particularly if it becomes apparent that you will always change your opinion to coincide with that of a senior manager – you needn't stick mulishly to your first opinion. You can allow yourself to be convinced of the validity of another viewpoint – otherwise there is little point in ever exchanging views.

If you are asked to make a *recommendation*, you have to take your thinking processes a stage further. You must assess the information you have gathered and reach a conclusion as to the line of action you feel should be taken. In other words, you have to be prepared to believe sufficiently in your opinion to be able to recommend that it should be acted upon.

The most testing exercise, of course, is the making of a decision. Making a recommendation involves only limited responsibility, whereas making a decision involves almost complete responsibility. Some decisions are relatively easy to make; others, particularly those which involve solving a problem, are far more difficult.

Approaches to problem solving

Obviously different problems need to be dealt with in different ways. Sometimes the method you use will be subjective. On other occasions, however, you may want to take a more analytical approach.

Creative problem solving

Creative problem solving deals with open-ended problems that have no single correct answer – such as a discussion about the possible length of a recession. It also deals with problems that seem unique – although it is interesting to note that one management writer, Peter Drucker, discovered that very few problems are unique or even unusual. His research showed that over 90 per cent of decisions made by the management of a large company over a five-year period were 'typical'.

Analytical problem solving

Analytical problem solving deals with:

- problems that do have a correct solution; e.g. planning the budget
- problems for which there are known solutions; e.g. established disciplinary procedures.

Shared problem solving

You need also to decide whether you want to solve the problem on your own or whether you want to request the assistance of your colleagues.

Problem solving can be a lonely process. It needn't be if you can count on some assistance from your immediate line manager, your colleagues and also your staff. Knowing how and when to do this has been the subject of much research. H. A. Simon developed what he called the *area of acceptance*. If your staff are likely to accept your decision without being involved, it will be inside their area of acceptance. If they are unlikely to do so, it is outside that area. He also developed two tests to identify whether a situation falls within or outside the area:

- The test of *relevance*. Do your employees have a personal stake in the decision outcome?
- The test of *expertise*. Do they have any expertise which may assist you in making a decision?

Note that this is similar to Barnard's *zone of indifference*, discussed in Element 1.2, page 75, and Element 4.1, page 327.

THEORY INTO PRACTICE

Using as an example the problem of whether or not to employ agency staff, consider whether or not you think:

a existing staff would be likely to feel that they had a personal stake in the outcome of a decision relating to the employment of agency staff, and
b they would be likely to be able to provide any relevant expertise.

The advantages and disadvantages of participative decision making have been the subject of much research. For example, the management writers Morris and Sashkin concentrated on the effect the amount of time available for making the decision may have on the involvement of employees in the process. Vroom and Yetton developed a 'decision tree approach' for identifying the optimum decision style a manager would find suitable in a particular situation:

- make the decision alone?
- obtain information from others, then make the decision?
- ask for individual advice, then decide whether to use it?
- ask for advice from a group, then decide whether to use it?

Decisions made within own area of responsibility

When you are faced with making a decision relating to your own area of responsibility, it is useful to have some idea of the recommended stages for solving the problem. One approach is given below. An alternative model is given in Chapter 7, page 579.

Stage 1 – Analysis of the problem

Ideally you should first of all outline the problem, determining why it is a problem. You should also define the problem as *factually* as possible using costings, statistics and other detailed information.

If you are carrying out this analysis with a large group you may feel that the group should split into smaller subgroups for 5 to 10 minutes to allow them to discuss the problem and report back any views to the meeting. After the ensuing discussion you should be in a position to summarise the key factors (even if they are ones you prepared earlier!).

Stage 2 – Suggestions of options

Much depends on your approach. If you decide on the creative approach you should be prepared to:

- 'play with' the problem from a number of different angles
- deal with a number of different aspects at one time, rejecting or adding to them at will
- cope with – and tolerate – emotions (if the problem solving is a group exercise).

If, however, you want to deal with the problem analytically, you should ensure that you:

- present the problem, both to yourself and others, as a series of staged issues
- use your chairing skills in a problem-solving meeting to prevent anything but the topic in hand being discussed.

Stage 3 – Evaluation of the options

Four criteria for evaluating possible options, suggested by Peter Drucker, are:

- the risk in relation to the expected outcome
- the effort required
- the desired rate of change
- the availability of resources – both human and physical.

What you may also have to determine at this stage is whether or not certain options will be totally unacceptable to your senior management. If they are, there is little point pursuing them.

Suppose you are faced with the problem of increasing absenteeism and unpunctuality at the workplace. You have certain options open to you:

- to improve your monitoring systems so that you know immediately when and how often someone is absent or late
- to institute certain disciplinary measures
- to introduce a reward mechanism, such as the payment of a good attendance bonus
- to organise a series of staff training sessions outlining the potentially damaging consequences for both the individual and the organisation should the levels of absence and unpunctuality continue.

You are then in a position to assess the possible consequences of each option:

- Improvement of monitoring systems. Will the new procedures offend those who are good attenders and be ignored by those who are not? Who will carry out those procedures and how often? What costs will be involved?
- Disciplinary measures. Does the organisation have any set procedures? Are you sure you will be able to gather together sufficient evidence about the staff you want to discipline? If not, the exercise is pointless. What will be the union reaction?
- Reward mechanisms. What form will they take? How much will they cost? Whose approval has to be obtained?
- Staff training sessions. How effective are they likely to be? What will they cost?

Obviously you may decide on more than one option. By following a process of elimination, however, you should be able to feel more confident that (a) the issue has been fully addressed and (b) you will be able to justify it to your line manager.

---

1 This exercise is often referred to as a cost-effectiveness (or cost–benefit) analysis. Whereas a traditional marginal analysis exercise considers cost factors only, a cost-effectiveness exercise concentrates on weighing the potential benefits of each option against the potential cost so that a comparison can be made in terms of overall advantage.

2 If you are problem solving in a group, a useful method for you to use at this stage is to list the options proposed on a flip chart or OHT together with their advantages and disadvantages. This enables you to concentrate the discussion on the major issues and to lead the members slowly but surely towards making a decision about possible solutions.

Stage 4 – Making the decision

Before making a final decision, you should stand back from it if possible to assess:

- what impact the decision will have – on members of staff, on the working practices, on the department, on the organisation itself, etc.
- how much it will cost to implement
- what assistance will be needed in implementing the decision
- what resources may be needed
- any other action that may need to be taken.

Once having made your decision, learn to live with it. Constantly re-addressing the same problem will solve nothing and will add considerably to your levels of stress! Even so, that should not preclude you from assessing the consequences of that decision after a period of time to assess the extent of its success or failure. You can do this formally – there should, for instance, be a formal periodic review built into any planning process to test the validity of any decisions made during that period. Equally, however, you can review a decision informally – particularly if it is one which is of some importance to you or one which has caused you some concern.

Consider the following scenario. You decide to recommend that your department buys a particular make of photocopier. It proves to be a poor decision. Your manager asks you for an explanation. You can analyse the decision-making process you used to see what went wrong. Figure 5.2.2 gives an example of the type of aide mémoire you can prepare for yourself to assist you in the process.

```
Decision review
Decision: . . . . . . . . . . . . . . . . . . . .
Date made: . . . . . . . . . . . . . . . . . . .
Date reviewed: . . . . . . . . . . . . . . . . .
                                         YES      NO
1  Was the right decision taken?
2  If not, was it incorrect because
   ● all the necessary information
     was not obtained?
   ● the full extent of the problem
     was not ascertained?
   ● the problem was not broken down
     into manageable pieces?
   ● potential constraints were not
     identified?
   ● consultation with all relevant
     personnel was not carried out?
   ● options were not identified
     and analysed?
   ● any other factor(s)?
```

Figure 5.2.2 An aide mémoire for a decision review

Decisions made in consultation with others outside your own area of responsibility

On occasions you may be expected to make either an individual or a participative decision outside your own area of responsibility. Suppose, for instance, there are three departments, all of them having their individual reception areas. You are asked to look into the possibility of centralising all reception facilities on the ground floor. Obviously you should analyse the problem in the usual way and evaluate possible options, but you should remember that in this instance your task will be made more complicated because, at each stage, you have to consult a number of key people to gain their collaboration. It can be a situation fraught with difficulty.

In such circumstances you should pay extra attention to making certain that your terms of reference are clear. Can you make a decision or are you expected only to recommend a course of action? Do you report back to your own senior manager or direct to someone else? What do you do if someone in another department flatly refuses to cooperate?

Other points to note are:

- Keep everyone informed as fully as possible at each stage.
- Allow more time for feedback.

- Encourage different forms of feedback – orally, by e-mail, via a senior manager, etc. – to avoid the accusation that you are railroading a decision through.
- Document the process at each stage to determine major stumbling blocks, individual concerns, etc.

THEORY INTO PRACTICE

Herbert A. Simon, mentioned on page 445, won the Nobel Prize in 1978 in Economic Science for his work on decision-making processes in economic organisations. A major work was his *Models of Man*. Research this book in your library, in preparation for Units 6 and 7, and find out what Simon had to say about the difference between programmed and non-programmed decisions. At the end of Units 6 and 7 you should be able to relate these to 'hard' and 'soft' problems and systems.

Legal and regulatory requirements relating to the transfer of information

It is likely that many of your decisions will be about your staff. Some decisions are simple, others are more far-reaching. The arrangement of the teabreak rota, for instance, may cause staff some momentary irritation but no more. Alterations to a job description may cause much greater concern. In such a case, therefore, you will almost certainly have put in writing not only the changes made but also the reasons for those changes, and you may have recorded those reasons in the – probably computerised – personnel file of the relevant member of staff. What you also have to do, however, is to make sure that in such circumstances you are not in breach of any provision of the Data Protection Act 1984.

Breach of confidentiality is a topic that has already been discussed (see Chapter 3, page 258). However, nowadays, the issue of confidentiality is much more far-reaching and encompasses the right of the individual in certain circumstances to know what has been recorded about him or her. Indeed it has become part of the debate about 'socially responsible' management and its obligation to employees, a debate that has become more prominent in recent years given the decrease in trade union membership.

Statutory requirements

The Data Protection Act 1984

The Data Protection Act attempts to address at least part of the issue by requiring all organisations to register with the Data Protection Registrar if they want to store on a computer database:

a   any data relating to an identified person ...

b   which includes an expression of opinion about that individual ...

c   but not an indication of the intentions of the data user in respect of that individual ...

Even though moral and ethical issues did influence the government's decision to introduce the Act, the main reason for its doing so was to avoid commercial isolation. In 1981 the UK became a signatory to the Council of Europe Convention on Data Protection which permitted ratifying countries to prohibit the transfer of personal data to countries without comparable data protection legislation. Failure to introduce such legislation would therefore have caused great difficulties for those British organisations with international interests.

Any data stored on a database must be:

- obtained and processed fairly
- held only for lawful purposes
- used or disclosed only in a manner compatible with specified purposes
- adequate, relevant and not excessive in relation to purpose
- accurate and kept up to date
- not kept longer than necessary for the specified purpose
- protected against unauthorised access and accidental loss
- available to the individual for inspection and, where appropriate, correction or erasure.

In one case, a serving police officer twice made use of the national police computer to check the registration numbers of vehicles owned by debtors of clients of a debt collection company owned by a friend. He was charged with 'using' personal data held within the memory of the computer for a purpose other than that permitted by the Act. However, he claimed that he had merely looked at the computer screen and had not passed on the information to his friend. The court held that the Act had not been breached. In order for a breach to occur, 'use' had to be made of the information. Looking at a computer screen or even making a printout was not 'using' the information but simply transferring it into a different form prior to *possible* use being made of it. As there was no evidence that the police officer had actually passed on the information to his friend, the charge was dismissed.

Anyone who suffers damage as a result of *inaccurate data* is entitled to claim compensation from the person responsible for the error. The two defences open to the data user are that:

- reasonable care was taken to ensure that the data was accurate, or
- the data was obtained from the data subject and there is an indication that the data was received in that form by the data user.

A person, who suffers damage as a result of the *loss, destruction or unauthorised disclosure of data* is also entitled to bring an action for compensation, other than in certain limited circumstances. Again, however, it is a defence to prove that reasonable care was taken to prevent the loss, destruction, disclosure or unauthorised access.

EC Directive on the Right of Privacy

The protection offered by the Data Protection Act has been extended in certain areas by the introduction of the EC Directive 95/46 which applies to the processing of personal data whether stored on a database or elsewhere. What it does, of course, is to iron out the current anomaly whereby information kept on a database is subject to statutory restrictions whereas that in a filing cabinet is not. Member states are compelled to implement the directive no later than October 1998, although the processing of data already held in manual filing systems can be delayed for up to 12 years from the date of the adoption.

The Directive also places more severe restrictions on the circumstances in which data can be processed to reveal racial or ethnic origin, political opinions, religious or philosophical beliefs, trade union membership and details of health or sex life.

Providing evidence in support of arguments

Administrators have to be prepared to justify any decision or recommendation that they make both to their senior managers and to their staff. You have just been advised to work through a set process to make sure that you reach a rational decision. However, even though at the end of that process *you* might be convinced that you are correct, you still have to persuade others. Therefore, what you should have been doing throughout the process is gathering evidence to support your case. Such evidence is available in many different formats.

Types of data

- *Primary data* – one definition of which is any raw data you collect yourself. This could be by direct observation, by interview, through the use of a questionnaire, etc. The advantage of such data is that it can be tailored to your precise requirements. Primary data can, however, be very time-consuming both to collect and to analyse.
- *Secondary data* – which is collected by others. Obviously this encompasses a wide variety of sources of reference which allows you to access much more information than you could collect yourself. Equally, however, you may not be as certain of its validity as you are of your primary data.
- *Deliberate data* – which is produced for the attention of future researchers.
- *Inadvertent data* – which is used by the researcher for some purpose other than that originally intended.
- *Unwitting data* - which may, for example, be contained in a speech, the main thrust of which is *witting*; i.e. intended, but may also contain some innuendoes or assumptions.
- *Tertiary data* – which is the source of sources; i.e. information you can use at the start of any information gathering exercise to direct you towards more specific data.
- *Quantitative data* – which concentrates on definable facts and figures and is normally quite considerable in volume.
- *Qualitative data* – which is more subjective and involve perceptions, attitudes and opinions.
- *Textual data* – which refers to worded descriptions; e.g. a quotation from an article or an interview. Sometimes, however, such data may be unreliable if, for instance, the quote is from someone with a grievance or an axe to grind.

- *Nominal or categorical data* – which has been subject to some form of classification; e.g. country of origin, type of organisation, etc.
- *Ordinal or ranked data* – where it is possible to make some comparisons between ranked categories; e.g. if different types of computers are classified as being of excellent, good, average or poor quality.

Generally speaking the more formal the situation and the more important the decision, the more evidence will be required. Indeed, if you have been asked to submit your recommendations in report form, you will be expected to include a section on your sources of information so that the person reading it can be assured that you have carried out a full investigation. In your report about the employment of agency staff, you could, for instance, have included in that section:

- primary evidence such as notes of interviews of agency staff, previous experience of employment of agency staff, letters from agencies in reply to your request for information, comments from staff giving their views, etc.
- secondary evidence such as information obtained from a textbook, journal or library information database.

In compiling a report, you may have to follow certain conventions concerning the way in which you present the information researched. You will almost certainly, for instance, have to state your sources of reference either in the form of footnotes or a bibliography.

Unless house rules prevail, a variety of approaches is acceptable. One method is to put footnotes at the end of each page. An alternative is to present them at the end of each section or even at the end of the full report. In each case the information should contain: the name of the author – normally surname first and then first name or initial; the title of a book; the title of a journal article, the title of the journal itself and its volume number; the date – the year if a textbook, the month and year if a journal; the page number(s).

THEORY INTO PRACTICE

Research the rules of compiling a bibliography to make yourself aware of the general format to be used.

Use of questionnaires

There may be occasions when you want to use the results of a questionnaire as evidence. The preparation of such a questionnaire can be somewhat complicated and, unless it is very limited in scope, is normally compiled by R&D or marketing personnel. However, if you have decided to canvass the views of your staff on a particular issue, you can make use of the questionnaire format and record its findings as evidence to support your proposed course of action. There are points to remember:

- Avoid preconceptions. Even if you are pretty sure that the staff will, for instance, not be in favour of a restructuring of the department, you should still try to frame the questions in as unbiased a manner as possible. You might ask your staff to list (a) the advantages and (b) the disadvantages rather than asking them what concerns they may have about it.

- Make the questions clear. Asking staff what effect they think the fall in profits may have on their department may provoke very different – and probably meaningless – responses. Asking them what suggestions they have to make as regards departmental economies given that the organisation has made a loss in the previous year, may lead to more helpful suggestions.
- Avoid asking staff to give a yes/no answer to questions which are too complex for such an approach, such as 'Do you agree that the fall in profits leaves us with no alternative but to make departmental redundancies? Answer Yes/No'.

Minutes of meetings as evidence

The recording of meetings in minute or note form has already been discussed in Element 5.1. Obviously the major reason for their being recorded is to act as a record of what has been agreed and the fact that they have to be approved at the following meeting will provide subsequent evidence of that agreement. In very formal minutes, however, the contents of which may be produced as evidence in a number of different arenas including the courts, there may be certain additional safeguards. On the very rare occasion where minutes are still recorded in minute books, any alterations to them must be initialled and signed by the chairperson and the minutes themselves must be kept in a secure place (e.g. a bank vault or safe) to prevent their being tampered with at a later date. In the far more likely scenario of their being word-processed, the normal rules relating to the security of any computer-based information apply.

1 Despite all precautions, the courts have traditionally been reluctant to accept computer disks as evidence, given the suspicion that they are less tamperproof than a signed and initialled, paper-based set of minutes.

2 Most evidence should be in written form – otherwise it is inconclusive. However, not all decisions are of major importance. If, for instance, you want to make a change to the way in which lunchbreaks are organised, you can reach an informal agreement with your staff and the very fact that they comply with it is evidence that they have agreed to your decision. In legal terms they have shown their agreement to the variation in the terms and conditions of their employment by their 'conduct'.

Element 5.3

Prepare and present management information to facilitate decision making

Types of management information

The provision of information is now big business and the number of sources to which you can make reference is enormous. In reality, of course, the very nature of your work is likely to limit the types and sources of information to which you need to refer on an everyday basis. If you work in the social services you are unlikely to need to check share prices on a daily basis; if you work in a stockbroker firm, the latest figures on juvenile crime will be of only marginal interest, and so on. If, however, you work in a commercial organisation, you may feel that you need access to certain sources of information of a regular basis. Look at the following scenario.

You work for a firm that manufactures wall-coverings and paint. Recently sales have been falling and the organisation is barely making a profit despite a recent price increase. The number of products manufactured has also fallen; and although no-one seems to know exactly why that has happened, there has been some staff discontent about the general working conditions, the levels of pay and the monotonous nature of the work. Turnover amongst the production supervisory staff has also been high. There are difficulties in recruiting suitable new staff particularly amongst the younger age-groups. The senior management team decides to hold a series of high-level meetings at which they intend to draw up a strategy to reverse the downward trend in sales. One of their preliminary requests to your senior manager is to provide them with certain information.

Financial forecasts and expenditure

First of all, the management team wants to know how their competitors are faring financially. In this instance, you could consult the Companies Registration Office (Companies House) at which all UK and most EU companies are required to file certain documents – in London if an English company, in Cardiff if a Welsh company, in Edinburgh if a Scottish company and in Belfast if a Northern Ireland company. The information such documents must contain includes the name of the company, the names of its directors, the date of its incorporation, its annual accounts and its annual return.

Alternatively, if the company is a UK or EU quoted company (i.e. listed as a public company on the Stock Exchange) you could obtain an annual report free of charge from the company or its registrar simply because by law it must provide such information on request. You might find this a more fruitful avenue to explore given that many companies use their annual report as a marketing tool and include in it a lot of additional information about products, subsidiary companies and future plans together with the chairperson's annual statement.

You may also want to consult an appropriate database such as ICC or Jordans. For further information see page 459.

The expansion of the Internet has led to increased availability of company information given that many companies now use it – and in particular the World Wide Web – for marketing purposes. If they put their own 'home pages' on the Web they may include not only their annual report but also more detailed product information and advertising and promotional material.

Research results

You are then asked to research the latest thinking on good industrial relations practices – to see if they can be used by your organisation to improve staff morale and consequently to reduce the high turnover. As a first step you may again access the Internet or carry out a preliminary library database search for newspaper or journal articles on the topic. You may want to trawl through recent issues of journals such as the *Human Resource Management Journal, Industrial Relations Journal, People Management* or *Personnel Managers' Factbook*. It might help you also to contact a professional association such as the IPD to see if it has published any relevant material. In addition you might be able to access relevant academic research usually first published in the form of a working paper and subsequently published formally in an academic or business journal.

Productivity forecasts and outcomes

Decreased productivity is obviously worrying your senior management team. What may worry them even more is to find that other organisations of a similar size and manufacturing a similar product are not in the same position. If you are asked to find out whether or not that is the case, you may first of all need to check a company directory such as *Kompass, Kellys* or *The Stock Exchange Yearbook* for general information. You can then carry out further research into the relevant companies. Again you may be able to find the information you require by looking at the relevant annual reports or by consulting databases such as Jordans or ICC.

Economic and social trends and influences

One of the senior management team is anxious to have a perspective on the broader issues that may affect the operation of the organisation. He wants to know, for instance, what effect the recession is having on sales, whether the product prices are set at the right level, and whether the failure to recruit younger people is the result of a general lack of interest in manufacturing. In such a case you may want to consult the retail price index, consumer prices, producer prices (i.e. inflation rates in the manufacturing industries), balance of payments, etc. – which will not only give you useful general information but also assist in financial forecasting. You may also want to make use of the material published by HMSO, the Economist Intelligence Unit, the International Monetary Fund or the OECD. In addition you may need to consult publications such as *The Monthly Digest, Economic Trends,* the *Annual Abstract of Statistics* or *Social Trends*. Economic and social forecasting forms a regular part of academic research, and such forecasts (from, for instance, the London Business School, Henley or Cambridge) are regularly published in journals or reported in the press. You may find a particularly relevant piece of research in one of them.

For more detailed information on all these sources see further page 456.

Sources of management information

Internal sources

Often, one of the most direct ways of obtaining information is from internal sources.

- Large organisations have their own libraries or information centres which contain collections of directories and other reference material such as reports, press cuttings, journals, textbooks, relevant legislation, etc.

- In smaller and medium-sized organisations, much of the same material may be available but it will be in the hands of certain key individuals. In this case, much depends on your knowledge of your own organisation and it is certainly worth your while to ensure that your knowledge is sufficient to allow you to access any available expertise.

Another useful source of reference can be your clients or customers. If you work in an accountant's office and have a client who happens to be the manager of a Computer Services department, he or she may be a useful first point of contact if you intend to invest in a computer network. If you are a college administrator, you might be able to make use of the relevant experience of virtually any of the part-time day-release students sponsored by their employers – and so on.

> Many organisations collect a variety of information in the course of a particular audit trail or strategic planning process. If such information is properly indexed, it can often form a useful database for other purposes.

External sources

Library services

Many regional public libraries have good collections of business and management material which can be accessed either free or subject to a small charge. Examples include the City Business and Westminster Central Reference Libraries in London, as well as extensive collections in other cities such as Manchester, Sheffield, Birmingham and Liverpool.

Failing that initial source of reference, you may then want to consider using the services of 'information brokers' who can access information for you on payment of a fee. A similar service is provided by certain academic institutions such as the London and Manchester Business Schools, newspapers such as the *Financial Times* and certain trade associations.

Trade associations and professional bodies

Both trade associations and professional bodies can provide information specifically tailored to the requirements of your organisation. Examples include the Leatherhead Food Research Association, the Furniture Industry Research Association, PIRA (Paper and Packaging) and RAPRA (Rubber and Plastics). In most cases you have to be a member of the association or body, although some of the larger ones allow access by non-members.

Government departments

Government departments can provide a vast amount of information on topics such as company legislation, industry-specific legislation, business and economic statistics, etc. The Monopolies and Mergers Commission Reports also provide in-depth studies on specific industries. In addition, there are a number of government department libraries which can be accessed by the public, one being the Export Market Information Centre which is part of the Department of Trade and Industry (DTI). Statistical information can be provided by the Office for National Statistics (ONS).

> Although much of this information was published in the government's *Business Monitor* series, this series is now published commercially and has become too expensive for many libraries to obtain. The majority of the remaining official information is published by HMSO.

THEORY INTO PRACTICE

The Single European Act 1986 has had major repercussions on the way in which many organisations operate. However, many of them, particularly the small to medium-sized enterprises, are still not sure of the extent of the repercussions. Official documentation, however, can be obtained from a number of sources.

- The Official Publications Office in Luxembourg provides a catalogue of publications on a regular basis free of charge.
- Eurostat, the statistical office of the EU, produces its own catalogue of official statistical publications.
- A number of academic libraries are designated as European Documentation Centres, holding collections of European publications.
- There are a number of Deposit Libraries, including the British Library and Westminster Central Reference Library.
- There are London-based libraries of the European Commission and European Parliament.

In addition the European Commission has set up a number of Euro Info Centres in the UK designed to help small and medium-sized businesses in areas such as taxation, research and development, exporting, standards, company formation, Directives applicable to a specific product, etc.

a Find out the address of your nearest Euro Info Centre.
b Consider which of the above issues may be of significance to your organisation and contact the Centre for further information.

Paper-based sources

Some of the paper-based sources of information available to you have already been discussed in Chapter 3. Other initial sources of management information include directories, newspapers, trade journals, market research reports, and statistical information.

Directories

These are often useful as a first source of reference and quite frequently provide a guide to other, more specific sources. Company directories such as *Kompass, Kellys, Key British Enterprises, the Stock Exchange Yearbook* and *Macmillans Unquoted Companies* can be used to gather information such as names, addresses, contact numbers, names of directors, company products, geographical areas, etc. This data can then be used to acquire further information on selected companies.

Factual information on topics such as consumer expenditure, market shares for leading brands and advertising expenditure, can be found in directories such as *Euromonitor's European and International Marketing Data and Statistics* or booklets published by the Advertising Association, Zenith Media or NTC publications. Publishers producing market research reports include *Marketsearch, Marketing Surveys Index* and *Findex* (the last two of which can be searched online on Profile and Dialog respectively).

Trade and professional directories provide information on associations in specific sectors. Trade-specific directories, normally published by trade associations, list companies in the sector and provide market information including statistics.

Publishers' guides give publisher information for trade journals in specific sectors providing specific information on individual industries.

Newspapers

Newspapers such as the *Financial Times* can provide a quantity of up-to-date information and can act as an initial source of reference in relation to recently published reports, surveys, sets of statistics, etc. Use can also be made of agencies that provide regular press cuttings on specific issues.

In addition, there are a number of 'real time' services which can provide information on events as they are happening through a personal computer via a newsfeed.

Trade journals

Trade journals cover a wide range of both industries and products and often contain buyers' guides and classified company listings. They can also act as a preliminary source of reference about specialists in different fields.

Market research reports

Market research reports are available on almost any given sector. Most business libraries will hold reports published by Keynote (ICC), MSI, Jordans, Euromonitor and Economist Intelligence Unit. Information generally obtainable from them includes the state of the market, the major players, their brand shares, forecasts and future prospects, and a financial analysis of the biggest companies in the sector.

Statistical information

The main UK body is the Office for National Statistics (ONS) which co-ordinates the statistical output of government departments and publishes:

- general compilations of data such as the *Monthly Digest, Economic Trends* and the *Annual Abstract of Statistics*
- specific titles such as *Social Trends* and the UK *Balance of Payments (Pink Book)*.

International organisations such as the International Monetary Fund, Eurostat (EU), OECD and the UN also publish statistical information as do banks, trade associations and professional bodies – albeit in relation to very specific topics.

Electronic sources (databases)

Electronic sources of information are rapidly overtaking the more conventional paper-based sources, and the majority of publishers of business and management information now provide online services via a computer terminal and telephone line. The following are a selection of the many different types of database.

- *Full-text databases* contain articles and other documents in their entirety, from journals, newspapers and market-research reports. Major databases include Textline (available on most major hosts – Dialog, Datastar, Profile, Nexis etc.), Nexis-Lexis, NewsNet, FT Profile (UK) and Profound.
- *Abstract databases* provide summaries of articles and full bibliographic details. Databases include the IAC suite covering internationally produced trade journals and newsletters, and ABI-Inform which gives details of management issues in companies and business.
- *Bibliography databases* provide publication details of books, journals and reports. Examples include the British Library Blaiseline Databases and the Marketing Surveys Index (MSI).
- *Company databases* provide the same type of information as paper-based company directories but do so in more detail. ICC and Jordans both produce databases giving details of all companies registered in the UK at Companies House. They also include information on defunct companies.
- *Company finance databases* which provide profit and loss and balance sheet information over a number of years for both quoted and private larger companies, together with information on company history, directors, major shareholders, business ratios, etc. Again ICC and Jordans produce such databases.
- *Statistical databases* provide information on share prices, company accounts, interest rates, exchange rates, financial futures, commodities and economic series. Datastream and WEFA are major providers in this area. Other specialist providers include CCN and Dun and Bradstreet which provide credit ratings on companies, IDD which gives information on mergers and acquisitions, and EKOD which specialises in European Company information.

THEORY INTO PRACTICE

Figure 5.3.1 lists some of the advantages of searching for your information online. Consider:

a   the extent to which you could make use of an online system in your present job
b   the disadvantages of such a system – both in general and in respect of your own workplace.

- *Speed of access.*
- *Flexibility.* You can use a number of different criteria to access the information you want; e.g. companies of a specific size, in a specific geographical area, in a particular industry, etc.
- *Wider search areas.* It is normally easier to interrogate a computer database with a number of speculative search titles than it is to check through a large number of paper-based indexes.
- *Uniformity.* Searching for data is becoming increasingly standardised and the more sophisticated systems can search across a number of different databases at the same time.

Figure 5.3.1 Advantages of using online sources of information

Preparing information from a variety of sources

Raw data is very rarely fit to be presented in its original state. If, for instance, you have been asked to obtain some information about the financial viability of an organisation, you will probably have carried out a number of information searches including scanning the library database, looking at back copies of relevant journals and newspapers, contacting external agencies, etc. At the end of that process you will have a file full of notes, photocopies, scribbled diagrams, etc. Simply putting that file on the desk of your line manager with an attached compliment slip is not the best way to enhance your prospects of promotion! What you should do, of course, is to re-sort that information into a more acceptable format – but in order to do that you have first of all to prepare the information you intend to use as follows.

- Determine the format to be used – a report, a memorandum, notes for a discussion group, etc.
- Determine the extent of your terms of reference. Are you merely presenting the information or are you expected to pass an opinion or make a recommendation about it?
- Sort the information into appropriate groupings. A useful approach is to prepare a set of folders with relevant headings in which you can file the individual notes and papers.
- Check that all the information has a relevant reference – the name of the agency, the author, title and date of the publication, etc.
- Check to see if there are any obvious gaps in your knowledge that might involve you in further research.
- Decide what is relevant and what is irrelevant.
- Check whether or not it is up to date.
- Decide what has to be included in full, what in summarised form and what as a footnote or reference.

The more complex the information, the more necessary it is for you to be able to index it properly. Otherwise, significant pieces of information can be lost in a welter of other, less relevant, data. The time you take in labelling your files and placing papers under subject headings, or in chronological order, is definitely time well spent.

Summarising information

It is highly unlikely that you will be able to prepare information from a variety of sources without at some stage using your summarising skills, given that part of your remit will almost certainly be to present the information in a concise and readable form. You are probably quite confident in this area, but if not it is worth consulting one of a number of standard texts which outline the basic procedures to be followed. What you should first of all decide upon is the type of summary you want to use. You may want it to be a straightforward summary involving the following steps:

- skim-reading the document
- listing the main points in note form
- checking back with the original
- subgrouping all relevant points – which may have been scattered throughout the original document
- checking and including source details where relevant
- compiling the initial draft
- checking it against the original
- checking grammar, spelling, tense, sentence as opposed to note form
- preparing the final format.

You may want to summarise the information in a more user-friendly form, particularly if you are using it for staff development or marketing purposes. In such a case, although you may still have to take the same preparatory steps, you may wish to present the final summary as a series of bullet points or even in diagrammatic form. For further information on modes of presentation, see page 468.

One method of determining whether or not your finished effort is clear to your audience is to subject it to the 'fog index' test:

1 Take six consecutive sentences at random from what you have written.
2 Count the total number of words in the selected sentences and also the number which have three or more syllables. Express this as a percentage.
3 Divide the total number of words by 6 to give the average sentence length. Add this average length to the percentage of long words and multiply by 0.4. If your answer is greater than 12, your writing is 'foggy'.

If you feel this sort of calculation is beyond you, check to see whether your word-processor has an automatic fog index calculator. Some do.

Organising and interpreting management information

Organising information using diagrams

The more complicated the information you wish to impart, the more essential it is that you organise and present it clearly and concisely. One useful method of organising management information – before you decide on its eventual presentation – is by means of a diagram. There are several formats from which you can choose.

Relevance trees

Suppose, for instance, you work for a small organisation which, for the first time, is facing a potential redundancy situation. No-one knows what procedures are involved or what possible consequences there may be. You are asked to make further enquiries and to report back. What you might do in such a situation is to prepare a diagram – described by the management writer, Jantsch, as a 'relevance tree' – to:

- display multiple interrelationships – which is often difficult to do in written form
- assist in the planning process where you have been asked to prepare a report on a topic which involves a series of stages and several different issues.

If you construct a relevance tree encompassing all these elements you will have created a 'working model' which can then be used to compile the report itself. Figure 5.3.2 is an example of what your relevance tree might look like after your first draft.

Another advantage of the relevance tree is that it can be used to highlight key items of information extracted from larger and more complex documents.

Mind maps

Another type of diagram, advocated by the writer Tony Buzan, is the 'mind map' in which you start in the centre of the page with a word or phrase indicating your main idea or central theme and then branch out with each sub-theme taking a separate branch. You can then add as many sub-themes as you wish. As with the relevance tree, the advantages of such an approach are that:

- the central idea is more clearly defined
- position indicates importance – items nearer the centre are more important than items nearer the periphery
- proximity and connections show links between key concepts
- any review of the information is easily carried out
- the structure allows for easy addition of new information
- new ideas can be stimulated each time the map is consulted.

If, therefore, you have been asked to look into the possibility of purchasing a computer network, your initial mind map might resemble that in Figure 5.3.3. You would then be in a position to enter into the second planning stage.

Relationship diagrams

A relationship diagram, although similar to a mind map, does not require you to start with the main idea. It consists of 'words' sometimes enclosed in circles, denoting factors in a situation, and 'lines' showing some sort of relationship between them. By constructing such a diagram, it is possible to

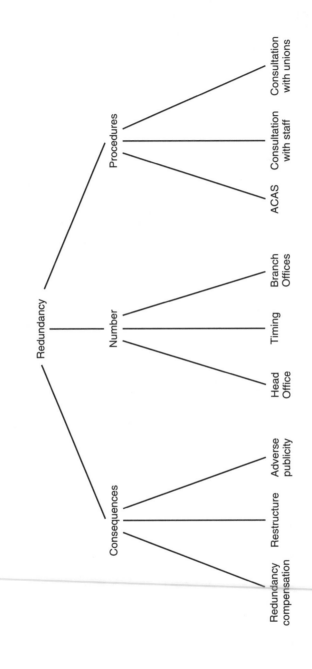

Figure 5.3.2 Example of a relevance tree

Figure 5.3.3 Example of a mind map

identify key groupings of factors, which may help you to progress to a mind map. Figure 5.3.4 outlines the steps you might have taken before compiling the mind map set out in Figure 5.3.3.

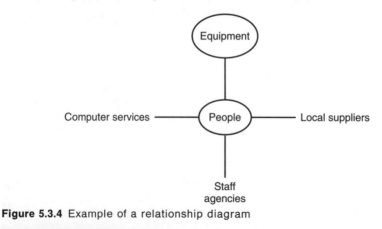

Figure 5.3.4 Example of a relationship diagram

1 Another type of diagram – the 'fishbone' – has already been discussed in relation to problem solving. If necessary, refer back to page 439).

2 One rather restricted diagrammatic technique is known as 'rich pictures', whereby pictures or cartoons (e.g. stick men, £££ signs) are used alongside words. It is a technique sometimes used when a group is working on a plan and the idea is to encourage participation and to make certain complex or technical ideas seem less daunting. See also Chapter 6, page 489.

THEORY INTO PRACTICE

Other types of diagram, normally compiled by technical personnel, include:

- systems maps
- Venn diagrams
- flow charts
- algorithms.

Check to see whether any are in use in your own workplace and, if so, how they could assist you in your own work.

Interpreting information

The higher up the organisational ladder you climb, the more complicated may be the information you have to absorb and the tighter the deadlines you may have to meet. Tempting though it may be, it is unwise and even dangerous to try to save time by including in any document you are preparing information which you do not fully understand or which you know may confuse the readers. In the first instance, you will look foolish if you are challenged and are unable to respond. In the second instance, you are not likely to achieve your purpose in persuading, informing, exciting, or convincing your audience if they don't understand what you are talking about.

Understanding a piece of prose is normally a matter of breaking it down into manageable 'chunks'. Suppose, for instance, you want to make reference to the following information in a report to your manager on the need for her to be aware of the tax implications if she chooses to remain in the UK or spend part of her time abroad.

'Residence of a taxpayer is not defined in the UK tax statutes so that the meaning is largely determined by case law and the practical rules which have been developed by the Inland Revenue. Prima facie, the factors to be taken into consideration in determining whether or not an individual is resident in the UK are his or her physical presence in the UK during the tax year. This is usually a prerequisite so that if someone does not actually stay in the UK during a tax year, he or she is not likely to be considered resident. If he or she is present in the UK for at least six months (183 days) then he or she is deemed to be resident. A count is made of the total number of days, whether or not there are successive visits, with the days of arrival and departure being ignored (s.336 TA 1988). A permanent abode in the UK is not necessary in order for a person to become resident. Thus a person who lives in a hotel but works in the UK for more than six months in any tax year would be deemed to be resident. However, if he or she has accommodation available for use in the UK then he or she is deemed to be resident in the year in which he or she sets foot inside the UK whether or not he or she owns the accommodation. This, however, is disregarded where the individual works full time in an employment, the duties of which are carried out wholly outside the UK or the individual carries on a trade or a profession wholly outside the UK.'

You may or may not instantly comprehend the meaning of the above passage. If you do, you can start to summarise it immediately. If you do not, you then have to adopt other strategies:

- Skim-read the passage in much the same way as you would do if you were preparing to summarise it.
- Try to identify the general sense.
- Identify any unfamiliar vocabulary or abbreviations, such as s.336 TA 1988.
- Don't be proud! If possible, ask someone who has some knowledge in this area to explain in general terms what the passage means.
- Take each section of the passage piece by piece and try to understand it. Make a brief note if necessary.
- List all the points you understand as you go along.
- When you have finished, re-look at your efforts and try to ascertain whether or not you feel you have a full (or at least fuller) understanding of the issue. Sometimes it is useful to pretend to be explaining its meaning to someone else by talking aloud to yourself – or actually to find someone who will listen to you and ask a few questions. You'll then be able to gauge very quickly the extent of your knowledge.

Interpreting statistics

Difficult though the foregoing exercise can be, it may be even more difficult if the information you are trying to interpret is presented in a statistical format. Even so, the same rules apply. In addition, you may find the following helpful.

- Look carefully at the headings and/or accompanying textual explanations. Often these give both a commentary on and a rationale for the figures.
- Try to spot extremes – what is the highest figure given and what is the lowest? Is there an obvious reason for this?
- Make comparisons – are the figures similar to or different from those of last year? Again, is there an obvious reason?
- Spot trends – are the figures always lower at one time of the year or in one particular area? If so, why?
- Use your knowledge and/or experience to determine possible reasons for the trends. If, however, you don't have a lot of expertise in a particular area, find someone who has and discuss possible interpretations with him or her.

An important point for you to remember *before* you begin any such assessments is that you should be prepared to test out in general terms the validity of any figures presented to you, particularly if they are prepared by one of your staff. Obviously if the figures themselves are incorrect, any subsequent interpretation of them is fallacious.

THEORY INTO PRACTICE

You are the senior administrator in the Administration department of a medium-sized organisation. There are two photocopiers in the department – one in the main office and one in the reception area. Recent photocopying bills are rather high and you therefore ask your assistant to produce some figures showing how many copies have been produced by each machine during the past three weeks. He gives you the following breakdown.

		Photocopier (main office)	Photocopier (reception)
M	1st	1420	3442
T	2nd	1340	3210
W	3rd	1520	3178
T	4th	1480	2987
F	5th	1180	3123
Sub total		6940	15940
M	8th	1560	3269
T	9th	1770	3311
W	10th	1560	7672
T	11th	1240	3126
F	12th	1910	3471
Sub total		8040	20849
M	15th	1110	3672
T	16th	1620	3672
W	17th	1220	3873
T	18th	1350	3026
F	19th	1510	3526
Sub total		6813	17769
Main total		21793	54558

Fortunately you are aware that he is not over-numerate. Nor has he prepared the figures on a spreadsheet. Before taking any action on the figures, you therefore decide to have a look at them to see if they make sense. There are certain anomalies. Consider what they may be and then compare your list with that on page 469.

Presenting management information

You should never underestimate the importance of well-presented material. As any publicist will tell you, the most mediocre material can be transformed by the way in which it is presented – and the most critical audience can consequently be won over.

You should be familiar with the house rules of your organisation on how you should prepare correspondence and write reports. If no such rules exist, you will probably have developed your own methods of presentation.

THEORY INTO PRACTICE

a Review the style of presentation you use for letters, memoranda, notices and reports. Try to determine if you think it can be improved in any respect.

b Compare the method of presentation you use when preparing a report with the example given in Figure 5.3.5, and assess the advantages and disadvantages of each format.

● Frontispiece	Heading or brief summary
● Introduction	Terms of reference which define the problem and what the report writer has been asked to do
● Procedures	Methods of collecting information
● Findings	A factual statement (with no opinions included at this stage)
● Conclusions	A brief statement which should follow logically from the findings
● Recommendations	Specific proposals (including any financial, physical or HR implications)
● Bibliography	
● Appendices	
● Signature and date	

Figure 5.3.5 A typical report structure

c Compare the checklist you use to scrutinise a draft report before submitting it with the following list to see how closely the two match:

- Is the heading self-explanatory?
- Are the terms of reference complete?
- Have you included all the procedures you followed?
- Is the meaning of the report clear throughout? Could any of the more complex passages be simplified?
- Do all the tables and diagrams make sense? Have they suitable headings and footnotes? Is there any other material that would be better presented in tabular rather than descriptive form?
- Is the report generally well written? Have you used the correct tense, spelling, punctuation? Have you remembered to use a spellcheck?

- Is the referencing clear? Have you missed out anything vital?
- Are your conclusions based on evidence? Have you made any claims you cannot substantiate?
- Have you avoided any evidence of bias?
- Are your recommendations feasible – or are they merely flights of fancy?
- Have you included (a) insufficient (b) too many appendices?

General principles

No matter what the house style, there are certain standard rules which should be followed to ensure that the finished document is easy to use.

- Unless it is essential to do otherwise, use short rather than long sentences.
- Avoid long passages of unbroken text. Use a sensible paragraphing system.
- Where relevant, use numbers or bullet points.
- Use headings and subheadings as appropriate.
- In other than the most formal of documents, consider the use of bold, italics, different sizes of type, etc. – although be careful not to overdo it!
- Present certain information in tabular, chart or graph form rather than as text (see below).

ANSWER TO 'THEORY INTO PRACTICE' EXCERSISE ON PAGE 467

The following could have caused you some concern:

a The fact that all the figures in the first column end with a nought. Has your assistant rounded them off to the nearest 10 but omitted to do so in the second column?

b The obvious miscalculation of the final subtotal and total in the first column.

c The sudden increase in the number of photocopies made on the reception photocopier on Wednesday the 10th. Is there a reason for that or is it a mistake?

d On the 15th and 16th exactly the same figures are shown in the second column. Is this merely a coincidence or has the same figure been put in twice by mistake?

Tabular presentations

If you want to present information other than in narrative form you can choose to display it in tabular form – particularly if you want to simplify certain information for the reader. Sometimes, however, making something simple can actually be rather difficult. Take the following example. You want to present the information in tabular form:

'In 1997 the sales of fiction contributed £93 000 to the overall profit of the company. The sales of non-fiction also increased to £68 000. The corresponding figures in 1995 and 1996 were, respectively, £70 000/£20 000 and £82 000/£46 000.'

You draft out the first table as in Figure 5.3.6A. You then want to make a comparison with the previous two years and therefore expand the original table as shown in Figure 5.3.6B. Now you have chosen to omit the '000s and the £ signs and append instead an appropriate footnote. You have also included your source of reference.

Suppose, however, you wish to extend the table still further to include a comparison with the *projected* profits in each year. One way to do this is shown in Figure 5.3.6C.

A
Profits made on fiction and non-fiction in 1997

	£
Fiction	93 000
Non-fiction	68 000

B
Profits made on fiction and non-fiction between 1995 and 1997

Year	Fiction	Non-fiction
1995	70	20
1996	82	46
1997	93	68

All figures in £000s.
(Source: Company Report 1997)

C
Profits made on fiction and non-fiction between 1995 and 1997 (compared with the projected figures)

Year	Fiction	Non-fiction	Totals
1995	70 (78)	20 (22)	90 (100)
1996	82 (64)	46 (36)	128 (100)
1997	93 (58)	68 (42)	161 (100)

All figures in £000s.
Projected figures are in brackets.

(Source: Company Report 1997)

Figure 5.3.6 Tabular representations for the example in the text

---

For examples of good practice in the preparation of tables, see publications such as the *Monthly Digest, Economic Trends* and the *Annual Abstract of Statistics.*

Graphical presentations

In certain circumstances you may wish to present information more graphically. Various examples of diagrams have been given on pages 461–464. Another type of diagram is the *pictogram*, which combines simplicity with an eye-catching presentation – but which is obviously very limited in use and can be open to misinterpretation.

Figure 5.3.7 shows pictorially the sales of non-fiction books in 1995, 1996 and 1997, corresponding to the example in Figure 5.3.6. Each 'book' represents £10 000 profit:

1995:	two books
1996:	four and a half books
1997:	Nearly seven books.

NON-FICTION PROFITS 1995 – 1997

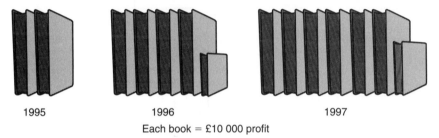

| 1995 | 1996 | 1997 |

Each book = £10 000 profit

Figure 5.3.7 Example of a pictogram

The general trend can be perceived but in no great detail. What may of more significance, however, is the fact that by altering the nature of the pictogram the actual results may be distorted. Suppose, for instance, the increase in profits had been from £20 000 to £40 000. This increase could be depicted by one book alongside another book twice its height. If however, in addition, the book is depicted as twice the *width*, this could give the impression that an even greater profit had been achieved than was actually the case – a doubling in two dimensions. If three-dimensional techniques are used then the size will be trebly increased.

Pie charts, line graphs and bar charts

Other traditional methods of graphical presentation include:

- the pie chart
- the line or multiline graph
- the bar chart or histogram.

See Figure 5.3.8 for examples.

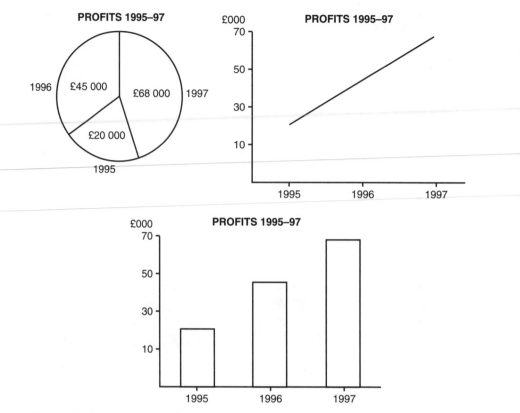

Figure 5.3.8 A pie chart, a line chart and a bar chart

Look in one of the sources *Monthly Digest*, *Economic Trends* or *Annual Abstract of Statistics* for examples of the different types of charts and graphs. Select one example of each and consider:

a the effectiveness of the presentation in assisting the reader to understand the information it portrays

b the types of information which, you feel, would not lend themselves to this method of presentation.

Computer graphics

At some stage in your career you will almost certainly have access to computer graphics, the generic term for the process which uses a computer to generate text, figures, logos, symbols and other graphic images. You can display the computer-generated images on your workstation monitor and can use the computer program to pick out the images, size, shape, style, colour, etc. you require. When you are satisfied with the result on screen, you can capture it on disk. Once you have done so, you can choose from a variety of outputs to enable you and your audience to view the images.

- *Film recorders* are used to create high-quality slides from the computer.
- *Large-screen monitors* resemble domestic televisions except that they are capable of providing far better quality images.
- *CRT projectors* are TV projectors to enable you to display TV images on to a large screen.
- *LCD projection panels* can be fitted on to an OHP and project full-colour data and graphics images.
- *Printers* can produce hard copy. Examples are dye sublimation printers used where true colour output is essential (e.g. 3D design and CAD applications); thermal transfer printers commonly used to produce colour OHP acetates and colour handouts; and inkjet printers used to provide colour copies for internal presentations or prior to the use of more expensive forms of output.

> The latest multimedia technology allows you to integrate and mix video, computer graphics, computer-generated animation and text with CD quality sound to produce complete shows and presentations. Multimedia software is available from various computer software manufacturers.

Oral presentations

Unless you are an extrovert, standing up in front of a group of people isn't easy. Indeed, good presenters are extremely rare if recent research is to be believed. One survey revealed that the most common complaints made by members of an audience were that the speaker:

- was inaudible
- spoke in a monotone almost guaranteed to send half the audience to sleep and the other half to the door
- simply read out notes without pausing
- muddled the content so much that no-one could grasp the sense of what was being said
- told the audience what they knew already
- used no visual aids
- used inadequate visual aids (e.g. illegible OHTs and/or handouts)
- mistimed the length – either by finishing well before the prescribed end or by rushing through half the material in the last two minutes of the presentation
- either permitted no interaction with the audience or handled such interaction badly
- had made no attempt to see that the surroundings were suitable (e.g. the right size of room, the right temperature, adequate furniture, etc.).

It is probably fair to say that in each of the above circumstances the speaker failed to clarify a particular issue or to persuade the audience of the wisdom of pursuing a particular course of action – even though he or she may have done hours of research and may indeed have prepared a very good case. Consequently if you want to make an oral presentation you would be well advised to make certain that you adhere to certain basic principles.

Suppose, for instance, that you work for a firm of accountants and are asked by one of the senior partners to come up with some ideas for a reorganisation of the administrative staff. What you do first of all, of course, is to gather together the relevant information and decide on the suggestions you are going to make. You then consider *how* to present those suggestions and decide on an oral presentation to the partners at their next meeting. You therefore address the *order* in which you want to present your material and then the way in which you intend to *deliver* it.

Order of presentation

If you already know and are known by all the people present you need not introduce yourself. What you should do, however, is to:

- introduce the topic
- explain your objectives
- say how long you expect the presentation to last
- say how you expect to deal with questions – whether you want the audience to ask questions during the course of the presentation or whether you would prefer that they waited until the end.

After this introduction comes the *main section* of your presentation. Outline the issue and indicate what you think are the main factors. Where possible give evidence to support your views. In many cases you might want to follow the written report format: terms of reference (as your introduction), the procedures you have followed, your findings and then your recommendations. What you have to do in addition, however, is to make clear to your audience at the end of each section that you are moving on to the next. Otherwise you may create confusion. Obviously you could assist that process with the use of visual aids.

Finally, *summarise* your key points (again with the use of visual aids if appropriate) and emphasise any recommendations you wish to make. Thank your audience and ask for comments or questions.

Method of delivery

It was once said of a famous actor that if he had to order a meal in a restaurant he rehearsed beforehand what he would say and how he would go about saying it. He knew that appearing to be natural is an art that needs to be practised! The same principle applies to making a presentation. Personality does come into it of course, and some people do feel more confident than others when talking in public. However, it is a skill that can be learned, however doubtful you may feel at first. Some initial self-diagnosis can help.

THEORY INTO PRACTICE

1 Read the questionnaire in Figure 5.3.9 and consider what your response would be to each of the questions.
2 If you have answered 'No' to any of the questions make sure that at your next presentation you pay particular attention to trying to overcome that problem.

Oral presentations questionnaire

Answer Yes or No to each question.

Relationship with audience

a   Do you make regular eye contact with your audience?

b   Do you check at intervals that you are on the right lines and that everyone appears to be understanding what you are saying?

c   Do you treat questions with courtesy and avoid antagonising the questioner by making him or her look inadequate?

d   Do you sound confident but yet relaxed and friendly?

Comprehension

e   Do you speak clearly and vary your tone?

f   Do you avoid dropping your voice at the end of each sentence?

g   Do you make certain that you avoid turning your back to your audience when speaking?

h   Do you use short sentences and straightforward language?

i   Do you avoid jargon?

j   Do you read through your presentation to make sure that there is a difference in the language you use for speaking compared with your writing?

Interest

k   Do you make use of effective visual aids?

l   Do you avoid presenting the audience with a mass of detail?

m   Do you make sure that any *detailed* handout is given to the audience after, not before, the presentation to make sure that they are listening to you rather than flicking through the handout?

Organisation

n   Do you always use notes or crib cards?

o   Are they brief and clearly numbered?

p   Do you mark the point at which you will be using each visual aid?

Figure 5.3.9 An example of a self-diagnosis questionnaire

Handling questions during oral presentations

Imagine that during the course of the presentation to the partners considered above, you are asked several questions. First, you are in the midst of talking about the advantages of accommodating all the filing equipment in one area, when one of the partners asks you whether or not she can still have her own PA. Another partner asks you whether your suggestion of allowing two people to job-share one post has any legal implications. You don't know. One of the older partners is obviously unhappy about the suggestions you are making and asks you outright why he should take any notice of what you are saying. The most recent partner, who wants to make a name for herself, persists in posing alternatives to all your suggestions – most of which you feel will be unworkable.

In these circumstances you should *stay calm* and consider the following guidelines:

- Do not allow yourself to be sidetracked into a long discussion about an irrelevant point or one which affects only one member of your audience. It is far better to tell the questioner that you will discuss the point further after the presentation. Take the same line if the questioner is not making himself or herself clear and you can feel the rest of your audience getting restive as you struggle to understand what is being said.

- Do not pretend you know the answer to a question when you don't. Admit you don't know but say you will find out.
- Do not respond to rudeness with rudeness. Quite often, if the rudeness is blatant the other members of the audience will come to your assistance. Otherwise respond briefly and then ask for other comments.
- Do not go on the defensive if your views are challenged. Take the contrasting viewpoint seriously and try, if possible, to reach some consensus of opinion – even if you have to say something like 'Of course, even the experts differ on that point' or 'I agree there are several ways of solving the problem – I was merely referring to the one I thought the most appropriate in this situation'.

The more experienced you become at giving presentations, the more adept you will become at handling questions. Whatever your level of ability in this respect, however, you should always have in mind a time limit. The effect of a good presentation can be ruined if the question and answer session is allowed to go on too long and the audience leaves feeling that more questions have been asked than solutions provided.

To remind yourself of the way in which you should *ask* questions, refer back to page 423.

Use of visual aids in oral presentations

Even the most gifted speaker will find it difficult to maintain the attention of an audience simply by talking to them over other than a very limited period. Visual aids are a way of maintaining that attention.

The simplest form of visual aid is probably a handout – provided it is short, such as a list of bullet points to which you can draw the attention of your audience as you speak. Graphs, charts or diagrams can be included.

Showing a series of overhead transparencies at a presentation is probably the most widely used form of visual aid. However, when preparing them, there are certain rules you should follow:

- Make certain that the room in which you are going to make the presentation allows you to make effective use of an overhead projector. It must be the right size, free from pillars or other obstacles to viewing, and capable of allowing a screen to be used (unless there is a convenient whiteboard or patch of wall – which, even so, is a second best alternative).
- Avoid putting too much on to a slide or OHT. It is not a suitable medium to display whole tables of figures or pages of text from a book or report. Avoid also the over use of colour – you want to keep the audience's attention, not distract them entirely.

- Make use of modern techniques where possible. Most modern photocopiers will photocopy on to special acetate and will allow you to enlarge your original if your word-processor fonts are too small. You can also superimpose slides to build up from a simple picture to a complex one – rather than sliding a sheet of paper down the OHT to reveal one portion at a time and so on.

If you have no access to an OHP, then prepared flipchart sheets can be a substitute. If you want to add to the prepared sheets, remember to leave blank sheets at the appropriate points – and preferably ask a colleague to turn the sheets over for you.

You can use video clips – provided you have taken the trouble to identify small key areas lasting no longer than a few minutes.

Finally, you can use an actual object. If, for instance, you are trying to convince an audience that the installation of telephone answering machines will make the organisation more effective, a brief demonstration of one of the machines will make a far greater impression than distributing a handout listing its advantages.

THEORY INTO PRACTICE

When your organisation revises its policy on fringe benefits, you decide to convey that information to your staff by means of an oral presentation at the weekly staff meeting. You are rather an inexperienced presenter and the presentation does not go well. You have prepared a very good set of notes, but as you deliver them to your staff you realise that some of them are not listening; others can't follow you. You realise also that you are talking too much and that you are in danger of running out of time. You speed up and consequently lose the section of the staff who, until then, were managing to understand you. Your OHTs don't seem to help. Consider what action you will take at any subsequent presentation to prevent the same problems from occurring again.

Presenting management information in response to requests from decision makers outside your own area of responsibility

The same general principles apply if you are asked to make a presentation to staff outside your own department. In this case, office politics may play a part. You will probably have sufficient standing with your own staff or colleagues to be able to rely upon their support and can expect them to give you the courtesy of their attention. If you are making a presentation outside your own area you cannot necessarily rely on the same loyalty. Indeed you may experience quite the reverse – from, for instance, an ambitious colleague from another department, who sees your making a successful presentation a threat to his or her chances of future promotion. It is even more essential, therefore, that you prepare thoroughly, that your visual aids are good and that you can withstand a potentially hostile question and answering session. It might also be an idea for you to ask for some of your allies to support you in making the presentation – to share part of the presentation, to act as back-up at question time, etc. On the plus side, you will have the right to feel pleased if you do make a successful cross-organisational presentation in the presence of members of the senior management who may have some influence over your career prospects.

Legal and regulatory requirements relating to the transfer of information

The invention of the photocopier has resulted in considerable benefits for the harassed administrator. No longer has he/she to employ an army of clerks to transcribe or summarise information – the press of a button can result in the production of any number of copies which, combined with the use of a marker pen to highlight points of significance, can make the transfer of information to a large number of people extremely easy. The only non-statutory legal restriction about which the administrator should be aware is the need to avoid breach of confidentiality (if, for instance, the information could be regarded as a trade secret) or republication of a possible libel. Look back to pages 258, 430 and 449 for further details.

Statutory requirements – the Copyright, Designs and Patents Act 1988

A lot of people make their living by writing or composing – and, given the chance, a lot more might make their living by reproducing the finished result under their own name. The problem is not new – at the first performance of each play written by William Shakespeare, there were copyists present who were paid to write down as much as they could by rival actors' companies so that they could perform a version of the original on subsequent nights. At that time, Shakespeare had little comeback – nowadays he might have. The Copyright, Designs and Patents Act 1988 attempts to protect the independent skill, labour and effort which has been expended in producing a work by preventing others from helping themselves to too large a proportion of that effort.

Copyright arises *automatically* without the need for registration or other formality. It is, however, common to see published work carrying the copyright symbol ©. Whilst this is not necessary in order to obtain copyright protection in the UK, the use of the symbol in conjunction with the name of the copyright owner and the year of first publication has three purposes:

- It confers protection under the terms of Universal Copyright Convention 1952 in a number of other countries, including the USA, without the need for any other formality.
- It raises a number of presumptions as to the authorship of the work, ownership of the copyright and date of first publication (although these presumptions may be rebutted by appropriate evidence to the contrary).
- It serves as a reminder of the rights of the copyright owner and a warning against infringement.

The Act affords legal protection to the creators of certain kinds of materials; i.e. original literary, dramatic, musical or artistic works (including computer programs), sound recordings, films, broadcasts or cable programmes and typographical arrangements of published works. The duration of the protection has been extended by 1996 EU regulations to 70 years after the end of the year of an author's death.

> 1 The law of copyright does not protect *ideas*. In one case, the plaintiff claimed damages from the defendant for infringement of his copyright in the scripts and dramatic format of the television show *Opportunity Knocks*. The plaintiff complained that certain catchphrases such as 'For X Opportunity Knocks' and the use of a 'clapometer' to measure audience reaction had been originated by him and that their use by others without permission breached copyright. The Privy Council, however, held that the catchphrase and clapometer did no more than express a general idea or concept for use in talent contests and were therefore not the subject of copyright.
>
> 2 Copying a product that has been manufactured from drawings amounts indirectly to copying the drawings and is an infringement of copyright. In one case, a dress designer saw another designer's samples at an exhibition and later marketed dresses that were a copy both in materials and design. It was held that although the *dresses* themselves were not protected by copyright, the *sketches*, which the designer had copied, were.

The Act also introduced certain 'moral rights':

- the right to be identified as the author of a particular work
- the right not to have a work subjected to derogatory treatment amounting to a distortion or mutilation of the work.

Copyright will not be infringed if copied parts of the work are used for:

- an individual's research or private study
- criticism or review of a work – provided the identity of the author and the title of the work are acknowledged
- the reporting of current events provided the identity of the author is acknowledged
- incidental inclusion of any work in an artistic work, sound recording, broadcast or cable programme
- educational use (but see page 480 for discussion on use of software)
- libraries and archives – see the Copyright (Libraries and Archivists) (Copying of Copyright Material) Regulations 1989 for further information
- the reporting of parliamentary or judicial proceedings, the proceedings of a Royal Commission or statutory enquiry
- abstracts.

Implications for administrators

The UK has the tightest copyright legislation in the world and to contravene the law in this area means to risk prosecution. The problem for administrators, however, is that the Act itself is rather difficult to interpret and there may be occasions when it is breached unknowingly. Fortunately various organisations are able to help.

- *The Copyright Licensing Agency* (CLA) licenses institutions for reprographic copying from books, journals and periodicals.
- *The Performing Rights Society* (PRS) administers the performing rights in copyright music on behalf of composers and music publishers, both British and international. The performing rights are defined as the right to perform music in public either 'live' or by mechanical means, as well as the right to broadcast music.
- *Phonographic Performance Ltd* (PPL) administers the public performance and broadcasting rights in sound recordings on behalf of record companies and their artists.
- *The Newspaper Licensing Agency* (NLA) was set up in January 1996 to allow organisations to make multiple copies from newspapers (although News International Group and regional newspapers are not covered by the scheme).
- *The Educational Recording Agency* (ERA) issues blanket licences to educational establishments covering off-air use of broadcast and cable programmes for the purpose of educational instruction.
- *The Design and Artists Copyright Agency* has a slide licensing scheme.

THEORY INTO PRACTICE

Most managers and administrators are aware of the penalties that can be incurred through breach of copyright. Unfortunately, however, many members of staff may not be equally concerned and those with unrestricted access to a photocopier might cheerfully flout the law by photocopying in bulk large sections of books, journals or newspapers. Given that on average every ten days one company is caught in breach of copyright and confronted with the threat of legal proceedings, consider what action you might take to make sure that (a) all staff recognise the dangers of breaking the law and (b) you can check that they are obeying your instructions.

Computer software

Software licensing is a particularly sensitive area. Since national and international intellectual property legislation does not at present fully protect the use of works in electronic form, many of the legal rights of the owners of such software are based on the terms of an individual contract. Normally, therefore, an organisation, as an end-user, will purchase a licence and not the software itself, which always belongs to the creator company. Consequently the organisation must ensure that it invests in the appropriate multi-user licence without which the product cannot be copied on to more than one machine or networked, without infringing the licensing agreement and copyright law.

The type of licence granted can differ from organisation to organisation. Some suppliers such as Microsoft and Novell offer discount 'select agreements' for businesses and educational institutions, whereby the software buyer gains a number of units for each product purchased during the course of a year, which permit the purchase of extra licences at a saving of around 50 per cent on normal costs. In addition, some companies such as Microsoft offer student discounts on licensed software. CD–ROMs tend to work on a stand-alone basis although some are sold for multiple users. Many, however, allow no more than 50 people to use the CD–ROM concurrently.

The Business Software Alliance (BSA) is a global organisation whose terms of reference are to eradicate illegal copying of software – 'software piracy'. It suggests that it is good management practice to have a software audit and to repeat this annually particularly since substantial penalties are imposed on users of illegal software – the current maximum penalty is up to two years' imprisonment or an unlimited fine.

THEORY INTO PRACTICE

For further information consult *A Pocket Directory of Organisations Involved in the Administration of Copyright and Rights in Performances*, The Copyright Licensing Agency, The British Copyright Council, 29 Berners Street, London W1P 4AA.

Verifying the validity of information and its sources

Reference has already been made to ways of providing evidence in support of arguments and ways of obtaining and validating information. Many of the same procedures apply if you want to make sure that information you wish to use in the decision-making process is in fact valid. What you might also want to do, however, is to undertake a critical analysis of the actual *document* upon which you wish to base that particular decision.

The analysis of documents can be divided into *external* and *internal* criticism. External criticism aims to discover whether a document is both genuine (not forged) and authentic (a truthful report of what it purports to be). More importantly, perhaps, internal criticism involves a more detailed examination of the document itself.

Suppose, for instance, you have been asked to write a report recommending the use of the services of a local firm of accountants. You have obtained information from a number of firms and now have to decide whom to recommend. You have established that the information is both genuine and authentic – what ideally you should now do in each individual case is the following.

1 Examine the document and determine what it says. Does it answer the questions you asked? Does it back up any statements with certain verifiable evidence? For example, if it states that the firm is the largest or longest established in the area, does it provide information in support of that statement?

2 Determine who wrote it. Is it a document prepared by one of the senior partners in direct response to your query, or does it contain general

information which is obviously sent out in response to almost every initial enquiry? Is it a current document – or has it been compiled some time ago?

3   Check on its completeness. It might be that you have asked some rather testing questions in your initial request for information and that some of the firms want to 'forget' to answer those questions because they feel it might put them at a disadvantage. More simply, certain queries may have been overlooked.

4   Draw comparisons. There may be many reasons for one response differing very obviously from the rest. It may indicate, for instance, that the firm in question is very much better than the others in the use of its initiative and its approach to clients. On the other hand, it may indicate that it is out of its depth and does not know how to respond in the required format.

Remember the axiom 'look at the person, not the words'. Where relevant, try to find out as much as possible about the author of any document. If, for instance, you are aware that he or she has decided political views or is known to have a particular axe to grind, you should obviously bear that in mind when reading the document. Conversely, if he or she is a known expert in a particular area, you may feel confident about accepting the opinions offered on a particular issue.

THEORY INTO PRACTICE

You read an article on a topic about which you know very little. It is written in a sensible and logical manner and seems to contain the answers to most of your questions. Before you include that information in a report you are writing for your line manager, however, you learn that the author is known for his highly controversial views on certain issues. Consider what action you would take.

Element 6.1

Identify the needs of an organisation for systems and procedures

Thinking in systems – or taking a systems approach – is nothing new. After all, we are familiar with concepts such as the solar system, our respiratory system and political systems. Expressions such as 'It's a crazy system' or 'We need a different system' are commonly used in everyday life. We may go shopping to buy an audio system or a computer system. However, many people who talk about 'systems' are often unable to define what they mean by this term – or to tell you where 'procedures' fit in to the concept.

Yet to be able to plan or design a system you should not only know what you are doing, but why you are doing it! There is little point in 'thinking in systems' if you have no clear idea about the aim of the exercise. If you become a systems fanatic, the danger is that you preach your new-found skills to others in a desperate attempt to make them converts. This may be useful but you should note that systems and procedures have drawbacks as well as benefits. They are not a panacea for all ills, nor will they provide you with a foolproof way of organising and controlling your administrative responsibilities. In addition, even the best system will fail if no-one believes in it or agrees with it. However, as a method of analysis and a strategy for improving the design and control of a variety of operations, having the ability to take a systems approach is an extremely useful addition to the repertoire of any manager or administrator.

A systems theorist will tell you that almost anything can be described as a system. By this definition, a bee becomes a system for making honey, a burglar alarm becomes a system for protecting property – and this chapter becomes a system for helping you to learn about systems and procedures. If it operates effectively then the output – or result – will be a reader who not only understands the concepts but is keen to put them into practice. However, as you will quickly learn, systems are also dependent upon their inputs – which, in this case, relates to the quality and accuracy of this text and the application of you, the reader. If you are keen and eager to learn, then the output will be considerably different from that likely to result if you are not. You may wish to bear this in mind as you read more about systems and procedures!

Types of systems and procedures

Credit for the original idea of systems theory is generally accorded to Ludwig von Bertalanffy, a biologist, who was the first to describe living organisms as functioning systems. Later, Bertalanffy broadened this concept to cover other types of organisms, and by the 1950s a variety of papers were being published – mainly in America at that time – on the relevance of systems theory to the management of organisations.

Today systems theory is widely accepted as a valuable framework or philosophy for solving problems relating to complex systems – such as modern organisations. Systems theory provides a method for looking at an organisation as a whole unit – yet one which is part of a wider and constantly changing environment. All complex systems are comprised of subsystems, which are interrelated and interact and influence each other so that changes to one subsystem have spinoff effects to other subsystems and to the system as a whole. As an example, we can describe individual planets as subsystems of the solar system, the climate system as a subsystem of the Earth, and so on. Environmental issues have made us fully aware that changing one subsystem – the ecological balance – has affects on other subsystems.

Many of the specialist terms traditionally used by systems designers, such as input, output, feedback and control, have now found their way into general usage – as have the terms 'systems' and 'procedures'. In addition, the value of thinking in systems has been proved in areas as diverse as space exploration, environmental forecasting and economic modelling.

This unit concentrates upon the types of systems you will meet in organisations and gives practical advice on planning and designing these to meet identified needs. At the same time it introduces you to the theory behind some aspects of system design and implementation so that you can more accurately judge the usefulness of employing this approach yourself.

What is a system?

Russell Ackoff, an early advocate of systems theory, described a system as a 'set of interrelated elements'. On its own, however, this is insufficient to enable you to comprehend what is meant by the term. Others have described systems as sets of component parts which are brought and used together to meet the needs of the users. An Open University definition is more precise, stating that a system has four distinct components:

- A system is an assembly of parts or components existing together in an organised way.
- The assembly is of particular human interest.
- Parts are affected by being in the system – they change if they leave.
- The assembly does something – it has an aim.

To illustrate this, think of a clock as a system for telling the time. The assembly of the components is critical – unless they are ordered accurately the clock will not function (or function effectively). The assembly is of interest to humans because it serves a purpose, it tells the time. The parts only function in the way they do because they are part of the system – removed from the clock they are simply isolated components. The aim of the assembly is to monitor, record and display the time *accurately*.

If a clock were developed which worked on the principle of perpetual motion then this would be a completely *closed system*. It would need no inputs from the environment to function. However, even the most basic clock needs a battery (or requires winding, which involves a human input). This means that the clock is an *open system*, and relies on an input from outside the process to be able to give the correct output, ie the time. This can be illustrated quite simply by a basic systems diagram as shown in Figure 6.1.1.

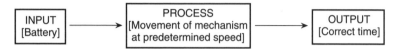

Figure 6.1.1 A basic systems diagram

The only truly closed system is a sealed chemical reaction or experiment. Every other system is open in that there is some interaction with the environment outside the system. At one time, it used to be held that Trappist monks, or even high-security prisons such as Alcatraz, were closed systems but this is not true. Even Trappist monks have some inputs from outside (albeit only minimal) and prisons hire staff and buy supplies like any other organisation.

Although all organisations are open systems, they differ in their *degree* of openness (or responsiveness). Thus a retail superstore is more open than a convent, a car manufacturer is more open than a funeral director. However, the trend today is towards greater interaction with the environment and concern for stakeholders: tobacco companies have to cope with the health lobby and the anti-smoking lobby; Shell has had to learn to cope with the environmental lobby and the human rights lobby. In systems terms we therefore say the *systems boundary* is more *flexible* – and more apt to shift or change position.

THEORY INTO PRACTICE

1 Consider how you would draw a basic systems diagram for each of the following:
   a a central heating system
   b a photocopying system
   c the human respiratory system.
2 If a clock can be described as 'a system for displaying the correct time', how would you describe each of the systems listed in (1) above?
3 Consider the degree of interaction and responsiveness between your organisation and its environment, i.e. its degree of openness and the flexibility of its boundary. You may also like to consider whether this is becoming more or less flexible with time.

Open-loop and closed-loop systems

A car can be described as a system of personal transportation using an internal combustion engine. The main input is fuel, the process is that of combustion, and there are outputs – power (which you want) and noise and exhaust gases (which you don't). You can vary the outputs by the type of inputs you purchase (as anyone who has ever put petrol into a diesel engine in error will know!) and by the degree of pressure you put on the accelerator, which varies the amount of fuel the engine receives. The greater the pressure, normally the faster you will go. Technically, only the capability of the engine limits the speed achieved. The systems diagram to illustrate this process is shown in Figure 6.1.2. You should note that there is no *mechanical* link between the output and the input or process, and this is therefore described as an *open-loop system*.

Figure 6.1.2 An open-loop system

However, some systems have automatic control subsystems which monitor the amount of output and then vary the input automatically. An example would be the installation of a tachometer on your car which regulated your speed. The function of the tachometer would be to operate as a control subsystem to measure your speed and then regulate the input to keep the output between predetermined limits. This is illustrated in Figure 6.1.3. Because we have now 'closed' the feedback loop, this is termed a *closed-loop system*. This concept is developed further later in this chapter.

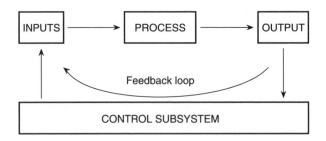

Figure 6.1.3 A closed-loop system

Some systems are *deterministic*. In this case we can calculate what output will be produced from a particular input. Your car is a deterministic system, with a fairly predictable output mainly depending upon the size of the engine. This type of system is sometimes termed a *hard system* because it uses *hard* (unequivocal, quantitative) *data* to calculate and predict the output – often by using mathematical formulae.

Other systems are non-deterministic. The technical term for this is *stochastic systems*. Examples include the economic system, political systems and traffic systems. Frequently (but not always) stochastic systems have the added, unpredictable ingredient of *people* – who either form uncertain inputs or who interact in unpredictable ways at the process stage. Such systems are sometimes known as *soft systems* because predicting their behaviour involves using *soft data* (thoughts, ideas, assumptions, opinions – all of which are qualitative) and outputs are therefore less easy to forecast. Do note, however, that not all stochastic systems involve people – the weather system is notoriously unpredictable and changeable even without the influence of human beings!

THEORY INTO PRACTICE

1 Imagine you fit a thermostat to your central heating system. Draw a closed-loop system diagram to illustrate how this would monitor the feedback and affect the input.
2 Identify whether each of the following is a deterministic or stochastic system, and give a reason for your decision in each case.
   a   an audio system
   b   a hospital
   c   a washing machine
   d   a university
   e   a bicycle.
3 In each of the examples given in (2) above, try to identify the inputs and desired outputs and then describe the process in systems terms (e.g. an audio system is a system for ...).

Business organisations and systems

A business organisation can be viewed as a system where a variety of inputs or resources are brought together and then organised and coordinated at the processing stage to produce outputs which accord to the organisational objectives. The term 'system' implies planned order and a methodical arrangement. However, as a system, each organisation is also part of several larger or *suprasystems*. For instance, your own organisation could be described as belonging to the national system of business organisations, as part of a specific industry-wide system (e.g. the newspaper industry or the pharmaceutical industry), as part of a federation of employers, and so on. This is looking upwards and outwards at larger systems of which your organisation is a part. Between your system and the external environment is your *systems boundary*, which determines the edge of one system and the start of another. As you will see later, identifying where the boundary should be placed is sometimes difficult and can affect our perception of a particular system.

If you look downwards and inwards at the organisation you can also identify different subsystems. These can be grouped in various ways, such as:

- broadly – as production or service systems
- more narrowly, according to the grouping criteria used in your organisation, eg departmental subsystems (functional areas), project subsystems (project areas), product subsystems (product areas), customer subsystems (customer areas) or geographic subsystems (geographic areas).
- in relation to hierarchical level, such as at strategic level (top management), tactical level (middle management) or operational level (first-line management).

You could therefore represent your organisation as a system in a variety of ways, depending upon how you perceive it. Indeed, if you perceive your organisation as 'a social system for staff' you would place the emphasis considerably differently than if you perceive it as a system for producing widgets. This should give you your first insight into a key issue about systems theory. You may disagree strongly with someone about how a system should operate, and the reason for this disagreement will often stem from the fact that you are viewing the system differently. The first stage, therefore, is to define what it is that you want the system to do, and where the system starts and ends. Only when you are in agreement about this can you proceed towards achieving your objective.

THEORY INTO PRACTICE

1 You have already met several systems terms in this chapter. Check that you understand what each of these mean by referring to the summary list given in Figure 6.1.4.

2 A motor car can be seen as part of a suprasystem which involves other cars and traffic and the overall road system. Identify how extending the boundary to include these aspects would assist you in analysing more precisely the performance of a particular car.

3 Your organisation has decided to review its security system. There is disagreement about the role of the health and safety officer in this process. She says she does not see security as part of her remit – even though she is responsible for coordinating the reports of the security guards.

   a   How would accurately defining the boundary of the system help in clarifying this issue?

   b   How would you define the components of the security system in place in your own organisation?

   c   If you were to compare your perception of the security system with that of other people in the organisation, how do you think the system boundary might vary – and why?

System	An organised assembly of elements forming a complex whole
Open system	A system that interacts with its environment
Closed system	A system that does not interact with its environment
System boundary	The dividing line that separates a system from its environment

Inputs	The ingredients that are put into the system, e.g. capital, labour, raw materials, expertise, management, customer information, etc.
Process	The transformation sequence or operation that converts inputs into outputs
Outputs	The goods and services that result from the process
Feedback	Information on the type or quality of outputs, which is fed back to influence the inputs or process
Closed-loop system	A system where feedback is linked to the system to adjust the inputs
Open-loop system	A system where there is no link between feedback and inputs
Subsystems	Parts that make up the whole system
Suprasystems	Large systems of which a smaller system is a part
Deterministic system	A system where the outputs can be predictably calculated from a given level of inputs
Stochastic system	A system where the outputs cannot be predictably determined from the inputs
Hard data	Objective, quantifiable data
Soft data	Subjective, qualitative data

Figure 6.1.4 Terms used in systems theory

There are several techniques you can use to help you to determine the extent of an existing system.

- A brainstorming session with other people will produce a long list from which you can usually extract those elements that are essential.
- You can view the system from different perspectives and then decide:
  - the inputs and outputs in each case
  - which inputs are dependent upon other people's outputs
  - at which point you wish to draw the boundary.
- You can illustrate your ideas graphically as a *rich picture*. One person, asked to do this for his department, represented his boss as an ostrich with its head in the sand, another group of staff as defenders of a castle wall, his own colleagues as firing arrows which never pierced the castle walls (or hit anyone), and himself as flat on the ground between the arrows and the wall (see Figure 6.1.5). This might have given people only a vague idea of what the system was trying to achieve, but it certainly illustrated its weaknesses!

Figure 6.1.5 One example of a rich picture

1 Identify at least one system in operation in your organisation where the inputs to this system are dependent upon outputs from other people.
2 Draw a rich picture (or visualise, if you are no artist) to show your own representation of your unit or department as a system. Try to do this by instinct after thinking about the people and the job for a few moments. One technique involves representing people by their key characteristics (your boss, for instance, could be anything from a stick of rock to a spider leering at you from its web). See if this technique gives you any insights into how you perceive your departmental system.

Types of systems

There have been several attempts by academics to categorise and classify types of systems. The Open University, in 1980, classified systems as follows:

- *Evolved systems* are those where the objectives emerge from the evolutionary process (a bee would obviously come into this category, as would some social systems).
- *Designed systems* are those that have been created by humankind to achieve specific objectives (computer systems are an obvious example, so are economic and political systems).
- *Model systems* are 'invisible' systems that represent messy situations which are usually poorly understood. Many organisational systems can be described as falling into this category, such as management systems and information systems, given the disagreements that occur in organisations on the reasons for a system and what it is hoping to achieve. It is this type of system that pictorial diagrams can sometimes best illustrate.

P. Checkland, in *Systems Thinking, Systems Practice*, suggested a different classification as follows.

- *Natural systems* include all biological systems such as trees, insects and human beings.
- *Designed physical systems* are typified by cookers, computers and audio systems.
- *Designed abstract systems* relate to philosophical approaches or scientific systems, such as modernism or postmodernism, Marxism and monetarism.
- *Human activity systems* are exemplified by traffic systems, voting systems, communication systems and management systems.

In organisations you are likely to find that there are a number of designed physical systems in use – particularly in a production environment – but that most of the systems with which you are involved as an administrator are in the last category.

Charles Handy, in *Understanding Organisations*, divided systems as follows.

- *Adaptive systems* exist to assist the organisation to interact with its environment. These are the systems concerned with the strategic aims and objectives of the organisation and its future policies.
- *Operating systems* focus on the daily operations that exist to produce the goods or service, and to provide the specialist expertise required from support areas such as marketing and finance.
- *Maintenance systems* are designed to keep the organisation operating effectively. These include not only obvious systems such as machine and equipment maintenance, but also relate to the maintenance of people and the coordinating systems which exist between different operational groups and sections. By this definition, wage, disciplinary and grievance systems would fall into this category as they are all linked to the reward and control of staff, as would health and safety and security systems.
- *Information systems* function as the backbone to all the other systems – providing the structure on which everything else is built. Another way of looking at information systems is to regard them as the nervous system of the organisation – responsive to a variety of sensory inputs from different directions, all of which should affect the output. From this perspective, a *communications system* is a subsystem of an information system.

For the purpose of your studies, however, you need to consider systems under two broad headings *operational systems* and *organisational systems*.

Operational systems

These relate to the daily functions carried out by production. They can also be seen to include all the support activities carried out by different sections of the organisation to fulfil the broad role of satisfying the customer (see Figure 4.2.2, page 340). *At its broadest*, this therefore includes:

- customer service functions
- computer support
- purchasing and stock control
- throughput and processing of goods
- distribution and logistics
- sales and advertising
- finance and accounting – basic billing functions.

However, a narrower definition would see operational systems as purely those which are concerned with production and the transformation of inputs into processed or finished outputs.

Organisational systems

These relate to the systems that exist for planning, decision-making, coordinating and controlling activities across the organisation. They include Handy's adaptive systems, maintenance systems, information systems and communication systems, as well as any management systems that are in place. They also include many administrative systems devised to coordinate and control a variety of cross-functional activities.

As ever, this is a problem in drawing boundaries. Where do operational systems end and organisational systems begin? It is suggested that, at this stage, you merely note the difficulty of precisely classifying systems and try to categorise some of the existing systems you can recognise in your own organisation

What are procedures?

Basically, procedures are step-by-step guides for action which regulate behaviour, remove uncertainty and ensure conformity and consistency in the performance of a task. The aim is to reduce thinking time, eliminate the need to make choices and decisions, and improve quality. This frees up time for more productive work and more crucial decisions relating to 'one-off' events. For that reason, the major benefit of procedures is to formulate a series of steps for performing routine, regularly occurring tasks, particularly in repetitive situations. Procedures are not usually suitable for use in one-off or exceptional situations.

The link between systems and procedures

Probably the best way of viewing the link between systems and procedures is to see a system as the bridge between inputs and outputs, with the procedures as the supports which hold the bridge in place (see Figure 6.1.6). Procedures can help to regulate the level and quality of inputs, the operation of the process, and the standard of the outputs. They also help to ensure that operations are carried out according to the policies of the organisation and in accordance with any rules or restrictions that are in place.

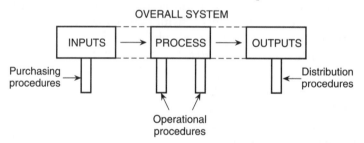

Figure 6.1.6 Illustrating how procedures 'support' an organisational system

Here are some obvious examples from everyday life of the link between the two.

- When you use a transport system you follow specific procedures for buying a ticket, queuing for a bus, boarding an airplane, buying refreshments on a train.
- If you drive a car on the road system, you follow detailed procedures for each manoeuvre you make or for changing from one road to another. You also have to do as you are instructed in given situations.
- If you use the national health system you will follow certain procedures for making a doctor's appointment, obtaining a prescription, calling an ambulance in an emergency.

All these procedures exist because they eliminate variety and standardise the particular elements of a much larger system. This makes the system itself function more effectively as there is less 'wastage' at any stage – of time, effort or resources. In addition, control is made easier. This point is developed further in the next section.

Types of procedures

It is possible to categorise or classify procedures in different ways, either according to function or according to the degree of prescriptiveness required.

If procedures are considered in relation to function, then a long list emerges, including:

- safety procedures
- quality procedures
- financial procedures
- administrative procedures
- personnel procedures
- operating procedures

and so on. These can be subdivided, so that under 'administrative procedures' you could devise a list which included:

- reception procedures
- customer service procedures
- telephone procedures
- filing procedures
- computer procedures.

These could be subdivided again – so that, for instance, computer procedures are divided into those concerned with:

- logging-on
- logging-off
- saving files
- creating directories

and so on! Probably an easier way to typify procedures is therefore to take a more holistic approach and to look at the way procedures can be categorised *in terms of their effect on the user*. In this way we can determine that:

- Some procedures are informal, whilst others are extremely formalised.
- Some procedures are documented, others are not.
- Some procedures are simple, others can be extremely complex.
- Procedures may be suggested or recommended (in which case they act as guidelines) or prescribed or mandatory (in which case the procedure, in effect, is similar to a list of rules).

Figure 6.1.7 illustrates the fact that the more *prescriptive* a procedure the more likely it is to be documented, and the more likely it will be formalised. In this case, the degree of initiative and variance allowed by the user is tightly restricted or almost negligible. Ideally, this should be because the repercussions of *not* following the procedure could be extremely serious. However, it is very rare that there is no room for manoeuvre or discretion at all by the user, as emergencies may occur which have to be handled and which the procedure cannot determine.

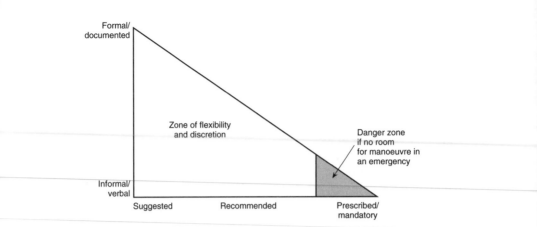

Figure 6.1.7 Types of procedures and prescriptiveness

The following examples may make the distinctions between different types of procedures rather clearer.

Some actions take place without any agreed procedures at all – I do something my way and you do it your way. Only if the actions of one of us affect the other are we likely to try to work out a compromise procedure. You may note from your personal life that learning to live with someone usually involves a considerable amount of negotiating compromise procedures.

In other cases, there are suggested procedures for doing something. As a child you were shown the suggested procedure for tying your shoelaces and fastening your school tie. When you started work your colleagues may have suggested procedures for contacting certain people, organising your work or doing the photocopying. Again there were no penalties for non-compliance but you may have found that you saved time by learning from other people. Suggested procedures are usually verbal and informal.

In many areas of our lives we learn to follow recommended procedures or guidelines. These may not be written down, simply because 'everyone knows what to do'. These can range from social actions (such as queuing for a bus) to going through a checkout at a supermarket, to checking in luggage at an airport. Sometimes, organisations put up notices to guide newcomers faced with unfamiliar situations, such as using a cash machine for the first time. Usually, we quickly learn that we gain more by following these procedures than by not doing so – therefore we are motivated to comply. It is worth noting, however, that if you find a *more effective* way of carrying out an operation, you may choose to abandon the guidelines. For instance, you may find a faster way of doing a job by using your own methods.

A prescribed or mandatory procedure is one you *must* follow. Non-compliance may result in some form of punishment – from a formal warning to a fine or even legal action taken against you. This is usually because non-compliance can seriously inconvenience or even endanger other people as well as yourself. There may be occasions when you can argue that a *minor* deviation was essential or non-consequential and you may be excused (such as driving at 33 mph in a 30 mph zone) but these will be exceptions and cannot be relied upon.

The dangers of being too prescriptive

Inexperienced writers of procedures may insist on a level of prescriptiveness that does not accord to the degree of compliance actually required, *or* insist that no variations can be allowed when these are actually needed. This has three main drawbacks.

- Staff operating the procedure are apt to consider it restrictive and bureaucratic. They may be discouraged from suggesting better ways of doing things or simplifying procedures. Alternatively, they may use the procedure as an 'excuse' for not showing initiative, even when this is required.
- It is rarely the case that procedures are foolproof, cover all situations or never need changing. This is particularly the case if the person who designed or who is responsible for reviewing a procedure does not operate it him/herself and regularly obtain feedback from the users.
- Users who disagree with the procedure in force or who feel frustrated or threatened by it are often tempted to employ avoidance tactics. These will become more overt if users discover that threatened punishments for non-compliance do not materialise. Strategies include a variety of game-playing tactics, looking for loopholes, finding exceptions not covered by the procedure, questioning the meaning of the procedure and claiming ignorance or misunderstanding. Such tactics can subvert the best attempts of any procedure writer as well as deluge him or her with a battery of queries, complaints and problems to solve.

THEORY INTO PRACTICE

1 In your own workplace, identify one example of:
   a a suggested procedure
   b a recommended procedure or set of guidelines
   c a prescribed or mandatory procedure
2 To what extent do you agree, or disagree, with the level of prescriptiveness required for your example in (1c) above?
3 A new and inexperienced Health and Safety Officer is deluging the organisation with prescriptive procedures to be followed by all staff. The MD feels his hands are tied as he knows little about the detail of health and safety and is concerned about operating unlawfully in any area.
   a What are the dangers in this approach by the Health and Safety Officer?
   b What, in your view, could be done to control the situation?

Identifying the need for systems and procedures

Why have a system?

The need for a system usually arises when:

- it is possible to simplify or automate certain operations
- organisational operations must be coordinated, improved or expanded
- greater control is needed over a certain area
- a reorganisation or restructuring has meant that groupings of activities are now different
- changes or new regulations have resulted in different working practices in certain areas or new operations entirely
- technological developments have resulted in new or different working practices
- there is a problem to solve
- any combination of these.

The need for a new system may be highlighted by decision-makers who want information on certain activities, which is not currently available from existing systems. The importance of liaison with users is addressed in the next main section.

Identifying the need for a procedure

A procedure is necessary when an activity is routinely carried out by different people, and where quality of delivery and time are both an issue. This should relate to the majority of activities in an organisation. The only way in which quality can be assured is to make sure that performance is standardised and that the correct tasks are being undertaken in the right order.

As an example, individuals may be involved in reporting accidents – though not too frequently, it is hoped! Obtaining the correct information promptly is essential. Therefore there will be a procedure to follow for those who witness an accident. Details of the procedure should be readily available to all staff. The documenting of the procedure means that those responsible for collecting the data on accidents can know what is required after each accident and those who submit it know what must be provided. This saves staff having to chase up the information each time, or sit down and interview each witness.

It is normal for new procedures to be required when working practices change or when a new system is devised. Existing procedures should be reviewed regularly to ensure that they are relevant and appropriate. If feedback from users is encouraged and is part of the overall ethos of the organisation, then staff will be encouraged to comment upon procedures they consider to be outdated, ineffective or inappropriate, so that these can be reviewed. If feedback is not encouraged then administrators will have a more difficult task.

Benefits of systems and procedures

A key aim of introducing a system is to obtain *synergy*, where the whole is greater than the sum of the individual parts. This means that by linking a series of actions into a process, and coordinating these, there are distinct benefits to be gained. Many administrative systems, for instance, are devised because of the need to link tasks and activities – from operations in the company mail room or reprographics unit to the processing and payment of purchase orders.

A list of benefits to be gained by taking a systems approach is given in Figure 6.1.8. Most of these are self-explanatory. However, a system will give benefits to users only if it is well planned, skilfully designed, achieves its goal(s) and is regularly reviewed. These points are dealt with later in this chapter and the next.

However, certain areas are worthy of further discussion here, particularly those relating to *efficiency* and *effectiveness*, *control* and *quality improvements*.

- It is applicable to all types of organisations and all types of operations.
- It provides a means for planning on a unified and focused basis to maximise coordination opportunities.
- It enables the organisation to be considered from different perspectives, depending upon the positioning of the boundary.
- The concept of an open system that interacts with the environment helps managers to plan how to adapt to change.
- It brings together disparate activities into a concentrated and organised 'whole' to create synergy.
- It enables goals to be identified and set for a linked set of activities.
- It provides a flow of activities to be linked rationally to achieve objectives.
- It enables critical points of control to be established and monitored for rapid and accurate problem-solving.
- It enables inputs to be analysed and utilised more effectively.
- It provides a management tool for continuous improvement.

Figure 6.1.8 Advantages of the systems approach

Efficiency and effectiveness

The purpose of introducing a system is always to improve either the *efficiency* or *effectiveness* of the organisation – preferably both.

Efficiency is concerned with the ratio of inputs to outputs – that is, the value obtained from any given level of resources. Effectiveness is concerned with the success of the system in meeting its objectives. This may include obtaining greater control over operations, achieving faster throughput, improving quality. There is a degree of trade-off between the two in most systems in that increased efficiency can lead to decreased effectiveness, and vice versa. An *optimal* system is one where the highest level of effectiveness is achieved from an acceptable level of inputs. One where effectiveness is not achieved is sub-optimal, one where resources are wasted is inefficient.

An optimal system is achieved only if the goals or objectives specified are appropriate and the system is designed to achieve these goals. For instance, if you were designing a supermarket cashpoint system with the goal of 'processing sales accurately' you might concentrate on achieving this by installing automated cash points with barcode readers linked to a computerised stock control and management information system. You would no doubt call for staff training for the processing of items. In an attempt to maximise efficiency you might analyse the number of customers in your store at certain times, and create a model using queuing techniques to decide your staff rota. This would make sure that you never had more cash tills operating than necessary, and would therefore keep your wage bill down. You would probably achieve an efficient system linked to the goal you had been set.

You would, however, be guilty of completely ignoring the needs of your customers – which were outside the boundary of your system. You might, for instance, identify that customers become disenchanted rather rapidly if they have to queue at checkouts – particularly when they can see that others are not staffed. In addition, a fast and *efficient* checkout person may have little time or inclination to improve customer relations. If this occurs then it is likely that many customers will take their business elsewhere, in which case the 'efficient system' becomes markedly inefficient in the long run.

To incorporate effectiveness and efficiency often means viewing the system rather differently. If the boundary is extended to include the customers, and the system goal is adjusted to become 'processing sales accurately whilst maximising customer relations', this would point to a rather different system. In 1996 Tesco instigated a new checkout system whereby, whenever there was a situation where more than one person was queuing at each till, another till was opened until all were functioning. This implies multiskilled staff – which obviously has training implications – who can be transferred from one duty to another as the need arises. Tesco also introduced packers to assist throughput of shoppers. Both policies were introduced as positive customer benefits. In a sense this system is simpler – there is no need for elaborate modelling and queuing theories; basic observation and adequate staffing support is all that is necessary. This is then a system which looks at the problem from the customer's point of view – and incorporates quality service and effectiveness as well as efficiency.

J. A. Penn, whose specialism is information systems, gave a rather broader interpretation of efficiency and effectiveness than the one above. For Penn, increased speed of operation and improved transmission of communications both count as *efficiency gains*. Improved control, lower costs of monitoring staff and greater competitive advantage are classed as *effectiveness gains*. Systems may be designed or redesigned to achieve any of these objectives. If we apply Penn's analysis to our checkout example, we see that increasing till throughput and improving the speed and accuracy of data capture will produce cost savings in relation to the operating system alone. The additional benefits – Penn's effectiveness gains – are improvements felt at managerial or organisational level.

The control function

Control is a key feature of our lives. This can be as basic as ensuring a meal is properly cooked, or as complex as controlling our expenditure so that we can afford a good holiday. The same applies to our working environment. All organisations have particular goals they wish to achieve linked to the strategic plan. You have particular goals you are charged to achieve as part of your operational responsibilities. Unless you monitor and control the progress of the activities which relate to these on a regular basis, then you will fail to achieve your goals. If you do not operate any controls then you only achieve your goal by luck, rather than by good management. Control involves a systematic effort to compare actual performance with planned performance, by obtaining regular feedback and then comparing this with predetermined standards and objectives. If there is any deviation from the plan then corrective action must be taken, either by adjusting the inputs or by altering the plan.

Control and hard systems

You already know the difference between open-loop and closed-loop systems (see page 486) and you were introduced to the concept of a control subsystem on the same page. It is possible to illustrate this more precisely by adding a few refinements to the diagram. To do this we will look at a simple example.

A firm sells two types of tumbler dryer. The first type has a simple timer device so that the user can set the time. This is an open-loop system as the machine will run its course until the set time has elapsed. The only way the system can be influenced is by the user, who may open the door to check whether the items are dry (i.e. he/she obtains *feedback*). By feeling the clothes the user becomes a *sensor* – and measures the degree of dryness. He/she then compares the dryness sensed with the dryness expected. In systems theory, this is operating as a *comparator*. Finally, if the clothes are still damp, the user may reset the switch or timer – which is the *actuator* that controls the inputs. Figure 6.1.9 shows this process diagrammatically.

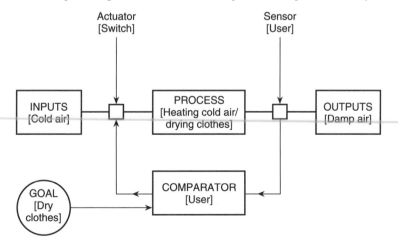

Figure 6.1.9 The tumble-dryer control process

An alternative would be to buy the second type of dryer where the sensor, comparator and actuator have been installed by the manufacturer. In this case the machine is more sophisticated. It has been preset to register the humidity level inside the dryer – and these features can operate on a more sensitive level than a user to stop the machine before the clothes become too dry. Throughout the process the machine senses the existing humidity level and compares this with its programmed setting. If they do not agree the process continues. When they agree the actuator turns off the machine. This saves the user from the necessity of constantly monitoring the system.

At this point it is worth noting that if the user does not agree with the settings he/she can usually override them. A microwave oven can be bought with similar preprogrammed settings. If the user considers these result in food which is overcooked then it is likely the settings will be overridden – with the user replacing him/herself as the sensor/comparator/actuator.

THEORY INTO PRACTICE

Many pieces of equipment in operation in your organisation work on similar principles, for instance a fax machine, a franking machine, a photocopier, and a telephone switchboard. In each of these cases, consider:

a the system in use
b the goal of the system
c the degree to which the control process is automated
d the degree to which operators may override this process – and the problems this may cause!

Control and soft systems

If operators can override sophisticated controls on basic operating systems, you may like to consider for a moment the degree of havoc they can wreak on more complex 'soft' systems where there is a mixture of man and machine involved in all parts of the system. Issues to think about include the following.

- There may be disagreement on objectives or goals (or the purpose of the system). *Goal ambiguity* may exist when various people have different goals they wish to achieve for personal reasons.
- There may be multiple goals, which just one system is incapable of achieving.
- There may be no accurate or precise methods of sensing or obtaining the information or data necessary for control purposes.
- The information or data, once gathered, may be difficult to compare with the goal. Perhaps a huge amount of data is produced, not all of which is relevant to the goal.
- The reported data may be interpreted one way by some people and a different way by other people.
- There may be no satisfactory means to be found for influencing or improving the process, or an unsatisfactory strategy may be used (i.e. an inappropriate actuator identified).

Control in practice

Control can be a time-consuming business. It is possible, for instance, to see yourself as the sensor, comparator and actuator, and to monitor the operations of your section by 'walking the job', sampling the throughput of work, obtaining feedback from other departments, talking to the staff and asking for regular reports. However, this would involve a considerable amount of effort to check many routine operations. In addition, it would probably irritate your staff. Visualising your section as a system that serves the needs of internal and external customers efficiently and effectively, and devising this in such a way that there is routine feedback on key objectives, means that you are free to undertake other tasks – and can, instead, monitor *variances* from expected performance. In other words, you can operate by the principle of *management by exception* and practise *time management* to a greater degree.

To control your section in this way you need regular information on operations. This means deciding:

- what must be measured
- how it will be measured
- what variances are acceptable
- what corrective action can be taken.

What must be measured

There is a danger in trying to control every function of a system, or in selecting the wrong functions to control. There is little point, for instance, in selecting functions which do not relate to overall organisational objectives which, in turn, are usually linked to profit. Otherwise you might find yourself arguing that you are successfully achieving your throughput objective whilst your directors are more concerned that staff costs or overheads are rising month by month. There must therefore be a direct correlation between the functions selected for measurement and your own major responsibility areas. Generally several measures are required to give an overview of all key performance characteristics.

How it will be measured

Obtaining too much information or information that is too detailed hampers, rather than assists, control. At each progressively senior level of the organisation the degree of detail should reduce, given that at senior level monitoring is taking place over a wide range of activities. Line by line monitoring also reduces flexibility as there is no opportunity to 'trade off' a short-term problem against a long-term progressive improvement. For this reason an objective overview is required.

Detailed information is also costly to collect, which is why many feedback systems are designed to incorporate regular sampling of results rather than provide continuous feedback. However, care must be taken in relation to the spacing of sampling, the timeliness of the information and the external factors which may apply. The quicker the signalling of a problem, the more promptly corrective action can be taken. In operational terms, the worst time feedback can occur is when there is a 'half cycle delay', as this gives completely inaccurate feedback. Sampling over a period of time usually gives 'trend' signals which assist anticipation.

> This concept is probably easier to understand if you consider how experience assists you in making decisions. For instance, you may realise that walking through reception at 10 am gives a false impression because two members of staff are absent on coffee break at that time. This does not matter if you also know that reception is usually quiet at that hour, that your staff are following recommended procedures in not drinking coffee where they can be seen by customers, and the receptionist has the ability to call for assistance if required from the main office during that time. The picture might be rather different for someone seeing that moment's staffing level in isolation.

Acceptable variations

A clear statement of the expected norms and standards for operation must be made, bearing in mind available inputs and required outputs. These are often expressed as 'benchmarks' for successful operation (see also page 532). Obviously, a mailroom consisting of one junior operator with the minimum of equipment cannot provide the same throughput as that obtainable by a mechanised, sophisticated operation with specially trained staff. Therefore any benchmarks must be devised by comparing like with like to give a realistic performance standard.

It has often been suggested that staff should have an input into setting their own goals, as they will then be more committed to achieving them. This is the philosophy on which techniques such as *management by objectives* are based. Imposed targets and standards are generally less acceptable than those which are negotiated and jointly agreed.

Differences between standard performance and actual performance must be analysed to obtain information on the scale of the variations – both in terms of degree of fluctuation and the time period over which these occur. Minor fluctuations or temporary or short-term difficulties usually indicate a situation where corrective inputs are required. Long-term trends are more significant and usually indicate that more radical corrective action is required.

Corrective action

A section which consistently fails to meet its targets with significant differences on a regular basis is clearly operating a system that is out of control. At this point either the objectives need to be re-evaluated or the system redesigned, otherwise the system will break down altogether. Many system problems occur because of a poor design, or because the system is no longer appropriate. However, there is a marked tendency for serious system problems to be addressed by making minor changes (often to the control subsystem) – which irritate users and are not successful for any length of time. These are sometimes termed *incremental adjustments*.

The problem for administrators is that many of the systems for which they are responsible involve human activity. There are often unspecific objectives, characteristics that are difficult to measure, characteristics that do not represent effective performance or which rely on impressionistic measurement and qualitative standards. There is also the problem of the human reaction to imposing controls or changing work patterns, which can range from open defiance to subversive tactics, and the difficulty of obtaining timely and appropriate information to inform decision-making. Positive leadership skills to maximise motivation and user participation are essential ingredients for success.

THEORY INTO PRACTICE

The arguments given above are easier to understand with an example. Read the following case study and answer the questions that follow – visualising your section as a 'system' which processes information to provide reports and returns. Then compare your answers with the commentary in the next subsection.

Staff shortages and absences have meant there have been several problems with reports and returns from your section produced after the specified deadline. You have now been asked to obtain and submit the absence and lateness statistics for all the staff in your department. There is speculation over why management want these figures – particularly the latter. You are concerned at present about staff morale. You are aware that staff turnover has increased over the past year, although not as much in your section as in others. However, you also know job opportunities have increased in the area and that several new organisations are offering higher salaries. Moreover, several vacancies have not been filled and the existing staff are working twice as hard to try to complete all the work that is coming in. Many are demotivated and depressed, feeling their efforts are unrecognised and unrewarded by management.

You duly obtain the information and submit it to your line manager. At the next departmental meeting you are informed that the company is tightening up the procedures to be followed if staff are late or absent and disciplinary action will be taken more often against repeat offenders. You are incensed and consider that such threats will demotivate staff even further. You argue that management are out of touch and living in an ivory tower, which annoys your boss. His view is that many staff are letting themselves and the rest of the team down through constant absenteeism which is contributing to an excessive workload for everyone else. He considers that his job, and yours, is to ensure they produce the reports on time.

1 To what extent did goal ambiguity contribute to the problem at the outset?
2 To what extent was the data provided insufficient or inappropriate?
3 What data would have been required to 'sense' the operation of the system more effectively?
4 To what extent was the 'comparative' process deficient?
5 What is the management using as an actuator?
6 What do you think should be used as an actuator?
7 How could the problem have been avoided?
8 How will you attempt to solve the problem?

Quality improvements

If a mechanical or hard system is not working properly then engineers will test the operation of the sensor, comparator and actuator. In some cases a machine with multiple goals will have multiple sensors, comparators and actuators – though it is a clever designer who tries to make one component undertake several roles! If a system involving people starts to break down, a less disciplined approach is used – which sometimes accentuates, rather than solves, the problem.

The whole aim of using systems is to apply a more disciplined approach to controlling problem areas – by identifying more precisely where the problems are occurring and then taking appropriate action. Problems can occur at the input stage, at the process stage, at the sensor point, at the comparator point, with goals, and/or with the actuator.

In the case study given above, an accurate diagnosis would have pointed to the following.

- There were too few inputs to undertake the process effectively (i.e. staff shortages, time available for report/return completion).
- The outputs were being affected by the number of inputs and *only possibly* by the hours staff work or their commitment.
- The sensor was quantitative (often preferred by management because such data is unambiguous) and therefore only related to time spent rather than effort or commitment. This therefore only sensed part of the operation.
- The comparative process neglected to consider other factors that affected staff, e.g. alternative jobs/wage rates. From that point of view, it could be said the systems boundary should have been extended.
- The actuator was a disciplinary one, rather than a motivational one. It might actually decrease inputs rather than increase them.
- The actuator was concerned with individual behaviour patterns. Soft systems are usually measured and controlled more accurately if *group* performance is measured (given that one individual may have a good day whilst another is having a bad day). A broader measure therefore provides a more reliable picture.
- In effect, management were trying to 'mend' a soft system by treating it as a hard system instead of viewing the system as a whole and remembering the 'people' aspect.

It could therefore be argued that by *accurately* identifying the system and the control function, the correct information would have been obtained, pertinent signals recorded and appropriate action taken. This is therefore a systems design problem, rather than a staff problem. Identifying how to improve the system would therefore be more effective than trying to increase the control aspect of the existing system. Systems design is covered in detail in Element 6.2.

System designers go to considerable trouble to try to minimise undesirable outputs. Scientists have been working for two years at Cern, the European particle physics laboratory in Geneva, to try to devise a nuclear reactor that can 'burn' atomic waste. Not only would this have no undesirable outputs, it could also be used to consume vast quantities of plutonium and other highly radioactive materials stockpiled around the world.

In your own organisation, try to identify at least two systems that give a negative output as well as a positive output. What suggestions could you make to minimise or eliminate the first and maximise the second? (If you cannot find any such systems, some ideas may be more forthcoming after you have read Chapters 6 and 7.)

There are drawbacks to organisations taking goals as unalterable rather than as negotiating points. Assume that your goal is to improve the workflow in your section. You think that the best way to achieve this will be to appeal to staff goodwill, or to threaten them, whichever is your nature. You then find that your pleas or threats are having no effect. If you are sensible and prepared to own up to being wrong occasionally, then you will question your strategy – rather than keep repeating it.

Chris Argyris called this *double-loop learning* – where failure to achieve the goal by taking a particular action results in questioning the type of action being taken. This is in contrast to *single-loop learning* where the same type of action is repeated time and again without effect (see Figure 6.1.10).

Although this may seem obvious at a personal level, it is amazing how many times people will continue to repeat an activity or strategy which is patently ineffective in achieving their goal. How many times, for instance, are you asked for the same type of information in a different guise, or told to make particular modifications to an operation – even though you know from experience that these do not work? It is as if the single loop develops a magnetic pull or fascination which, through habitual behaviour, cannot be discarded.

Ways of negotiating and agreeing needs

Often, one of the first stages in devising a complex system is to undertake a *feasibility study*. This indicates whether or not the original perceived need for a system is accurate and identifies the possible alternatives. It will also help in determining the boundaries of the system. However, for this to provide a sound indication of what is required and for realistic alternatives to be put forward, it is important that the needs and opinions of users are sought and that objective data relating to the system is obtained.

The importance of user agreement in soft systems and associated procedures has been indicated at several points so far. Its value is such that today this is generally undertaken at an early stage in a *system design life-cycle*, as illustrated in Figure 6.1.11 on page 507.

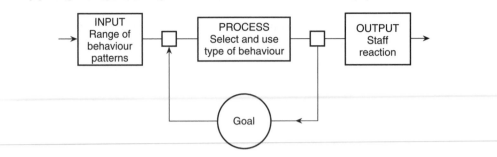

(a) Single-loop learning

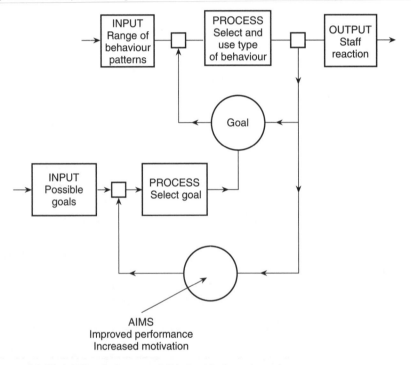

(b) Double-loop learning

Figure 6.1.10 (a) Single-loop and (b) double-loop learning

The role of users

The original providers of 'systems' in organisations were computer specialists who, in the early days, had an unfortunate tendency to use their expertise and jargon as a protective barrier to separate them from perceived philistines in the other parts of the organisation! This tended to result in the design of systems that were extremely computer-friendly but inordinately unfriendly for the users, who were unable to obtain the type of information they required quickly and easily and/or in a format they could understand.

Thankfully, those days have long since passed in the vast majority of organisations. There is now a broad acknowledgement that the

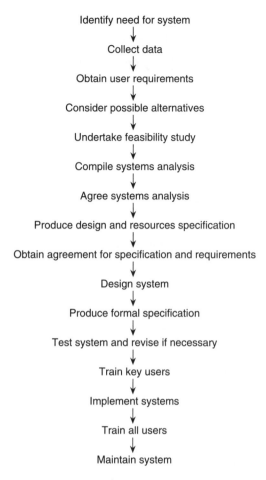

Identify need for system
↓
Collect data
↓
Obtain user requirements
↓
Consider possible alternatives
↓
Undertake feasibility study
↓
Compile systems analysis
↓
Agree systems analysis
↓
Produce design and resources specification
↓
Obtain agreement for specification and requirements
↓
Design system
↓
Produce formal specification
↓
Test system and revise if necessary
↓
Train key users
↓
Implement systems
↓
Train all users
↓
Maintain system

Figure 6.1.11 A system life-cycle

involvement of users not only improves the original concept but also creates a positive atmosphere for any changes that have to be made and a joint commitment to ensuring they are implemented successfully.

It is impossible for one person to design a system or a set of procedures that will meet the needs of all users (or achieve the best compromise). This is even true if the designer is an expert in the particular area to which the system or procedure will relate. At a basic level, there are few people who understand the job role and operational needs of their colleagues in any depth – let alone to an extent where they can second-guess their perceptions, attitudes to change and motivational stance. If the system relates to an area where the designer is uncertain of the objectives or unfamiliar with certain aspects of the process, the type of inputs being used and/or the outputs required, then the task becomes an impossibility.

Users are frequently requested not only to give their views and opinions on an existing system, and their needs in relation to any new or revised system, but also to assist in the providing of data to inform the process of analysing current working practices. This may be collected on a *data collection form* which specifies the type of data obtained, by whom it was obtained, when and where.

User involvement has been well documented in several studies. The following are some of the conclusions.

- User satisfaction is greater when users are given the opportunity to make a substantial input at the design stage.
- Users are less likely to see new systems and procedures, or amended systems and procedures, as a threat if they are involved with the changes.
- It is easier to build in quality at each stage of the process or procedure if users actively contribute.
- User involvement normally shortens the timespan between design and implementation – as less 'testing and review' is required.
- Users should be treated as 'internal customers', with their needs as critical to systems and procedure designers as if they were external customers.
- Involving users implies a shared responsibility – as users are charged with making the designers aware of what they require.
- Users are often better placed to identify problems and difficulties with existing or proposed systems and procedures than are designers. Additionally, they may identify unwelcome outputs which would result from a particular system.

Much will depend upon the ethos and culture of the organisation, the management style, the extent to which users feel their participation is genuinely required, and the specialist expertise required in designing a particular system or procedure. Only if they feel their contribution will be valued are users likely to give their commitment.

The degree of user involvement and the method of obtaining this can vary considerably. At one extreme there can be a basic one-way communications system of information disseminated by newsletter, memo, e-mail or briefing session. At the other extreme is what E. Mumford called Participative Systems Design, where full responsibility for the system is given to the employees who will have to work it. Between these extremes there are the following:

- With *consultative participation*, the majority of decisions are made by the system designer. The users are involved purely in assisting in defining objectives and suggesting the final format of the system or procedure.
- With *representative participation*, user representatives either work with the designers or form part of a steering group or committee to influence the process.
- With *consensus participation*, users or user groups are involved continuously throughout the design and testing process.

Note that there is *no one ideal method*. Much will depend upon the system or procedure, the degree to which technical knowledge (of systems or writing procedures) and expert knowledge (of the particular process or activity) is required. An experienced designer may obtain a high degree of user input at the initial stages and then take a more autocratic stance over the technical design. A more democratic role is then taken over testing and implementation. Generally, however, there is a trend towards increasing participation by users at all stages, with the recognition not only of the rights of the users, but also of the contribution they can make and the benefits in terms of system or procedure design and the motivation of staff. It is generally accepted that the type of user groups to be established and the formality of their brief will depend largely on the organisation culture. It is usually best if all stakeholders are involved to some degree. Where this is impractical, those selected should have good relationships with the colleagues and groups they represent, their views must be considered credible because of their knowledge, expertise, interest or past experience, and there must be good communications between members of the user group and other staff. In some cases user groups may vary – with one, say, being set up to examine technical issues and another to examine the documentation or other practical aspects.

Dealing with users is not always plain sailing, and various types of problems have been identified.

- There can be a disparity between the influence, control and power positions of various users, which surfaces in group meetings. This is exacerbated if the organisation has a predominately hierarchical structure and culture and those with the most power are not necessarily those with the most knowledge or interest.
- Users can be unclear about their requirements at the start of a project. They may then gain a greater appreciation of what can be done and change their minds about what they require. This can create problems and frustrations for the designer.
- There may be a communication gap between users and specialists – particularly when there are complex technical problems or a variety of restrictions or regulations to take into account.
- Becoming a member of a user group requires a change of stance from active user to reflective overviewer. Many users may find difficulty in making this transition unless they are given adequate time and assistance.
- Users have conflicting needs and there may be difficulties in making choices, recognising trade-offs and converting common needs into feasible and achievable objectives.
- Conflicts and disagreements may arise. Interestingly these are usually on minor issues – probably because everyone can understand these easily.
- The larger the group the more time the process of consulting with users is likely to take. This can create delays and exacerbate problems with tight deadlines.
- On a very practical level, organising regular joint meeting times may be difficult, particular if cross-functional staff are involved or if everyone from one department is a user and yet coverage for routine tasks is required.

A major problem may arise if users perceive a hidden goal of management to be incompatible with their own goals. For instance, they may conclude that a proposed system will result in fewer staff being required and that the effect could be redundancy or short-time working. At this point they are likely to withdraw their cooperation altogether.

However, from a designer's point of view there is a distinct psychological edge to be gained by involving users, in that, even if their joint contributions do not overly influence the design, the mere act of involving them usually increases acceptability and helps in the planning and implementation process.

> A famous management case study is the systems design problem faced by Trist and Bamforth who investigated the lower productivity and decreased satisfaction being displayed by miners following the introduction of technological innovations in a mining operation. The original small, closely knit groups had been reorganised into larger groups with a broader task remit. The result was not only reduced productivity but also a higher accident rate and greater turnover. Trist and Bamforth reintroduced several of the key features of the original small workgroups with dramatic improvements to morale and productivity. They concluded that a technological approach was inappropriate, because social systems and interactions had also to be considered. This is often termed a *sociotechnical approach.*

The role of decision-makers

In some cases the decision-makers and the users will be the same people. This, for instance, is the case where an information system will be supplying data to all levels of the organisation, or where a system involves several functional areas and support staff. In the case of the latter, support by senior management is essential to obtain agreement across all the different areas. In other cases, decision-makers are not key users, but may have a decisive role in agreeing resource allocation or in obtaining approval for radical suggestions for change.

Generally, if a serious review of existing systems is being carried out, called a *systems audit*, or if a radically new system is being designed, it is sensible for a senior manager to be given the responsibility to ensure that this is undertaken successfully. Even if the planned system or procedure is less far-reaching, it is only good sense and common courtesy to ensure that your line manager is aware of any changes you are proposing and to ensure that you do not exceed your own authority. Quite often, the additional experience of senior managers and/or the fact that they can take a more global view of any proposed system or procedures and its broader implications can usefully inform the design. In this case, they become a source of specialist advice in addition to being a mentor and/or approver.

The help of an experienced decision-maker or adviser can be very useful if you are faced with several alternative options for meeting user needs. Quite often the designer will be asked to undertake a feasibility study to evaluate each option against:

- the economic costs and benefits (including development and training costs, the acquisition of any equipment or materials)
- the technical issues (including existing technical competence of operators, capacity and capability of existing equipment, etc.)
- operational issues (including a review of existing systems and procedures, staff attitudes to the proposals, an objective evaluation of the need for change, suggestions on the best way to proceed with design and implementation)
- organisational strategy and objectives as a whole.

Needs and organisational objectives

One problem with obtaining views from users and decision-makers is that you may well end up with a diversity of opinions and a range of recommendations which are impossible to reconcile. If you have committed yourself to a participatory approach, you will have raised expectations in all quarters and now be faced with having to satisfy some and disappoint others. This is demotivational for anyone who made a positive contribution at the outset.

This type of problem is less frequently encountered, however, in organisations that design systems and procedures linked to their strategic plans and organisational objectives. Firstly the business strategy should be explicit and known to all staff. Secondly, resources should be known to be allocated towards achieving organisational objectives. The logical starting point is then to identify:

- the aim or goal of the system or procedure
- the relationship between this system or set of procedures and any others that exist
- the way in which the planned system or procedure 'fits' with the overall strategy and specific objectives that relate to this area
- the components that cannot be changed (e.g. level of manpower, space or accommodation, type of outputs required)
- the components that can be changed (e.g. type of equipment, location of process, skills and expertise of staff)
- the components or outcomes that must be changed (e.g. quality of output, speed of throughput)
- the restrictions that apply to any systems or procedures (e.g. company policy guidelines, company rules, external legislation and regulations).

There is then a general consensus point from which to start negotiations on user needs and requirements. This does not guarantee an end to potential conflict but should at least contain the areas over which disagreements are likely to emerge, limit the range of possible options to those which would seriously merit a full feasibility study, and keep user expectations to a realistic level.

Types and sources of specialist advice

One benefit of obtaining participation from users is that you will gain from the variety of expertise from different operational areas. This gives you specialist advice which is invaluable at the design and implementation stage. However, many types of systems and procedures are related to areas where additional specialist advice is required – either from inside or outside the organisation.

It is normally the case that specialist advice is required when the system or procedures will involve:

- a specialist area
- personnel from a variety of functional areas in the organisation
- current or emerging legal or regulatory requirements
- technical support or information
- external organisations (e.g. suppliers or distributors)
- specific standards or external assessment.

Internal specialist advice

The degree to which this is *available* in-house will depend upon the size of organisation, the specialisation of job roles, the degree of contracting-out or outsourcing, and the range of functions and operations carried out within the organisation. The degree to which it is *required* will depend upon your own job role and specialist expertise, the type of system or procedure you are designing and its implications, the level of expertise you already have, and the expertise of any user group you have formed.

As examples, internal specialist advice may be available to inform each of the following, although the list is by no means exhaustive:

- exporting and shipping procedures
- health and safety procedures
- security systems and procedures
- financial recording systems for auditing purposes
- technical operating systems and procedures
- disciplinary and grievance procedures
- computer-based systems and procedures
- transport and logistical procedures
- computer information systems.

In addition to asking for advice from people within the organisation, a wealth of information can usually be found by looking at company documentation, copies of existing or previous systems or procedures, manuals and reference books relating to equipment or current systems. You should also note that in a large organisation it is quite possible that a good system to achieve the same aim is in operation in another department! Good internal communications, coordinating links between functional areas and a culture of sharing best practice are the most effective ways of ensuring that everyone can benefit from the learning curves that have been experienced in other areas.

External specialist advice

If you work for a small firm, it is likely that much of the expertise required for the areas listed above will be accessible to you only if you go outside the company. You may then need to contact the Health and Safety Executive for advice on safety procedures, a solicitor for information on employment procedures, and a security association or the local police for assistance on security systems. Even in a large organisation, if you have any suspicion that the information you have received internally may not be totally accurate or up-to-date then you would be sensible to check with an outside expert. For instance, it is doubtful if you could automatically assume that anyone will have current knowledge of environmental health or data protection requirements, unless your organisation employs a specialist to cover this area.

Quite often a useful starting point may be your own trade association or local Training and Enterprise Council. If you are completely stuck then visit your local library, find the name of an organisation which oversees that particular area and telephone them. They may well advise you to contact a regional office or a different organisation, but at least you are now in a position to work your way downwards.

In many cases you may be able to obtain a broader viewpoint if you are on good terms with other non-competing organisations in your area, your suppliers, your business customers or even competing organisations outside your own locality. Visiting another company can often give you useful insights into different ways of working and organising tasks to achieve objectives. In a similar way, if you have a network of contacts in other organisations you may be able to obtain useful pointers from them to help you on your way.

Many organisations consider registering to achieve a BSI Quality Assurance award – such as ISO 9000. This is a series of standards which can be applied to a range of businesses – from manufacturing plants to the service sector, from professional associations to local government. The standards provide a framework for management systems, procedures and work instructions. Most organisations start by preparing a quality manual which documents the systems and procedures in operation. Regular internal audits are required to ensure that the system is still functioning as documented and to identify any improvements that could be made.

At Registration each organisation is nominated a Client Manager who gives support and guidance as the manual and other documentation are being prepared. In addition there are materials to help, such as ISO 10013, which gives guidance on creating a quality manual. Support is also provided by local Training and Enterprise Councils to member companies.

THEORY INTO PRACTICE

1 Find out more about ISO 9000 and the benefit of quality systems by contacting the BSI Customer Helpline on 01908 288007 and asking for their information pack.
2 You work for a small company which is involved in bottling and packaging fruit juice. Your MD has become fixated with the thought of a major crisis affecting the company – another local firm was massacred in the press following product contamination through a machine fault. The firm in question handled the crisis badly, neglecting to recall its products promptly and denying the crisis existed until it was forced to change its stance following an investigation by the local press. Your boss has been charged with the task of designing a set of procedures for crisis handling, but doesn't know where to start. What *internal* and *external* specialist advice do you consider would be required, and where would you obtain it?

Specifying systems and procedures

Drafting a specification is usually the second stage of the systems development process. From a practical point of view, this may be difficult to isolate as a distinct stage in the process unless you are involved in major projects. Additionally, you will often find that system development is more iterative than sequential. This aspect is discussed in more detail in Element 6.2. However, drawing up a specification at a relatively early part of the process helps to clarify what exactly is required and what the system is intended to do.

Specifications appear in many different forms. Assume you are buying a new car. You could specify the exact make or model (because you know exactly what you want); or you could write down your detailed requirements for the car, which might include: the functions you wish it to perform (speed, performance, fuel-consumption), the form you wish it to take (size, shape, colour, etc.), its fitness for a particular purpose (taking the children to school, carrying the shopping), the generally agreed standards to which you require it to conform (e.g. safety features, car alarm), and any additional specified standards (e.g. full service history, ISO 9000 accredited supplier).

Systems specifications

When you are specifying a system, the above aspects translate into identifying or describing:

- the objectives of the system
- the relationships between each part of the system
- the proposed installation instructions (to make it fit for the purpose)
- the standards which it must achieve.

For a mechanical system you may be expected to give a breakdown of the specifications to include function, form, fitness for purpose, technical design, manufacturing construction, quality, reliability, conditions for use, and servicing schedules. As an obvious example, consider the type of investigations you would undertake and discussions you would or *should* have if you were negotiating the installation of new photocopying equipment throughout the organisation. You would have every right to obtain detailed specifications on alternative types of equipment and to investigate machines and suppliers for reliability and servicing by reading journals such as *What to Buy for Business* and other user guides.

The situation is little different if you are trying to specify a soft system which involves people and processes, rather than equipment. In this case, the technical design links to the way in which you will design the system (see Element 6.2), conditions for use relate to the circumstances covered by the system, and servicing schedules relate to the number of times you will obtain feedback and review the system (see Element 7.2).

Systems specifications may be produced in a variety of formats. They may be as basic as a simple checklist, or include design charts, diagrams, structured or unstructured written documents, photographs or data obtained from observational visits. Ideally they should be complete, consistent, unambiguous and accurate, to be used as a basis for the designer, who simply checks, at each stage, that he or she is fulfilling the specification. This helps to avoid errors at the early stages which can be expensive to rectify later. However, this approach is more suited to simple systems or hard systems than soft systems incorporating complex problems. A difficulty occurs when users are unsure of their objectives, problems are as yet unknown and the needs of different groups of users are at variance. In this case the original specification must include flexibility options, so that as both users and designers move up the learning curve the system can be improved from the original conception. Frequently a useful starting point is to undertake a *systems analysis*, preferably after consultation with potential users, which outlines the key points to be borne in mind. In this case, preparation of an exact specification is undertaken in conjunction with the system design process (see Figure 6.1.11 on page 507).

Procedural specifications

These specifications state the actions to be taken and the specific sequence in which they will be undertaken to convert precise inputs (of energy, materials, information, knowledge or received wisdom) from one form or place to another. They also include decision points which cause some steps to be included or omitted.

Procedural specifications may be available in many forms. In some cases it may be specified that new recruits can learn by 'sitting next to Nellie', in another case a procedure chart, a flow chart or a written procedure document may be produced. The specifications can have different levels of detail. Experienced staff would not require detailed instructions on how to send a fax – a new recruit might need this help.

As with systems, procedures can usually be broken down into *procedural subroutines*. At the design stage these must be cross-referenced to show how the procedure will operate in its entirety.

Cars, computer systems and even aeroplanes are defined and designed by this process. The systems and procedures are analysed and a synthesis of all the required components is undertaken.

By the same token, working out the detailed specifications of any system or procedure you are planning enables you to check more precisely the resources you require and to plan a realistic timescale for implementation.

THEORY INTO PRACTICE

A senior administrator in a large organisation was asked to suggest a revised system for the processing of expense claim forms in the organisation. The senior managers were concerned that:

- expenses for the past year were over the budget allocation
- expense claims were being submitted infrequently, which was causing cash flow problems
- there were complaints from finance staff and administrators about the number of forms that could not be processed without clarification because of errors or omissions
- there were complaints from users about late payments and the design of the existing form, which many said was over-complicated.

A data collection form was prepared and a system analysis was conducted following initial investigations and consultations with users. These are shown in Figures 6.1.12 and 6.1.13. Examine these documents carefully, as this particular scenario is developed further in the next element, which relates to system and procedure design.

DATA COLLECTION EXERCISE: SAMPLING COMPLETED EXPENSE FORMS					
			Type of discrepancy		
Reason for discrepancy	Missing receipts	Unreadable claim	Wrong calculations	Expense not allowable	Over budget
Misunderstood claim form					
Misunderstood system					
Carelessness					
Rushed completion					
Other (please specify)					

Total forms sampled . . . .

Total forms rejected . . . .

Total forms with claims from previous month or earlier . . . .

Date data collected . . . .

Place of collection . . . .

Signature . . . .

Figure 6.1.12 A data collection form

Figure 6.1.13 System analysis for processing expense claims

Aim

To introduce an improved system for processing expense claims.

Objectives of system

1   To ensure expense claims are checked thoroughly and any errors identified and corrected.
2   To minimise delays and additional processing work caused by incorrect completion.
3   To improve the prompt submission and throughput of expense claims per month to meet cash-flow objectives.
4   To process expense claims to monthly deadlines for payment.
5   To monitor expenditure on expenses to ensure this is within budget levels.
6   To ensure all appropriate tax relief is recorded and claimed by the organisation.
7   To simplify the process for users.
8   To produce auditable records.

Constraints

1   Inland Revenue regulations limit allowable expenses unless specific dispensation has been negotiated beforehand.
2   Expenses can be allowed by the company to employees even if they do not attract tax relief.
3   Regulations on expenses can change frequently. Up-to-date information is required from the Inland Revenue/Company Accountant.

Investigation

To obtain information on:

1   Current expenses system
    a)   departmental procedures
    b)   finance procedures
    c)   authorisation procedures.
2   Difficulties for users, departmental administrators and finance staff.
3   Financial records to obtain data on expenditure to budget and cash flow records.
4   Staff attitudes towards any proposed new system.

Alternative suggestions

1   Decentralise expenses processing to departmental level, with administrators given authority to check and pass expenses. Departmental managers to countersign claims over £100 per month. Finance staff process only for payment and tax records.
2   Administrators responsible for checking expenses against pre-agreed staff limits, processing of expense claims to be undertaken by finance staff.
3   Departmental managers responsible for authorising expenses against departmental budgets. Administrators to check expenses, finance staff to process.

Requirements

1 Data on existing system plus identification of problem areas.
2 Analysis of current expenses documentation and user perceptions.
3 Data on current levels of expenditure on different types of expenses.
4 Procedures for departmental managers, administrators, finance staff and users of new system.
5 Procedures for monitoring correct form completion and expenditure against budget of new system.

Results of investigation

1 Only 15 per cent of staff submit expense claims regularly each month. 50 per cent submit claims every 3 months and 35 per cent only on a six monthly basis. This results in cash flow problems.
2 Last year, expenditure on entertainment and subsistence was 35 per cent over budget whilst expenditure on travel was 10 per cent below budget. Minimal variance was experienced for expenditure on other categories.
3 Seasonal variations in trade mean there is a higher demand for expense claims in the months of March–June and September–November. The current monthly budget allocation system does not allow for this.
4 Many staff consider that expense forms should be simplified to aid completion. It is because the task is often seen as complex and onerous that it is put off until a considerable claim has amassed.
5 There is no responsibility for individual stages of the processing procedure, with the result that queries are not referred promptly for clarification. There can often be delays obtaining answers to queries. This results in late or delayed payments.
6 Departmental managers complain at having to authorise all claims, even if for very small amounts.

Recommended system following user consultation

1 Expense claim submission dates (per month) are published each December by finance for each month of the following year. These dates are scheduled for the return of checked expense claims to Finance department by about the 10th of each month to reduce the burden on finance staff at the end of the month.
2 Expenses submitted by the due date in week one are guaranteed for payment by the end of week four, unless there are serious errors or omissions.
3 The expense claim form is revised and simplified.
4 Completed forms, plus receipts, to be submitted to the department's Administrator one week before the finance deadline. The Administrator to be responsible for checking claim forms for accuracy and referring queries promptly back to the originator.
5 The Administrator to keep records for each member of staff to remind those who fail to submit a form that this is due, and to check that this is submitted the following month.

6   Administrators to be responsible for sanctioning expenses under £100 per month. Above that figure, the claim to be countersigned by the departmental manager.

7   The Administrator to keep records of expense claims relative to departmental budgets.

8   Staff requiring additional expense allowances in any month to bid for these on a special claim form through Administrators (if under £100) and through departmental managers if over £100. Where possible this bid should be submitted the month prior to the expense being incurred.

9   Finance staff to be responsible for entering cost codes, recording expenses, recording reclaimable VAT amounts, keeping auditable records and making payments by the end of week four.

10 Finance department responsibility to be devolved to one member of staff and one back-up member of staff. This person to be trained to answer departmental queries regarding allowable and non-allowable expenses or to be responsible for referring such queries to the Finance Manager.

Queries/possible problems

1   Can tasks be handled by finance and by departmental administrators with existing staffing and workload?

2   Encouragement for staff to submit claims promptly may not be sufficient to generate claims monthly.

3   To what extent could computerised records and processing assist throughput?

Recommendations

System to be designed and discussed with administrators, finance staff and other users then tested before full implementation. Recommend review after 3 months to ascertain if objectives are being achieved or if further measures required.

Procedures for obtaining approval for specialist advice

If you are in the business of planning systems and procedures then you should certainly be aware of those that already exist in your organisation. In some cases, these may affect or constrain your own activities.

- There may be specified ways in which all new systems and procedures must be documented (see Element 6.2)
- There may be specified approval procedures that must be followed before any draft procedure can be implemented (see Element 7.1)
- There may be nominated staff with overall responsibility for certain areas relating to your planned system or procedure.
- There may be specific organisational procedures to follow for obtaining approval for specialist advice.
- Company policy may specify the areas where external advice *must* be sought.

It is tempting to think that such systems and procedures have been designed simply to make your life more complicated and are little more than bureaucratic encumbrances. However, they are often essential, particularly in large organisations as a coordinating device to prevent duplication of effort and to ensure that all the organisational systems operate in harmony. It is also the case that new or inexperienced staff could operate as 'rogue viruses' by introducing new untested systems or procedures which actually disrupt existing ones. If your organisation operates to ISO 9000 standards it will be essential for all systems and procedures to be part of the overall system and documented accordingly. In a very small organisation, of course, it is likely that you will have a freer hand to make and develop your own contacts – provided your line manager knows what you are doing!

Frequently, too, expert advice may be available in-house which is unknown to some staff. There is also the danger, if external contact is uncoordinated, that existing networks and contacts may exist that are either not used as they should be or are too frequently contacted by diverse staff – which creates a very poor impression. For this reason, you may need to talk through your proposals with your line manager and obtain clearance to make contact with specialists, or may even have to hand over this part of the task to someone whose job it is to obtain this type of information. The benefit in the latter case is that you are no longer (technically) responsible for its quality or accuracy. However, you may feel that your moral stance is a little different!

THEORY INTO PRACTICE

1 Investigate the procedures you would have to follow in your own organisation to:
   a obtain specialist advice from a senior colleague in a different department
   b obtain advice on employment legislation if you were drafting new recruitment procedures.
2 If you were investigating the best method of processing expense forms in your organisation, what specialist advice would you require from inside and outside your organisation? What procedures would you have to follow before you could obtain this information?

Element 6.2

Design and agree systems and procedures to meet organisational needs

Since the main reason why some systems and procedures are ineffective or inefficient is because of design problems rather than 'people' problems, the onus on the designer is considerable. You should already appreciate that the first stage in setting up any system or procedure is to define and agree your aims, goals or objectives with both users and decision-makers. However, before you start actually to design your system or procedure it is important to appreciate the characteristics of a good system and the type of problems caused by one which has been badly designed.

This element covers the various approaches to the design of systems and procedures and then looks, more practically, at how these can be applied to administrative systems and procedures. The documentation which relates to the design process is covered briefly, given that this is often open to individual interpretation, unless the procedures must accord to specific requirements, such as for ISO 9000. You will also be introduced to the type of legal and regulatory requirements which may constrain your attempts.

Identifying effective and ineffective systems

Characteristics of an effective system or procedure

To design an effective system or procedure it is first important to appreciate what constitutes its effectiveness. Users evaluate a system or procedure as 'good' or 'bad' in relation to its ability to assist them in achieving objectives quickly and easily. For a designer, it is important to have a more in-depth and a broader appreciation of this aspect.

In Element 6.1 a bee was described as a system for producing honey. To be more precise, we should have limited this definition purely to the types of bees that produce honey, but the example is useful enough for our purpose. A bee colony is an extremely effective and efficient system – and undertakes several very streamlined procedures!

As a system, a bee colony:

- is economic – bees eat little and work hard
- is simple – even children understand quickly what bees do
- is flexible and can adapt to its environment (for example, if there are no flowers bees will happily sample clover instead)
- is reliable – the only factor that would affect this is bad weather or severe cold
- is portable – if you move the queen, the bees will follow to another hive
- is secure – and has defence mechanisms to prove it!
- is durable – if one bee dies then other bees take its place
- is well integrated with its environment – and utilises this to fulfil its objectives
- is competent – the division of labour in the hive assures the continuance of the system as a whole
- rewards users (i.e. bees pollinate flowers) and has no undesirable outputs.

If you ever design a system which is quite as efficient and effective then you should congratulate yourself. In fact, if you look at many natural systems as a designer, you soon become very impressed – if not overawed. To date humankind is still struggling to invent a perfect system. As consolation, you may take comfort from the fact that some think the bee would be an even better system if utilising its sting was not an instant method of committing suicide.

As a procedure, a bee colony:

- follows a known routine (whether as workers, drones or a queen)
- follows a routine that supports other routines (the hive operates for the collective good)
- undertakes each task purposefully and efficiently
- follows a routine which allows for individual initiative (e.g. in selecting the best flowers)
- communicates useful information related to the task to others (by doing a 'dance' in the hive to show others where more flowers with pollen and nectar are to be found).

The basic points to remember from this are that, as a general rule, the more simple and uncomplicated you make systems and procedures the better for everyone. The more you allow for individual contributions from users and give them scope to use their initiative, the better; the less inclined you are to keep 'tweaking' an effective system or procedure, the less you will irritate people. To use an old expression, 'If it ain't broke, don't fix it.'

Results of ineffective systems and procedures

It is easier to define an ineffective system or procedure if you look at the problems that can be caused, such as:

with systems
- an inability to solve the problem
- not addressing the real needs of users
- conflicting with other organisational aims and objectives
- excessive design costs
- hidden costs
- undesirable outcomes and side-effects
- ineffective control mechanisms (or none at all)

with procedures
- confusion over who does what
- miscommunications and misunderstandings
- conflict with other organisational procedures or departments
- problems, side-effects and deviations from the norm not considered
- lack of documentation – or too much of it!

These difficulties are usually caused because there has been a failure to identify the problem, the needs of users or the needs of the wider organisation; the designer is inexperienced and/or has misinterpreted the problem or needs of the users; the specification is inflexible (or there is no specification at all); changing external events are ignored; the system or procedure is implemented without testing; or the system or procedure has been developed for all the wrong reasons – such as political gain, managerial ambition, to enforce control or status or to prove technical competitiveness.

A college was concerned that its room utilisation procedures should be effective. Timetables on the central computer system showed 97 per cent utilisation of all rooms, but it was decided that this system alone was ineffective in monitoring usage. The Principal was concerned that rooms were empty when he walked down corridors, yet middle managers were always requesting more accommodation.

It was decided to check utilisation by employing a firm of outside consultants for one week. The consultants would walk around the building every hour, checking how many students were in each room. This would be compared against the timetable listings.

The consultants' report showed that actual utilisation was extremely variable – particularly in the block used by adult students. A high of 95 per cent was reported only for 11 am to 12 noon and 1 pm to 2 pm. Several rooms were completely empty mid-morning and mid-afternoon, between 9 am and 10 am, after 3 pm and on Friday afternoons.

The Principal used this information as the basis for a decision to postpone plans to build an extension for adult students.

1 To what degree do you consider the idea of bringing in consultants for monitoring room usage was efficient and effective?
2 What deficiencies can you identify with the system?
3 Should the Principal have been surprised when staff protested strongly about the survey and his actions? Give a reason for your answer.
4 What system would you have recommended and why?

Obviously, computerisation can be used to improve the processing of many operations and to speed up many systems and procedures. This is one reason why organisations are willing to spend so much on computer developments. According to the latest figures, spending on IT systems was £390 billion in 1996 – a higher level of investment than on production equipment and manufacturing plants.

However, some of the most widespread system disasters have involved IT hardware and software – when the computers 'go down' and so disrupt operations.

According to Professor Chris Clegg of Sheffield University, between 80 and 90 per cent of IT investments do not meet their performance targets. Eighty per cent of systems are delivered late and over budget, 40 per cent fail or are abandoned, less than 25 per cent combine business and technology objectives successfully. This leaves only 10 per cent to 20 per cent which successfully meet all their criteria.

One recent catastrophe has affected the National Health Service, with a series of controversies associated with the introduction of computers. One of the main problems has been the failure of different systems to relate to each other. In other cases the problems have ranged from inadequate cost-benefit appraisals and the difficulties of adding on new systems to older and larger systems.

Types of systems and procedures

Classifications for systems and procedures were discussed in Element 6.1. However, when you are approaching systems and procedures from a design perspective you may wish to classify them less theoretically.

- Some are completely new and some are a 'redesign' of an existing system or procedure.
- Some must be relatively rigid, others can be much more flexible. Flexible systems are required when the environment in which they are contained is rapidly changing. Potential changes need to be considered before you even start your design. Flexible procedures can be agreed if the consequences of different types of action will be unimportant.
- Some systems and procedures are production-oriented and some are service-oriented. A reprographics unit, seen as a 'system for producing printed documents' and its associated procedures, could be viewed as the former and a reception facility and interaction with customers as the latter.
- You could consider the degree of human involvement in the system and the points at which variable actions and attitudes of staff could affect the outcome.
- You could consider the degree to which your system or procedure interacts or overlaps with existing systems and procedures.

Undertaking an analysis of a system enables you to identify the most applicable place to site your boundary, and helps you to identify inputs and outputs. It also helps to guide you towards linking it with other established systems and procedures and to identify accurately the level of prescriptiveness required.

Designing systems and procedures to meet specified needs

There are various common approaches to the designing of systems and procedures. No one approach is always correct or always wrong – it very much depends upon your experience, the type of system or procedure you are trying to design and the circumstances.

With a *top-down* approach you start with the system's goals, objectives and boundary and work downwards to consider the detail. With a procedure, you start with the overall plan and then break it into segments. This is often the easiest way for beginners but is not always effective, as it means addressing the more complex issues first! It is often only suitable for a simple system or procedure when there is no danger of change mid-way and when you are certain you know what will be needed and practical at user level.

A *bottom-up approach* starts by examining the inputs, outputs and process and then moves upwards to consider the whole system and its objectives. For a procedure, it starts with examining current procedures and actions and building on these. Some designers consider this approach is more appropriate because the needs of users are considered in more detail at the outset. There is also a greater likelihood that the new system or procedure will match what really happens (provided you want to keep the status quo!). The danger is that when everything is put together the complete system may malfunction or the various parts of the procedure may not dovetail neatly or effectively.

With the *critical first design* approach the most critical aspect of the system or procedure is considered first. This may be the solving of a particular problem, or the achievement of one particular objective, or the coordination of the operations of two different departments. In this case the designer may draw up a 'ranking list' of all the aims and objectives and identify those that must be achieved, those that are mutually exclusive and those that would be too costly to achieve.

THEORY INTO PRACTICE

Which of the above approaches is being taken in each of the following?

a A member of staff buys a Powerpoint package and then asks you how it could be used to the department's advantage.

b A scientist works for years to eliminate an undesirable (toxic) output associated with a chemical process.

c The Principal's actions in the THEORY INTO PRACTICE case study on page 524.

Practical approaches to system design

The best approach depends upon the circumstances that apply in a given situation.

The traditional (sequential) approach

This usually involves a series of actions, as shown in Figure 6.2.1. The initial emphasis is on investigating options and possibilities, through:

- defining the problem, identifying what is required and the likely advantages of each option
- drawing up a feasibility study to assess potential costs and benefits and to identify resource constraints and requirements (at this stage any restrictions or rules concerning use or application must be incorporated)
- determining user requirements through observation, analysis of current systems and procedures, meetings and individual interviews
- drawing up a design specification which incorporates required resources and takes account of predetermined timescales and realistic costs (any discrepancies may then be referred back to the potential users for discussion and clarification).

Finally, key requirements are analysed to produce a final specification, which may be amended after the design process has been completed.

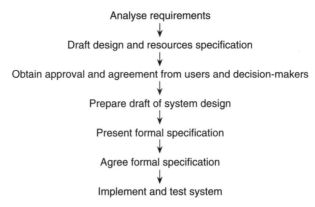

Analyse requirements
↓
Draft design and resources specification
↓
Obtain approval and agreement from users and decision-makers
↓
Prepare draft of system design
↓
Present formal specification
↓
Agree formal specification
↓
Implement and test system

Figure 6.2.1 A sequential approach to systems design

The presumption behind this approach is that systems design is a sequential process in which all planning is undertaken at the outset, before any trials or implementation. Whilst this is appropriate if users know exactly what they want or if an existing (successful) system is being updated, this approach is less successful on other occasions. Often, some user requirements are not known until later. In addition, if problems are only discovered on implementation they may be both costly and difficult to rectify and result in poor staff morale or, even worse, missed opportunities because of the delays involved.

Iteration

This approach assumes that the process of systems design is more fluid, with each stage being 'revisited' on several occasions for additional clarification on objectives, aims and methods of achievement. It may, for instance, be found that some user objectives are in conflict with each other or that some users do not possess all the required knowledge to make 'final' decisions at the outset. This approach allows for reworking – and users can be consulted at any point to inform systems design and development. Whilst this is often more effective for completely new or revolutionary systems – or for new designers – the problem is one of wasted resources if several earlier attempts have to be rejected.

User validation

This reverts to the sequential approach but allows for users to check and agree *each stage*. It requires time for the users, which leads to additional use of resources and therefore additional costs. In addition, the users need to understand the specification and the aims of the designers. Additional time may be required to 'translate' and communicate these objectives to users unfamiliar with any specialist terminology or jargon used. However, the benefits are increased participation, the ability to deal with constantly changing requirements, and an increase in acceptability and perceived usability by users.

Incremental evolution

In this case the system is broken into separate parts, each of which is introduced separately. Each is checked and refined and then 'builds' on to earlier parts of the system. Each stage of development, testing and learning informs the next. The key role of the designer is keeping the overall picture in mind, related to how the whole system will function and how each part is integrated. This can be a useful technique for tackling the design of a complex system which affects many aspects of the organisation. It also makes learning easier for the users, but the time taken to complete the project is longer.

Prototyping

This approach involves designing a key part of the system and then testing it. If this is successful then the prototype forms the nucleus for the remainder of the system. This approach is often preferred by users who want to test an 'actual' system and its associated documentation rather than review and comment on a specification – which may, to them, be relatively unintelligible. However, the fact that the system has to be more developed before user feedback can be obtained obviously adds to the costs of development. This type of approach is appropriate if designers require input by users in relation to the correction of errors, or to clarify or define their requirements in a changing environment, or where technology is constantly changing.

THEORY INTO PRACTICE

1 Which of the above approaches would you use in the following circumstances?
   a You want user feedback on your proposed operating system and relevant documentation.
   b You are redesigning a basic, simple system.
   c You want user approval at each stage of the design process.
   d You want to make a complex system easier to learn and understand.
   e You are an inexperienced designer, working with a new user group, to design a system that may need changing at each stage of its development.
2 Obviously, all the approaches covered in this section can equally be used when writing procedures. As a check, read through each description, noting the situations in which each approach should best be used. You may like to note that the sequential approach to designing procedures is often much shorter and more abbreviated than for a system, particularly if you are simply updating an existing, effective procedure.

Ways of specifying systems and procedures

The aim of the specification is to be a precise description of the desired system. However, it must be understandable to all who read it, so it must be drawn up in language that is readily understandable. For complex systems, a specification may be drawn up:

- as a draft, after the feasibility study has been completed
- as a design specification to ensure that the designer keeps to the agreed brief
- as a formal document, after design, for future reference.

The specification may therefore go through several redrafts. The advantage of allowing for this is that flexibility is retained at the design stage. However, it is important to ascertain to what extent you can exceed or amend the agreed brief or the agreed design specification during the design process. If you treat your first submission as a rough guide whereas your line manager equates it to a tablet of stone, then you might have something of a problem on your hands later!

The specification must state what is required to operate the system or procedure, the attributes each requirement must possess, and the essential and desirable relationships between the requirements. In a nutshell, the specification must:

- include all the essential information
- be exact and precise
- describe the system or procedure in such a way that it is easily understandable by potential users
- take account of any rules, regulations or policies that will restrict operations
- clearly identify the potential timescale for implementation and the estimated costs of implementation.

The format is immaterial – unless your organisation has an agreed policy on the way such specifications are designed and submitted. In some cases the specification may be presented orally, with appropriate visual aids. Sometimes a written report may be more suitable. If you are proposing to implement a straightforward procedure which is simple, inexpensive (or even cost-saving) and limited only to your own section, a brief verbal exchange with your own line manager and further consultation with your users may suffice.

Types and sources of information required in drawing up specifications

If we assume that you are following the system life-cycle illustrated in Figure 6.1.11 on page 507, then you will have already amassed a variety of information on your proposed system or procedure, including:

- documentation relating to any existing systems or procedures that:
  - will interact or overlap with your own
  - are subject to the current review
- documentation on any company policies, rules or regulations or statutory requirements that will affect your system or procedure
- notes (or minutes) from meetings with user groups outlining the discussions that took place and the conclusions reached
- data collected from investigations into existing systems and procedures (or comparative systems and procedures in other organisations) or into problem areas
- copies of any feasibility studies you were asked to undertake
- your own notes – ideally with your own ideas and plans

- notes made from discussions with internal and external specialists
- quotations, estimates and specifications from outside suppliers (ideally with your own evaluations attached).

It is useful to date all this information and to make it clear on each document where your 'source' is based – in case you need further clarification at a later date. Equally, any documents you send out should be clearly dated with a copy of the circulation list attached. Eventually, you will be able to add the specification and your draft and final designs to these documents to provide a full information file on the project you are undertaking. This is not only helpful in the future, if the system or procedure is later reviewed, but is extremely useful if you find yourself later trying to solve a similar problem in another area, or if you have to 'backtrack' at a later stage because users change their minds (or cannot remember what they agreed to earlier).

---

1   If you are contracting out the designing of a new system to an external consultancy, you should certainly keep all documents safely. This is because a legal contract will exist between you and the supplier. If the system fails to work satisfactorily then you may need all the evidence you can muster to argue your case.

2   A major difficulty with complex systems can occur if the designer or main user leaves the organisation and no-one can answer important questions relating to its potential applications. Making sure there is a clear reference file which can be accessed by anyone makes it much easier for any new staff member, with the appropriate expertise, quickly to understand what is happening .

Types and sources of specialist advice

Obtaining specialist advice, both internally and externally, was dealt with in Element 6.1, pages 512–514. However, it is worth noting that by the time you have worked through preparing a feasibility study, amending your original ideas and obtaining resource approval, and have arrived at the stage of preparing your design specification, then there may be a need to revisit some of your earlier sources of expertise. This might be necessary to clarify certain issues now that you have become more certain of your objectives and how you will achieve them. You may also want to check that any resource quotations still stand – particularly if agreement has taken several months to obtain. An interesting anomaly is that in some areas (such as computer hardware) you might actually find that prices have fallen since you first obtained a quotation! Whilst this might sound marvellous, the practicalities of reworking all your costings and then resubmitting these might mean the idea has rather less appeal.

You may also be keen to obtain advice and assistance from any experienced systems designers in the organisation – particularly if the project with which you are involved is very complex. The skills you will need to learn include:

- techniques for analysing the myriad of data you have acquired
- techniques for identifying the best method of monitoring and controlling your proposed system or procedure
- methods of drafting a system specification and a set of procedures in a clearly understandable form for users
- learning how to prepare a user manual.

In addition, you will need to check that you are following organisational procedures for preparing and submitting any documentation.

The remainder of this section is intended to give you guidance on the first three of these skills – although it is much easier to acquire the knowledge and apply it in your own workplace if you can consult someone who is experienced and who is prepared to be your guide and mentor on the first occasion. You should note that user manuals are dealt with in Chapter 7.

Analysing data

Before you prepare a design specification you will need to analyse the data you have obtained and stored carefully in your information file. Some organisations have specially formatted *data collection forms* for this purpose. In other cases, the format is up to you. You have already met an example of a data collection form in Figure 6.1.12, page 517.

When analysing data be careful not to prejudge the issue and form a conclusion first and then try to make the data justify your initial assumptions! If possible, try to suspend any form of judgement until you have obtained as much information as possible. If there is any doubt in your mind then perhaps you have obtained insufficient detail, or asked the wrong questions, and will have to go back to the source for more information.

Many people find it easier to analyse data relating to hard systems than soft systems. This is because numerical data can be recorded on graphs and charts or analysed mathematically to identify relationships and correlations. Soft systems, in contrast, result in qualitative views, opinions and descriptions which are more difficult to process. However, some useful techniques do exist for 'managing' this process.

Affinity analysis

This is useful for classifying user ideas, opinions or concerns. After initial discussions or a brainstorming session with users, the main categories of concern or main headings to describe common problems are identified. Flip charts are ideal for this purpose. In the earlier case study on expense claims (pages 516–520), we might find that user concerns could be grouped under:

- the processing of expense claims
- the documentation in existence
- the method in which claims, queries and problems are handled
- the skills and attitudes of administrators
- the skills and attitudes of users
- the skills and attitudes of finance staff.

Fishbone diagram

From this information a cause-and-effect diagram can be drawn. This is sometimes described as a *fishbone diagram*, which you first met in Chapter 5, page 439. Using this technique, the causes relating to each type of concern are identified. If you find yourself in the situation where dozens of causes are suggested, then you need some way of paring these down into a usable number. It is normal to limit the number allowed to a maximum of those five or six that will have the greatest influence on the effect you are investigating. You can insert lower-level causes which significantly contribute to a problem through making an insert arrow on a particular cause line.

Figure 6.2.2 shows a fishbone diagram that might be drawn after initial discussions with users of the existing expense claim system. The aim of the discussion was to identify the main contributory causes that created delays in the processing of expense claims.

You should note that some designers prefer to start by considering the various factors that could contribute to possible causes under particular categories, such as existing systems, equipment, methods of working, personnel, forms to complete, level of knowledge of staff (i.e. a top-down approach). Alternatively you could brainstorm all possible causes before organising them into groups and subgroups (i.e. a bottom-up approach). This can be done by the group or by yourself as an individual if you understand the problems well enough. However, in this case the draft diagram should then be referred back to users to ensure that all their comments and suggestions have been included. A cause-and-effect diagram should be constantly fluid – so that additional information can be added at any stage of the development process as further knowledge comes to light.

Tree diagram

A different technique is to produce a *tree diagram* which shows the relationships between a particular topic and its constituent elements (see Figure 6.2.3). A tree diagram is helpful because it shows both logical and sequential links in a process. It is usual to start by writing the topic at the left-hand side, then branching the major categories to the right. These can then be subdivided into different elements and subelements. Again it is useful to undertake this exercise as a group. Alternatively, you may draft out the tree diagram yourself, following group discussions, and then take it back to the user group for agreement.

Monitoring and controlling the system

Monitoring must always be undertaken against predetermined standards which are well known by all system users. If you are concerned about setting realistic standards then a useful technique is *benchmarking*, where you compare a process against the standards achieved by recognised leaders in the field. Whilst this technique is mainly applied to customer-focused activities, it can also be used to set realistic targets for any internal system or procedure. The difficulty, however, may be in obtaining benchmarks

Figure 6.2.2 Cause-and-effect or fishbone diagram

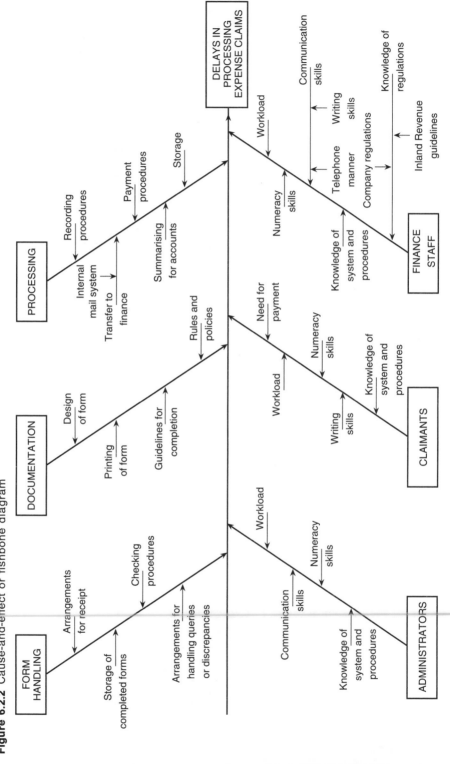

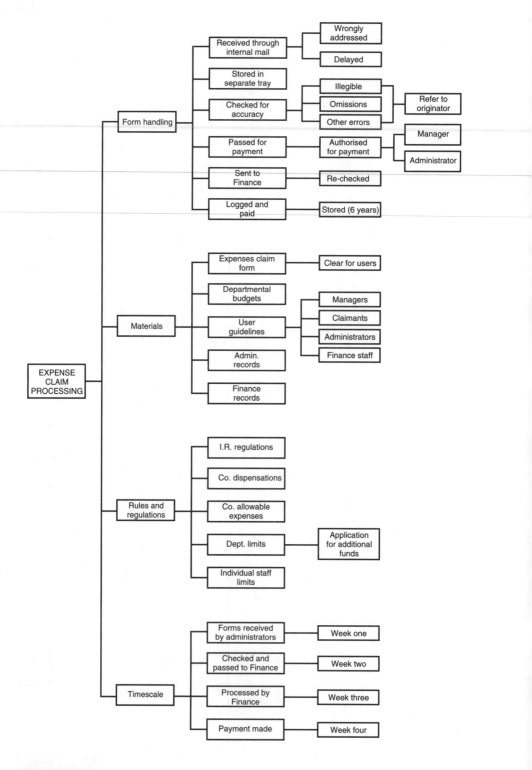

Figure 6.2.3 Tree diagram

against which you can compare your internal operation performance results. Ideally you will obtain these through personal contacts, interviews, professional contacts or your specialist advisers. Certainly, in the field of expense submissions, you should expect to be given guidance in the standards you could realistically set or expect from your company accountants or auditors. You should also expect to hold discussions on the range and type of variances that will be acceptable, as well as considering the type of corrective action that would be both appropriate and acceptable to staff.

The main point is to identify the type of reports and data that will give you accurate and prompt information on performance against standards. It is also important that you know who is collecting this information and how often. Finally, the methods used to monitor and measure outputs, the objectives, the standards and the allowable variances must be clearly communicated to everyone. Setting up a system that enables the key information to be gathered and monitored routinely, so that only exceptions are reported upwards, makes life easier for everyone.

THEORY INTO PRACTICE

Common mistakes made by new designers include:

- asking for too much information too often
- asking for information that is not linked to the objectives
- monitoring too tightly
- forgetting to monitor altogether once the system is in place!

Look back to the system analysis in Figure 6.1.13 on page 518 which identified the objectives of the redesigned expenses system. Then reread the notes on control in Element 6.1 (pages 499–503). From this, what information would you select as your control data for this new system, and why?

Drafting systems specifications and procedures

Writing over-complicated specifications and elaborate procedures is usually a time-wasting and demotivating exercise for both designers and users. Imagine yourself in the shoes of a user who is obliged to read a long document that gives a mass of complicated technical detail. The end result can range from fear or boredom through to aggression or apathy.

In many cases, particularly for administrative systems, such a level of detail is unnecessary. If you were writing a specification for a traffic management system around Heathrow then the situation would be rather different! Administrative procedures should be kept as straightforward as possible, so that they can act as a rapid *aide mémoire* for users.

One method of drafting out a system is to draw up a *user process chart*, as shown in Figure 6.2.4. This shows the interactions between different users with the sequence of activities clearly indicated. The chart also shows the

Figure 6.2.4 User process chart: expenses system

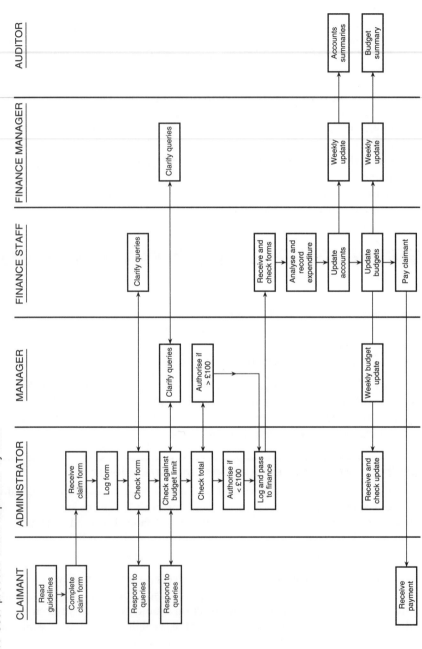

areas of responsibility for the various parties involved. The chart then needs to be agreed before being finalised. To fulfil the remit for the system specification, a document may be attached to this giving additional details required on resources, timescale for implementation (see also Chapter 7) and any further costs and benefits that have been identified (see page 514 for further details of specifications).

A procedure is normally drawn up by creating a *flow chart*. Certain conventions are used to indicate the different types of activity and these are shown in Figure 6.2.5. A flow chart is simply a pictorial representation of the steps in a process. For many administrative procedures your staff may prefer to receive a simple checklist – particularly if they are more familiar with text than graphics. Again it is usual to draft out the document first and then discuss it with potential users before making any necessary amendments.

Any written procedures or flow charts to accompany, inform and control a system are usually attached to the system's specification for final submission and agreement with decision-makers.

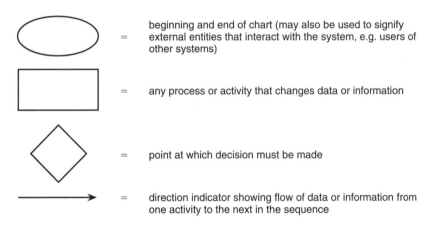

Figure 6.2.5 Flow chart symbols

1 Figure 6.2.6 shows a draft flow chart for administrators operating the new expenses procedure. Check that you can identify the various activities, the points at which decisions are made and the route to follow. Figure 6.2.7 shows a step-by-step written procedure for drawing a flow chart. Use this to draft a flow chart yourself for any procedure with which you are familiar.

2 Assume that when you show the procedure to the administrative staff they argue that it would be more sensible to check if a claim is within the budget limit *before* checking the form for accuracy, given that some forms over budget may be rejected by the manager. Redraw the flow chart making this change.

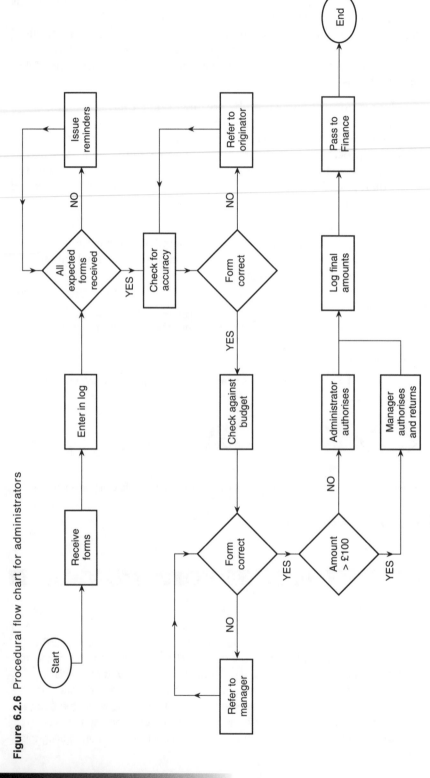

Figure 6.2.6 Procedural flow chart for administrators

1	Identify the beginning and the end of the process.
2	Consider the overall process from beginning to end. If the process is one that is already in existence, then either obtain a full description from the user or observe it in operation.
3	Identify the various steps and define these in terms of activities, decisions, inputs and outputs.
4	Draft out the flow chart.
5	Test the flow chart yourself by working through it, considering alternatives that do or may occur.
6	Review the draft flow chart with any existing or potential users.
7	Amend the draft flow chart, incorporating any agreed improvements.
8	Test the flow chart against existing practices or against a 'dry run' of the new procedure.
9	Make any final amendments.
10	Date the flow chart, issue to all users, file a copy for future reference.

Figure 6.2.7 Procedure for designing a flow chart

An organisation's procedures for obtaining approval for specialist advice

You should note that this topic was covered in Element 6.1 on pages 520–521. However, it is possible that you may want to clarify additional issues or existing issues with internal and external specialists throughout the design process – particularly if you are adopting an iterative or user validation approach. If you are involved in regular review sessions then it is always sensible to ensure that your own line manager knows what is happening or what you intend to do, before you do it. This is particularly important if prior knowledge by others of the system or procedure with which you are involved could result in unfavourable outcomes. This could occur if it:

- is politically sensitive (managerially or departmentally)
- may involve contentious issues which are as yet unresolved with users
- is confidential
- could result in press speculation.

This does not mean that specialist advice cannot be obtained. It does mean that you would have to be more careful about whom you contact and the details and information you provide. Obvious examples of potentially problematic systems and procedures include:

- consultation with employment lawyers on redundancy procedures
- potential systems concerned with departmental restructuring and reorganisation
- procedures concerned with research and design projects and associated press releases
- public sector systems and procedures that will affect consumers or users of the service

- a system or procedure your own manager wants to introduce to gain political advantage over another department.

Another danger of which you should be aware is that of asking people for advice and then ignoring it! People who have given freely of their time and expertise are apt to feel rather aggrieved if their suggestions are discounted, even if there is good reason for this. If anything later goes wrong, they are likely to want to put their views forward, if only to justify their own position. On occasion, therefore, it may be better not to ask unless you are certain you will want to take account of the information and advice you receive.

> The fire that occurred in the Channel Tunnel in November 1996 was the subject of judicial inquiries on both sides of the Channel. The report by the Channel Tunnel Safety Authority identified that several problems occurred because of over-complicated safety procedures and a lack of staff training. The Fire Brigades Union also criticised the design of the open lattice wagons, which it had constantly opposed since their inception. In addition, the Chief and Assistant Chief Fire Officers' Association urged an urgent redesign. The Fire Brigades Union threatened that if this were not done, they might let a future fire burn itself out once people had been evacuated. This is clearly a case where a company is feeling the effects of ignoring previously given specialist advice.

Legal and regulatory requirements concerning systems and procedures

Designers of systems and procedures rarely have total freedom to specify exactly what they want without any restrictions at all.

- Systems and procedures relating to the recruitment, training, promotion or dismissal of staff must take account of current employment legislation.
- Those relating to salary increases and job evaluation schemes must conform to the requirements of the Equal Pay Act 1970 and the Equal Pay (Amendment) Regulations 1983.
- Health and safety systems and procedures are subject to a wide range of legislation, depending upon the particular issue involved.
- Those relating to data stored on a computer system must take into account the Data Protection Act 1994; and, from 1998, those relating to paper records have to incorporate the requirements of the Data Protection Directive (EU) 1995.
- Those that concern consumer goods and services and relationships with consumers and suppliers should be drawn up in accordance with the requirements of the appropriate consumer or competition legislation.

- Systems and procedures that relate to the external or internal operations of the organisation itself, its shareholders and its financial situation must fulfil all the legal obligations of the enterprise, either as set out in the Companies Acts or in any public sector terms of reference.

All these types of legislation have been considered in depth in earlier chapters. However, a further area that is having to be considered to a greater extent by most organisations relates to environmental issues. Any systems or procedures you devise with environmental implications are likely to be constrained or controlled by a variety of Acts and regulations, including the Environmental Protection Act 1990, the Radioactive Substances Act 1993, the Environment Act 1995 and Special Waste Regulations 1996. Actions by the European Union to regulate pollution, improve water quality and improve environmental standards have resulted in over 25 environmental directives over the past few years.

Advice and information on, and the monitoring of, organisational and public activities is undertaken by the Environment Agency, which is sponsored by the Department of the Environment and operates at regional level. It is mainly concerned with areas such as pollution control, water resources (including abstraction and potential contamination), conservation and flood control. It advises businesses on issues such as air pollutants, water pollutants, radioactive material disposal, waste regulations and recycling. Many environmental matters are also controlled by local authorities, including noise, litter and air pollution and planning permission – particularly where the general public or small businesses are concerned.

Proactive environmental policies are being followed by an increasing number of business organisations, given the pressure by environmental groups and the adverse publicity that results if breaches are uncovered. In future it may even be the case that companies showing greater concern over these issues find their profits increasing. Several reports submitted to the government are proposing that the taxation system should be adjusted to penalise bad practice and to reward good. One study by the Institute for Public Policy Research has claimed that more than £20 billion a year could be raised through higher taxes on pollution and waste. Two papers submitted by research fellows at the Institute for European Environmental Policy are proposing measures to encourage more environmentally friendly travel, including escalating fuel duty to reduce needless car journeys and to encourage greater use of public transport. If these suggestions are implemented, you may find you have to urgently redraft guidelines on company travel procedures – as well as on environmental concerns!

In any case where legal or regulatory requirements affect the design of your systems or procedures this must be communicated to all decision-makers and users. This is so that, firstly, amendments and alterations are not suggested to areas which cannot or must not be changed; and secondly, because it is almost guaranteed that these requirements will increase the prescriptiveness of any procedures you write and staff must know the reason why these are mandatory, rather than simply be given unsupported directives to follow.

1   Everyone has a legal 'duty of care' to keep household, commercial or
    industrial waste safe at every point of processing. This relates to the points
    at which waste is produced, stored, transported, treated, recycled or
    disposed of. This means that if you pass waste to someone not authorised
    to receive it, you are legally liable.

2   The EU Directive on Packaging and Packaging Waste states that at least 50
    per cent of UK packaging waste must be recycled or otherwise recovered
    and re-utilised by year 2001. The Producer Responsibility Obligations
    (Packaging Waste) Regulations 1997 ensure that the costs of producing,
    using and disposing of packaging fall directly on those who produce or use
    it. If you are involved in the packaging industry in any way you should check
    whether your organisation should be registered with the Environmental
    Agency or should become a member of a business membership
    compliance scheme which takes responsibility for your legal obligations
    under this Directive.

THEORY INTO PRACTICE

Find out the systems and procedures in your organisation to promote
environmentally friendly practices. A useful area to start looking is your stationery
purchasing procedures and the way in which waste paper is handled and
collected. Does your organisation promote recycling, for example? A key area in
most organisations is photocopying. Not only is a vast amount of paper purchased
but most organisations collect an enormous quantity of spoiled paper through
misalignment, paper jams and other operational and machine faults.

Usually, waste paper that is merely scrapped or discarded can be classified as an
undesirable output – particularly if it is stored in such a way that it is also a *fire
hazard*. Introducing better procedures to process this could therefore eliminate two
negative outcomes in one stroke!

Procedures for agreeing designs and specifications

Your organisation probably has specific procedures in place to control:

● the way in which procedures are produced and documented
● the way in which procedures must be agreed.

As an example, it is usual for organisations designing procedures to conform
with ISO 9000 requirements to draw up a front sheet or title page giving
details of the designer and approver and numbering the procedure for
reference. This process is undertaken to prevent unauthorised procedures
being introduced. The front sheet may also include a brief description of
the procedure, its intended outcome, its scope (i.e. where and when to
apply the procedure) and whether it is mandatory or a guideline. An
example is shown in Figure 6.2.8. In this case the example used is very
specific and there are no occasions identified when the procedure would not

be implemented. The situation may be less clear-cut in other instances –
such as when to apply disciplinary procedures. Then more detailed
information on the intended scope of the procedure would be included.

RICHARDS AND WEBB PLC
OFFICIAL MANDATORY PROCEDURE TITLE: EXPENSE CLAIM PROCEDURES NO: 164/C DATE: 3 MAY 199–
DESCRIPTION OF PROCEDURE Procedure for handling, checking and processing completed expense claims prior to payment
OUTCOME OF PROCEDURE To achieve prompt and thorough checking and processing of all expense claims
SCOPE OF PROCEDURE To be applied when processing all expense claims without exception

Designed by:	Approved by:	Implemented from:

Figure 6.2.8 Example of a title page for a formal procedure

The agreement procedure is also strictly controlled to ensure that no
systems or procedures are implemented which have not been rigorously
checked and tested beforehand, or which do not conform to organisational
policies and objectives and any legal or regulatory requirements. This also
ensures that agreement with users, specialist advisers and decision-makers
has been reached before the design agreement stage. As with any system or
procedure, the aim is to control a particular process – in this case the
devising, designing, specifying and agreeing of systems and procedures.

Small organisations are less likely to operate formal agreement procedures
than are large organisations or those that are publicly accountable. In the
case of the former, the suggested designs and specifications may be the
subject of an informal discussion group concerning key users and decision-
makers as well as the designer, who may be expected to give a brief
presentation and overview of his or her proposals. It is useful to circulate
brief details of the proposals before the discussion so that those involved
have a basic understanding of the concept, which saves time on the day.
Obviously, if – as a designer – you have been working closely with your
user group and decision-makers from the outset, it is sensible to assume that
this discussion will contain no surprises but simply be the next stage in the
process. Whilst you may have to be prepared to field some unexpected
questions and to make some adjustments from suggestions received, often
an informal meeting such as this is merely a 'rubber-stamping' process
rather than an in-depth inquisition.

The opposite may be true if you work in a very large organisation with a large number of external stakeholders, if you are involved in the designing of particularly contentious or highly political proposals, or if certain groups are antagonistic towards your ideas. You may find that you are in a position of having to present and defend your suggestions before a large group of people, some of whom may be unfamiliar with your existing operations and procedures. It is to be hoped that in this situation you will have more than adequate support and assistance from your own line manager, and you should have prepared your case well in advance.

If you work in a highly political and competitive environment then it is sometimes more pragmatic not to spend too much time dotting every 'i' and crossing every 't' of your proposals if this means that your sense of ownership will be so great that you will be devastated if they are rejected. In such an organisational culture, a philosophical approach is often the only way to survive.

A more common problem for organisations that use a committee style of agreement process is that the range of suggestions for amendments can be fairly wide. However, these are more containable if you are present to argue your case and to answer questions and queries as they arise. The worst-case scenario is having to submit your proposals for due consideration when you will not or cannot be present to justify the decisions you have made. In this case your working documents must be of first-rate standard with clear cross-references where these are required. It is also useful to write a brief summary page which contains all the main information. (If the committee is hard-pressed, this may be all that they read!)

One tactic for dealing with a highly critical manager was successfully used by his administrator on a number of occasions. Knowing that her boss liked to find at least one or two faults to justify his existence, the administrator deliberately incorporated at least two clangers or grammatical errors into every document. The manager was so distracted finding and correcting these that he usually left the content untouched. However, this is not a tactic to be recommended!

Testing systems and procedures before implementation

A group or committee that is hesitant about giving its full backing to a suggested system or procedure may insist upon a period of 'testing and review' before implementation. This is particularly the case if there has been some opposition towards its introduction or if doubts have been expressed that all likely contingencies and ramifications have been covered. The aim of testing a system or procedure is to provide a 'dry run' to demonstrate that the behaviour of the system or the outcome of the procedure is the same as was proposed in the specification (see also the prototype approach on page 528).

In addition to committee or group requirements there are other very sensible reasons for suggesting this course of action. The following are examples.

- The designer is new to systems or procedures or new to the organisation.
- The system or procedure is highly complex.
- The cooperation of several different user groups is required.
- The designer or potential users feel that further feedback could usefully inform the process.
- The documentation is considerable and could usefully be revised by users testing the system.
- The system or procedure interacts with other existing systems or procedures to a considerable extent and the effect of this interaction is still unknown.
- The new system or procedure involves considerable costs if implemented across the whole organisation. Testing it in one area means there is less danger of wasted investment.
- It is difficult to determine the time-period for implementation. Testing would mean that this could be calculated more accurately.
- The system is crucial to organisational operations and failure would create severe disruption or unwelcome publicity. This is the reason why computerised payroll systems are usually introduced *in tandem* with manual systems at the outset, and why new systems and procedures that will involve customers and clients are usually tested thoroughly before 'going public'.
- The system or procedure is one that would only be implemented in an emergency (such as a fire procedure or a product recall procedure). In this case, testing, 'dry runs' and simulation are the only methods by which problems can be ironed out and staff training can take place.

The main difficulty arises when time is short. In this case there is a tendency in many organisations to neglect or abandon testing altogether. This may not matter with a simple or straightforward procedure. However, if the procedure concerns an important area, or if it relates to other procedures, or if a complex system is involved, then there may be serious consequences. It is arguable that if Eurochunnel had tested its safety procedures more rigorously the problems it experienced when a fire broke out would not have arisen – or at least, not to the extent they did.

If users are involved in the testing process it is important that they receive a clear brief as to their own contribution and the depth of analysis and comment that is expected. They must also be given time to undertake the task. Often a time limit is put on the testing process and the range of activities is limited to normal operations. Otherwise the delays incurred by in-depth testing against all possible criteria may be too costly if the system or procedure has to be constantly reworked and redesigned.

Your systems designer is thinking of introducing a new e-mail software package for staff. He considers this will be more beneficial as the updated software contains several new functions, even though the system is more complicated to use than the one currently installed on the network.

1 To what degree do you think that testing would be essential before the company invests in the upgraded software?
2 Who would you involve in the testing process, and why?
3 What limits or remits do you think should be given to the testers, and why?
4 Identify one example of a system or procedure in your organisation which:
   a   should have been tested but was not (or should have been tested more thoroughly than it was)
   b   required no testing.
   What was the consequence of the approach taken in (a) above?

Implement, evaluate and improve organisational systems and procedures

Element 7.1

Organise the implementation of systems and procedures

At the implementation stage it is assumed that plans and designs have been agreed by users and accepted by senior management, and that the system specification, which incorporates costs, timescale and benefits, has also been finalised.

This element examines the process undertaken to facilitate the implementation of a new or revised system or procedure so that minimal problems and disruptions to current work activities are experienced. As with many operations, the devil often lies in the detail, and these can only be considered in depth if the implementation process is itself carefully planned. If it is neglected, rushed or skimped then unexpected problems and disturbances are almost guaranteed.

Types of systems and procedures

You have already met several classifications of systems and procedures in Elements 6.1 (pages 490–491) and 6.2 (page 525). At the stage of planning implementation you can consider systems and procedures as:

- hard or soft
- operational or organisational
- completely new or redesigned
- recommended or mandatory
- simple or complex
- 'one-off' or involving ongoing continuous development
- internally focused or involving other stakeholders.

The reason for this type of analysis is to facilitate the identification of the major areas that must be considered at the implementation stage to minimise any difficulties, and to enable you to devise subsystems to deal with these at the outset. The analysis will also give useful guidance on the timescale for implementation and the resources you are likely to require.

Soft systems and procedures present more difficulties in implementation than *hard* systems and procedures because they involve less tangible issues, mainly relating to people. There are therefore user attitudes and existing skills and knowledge to take into account. On a scale of one to ten of 'softness', changing the stock procedure in the stationery store might rank as level 1 or 2, changing the office layout may rank as between 4 and 6 (depending upon the degree of change people will experience to their work group and working environment), and reorganising and restructuring the whole department to incorporate a new computer system may rank as 8 to 10. The higher the ranking, the greater consideration you must give to human needs, concerns and issues and the more emphasis you must place on excellent communications systems and comprehensive user support.

Operational systems or procedures are likely to be more constrained than those that are *organisational* – which may cross several boundaries and involve more cross-functional staff. If, for instance, you are introducing a new operating system which will affect only a small group of users, the training can be specifically geared to their particular needs and linked to their existing knowledge. If the new system or procedure involves virtually all employees in the organisation then the training requirements will be more varied and less easy to identify.

A *new* system or procedure has the disadvantage that users need to be encouraged to change their working practices completely. However, whilst there may be less new 'learning' for a *revised* system or procedure, staff do need to be encouraged to 'unlearn' existing practices.

Recommended practices or revised guidelines will need less monitoring in the early stages than *specified* or *mandatory* systems or procedures. In this case more detailed support and training is required by users.

Complex systems and procedures will need greater consideration and may be 'phased in' rather than introduced quickly so that possible difficulties can be evaluated and users can be acquainted with new methods of working on a more gradual timescale. The different implementation options available are discussed on pages 553–556.

Once *'one-off'* projects go live, there is usually a disbanding of any user groups – at least after an initial feedback and evaluation process (see Element 7.2). After that stage, the system or procedure may be virtually ignored until the next review is scheduled or the next systems audit takes place. In many organisations today, this approach has been rejected for all but the most basic systems, and there is a move towards *ongoing evolution and development* – more often known as *continuous improvement*. In this case, a user group may be maintained, even if in a diminished form. This is particularly the case where technological developments, product changes or external pressures constantly affect user needs. This aspect is discussed in more detail in Element 7.2.

Obviously all systems and procedures should be carefully tested and checked before implementation. A system that is clearly unworkable from day one destroys the confidence of users and the credibility of the designer and the design team. If the system or procedure is one that will also be used by *external stakeholders*, such as suppliers or customers, the organisation as a whole 'loses face' if the system crashes spectacularly – particularly if this is accompanied by adverse press publicity.

The Hoover company never fully recovered its image following its handling of a free flights offer. Not only were there inadequate systems in place to cope with the dramatic demand for free tickets, but the system itself was designed to put customers through a whole series of 'hoops' before they could qualify. To make matters worse, the company had no system in place for dealing with the ensuing crisis, and ignored or disclaimed press accusations of mismanagement and mishandling.

THEORY INTO PRACTICE

The unlearning and relearning process relating to revised systems and procedures has clear links with the 'unfreezing, changing and refreezing' strategies put forward by Kurt Lewin and described in Chapter 4. You may find it useful at this stage to refresh your memory on change management and the various reactions of individuals to change by referring back to pages 298–299.

Types and uses of implementation action plans

An implementation action plan is, quite literally, a plan of action that describes the process of implementation in some detail against a prearranged timeframe. Ideally it should also contain:

- information on the method of implementation to be used (often with a brief justification) – see pages 552–556
- details of the preparations that must be completed before implementation takes place
- information regarding the staff who will be involved in the implementation process and at what stage various groups of staff will be affected
- notes on supporting documentation and when and to whom this must be issued
- details of training requirements and how training will be undertaken
- information on other types of user support, such as help lines, memory joggers and section experts.

It is usual to prepare the action plan in consultation with users and decision-makers, as their support is often critical for successful implementation. Obviously, if 'users' implies all employees then it may be practical only to involve key users when gaining agreement for the action plan, and to utilise their support and knowledge by asking for their help in disseminating the information to other users in their particular sections or work groups.

Planning for implementation

Before the action plan can be completed, you would need to have considered, negotiated and agreed various issues, including the following.

- Is any refurbishment or redecoration required of working areas?
- Are there any equipment and installation requirements?
- Do you need any material resources, such as printed forms or other documentation? Bear in mind that if these are still in a developmental phase you may prefer to draft them in-house. It is plainly wasteful to arrange for external printing to be carried out until all documents have been finalised.
- Are any storage facilities required (and associated equipment and materials)?
- Will there be any changes to individual work activities and job contents, with implications for staff grading and pay scales?
- Will there be any adjustments in current working practices and workflow?
- What will be the length of time required for the dissemination of information? How will this dissemination process take place? (Remember, this will take longer and consist of different processes if external stakeholders are involved, particularly customers.)
- What will be the training requirements of users – both the 'who' and the 'how'? The first implies both the number of staff and any selection procedures that may be instigated; the second relates to the degree and level of training. For instance, should this be purely basic or to advanced level to facilitate continuous feedback and ongoing development?
- What will be the criteria for assessing the effectiveness of the system – both short-term and long-term?
- To what degree will the system be final when it is first implemented?
- How will the introduction of the new system or procedure be communicated to users?

Many of these issues should have been ongoing considerations since the design stage, others may be raised only later in the process. The basic point is that the more comprehensive your planning the less danger there is that something is left to chance. Implementation characterises the integration of all the system inputs simultaneously. This can be undertaken smoothly and harmoniously only if there are no potentially rogue aspects which have been overlooked.

Techniques for implementation planning

A variety of techniques can be used for planning all the aspects of implementation and for working out an appropriate timescale. In each case you are attempting to identify:

- the most appropriate order for sequencing the tasks
- which tasks can be carried out simultaneously and which must be sequential
- the total length of time required for implementation
- the resources that will be needed
- key areas of responsibility.

Flow charts

If the implementation process is reasonably straightforward you could design a flow chart that identifies the sequence of operations and the points at which decisions must be made – similar to the flow chart illustrated in Figure 6.2.6 on page 538.

Control charts

Another technique is to create a chart or planner that identifies the length of time and resources required for each part of the operation. This can be designed to show both sequential and concurrent activities and to display the earliest possible completion time. An example is shown in Figure 7.1.1. One type, known as a Gantt chart, enables actual performance to be plotted against planned performance so that this can be monitored more easily.

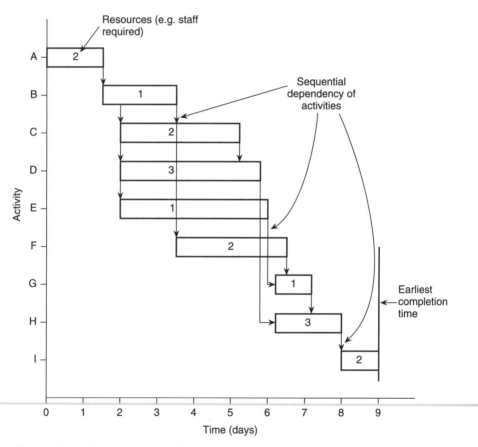

Figure 7.1.1 Example of a control chart

Critical path analysis

This technique involves identifying the various parts of the implementation process in a logical order and charting the maximum time period required. This is known as *critical path analysis* (CPA) – a variation is the *program evaluation and review technique* (PERT). In CPA, a chart is created which displays the relationships between the parts or phases of a project, with key activities identified according to anticipated time requirements. At this point the path requiring the *longest* time to accomplish is designated as the critical path. Any changes encountered on this path will either shorten or lengthen the entire project (and may contribute significantly to increased costs or cost savings).

A basic CPA diagram is shown in Figure 7.1.2. Note that the activities are often described in a key, rather than written on the actual diagram.

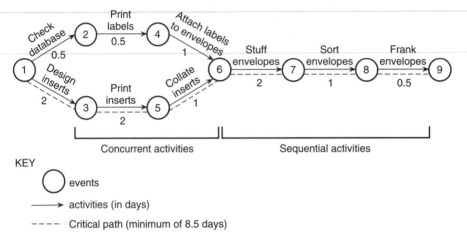

Figure 7.1.2 Critical path analysis for sending a mailshot

The implementation action plan

The information obtained from one of the foregoing charts or diagrams is agreed and then transferred to the *implementation action plan*. The format of this may be specified in some organisations, in others it is more variable. Quite often a simple columnar format is used showing the activity, the time period and the person responsible for undertaking the activity. An extract from such an action plan, drawn up from the CPA diagram in Figure 7.1.2, is shown in Figure 7.1.3. Note that a final column is provided for comments and updating – in other words to record actual events rather than planned events. This is useful for noting points that may have been overlooked or later significantly altered the plan. In this case, after implementation has been completed and the action plan consigned to the project file, it contains sufficient information to be used as a basis for future decision making related to similar projects.

A wide variety of software programs are available to help in the planning and scheduling of projects that incorporate a range of different activities, all of which must be integrated smoothly. For general project management, Microsoft's Project is ideal as it contains extensive planning and analysis facilities – including CPA. In other cases, statistical software such as Arcus' ProStat or Minitab may be more suitable.

Activity	Scheduled start time/date	Scheduled completion time/date	Staff member	Comments
Check database	0900/ 10.6.9-	1200/ 10.6.9-	JA	
Design inserts	10.6.9-	12.6.9-	DB	
Print database labels	1300/ 10.6.9-	1700/ 10.6.9-	JA	*Format incompatible with system; referred to Computer Services for conversion.*
Print inserts	12.6.9-	14.6.9-	CK	*Took $1\frac{1}{2}$ days; see attached spec, for future copies.*

Figure 7.1.3   Extract from an implementation action plan

Find out whether your organisation insists upon a particular format for implementation action plans or whether you would have a free hand with any such plans you wish to create or design.

Integrating the installation of systems and procedures with existing work flows and conditions

One problem for system developers is that, particularly when they have expended considerable effort on a complex project, they can become so immersed in the design and implementation that they forget the day-to-day operations being carried on by other staff. In reality, this is less likely to occur if, as an administrator, you are designing or revising a system or procedure for your own section. It is far more likely that *you* have been expected to do this job alongside your other duties – rather than undertaking systems design and implementation as a completely separate activity. You are more likely to be affected by this mentality if you work as part of a cross-functional specialist system design team and have less appreciation of the daily jobs being carried out by the end-users.

A good illustration of planning for the installation of new systems and procedures to link with existing conditions is that of architects and site engineers responsible for the introduction of new road systems. New road building must be planned and scheduled at the same time as schemes are devised for keeping the traffic moving. Diversions are usually kept to a minimum. The planners may use one diversion for traffic whilst building one stage of a new road, and then utilise the new section whilst the next one is completed. Alternatively, they may close a road completely for a short period and divert traffic away from it. In France, motorway contractors often build in discrete sections and link each stage to the existing road system until eventually the whole road is converted (see Figure 7.1.4). In Britain, we tend to build a new motorway in one go, and on the day after its completion open it in a blaze of publicity.

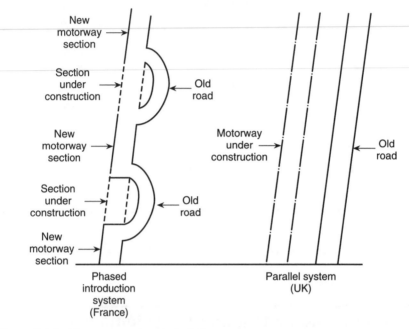

Figure 7.1.4 Two approaches to building motorways

In a similar way, you have a variety of choices on the method to use for implementation. You should note that whilst the following descriptions concentrate on systems implementation, to a lesser degree they are equally applicable to the implementation of procedures.

Parallel systems

In this case both the old and the new systems operate in parallel until the new system has been completed and satisfactorily 'debugged'. At the very least, there is a short 'overlap' period.

Advantages
- useful for providing fallback when a critical system is being changed (e.g. manual to computerised payroll system)
- helpful for external users (e.g. customers or clients) who may not have received any information on the new system
- almost essential if external users have paid for any type of privilege associated with the old system
- enables extending testing time whilst operations continue.

Disadvantages
- resource-heavy (often doubling staff requirements)
- confusing for staff
- may be completely impossible or impractical.

Phased introduction

This method allows the new system to be introduced in 'phases' – which may or may not be sequential.

Advantages
- useful for implementing a complex system or complicated series of subsystems
- reduces the time lag between finalisation of the design and introduction of the system
- enables users to become familiar with the new system on a 'step-by-step' basis
- the debugging or improvement of each phase, following feedback, can inform the next *before* its subsequent implementation.

Disadvantages
- users may become demotivated if they perceive a constant state of change
- overall timescale is difficult to plan – much depends upon problems encountered during each phased implementation
- can be difficult to identify separate, roughly 'equal' phases
- can be difficult to plan for smooth links between phases – overall operational success may be measurable only on completion.

Pilot scheme or 'dummy run'

In this method the system is finalised and tested by the designer and then given to key users to test further. Their feedback then informs the final design before full implementation. A variation of this approach is *partial implementation* when a new system is introduced section by section or department by department. In this case the 'user group' is determined on an organisation basis rather than selected by the designer for technical competence, keen interest or appreciation of the implications. Ideally, any trials will include some form of *stress testing* – so that the ability of the system to operate when having to cope with abnormal work loads or requests is tested as well as its capability for dealing with a normal range of activities.

Advantages
- key users or a test group can assist in debugging and finding errors to inform the final system
- useful suggestions are often received to inform future/further development
- method provides 'internal experts' who can then cascade or train other users
- useful when the final requirements of users are not fully known at the design stage.

Disadvantages
- needs of key users or test group may not be representative of all user groups
- time and resources required by testers
- testers must volunteer and have positive attitude for success; imposed testing often results in a 'Why us?' attitude and negative feedback
- dummy runs may not identify key organisational or cross-functional needs.

Overnight change

Tom Peters is keen on emphasising that change 'happens tomorrow or not at all'. Whilst the sentiments behind this statement may be appreciated, major change cannot always be so well planned that it can happen overnight. However, this approach does avoid the pitfall of 'good intentions' that come to naught – even if it can be equated with the short, sharp shock treatment!

Advantages
- users have no choice but to conform to new requirements
- reduces arguments and disagreements over minor points and perceived difficulties
- most economical method.

Disadvantages
- strong risk of chaos and losing face if it crashes
- high level of user support required both pre- and post-implementation
- costly mistakes may be made in the early days
- debugging more expensive and difficult following mass implementation.

THEORY INTO PRACTICE

For each of the following systems and procedures, identify (a) which method(s) you consider most suitable for implementation, (b) which methods you consider might be appropriate but are not ideal, and (c) which methods are definitely unsuitable. In each case be prepared to justify your choice. Then discuss your ideas with your adviser or assessor:

a a new computerised management information system across the whole organisation

b a revised customer service procedure for dealing with serious complaints

c a computerised stock control system for departmental stationery stocks

d a new procedure for recording and monitoring staff holiday entitlements

e a new switchboard and internal telephone/fax by computer system which incorporates ISDN services and Internet availability

f a new electronic filing system with its associated high-tech equipment including scanners, computers and relevant software.

Providing guidance for implementing systems and procedures

The type of guidance required at the implementation stage will depend upon:

- the degree to which users have been involved in the design and negotiation processes
- the number, disparity and type of users
- the degree of knowledge required by users
- the time period for implementation and method chosen
- the complexity of the system or procedure
- the culture or ethos of the organisation
- the degree of trauma involved with the change.

With the best will in the world, it is impossible to involve all users at all stages if you are involved in the design and implementation of a complex organisational system. It is also completely impractical if your new system or procedure will involve all your actual and potential customers!

Considering the user

There is a vast difference between the type of guidance required by a person who is a technical specialist and one who is a relatively uninformed customer. A navigational guidance system would be perfectly understandable if you had spent several years being trained and educated to an appropriate standard by the armed forces or were an expert in this area. To everyone else it would probably be virtually incomprehensible. For that reason the way in which the guidance is structured, designed and written must take into consideration previous knowledge and the degree to which understanding the new system is required.

As an example, consider the welfare benefits system. If you are not in receipt of benefits you simply need to know it exists and have a broad appreciation of what is available and who to contact for more information if you need it. If you are in receipt of benefits, you need to know the rules that apply to you and how to claim. If you are employed by the benefits office you need a far greater appreciation of the 'grey areas' and how to interpret the regulations. The vocabulary and style of writing, depth of information, type of graphics, method of communication and sheer volume of information will vary in each case.

Considering the time-period and complexity of the system or procedure

Ideally, guidance and communication will be a staged process – particularly for a complex system or procedure that is being introduced in one fell swoop. With a simple system or a basic revision to an existing system you may find that a brief training session and a user checklist/*aide mémoire* are all that is required. For a sophisticated system you may need some or all of the following stages in place.

- Initially basic information is provided to all possible users. This may consist simply of details of the system or procedure that is about to change, *why* it is changing and when the change will take place. Giving the reason and identifying the benefits normally helps to facilitate acceptance and reduces negativity. Write this document from the users' perspective – each of whom will be wondering 'what's in it for me?'
- The next stage is often to issue a timescale for the implementation of each stage of the new system – or the completion date for implementation. Make this realistic and keep to it! Otherwise you are safer to be non-committal about end-dates.
- Issue information about how guidance will be provided, the materials that will be issued and the specific training activities that have been arranged.
- Issue guidance and implement training plans (see the next main section).
- Obtain feedback on the success (or otherwise) of training activities. Remedy any deficiencies.

Post-implementation

- Provide helplines, on-screen support and/or assistance from internal or cross-functional experts from the date the system or procedure goes 'live'.
- Issue comprehensive user manuals for future reference.

Considering the culture and ethos of the organisation

It is a sad fact that, despite the reams of advice given by management experts on the importance and benefits of staff consultation and participation, in some organisations the emphasis is more on the stick than the carrot. This may be tolerated relatively amicably if systems changes have normally been found to have benefits for users, making their jobs easier or more interesting. However, if autocratic or 'Big Brother' management has been coupled with systems incompetence or the constant tinkering with existing systems to improve monitoring and control, or to reduce costs above all, then staff may have become totally disillusioned and disenchanted with the whole process. In this case, you are likely to have something of a problem on your hands. This is particularly so if only a few or even no potential end-users have been involved at any stage of the design process – so that the first communication they receive is a management edict saying what must be done and by when. Reactions can range from annoyance to rage and from apathy to active dissension.

It may be of some comfort for you to know that generally staff are more affected by their daily surroundings and the atmosphere in their own particular environment than by the machinations of senior management. If, therefore, you are introducing a system or procedure that affects only your own staff or department, then issuing comprehensive and timely guidance and promoting the positive benefits of the new practice may be all you need to obtain staff support.

Considering the trauma

Radical change, which threatens people's jobs, is probably the most traumatic type of event experienced in the workplace. If a new system is likely to result in redundancies or a severe disruption to previous work patterns, work groups or status, then there will undoubtedly be considerable resistance. Indeed, studies have shown that, in a redundancy situation, staff who are *not* selected are often badly affected by guilt when their colleagues lose their jobs and perceive taking on duties previously undertaken by their colleagues as disloyal and tantamount to collaboration with the enemy.

To try to reduce the trauma, many of the more caring organisations have introduced counselling sessions and have been prepared to pay for outplacement counselling – aimed at helping redundant staff to find new jobs more quickly. Professional counselling services may also be made available for staff who have to remain and who are concerned about their ex-colleagues, worried about their own job security and their ability to cope with new or increased responsibilities. From a slightly different perspective, this type of activity can also be classified as 'support'.

THEORY INTO PRACTICE

An educational establishment wanted to monitor staff holiday entitlement more tightly. It also wanted to ensure that all academic areas were covered over the summer to ensure that enquiries were handled both promptly and accurately. Unfortunately, the 'message' communicated to staff focused on the first objective, rather than the second.

Each member of staff was entitled to up to four consecutive weeks' holiday over an eight-week period. To obtain full coverage of each department, ideally staff cooperation was required so that not all staff would take their four weeks' holiday in consecutive weeks. However, this aspect was ignored at the planning stage. Instead, a grid was devised (see Figure 7.1.5) into which staff were instructed to enter their initials to show their holidays. At the time the grid was issued many people had still to make their arrangements. In addition, there was no indication on the grid whether initials should be entered on the weeks staff would be in or out. The result was total confusion. During the summer, when managers tried to monitor the system, they found that staff gave one of three reasons for not following the rota:

a their own plans had changed unexpectedly

b they had been asked to come in at the last minute to cope in an emergency

c they had entered their initials in the wrong way.

This made the system virtually unworkable and unenforceable. If you were given the job of completely redesigning the system for the following year *and making it acceptable to staff*, what would you do, and why?

HOLIDAY ROTA/DEPARTMENTAL COVER

Please complete with your initials.

Note that all staff are entitled to a maximum of 4 consecutive weeks.
All departments must be covered for each week.

w/c 6/7	w/c 13/7	w/c 20/7	w/c 27/7	w/c 3/8	w/c 10/8	w/c 17/8	w/c 24/8

Figure 7.1.5 An imprecise system

Types of training support

The type of training and training support materials required for potential users will obviously vary depending upon the complexity of the system or procedure and the planned method of implementation. In some circumstances specific training provision will be required, in other cases this may not be necessary. In other cases, comprehensive documentation or formal guidelines may be required. At a basic level, a brief checklist may suffice.

Training provision

Issues to consider include:

- whether specific training provision is required
- whether informal or formal training sessions are more appropriate
- whether training support should take place on an individual, random group, working group or team basis
- whether user needs can be covered in one session or whether a series of training sessions need to be arranged
- whether different types of sessions should be held for different types of users
- the type of support materials required.

Other key considerations include the following.

Who should do the training

Bear in mind that anyone responsible for carrying out the training needs to be fully competent and conversant with the new system and procedures, sympathetic to user needs, 'acceptable' to users (in terms of professional credibility and style) and able to communicate with users effectively. A technical specialist may be excellent from the knowledge and skills perspective but find it difficult to make him or herself clearly understood. A good communicator or experienced trainer may not have the requisite background knowledge. However, the choice of trainer is often crucial to the success of the sessions.

When to carry out training

Ideally there should be adequate training before the system or procedure is introduced, followed by backup and review sessions later. However, 'when' also encompasses times and days. You may find you have less than active support from staff if the only time you can find when everyone is available is during lunchtime every day for a week or between 6 pm and 7 pm each evening! If you are trying to train staff to use a vital new system or procedure, then it is important that consideration be given to releasing staff from their operational duties to undertake training activities during normal working hours, which has obvious cost implications.

How the training should be organised

A wide range of activities are available (see Figure 7.1.6) and obviously the most appropriate for the situation should be selected.

Where the training sessions should be held

The environment can be important – even the layout of the seats might affect learner attitudes. A formal 'cinema' style seating arrangement implies a 'tell' approach, whereas more informal groupings of chairs indicate a more participative atmosphere.

- One-to-one tuition from an experienced colleague ('sitting with Nellie')
- Demonstration and practice ('tell/show/do' sessions)
- Computer-based training
- Seminars and/or workshops
- Coaching
- Videos
- Structured activities
- Role-plays and CCTV feedback

Figure 7.1.6 Training and learning support activities

Preparations prior to the start of the training sessions

These include:

- booking the accommodation (if necessary)
- organising for essential equipment to be available (particularly important if computers and relevant software must be available)

- arranging for suitable resources, such as flipchart, overhead projector, whiteboard, video and CCTV
- designing and preparing handouts, training manuals or user manuals
- deciding the content to be covered in each training session
- deciding how you will evaluate the success or failure of each training session in meeting its objectives.

Do be aware that there is a limit to the amount of information people can understand and remember at one session. It is therefore useful to prepare a summary of the main information for participants to take away with them afterwards. This can be supplemented with more in-depth materials later, which can be made available at the point of operation.

You cannot evaluate the success of a training session unless you are clear about:

- the objectives of each session
- the outcomes you wish to achieve
- the type of evidence you will accept to prove that the training has been successful.

Various methods are used to obtain this evidence. On NVQ schemes, such as the one you are following, documentary and verbal evidence is required and this may be supplemented with witness testimony and observational reports. You may be satisfied by setting a practical activity, a role-play or a simulation and observing how satisfactorily staff perform these activities. Some training programmes are evaluated through the completion of questionnaires by participants at the end of each session. The design of these questionnaires is critical to their value. Those with very general questions, quickly answered by ticking a box, are usually less informative than those that require more detailed consideration by participants – although the latter are often skimped if they are issued at the end of a full day of training. Do bear in mind, however, that if several people report that there are certain key issues they do not understand, it will be up to you to rectify the problem!

Training support materials

The most common type of support material is a user manual which includes any formal guidelines users must follow. Most people are familiar with support materials – they are provided routinely with household and electrical appliances, cars, computers and audio/visual equipment. In some cases, a simple booklet or leaflet or even one-page instruction sheet is sufficient. 'Formal guidelines' (often linked to health and safety) may be highlighted or illustrated for emphasis. However, from personal experience, everyone knows the difference between the manual or booklet that is user-friendly and the one that is not – the latter is usually consigned to a dusty shelf after a few fruitless attempts at fathoming its contents. The difficulty often occurs when the manual or information sheet has been written by a technical specialist with little appreciation of the needs of others. There are basic rules to follow to avoid this problem:

- Keep manuals or information sheets as short and simple as possible.
- Include important guidelines or formal guidelines at the start and highlight these clearly.
- Use a new page for each operation and number the pages.
- Use clear headings and bullet points for a sequence of events – or a flow chart – to avoid 'wordy' explanations.
- Use clear, simple English and avoid jargon and pretentious phrases.
- Have clear sections with a contents page at the start and, if necessary, a short index at the end.
- Include graphics where these would make points clearer.
- Adopt a logical sequence, such as:
  - start with routine operations
  - progress to more complex situations
  - include a 'trouble-shooting' ('what to do when something goes wrong') guide
  - give details of further backup and support available (e.g. user helplines, departmental experts who can be contacted, etc.).
- Include a 'suggestions' form, which users can return if they spot a way in which your system or procedure can instantly be improved beyond all recognition! This is particularly useful if the system or procedure will be subject to continuous or ongoing development.

In addition, the presentation must be such that it is not only *easy* to read, it positively asks to be used!

There have been many criticisms of the new system of self-assessment that has been introduced by the Inland Revenue. One of the main unions representing Inland Revenue staff, the Public Services, Tax and Commerce Union, has reported that in some areas approximately half of the 8.5 million new tax returns sent back by the public have been incorrectly completed – resulting in a hugely increased workload for staff trying to check and return the forms. A common problem appears to be taxpayers leaving parts of their return blank or adding unacceptable comments, such as 'see P60' or 'please refer to employer'. Others have been more creative and tried to adapt the form for their own needs by writing their own questions and drawing in their own boxes!

The problem has been exacerbated by the fact that there were over 15 000 redundancies in the Inland Revenue service between 1992 and 1997 – increasing the burden on remaining staff and making it extremely difficult for them to cope with the new system. However, other problems have allegedly been caused by:

- the Revenue overestimating people's ability to deal with a very complicated form
- setting penalties for late completion, which has resulted in taxpayers rushing to complete and return the forms
- complicated procedures for calculating tax (according to several authorities, the *Tax Calculation Guide* – issued with the form – is neither logical nor easy to understand by anyone who is neither a professional accountant or has a natural aptitude for complex calculations)

- delays in installing the software to enable tax returns to be processed
- no additional time or resources for staff to cope with their day-to-day work plus the additional workload.

To help taxpayers the Revenue have installed a helpline on 0645 000444. Accountants, in every high street in Britain, are also busier than ever giving advice and assistance to their clients.

THEORY INTO PRACTICE

Try to obtain a copy of a self-assessment form and *Tax Calculation Guide*. Evaluate the form and the support materials and give your opinion on whether you think:

a such a system was so complicated it was doomed to failure at the outset

b the system is feasible, but the support materials require a complete review

c the support materials are appropriate in every respect.

Compare your answer with the views of your adviser or assessor.

Legal and regulatory requirements relating to implementation

The main requirements were discussed at the end of Element 6.2 on pages 540–542. However, when you are planning the implementation of systems and procedures and organising training provision for end-users, frequently the two main areas you need to consider are those relating to health and safety and to data protection and security of information.

Health and safety

In this context you should be concerned with health and safety issues during training activities. This topic was covered comprehensively in Element 1.2.

Data protection

In this context you should be concerned with the confidentiality of information which users can access during training, particularly if this is held on computer. Computer training sessions also need to be carefully controlled to prevent new users failing to follow procedures implemented to reduce the possibility of viruses being introduced on to the system or the system being susceptible to 'hacking'. Apparently, however, the biggest problem for many organisations involved in computer-based training sessions is new users surfing the Internet!

Equal opportunities

A final area to consider when scheduling implementation or arranging training is that of equal opportunities. If you work in a politically sensitive organisation it may be sensible to work out your user rota so that you cannot be accused of discriminating against any particular groups at the implementation or training stages.

Legal and regulatory considerations relating to training were covered fully in Element 1.1 on pages 49–52. Turn back to that section now and refresh your memory on the key requirements to bear in mind at this stage of your systems process.

Element 7.2

Evaluate the effectiveness of systems and procedures, and identify opportunities for improvement

It may be tempting to see this as the last stage in the process of systems or procedural development. In truth, experienced practitioners will tell you that *good* systems and procedures are so regularly evaluated and re-evaluated that the process is virtually unending. Therefore, all the best systems and procedures are the result of an ongoing process of feedback and readjustment by which means they are constantly improved or recustomised for new and emerging user needs.

This element covers the reasons why feedback is necessary, the methods that can be used to obtain it, strategies to use when evaluating feedback, and how suggestions can be utilised effectively to inform the development process. The aim is to monitor organisational systems and procedures to achieve better quality and a faster work throughput, to increase 'added value' to users and customers, to cope with change, and to foster the *kaizan* system of continuous improvement.

Types of systems and procedures

One basic way of categorising systems and procedures in this context is to describe them as those that are relatively easy to monitor and control and those that are not. Whilst this may seem rather trite, it enables you to move towards a more sophisticated delineation.

Figure 7.2.1 shows systems and procedures divided into four broad categories.

- *Discrete*. An operational system or procedure may be discrete and static. In this case it relates only to your own area of responsibility and the remit rarely changes. Indeed, you might be the only person who uses it! This is the easiest system to monitor and control.
- *Multifunctional*. At organisational level, too, there will be systems and procedures which are relatively static and unchanging and used by staff from a variety of departments. An obvious example is the internal mail system. This, too, should only need routine monitoring and control.
- *Developmental*. At operational level, you may be involved in implementing more dynamic systems and procedures. In this case there is a greater likelihood of change, through internal or external

pressures. Examples include systems and procedures related to information technology, where change occurs regularly because of increasingly sophisticated hardware and software and/or because of changing user needs. In this case there is a greater emphasis on continuous monitoring and control.

- *Evolutionary*. Finally, at organisational level, there are complex systems and procedures which are used by a variety of people, all with varying needs, and where the needs of users are constantly evolving and the type of system or procedures may frequently change. An example is a computerised management information system which is used by a vast number of staff for different reasons and where the demands for information may be subject to frequent revisions.

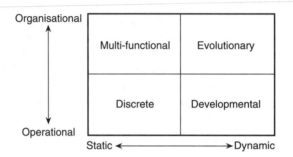

Figure 7.2.1 Types of systems and procedures

Unless you are a systems specialist, it is unlikely that you will be asked to take sole responsibility for evaluating and improving the latter. However, certainly within your own area of responsibility it is likely that you will be expected to undertake this type of task, particularly for systems you have designed and implemented. Secondly, you may also be asked to contribute towards the evaluation and improvement of more complex systems and procedures – especially if you work for an organisation where user suggestions, initiatives and contributions are actively welcomed, or where an organisational system or procedure links to your own area of expertise or an area in which you have a particular interest.

The basic points you should note at this stage include the following.

- Relatively static systems and procedures may be subject to periodic reviews for updating purposes. Apart from these instances they may be left alone.
- Dynamic systems and procedures, on the other hand, may be reviewed regularly or even on an ongoing basis, with specialist staff employed solely for this purpose.
- Operational systems and procedures are often concerned with day-to-day output and quality. In this case, monitoring relates to whether staff are carrying out their duties effectively and to the deadlines specified. At regular intervals you may also be expected to evaluate the efficiency of these systems in relation to costs and the ratio of inputs to outputs. A

problem with the system obviously must be corrected, but finding there is a problem does not usually indicate a major emergency.

- Organisational systems and procedures frequently incorporate wider ramifications, particularly where they are concerned with providing information or communications to the whole organisation and are essential for achieving organisational plans and targets. In this case, there are concerns relating to the control of the organisation *per se*. If the budgeting system fails or the computer network crashes in a big way then the consequences can be extremely serious. In this case, not only must emergency procedures be implemented immediately but fundamental design changes may be indicated to prevent the problem recurring. This has associated resource implications.

A system or procedure that is constantly changing is difficult to measure with any precision because the state in which it exists is never the same. It is like shooting at a moving target! As an example, imagine you are watching a cricket match and someone asks you for the score. Within seconds of reporting this accurately the total number of runs may have changed, so your 'report' was only accurate for a very short time-period. Therefore you may need a different method of accurately describing the state of the system at any given moment, such as by identifying the objectives that comprise it. This concept is known as the *state–space approach*. Thus the reprographics system may be defined at any moment by the number of machines, operators, amount of paper, work in progress levels, etc. The *update process* is any process that changes the system, such as the addition of an extra machine or member of staff or the undertaking of different tasks which reduces the work-in-progress levels. This approach may be suitable only for a discrete system because the different states can be measured and compared. For a truly continuous system that changes very rapidly it may not be appropriate, as the state in which it existed previously may not be known – such as the amount of traffic on a busy road junction.

THEORY INTO PRACTICE

Viruses cause havoc in organisations that hold critical information on computer. These days, this means virtually every company. The additional problem of Internet access is the danger of downloading a virus – and warnings are often e-mailed to users to warn them of the danger. Most organisations wisely invest in virus detection packages to help to minimise the problem. Otherwise they run the risk of having a large number of files erased or contaminated. Whilst the cost of replacement is huge, the difficulties of operating without a major information base are enormous and can lead to lost opportunities and lost business.

Check the systems and procedures in your organisation to prevent contamination of your computer system by a virus. Find out how often these are reviewed to check that they cope with newly identified viruses. If no systems are in place, this could be the first area you volunteer to investigate. Over time, you could save your company from a major disaster and from substantial financial loss.

Obtaining feedback on the effectiveness of systems and procedures

Systems and procedures need re-evaluating at regular intervals for a variety of reasons.

- External changes can mean a different system or procedure is required, for economic, technological, social or political reasons. They can encompass new laws and regulations which affect existing systems and procedures (see also pages 581–584).
- Users are on a learning curve. After the system or procedure has been in operation for some time there is a greater appreciation of its capabilities and how it can be developed to meet new or additional needs.
- Many new systems and procedures need 'debugging' at the outset, and some problems are identified only after the system or procedure has been operating for some time. It is often the case, for instance, that a system or procedure is seen as being inflexible or incapable of coping with problem situations that are encountered only after the original implementation process has been accomplished.
- A system or procedure may be considered unworkable or lose credibility because of inaccurate information or because it creates more problems than it solves. In this case a complete redesign may be required.

THEORY INTO PRACTICE

A useful 'test' for the effectiveness of a computerised information system is shown in Figure 7.2.2. Either score an information system in operation in your own workplace against this checklist, or redesign the checklist to customise it for a system or procedure you are currently reviewing. Note that a low score signals that a re-evaluation is well overdue in the area you have chosen.

Allocate each answer with a score of 1–5, where 1 = poor, 2 = fair, 3 = average, 4 = good, 5 = excellent.

1 The information provided is accurate.
2 The information provided is useful.
3 The information is provided promptly.
4 The information is in a form that is readily understandable.
5 I can clarify questionable issues quickly.
6 Information can be updated quickly and easily.
7 The system is flexible and meets changing needs.
8 I am given guidance on areas where problems are being encountered.
9 The system enables me to control key areas of my job more easily.
10 The system is not overly prescriptive.

Figure 7.2.2 Checklist for an effective information system

Monitoring and controlling systems and procedures

You will remember that for control to be effective it must link to the objectives of the system or procedure. Quite simply, it is impossible to establish satisfactory criteria for evaluation if the whole purpose is hazy or unclear.

Obtaining feedback on the appropriate criteria is absolutely essential if you are to measure the effectiveness of the system or procedure (e.g. its 'quality' objectives) and its efficiency (e.g. its ratio of input to output objectives). You also need to know the relationship between the system and organisational policies, rules and regulations. Examples include systems and procedures for allowing credit, which should link to the company's credit policies, and systems and procedures for accepting returns, which should dovetail with the company policy on returned goods.

The first stage is to select the characteristics you wish to assess. These must correlate with the main objectives, and your life will be easier if these are both measurable and capable of being isolated. Ideally, these will have already been specified as part of the design process and clear, measurable targets will already be in place. However, quantitative measures and targets are not always appropriate. (In New York, when the police were faced with measurable arrest targets, they reacted by locking up virtually everyone they could find!) If you work in the public sector, you may find appropriate measurable targets very difficult to isolate. Considering a doctor to be efficient because he or she can see 100 patients in an hour has obvious flaws! Generally you will need to identify several aspects, such as:

- speed of work
- quality of work
- resources used
- standards of service

and will attach suitable measurements of control to each one. This may include such aspects as waiting time, safety issues, turn-round time, etc. It is also important to note that obtaining customer feedback is an important part of any system or procedure that directly affects customers as users. Staff perceptions, for instance, of customer waiting time or inconvenience may be rather different from those of the customers themselves.

In addition, bearing in mind that you are evaluating the actual system or procedure, it is a good idea to identify a method of evaluating user opinions on the 'usability' or 'user-friendliness' of the system or procedure itself. Bear in mind that you need also to determine the standards you expect the system to reach. This should be done *before* obtaining feedback – otherwise there is a huge temptation to 'massage' your findings to fit the standards you hope to obtain. The objective approach means you will have pre-set these according to internal/external benchmarks, specific target ratios or records of past performance. These should relate, in turn, to the agreed budget and proposed costs and benefits identified at the time the system or procedure was designed.

At this stage you have to determine:

- how to obtain the feedback
- how to assess that the feedback is both valid and reliable.

You should also note that your aim is not just to measure performance but to control your system. Your focus is on identifying improvements and constructive ways of bringing performance up to standard, rather than dwelling on past failures and problems.

Methods of obtaining feedback

Feedback can be obtained by both formal and informal methods.

Formal methods include:

- devising and issuing questionnaires to users
- undertaking an in-depth cost–benefit analysis
- holding a formal review meeting
- setting up an evaluation/review group.

These types of method are appropriate for a formal annual review or if a systems audit is being undertaken. However, it is a rather dangerous and complacent practice to ignore a system or procedure until a formal review takes place. For that reason, there are also occasions on which you will wish to obtain more regular, informal feedback from users – particularly those in your own area of responsibility.

Informal methods include:

- talking to users
- observation of working practices
- informal discussion groups
- using the system or procedure yourself.

The difficulty with informal methods is that they are less precise and more open to individual interpretations by users – particularly if there is no set agenda. The dangers to be aware of include forceful individuals deflecting interest away from general issues to pursue their own interests, a free-ranging discussion that encourages feedback but is almost impossible to control, and conflict of opinions. It is therefore sensible to identify the main areas on which you require feedback and communicate these first – both to contain any discussions and to focus them on critical areas of importance. This can then be followed with an 'any other business' general feedback session for less crucial areas.

A checklist for system designers to use as an evaluation tool is shown in Figure 7.2.3. This gives an indication of the areas that can be assessed. However, it is not exhaustive and would require customising for particular systems and procedures that you are evaluating.

1 The system is economically realistic.
2 Control is concentrated on key strategic activities.
3 The system links with existing workflow activities.
4 The system clearly links with organisational policies and practices.
5 The system regularly achieves its goal(s).
6 The system has positive links with other systems and procedures in operation.
7 The system is suitable for the purpose for which it was designed.
8 The system has been accepted by users.
9 The system is regularly used by users and managers.
10 Users understand the system and obtain clear benefits from its operation.
11 Feedback from users is positive.
12 The system has improved the quality and timeliness of information available.
13 It is clear where responsibility lies for the re-evaluation and control functions linked to the system.
14 The control aspects are clearly understood by all users.

Figure 7.2.3 Checklist for system designers

Validity of feedback

Validity is an interesting concept. It means that any arguments put forward are based on sound reasoning and contain no misconceptions or assumptions. Given there are a variety of misconceptions about systems, it is interesting to investigate validity from this viewpoint.

Assume you are talking to three colleagues who have different views about systems:

TOM   All systems are rubbish. We had them at my last place and they never worked. Let's not waste our time on this.

DICK   No, no – the more systems the better. That way everyone knows what to do. The more systems we have, the better the organisation will be run.

HARRY   Surely there's a time and a place for systems? A good system, at the right time will help provided it is well designed and not overly prescriptive. A bad system can make matters worse, not better.

Your tendencies ought to lean towards agreeing with Harry more than his colleagues! In fact, although you may instinctively feel that both Tom and Dick are each prejudiced in their own ways, you could also argue that each is putting forward an invalid argument. Both of their statements start with a broad generalisation or sweeping statement, rather than a precise definition. The second statement may be either true or false but the third is an invalid conclusion drawn from the assumption that both of the foregoing statements are completely accurate in every respect. You may also find that people have a tendency to introduce irrelevancies into statements which support their assumptions. These, too, should be discounted.

Validity can be measured by the degree to which statements are accurate, precise, logical and can be tested for accuracy and applicability in a wide variety of circumstances. By this measure, although you may support Harry's views, he would fail the test for validity because he is putting forward a personal viewpoint which is bereft of data to back up his arguments. If this information was supplied in a later explanation you could accept his statements as valid.

Reliability of feedback

Reliability relates to the ability of an item to perform in the same way on a large number of occasions. If you were testing a car for reliability, for instance, you would drive under a range of different conditions, note down the performance and then describe its reliability in relation to the number of times it failed to perform, performed adequately or performed well. In layman's terms you may describe the car as 'reliable, dependable – can be trusted to perform in a variety of conditions'.

System reliability is obviously important. We have already discussed the danger of systems that are unreliable, fail to perform or crash creating major problems. However, to ascertain whether feedback is useful, you also need to assess the data or information you are receiving for reliability. The techniques that can be used to assess reliability are described in the next section.

Ways of evaluating feedback

Feedback is usually *positive* or *negative*, but rarely neutral. It can comprise hard or soft data, that is, facts and figures or suggestions and opinions.

Analysing hard data

Detailed techniques for undertaking statistical analysis, calculating probability factors and mathematically processing data are beyond the scope of this book. However, it is worth noting some of the main points relating to the analysis of hard data to test for accuracy and reliability.

Testing for reliability requires the collection of data to assess performance over a period of time. This enables the mean, or average, level of performance to be identified. Generally, a more accurate picture is obtained through the compilation of a *frequency distribution table* which illustrates the actual patterns of performance more precisely and minimises errors of assumption.

A range of data collection techniques are available. These include consideration of the total number to be sampled, method of sampling, identifying whether the sample selected is representative of the total, and deciding whether a control group should be established. The frequency with which data is collected will vary depending upon its type, importance and usage. An additional option is whether historic data should be examined to test the reliability of current data.

Data can be weighted, so that the most important data is given additional importance in any mathematical calculations. A similar technique is to prepare a *Pareto diagram* which concentrates on the items that contribute most to the final effect. Ideally these should represent the key *performance indicators* or *targets* to be achieved.

Plotted data has a tendency to show a *normal curve of distribution* (see Figure 7.2.4). This illustrates a few cases of extremely low or high performance and a high level of median performance. A skewed curve often indicates something unusual is occurring and usually needs investigation.

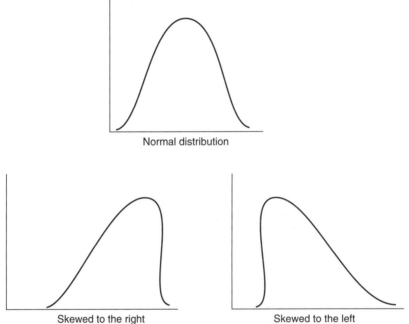

Normal distribution

Skewed to the right   Skewed to the left

Figure 7.2.4 Distributions

Correlation analysis is undertaken to identify the relationship between two sets of variables. This usually means drawing a *scatter graph* to confirm or disprove the relationship. A positive correlation means that the two are related and if one increases so will the other. A negative correlation indicates that as one increases the other will decrease. In some cases there may be no correlation or relationship at all (see Figure 7.2.5).

The *Pareto effect* is often known as the 80/20 rule and can be applied to a wide range of situations. For instance, 80 per cent of the world's wealth is owned by 20 per cent of the population, 20 per cent of the clothes in your wardrobe you wear 80 per cent of the time, and 20 per cent of the items in any stock inventory usually account for 80 per cent of the turnover. By concentrating upon feedback relating to the Pareto items in the stock inventory, greater control can be achieved quickly and more easily.

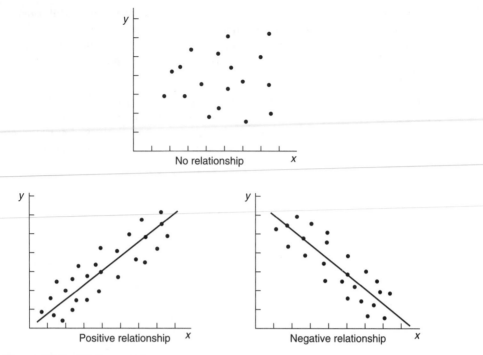

Figure 7.2.5   Scatter graphs

THEORY INTO PRACTICE

If a group of pupils are taking an examination, it is usual for the results to display a normal curve of distribution. A curve skewed to the right indicates that either the examination was easy, the teacher was excellent or the pupils were all of above-average ability. A curve skewed to the left would imply the opposite. Your perception on what should be done about this would depend upon whether the figures were national or from one school, and whether you were a pupil, teacher, head or examining board official.

Assume you have systematically obtained data on work throughput in your department per day and have found (a) a curve skewed to the right, or (b) a curve skewed to the left.

1 What do you consider this would imply, in *each* case?
2 How might your judgement be affected if your department's performance were significantly better than other departments?
3 How might your perception differ if you were a member of staff, the departmental manager, the manager of a different department, or the Chief Executive or MD?

Analysing soft data

Soft data is more difficult to test for accuracy and reliability, although you can borrow some of the techniques above, such as correlation analysis.

However, in this case you are more likely to be scrutinising the source of the data rather than the content of the information – and testing this for reliability. If the person who provides the opinion or judgement is very experienced, is not easily prone to exaggeration and has given you excellent information in the past, then – in your mind – there will be a positive correlation between that person and the reliability of their feedback. With some other individuals you may have no past experience (there is therefore no definitive relationship) or you may have been badly misinformed on a number of occasions, leading to a definite negative correlation. You will hold the same perceptions about other types of sources, such as filing systems, computer systems, departments and external advisers.

Whilst you are unlikely to keep a scatter graph for every time you receive information from a particular source, it is worth noting that the technique of *triangulation* is useful for assessing reliability of feedback. When you receive information that is questionable, test it with as many reliable sources as are realistically possible to see if you receive confirmation or otherwise. One danger is that you will receive the same information on several occasions, but it all emanates from one unsound source! You should also be aware that there is a significant difference between facts and opinions. In particular you must be careful to discriminate between:

- independent, uniform and objective facts which substantiate opinions
- opinions that have no facts to support them
- facts that have been manipulated, twisted or distorted to support a particular opinion (this is the strategy of an experienced operator – who may be prepared to supply facts, but only those that prove their own previously formed opinion!).

Remember that you are looking for objective and comprehensive factual evidence or collective opinions based on sound facts wherever possible.

> An experienced salesperson with an American company alleged that there was a high correlation between the sale of nappies and beer. He was laughed at by his colleagues until the data was analysed and supported his findings. Later investigations proved that this occurred only when the two products were sited close together in sales outlets. It transpired that men asked to babysit or to buy baby things treated themselves to a 6-pack or a can as a reward!

Identifying and evaluating improvements to systems and procedures

The range of improvements you are likely to recommend must be compatible with the overall objectives and policies of both the organisation and the original system or procedure specification which was submitted. Generally, you are likely to recommend one of the following types of improvements:

- *corrective action* – to rectify specific problems and errors in the original system or procedure

- *adaptive action* – to change the system or procedure to cope with new requirements such as legislative or regulatory amendments
- *continuous improvement* – to review the system or procedure constantly, to improve efficiency and enhance performance overall.

Corrective action

The sequence of activities to ensure that each system or procedure is improved involves:

- identifying problems and difficulties encountered by users
- isolating each problem or difficulty in order to establish its severity and identify the most appropriate improvements in each case
- investigating problems and possible causes to identify the degree to which adjustments are essential and the degree to which they are justified
- identifying and implementing appropriate and cost-effective methods of making improvements.

The system or procedure must then be re-evaluated to check that the improvement has been achieved as planned.

Identifying and isolating problems or difficulties

The issues identified following the feedback evaluation process described in the previous section are a major remit of any review activities, or any evaluation or user group concerned with the development and improvement of the system or procedure as a whole.

Isolating problems or difficulties is essential if any improvements are to be successful. The danger in omitting this stage is that the system or procedure is viewed as 'needing improvements', and the solution is one of 'incremental tampering', which may solve one problem and instantly create another. Isolating a problem means that accurate causal links can be established and the *effects* of making any changes are viewed in relation to their interaction with other parts of the system or procedure.

In an earlier section, for example, you were invited to evaluate the user documentation for the Inland Revenue self-assessment system. Several problems were being experienced with incorrect form completion and processing. However, investigation showed that some mistakes on the form could easily be rectified by Inland Revenue staff at the inputting stage. Others could not. If all the problems had been identified in the same way, the solution could have been to return *all* incorrect forms to the originators. By isolating the problems in terms of 'types of errors', different – and more appropriate – solutions were suggested in each case.

Investigating problems and causes

You would hardly reorganise the mailroom system in your organisation because it failed to operate on the day of a mail strike, or put the entire department through a retraining session because a temporary employee made a mistake completing a form. Whilst these examples are extreme, they illustrate the need to identify the *cause* of a particular problem, establish the likelihood of its recurrence, and identify cost-effective methods of improving the situation. From that perspective, key factors include:

- the severity of the problem (i.e. whether it is superficial or critical in relation to key performance indicators)
- the frequency with which the problem occurs in relation to the frequency with which it could be expected to occur or could be tolerated
- whether or not the problem could have been foreseen
- whether it was created by factors internal to the system, internal to the organisation or external.

Some problems may have multiple causes. For instance, delays in work throughput could be caused by increased demand, more complex activities or staff absence. Staff absence may be through sickness, a high level of staff turnover or annual holiday entitlement. A flu epidemic cannot be foreseen but *some* absences through sickness can be expected, and annual holidays should be scheduled in advance. The implication for system evaluators is therefore different in each case. Failure to meet targets may be for a variety of reasons – including inappropriate target setting, unrealistic standards of achievement, inadequate support for staff or unforeseeable external events. Only after all the possible causes have been identified and the implications fully discussed should possible solutions be considered.

There is an unfortunate tendency in organisations for:

- solutions to be suggested (and even implemented) before causes have been fully investigated – this amounts to 'jumping to conclusions'
- numerical data to be accorded greater importance than other facts and supported opinions
- external factors to be ignored or discounted because they are less 'controllable'.

A recent paper published by accountants Price Waterhouse on 'value reporting' argues that companies often lose out when financial and quantifiable targets are seen as the only aspects that are important. This is substantiated by Robert Kaplan and David Norton in their recent book *The Balanced Scorecard*, which argues for a better mix of performance measures. According to the authors, some of these should be financial, others should be related to customer service and other factors. However, all should be expressed in quantitative terms. A further study by KPMG confirmed that customer service is often neglected to satisfy the needs of the accountants. The argument is that successful management incorporates understanding, judgement and instinct and there is scope for recognising that not everything of value is necessarily measurable. The key is finding the balance.

Recommending improvements

It is fairly obvious that if the cause of a particular problem has been correctly analysed then it is a logical step to identify and suggest an appropriate improvement. However, in many cases there are 'trade-offs' between an improvement in one area and a deterioration in another.

An example is the old chestnut of 'quantity' versus 'quality'. If it is decided to improve throughput through making staff work more quickly, then staff may well argue that quality will suffer – and vice versa. In some cases, too, identifying the cause may give you another problem rather than suggest a solution! If throughput is down in the reprographics section because staff are fatigued, then cracking the whip is hardly likely to be effective. If throughput is down because of constant equipment breakdowns and yet there is no money available for replacements at present, then the most obvious improvement may be unacceptable. It is rather like the manager who said that the only way he could improve productivity was to sack all the staff and start again! If you inherit a motley, disorganised and disparate crew of staff then you may have some sympathy with his views.

In most cases, you will be expected to recommend improvements with the minimum of additional resources. If this also requires behavioural changes of your staff it may be the easiest area to identify and the most difficult to solve.

Evaluating improvements

There is no point in implementing improvements if you forget to check whether or not these have been effective. In a sense, this is a variation on double-loop feedback to which you were introduced on pages 505–506. In this case, however, rather than re-evaluating the goal you are re-evaluating the improvement you made to check that it was satisfactory (see Figure 7.2.6).

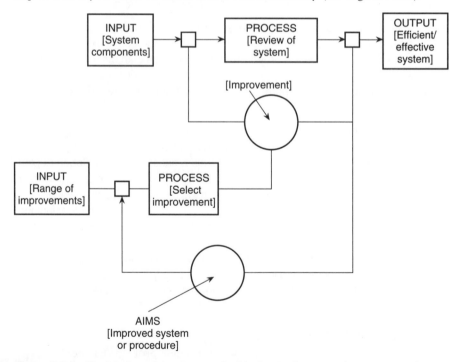

Figure 7.2.6 Double-loop learning applied to improving a system or procedure

J. G. March, in *Theories of Choice and Making Decisions*, argued that decisions to solve problems are often made in one of five ways.

The *rational approach* implies collecting every possible piece of information, analysing it objectively, making a rational decision, evaluating every possible outcome and proposing appropriate action. In reality this is virtually impossible to achieve. Quite apart from the time constraints that are normally in operation, it is virtually impossible to obtain and analyse every scrap of information that would influence a decision. For that reason, decision-makers often opt for a different method.

Bounded rationality is the common-sense approach. It relates to obtaining as much information as possible, adding to this with relevant views and opinions and then making the 'best possible' decision in the time available. Most decision-makers have considerable empathy with this viewpoint and feel that it accords with their own experiences.

Rules and precedents is the method used when decisions are based on previous actions and cases, and when detailed consideration is given to the organisational rules and limitations that would apply to different courses of action. This method is used to justify decisions in a wide variety of bureaucratic organisations and in cases where individual initiatives are discouraged or criticised. It is the safe and expedient alternative in this type of situation.

Symbolic action is the choice of those who want to reward the popular view or have the time to contemplate the best way of reaching a compromise solution. In this case the views of users would be obtained and studied and their reactions to possible improvements considered in detail. The method they would prefer is the one that would be recommended.

Garbage can analysis is used more often than you may realise! In this approach, the decision-maker is faced with a stack of problems to solve, some of which conflict, some of which are urgent and many of which seem unsolvable at any given moment of time. Information also arrives in random order, some of it useful, some less so. In this case the decision-maker restricts his or her activities to solving the most pressing problems and does this by matching up information and problems to find the most pragmatic solution in the time available.

Adaptive action

When you recommend adaptive action, the review group or user group is charged with the task of identifying the particular changes that have occurred which mean that a system or procedure needs updating. The most difficult part of the task is in identifying the likelihood of *future* changes, forecasting how these will take place, and planning the best way of changing the system or procedure to take these into account. The more flexibility and adaptability is designed into a system or procedure, the easier it is to update it.

A brainstorming session may be needed to identify external factors, using the PEST technique of identifying political, economic, social and technological areas of change. SWOT analysis may be undertaken to identify both internal and external areas that can be viewed as strengths, weaknesses, opportunities and threats to the organisation. These are then applied to existing systems and procedures to see if they can usefully inform adaptive action.

There may be a need to consult specialist advisers for updates in certain areas or to obtain their advice and expertise. This issue is covered in more depth below.

Continuous improvement

Continuous improvement is a combination of both corrective and adaptive action. Problems, errors and difficulties are identified and remedied at the same time as the system or procedure is continually updated. Whilst no system can ever be perfect, a continuous review process has this as its ultimate goal. This means regularly reviewing inputs, outputs and process and regularly reappraising the control process and the way control is achieved.

Despite the obvious benefits from this approach, there appear to be few documented cases of organisations that routinely recognise the need for a continuous feedback loop which links the emergent needs of users with the system or procedural changes required. L. Damodaran suggested that criteria for system acceptability should include the following factors:

- the quality of the system in relation to its purpose (sometimes called *task fit*)
- the ease of use of the system
- the effectiveness of user support
- an assessment of indirect factors and consequences (such as effect on job content and related systems and procedures).

Whilst Damodaran was primarily concerned with computerised information systems, the applicability of these criteria and the importance of continual evaluation to encourage organisational learning and facilitate proactive and positive system development is obvious.

THEORY INTO PRACTICE

Identify a system or procedure in your own workplace where problems were seen and improvements were made.

1 Which of March's approaches do you consider was used in recommending these particular improvements?

2 Would the recommended improvements have been different if any of his alternative approaches had been taken?

3 Which approach to decision-making do you think you tend towards? What facts can you provide to support your position?

4 In the system or procedure you identified, do you consider the improvements were appropriate and effective? What evidence could you provide to substantiate your view?

Legal and regulatory requirements relating to implementation

The greatest difficulty for evaluators is keeping up-to-date with the statutory regulations and organisational policies and requirements that affect systems and procedures. In Chapter 6 you were introduced to the importance of obtaining specialist advice – either internally or externally – when systems and procedures encompassed legal or regulatory areas. In this chapter you have been introduced to the way in which external factors can affect systems and procedures. In some cases changes in legal and regulatory areas trigger a review of existing systems and procedures. In other cases, they do not. It can be tempting for evaluators to forget that laws, directives and regulations are regularly amended or changed and that such changes will have to be incorporated into any revisions or improvements that are made.

The speed of change in this area is considerable and can be alarming to the uninitiated. In any given year there are many examples of Directives and Acts of Parliament that directly affect business activities, in addition to actions by pressure groups which influence business policies in many areas. Many of the changes introduced during 1997 and issues currently being debated have been incorporated into this book. However, at the time of writing, there are many further plans and issues that may come to fruition:

- a new private member's bill by Labour MP Linda Perham, backed by Age Concern, to restrict ageism in advertisements and recruitment procedures
- a new European Directive on the rights of part-time employees
- a Green Paper on plans to introduce a statutory right for small firms to charge interest on late payment of invoices
- government action to regulate the ratio of profits to investment of privatised industries and utilities and to monitor the bonus payments of directors
- closer regulation of various sectors of business, including the financial services industry, estate agents and will-writing firms
- increased pressure and a greater number of legal challenges on insurance companies which use technicalities as an excuse for non-payment
- additional pressure on organisations to review customer service practices and procedures to take account of the requirements of the Disability Discrimination Act

- a review of competition policy with government proposals to prohibit anti-competitive behaviour, including cartels, predatory pricing and the abuse of market power
- a European Directive that introduces new rights for workers to be consulted about changes to their employment conditions
- legislation to protect employees' rights to form a trade union
- the proposal of a minimum wage following deliberations by the Low Pay Commission
- proposals to change the law on advertising to outlaw tobacco advertising
- increasingly 'green' policies, backed by taxation, to include new transport policies and stricter targets to reduce carbon monoxide emissions
- greater pressures for organisations to undertake environmental and ethical audits on company policies and practices.

These are quite apart from new legislation on workers' councils, paternity leave and data protection, specific actions and recommendations by regulators and additional future proposals and planned Directives put forward by the European Union.

A change in the law has given campaigning groups the right to take legal action on behalf of those whose rights have been infringed, such as by challenging unfair contracts designed to ensnare customers or give sellers too much power. This means that bodies such as the Consumers Association can seek an injunction against the sale of dangerous products, environmental groups could take action against 'cowboys' who dump toxic waste at landfill sites, and housing groups can challenge the actions of local authorities, estate agents and builders on behalf of their members. Until the change, only named individuals could take cases to court.

The government sees this action as empowering consumers to mount legal protests in key areas. It is forecast that the most immediate areas of attack will include mobile phone agreements, employment contracts and holiday booking forms – unless, of course, organisations voluntarily review any dubious areas as a matter of urgency before they are forced to do so.

Keeping one step ahead

If you are concerned about your ability to stay up-to-date with current legal and regulatory requirements and interpret these correctly so that you maintain compliance, it is strongly suggested that you select Unit 10 as your option for this award. This unit deals in depth with the issue and provides important information to inform your investigations. In the meantime, you could use the checklist illustrated in Figure 7.2.7 as a first step to assessing the areas where additional research is likely to be required.

1 Does the system or procedure relate to specific legal areas affected by
   - company law
   - consumer law
   - employment protection legislation
   - health and safety
   - environmental legislation
   - competition law?
2 Are new EU Directives planned to extend or amend relevant areas?
3 Does the system or procedure require the storage or transmission of personal information on computer, by the Internet, or in structured paper files?
4 Is the system or procedure affected by any long-term contracts or agreements with suppliers?
5 Is your particular industry subject to changing government policies or the actions of government-appointed regulators?
6 Do you have to follow specific guidelines to comply with ISO 9000 accreditation? Have you a copy of the most up-to-date requirements?
7 Does the system or procedure affect customers and clients and are any based in non-UK territories where specific legal requirements and regulations will affect your operations?
8 Have there been recent press reports on legal or regulatory changes which could affect your system or procedure?
9 Are there any company policies relating to these areas that need to be taken into account? Have these been revised in any way?
10 Have you checked your assumptions on all these areas with a specialist adviser either within your organisation or outside it?

Figure 7.2.7   Checklist for legal and regulatory changes

An important issue is 'the millennium bug' or computer timebomb facing many organisations at midnight on 31 December 1999. In a recent report, the Chairman of Boots the Chemist, Sir Michael Angus, reported that rewriting the computer software for his organisation would take 300 staff-years and cost up to £10 million.

The timebomb affects both hardware and software produced mainly before 1995, when programmers shortsightedly used a two-digit code for the year – so that after 99 it will revert to 00 – which will cause any archived computer files to 'expire' after 1999. Another problem is the installation of a particular chip that will cause a computer to reset automatically to 4 January 1980 at the end of 1999. The problem is not, however, restricted to the turn of the century. One consignment of canned goods has already had to be destroyed by a retailer, when it was found that the computer system had printed the expiry date as 1904 rather than 2004. There are obvious implications for organisations undertaking forecasting and planning on an annual basis, which will have to make arrangements well before 1 January 1999 for their systems to cope. Action recommended by the experts includes

- checking contracts with suppliers or maintenance contractors to make sure there are no exclusion clauses which mean that expert assistance will not be available or that the onus is completely on the customer
- checking to ensure that no pre-1995 DOS software or bespoke software is in operation
- ensuring that no PCs have pre-1995 ROM-BIOS chips installed
- checking how the millennium date will affect archived files
- contacting suppliers of existing hardware and software to check that all information which is 'date sensitive' on their systems will be able to cope with the millennium
- contacting specialists for advice and information
- making plans to modify and change systems *at least* one year in advance of the date change.

THEORY INTO PRACTICE

Recent surveys have revealed that 72 per cent of senior managers are unaware of these problems or consider there cannot possibly be any difficulties because new hardware and application software has been purchased. The recommendation is that anyone who is doubtful in any way should contact the National Computing Centre on 0161 228 6333 for impartial advice.

1 Find out what plans your organisation has made to re-evaluate its computerised systems and procedures in the light of the millennium problem.
2 Identify the methods you could use to obtain current feedback on your existing system and the type of improvements required.
3 If you are studying for this award *post* 2000, you may find it useful and informative to evaluate the extent to which your organisation obtained feedback on opportunities for improvement to its systems and, where appropriate, implemented these promptly and effectively.

8 Contract for the supply of resources and services

Element 8.1

Negotiate contracts for resources and services

This unit concentrates upon contracting for the supply of goods and services, and it is assumed that if you have chosen to study it you are already working in an appropriate area – even if it is not an area devoted solely to purchasing and supply. What you will be required to do is to take a situation check and to compare and contrast your workplace and its systems with those commonly used in other areas. You may also find it useful to re-read the general provisions relating to physical resources set out in Chapter 2.

Your own work role and responsibilities

The general responsibilities of administrators have already been discussed. This element discusses in more detail some specific duties relating to contracting for resources and services.

To choose this unit as an option you must be working in an area that gives you the appropriate level of responsibility to allow you to achieve the competences expected of a level 4 NVQ candidate. Consequently, it may be useful for you to be aware of the competences set and approved by the Chartered Institute of Purchasing and Supply for its level 4 qualification in Purchasing, particularly the competences that relate to the negotiation of contracts for the supply of services and resources. Not only does it require candidates to show a marked level of competence in:

- contributing to the health and safety of the working environment
- creating and maintaining appropriate professional relationships with other people
- contributing to the maintenance of systems for security and confidentiality
- contributing to organisational strategy

it also requires them to show the same level of competence in:

- selecting a supplier for specified supplies
- contracting for supply
- determining conditions in the market for suppliers
- determining potential suppliers through vendor evaluation
- optimising the supplier base
- entering into strategic sourcing arrangements
- contributing to the establishment and integration of purchasing related systems

- establishing and maintaining databases of purchasing/stores and management information
- obtaining improvements in supplier performance
- establishing and evaluating current and future requirements for supply
- developing the effectiveness of purchasing operations.

THEORY INTO PRACTICE

Obviously, much depends on your own work area as to the extent to which you are engaged in these activities. At this stage, it may be a good idea for you to look at your job description and compare it with that in Figure 8.1.1, which outlines a specimen job description of a project purchasing administrator whose duties and responsibilities would probably be assessed as being of NVQ level 4 standard. Analyse:

- how closely it resembles your job description
- what the differences are – bearing in mind that your job description may be much less specialised
- who else, if anyone, in your organisation is expected to carry out some – or all – of the duties described
- why your job description includes/omits some of the items
- whether you think these additions/omissions are justifiable in the light of the work you actually carry out.

- To report directly to the senior manager and to liaise with other project managers
- To provide a full purchasing service to the senior manager, including
  - subcontracting
  - ordering
  - expediting
  - inspecting
- To represent the senior manager at meetings with clients
- To prepare purchasing procedures, to agree them with the senior manager and the client, and to ensure that they are carried out
- To supervise the rest of the staff in the team
- To agree the staffing for the project with the senior manager
- To supervise
  - the preparation of conditions of contract and subcontract
  - the list of suppliers and subcontractors
  - the inspection procedures
  - the shipping documentation
  - all other documentation
- Where relevant, to agree with the client the names of firms to be invited to tender and to attend the opening of tenders meetings where applicable
- To monitor and review the progress of the work, including attending monthly review meetings and preparing monthly purchasing status reports
- To check and sign bid summaries before submission to the client and senior manager

---

- To supervise the ordering of supplies
- To ensure that copies of purchase orders, correspondence and any other appropriate documents are forwarded to the senior manager, client and any other relevant personnel
- To obtain schedules of work from suppliers and subcontractors
- To make sure that any negotiations are properly carried out
- To ensure that invoice queries are dealt with promptly
- To carry out any other duties as may reasonably be required.

Figure 8.1.1 Specimen job description for a project purchasing administrator

Scope and limits of your own authority to negotiate contracts

Negotiating contracts for resources and services is a specialised role and one for which you will probably have received specific training. However, almost certainly there will be limits imposed on the extent of your authority to finalise any deal.

1 Determine how far through the contracting process you can proceed without having to refer upwards to a senior member of staff.
2 Determine also whether the limits on your authority are written down and specific, or whether they have been agreed as a result of an informal arrangement between you and your senior manager. Assess the advantages and disadvantages of each approach.

Types and sources of specifications for the supply of resources and services

Each time you place an order for a certain type of physical resource or an advertisement for a certain type of employee, you have a fair idea of what you want. Sometimes, however, you need more than just a general 'idea', particularly if the goods you are ordering are required for production purposes or the post you are advertising is for a high-level, technically qualified specialist. In such circumstances you need a detailed specification of what you require. There are various ways of approaching specifications.

The use of a brand name

The quickest and easiest method of specifying what you want is to ask for it by its brand name. Indeed in some cases you may have little choice, such as:

- when the process is secret
- when a patent is involved
- when only small quantities are required, making the production of a detailed specification uneconomic
- when testing by the buyer is impracticable

- when the brand has been used successfully before and is requested by the relevant staff.

Bear in mind, however, that brand-named items may cost more than unbranded alternatives, and if they are used to the exclusion of all others there is the danger that they will become a monopoly.

This type of transaction is protected by section 13 of the Sale of Goods Act 1979 (SGA) as amended by the Sale and Supply of Goods Act 1994 (SSGA), which states that where there is a sale of goods by description, there is an implied condition that the goods shall correspond with the description. The courts have given a wide meaning to the term a 'sale by description' to include:

- sales of purely generic goods (e.g. 20 cotton nightdresses)
- sales of specific goods the buyer has not seen (e.g. a 1935 grandfather clock)
- sales of specific goods the buyer has seen if they are sold as goods answering a description (e.g. Scottish whisky)
- goods selected by the buyer at a self-service store or supermarket (section 13.3 of the SGA states that a sale of goods is not prevented from being a sale by description by reason only that, being exposed for sale or hire, they are selected by the buyer).

Note, however, that if a seller tells you that – although describing a particular item – he or she is making no representations about it and you must exercise your own judgement, you cannot rely upon the Acts' protection. In one case a seller told the buyer that he had come to sell two paintings, one of which was by a well-known artist. He also said, however, that he was not an expert in this field. It was held, therefore, that it was *not* a sale by description.

The use of a sample

Instead of describing by name the type of product you want, you can choose to give the potential supplier a sample of, for instance, goods previously supplied. Alternatively the supplier could provide you with a sample of the goods he or she intends to supply if an order is placed. If you go down this route, remember to keep the sample in case there are any ensuing problems. Section 15 of the SGA as amended by SSGA 1994 provides that:

- the bulk must correspond with the sample in quality
- the goods must be free from any defect making their quality unsatisfactory which a reasonable examination of the sample would not reveal.

A performance specification

A further possibility, particularly if a sample is not available, is to prepare a performance specification giving a clear indication of the purpose, function, application and performance expected of the resource or service. Obviously this is the most useful method if, for instance, you want to purchase an item such as a set of machine tools about which you may have little knowledge.

One of the advantages of a performance specification is that it is protected by Section 14(3) of the SGA as amended by the SSGA 1994 which states that, where the seller sells goods in the course of a business and the buyer, expressly or by implication, makes known to the seller any particular purpose for which the goods are being bought, there is an *implied* term that the goods supplied under the contract are reasonably fit for that purpose. In *Priest v Last* [1903] 2KB 148, for instance, a man bought a hot-water bottle for his wife, who was subsequently scalded when it burst. He was held entitled to damages because he had relied on the seller's skill and judgement. The hot-water bottle had been used for its obvious purpose and it therefore did not matter that he had not specifically told the chemist what use he intended to make of it.

- Where the seller has no say in the selection of his or her stock – for example in a franchised business – and the customer is aware of that fact, the seller will not be liable under this section. However, he or she would still be liable under section 14(2) of the SGA, which states that where the seller sells goods in the course of a business there is an implied term that the goods supplied under the contract are of satisfactory quality.
- The implied term of 'satisfactory quality' also applies to additional items supplied under the contract, such as packaging, containers, instructions, etc.

A conformance specification

This type of specification concerns the product itself, not its application. It is normally used where, for instance, items are required for incorporation in the assembly of a product, or where a certain chemical is required for a production process. In such circumstances you must lay down in the specification the precise requirements to be met by the supplier.

- Most technical contracts contain a clause dealing with the effect of non-performance through failure to conform to the specification. Non-compliance with a specification can lead either to a valid repudiation of the contract, or to an action for breach of contract and a subsequent claim for damages. It can also lead to a defence against a claim that the agreed payment has not been made.
- Business equipment journals often draw up their own specifications to compare the features of a particular range of equipment. In one issue of *What to Buy*, for instance, a number of different projectors were measured against nine criteria.

Preparation of specifications

A specification communicates to the supplier exactly what you wish to have supplied, and provides criteria against which the goods or services actually supplied can be compared, so it is worth taking some time in preparing one.

The contents will vary according to the type of specification you are preparing and your own role. In the case of a simple item you may content yourself with a brief description, or the completion of a pro forma which lists the main issues – price, size, style, design, compatibility, etc.

Technical specifications

Where the goods or services required are more complex, the specification must reflect that complexity. You – or, more probably, one of your technical experts – have to prepare a *technical* specification. Such a specification may cover all or some of the following.

- *Formalities.* These may be a list of contents, rationale, statement of terms of reference, definitions of terminology, reference to relevant authorities and documents such as statutory regulations, national and international standards, etc.
- *Purpose.* This is the purpose for which the equipment or material is intended.
- *Environment.* This covers the conditions in which the item or material is to be installed, used, manufactured or stored.
- *Characteristics.* As this is, of course, the most vital part of the document, you might want to make use of samples, drawings, models, etc. to illustrate your requirements. You must also ensure that you include details of:
  - properties, such as strength, dimensions, weight, etc., with tolerances given where relevant
  - any required interchangeability
  - materials and their properties (including any permissible variability)
  - any specific requirements such as heat treatment
  - appearance, texture, finish
  - identification marks, operating symbols on controls, weight, safety indications, etc.
  - method of marking.
- *Performance.* This might cover:
  - performance under specified conditions
  - the test methods and equipment for assessing performance and where, how and by whom carried out
  - criteria for passing tests
  - conditions for acceptance
  - any reports, test schedules or certificates required.
- *Durability, reliability and estimated life.* There may be recognised ways of expressing these, such as 'mean time to failure' or 'guaranteed error-free'.
- *Quality control mechanisms.* These may cover procedures to check compliance with the specification, such as
  - the method of checking
  - production tests on raw materials, components, subassemblies and assemblies
  - evidence of compliance, such as supplier's certificate, independent certification scheme, etc.

- inspection facilities required by user
- instructions regarding reject material or items
- instructions regarding modification of process
- position of subcontractors in quality control procedures.

- *Packaging*. This could cover:
  - specifications
  - condition in which the item is to be supplied – (how packaged, etc.)
  - recommended maximum period of storage
  - marking of packaging
  - instructions for use.

> The Shropshire Fire Service wanted to purchase a new turntable-ladder fire engine. The fire engine was a new design, and two similar ones, supplied to Derbyshire Fire Service had proved to have some flaws. Consequently they were changed, the changes being known as 'Derbyshire modifications'. Shropshire Fire Service asked the company at the post-tender stage to vary the specifications to incorporate the modifications. This was agreed but the modifications were never made and the engine was built to the original specification. The company was prosecuted under the Trade Descriptions Act 1968 because the vehicle did not comply with the amended specification.

Specifications for capital equipment

If a capital item is required, the specification is sometimes split into a *general requirements* section (which tends to be relatively constant) and a *particular requirements* part which comprises:

- a section on the required equipment, services or works
- a site details section giving relevant information about the location that could affect the design and performance of the capital item
- a section on additional information required from the seller.

In some instances a printed pro forma can be used as in Figure 8.1.2, in which column A describes the requirements, column B indicates whether or not they are relevant in this particular instance, column C allows the seller to state how far he or she can comply with the requirements, and column D is left blank for the buyer to complete when he or she is satisfied that the requirement has been met.

A: Overall performance requirements	B	C	D
1 Equipment must be suitable for outdoor use	Yes	Yes	
2 Must have a minimum service life	3 yrs	5 yrs	
etc.			

Figure 8.1.2 Extract from a capital equipment specification

One professor of computing research maintains that modern gadgets are making consumers' lives harder, not easier, because the instructions for their use are so complex. He blames the complicated specifications drawn up by the internal engineering teams in large companies, which are issued to publicity houses to simplify even though they may never have seen the items in question.

Specifications for services

The list of services you may need to buy is almost endless – accountancy, advertising, marketing, catering, cleaning, decorating, design, legal, security, training, etc. Preparation of the necessary specifications requires an approach that is different from that for physical resources.

Obviously, services are intangible. They cannot be stored or stockpiled (although you may argue that payment of a retainer is a type of 'stockpiling'). Consequently they must be provided at the exact time of need. It is of little use arranging a training session for your staff at a time when the training consultant cannot attend, or requiring a security presence at a particular function when the security guard will not be available until the following week.

You can touch, feel and weigh goods, but not services. How do you know that you have obtained value for money when you ask a computer consultant to recommend a new computer network, or a solicitor to advise on how to implement a redundancy procedure?

When you buy goods it is usually easy to ascertain that the contract has been fulfilled; i.e. the goods have been delivered at the right time, in the right quantity and of the right quality. It is less easy with some services. Suppose, for example, you negotiate with a gardener to carry out a landscaping project: when are you going to decide that the contract has been completed – when the last plant has been planted, when the seedling becomes a tree?

THEORY INTO PRACTICE

All these problems have a solution – otherwise contracting for services would be a dying art. Consider how you would overcome the difficulties just outlined when submitting a specification for a service you require at your workplace.

Preparation of job specifications

There are certain similarities between the processes involved in purchasing goods and in recruiting staff. Just as you should have a clear understanding of exactly what type of goods to order, so too should you have the same understanding of the type of employee you require. If you are interviewing someone for work in your own field, this part of the exercise should not prove difficult. If, however, you are interviewing someone whose skills and qualifications are totally different, to carry out work in which you have no personal expertise, a precise job specification becomes a necessity.

Some organisations have job specifications on file for every position in the organisation. These contain well-developed criteria to assist the interviewer to determine the suitability of an applicant for a particular job. Other organisations make little use of them. Check the situation in your own organisation, and consider how such specifications either assist or would assist the interviewing process.

Developing organisational criteria

Some organisations develop their own criteria by means of group discussions amongst senior management, who are required to decide on the basic characteristics they want in a workforce – flexibility, motivation, technical skill, social skill, confidence, etc.

A more sophisticated approach is one in which a team of psychologists interviews individual managers or key personnel to assess how they structure their own 'perceptual maps' of the organisation or specific roles in it to create a *repertory grid*. You first met this technique in Chapter 1. In this case, the interviewee is asked to name ten key people. These names are called 'elements' and comprise the horizontal side of a grid or matrix. The interviewee is then asked to consider three of these elements, saying in which respect any two are similar but different from the third. How he or she describes the similarity and difference will indicate one of the ways in which that person 'construes' the environment. One interviewee may, for instance, choose three people, two of whom are hard-working and one is not. Thus hard-working/lazy would be labelled as a *construct* and entered as the first line on the vertical dimension of the grid. The interviewee is then asked to rate each of the remaining seven names as closest to either hard-working or lazy. Another three names are then compared to produce another construct, which becomes the second item on the vertical dimension. The comparison is continued until all the combinations of names are exhausted. The result is a grid, where the vertical axis is a list of constructs showing how the interviewee classifies his or her work environment. These are each related to the managers or roles listed on the horizontal axis. The organisational criteria can then be identified by examining the grids of a number of managers in the organisation.

Research has been carried out into the use of these grids by V. Stewart and A. Stewart, and by G. A. Kelly. See further *Business Applications of Repertory Grids* (McGraw-Hill, 1978) and *The Psychology of Personnel Constructs* (Norton, 1955).

Developing functional or departmental criteria

Many recruiters like something more specific than organisational criteria with which to work, preferring to have criteria laid down for each department or SBU. Certain departments require staff with technical skills and little more, whereas others demand not only specific skills but also skills of communication or dealing with people.

Developing individual job criteria

Different organisations use varying terminology to describe the parts of the recruitment process. Most, however, distinguish between a *job description* which relates to the work required of a particular person in a particular job, a *job specification* which relates purely to the job itself, and a *job analysis* which either specifies in more precise detail the job itself or combines this with a *personnel specification* outlining the type of person most likely to be successful in it.

> When drawing up a job specification you should be cautious with vague terms such as 'liaise', 'coordinate', etc. Otherwise you or the manager concerned may have some difficulty in determining accountability when setting or checking on targets.

Possibly the most widely used approach involves drafting a detailed specification that covers both the job itself and the person who might best be employed in it. If you are asked to compile such a job and personnel specification, you should address the following issues.

- *Job title.* Give a formal job title, together with its departmental and geographical location. Does a distinction need to be made between a trainee and a fully trained person?
- *Job context.* How does the job relate to other jobs? How is it linked to the overall objectives of the department or organisation?
- *Main duties.* List the main duties and responsibilities of the job, derived either through discussion with existing employees and their supervisors or by observation of the work carried out. Has any account been taken of recent appraisal reports which may contain an updated set of duties? Are all the duties listed without any account being taken of order of importance or priority? Is a supervisory role distinguished sufficiently clearly from that of a subordinate? Is some distinction made between the most and the least difficult duties – to enable the interviewer to probe these areas with the interviewee?
- *Features of the work.* Is the work heavy, monotonous, dangerous? Is the workplace dark, dusty, damp, hot, cold? Is the work solitary or is it undertaken as part of a team? Is there considerable or only slight supervision? Is the prevailing atmosphere one of cooperation or competition?
- *Criteria used in evaluation.* What criteria are used in evaluating job performance? What is regarded as 'normal' working performance? Are the criteria linked to promotion prospects?
- *Attainment.* What skills and knowledge are required? What educational and occupational experience is necessary?
- *Aptitudes.* What abilities are required? Are there any particular aptitudes necessary for the job in question?
- *Physical requirements.* Is there a height requirement? Should applicants be free from disability in limb movement, colour blindness, etc.? Is age a factor?

- *Personality characteristics.* Should the applicant be precise and patient, confident and outgoing, self-reliant, possessing leadership characteristics, able to work as a member of a team, etc.?
- *Interests.* Might interests outside work be relevant for successful performance of this job?
- *External constraints.* Has the applicant to be prepared to work away from home, to work antisocial hours, to take holidays that do not coincide with school holidays, etc.?

One way of evaluating the relative significance of each of the tasks listed in a job analysis is to use a *main duties weighting formula*, which provides a weighting on a scale of 1 to 3. The high-weighting duties are those upon which the recruiter should concentrate most.

In order to determine these weightings you can either make use of the 'construct' grid (as already discussed in relation to the formulation of organisational criteria), or take a more behavioural approach – writing a description of the job in such a way that recruiters can identify and examine past behaviour of applicants in order to define desired future behaviour. If, for instance, you wish to employ a security guard you may identify skills such as stamina, willingness to work hard and accept unsocial hours, ability to communicate, physical strength, trustworthiness and self-reliance – simply because previous successful holders of the post have shown such characteristics. Alternatively you may decide to use an 'accomplishment record inventory' compiled as a result of asking a large sample of job holders to identify the major accomplishments of their job. You may also wish to introduce the concept of 'competences' to describe the practical capabilities required of each potential job holder.

THEORY INTO PRACTICE

The management writer Tom Peters advocates the use of 'soft values', such as teamwork potential, in job specifications. Assume that you are about to write a specification for a job vacancy in your own area of work. Consider what values you think the job needs and the questions you would ask at interview to try to determine whether or not the applicants possess such values.

An organisation's procedures and policies relating to contracts

Your organisation's strategic plan should give you some general guidelines on the policies and procedures to implement during the negotiation of contracts for both resources and services.

Although these policies differ from organisation to organisation, there are generally certain similarities. Most policies, for instance, specify the level of authority necessary before a member of staff is able to enter a binding contract for resources or services. Many also specify certain financial limits above which the contracting process has to be carried out by a more senior member of staff. By their very nature, however, policies tend to be broad-brush. What must also be instituted alongside them are the procedures to be used to ensure that the policies are correctly implemented.

Contracts for obtaining resources and services

When negotiating contracts for resources or services you may be required to implement at least some of the following procedures.

- Complete certain standard legal documents (for further discussion on this issue see page 616).
- Consult the Production department or other relevant staff before any negotiations take place, to ascertain:
  - the *quantity* of goods or service required
  - the essential *quality* of those goods or service
  - the *time limit* by which the goods have to be delivered or the service rendered
  - the *price bands* in which you have to negotiate.
- Draw up an action plan prior to any further discussions.
- Consult specialists (e.g. a solicitor on a retainer basis in case you encounter legal problems outside your area of expertise).
- Follow a specific procedure if you are trying to resolve any difficulties during the negotiation of a contract for technical or specialised goods or resources (e.g. an argument about the capabilities of a piece of technical equipment).
- Refer back (if necessary) to your senior manager when the initial contract has been drawn up but before any final agreement has been reached.
- Communicate any agreement reached to the relevant personnel.
- Monitor and review the contract to see that its terms have been fulfilled (see further page 641).

Contracts for providing resources and services

If you have to negotiate a contract under which your organisation is to provide certain resources or services, you will probably be expected to follow much the same procedures as above. The main difference, of course, is that you will discuss terms relating to quantity, quality, time and price with the potential client rather than with members of your own organisation. This may involve a longer negotiation process. You may, for instance, have to be prepared to enter into a dialogue with your Production staff to check that the client's requirements can actually be met, and to follow the requisite procedures should there be any perceived difficulties in doing so.

THEORY INTO PRACTICE

1 Where relevant, check your organisation's procedures for negotiating a contract for the supply or provision of resources and services, and compare them with the list just given.
2 If no such procedures exist, try to assess how helpful the above list would be to you in any negotiations you have to carry out.

An organisation's procedures and policies for conditions of supply

The major policy decision facing most organisations in relation to conditions of supply is whether to centralise or decentralise the function. Once that decision has been made, procedures can be established to ensure an effective supply system.

Purchasing activities tend to fall into three main phases, each of which is accompanied by a set of procedures involving the preparation and completion of a standard set of documents.

The notification phase

If your organisation channels its supply requirements through a Purchasing department, obviously that department will buy on behalf of the rest of the organisation and must therefore be notified when any purchase is required. Even if the system is decentralised, there may still be a need for individual members of staff to notify the person responsible for negotiating the contract and ordering the supplies.

The first stage in the process is normally the completion of a *requisition form* – either manually, or more frequently nowadays by means of a computerised pro forma. This not only outlines the requirement but also acts as authorisation for the expenditure and as a record for audit and future reference. Once completed the requisition form should be date-stamped and passed to the person authorised to make the purchase. He or she checks that the request has been properly authorised and if necessary also checks that it has been signed by an authorised signatory.

THEORY INTO PRACTICE

1 Check the procedures for notifying a requirement in your own organisation, and assess their effectiveness.
2 Consider how you would deal with the following situations if you were responsible for approving and processing requisitions from members of staff, some of whom may be senior to you:
   a a manager who, rather than completing the required requisition form, telephones you to say that he must have some goods as a matter of urgency or production of a particular item will cease
   b a manager who insists on using a certain supplier even though you feel that another one will give better value.
   c a senior manager who sends in requisition forms that are apparently authorised by her line manager but whose signature you feel may be forged
   d a manager who complains about having to complete a requisition form each time he wants a particular item that is frequently required
   e a manager who always orders too large a quantity of goods because she is worried about stocks running out.

If you work in an engineering firm you may have to deal with a bill of materials or parts list which serves much the same purpose as a purchase requisition. A parts list is generally attached to, or included in, a drawing which the buyer must check and subsequently indicate in the order number column whether the part is to be provided from stock or purchased externally. In the latter case the purchase order number will be entered before the drawing is passed to production control for subsequent issue to the manufacturing department when the items have been received.

The ordering phase

Once you have received a requisition, you should check it to see whether:

- it is accurate
- it conforms to any company-imposed specifications
- the item requested has been purchased previously – and if so, in what quantities and from what supplier.

Selecting the supplier

Chapters 2 and 4 introduced you to the various relationships which exist between organisations and their suppliers. If you have to choose a supplier the simplest situation is where you can use one who has supplied goods or services previously and has proved satisfactory. Even so, it is normally good practice at periodic intervals to contact other suppliers to check what else is on offer.

Where you are making your first purchase, you may have to follow certain procedures. You may be required to send a pre-printed purchase enquiry or 'request for quotation' form to prospective suppliers, requesting information about price, quality, delivery, other terms and conditions, etc. When large sums are involved you can include on the form a request for prices for a number of different options which can form the basis for future negotiations. Although individual company policies differ, you may be expected to contact at least three suppliers each time a new product is required so that a comparison can be made of the responses.

On occasions you may also want to ask potential suppliers to provide a detailed cost analysis. This is probably unnecessary if independent suppliers are competing for the contract, but it is useful if your organisation depends on just one or two suppliers and cannot therefore rely upon natural competition to keep prices down.

Placing the order

The most important thing to remember is that any order you place becomes a legal contract, and so this is almost certainly an area in which there will be established procedures to follow. Indeed, it is normal practice for an organisation to insist that all orders be placed by means of an official order form. The form is usually multi-part with copies for the relevant departments and the supplier. Some organisations may expect you to send two copies to the supplier. The supplier signs and returns the second copy, marked 'Acknowledgement', to show that the order has been received and accepted.

If the contract covers more than one order you may also be expected to use:

- the regular purchase order form for the contract itself, and additional forms for the orders – known as call-offs, contract releases or delivery instructions; or
- a special form for the contract agreement and the regular order form for the goods; or
- the same purchase order form for both, in which are included words such as 'This is an order against contract number …'.

Other types of order

A *period order* normally covers one year's requirements. Renewal dates are usually staggered so that not all contracts come up for renewal at the same time. Some organisations contract for 50 per cent of their estimated annual requirement and their actual requirements are ordered against this contract as the need arises.

A *blanket order* may be placed with a local supplier for the supply of a large number of maintenance, repair and operating items. This cuts down paperwork by consolidating all the requirements into a single agreement, and by arranging for a single monthly invoice.

THEORY INTO PRACTICE

Many organisations set out their policies and procedures in a *purchasing manual*. This might contain:

- *general* policies stating the objectives and responsibilities of the purchasing department or of the individuals expected to negotiate for resources and services
- *consequential* policies stating how the general policies apply to specific activities such as the selection of suppliers
- the procedures to be followed, such as the sequence of actions by which goods should be ordered
- guidance to those responsible for carrying out the policies or procedures
- detailed rules relating to the conduct of staff.

1 If you are expected to comply with the requirements of such a manual, assess how effective it is in assisting you in your work.

2 If you do not have a purchasing manual, consider the advantages one might bring to your job.

The completion phase

If you are supplying goods, it is accepted practice to notify the buyer that they are on their way by means of an *advice note* or *dispatch note*. How the note is dealt with depends on the procedures favoured by individual organisations.

If your organisation has a purchasing progress section, the note will probably be routed to it for a daily check on when goods actually arrive. Otherwise that responsibility has to be taken by the individual department or SBU.

The supplier can make use of the information on the advice note to prepare the appropriate invoice. Some suppliers include the advice note as part of their invoice set; others prepare both an invoice and an advice note when they receive an order, whilst at the same time preparing their own works order to initiate the manufacture of the product.

When the goods are received you should arrange for them to be checked for quantity and quality against both the purchase order and the advice note. Although nowadays most information is keyed directly into a computer at the receiving point, some organisations still produce a 'goods received note' (GRN) which is usually prepared in duplicate or triplicate and is serially numbered. Alternatively you can send back to the supplier a copy of the purchase order showing the goods as having been received.

THEORY INTO PRACTICE

1 Look at the procedures in your own organisation for ordering and receiving goods (including the extent to which procedures are computerised). Compare these with the standard procedures just outlined. Consider the reasons for any difference in approach.
2 Check how often you contact new suppliers to gauge their product range, and what procedure, if any, you use to reassess your regular suppliers.

Some organisations simplify the whole ordering system by placing contracts centrally but orders locally, using a simple release form like a stores requisition. Suppliers deliver direct to the department or SBU concerned so that very little stock needs to be kept, and a simple bulk invoice is submitted periodically, usually monthly.

A few organisations use a blank-cheque order system. The company's order form includes a blank cheque for the supplier to complete. The supplier arranges for the order to be fulfilled and dispatched. At the same time he or she completes the cheque portion with the relevant net invoice total and deposits it at the bank. He or she is expected to deliver the ordered amount at the agreed time, together with an advice document which the buyer uses for audit purposes.

Under another arrangement, the supplier will deposit goods with the buyer, which the latter pays for as and when he or she uses them. The supplier periodically checks the number of items in stock and replenishes them to an agreed level. A single contract covers the agreed period, indicating the price of each item against a code and description. Invoices are paid against this contract.

Legal and regulatory requirements relating to contracts

A commercial contract is treated by the courts in the same way as any other contract and you must therefore comply with the usual *non-statutory requirements*. Since much of the information it contains will be considered sensitive, you should also take care to ensure that there is no breach of confidentiality, the legal position in relation to which has already been discussed.

Statutory requirements

Before entering into any contractual negotiations, you should be aware of the general legal climate in which you are operating. Although the bulk of the statutory legislation relating to the sale of resources and services is dealt with on page 629, you should know, for instance, that legislation exists to monitor potential monopoly situations, to prevent unfair mergers, to curb potentially restrictive practices, and to prevent anti-competitive practices. *Anti-competition legislation* is the subject of the remainder of this section.

The Fair Trading Act 1973

Under this legislation the Secretary of State and the Director General of Fair Trading have discretionary powers to refer to the Monopolies and Mergers Commission (MMC) cases of the supply or purchase of goods or services in the UK where it appears that a monopoly situation exists. A monopoly is generally held to exist if one company or group of companies accounts for at least 25 per cent of the market (whether as buyer or seller). If it is held that the monopoly is likely to have an adverse effect on consumer rights, the company or group may be required to cut prices or implement other recommendations. Similarly, the Commission may investigate any mergers which would create or enhance a market share of 25 per cent or more in the UK or a substantial part of the UK.

The Competition Act 1980

This applies to companies with an annual turnover of more than £5 million or controlling more than 25 per cent of the market. It gives the Office of Fair Trading (OFT) investigative powers to control possible anti-competitive practices in the supply and acquisition of goods or services. For further discussion on the OFT, see Chapter 2.

A recent example of MMC involvement was an investigation into the prices of CDs in the UK, compared with those in the USA. *Which?* magazine compared the prices of six different CDs and found that the US prices were on average 17 per cent lower than UK prices. The average pre-tax price of The Beatles' *Abbey Road* CD was £13.05 in the UK and the equivalent of £10.44 in the USA. Two years previously, however, the MMC had ruled the differences to be acceptable and did not change its position.

Another investigation into alleged price-fixing, this time in the market for household electrical goods, culminated in an MMC recommendation that suppliers should no longer be allowed to set retail prices on televisions, washing machines and other electrical goods. The head of policy research at the Consumers Association welcomed the report and indicated that the Association's research had also revealed 'considerable evidence of price-fixing in the industry, which keeps prices high'. Somewhat predictably the major manufacturers insisted that the MMC had not taken all the evidence into account, and that issues of service and product support had been ignored. In addition it was argued that as very few electrical retailers make reasonable profits selling goods, if they were engaged in price-fixing they were doing so very badly!

The Restrictive Trade Practices Acts

These Acts regulate agreements between business owners and traders to control or regulate prices or output. Such agreements are considered to be void and contrary to public policy unless they can be shown to be in the public interest, so the Restrictive Trade Practices Acts of 1976 and 1977 along with the Resale Prices Act 1976 impose certain restrictions upon them. They must be registered with the Director General of Fair Trading and must then be shown in the Restrictive Practices Court to be in the public interest.

Sole trading (Solus) agreements

Although these are regarded prima facie as being contrary to public policy, they are permissible particularly where they represent standard practice in an industry. They must, however, be subject to the reasonableness test. Where it appears that an agreement is too one-sided, it will be held to be void. In *Schroeder Music Publishing Co. Ltd v Macaulay* [1974] 1WLR 1308 a contract had been drawn up between a young musician and a firm of music publishers, which was very much to the disadvantage of the musician. This was held to be unreasonable because, given the nature of the music industry, the parties were not in an equal bargaining position. Similarly in *Esso Petroleum Co. Ltd v Harper's Garage (Stourport) Ltd* [1968] AC 269, the garage-owner owned two garages both of which were subject to two solus agreements with the plaintiff petroleum company – one for four years and five months and the other for 21 years. After prolonged but unsuccessful negotiations to extricate himself from the agreement, the garage-owner then started to sell a different brand of petrol. The petroleum company sought an injunction to enforce the agreement. The House of Lords held that although the shorter agreement was reasonable, and therefore valid, the longer agreement was too long and could not be enforced.

Not all attempts to break a sole trading agreement are successful. The singer George Michael lost his action against his employers, the Sony Corporation, when he complained that the terms of his contract were too onerous. The court felt that:

- when he entered into the contract he had been on equal terms with his employer
- prior to signing it he had received professional advice

- he had been paid very handsomely under the agreement.

Because of the potential legal problems in this area, most music publishing and recording companies now make arrangements for recording artists to be given professional legal and financial advice before signing a contract.

Future restrictions in the UK

Despite all the existing restrictions, it is predicted that the present government will institute the biggest reform of competition policy in more than 20 years. In a Green Paper *Tackling Cartels and the Abuse of Market Powers* (now incorporated into the Competition Bill) it outlines new investigative powers for the OFT, outlawing cartels and introducing fines for companies breaking the anti-cartel rules. It also plans to ban 'unfair' behaviour such as predatory pricing by companies dominating a particular market.

Whereas European law allows for immediate fines totalling 10 per cent of turnover if a company transgresses an anti-competition law, UK authorities cannot impose fines. A company can only be fined for contempt if an undertaking given to a court is subsequently broken.

UK competition legislation is subject to that of the EU and in particular the relevant articles of the Treaty of Rome (see Figure 8.1.3).

Article 85 (i)
With certain limited exemptions, agreements are prohibited which permit:
- the direct or indirect fixing of purchase or selling prices
- the limitation or control of production, markets, technical development or investment
- market sharing or sharing of sources of supply
- the application to parties to transactions of unequal terms in respect of equivalent supplies, thereby placing them at a competitive disadvantage
- the subjecting of the conclusions of a contract to the acceptance by a party of additional supplies, which, either by their nature or according to commercial usage, have no connection with the contract.

Article 86
Action by an enterprise to take improper advantage of a dominant position is prohibited; i.e the direct or indirect imposition of any inequitable purchase or selling prices or of any other inequitable trade conditions.

Figure 8.1.3 Two relevant articles of the Treaty of Rome

Ways of negotiating contracts

This section develops further the negotiating techniques to which you were introduced in Chapter 4. Consider the following scenario. You want to find out whether a new printer for your computer can be delivered by the following Wednesday. You pick up the telephone and ask the sales representative of an organisation whether this is possible. He is uncertain and asks you whether you would be prepared to wait another week. You say that you are prepared to give him until the Friday to make the delivery. He agrees. You ask whether any discount will be made to you as a regular customer. He says that the latest offer of 12 per cent discount ends tomorrow. You ask him to reconsider and eventually he agrees that you can have a 10 per cent discount.

This simple episode involved a series of negotiations, resulting in you persuading the salesperson to agree to most of your proposals. However, no matter how experienced you are, there are certain basic rules you should follow in negotiations.

Your first step should be to recognise your negotiating position:

- Are you a buyer or a seller?
- Are you negotiating for goods or services?
- Do you want to negotiate a commercial contract or an employment contract?
- Are you initiating the proceedings or responding to them?

At this stage you should also try to assess how *strong* your position is. Suppose you want to order some goods from a supplier. You will be in a strong position if:

- you do not need them urgently
- you know the supplier is anxious to make the deal
- there are a number of suppliers who can provide the goods or a suitable alternative
- you know you are one of only a few customers
- you have a good reputation for paying on time.

On the other hand, the supplier will be in a strong position if:

- it is known that you must have the goods
- the supplier has a monopoly or near-monopoly on the goods in question
- the supplier already has a healthy order book.

Negotiations tend to cover a predictable and relatively small number of issues. See Figures 8.1.4 and 8.1.5 for an outline of the most common of these issues.

Price
- the type of pricing agreement
- modifications to quoted or existing prices
- quantity, cash and/or trade discount
- credit terms
- delivery charge
- basis on which price increases are to be determined
- trade-in allowances

- charges for use of patents owned by the supplier
- sharing of savings due to improved design or production factors
- compensation for cancelled orders

Delivery
- road, rail, air or sea
- time of delivery
- delivery to specified sites
- buyer's warranties in respect of rejected goods or late delivery

Quality
- acceptable quality levels
- supply of samples
- methods and place of inspection
- conditions or warranties
- amendments to specifications

Figure 8.1.4 Common issues arising in negotiations for the supply of goods

Payment
- weekly or monthly
- salary scale
- superannuation scheme
- bonus payments
- productivity payments
- overtime
- performance-related pay
- share options
- sickness pay
- private medical scheme
- holiday pay
- pension rights

Conditions of employment
- place of work
- hours of work
- maternity/paternity leave
- crèche facilities
- training/promotion opportunities
- company car

Figure 8.1.5 Common issues arising in negotiations for the supply of services

General principles of negotiation

At the start you may not know the relative strength of your bargaining position. You have to try to find that out during the negotiation. Remember certain general principles.

- Don't bargain if you don't have to bargain. If you are certain that you can get what you want, don't negotiate – merely state your terms.
- Don't look too eager to make a deal. Otherwise you give the impression that you are desperate.
- Don't make it look too easy, even if you want to agree to a deal. If someone thinks they have wrung a good deal out of you, so much the better.
- Leave yourself some room for manoeuvre. If, for instance, you are keen to recruit a really good PA, be careful not to indicate straight away all the benefits you are prepared to offer. Save some in case you need to persuade the most suitable applicant to accept your offer by increasing the package of benefits available to him or her.
- Avoid being considered untrustworthy. Some of the most skilful negotiators have faced each other over the negotiating table for many years – and both they and their clients nearly always leave feeling that they have negotiated a good deal. If those negotiators didn't trust one another not to go beyond a certain level of tolerance there would be few occasions when all parties felt satisfied.
- Don't talk too much. By doing so, you may unwittingly reveal more than you intend – and allow the other person to keep potentially vital information undisclosed.

It is sometimes recommended that your preparations should go further and that you should actively seek to undermine those with whom you are about to negotiate – by, for instance, making certain complaints about the service they offer prior to the start of the negotiation. The idea is that they will then be more inclined to negotiate to avoid a recurrence of these complaints. However, this is a game that two can play and you have to be careful that you are not subsequently on the receiving end of such a tactic.

THEORY INTO PRACTICE

The management writers Rackham and Carlisle argue that there are three criteria for a successful negotiator. He or she should:

- be rated as effective by both sides
- have a good track record
- have a low incidence of failure.

That's fine for the experienced negotiator. However, what about the would-be negotiator who cannot prove that he or she matches those criteria? Consider what criteria you would use to try to determine whether someone has the potential to be a good negotiator.

Phases in negotiations

There are normally three phases in any negotiating process: the pre-negotiation phase; the meeting phase – which consists of both introductory and discussion stages; and the post-negotiation phase.

The pre-negotiation phase

At the outset you must determine what you want and how far you are prepared to compromise. Imagine that you are at an auction and have seen something for which you wish to bid. Ideally you should decide both the price you would like to pay and the maximum price you would be prepared to pay. In exceptional circumstances, however, you might be prepared to increase the price you are willing to pay, or you might decide not to buy, even though the asking price is lower than you expected.

Establishing your objectives

Imagine that you have been asked to get the best deal possible on an order for new canteen equipment. Ideally you should ask yourself three questions:

1   *What do I want?* For example, do I want the lowest possible price regardless of any other factor? Am I really after a larger discount from my usual supplier? Must I have quick delivery? Do I want better quality? Do I want to give this order to a particular firm to cement what is proving to be a very successful relationship?

2   *If I have several wants, which is the most important?* Do I want the lowest possible price no matter what? Do I prefer to have higher-quality goods at a higher price? Will I accept lower-quality goods if I am promised a discount? Will I accept goods of any quality provided they are delivered the next day?

3   *What are my limits?* How high a price am I prepared to pay before deciding that there is no deal? How long am I prepared to wait for delivery? How far am I prepared to compromise to maintain good relations with the supplier?

You might also want to decide:

●   the order in which you want to negotiate – do you want to negotiate for the complete range of equipment, or do you want to concentrate on one major item to see whether or not it is worth proceeding any further?
●   what your attitude is going to be – are you going to take a reasonable or authoritative approach?
●   whether you want to make or receive the first offer
●   what sort of approach the seller may have – have you dealt with the firm before, or is it a new supplier whose tactics may differ?

Several books have been written about the preparations that should take place prior to the start of industrial relations negotiations. The same principles can be applied to negotiating for resources. Suppose you want to buy a piece of office equipment. Your budget is limited, and although you are willing to pay about £150 for the equipment, ideally you would like it for about £140. Your absolute limit, however, is £160 (your fallback position). You realise, of course, that the seller of the equipment will be using reverse tactics. He or she would ideally like to sell the equipment to you for as much as possible, hoping to get you to pay £160. However, the absolute minimum to which he or she could agree would be £140. This is set out in diagrammatic terms in Figure 8.1.6.

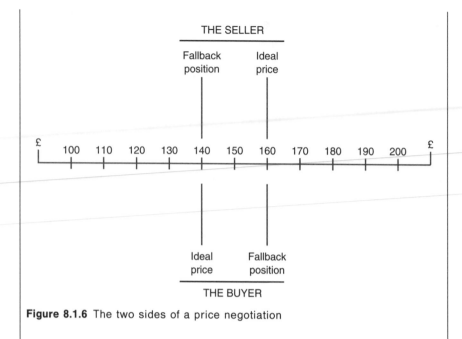

Figure 8.1.6 The two sides of a price negotiation

When planning a purchase of any significance, therefore, you could make use of such a device to clarify what your ideal price, realistic price and fallback positions are likely to be. You are then less likely to be panicked into agreeing to a totally unfavourable deal. Remember, however, that unless the other party is desperate, being too greedy won't work. If your ideal price is too far below any realistic level then there is little point in even beginning the exercise because you will never reach an agreement.

Collection of information

In order to decide on your objectives you must be prepared to spend some time collecting relevant facts. Consider the following scenarios.

- Your organisation supplies photocopying equipment to a number of small firms on a rental basis. Periodically the agreements have to be renegotiated. Consequently before entering into any negotiations with these firms you should acquaint yourself with:
  - the duration of the current agreement
  - the current rental costs
  - the cost of maintenance (call-out costs plus repair costs)
  - whether the number of photocopies exceeds or is below the limit agreed
  - any disputes that have occurred during the period in question
  - any instances of non- or late payments
- You have been asked to arrange for the regular supply of computer consumables to the Computer Services department. Before entering into negotiations with potential suppliers you need to determine:
  - the brands of the goods

- how frequently you want the deliveries to be made, in what quantity, at what times and to whom
- whether or not you will accept part or late delivery
- whether or not you will accept substitute brands.

At this stage ask yourself the question 'what if?' to ensure that you have collected *all* the information you require. Suppose, for example, you want to buy a computer. Before entering into any negotiations what you should do ideally is to ask yourself:

What if

the price is too high?
it doesn't arrive on time?
it doesn't do what the salesperson promised?
it does some but not all of what the salesperson promised?
it is too slow?
it breaks down?
it needs updating?
it isn't compatible with the network?
the manual is too complicated to understand?

You should then try to provide the answers that you would find satisfactory – and bear them in mind when asking the salesperson the questions.

The meeting phase

General principles

Most meetings can be broken down into four parts:

- the establishment of an agenda, and the rules of conduct
- the identification of problems and issues, and of a settlement 'range'
- modification of the range and solving of problems
- closure and agreement.

Ideally you should try to confine the initial stages of negotiation to agreeing on what you are trying to achieve and, if possible, within what parameters – including how long you expect the meeting to take and the next steps, if any, if no agreement is reached during that period. You should also try to:

- establish an atmosphere that lends itself to reaching an agreement
- test the other party's position – does he or she seem willing to negotiate, or is it obvious that there is going to be some resistance?

In most negotiations one party makes some form of presentation to the other, in varying degrees of formality. If you are the one who is expected to 'sell' either the product or service, remember the following principles.

- Don't engage in a long monologue. If you do, the other party will switch off when, ideally, what you want is feedback on what you are saying.

- Keep the facts simple, and remember that most people can absorb only a limited number of facts at one time. Where possible, use visual aids – catalogues, samples, etc. Remember the old adage: 'Tell them what you are going to tell them; tell them; and then tell them what you have just told them.'
- Try to create a climate of confidence. The other party wants to be reassured that you are someone trustworthy enough to deal with. Include some anecdote at the beginning of the session which illustrates such reliability: 'I believe you know Martin. I've dealt with him for years'. However, make certain you can't be caught out with incorrect facts and figures. Telling lies is dangerous. If you are caught out you look a fool and your credibility is totally undermined.
- Shape the presentation towards the anticipated reactions of the other party. If you think he or she may react unfavourably towards a certain issue, think ahead and have your argument rehearsed should an objection be raised. Emphasise the benefits you think will be most appealing.
- Try never to be forced on to the defensive. If you have a genuine weakness in your case and the other party notices it, it is far better for you to admit it but to point out that, overall, the strengths outweigh the weaknesses.
- Be prepared to give the other party time, particularly if the negotiation involves either a very delicate issue or the expenditure of a large sum of money. Signal your intentions at the first meeting to let him or her get used to the idea, and then ask for a further meeting.

A technique sometimes used by organisations faced with the prospect of making some staff redundant is to first of all make sure that the office grapevine picks up the news that there are likely to be some redundancies in the near future. Senior managers then express concern in various forums about the financial position of the organisation or a particular area of it. The union is consulted and an intimation given that the problem is serious and that the number of redundancies may be considerable. Certain targetted individuals are asked if they have considered early retirement or other jobs. By the time the need to make people redundant arises, the workforce have become resigned to the idea. Indeed there may be relief that the number of redundancies is not as great as anticipated – and some people will already have left, thus reducing the size of the problem.

Handling price negotiations

Negotiating price is potentially difficult for a new negotiator. Many people find haggling over price embarrassing – even though they might be haggling for their organisation and not themselves. In certain arenas – such as the performing arts – people employ agents to do the haggling for them. If, however, you are not in that position you may be interested in the following tips drawn up by a seasoned negotiator.

Try to ensure that the other party makes the first bid. This lets you know the limit of his or her expectations. Remember, however, that in certain circumstances this is an unrealistic expectation. Many organisations, for instance, have a training budget and ask private training providers to tender for training contracts. Ideal though it may be for the providers to know how much the organisation is prepared to pay, so that a bid can be framed around that amount, they are very unlikely to be able to find out this information. The organisation will generally assume that if the provider knows how much money is available, he or she will 'bid up' to that amount.

When discussing price, try to keep within the level of expectations. If at the outset you ask for too high a price, or indicate that you are willing to pay only a very low price, then you lose contact with the other party who is uneasy at even attempting to negotiate further.

If you have to state a price, do so *without* using the words 'or near offer'. Otherwise you are letting all potential buyers know that you have no real expectations of getting the price you are asking.

If a buyer asks you whether a price is negotiable you may find yourself in some difficulty. If you say 'yes' then it is known that you are prepared to bargain downwards. If you say 'no' then you may lose a sale. In the case of a sale of goods there is no easy solution. In the case of a sale of services (i.e. a contract of employment) you may be able to deal with the situation by saying, for instance, 'It depends on what else there is on offer. Are there are any other fringe benefits?'

If you are asked to give a quotation, give a total figure where possible rather than a cost breakdown, to allow yourself more room for manoeuvre. Obviously if you are *asking* for a quote, insist on such a breakdown.

> Experienced negotiators refuse to believe that there is such a thing as a fixed price. Instead they believe that if you change the deal you change the price. For example, you could:
>
> ● negotiate to pick up and install the goods yourself instead of paying delivery and/or installation charges
> ● agree to forego the parts and labour warranty
> ● ask whether there is a 'good as new' but slightly damaged item, as opposed to a brand-new one
> ● intimate that you may be willing to place all your business with that firm for a particular period.

THEORY INTO PRACTICE

A second-hand car is for sale. It is very rusty and is obviously not going to pass its next MOT. However, it is one of the few specimens of that old model at present on the market and could possibly be considered a collector's item. Consider how you would advise (a) the buyer and (b) the seller to negotiate the best possible deal.

Negotiating behaviour

The ways in which members of meetings and groups interact have already been discussed (see Chapter 5). When you start negotiations with your opposite number, you may have to demonstrate some of the same skills – but you will almost certainly have to demonstrate others.

Most of these types of behaviour are 'up front' and can be responded to accordingly. You may encounter difficulties, however, when the other party starts to break the unspoken rules by indulging in what one management writer has described as 'ploys'.

THEORY INTO PRACTICE

Before being tempted to retaliate in kind, read the following scenario in which two administrators try to 'negotiate' for the services of a clerical assistant who has been employed to work for both of them. Consider what 'ploys' you think may have been used by both negotiators, and compare your answer with that suggested on page 613.

LORCAN   Look, we can't be sitting here all day arguing about it. We'll have to come to a decision in the next half hour or forget the whole thing.

DEVLA   I don't know why you can't agree to letting Aileen work for me in the mornings and you in the afternoons.

LORCAN   OK, to speed things up, I'll agree to let Aileen work for you every morning except Friday – oh, and except the last Thursday of every month when we're always frantically busy.

DEVLA   I have to warn you that I've already been assured by the departmental manager that she'll back me in whatever I want – and you know how much influence she has on the group manager.

LORCAN   You'll be very sorry if you do try to go behind my back. I've important friends too.

DEVLA   You've already lost one or two battles you know – be careful that you don't lose another one or your reputation will take a knock.

LORCAN   Calm down. I've one or two contacts in Personnel and I happen to know that another clerical assistant is going to be appointed in your area within the next few weeks. There's no point you making elaborate arrangements for job sharing if they are only going to be in place for a short time.

DEVLA   Perhaps you're right – but I can't make a final decision until I have a word with my manager.

The post-negotiation phase

Once an agreement is reached the inexperienced negotiator breathes a sigh of relief. More experienced negotiators, however, are less relaxed. They know that what is apparently agreed to in the negotiation room can be forgotten or distorted after the meeting finishes. There are some ways around this.

- Write down what has been agreed – preferably at the meeting itself, or as soon as possible afterwards.
- Try to be the one who draws up the draft agreement – despite the extra work. This will clarify your thoughts as to what has been agreed much more surely than merely reading through a draft prepared by someone else.
- Make certain that all appropriate people in your organisation know about the deal. They can then take appropriate actions.
- Ensure that the draft agreement becomes a formal agreement.

Also, take some time to evaluate the process, particularly if you are a new negotiator. There are bound to be things you think could be improved, and it will certainly help you in ensuing negotiations if you have made a note to yourself of pitfalls to avoid, examples of good practice to be repeated, etc. Some negotiators keep detailed information on their opposite numbers – what their strengths and weaknesses are, etc. – and update their information file at the close of each negotiation. Much depends, of course, on how often and at what level you are expected to negotiate.

ANSWER TO 'THEORY INTO PRACTICE' EXERCISE ON PAGE 612

The ploys used include:

'Time's getting on' (If you don't settle now, you'll miss out)
'Believe it or not' (I'm holding all the cards)
'Do it or else' (You'll be sorry if you don't)
'Think of your reputation' (You'll have no street cred if you do/don't agree)
'Trust me' (You know I wouldn't pull a fast one)
'Beyond my remit' (I'll have to consult someone else)

THEORY INTO PRACTICE

Consider whether you think negotiating for the best deal possible – even if you know you could afford more, or if you realise your opposite number is in a weak bargaining position – is totally ethical. What justification, if any, do you think you might have in doing so?

Obtaining specialist advice on contracts

It is essential to feel confident that you are negotiating with a suitable – and trustworthy – supplier. Otherwise any agreement you negotiate will be high-risk. As you become more experienced in this area, you are likely to build up a series of long-standing relationships with a number of reputable suppliers. When you first begin, however, you may find it useful to obtain advice and information from various sources.

Within your organisation, you can:

- consult more experienced colleagues

- check past records and consult appropriate databases or, in some limited cases, research in the company library
- use, where relevant, the organisation's approved list (i.e. its list of suppliers who have been assessed and approved (for further information on supplier assessment, look back to Chapter 2).

Outside the organisation, you can:

- check trade directories, trade journals, etc.
- communicate with fellow professionals in the same field
- talk to suppliers' representatives, or attend relevant exhibitions at which the terms and conditions of supply offered by a number of suppliers can be compared
- make use of sourcing services (i.e. agencies providing information about potential sources of supply and the reliability of the suppliers).

THEORY INTO PRACTICE

Difficult though it may be to check that a UK supplier is sufficiently reliable to allow you to feel confident in negotiating a contract, it is even more difficult when the supplier is overseas. Investigate what procedures, if any, are in place in your own organisation to check on overseas suppliers.

Element 8.2
Contract for resources and services

Your own work role and responsibilities

If you are expected to take responsibility for agreeing contracts, that should have been made clear at your job interview and be in your job description. Contracting may form the sole basis of your work or be one of several responsibilities you have. If you are in a large manufacturing or services organisation with the purchasing of supplies forming a major part of the operation, you could be one of a number of people involved; in a smaller organisation you might have the whole responsibility.

Contracting does involve considerable responsibility because if you make a mistake it can be very costly for a variety of reasons:

- in lost time – if the goods are of the wrong quality or quantity and reordering is necessary
- in loss of customer satisfaction
- in purely monetary terms, if you have agreed too high a price as a buyer or too low a price as a seller
- in terms of the expense involved in any legal action.

Assess your own responsibility for agreeing contracts, and consider:

a what qualities you have had to develop to assist you to cope with that responsibility

b any difficulties you feel you may need to overcome, and how you intend to overcome them.

The scope and limits of your own authority to agree contracts

In Element 8.1 you were asked to consider the limits of your responsibility in negotiating a contract (see page 587). The same considerations apply to the limits placed upon your authority to *agree* a contract. You must, however, also be aware of the way in which you are perceived by the other party to the contract. If you appear to have the authority to agree the contract, the courts may hold that you are an *agent* for your organisation and that you have bound your organisation by any decision you reach. Figure 8.2.1 gives a brief summary of the law of agency – study this and consider to what extent you fall into the agent category in your job.

- An agent is a person who is empowered to represent another legal party – known as a *principal*. He or she has the authority to act on behalf of that principal in any dealings with anyone else – normally termed a *third party*.
- If an agent contracts with a third party on behalf of a principal, he or she impliedly guarantees that the principal exists and that he or she has that person's authority to act as an agent.
- The duties of an agent are:
  - to perform the undertaking according to instructions
  - to exercise due care and skill
  - to carry out instructions personally
  - to account
  - not to permit a conflict of interests to arise
  - not to make a secret profit or misuse confidential information
  - not to take a bribe.
- The rights of an agent are:
  - to claim remuneration for services performed
  - to claim indemnity for all expenses legitimately incurred in the performance of services
  - to exercise a lien over property owned by the principal.
- Where the agent indicates that he or she is acting as agent, the general rule is that only the principal and third party have rights and obligations under the contract.

Figure 8.2.1 Basic principles of the law of agency

1 There are different classes of agent. Check that you are aware of the difference between:
 - a general agent
 - a del credere agent
 - a commission agent
 - a mercantile agent/factor.

2 Check that you are aware of the difference between *actual* authority and *apparent* authority.

3 Either find out or remind yourself of what is meant by the doctrine of *estoppel*.

Types, sources and formats of contract documents

Types of contract

Contracts for the supply of goods

Not surprisingly, the most common form of contract in the business world is for the supply of goods or services. This is defined in section 2(1) of the Sale of Goods Act 1979 as 'a contract by which the seller transfers or agrees to transfer the property in goods to the buyer for a money consideration called the price'.

There are variations on this type of contract. For example, in contracts of exchange and barter, no money changes hands. These cannot therefore be protected by the Sale of Goods Act, although the Supply of Goods and Services Act 1982 imposes certain statutory duties on the supplier.

Another variation is a contract for work and materials whose main purpose is the provision of a service. If, for instance, you have your hair cut, the main substance of the contract is the skill of the hair stylist; supply of the shampoo, conditioner, etc. are merely a secondary part of the contract.

In one case in the 1930s an artist was commissioned to paint a portrait. When a dispute arose between the painter and sitter, the Court of Appeal held that the contract was one for the painter's skill as an artist and not for the sale of goods (i.e. the finished portrait).

Contracts for the supply of goods on credit

Selling goods on credit is now an established part of commercial life. All forms of granting consumer credit are regulated by the Consumer Credit Act 1974, an outline of which is contained in Figure 8.2.2. There are a wide variety of ways of selling on credit.

● The Act governs the provision of credit under *regulated agreements*. A regulated agreement is defined as being a credit agreement between a supplier and a consumer, for a sum of less than a specified amount.

- Regulated agreements do *not* include: credit sale agreements for less than £50; land mortgages; running credit agreements; non-commercial credit agreements; credit agreements where the APR is less than 13 per cent; a credit agreement for the finance of international trade; a fixed-sum debtor–creditor–supplier agreement with four or fewer instalments.
- Sections 10–13 define:
  - running-account credit
  - fixed-account credit
  - restricted-use credit
  - unrestricted-use credit
  - debtor–creditor–supplier agreements
  - debtor–credit agreements.
- Sections 21–23 control the licensing and regulation of consumer credit agencies.
- Sections 43–47 control the advertising of consumer credit. The Consumer Credit Advertisement Regulations 1989 govern advertising published after 1 February 1990.
- Sections 87–101 outline the procedures to be followed and the remedies available to both parties in the case of termination or default.
- Sections 137–140 give the courts power to examine a credit agreement that has been made on exorbitant terms and, if the circumstances warrant it, to set aside the obligation, alter the terms of the agreement or require the creditor to repay all monies received.

Figure 8.2.2 Some features of the Consumer Credit Act 1974

Hire purchase

Hire purchase is essentially an agreement for the *hire* of goods for a certain period at the end of which the hirer chooses to purchase them from the owner. The hirer obtains the immediate use and enjoyment of the goods but does not become the owner until all the instalments have been paid.

THEORY INTO PRACTICE

Consider the distinction between a contract for the sale of goods and that of hire purchase. Consider also the likely consequences of such a distinction.

Conditional sale

A conditional sale is similar to a hire purchase agreement in that the customer obtains immediate possession of the goods in return for the payment of regular instalments. However, although the transfer of ownership occurs only when some specific condition is fulfilled, the buyer under a conditional sale agreement is committed to buy from the outset.

Credit sale

In this instance, ownership of the goods passes to the buyer at the start of the agreement.

Contracts of bailment

A contract of bailment arises when the owner of goods – known as the bailor – entrusts possession of them to another – the bailee – who has to take reasonable care of the goods whilst they are in his or her possession and who has to return them at the end of an agreed period or on request. Examples include handing clothes in at a dry-cleaner or depositing important documents with a bank. Also covered are hire agreements under which the owner of goods allows someone else to make use of them in return for regular rental payments – such as the monthly or yearly rental of a photocopier. Although the hirer has possession of the goods, he or she will never gain ownership.

> In business circles it is more usual to refer to the *leasing* rather than the *hiring* of equipment, and to agree a contract between the *lessor* and *lessee* rather than the *owner* and *hirer*.

Contracts for financial services

The relationship between a bank and its clients is contractual, and is covered to a large extent by statutes such as the Bills of Exchange Act 1882 and the Cheques Act 1957. Insurance contracts are also contracts for financial services, whereby an insurance company undertakes to provide financial compensation if the risk insured against actually occurs.

THEORY INTO PRACTICE

1 A major addition to the list of types of contract just outlined is, of course, the contract of employment. For further details look back to Chapter 2, page 177. Also check to see whether you employ the services of a private employment agency and, if so, under what type of contract.

2 Your organisation will have a contract or set of contracts relating to its premises – whether they be freehold, leasehold or rented. Investigate which type of contract exists.

Sources and formats of contracts

All contracts, no matter what their type or subject matter, have to include certain elements, and the law that lay down the legal formalities to be observed are both statutory and non-statutory. For a more detailed discussion, see Chapter 10.

Because there is such commonality of content, both commercial and employment contracts tend to follow a standard format. Consequently, even if you move to a different organisation you are unlikely to note a huge disparity in the way contracts are compiled. However, although you may expect that all the contracts will be in writing, the law of contract does not *require* them to be in that form other than in certain specific circumstances:

● The sale or transfer of land, where the Law of Property (Miscellaneous Provisions) Act 1989 requires that agreements must be in writing.

- Marine insurance, which is governed by the requirement of the Marine Insurance Act 1906 that only a written policy will be considered valid.
- Consumer credit agreements, the majority of which are governed by the Consumer Credit Act 1974, must be in writing. Under the provisions of this Act a hire purchase agreement made between a consumer and a business for a sum of less than a specified amount is called a regulated agreement and must not only be in written form but must also contain certain specified information.

Although certain contracts need not be in written form *initially*, if a dispute arises then there must be written evidence of the contract to enable a court to enforce it. Consequently a contract of guarantee – whereby the creditor sells goods to the debtor and the guarantor guarantees that the debtor will pay (thus making himself or herself secondarily liable for the debt) – need not be in writing at the beginning of the contract but must be in that form before a dispute can be settled.

Formats of contracts

The full content of a contract may not necessarily be contained in one document. A contract of employment can be an amalgam of the advertisement, the agreement made at the interview, the job description and the actual work carried out by the employee. A commercial contract can also consist of a variety of different documents. For instance, although a catalogue, price list, brochure or prospectus is in itself merely an 'invitation to treat' until a prospective buyer makes an offer to buy certain goods, if the supplier decides to accept that offer, the information in those documents can be held to form part of the resulting contract.

Standard form contracts

Most organisations do not want to waste time or money in compiling contracts from scratch each time they do business with a new or existing customer or supplier.

In addition, legal thinking has moved on slightly from the old position of examining the 'classical model' of a contract to see that the standard elements of offer, acceptance, consideration and intention are present, towards examining the commercial reality of each situation. Consequently there has been an increase in the use of standard form contracts on which are printed lists of standard terms and conditions. There are obvious advantages of such an approach:

- If the terms are contained in a written document, both parties are absolutely clear about what has been agreed.
- It is too time-consuming to negotiate individually each time.
- Once the contract has been drawn up, any future negotiations can be dealt with by relatively junior members of staff.
- It can minimise the risks of accidentally omitting important limitation or exclusion clauses.
- The other party is presented with what is almost a *fait accompli* with regard to the terms and conditions.

The following extract from a journal outlines some of the perceived *disadvantages* of a standard form contract.

'The standard form contract is fine for the supplier of any goods or services. He or she can blind the poor consumer with science and make certain that the terminology used is so technical, so complex and so long-winded that only a legal expert can fully understand it – and the exemption clauses such a contract generally contains are almost unbelievable. It's no use saying that the consumer should spend a couple of days trying to figure it out, or that he or she is perfectly free to go elsewhere if not satisfied. In the real world, 'shopping around' for a better deal isn't always easy – particularly if the consumer isn't in a particularly strong bargaining position. The whole concept of the freedom of contract is undermined by this type of document.'

1 Either from your own experience in dealing with standard form contracts, or after some more personal research, consider how far, if at all, you agree with the comments made in the article.
2 Consider any safeguards you think could be introduced to protect the consumer. (For further discussion on unfair exemption clauses, see page 630.)
3 You want to buy some goods and are given a standard form contract to sign. Some of the clauses concern you. What possible action do you think you should take (a) if you feel you are in a strong bargaining position, and (b) if you feel you are not?

Ways of ensuring protection in case of breach of contract

The legal remedies open to you should the other party to a contract fail to fulfil his or her part of the agreement are discussed on page 651. However, no matter what amount of legal recompense there might be if a breach does occur, you must ensure that there are procedures in place to try to prevent such a breach from occurring in the first place, mount a rescue operation if necessary. Ideally you should:

● vet all potential suppliers and, where relevant, check that they have the ISO 9000 registration.
● make certain that you do not place total reliance on one supplier, so that you always have another source of supply upon which to call.

In addition, you should ensure that the contract specifies any action the organisation will take and expect the other organisation to take should there be a breach, i.e. include clauses in which you reserve the right to:

● refuse to accept the goods
● return them for replacement or the receipt of a credit note
● require the supplier to send someone to your premises to inspect the goods and sort the faulty items from the correct ones
● negotiate a lower price for goods of less than the expected quality.

Assess the extent to which your organisation includes safeguards against breaches of contract, and how effective you think they are. Assess also the extent to which you think it pays equal attention to the potential consequences of any breach on your part.

An organisation's procedures and policies relating to contracts

If your organisation has a Legal department, any contracts you negotiate will probably have been drawn up by them and/or agreed by them before final signature. You may, however, still have the responsibility for processing those contracts. If there is no such department, your responsibility is likely to be greater. In that case you should seek specialist advice if in any doubt about the legal position, or consult your line manager.

Providing resources and services

If you are contracting to provide goods or services, you may be responsible for:

- preparing the initial draft contract – or completing a standard form contract
- sending the draft contract to the potential purchaser
- receiving back the contract as amended by the purchaser
- depending on your level of authority, either agreeing to the amendment, rejecting it, sending a counter offer or referring it to a senior manager for decision
- signing the final version and checking that it has been signed by the purchaser.

Obtaining resources and services

If you want to obtain resources or services, obviously you will follow the same procedures but with the roles reversed. You will state your requirements, the supplier will send you a draft contract for you to check and agree to or amend, and he or she will then have the opportunity to accept or reject your offer or to renegotiate.

'The battle of the forms'

A common problem in preparing and exchanging contracts is known as the 'battle of the forms', where both parties attempt to ensure that the contract is made on the basis of their standard conditions. This is most common where a contract of sale is involved and both seller and buyer are using printed stationery which has on the back their standard conditions of sale and purchase.

Suppose, for instance, you order goods from a supplier over the telephone. The supplier sends you a standard letter quoting £500 for sale and delivery of the product. The letter contains conditions of sale very favourable to the supplier. The quotation also states that if it is approved it will go ahead on the supplier's standard conditions. You order the goods on an order form which outlines your organisation's standard conditions of purchase. The supplier sends you the goods without any further written communication. Two questions then arise:

- Is there a contract; i.e. an offer, acceptance and intention?
- If so, on whose conditions has it been made?

In settling the issue, it is usual first to look at the *offer* that was made. Normally the supplier would be held to have made an offer (i.e. the quotation) and your order would be held to be a *counter* offer (*not* an acceptance) because it was not placed on the same terms as the offer.

Clearly, on this basis there would be no contract at all unless the seller later did something that amounted to an acceptance of your counter offer, or conversely, made yet a further counter offer which was then accepted by you.

If both of you remained silent then it is likely that there would be no contract until the supplier delivered the goods, or perhaps not until you had accepted them – depending on whether the seller in delivering the goods was accepting your latest counter offer or making a *further* counter offer on his or her own behalf. This would depend on the documentation accompanying the goods. Since in contracts made in this way there is often a gap between order and delivery, this will mean that in many cases, although the parties may *imagine* they have made a contract, they have not as yet done so and it is open to either party to withdraw.

In some cases it might be found that one of the parties has done something that could be treated as an acceptance. In one such case, a seller issued a quotation for the supply of a machine tool for £75 535 with delivery in 10 months. The buyer replied by placing an order. Both the quotation and the order were respectively seller's and buyer's standard conditions. A significant difference between the two was that the seller's conditions provided for price escalation which entitled him to charge his list price *at the date of delivery*. On receiving the buyer's order, the seller returned to the buyer a tear-off slip at the bottom of the buyer's order form which contained the words 'we accept your order on the terms and conditions thereon'. The Court of Appeal held that by returning the buyer's slip in this way, the seller accepted the buyer's counter offer, even though the slip was accompanied by a covering letter stating that the order had been entered into in accordance with the original offer.

THEORY INTO PRACTICE

1 Examine the procedures in place in your own organisation for the completion of contracts for resources and services, and try to assess whether they are sufficiently precise to avoid a 'battle of forms' problem developing.

2 In some countries the 'knockout doctrine' is used, whereby those provisions of the parties' standard conditions that are inconsistent with each other 'knock each other out', leaving only the provisions in which the parties are agreed. Consider whether or not such a doctrine should be introduced in the UK.

The content of contracts

It is equally important to make sure that you follow the correct organisational procedures when deciding on a contract's contents. As already discussed, the four basic issues are usually quantity, quality, time and price.

Contracting for the right quantity

When contracting for goods, the quantity you order will almost certainly depend on your organisation's approach to the amount of stock it wishes to carry. If it chooses to carry a considerable amount, you may have the advantage of being able to negotiate a reduced price because of bulk purchasing, and in such circumstances you may be involved in calculating economic order quantities (i.e. the size of order that minimises the total costs of purchasing and holding the stock).

If, on the other hand, your organisation operates a 'just-in-time' system, whereby stock is either produced or delivered in just the quantity required for the next stage in any process or project to be carried out, then you will be more interested in the time at which a small amount of stock can be delivered rather than the quantities. (For further discussion on these systems refer back to Chapter 2.)

Contracting for suitable quality

Although many implied terms relating to the quality of goods are now covered by statutory legislation, for various reasons – including the financial cost that may be incurred if you want to enforce your statutory rights – it is probable that your organisation will want to ensure that any contract for the supply of goods or services contains *express* reference to the quality level expected. If you have confidence in a particular brand name you may need only to specify that; or if you have confidence in a particular supplier you may feel that you need give only a brief description of your requirements. In other circumstances you should describe in far greater detail your exact requirements. A detailed specification becomes essential (for fuller discussion on this point look back to page 587).

Problems can occur when the item you are ordering is very expensive or very specialised or both, and you find yourself in a situation where you are not absolutely sure how to specify what quality you require. In such circumstances you can look for a supplier who complies with certain national and international standards, and specify those standards part of the contract.

Most developed countries have national standardisation bodies. Although the British Standards Institution (BSI) was the first, there are now more than 100 similar organisations belonging to the International Organisation for Standardisation (ISO) and the International Electrotechnical Commission (IEC). BSI not only represents the views of British industry on these bodies, it also presents the British view in the development of the European standards through the European standards organisations CEN and CENELEC.

- Since 1979 when the British Standard 5750 was first introduced, if a company becomes registered as meeting its requirements, then that company is recognised as being able to supply its goods or services to a stated level of quality. In 1987, the ISO developed the international equivalent known as the ISO 9000 series of five standards. In turn the BSI adopted, without amendment, the ISO 9000 as the new BS 5750. The ISO 9000 series was also adopted as the European standard EN 29000, and for all practical purposes, therefore, the standards are identical.
- Over 15 000 British Standards have been published, classified into one of the following standards programmes: Building and Civil Engineering; Materials and Chemicals; Engineering; Electrotechnical; Consumer Products and Services; Healthcare; Management Systems and DISC (information technology).

THEORY INTO PRACTICE

1 Investigate whether your organisation is registered as meeting the BS 5750 requirements. If it is not, what advantages do you think might accrue to it if it registered?
2 BS 5750 states that in establishing and maintaining an acceptable programme for quality, a supplier should also control the quality of the work of subcontractors. If appropriate, determine what procedures your organisation implements to ensure that its subcontractors comply with the same quality requirements as those of the main organisation. If your organisation does not have any such dealings, research into the procedures other organisations use. (You may want to check BS 5750, Part 4, for its guidance relating to the selection and control of subcontractors.)

Note that, although the BSI/ISO standards are employed by most major purchasing organisations in the UK as a benchmark for establishing quality, they do not apply to the actual *products* of the supplier, whether goods or services, but to the manner in which that supplier organises all aspects of his or her business that have a bearing on quality. It is therefore possible – although not perhaps probable – that you could insist in your contract that the supplier must be registered as having achieved BS 5750/ISO 9000 standards, and yet still receive goods or services that are faulty or unsuitable.

Contracting for delivery at the right time

Time is usually of the essence in the provision of goods or services, and it may be useful for you at this stage to re-read relevant sections of Chapter 3 to remind yourself of the need for forward planning, not only in this but also in other areas of your work.

One of the first steps you should take prior to framing an appropriate contractual term is to decide on the *lead time* you require for a particular item. Ideally what you should do is to work backwards from the date the product or service is required and attach a time limit to each stage in the process. If, for instance, you have to purchase a particular set of components and you establish that they are needed in two weeks' time, you would prepare a planner to include the time spent on:

- preparing the requisition and, if relevant, sending it to the purchasing department and arranging for it to be processed
- transmission of the order to the supplier
- completion of the order by the supplier
- transport of the order
- inspection and storage
- issuing to the relevant department.

THEORY INTO PRACTICE

1 It is often said that *consistency* of lead time is more important than its actual length. Consider whether you agree with that statement, and give reasons for your view.
2 Unless your organisation relies heavily on a just-in-time system, it will probably have established procedures for calculating re-order levels and buffer stocks in case the lead-time plan falters. Research into what they are and try to determine their effectiveness.

Contracting terms and methods of payment

One of the essential elements of a contract is the consideration involved, and you will almost certainly find that your organisation has very well-defined procedures in place to determine what price it is willing to pay for a particular product and the steps its staff should take to reach agreement over that price.

An organisation might require potential suppliers to submit their price lists right at the beginning of negotiations. What you can then do is compare the prices quoted, and possibly undertake some research as to the 'standard' price. You could, for example:

- consult trade journals containing information on UK prices and price trends for a wide range of materials and services
- access relevant databases.

When you have received a number of quotations your organisation may require you to complete a quotation analysis form, to compare the prices, packaging, delivery and any additional charges.

Most organisations have procedures in place to break down a quoted price into its constituent elements to determine the reasonableness of the proposed charge. Investigate the method used by your organisation to do this, and try to assess its effectiveness.

Another common practice is the submission of a tender or sealed bid. This is a formal procedure whereby you invite potential suppliers to make an offer of their terms, including price, for the supply of certain goods or services. If accepted, the offer forms the basis of a contract. There are various types of tendering process.

- In an *open tender*, prospective purchasers are invited to compete for a contract that is advertised in the press. Generally (although not always) the lowest tender is accepted.
- In a *restricted open tender*, prospective suppliers are invited to compete for a contract, the advertising of which is restricted to appropriate technical journals or local newspapers.
- With a *selective tender*, only those suppliers on an 'approved list' (who have previously been investigated) can take part.
- In a *serial tender*, prospective purchasers are requested, on an open or selective basis, to tender for an initial scheme on the understanding that, subject to satisfactory performance and unforeseen financial contingencies, a programme of work will be given to the successful contractor, the rates and prices for the first job being the basis of the rest of the programme.

Even though the aim of the tendering process is to produce the best price/quality combination, the Central Unit on Purchasing nevertheless recommends that a post-tender negotiating procedure should take place, particularly where:

- the order value is £100 000 or more
- the final evaluation does not produce an outstanding supplier
- clarification is needed about some terms or conditions
- it is a supply agreement for 12 months or more.

Public procurement in the EU takes place under the auspices of the GATT* (General Agreement on Tariffs and Trade) directives issued by the EU. The directives aim to extend public-sector purchasing across national boundaries, and require bodies subject to such directives to:

- advertise all purchasing requirements (in excess of a stated price threshold) in the EU's *Official Journal*
- award contracts following advertisement on the basis of non-discrimination between suppliers from different EU countries, with the aim of obtaining the best value for money
- follow the requisite procedures for 'open', 'restricted' or 'negotiated' tenders.

*Now known as the World Trade Organisation (WTO).

'Public procurement' covers not only government departments but also public authorities such as the police, education authorities and local authorities. If you work in one of these sectors, research the directives in more detail and check to see who is responsible for seeing that they are complied with.

Discount

One way in which you may be able to influence the price you pay is to include in the contract some reference to the discount you expect in particular circumstances:

- Prompt and/or cash payment can attract a discount. Note, however, that your organisation may well have a policy of settling invoices only after 30 days' grace, so that early payment may not be an option.
- If given a sufficiently large order, suppliers can often produce additional items at a marginal cost having recovered the overheads on the initial quantity. Bear in mind, however, that you will have to weigh the advantages of the lower price against the disadvantages of having to store more material than you need, thus incurring storage costs and also possible wastage.
- If you are a long-standing and valued customer you are in a good position to negotiate a lower price.
- Seasonal or promotional offers may be available. If you buy fuel, for example, you may be in a better position to negotiate a discount during the summer months. If you buy garden furniture you may be offered a discount during the winter, and so on. On certain occasions a supplier will publicise a 'special offer' which may be of particular interest to you.

'Always pick the supplier who quotes the lowest price and haggle afterwards about the level of service you require.' Consider to what extent you agree with that statement. Does the purchasing policy of your own organisation ever work along those lines?

Obtaining specialist advice on contracts

Within the organisation, the same sources of specialist advice apply to the making of contracts as to the negotiating of contracts. Look back to page 613 for the relevant information.

Outside the organisation

In this instance, a little knowledge is sometimes worse than none at all. You must feel confident that when you ask for advice from a particular source, it is going to be good advice. Consequently, unless your organisation employs its own legal staff, you may have to use the services of a firm of solicitors. If your relationship with a particular firm is long-standing and has proved successful, you should have few concerns.

Where you are looking for legal advice for the first time, you should check out the local firms by asking them to send you details of their experience in advising on commercial contracts and dealing with any resulting concerns. You should also try to find out from them whether they have other clients in the same line of business as you. Ideally – although this is not always possible – you should try to 'test' them out on a relatively trivial matter in the first instance to see how they perform.

If you feel that the advice you have been given has caused you to enter into an inappropriate contract or to incur a financial loss, you may be able to recoup some of those losses by suing your adviser for the advice he or she gave.

Prior to 1963, professional negligence was recognised only where a fiduciary duty existed between the two parties. However, in that year a case was heard concerning an advertising company that requested and received a credit reference for one of its clients from the client's bank, and on this basis allowed the client to have credit. The credit reference included a disclaimer enabling the bank to avoid any liability for its reference. The company's client then went into liquidation and the company sued the bank to recover its losses. It did not succeed because at that time the disclaimer was held to protect the bank from liability. However, it was established that a duty of care existed because there was a 'special relationship' between the two parties.

Other special relationships include those of a client with an architect, surveyor, building society or credit reference agency, but what constitutes such a relationship has been defined rather restrictively by the courts. In one case, for instance, it was held that accountants owed no duty of care to investors who might invest in companies on the basis of published accounts. It was, however, recognised that a different situation existed where accountants or directors *knew* that a particular person would be relying on given figures to assess the financial viability of a company for the purpose of making a takeover bid.

In addition, although property surveyors and valuers are not generally in a contractual relationship with a purchaser (the relationship being between the building society or other lender and the surveyor or valuer), the courts have held that if the professional carries out his or her work negligently then a duty of care will not have been met.

Neither solicitors nor barristers are liable in negligence for the work they carry out in court. Even so, they do owe a duty of care to their clients in other work that they are asked to carry out.

THEORY INTO PRACTICE

The Financial Services Act 1986 imposes restrictions on the way in which financial advisers are able to operate. Investigate its main provisions and assess whether it has any relevance for you.

Legal and regulatory requirements relating to contracts

Chapter 10 contains a brief outline of the initial requirements in the compilation of a contract. You should also be aware of certain contractual terms and their effect on the contractual relationship, and the way in which statutory law affects agreements.

Contractual terms

Misrepresentation

Even when a contract is not in written form, what the parties agree to must be clear and free from misrepresentation. If, for instance, the seller of some goods claims that they will perform a particular function, knowing that to be untrue, he/she is guilty of *fraudulent* misrepresentation. If the seller makes that statement without due care, then he/she is guilty of *negligent* misrepresentation. Even if the seller genuinely believes that the goods will perform that particular function, and they cannot, the result will be *innocent* misrepresentation. There are different remedies open to the buyer. (See further page 639 for the effect of such misrepresentations on a contract.)

- The law does try to keep a sense of proportion, however. If a statement is made which is obviously mere sales talk (a 'trader's puff') then there will be no legal remedy. If, for instance, a sales representative tells you that 'it is the snip of a lifetime' or a 'dream holiday', you would have difficulty in taking him or her to court on the basis of misrepresentation.
- Although a manufacturer is not a party to a contract between a supplier and purchaser (see page 632 for discussion of the doctrine of privity of contract), he/she may still be held to account in common law for any 'extravagant claims' made in an advertisement. One classic case involved a company promising in an advertisement to pay £100 to anyone who contracted 'flu after using its patent remedy three times daily for two weeks. The plaintiff used the remedy as directed but still caught 'flu. Even though the plaintiff had not bought a remedy directly from the company, it was held that there was a contract between them because all the essential requirements of offer, acceptance and consideration were present. Nowadays, of course, statutory law provides additional protection.

Conditions and warranties

Traditionally, contractual terms have been divided into *conditions* (major terms that are vital to the main purpose of the contract) and *warranties* (less important terms, breach of which does not go to the root of the contract). An interesting illustration of the difference between the two is that of a singer who was engaged to appear in an opera but was too ill to perform on the first night, and another singer who arrived at rehearsal three days later than agreed. In the first instance there was a breach of condition, in the second a breach of warranty.

In recent years the courts have realised that it is difficult to draw a distinction between conditions and warranties and have introduced the concept of *innominate terms* – intermediate terms to be assessed only in the light of the consequences of a breach. If a breach of a term results in severe loss, the injured party will be entitled to repudiate the contract. If it results in only minor loss, he/she will be able to claim only damages.

Express terms

In Chapter 2 there was some discussion of the difference between express and implied terms in a contract of employment. Such terms have equal importance in a commercial contract. This subsection deals with express terms and the next with implied terms.

The most common types of express terms in commercial contracts – particularly in standard form contracts – are exemption or exclusion clauses, liquidated damage clauses, and price variation clauses.

Exemption or exclusion clauses

Exemption clauses are express terms in a contract which try to remove or limit the responsibility of one party to the contract. You meet this type of clause if, for instance, you park your car in a car park and receive a ticket on which are printed the words 'Customers use this car park at their own risk', or if you receive some details of a property from an estate agent which say that the purchaser must satisfy himself or herself as to the validity of any statements about the property.

Given that UK law makes it clear that in general a contract agreed between two parties is of interest only to them, you might think that an exemption clause is binding no matter what the adverse consequences may be. However, the courts are uneasy about exemption clauses – it being felt that they are sometimes unfair – and have therefore introduced certain limitations on their use. Anyone wanting to insert such a clause must show that it truly forms an agreed part of the contract, ideally by being contained in a signed document. If it is in an unsigned document it must comply with certain conditions:

- The document must be regarded by a reasonable person as a contract and as such likely to contain exemption clauses. Thus when a holidaymaker was injured as a hired deckchair he sat on collapsed, he was able to sue the hirer for damages despite the fact that the ticket he had purchased contained an exemption clause for any injury caused. The Court of Appeal held that a reasonable person would assume that ticket to be a *receipt*, not a contract.
- Even if it is decided that the unsigned document *is* a contract, the person seeking to rely on the exemption clause must show that reasonable steps have been taken to give notice of the clause to the other party. In one famous case, Lord Denning made the point that the more unreasonable a clause is, the greater the notice that must be given of it. Indeed, he opined that in some cases such a clause should be printed in red ink with a red hand pointing to it!

Further safeguards against exemption clauses are included in the Unfair Contract Terms Act 1977 (supplemented by the Unfair Terms in Consumer Contracts Regulations 1994). Figure 8.2.3 gives a brief outline of their contents.

The purpose of the Act is to protect *consumers* when they enter into contracts with businesses. Business-to-business contracts remain subject to common law rules – unless they buy something outside their normal scope of business. The Act's main provisions are as follows.

- There can be no restriction or exclusion of liability for death or personal injury resulting from negligence.
- In the case of other loss or damage, there can be no restriction or exclusion of liability unless the term satisfies the requirement of reasonableness.
- Certain exclusion clauses will be void under any circumstances in a consumer transaction (e.g. exclusion of sections 12, 13, 14, 15 of the SGA.
- In the case of defective goods supplied for private use or consumption, there can be no exclusion of liability either in the contract or in the guarantee.

NOTE: *The Unfair Terms in Consumer Contracts Regulations 1994* is of particular relevance to standard form contracts where the consumer has had little influence over the terms. In such a case the requirement of 'good faith' applies, the guidelines for which are similar to the normal test of reasonableness.

Figure 8.2.3 Some features of the Unfair Contract Terms Act 1977

If a trader falls foul of the Unfair Contract Terms Act, he/she will face civil liability. However, the Consumer Transactions (Restrictions on Statements) Order 1976 (as amended) supplements the former Act by making it a *criminal* offence for a trader who continues to use exclusion clauses rendered void by the Act, by displaying notices such as 'No refunds', on the assumption that many consumers could be led to assume that they had no legal redress should the goods purchased prove unsatisfactory.

Liquidated damages clauses

Such clauses lay down the amount of damages that will be payable in the event of a breach of contract. For further discussion on this point, see page 658).

Price variation clauses

Some suppliers are very reluctant to be bound by a fixed price in case they have miscalculated increases in the cost of raw materials, overheads, etc. In such circumstances what they tend to do is to insert a term in the contract allowing a price variation under certain circumstances.

1 There are obvious dangers in signing a contract containing a price variation clause. Assess how your organisation deals with these clauses and how effective you think that action is.
2 Research the following cases and then draw up an *aide mémoire* for yourself summarising the main points.
   - *Olley v Marlborough Court Ltd* [1949] 1AER 127
   - *L'Estrange v Graucob Ltd* [1934] 2KB 394
   - *Parker v South Eastern Railway Co.* [1877] 2CPD 416
   - *Chapelton v Barry Urban District Council* [1940] 1AER 356
   - *Interfoto Picture Library Ltd v Stiletto Visual Programmes Ltd* [1988] 1AER 348
   - *J. Spurling Ltd v Bradshaw* [1956] 1WLR 461
   - *White v John Warwick Co. Ltd* [1953] 1WLR 1285
   - *Ailsa Craig Fishing Co. Ltd v Malvern Fishing Co. Ltd* [1983] 1AER 101
   - *Alexander v Railway Executive* [1951] 2AER 442
   - *Thomas National Transport (Melbourne) Pty Ltd and Pay v May and Baker (Australia) Pty Ltd* [1966] 2 Lloyd's Rep 347
   - *Mitchell (George)(Chesterhall) Ltd v Finney Lock Seeds Ltd* [1983] 1AER 108.

Implied terms

As already discussed, the courts will imply certain rights and obligations in a contract of employment. Although most of the implied terms of commercial contracts are covered by statutory law (see below), certain standard terms have also been implied by common law. For instance, the courts will imply a term into a lease of a furnished house that it will be reasonably fit for habitation at the start of the tenancy.

In common law, the doctrine of *privity of contract* means that a contract is made between two people or parties and the rights and duties thus created apply only to them. Consequently only the purchaser can take an action in contract in respect of a defective product. Similarly, a consumer's rights in contract are restricted to an action against the person who sold or supplied the goods. Statutory law, however, widens this responsibility quite considerably.

The sale of goods

The major statute relating to the sale of goods remains the Sale of Goods Act 1979 (SGA) as amended by the Sale and Supply of Goods Act 1994 (SSGA), although in recent years there have been a number of other statutes each relating to a specific aspect of consumer protection.

Although, as already discussed, two parties are generally free to agree a contract, the SGA provides that any agreement for the sale of goods will automatically include a number of conditions and warranties, the most important of which are the following.

Section 12 of the SGA

There is an implied condition on the part of the seller that in the case of a sale he/she has a right to sell the goods. If the seller cannot pass rights of ownership to the buyer, he/she will be liable for breach of a condition. In addition, s. 12(2) implies two warranties; i.e. that the goods are free from any third-party rights, and that the buyer will enjoy 'quiet possession of the goods'. Thus, the buyer of a stolen typewriter who brought an action under s. 12(2) was awarded its purchase price together with the cost of a repair she had carried out.

Section 13 of the SGA

As already discussed (see page 588), where there is a contract for the sale of goods by description – if, for instance, they are ordered from a catalogue – there is an implied condition that the goods will correspond with the description.

Although the courts seem prepared to enforce s.13 quite rigorously, sellers can sometimes avoid its terms by including in the contract words such as 'bought as seen' or 'sold as seen'. Beware, therefore, if you see such a phrase in any contract you are negotiating.

Section 14 of the SGA

Where the seller sells goods in the operation of a business, there is an implied term that the goods supplied under the contract are of satisfactory quality; i.e. that they meet the standard a reasonable person would regard as satisfactory. Criteria include their fitness for the purpose for which such goods are commonly supplied, their appearance and finish, their freedom from minor defects, their safety and their durability. Note, however, that the protection does not extend to any defects that have been specifically drawn to the buyer's attention, or to circumstances where the buyer has inspected the goods or the sample before making the contract.

When you purchase goods and rely on the skill of the seller in advising you that the goods will do what you want them to do, there is an implied term that that advice is sound. Where, however, you have any special requirements you must make them known to the seller prior to the contract. A woman with sensitive skin who bought a made-to-measure tweed coat, and who subsequently developed a skin complaint through wearing it, was unsuccessful in claiming damages because the coat would not have affected a person with a normal skin and she had not made her condition known to the seller.

Section 15 of the SGA

As already discussed, if the sale is by sample, the bulk of the goods must correspond with the sample and with the description.

THEORY INTO PRACTICE

1 Section 17 of the SGA provides that the property in goods passes when the parties *intend* it to pass. Section 18 sets out various rules designed to ascertain that intention. Section 19 provides that where the seller has reserved the right of disposal of the goods until some condition is fulfilled, ownership of the goods will not pass to the buyer until that condition is met. Section 20 states that, unless otherwise agreed, the goods remain at the seller's risk until the property in them is transferred to the buyer. Check the details of these sections, and some of the major cases in this area:

- *Re Anchor Line (Henderson Brothers) Ltd* [1936] 2AER 941
- *Tarling v Baxter* [1827] 6B&C 360
- *Underwood Ltd v Burgh Castle Brick and Cement Syndicate* [1922] 1KB 343
- *Genn v Winkel* [1911] AER 910
- *Poole v Smith's Car Sales (Balham) Ltd* [1962] 2AER 482
- *Healey v Howlett and Sons* [1917] 1KB 337
- *Aluminium Industrie Vaassen BV v Romalpa Aluminium Ltd* [1976] 2AER 552.

2 Sections 21–25 of the SGA detail the *exceptions* under which a person who buys in good faith may obtain good title to goods; i.e.
- sale in a market overt
- sale under a voidable title
- sale by a seller in possession after sale
- sale by a buyer in possession.

If you are, or are likely to be at some in the future, involved in any such negotiations, check to see what the Act says in more detail.

The supply of goods and services

The provisions of the SGA apply only to contracts where goods are sold for a money consideration. They do *not* cover:

- other methods of obtaining goods, such as by hire purchase, hire, barter, or work-and-materials contracts.
- the provision of services.

Hence the importance of the Supply of Goods and Services Act 1982 (SGSA), which is split into two parts. The first part deals with any goods or materials supplied and contains very similar information to that of SGA. The second part deals with the work, labour or services provided. Its principal provisions are the following.

Section 12 of the SGSA

A contract for the supply of services is one under which a person (the supplier) agrees to carry out a service. It does not apply to contracts of service in employment or to apprenticeships.

Section 13 of the SGSA

Where the supplier is acting in the course of a business there is an implied term that the supplier will carry out the service with reasonable care and skill.

Section 14 of the SGSA

Where the supplier is acting in the course of a business and the time for performance cannot be determined from the contract or ascertained by a course of dealing between the parties, there is an implied term that the supplier will carry out the service within a *reasonable* time. If, therefore, you take your car to a garage for a minor repair, it is reasonable to expect it to be kept for a few days but not for six months.

Section 15 of the SGSA

Where consideration cannot be determined by the contract or from a course of dealings between the parties, the customer will be expected to pay a *reasonable* charge for the service.

Section 16 of the SGSA

This section allows ss. 13–15 to be excluded by express agreement, provided the exclusion term complies with the reasonableness test under the Unfair Contract Terms Act 1977.

Consumer protection

If you are in business, the law has generally assumed that, on the whole, you are able to take care of yourself. However, that assumption has been somewhat 'softened' by the introduction of legislation designed to protect consumers from unscrupulous manufacturers and suppliers. Here we look at the Trade Descriptions Act 1968 (TDA) and the Consumer Protection Act 1987 (CPA). The latter covers both misleading price indications and consumer safety issues.

Section 1 of the TDA

This creates certain criminal offences relating to trade descriptions. Any person who, in the course of a trade or business, applies a false trade description (as defined by s. 2) to any goods shall be guilty of an offence. This 'catch-all' section was used in a case in which the defendants sold a watch to the plaintiffs that was described as a 'diver's watch' and hence waterproof. When the watch was put into water it stopped working. The defendants were found guilty of an offence.

Section 3 of the TDA

A false trade description is one that is false to *a material degree* or is misleading. Where, therefore, the false trade description is not material to the supplying of goods, an offence will not be committed. However, the courts have tended to favour the plaintiff in such circumstances, one example being that of a second-hand car dealer who described a car as being 'beautiful'. While the upper bodywork was good, the car was unroadworthy. Despite the defendant's argument that his statement was meant to refer only to the appearance of the car, the court convicted him of an offence on the grounds that it was reasonable to assume that the statement was meant to refer to the whole of the vehicle.

Section 14 of the TDA

This applies to false or misleading statements with regard to services, accommodation or facilities, provided it can be proved that the trader either knew that the statement was false or was 'reckless' as to its truth. A firm of tour operators published a brochure stating falsely that the rooms in a hotel were air-conditioned and showing a photograph of a room that was in fact in another hotel; it was held guilty of committing an offence – despite the fact that at the time of publication it was unaware that the description was false. Upon discovering the inaccuracy, it had informed its agents and those customers who had already booked, but a new customer had not been advised of the mistake. Consequently the firm was in breach as by that time it knew the description was false.

Sections 24 and 25 of the TDA

The defences available to a charge of breach of one of the provisions of the Act include:

- that the commission of the offence was due to a mistake, to reliance on information supplied, to an act of default of another person, to an accident or some other cause beyond the supplier's control
- that the supplier took all reasonable precautions and exercised all due diligence to avoid the commission of such an offence either by him or her personally or by any person under his or her control.

THEORY INTO PRACTICE

Read the following summary of a case and try to determine whether or not an offence has been committed. Check your answer with that on page 637. Note that the case was held before the introduction of the Consumer Protection Act 1987, sections 20 and 21 of which created the offence of giving a misleading price indication. For further information see below.

A store made a special offer on 'Radiant' washing powder and put up a poster offering specially marked 'Radiant' packets at a reduced price. When the store ran out of the specially marked packets, ordinary packets were put in their place but the poster was not taken down by the manager. The store was prosecuted.

Sections 20 and 21 of the CPA

Section 20 states that a person shall be guilty of an offence, if in the course of business, he/she gives a misleading price of any goods, services, accommodation or facilities. Section 21 gives a list of circumstances under which a misleading price indication may be made, such as where:

- a recommended price is quoted as being higher than it actually is
- false facts are used to determine the price
- the price covers matters in respect of which an additional charge is made
- a statement is made that the price of the goods is due to fall or rise, when in reality the supplier has no such expectation.

Sections 10 and 11 of the CPA

Section 10 states that a person shall be guilty of an offence if he/she supplies any consumer goods that fail to comply with the general safety requirements. The areas covered by section 11 include:

- the composition or contents, design, construction, finish or packing of goods
- approval of goods under this section
- any requirements as to inspection or testing
- any warnings, information or instructions to be provided with the goods
- any requirement relating to the provision of information to officials
- prohibitions on certain goods or materials.

- The Consumer Protection Act also introduced a range of strict liability offences, covering injury and damage caused by defective products. Consequently a person who suffers an injury or loss no longer needs to prove negligence. Where such an injury or loss occurs because of a defective product, the manufacturer or producer of the product will be liable unless he or she can rely upon one of the statutory defences under section 4 of the Act.
- The General Product Safety Regulations 1994 came into force in October 1994 and imposed a further statutory duty on the producers of goods to ensure that they are safe. However, they are applicable to producers of consumer goods only. Where goods are produced to be used solely in a commercial environment (e.g. goods produced by one business to be used in another) the Regulations do not apply.

ANSWER TO 'THEORY INTO PRACTICE' EXERCISE ON PAGE 636

The House of Lords ruled that the store had not committed an offence. The manager was held to be 'another person' under s. 24 and the store had in place reasonable precautions to prevent such an event happening.

THEORY INTO PRACTICE

In addition to the Consumer Credit Act, several other Acts create criminal offences relating to the supply of consumer goods:

- Weights and Measures Act 1985
- Food Safety Act 1990
- Road Traffic Act 1988
- Unsolicited Goods and Services Act 1971.

Depending on your area of work, check that you are aware of the possible effects these Acts may have on your business operation.

The government is becoming increasingly concerned about companies lending at high interest rates to people on low incomes, and in particular the so-called 'non-status' lenders who are more aggressive than the credit companies and who impose punitive charges if repayments are late. Some statutory restrictions are therefore expected to be introduced shortly.

Consequences of using inadequate contractual documentation

One possible consequence of using an inapplicable or inaccurately completed contract is that, although you think an agreement has been reached, nobody else does! Another is that you may indeed have reached an agreement but it is one that commits you to a set of conditions that may not be to your advantage but which are difficult to repudiate. In such circumstances you must either learn to live with the contract or – where applicable – claim that you made a mistake or that the supplier has induced you to enter the contract under a misapprehension.

Mistakes

Suppose, for instance, you make a mistake in the document. Generally speaking you will have to stand the consequences of that mistake. However, in certain circumstances a mistake will render a contract void:

- *Common mistake* – where both parties share the same mistake. In *Magee v Pennine Insurance* [1969] 2QB 507, for instance, a proposal form for car insurance was completed incorrectly by the plaintiff, Mr Magee. When the car was subsequently written off, the insurance company offered Magee £375 as a compromise on his claim. After he had accepted this offer, the company discovered the error and sought to repudiate the agreement. It was held that the agreement *could* be set aside.
- *Mutual mistake* – where the parties are at cross purposes; i.e. they have different views on the facts of the situation but neither realises it. In such circumstances the courts will try to decide which of the competing views would be taken by a 'reasonable' person, and the contract will be enforceable on those terms. If, however, they cannot do so, the contract will be void.
- *Unilateral mistake* – where only one of the parties to the agreement is mistaken as to the circumstances of the contract *and* the other party is aware of the fact. In such circumstances the contract will again be held to be void.

Mechanisms for dealing with mistakes

Fortunately, if you do make a mistake in a written document and want to try to correct it before the contract becomes void, you may be able to do so in one of two ways.

Rectification

Where the written document fails to state the actual intentions of the parties, it may be altered under the doctrine of rectification. In one case, for example, the plaintiff agreed to transfer his car hire business to his daughter in return for her agreeing to pay certain household expenses, although this was not stated in a later written contract. The father was held to be entitled to have the agreement rectified to include the terms agreed.

Non est factum

It is assumed that someone who signs a contract will have read, understood and agreed to its terms. Where, however, that person does so under a misapprehension as to its true nature, the law may permit him or her to claim 'non est factum'; i.e. that the document is not their deed. Note, however, that there must be some *fundamental* mistake rather than mere carelessness. Thus, where a 78-year-old widow who had broken her glasses signed a document without reading it, she was unable to claim 'non est factum' because she knew she was signing a deed of gift even though she did not realise its entire contents. On the other hand, a man who could not read and write but who signed what he thought was a guarantee relating to one part only of his son's business was able to plead 'non est factum' when it was discovered that the guarantee covered all aspects of his business.

Misrepresentation

When you want to buy goods or services, you may be strongly influenced by what the supplier tells you. If you are particularly impressed by what he or she says, you are obviously more likely to enter into a contract. The problem arises, however, when the supplier has not been totally truthful – either innocently or deliberately – in which case you may be able to claim that he or she has misrepresented the situation. Misrepresentation can be defined as a false statement of fact, made by one party before or at the time of the contract, which induces the other party to enter into the contract. If it occurs the contract is voidable and the innocent party may then rescind it or claim damages.

However, there is no general duty to disclose information, and silence does not generally amount to a representation. Where, therefore, you have not thought to ask a pertinent question, *the law will not protect you for having failed to do so.* Nor will the law protect you from 'sales puffs' or statements of opinion.

The statement in question must actually have induced you to enter the contract. It must therefore have been made to you directly and not through a third party, and you must actually have relied upon it. However, once you can show that you have relied upon it, the other party cannot claim that it was unreasonable for you to have done so. In one case, an inaccurate statement contained in auction particulars, and repeated by the auctioneer, was held to constitute a misrepresentation in spite of claims that it was unreasonable for anyone to allow themselves to be influenced by such a statement.

Such protection is helpful if you are the purchaser. If, however, you are the supplier, you will be more interested in the defences open to you should a claim of misrepresentation be made against you. If you are accused of fraudulent misrepresentation, you can, of course, try to prove that you honestly believed that any statement you made was true. However, you may still have to face a claim of negligent misrepresentation under the Misrepresentation Act 1967, which reverses the normal burden of proof and compels you to show that you had reasonable grounds for believing the statement to be true.

Requirements for accurate and valid completion of contractual documentation

The formalities to be observed when drawing up and exchanging a contract, and the consequences of doing so, have already been discussed. In addition you should always check that the contract is 'complete' (including date and signature) – otherwise it will not be legally binding. In one case, an agreement for the purchase of a van provided for the balance of the price to be paid over two years 'on hire purchase terms'. It was held that there was no agreement since it was uncertain what terms of payment were intended. Similarly the contract must not use 'non-essential' words – otherwise they will be disregarded. Thus, where a standard form contract contained the words 'usual conditions of acceptance apply', but no usual conditions of acceptance could be identified, the phrase was held to be meaningless.

Even where the contract seems technically complete, you should leave nothing to chance. However theoretically knowledgeable you might be about the law, if in practice you fail to read the contract thoroughly or to check the final document against any previous draft, you could find again that you have agreed to something you never intended. In such circumstances, the standard form contract has both advantages and disadvantages. The advantage, of course, is that you are likely to be familiar with its layout and with the majority of its contents and will quickly be able to spot any anomalies. The disadvantage is that you can be *too* familiar with it and skim-read it rather than reading it word by word. Your proof-reading skills are never more important than when checking a legal document.

Suppose, for instance, you are used to glancing through such a contract to check on the terms and conditions relating to delivery. You are used to wording such as:

> 'The supplier will deliver and unload the goods to the point of delivery stated overleaf not later than the date for delivery stated overleaf. Time shall be of the essence. The supplier recognises that late delivery may cause the company consequential loss, such as inability on the part of the company to meet other contractual commitments, and agrees to pay liquidated damages in compensation for such loss at the rate stated overleaf.'

The danger is that you might read the clause, note that it is a standard clause, and yet fail to check that the information stated 'overleaf' actually complies with your requirements – even though, of course, that information will be regarded as being part of the contract.

You might overlook the fact that a standard clause has been subtly altered. You may, for instance, be so used to a cancellation clause which entitles you to cancel the order by giving written notice that you fail to notice that another sentence has been added committing you to pay a cancellation charge.

Read through the following contractual clause at your normal speed and make a mental note of what it says. Then read it through much more carefully and check to see what, if anything you have overlooked. If nothing, excellent!

'It is the buyer's responsibility to ensure that all necessary approvals have been granted before manufacture commences. The company will assist in supplying drawings and calculations when requested to do so. No design work or calculations will be issued prior to the placing of a firm order or contract. An additional charge will be made for any design work or drawings required over and above those normally supplied by the company. It is the buyer's responsibility to satisfy himself or herself that the drawings, calculations and specifications are correct, as no responsibility for errors or omissions will be accepted by the company once the buyer has approved details submitted. The company's responsibility in any event is solely confined to its own manufactured components and does not extend to other products or components or overall structural or architectural considerations.'

Element 8.3

Monitor contractual performance

Your own work role and responsibilities

If you are responsible for negotiating and agreeing contracts it is more than likely that you are also responsible for monitoring their progress. However, you may have organised your work in such a way that, once you have carried out the initial work, you then delegate the monitoring task to one of your team. Obviously, you should be very sure of the capabilities of that person. If he or she fails to write up a set of minutes or to check that the monthly expenses claims have been submitted, that is annoying but not damaging. If, on the other hand, he or she fails to check the progress of an order so that a production line falls idle because of lack of materials, that is both annoying *and* damaging.

1 Consider those people in your organisation (possibly including yourself) who are responsible for monitoring contractual progress, and try to assess the extent of their:

- attention to detail
- persistence
- ability to implement successful planning and follow-up systems
- ability to look ahead and avert a possible crisis.

2 Where you feel that anyone lacks any of these qualities, consider what form of staff development you would suggest to help to improve their performance.

Scope and limits of your authority to monitor the meeting of contract conditions

In Element 8.1 you considered the limits placed on your authority to negotiate contracts. It might be, of course, that although you do not have complete authority to enter into a contract, you have the sole responsibility for seeing it completed. A major difficulty in this respect is that you may not be the only person involved in the contractual process. Suppose, for instance, you work in an organisation that relies heavily on the purchase of certain components for its production processes. During the whole contractual process, you have to liaise with a number of people within your own organisation as well as the suppliers themselves. You may have to negotiate initially with:

- the technical department responsible for drawing up that particular specification (you may need to know not only what primarily is required, but also whether any alternatives would be acceptable)
- the Production or 'user' department for its requirements as to delivery times, etc.
- the Finance department for information on essential documentation, desired methods of payment, etc.

Having completed the initial round of meetings, however, you or your deputy then have to make sure that the progress of the contract is notified to all relevant personnel. All is well if matters run smoothly. You are faced with problems, however, if the goods cannot be supplied on time or in the desired quantity, particularly since many of the people with whom you are likely to be dealing will not be subject to your control, or even that of your senior manager. Although ultimately, of course, you can invoke the protection of your senior manager and ask him or her to solve the problem, it is obviously preferable if you can avoid doing so other than in extreme circumstances. The following are some ways of doing this.

Keep everyone up to date on what is going on. Give them the information rather than relying on them to ask you. Ask for their assistance where possible. If, for instance, you are having great difficulty in obtaining goods of the right quality within the specified time limit, you may find that the Production department or other user may accept a substitute or suggest another solution.

Try to be *proactive* rather than merely reactive. Whilst the ultimate user may have the technical knowledge, he or she may not have your up-to-date knowledge of what is available on the market or of the idiosyncrasies of different suppliers. For instance, he or she might be unaware that a particular supplier is always late delivering the goods or always tries to vary the price agreed on the grounds of increased production costs. If you circulate this information on a regular basis, you may be able to avoid the problem of your heart sinking when a particular supplier is requested, because you know that you will have to constantly chivvy him or her to deliver the goods under the agreed terms.

Ways of monitoring contractual performance

Throughout this unit, emphasis is placed on the four major elements of most contracts for the supply of resources or services: quantity, quality, time, and terms and methods of payment. It is often good practice, therefore, to develop systems for monitoring a contract under those four headings.

Monitoring quantity

This is probably the easiest part of the contract to monitor, given that once the quantity has been negotiated that remains a fixed requirement. However, there are occasions when goods or services are delivered in instalments, and you must have in place an efficient inventory control system (possibly centred around the goods received note) to monitor both the amounts delivered and what is outstanding – measured each time, of course, against the last day of delivery.

THEORY INTO PRACTICE

Types of ordering policies include:

- blanket orders, grouping together many small requirements
- capacity booking orders, reserving supplier capacity for the production of various parts, used in conjunction with make-orders specifying later what parts are to be made
- period contracts, stating an estimated total quantity for the period and the agreed price, in conjunction with call-off orders stating the delivery date and quantity
- period contracts, specifying a series of delivery dates and quantities (e.g. 100 on the first day of every month)
- 'order-up-to' contracts, often used by stock controllers.

1 Either from experience or personal research, consider what control methods you could institute to ensure that you were able to monitor the progress of each of the above contracts.

2 Consider any other types of contract you use in your workplace and assess the effectiveness of your monitoring mechanisms in relation to them.

Monitoring quality

Monitoring quality is often more difficult than monitoring quantity. The law does offer some protection if, for example, the bulk of goods delivered does not match the quality of the sample. It also offers several remedies (see further page 588). Obviously, however, the sooner you become aware that what you have ordered – or what you are supplying – is not of acceptable quality, the sooner you can attempt to rectify the situation without having to resort to the law.

If, as already discussed, you contract with an ISO 9000 registered firm (see page 624), you can assume that at the very least it has systems in place for reviewing constantly the quality of its goods or services. If, on the other hand, you are the supplier and have obtained ISO 9000, you will be committed to instituting procedures designed to enable you to produce items of a consistent level of quality. Indeed, Part 2 of the BSI 's *Quality Assurance Handbook* devotes considerable attention to 'reliability and maintainability'.

You should ensure that you institute a series of checks on both incoming and outgoing goods. Many organisations select from three options.

The first option is *incoming inspection*. Items are inspected on delivery according to a specified accepted quality level (AQL). The results of the inspection are tabulated either by the Quality Control Department or the person to whom that task is delegated, and the information is sent to the receiver of the goods (whether it be the Purchasing department or an individual member of staff). Where an item does not meet the requirements it can then (if and as agreed):

- be returned for full credit
- be returned to the supplier at his or her expense for correction or replacement
- be repaired, with the expense of the repairs charged to the supplier
- be used, but a price reduction negotiated with the supplier
- be scrapped, with the scrap value being credited to the supplier.

Whatever the agreement, when goods are rejected the norm is to inform the supplier in writing and request confirmation of receipt of the advice. Where relevant a credit note should also be requested. In some systems, when the supplier has agreed to the goods being returned, he or she will issue a debit note.

The second option is *source inspection*. The purchaser either has resident inspectors at the supplier's organisation, or arranges for the inspectors to visit the supplier at regular intervals.

The third option is *source control*. The supplier is made totally responsible for supplying a product in accordance with a given specification and for reporting inspection results to the purchaser.

Some organisations, accustomed to ordering in bulk, use a 'sample' system of monitoring whereby a percentage of the goods delivered are tested at random to see that they match the quality requirements.

THEORY INTO PRACTICE

Obviously, inspection procedures differ from organisation to organisation, particularly in the smaller ones. Consider:

a the advantages and disadvantages of the procedures just outlined, and
b how they compare with the procedures in operation in your own organisation.

Consider also any improvements you could make to your own inspection procedures.

The more reputable the brand name of a product, the more likely it is that it will meet even the most stringent of inspections. To cut down the need for personal inspections you may therefore be wise to purchase or supply goods that come into one of the following categories:

- have the BSI Kitemark, which indicates that
  - BSI has tested samples of the product against the appropriate British Standard and has confirmed that the requirements of the standard have been met
  - BSI has assessed the manufacturer's quality management system
  - both company and product are subject to continual surveillance by BSI.
- have complied with a British or international standard specifically concerned with safety
- are part of the BSI Registered Stockists Scheme
- have been checked by the testing houses set up by some trade associations.

Monitoring time performance

In trying to ensure that deliveries are on time, make your supplier fully aware of your time schedule. You can do this by:

- checking out the supplier before entering into any contract (if necessary, look back to Chapter 2 for a more detailed discussion on this point)
- making lead times clear
- keeping the supplier updated with any relevant information
- avoiding rescheduling requirements other than in emergencies
- avoiding altering any of the specifications
- stating a definite delivery date (not ASAP or Urgent).

You should keep a record of how effective each supplier has been in delivering goods or services at the time agreed. One method sometimes used when suppliers are expected to make regular deliveries is to compile a chart that assesses delivery performance by calculating the percentage of deliveries in each period that are behind schedule. See Figure 8.3.1 for one example of such a pro forma.

Deliveries to date

Supplier	Deliveries	Late (%)	This period (%)	Past 2 years (%)

Figure 8.3.1 A pro forma to monitor delivery performance

Another very effective method of identifying non-compliance with contracts for the supply of goods is to use a computer system that allows you to check instantly:

- the value of forward commitments by date
- the value of business placed with any supplier
- outstanding orders from any supplier
- overdue orders from any supplier, with promised delivery dates
- details of any outstanding order by order number and/or by part number
- list of any goods currently below re-order levels.

A single check each day allows you to chart the progress of an order and to identify when and for how long it is overdue. The same type of system can, of course, be used for services.

> If you become aware that a supplier is having difficulty in delivering your order on time, it is of little use just crossing your fingers and hoping for the best. Ideally you should take action to try to improve matters by appointing someone to act as an *expeditor* to maintain close contact with the supplier and to 'chase' the progress of an order. The cost of such a function can be justified on the grounds of the additional costs incurred should goods *not* be delivered on time, or if legal proceedings have to be instituted because of non-delivery.

In many manufacturing organisations, the ordering of materials and components has to be synchronised with production requirements, in which case time is again of the essence. The process involves:

- drawing up a master production schedule which details the end-products to be completed week by week
- breaking the schedule down into lists of all the parts required to make each product (i.e. preparation of the parts list or bill of materials file)
- preparing an inventory file comprising the records of individual items in stock.

The information thus gathered is then incorporated into a materials-requirements planning package designed to calculate the requirements and lead times, and then to arrive at dates at which orders should be placed if the net requirements are to be available in time.

THEORY INTO PRACTICE

Despite all your precautions you may occasionally find that a sudden shortage of a key item has occurred. Consider (a) what procedures, if any, are in place in your organisation to remedy such a situation, and (b) any further action you could suggest.

Monitoring terms and methods of payment

Cash flow can become a big problem for many organisations, and it is therefore vital that money owed by customers be collected as soon as possible. However, it is equally important to recognise that failure to pay on time also has several disadvantages. Acquiring a reputation for being a late-payer or one who needs several reminders may have adverse repercussions if you want an urgent delivery, or if you are desperately looking for goods in short supply. You may also find that your organisation is not able to claim a discount for payment within a certain period, or that you have to pay interest when the agreed time for payment has elapsed.

Consequently, even if it is not your responsibility to oversee the payment or receipt of payment, you should nevertheless have systems in place to monitor that it is in fact taking place.

THEORY INTO PRACTICE

Obviously, such systems differ depending on the size and structure of the organisation. Check that you know who is responsible in your own workplace for ensuring payment – either to or from a supplier. Check also the procedures in operation to ensure that payment is made on time. Where possible, contrast the case of a good and a poor payer and try to determine the reason for this.

Types and sources of information relating to contractual performance

The various sources of information likely to assist you when negotiating and preparing contracts have already been discussed (see page 613).
Additionally, you may want to check whether the goods or services for which you are contracting are covered by an industry-wide code of practice, and if there is a problem to ask the association responsible for that code of practice for assistance.

Section 124(3) of the Fair Trading Act 1973 places a duty upon the Director General to encourage associations to prepare codes of practice for guidance in safeguarding and promoting the interests of consumers, and Figure 8.3.2 outlines some of the major participants.

ABTA (Association of British Travel Agents)
AMDEA (Association of Manufacturers of Domestic Electrical Appliances)
BDMA (British Direct Marketing Association Ltd)
CCA (Consumer Credit of the UK)
CCTA (Consumer Credit Trade Association)
DSA (Direct Selling Association)
FDF (Footwear Distributors Federation)
FLA (Finance and Leasing Association)
GGF (Glass and Glazing Federation)
LAPADA (Association of Art and Antique Dealers)
LPFA (London Personal Finance Association Ltd)
MOPA (Mail Order Publishers' Authority)
NAMSR (National Association of Multiple Shoe Repairers)
NCCF (National Consumer Credit Federation)

RETRA (Radio, Electrical and Television Retailers' Association)
RMIT (Retail Motor Industry Federation Ltd)
SMMT (Society of Motor Manufacturers and Traders)
SMTA (Scottish Motor Trade Association)
TSA (Textile Services Association Ltd)
VBRA (Vehicle Builders and Repairers Association)

Figure 8.3.2 Associations that issue codes of practice to their members

These codes provide you with an alternative source of consultation if a product or service proves unsatisfactory – before you resort to legal action. All the codes provide conciliation procedures, and most provide arbitration – although in the latter case the customer is generally required to pay a fee for the service. For further discussion about conciliation and arbitration procedures, see page 652.

It is difficult to determine whether consumer legislation, combined with the codes of practice, has improved the quality of resources and services. Recent statistics issued by the trading standards departments and Citizens Advice Bureaux indicate an upward trend in complaints, the majority being about motor vehicles, furniture and floor coverings, household appliances and electronic equipment.

Ombudsmen schemes

One perceived disadvantage of the conciliation schemes offered under most codes of practice is that they may not be completely impartial. However, another possible source of help for you if you are concerned about the outcome of a particular contract is to take advantage of the ombudsmen schemes. All of these are independent and in every case the service is free of charge. The British and Irish Ombudsman Association admits to membership only those people who satisfy the four criteria of independence, effectiveness, fairness and public accountability, and Figure 8.3.3 lists the main schemes in operation in the UK.

- Banking
- Broadcasting
- Building societies
- Estate agents
- Funeral directors
- Health services
- Insurance
- Investment
- Legal services
- Local government
- Parliamentary commissioner
- Pensions
- Personal investment
- Police complaints

Figure 8.3.3 Ombudsmen schemes

The extent of the jurisdiction of a particular ombudsman depends on the scheme. For example, the private-sector schemes do not usually cover all members of a particular industry. The Corporate Estate Agents Ombudsman is concerned only with the large chains of estate agents owned by banks, building societies and insurance companies and cannot deal with complaints against independent estate agents. Similarly the Insurance Ombudsman's Bureau can consider complaints against only those insurance companies and members of Lloyd's that are members of the Bureau. However, where the jurisdiction does extend, the ombudsman can not only make an individual ruling and award compensation, but also may well make a recommendation that certain business practices and procedures of the organisation in question be altered or improved.

> The ultimate sanction for many organisations is bad publicity. Every ombudsman publishes an annual report, which will normally give examples of complaints that have occurred in the previous year and statistics on the number and type of complaints, without naming the organisations involved. However, if an organisation were to fail to comply with a decision, in some schemes the ombudsman would have the power to name it.

Identifying non-compliance with contracts

Contracts for obtaining goods or services

In most cases it is relatively easy to determine whether goods you have received have been delivered on time and that a bill for the correct amount has been submitted. You will probably have picked up any slippage on delivery through the use of your inventory control system, and any delay in payment should be picked up by accounts staff.

It is often equally easy to determine whether the goods are 'of satisfactory quality'. Indeed, section 34 of the Sale of Goods Act 1979 (as amended by the SSGA 1994) states that, unless otherwise agreed, when the seller tenders delivery of the goods to the buyer, he or she is bound on request to afford the buyer a reasonable opportunity to examine the goods for the purpose of ascertaining whether they are in conformity with the contract and, in the case of a contract for sale by sample, of comparing the bulk with the sample. In one case the plaintiff received the shipping documents and paid the price for some goods prior to their arriving in England. Upon arrival, they were found to be unsatisfactory. The plaintiff argued that he had not had a reasonable opportunity to examine the goods. The defendant argued that he should have examined them at the port of departure. The court held, however, that the plaintiff could succeed – he had not had a *reasonable* chance to examine the goods.

Problems can sometimes arise when you receive goods that look OK, that have passed the initial inspection and that you therefore store for future use. It is only when you actually begin to use them that you discover certain defects. Suppose, for instance, you order a computer and specify that it must be able to carry out certain functions. You have no need to use one of these functions until some weeks after the computer has been installed, and it is only then that you discover that it is not equipped with that particular function. You may be able to claim certain remedies. However, you are still left with the situation that the computer doesn't fulfil your requirements. It is good practice, therefore, to try to assess whether you need to apply a more rigorous inspection procedure in the case of goods whose defects may otherwise be hidden. For the computer, for instance, you could have prepared a checklist of the functions requested and tested them out immediately on delivery of the equipment – even if you had no real intention of using all of them straight away.

Equally serious problems can occur where the contract you enter is one for services. Assessing the ability of a person to carry out a task is often more difficult than assessing the ability of a photocopier to print coloured copies! Even if you have carried out all the necessary formalities – preparation of a job description, detailed interview procedure, etc. – you may find that for some reason the employee does not live up to expectations. Again, time is of the essence. Bearing in mind that legally you are allowed to dismiss someone within a two-year period of commencing employment without incurring the risk of a claim for unfair dismissal (other than in certain specific circumstances), ideally you need to treat that as the probationary period. During that period, however, you should be instituting certain procedures to enable you to assess the progress of the new employee, (a) to determine whether any staff development or training is required, and (b) to collect any evidence should he or she prove to be unsatisfactory. (For a more detailed discussion on staff appraisal systems, look back to Chapters 1 and 2.)

Contracts for supplying goods or services

In the case of the supply of goods, your outgoing systems should mirror your incoming systems. If, on the other hand, you supply services, the problems of identifying possible non-compliance intensify, particularly since you want to be able to spot it before your client does!

If you have followed all the standard procedures in relation to the recruitment and interviewing of staff, you will at least have minimised the risk of taking on an unsatisfactory employee. However, problems can occur even with the most apparently satisfactory employee if, for instance, there is a personality clash with a particular manager or if there is a breakdown in communications and he or she turns up late, at a different time, without the requisite skills, etc. Most organisations that 'hire out' staff or a particular service keep very detailed records of:

- different organisational requirements (often with a 'profile' listing likes, dislikes, preferences, etc.)
- employee performance – normally on a task-by-task basis and evidenced by a short questionnaire completed by the client organisation.

If as a consequence you find, for instance, that one employee is constantly mentioned as being unpunctual, too slow, etc. you are provided with an indication that the contractual requirements are not being met and you therefore have an opportunity to remedy the situation.

Dealing with non-compliance

Quite frequently the contract itself will specify the action to be taken if there has been non-compliance in a number of areas. If it does not, and you are in the position of not having received the resources or services you require despite all your efforts of persuasion, you may have to resort to legal action to obtain either specific performance or damages (for further discussion see page 657). However, there are other options open to you.

Uncompleted contracts

If the contract has been partially completed, you may choose to accept that part – on the grounds that something is better than nothing – even though you are not *required* to accept part performance. In one case, for instance, a builder contracted to install a central heating system in return for a lump-sum payment. He installed it badly and it was estimated that a further sum would have to be spent on it to make it work properly. The householder refused to pay any money at all and was held entitled to do so by the court.

However, such a course of action would not be open to you if from the outset you intended the contract to be a series of agreements. If, for example, you enter into a contract for the delivery of some goods on the 1st, 10th and 20th of a particular month, then each agreement will constitute a separate contract. Consequently, if the goods are delivered on the 1st and the 10th but not the 20th, you will still be obliged to pay for the first two deliveries.

Again, if the contract has been *substantially* performed, a court may apply the 'quantum meruit' principle (i.e. based on what each party deserves). For example, if you offer an industrial cleaning service over a six-month period but fail on one occasion to send a cleaner to carry out the work, your customer may still be required to pay you for the work actually carried out. Be careful, however, of over-reliance on this protection. Traditionally the courts have been very reluctant, for instance, to apply the 'quantum meruit' principle to employees who, during industrial disputes, perform the majority of their contractual obligations but refuse to carry out one particular task (e.g. compulsory overtime, dealing with members of the public, etc.). In such circumstances the principle of non-payment for part performance is normally invoked.

THEORY INTO PRACTICE

Study sections 30 and 31 of the Sale of Goods Act 1979 (as amended by the SSGA 1994) for more information on this area.

Contract conditions not adhered to

If, despite all your efforts, you find that the contract has not been adhered to to your satisfaction, you may wish to invoke the *guarantee clause* contained in many commercial contracts; for example:

> 'Subject to compliance with certain conditions, the company will repair or replace (at its option) any components of the company's manufacture which fail owing to faulty materials or workmanship.'

One difficulty, however, is that guarantees are often designed to limit liability to such an extent that you will not be given full recompense for any breach. Some guarantees in contracts, for instance, add wording such as:

'The liability of the company under this guarantee shall be limited to the invoice value of the components replaced or repaired and the company shall not be liable for any consequential loss or damage howsoever caused. It shall be the duty of the customer to insure against such consequential loss and to hold the company harmless therefor.'

In such circumstances your organisation's representative may have to decide whether to refuse to accept the limitations of the guarantee and to enter into further negotiations with the supplier. Bear in mind, of course, that guarantees cannot eliminate your statutory rights – nor can they protect the supplier from statutory liability for his or her negligence. Indeed, you will often find that you are better off under the implied terms provided by the Sale of Goods Act than under a seller's guarantee.

THEORY INTO PRACTICE

Many organisations choose to insure against certain eventualities. Check to see what insurance cover – if any – your own organisation has as a protection against non-performance of a commercial contract.

Possibly your final step before resorting to legal action is to consider the use of *conciliation* or *arbitration* in cases where, for instance, there is a dispute about payment or quality. Mention has already been made of the various codes of practice in existence, and in such cases some provision is usually made for both conciliation and arbitration in the case of a dispute. For example, the Association of Mail Order Publishers' code of practice has a free conciliation scheme and, in addition, makes arrangements where necessary for arbitration by the Chartered Institute of Arbitrators.

However, you should note that the Consumer Arbitration Agreements Act 1988 specifies that any stipulation in an agreement with a consumer that future differences *must* be referred to arbitration cannot be enforced. An alternative, therefore, is the county court arbitration scheme introduced to deal with claims under a certain amount. The rationale is much the same as for an industrial tribunal and the proceedings are supposedly quicker, less formal and less expensive than proceedings in other courts. The strict rules of evidence do not apply, and unless the arbitrator orders otherwise, the hearing is held in private.

THEORY INTO PRACTICE

1 Remind yourself of the difference between conciliation and arbitration – particularly in relation to the extent to which they bind both parties.

2 For a brief outline of the conciliation and arbitration procedures offered by ACAS, in the case of an industrial as distinct from a commercial dispute, see Chapter 10, page 730.

3 The county court system is described in more detail in a series of leaflets available free of charge from the county courts. Obtain copies of them for possible future reference.

An organisation's procedures for varying contracts

A variation of the original contract may be by mutual consent or in some cases made unilaterally. In the first case, the contract will remain in existence in its new form. In the second case the party to the contract who has not agreed to the variation can claim that it has been breached. To avoid possible conflict, therefore, many commercial contracts contain some reference to possible variations – particularly in relation to costs – and how they are to be negotiated. For example:

> 'All quotations and estimates issued by the company are, unless otherwise stated, based on current costs of production (materials, hours and wages) and are subject to amendment on or after acceptance to meet any recognised rise or fall in such cost.'

Difficulties can occur when the proposed variation of the contract relates to price. There may be occasions on which you, either as the purchaser or the supplier, may want to ask for a price adjustment. Such a request may arise at the enquiry stage, where, for instance, a supplier quotes a higher price for goods than that previously quoted – in which case the purchaser has the choice to accept or reject it. It may also arise, however, during the course of the execution of the contract, or even on completion of the work, because:

- the purchaser has asked for a change (i.e. a variation) in the specification
- unforeseen costs have occurred
- inflation has affected wages, materials and other related costs.

In these circumstances it is good practice for both parties to follow a set procedure. This could be:

- to ensure that any adjustments are authorised by a senior manager
- to notify the adjustment to the relevant departments – Design, Estimating, Production, Accounts, etc.
- to confirm any adjustments in writing
- where a standard costing procedure is in operation, to monitor price adjustments and variances against standard material costs
- where adjustments are calculated in accordance with an agreed formula, to identify clearly the base date of both the original contract and the circumstances giving rise to the adjustment
- to ask the suppliers to provide data to justify price increases.

All is well if the two parties agree. Where they find difficulty in doing so, the purchaser may have to consider:

- looking for an alternative supplier
- looking for alternative materials
- checking to see whether it is worth producing the goods or service in-house (e.g. using in-house printing facilities rather than contracting out)
- a longer-term strategy requiring any future contracts to contain a clause specifying longer notification of any adjustments.

1 Most organisations allow their fixed-price agreements to be varied to encompass a redeterminable fixed price, a fixed price subject to certain adjustments, or a fixed price with incentives. Consider the system in operation in your own organisation and the reasons for that choice. Compare it with the other methods and assess the advantages and disadvantages of each.

2 Check also what procedures are in place should you and the seller not be able to agree over a proposed price adjustment.

Some commercial contracts contain a 'force majeure' clause stating, for instance, that if delivery is delayed by some cause *totally* outside the control of the supplier, then he/she shall give written notice of such cause within seven days of its occurrence and the company may then (but without prejudice to its other rights) 'allow such extra time for delivery as is reasonable under the circumstances'. The major problem, however, lies in deciding whether the problem is actually totally outside the control of the supplier and, if so, whether the contract should therefore be considered to be frustrated (see later).

Consequences of terminating contracts

Most of the major legal consequences of terminating contracts are dealt with on page 656. However, they are not the only consequences – a terminated contract can have both financial and marketing implications. If, for instance, you have failed to supply some goods or perform a service and the contract is terminated, possible consequences include:

- loss of future business
- bad publicity (word soon gets round if you are unreliable)
- administrative and production costs incurred by non-payment of the account
- laying-off of staff and/or a decline in morale
- adverse effects on any promotion prospects for those involved
- possible disciplinary action if a mistake has been made or negligence can be proved

The above list may sound like the story of the horse with a nail missing from its shoe causing the battle to be lost; but it is often true that if one contract is terminated for lack of performance, more tend to follow suit simply because there is a basic fault in the organisation's product, service or procedures.

If, on the other hand, it is the other party to the contract who causes its termination, the consequences may be almost equally far-reaching. For example, there may be:

- disruption to a vital schedule
- difficulties in maintaining a particular service until another supplier is found
- loss of *future* custom if, for instance, your production line is held up for want of a vital component
- laying-off of staff for the same reason
- the work involved in finding another, more suitable supplier.

THEORY INTO PRACTICE

1 Consider the possible consequences if:
   a you arrive at work one day to find a letter saying that the organisation with whom you contract for a frequently used component has gone out of business and the contract is therefore at an end
   b you receive a telephone call saying that a set of gifts for VIPs to be presented at the end of a prize-giving ceremony that evening cannot be delivered in time
   c you realise that you are not going to be able to send the total quantity of goods required by one particular customer.
2 In all three cases, consider what action you would take to try to minimise the possible consequences.

Recording variations and agreements

Recording all variations to a contract should form part of your overall procedure for monitoring the progress of that contract. The approach depends, of course, on the actual format of the contract.

If, for instance, you use your purchase order form as the basis of the contract, you will probably distribute copies of it to key personnel. When, therefore, you negotiate a variation to that contract, ideally the same mechanism should be used. Some organisations use the same multi-set format – although often in a different colour to indicate that it is a variation and not a new contract. Others convey the information by memo, with an attached circulation list to be initialled and dated by each person on that list. The circulation list is then attached to the original contract plus the variation, as evidence that all interested parties have been informed.

Variations to standard contracts are usually more formal, and result either in a complete 'amended' contract being exchanged between the parties, or a standard 'adjustment' form being completed and exchanged.

As already discussed, a frequent variation is that of price. In such circumstances it is standard practice to have a 'price adjustment' form agreed between the parties and completed as and when required. One option is to permit the seller to make adjustments to the contract price that he or she considers to be justified by cost increases, although the buyer is entitled to request independent evidence that the adjustment is correct. A second option is to agree a formula for index-linking the contract price (i.e. for adjusting it in line with changes in published indexes of cost available both to buyer and seller).

Legal and regulatory aspects

Most commercial contracts terminate automatically when the goods are delivered or the service is rendered in accordance with the agreed conditions. However, there are other occasions on which contracts end, with certain legal repercussions.

Frustration

There are times when a contract cannot be completed because of the influence of outside factors – or, in the case of a contract for personal services, because of illness or death. Thus, when someone hired a concert hall in order to hold a series of concerts but the hall burned down before they could take place, the contract was held to be *frustrated*. Similarly, when someone advertised that rooms in his flat were available to let to those who wanted to view the coronation procession of King Edward VII, the subsequent contracts were held frustrated when the procession was cancelled because of the king's illness. Another contract was held to be frustrated when a pianist was too ill to perform at a particular concert.

Frustration will not be held to have occurred in certain circumstances:

- *Where the agreement was impossible from the outset.* Where the two parties agree to do something that is not possible (e.g. where there is a contract for the sale of specific goods and the goods, without the knowledge of the seller, have perished at the time the contract was made) the contract is not frustrated. Instead, s. 6 of the Sale of Goods Act 1979 applies and the contract is held to be *void*. Section 7 covers a similar situation when the goods perish before the risk passes to the buyer.
- *Where a contract merely becomes too difficult or expensive to perform.* Just because a contract becomes very difficult or expensive is no reason for considering it frustrated. In one case the defendants had entered a contract to ship goods between Egypt and Hamburg. Because of a dispute, the route by which the goods were going to be transported was closed. The contract was not, however, frustrated since, difficult and expensive though the alternative route was, it was nevertheless still available.
- *Where there is provision in the contract for frustration.* If, for instance, a concert ticket contains a term that states that in the case of cancellation or postponement, money will be refunded, that provision stands in place of any claim for frustration.

- *Where one of the parties is responsible for the act that caused the frustration.* If someone carries out an act that prevents him or her from performing the contractual obligations, obviously frustration cannot then be claimed. If, for example, you agree to deliver some goods by sea and then sell the ship before the goods are transported, you cannot then claim the contract has been frustrated.
- *Contracts for the sale of land and leases.* Although not an absolute rule, it is normally the case that any contract for the sale of land and leases cannot be subject to frustration.

The effects of frustration

The rights and duties of each party should frustration occur are contained in the Law Reform (Frustrated Contracts) Act 1943, under which the following provisions apply:

- any money paid is recoverable
- any money due ceases to be payable
- expenses incurred prior to frustration may be recovered
- where there has been partial performance prior to frustration, and one party has received a valuable benefit, a 'quantum meruit' may be available to the other party.

Breach of contract

If a contract is frustrated, it is treated to a large extent as if it had never existed. Where, however, it is obvious that a contract does exist but that one party is in breach of it, certain remedies will be available to the other party. General information about contractual remedies is given in Chapter 10, but the following points relate more specifically to the consequences of breaching a contract for the sale of goods or services.

The first step to take is to decide whether it is a breach of a condition or of a warranty. Where a *condition* is breached, you can generally choose either to:

- continue the contract but claim damages, or
- repudiate the contract.

Where, however, a *warranty* is breached you are allowed only to claim damages. (But see page 630 for a discussion about the increase in the use of 'innominate terms'.)

If the other party to the contract makes it clear that he or she either cannot or will not carry out the agreement, you may then be able to claim an *anticipatory* breach. You can either sue for damages immediately or wait for the date of performance to arrive. In the latter case, however, you take the chance that a supervening act may occur rendering the contract void. If, for instance, someone places a series of newspaper advertisements with you and then changes his or her mind, you may be able to claim damages immediately or delay the claim until the date for the last advertisement. If, during that time, the newspaper closes down, however, the contract will be void.

Damages

A common-law right to claim damages is available for every breach of contract. Damages can be:

- *nominal* – awarded when, although there has been a breach, the breach has been minimal
- *substantial* – intended to put the injured party in the same financial position that he/she would have been in had the contract not been breached
- *exemplary* – where the court feels the breach or the conduct of the party initiating the breach justifies awarding the injured party damages above and beyond the financial loss incurred.

In addition, damages can be liquidated or unliquidated.

Liquidated damages

Many commercial contracts contain a provision as to what financial penalties – i.e. liquidated damages – should be paid in the event of a breach. To be valid, however, such a clause must be a genuine pre-estimate of the anticipated effect of the breach, and not a penalty clause which allows for the payment of a randomly arrived at large amount – in which case the court will ignore it.

THEORY INTO PRACTICE

In one well-known case in 1915, the plaintiffs supplied the defendants with tyres under a contract designed to achieve resale price maintenance. The contract provided that the defendants had to pay the plaintiffs £5 for every tyre they sold in breach of the agreement. When the defendants did sell tyres at less than the agreed price they then resisted the plaintiff's claim for the £5 per tyre, on the grounds that it represented a penalty clause. Consider what you think the court decided. Check your answer with that on page 659.

Unliquidated damages

Where the parties have made no provision for the level of damages to be awarded, the court will decide the amount to be paid. It will consider what loss has been suffered by the plaintiff. It will also need to decide what type of damage has occurred for which compensation is payable – economic loss, mental anguish, etc. – or nowadays, even mere discomfort. In one case the plaintiff was awarded damages because the hotel at which he had booked a holiday was way below his expectations.

THEORY INTO PRACTICE

The courts will also try to determine whether (a) the damage is too remote, and (b) whether the plaintiff has taken any steps to *mitigate* his or her losses. Research further into what the law requires in the latter situation.

Other remedies

Sometimes damages are an insufficient remedy. If you have ordered a supply of components which fails to arrive on time, and you are thus prevented from completing a valuable order, you may be content with monetary compensation. If, however, you want to buy a particular piece of land for redevelopment, damages would be of less use to you than an order for *specific performance*, whereby the court insists that the land be sold to you. Similarly the court might impose an *injunction*, ordering a person not to break his or her contractual obligation.

For obvious reasons, the courts are reluctant to enforce the doctrine of specific performance in the case of a contract for employment (see further page 754). However, on occasions they have issued injunctions to prevent an employee from breaking a contract with one employer to take up employment with another. In such a case, of course, they may be indirectly enforcing specific performance if the employee is thereby forced to continue working for the first employer. In one case an actress who attempted to break her contract with one film company and enter a contract with another was prevented from doing so. In her overcrowded profession, she would have had little option but to continue working for the first film company.

> Two common types of injunction are the *Mareva* injunction, which prevents a person from removing assets outside the jurisdiction of the English courts or disposing of assets within its jurisdiction; and the *Anton Piller* injunction, which may be awarded to a plaintiff's solicitor giving him or her the power to enter and search a defendant's premises for documents or other items. The purpose of this order is to prevent the defendant from destroying potential evidence.

The Sale of Goods Act 1979 deals separately with the remedies available to the buyer and the seller. The seller can take action on two fronts. He/she can claim *personal* remedies (i.e. an action for the contract price or damages for non-acceptance) and *real* remedies against the goods:

- a lien (the right to retain the property until the claim is satisfied)
- stoppage of goods in transit
- right of resale.

The buyer can claim damages for non-delivery or breach of warranty. He or she can also claim specific performance or the right of rejection.

For further information see sections 41–53 of the Act.

ANSWER TO 'THEORY INTO PRACTICE' EXERCISE ON PAGE 658

Even in 1915 when £5 per tyre represented a considerable sum, the court held that the provision was a genuine attempt to fix damages and was therefore not a penalty. It indicates the courts' reluctance to interfere with a contract agreed to apparently voluntarily between two parties.

9 Negotiate and control financial resources to meet operational plan

Element 9.1

Prepare financial estimates and negotiate financial resources to meet operational plan

It is assumed here that, since you have selected this option unit, negotiating and controlling financial resources for your own department or section is an integral part of your job. For that reason, as you read this chapter, you will find that rather more onus is placed upon you to investigate particular issues than you encountered in the mandatory units. This is partly because, by the time you are working on the option unit you should have gained a better appreciation of the requirements of the scheme, and also because the financial systems and procedures in operation in organisations vary quite considerably. However, you will also find that all the basic information is covered here to enable you to meet the knowledge and understanding criteria.

The acquisition, monitoring and control of organisational finance is crucial – not only for business profitability but also for its very survival. Finance, money, cash – call it what you will – is the oxygen that gives life to the business; starved of this essential fuel the business will slowly die. The critical importance of cash flow to business survival should be both understood and respected by all senior administrators – whether they are working for a small partnership, a large multinational or the local hospital trust.

The need for finance is not just at organisational level. Departments, divisions or units also need to acquire financial resources in order to function. Obtaining these means becoming involved in organisational procedures to validate and monitor their use. The larger a business and the more diverse its operations, the more complex these procedures are likely to become. As an emergency measure a sole trader can examine the latest bank balance (or, even better, the bank reconciliation statement) for a quick check that financial resources are available to pay for current requirements – though this is unlikely to be successful as a long-term operational strategy! For a large business, with diverse interests, a variety of operational costs and overheads and a myriad of conflicting demands for resources, such an approach would always be unmanageable. Without comprehensive and rigorous financial systems for managing financial affairs, the apportionment and allocation of resources would be on an irrational basis, with little or no consideration of the present and future needs of the business. Control would be sporadic, non-existent or ineffective, and the organisation would be unable to meet its key objectives on a systematic basis or to fulfil its statutory obligations relating to the provision of financial information.

For that reason, the larger the organisation becomes, the more likely it is that a variety of systems and procedures are in place to allocate, monitor and control financial resources. Understanding why these are in place, how they operate and how to speak the language of the organisation's financial controllers or gatekeepers is an essential weapon in the armoury of any self-respecting senior administrator.

Your own work role and responsibilities

You are likely to be involved in estimating and negotiating the financial resources you require if your responsibilities cover any combination of the following areas:

- purchase, renewal, leasing, rental or maintenance of office equipment
- purchase of office consumables
- planning of business travel, entertainment or special events
- hire or subcontracting of staff – either permanent or temporary
- refurbishment or re-equipping of offices or office areas
- costing of particular goods or services sold by the organisation
- monitoring of income received through the sale of particular goods and services
- preparation or provision of quotations to customers.

However, although only some of these activities may be part of your official job role, today it is arguable that all senior administrators should have a fundamental understanding of the basic concepts of financial management as well as the systems and controls in their own organisation. Knowing which systems are in place, *why* they are in place, how they operate and their strengths and weaknesses is crucial to managing your section's need for financial resources. Only if you understand the basis on which financial decisions are made can you effectively negotiate for the resources you require, accurately evaluate alternative courses of action, challenge false assumptions, submit a financial document which will stand rigorous scrutiny, and query any adverse decisions in a knowledgeable manner. This then places you in a stronger position to achieve your own departmental objectives.

Groucho Marx once quipped, 'I kept asking my accountant for information, but all he gave me was figures.' If you are to be an effective senior administrator you should be beyond staring incomprehensibly at a page of numbers or feeling inadequate because you fail to understand why some of your calculations and assumptions are being challenged. This requires a proactive strategy to develop your knowledge of financial issues, rather than a knee-jerk, defensive reaction to protect your position.

This section therefore provides a brief guide to the background of finance and financial management in business.

An organisation's financial structure

Figure 9.1.1 identifies the major elements of the financial structure of a typical organisation, and a brief explanation for each of the major areas is given below.

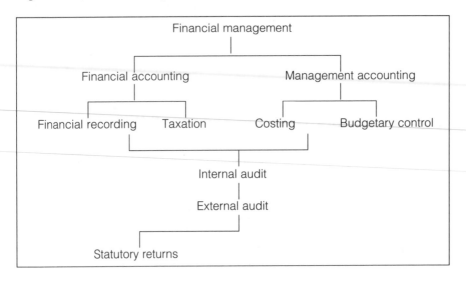

Figure 9.1.1 The components of financial management

Financial management

Key functions of financial management include the following:

- formulation of financial policy within the organisation
- use of acquisition and utilisation strategies to ensure that finance is available to meet organisational objectives linked to the strategic plan
- development and use of ethical investment policies to ensure that surplus funds are invested in accordance with organisational policies and future objectives
- use of investment appraisal techniques to ensure that finance is used in the most cost-efficient and ultimately beneficial manner
- interpretation, analysis and evaluation of current financial information to provide timely, accurate and informed advice to aid managerial decision-making
- the overseeing of external financial reporting activities to ensure that legal and regulatory requirements are met (this includes the preparation and submission of company accounts, the internal/external auditing functions and the payment of taxes)
- monitoring the control and use of funds throughout the organisation and providing feedback on organisational performance in relation to financial performance indicators appertaining to liquidity, efficiency, profit and investment
- advising on the future financial strategy of the organisation.

The role of the Finance Director (or equivalent) is therefore fundamental to the success of the business. The job requires a balance between the pessimistic stance of an accountant and the energy and optimism of an entrepreneur! Too cautious an approach will stifle the enterprise, whereas the dynamic marketeer may have to be restrained on occasion for the good of the whole.

In addition to financial expertise, technical competency and shrewd business skills, a further requirement of today's financial manager is IT literacy – not just in fundamental software applications but an in-depth grasp of the way in which computer systems can inform and control financial operations and decisions. Many organisations are finding to their cost that such a brief is not easy to fill.

Financial accounting

Financial accounting is concerned with the preparation of the company accounts required by law under the Companies Act 1985 (as amended by the Companies Act 1989); i.e. the profit and loss account and the balance sheet. Although it is not a statutory requirement, most organisations also prepare a cash flow statement which includes reports from the chairman, directors and auditors. In addition, a copy of the 'source and application of funds' statement may be included (see page 670). The Act also stipulates the recommended formats (there is a choice of two) for the main accounts and requires that comparative figures be shown for the previous year. These accounts are made available to all shareholders and filed with the Registrar of Companies in either Cardiff or Edinburgh. The Stock Exchange regulations also require listed companies to issue interim reports to shareholders.

The aim of the Act is to protect stakeholders by setting minimum disclosure requirements relating to the financial affairs of an organisation. This therefore presupposes that:

- the accounts give a 'true and fair view' of the organisation's activities
- the accounts can be interpreted to indicate the financial health (or otherwise) of the organisation.

The 'true and fair view' is a requirement of the Companies Act 1985, and this must be validated by the auditors who have inspected and checked the accounts. All accounts can be subjected to a variety of financial 'tests' or measures to check whether the company is over-trading (trying to achieve more than it is financially capable of doing), too highly geared (borrowing too much in relation to its share capital), or struggling to achieve adequate returns in relation to the capital that has been invested in the enterprise. However, whether the average stakeholder has the interest or expertise to interpret a set of complex accounts in this way is far more debatable. In reality, the financial press is more likely to undertake such an analysis.

Private companies are allowed some concessions under the Companies Act 1989, depending upon their size, and can submit abbreviated accounts if they meet certain criteria, although they must still provide shareholders with full accounts.

For the accounts to be prepared in the first place, the financial transactions that take place must be recorded accurately. Information is required on:

- sales, returns, debtors (who owe money), discounts, and unpaid (bad) debts
- purchases of goods to be sold and consumables, returns, creditors (to whom the company owes money), discounts
- stock levels and value
- purchases of capital items and depreciation of assets
- capital, bank balances, expenses (including staff wages and salaries), and drawings (i.e. owners' or partners' remuneration).

The normal procedure is to record all financial transactions in 'books of accounts' based on the time-honoured system of double-entry book-keeping. In the vast majority of organisations today this is usually a computerised operation.

- If you work for a small firm that is *not* a limited liability organisation, such as a solicitors' partnership or a sole trader, then the owner (or each partner) will be liable to pay *income tax* on his or her share of the net profit. All limited companies, however, are legally a distinct entity. The directors are therefore salaried employees and it is the organisation that is liable to pay *corporation tax* (CT) on the net profit. The directors are personally liable to pay income tax on their own earnings, just like any other salaried employee. The amount of corporation tax due is normally shown in the company's balance sheet as one of its current liabilities. An additional requirement is *advance corporation tax* (ACT) which is levied on dividends and eventually deducted from the CT due. ACT was in the news in 1997 when the Chancellor of the Exchequer announced the abolition of the ACT of 20 per cent on share dividends which could be reclaimed by pension fund and PEP managers.
- Many people are under the mistaken impression that the more profit made by an organisation in any one year, the better. This is not always true – as a heavy tax liability in one year might create severe cash-flow problems for the organisation in the following year. A key remit of a finance manager is to advise on strategies that will spread the burden of tax and keep it as low as possible. *Tax avoidance* tactics of this nature are not only perfectly legal but sensible business practice. However, *tax evasion* – which is evading the legal duty to pay tax – is illegal and punishable in law.

There is no legal requirement for companies to provide *employees* with a copy of the annual accounts. However, employees can inspect the copy of their employer's accounts lodged at Companies House. If you work for a private company you may find that only abbreviated accounts have been filed. Some organisations do prepare a set of accounts specifically for their employees, and appended notes to help understanding. Others go the extra mile and give a full presentation to employees to inform them of current financial issues, and allocate time for questions and answers.

The skills required for interpreting and understanding published accounts are outside the remit of this book. However, it is an aspect of personal development you should seriously consider if such documents are a foreign language to you! A variety of books for non-accountants has been written, all of which give basic information in layman's terms. Alternatively, if you have friends in the accounting profession or can acquire a mentor in your financial section this may be all you need.

THEORY INTO PRACTICE

1 Check whether employees in your organisation receive a copy of the accounts and, if possible, obtain a set of the financial statements and other reports issued at the end of the last financial year. If you are unable to obtain these, you can contact any listed public limited company and ask for a set.
2 Read the chairman's, directors' and auditors' reports and then glance through the accounts themselves. Either obtain a book that will help you to understand the entries in more detail, or lobby someone in your organisation to talk you through them and answer your questions.

Management accounting

Management accounting is concerned with the day-to-day and future management of finances – rather than the historic and statutory informational role of financial accounting. The fundamental purpose of a management accountant is to provide timely information to assist and inform management decision-making. It therefore incorporates techniques related to:

- preparation of budgets, and budgetary control
- cost accounting and costing systems
- production of performance reports and budget statements
- reporting and analysis of adverse and favourable variances in budget performance reports
- presentation of financial information in a form and style that is readily comprehensible and usable by management
- interpretation of information in the light of past performance, current events, future trends and organisational objectives, to guide managerial decisions.

However, it is important to note the link between management accounts and financial accounts. The former review, interpret and analyse the latter – but from a different perspective. This perspective closely relates to the planning strategies of the organisation.

Financial planning and planning strategies

An organisation may be faced with a fundamental economic problem of limited resources and seemingly unlimited wants. The Sales Manager might be convinced that if the organisation invests in setting up a telemarketing section this will pay for itself within two years; the Production Manager might be vehement that two machines must be replaced before the end of next year; R&D apparently urgently need an injection of cash for an exciting new project; the IT Manager might be adamant that the organisation must upgrade its computer facilities to remain competitive; and so on. Evaluating each of these requests is no easy matter. A wrong decision can result in money wasted on an unsuccessful project and missed opportunities in another area. For that reason, the allocation of financial resources is closely tied to the strategic, tactical and operational planning process for the organisation. The aim is to finance those events and activities that will most efficiently and effectively enable the organisation to achieve its strategic and corporate objectives in a methodical and planned manner, with due consideration for the total amount available for capital investment and general expenditure at any one time.

The planning process

In most organisations, planning is undertaken on a 'revolving' or 'rolling' basis, with future plans being determined and reviewed on a formal basis each year and current plans being monitored and reviewed on a more regular basis.

There are basically three levels of planning, and each links with the preparation and monitoring of financial plans and budgets as shown in Figure 9.1.2.

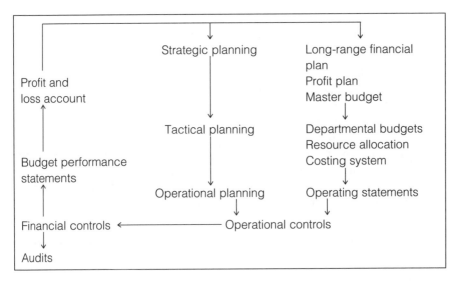

Figure 9.1.2 Financial planning and controls

Strategic planning

Strategic planning is concerned with the long-term plans of the enterprise. At this level, planning is undertaken by senior management who consider the internal and external environment to identify the strategic response of the enterprise to new challenges and opportunities, declining markets and changing demand for its products or services. The strategic plan is often projected for five years or beyond and the main objectives of the organisation must be identified against which the success or failure of the plan will be measured.

Most private-sector organisations identify profitability as a primary objective. Other objectives may include market share, global expansion, quality and customer service. Public-sector organisations (such as local authorities and health authorities) are normally accountable to government auditors for their investment and spending plans and will usually have objectives that incorporate a public service component and value for money for the taxpayer. However, in any organisation, for the objectives to be achieved, the strategic plan must be supported by prudent financial management which involves in-depth consideration and analysis of predicted cash flow and likely investment opportunities.

Once the organisational objectives have been determined, then the activities and events that must occur to enable these to be achieved have to be identified. Some of these will involve revenue, others will involve expenditure. It is at this point that techniques such as *cost–benefit analysis* and *investment appraisal* are used to determine which choices should be made, bearing in mind the total resources available. This process can result in some unpalatable decisions, particularly when choices between conflicting objectives must be made. A local authority which decides to cut social services to finance school building repairs; the football club which spends £1 million on a new player instead of building a new stand; and the hospital which closes a ward but buys a new computer system – are all likely to be challenged by those groups who disagree with the decision. In a private organisation, questions may be asked by shareholders and by other stakeholders such as employees, who may not agree with all the decisions that have been made – particularly if these result in cuts in their own area or the rejection of one department's pet project.

The result of this decision-making process is the compilation of a *long-range financial plan* which identifies the future revenue and expenditure of the organisation over, say, the next 3–5 years. You may find that your organisation uses a different term for this document, such as the *long-range budget* or *profit plan* (which gives details of expected revenue from different sections of the organisation). This document then informs the process of budgetary planning and control for the organisation as a whole and the *master budget* which is later prepared for the organisation.

Tactical planning

Tactical planning is usually undertaken at departmental level by departmental managers and middle managers – the aim being to determine the resources needed to enable them to achieve the objectives relating to their own area. Again, there are obvious resource implications which inform both the profit plan (in terms of units of production, labour costs, machinery and equipment, etc.) and the *departmental budgets* (see pages 671–2).

You should bear in mind that a key requirement of effective cost control and budgetary control is that there be a distinct *bottom-up* aspect to financial planning. There is no future for management in determining the objectives a manager must reach but denying him or her the resources needed to achieve them. This issue is dealt with in greater depth under *responsibility centres* in the next section.

Operational planning

Operational planning involves planning activities to ensure that the objectives are met at unit or section level. It is also concerned with the efficient use of resources allocated to the unit. Operational plans are usually formulated over an annual period and are specified in the *operating statement*, which is monitored and controlled rigorously. You should note that there is often a close link between the units or sections charged with meeting certain operational objectives and the responsibility centres discussed in the next section.

The term *opportunity cost* is used to describe the cost of an alternative that was forgone when a choice was made. The opportunity cost of reading this book at the moment could be an evening out for a meal, a night watching television or a weekend trip with friends. In financial terms, allocation of scarce resources in one area will always mean an opportunity is forgone in another. Minimising opportunity costs is therefore important at the planning stage. The difficulty is that the true opportunity cost may not be totally foreseeable at this stage. Consider the following.

- The recently privatised water companies have been criticised for giving high dividends to shareholders. The opportunity cost has been investment in renewing water mains, pipes and updating treatment works. The Labour government has been more critical of this policy than the previous government. Could this have been foreseen by the financial planners?
- Bill Gates originally decided there was little future in the Internet and minimised investment in developing this area. Virtually overnight he changed his mind because he calculated the opportunity cost for Microsoft of ignoring developments in this area would be too great. Will he be proved correct in the future?
- Many financial planners have recently had their fingers badly burned through the actions of environmental protestors. The Newbury bypass action groups and Manchester second-runway protestors have added greatly to the costs of both projects through the bills associated with actions to remove them. Could it be that, in the future, protestors will make such projects uneconomic?

THEORY INTO PRACTICE

Methods of forecasting and planning financial expenditure and preparing budgets are dealt with in more depth on pages 670–673. However, although a general guide is given in this book, you should note that the formats of budget documents, the methods of controlling and checking actual against planned performance, and the extent to which variances (overspends or underspends) are allowed or tolerated, vary tremendously between organisations.

In preparation for the subsequent sections, you are advised to obtain information on your organisation's budgeting system, the way in which it is monitored and controlled, and the degree to which your own line manager can influence its composition.

Scope and limits of your authority relating to financial resources

Senior administrators have a variety of responsibilities in relation to the control of financial resources. The scope of your own authority and independence in this area will depend on your job role, the degree to which you are involved in financial resource planning issues, and the costing and budgetary systems in place in your organisation.

Responsibility for financial areas is often determined through a system of *responsibility accounting* which recognises specific areas for responsibility and accountability within the organisational structure. Various types of areas can be determined.

- *Cost centres* relate to areas where managers are responsible for the expenses or costs under their control. The differentiation of cost control for those expenses outside the remit of an individual area is dealt with on pages 677–680.
- *Profit centres* are areas of the business where managers are responsible for *both* costs *and* revenues. This would apply, for instance, in a section which was responsible for the production and marketing of a product or service.
- *Investment centres* are areas where, in addition to costs and revenues, a manager is responsible for making certain capital investment decisions and would have an input into the size and type of investment. An example could be a branch outlet or subsidiary division where decision making has been delegated (decentralised) to those responsible for developing and operating the unit.

Obviously, the smaller the areas delineated for control, the larger the number of centres there will be.

The aim of declaring these areas *responsibility centres* is to link accountability with decision making. In other words, it is recognised that individual managers can be held responsible for performance only if they have the ability to make decisions relating to the control of costs and revenue. Otherwise, constant overruling from above would give a manager a perfect excuse for disclaiming any responsibility for results.

Your own scope and responsibility is therefore likely to link directly to the answers to the following questions.

- Does your organisation practise responsibility accounting? Some organisations still choose to keep financial decision making centralised, and impose – rather than negotiate – budget norms and restrictions, despite the wealth of evidence that this is often unsuccessful. This may also occur in medium-sized companies which started off with an entrepreneurial figurehead who made all the decisions and who is still firmly holding the reins.
- What type of centre do you work in? Are you involved simply with costs, or with costs and revenue or investment decisions as well?
- What is the size and type of your organisation? An organisation that produces standard items on a recurring basis is likely to have its costing and budgetary procedures more finely tuned than one providing highly customised or differentiated services at the leading edge of technology. Similarly, manufacturing organisations have been involved in costing procedures for many years, whereas for many public-sector organisations this is a relatively new concept.
- Do you hold your own budget or control a budget on behalf of your line manager? What is the degree of responsibility delegated to you?
- What are the specific procedures in your organisation for submitting bids for revenue and capital expenditures? What are the authorisation procedures which link to these? Do they depend on the level of expenditure?

In most organisations it is usual for specific authorisation procedures to be in place for the agreement and sanctioning of all expenditure. Often this is purely a case of each manager obtaining a signature from his or her own line manager, and this continues to the highest levels. In other cases, the type of authorisation required depends upon the level of expenditure required. If you are ever in any doubt about whether authorisation is required or whether a particular issue exceeds your own authority, it is *always* wise to err on the side of caution and obtain agreement in writing.

Because you may work in any of the three centres described above, for the rest of this chapter you will find these described by the 'umbrella term' of responsibility centres.

Sources of information relating to financial requirements

The financial requirements of the entire organisation are normally estimated and assembled into a variety of budgets and then compiled into the master budget. The master budget effectively consists of the sales, production, capital and cash budgets, in addition to a forecast balance sheet, budgeted profit and loss account and a 'source and application of funds' statement. The latter identifies the planned movements in assets, liabilities and capital and the effect on cash flow. It also explains where additional funds will be derived and the use to which they will be put. In most organisations, the budgetary procedure (or the procedure for the submission of bids or estimates for future financial resources) follows a regular set pattern and financial cycle, usually over a period of twelve months. However, the cycle can vary considerably in particularly fast-moving or longer-paced industries, such as the pop record industry and the construction industry respectively.

Generally, the first and crucial budget to be prepared is that concerning the *limiting factor* which has been determined by the organisation. For most private-sector organisations, the principal factor affecting all other budgets is that of sales – and in this case the sales budget would be calculated first. With certain public-sector organisations, such as universities and local authorities, the limiting factor may be related to government grants and other income sources, and this would be the limiting factor constraining expenditure. However, for the purpose of the example that follows, we will assume a commercial organisation that has an income determined by sales.

Budgets

Estimating sales activity

The sales budget must include details of the forecast number of units to be sold and the selling price. However, estimating sales demand may be extremely difficult, given that managers are being asked to forecast sales that may occur a year or more in the future. A variety of different forecasting techniques are used, but basically these can be divided into three:

- *quantitative estimates* based on the statistical analysis of previous sales patterns and general business and market trends
- *qualitative views* expressed by those responsible for sales, such as departmental heads, regional managers and representatives
- *market research* to ascertain more precise data on new or improved products.

Obtaining a mixture of facts and opinions gives a more rounded view of *any* type of forecast.

The production budget

In manufacturing industries, the next stage is to forecast the production budget. This involves examining the amount that ought to be produced in line with the sales forecast, and considering the amount of stocks held, current work-in-progress and stock requirements. Calculations also take place in relation to the amount of labour and raw materials needed to produce the required amounts, and the total overheads which must be included in the production budget (see Figure 9.1.3 on pages 676–677).

Additional budgets

The range of other budgets that are prepared depends upon the organisation in question, but may include:

- *service area budgets*, such as for administration, human resources and computer services (none of these areas is directly involved in the production or selling of goods but must be allocated specific expenditure levels)

- *policy area budgets*, such as research and development and capital expenditure (these budgets may be calculated over a longer period than normal operating budgets to take into account the long-term strategies of the organisation).

The cash budget

This is a crucial document that can be prepared only after all the other budgets have been drafted. It shows the effect of budgeted plans on the organisation's cash flow. Cash inflows and outflows are shown, not only for the overall budget period but also for sub-budget periods against which performance will be measured. The 'first pass' at the budget may show that there will be a projected deficit at particular periods. Management then have to choose between deferring certain plans or raising the additional finance that would be required. Equally, there may be periods where an overall surplus is indicated. In this case, management have to choose whether to spread the activities over a different timescale, or where to invest the surplus funds for best advantage.

The forecast cash budget may result in original plans having to be revised. Then, functional managers are charged with the task of reviewing their own budgets to accord with the essential cash-flow requirements. Only when these changes have been agreed can the master budget be finalised.

Sources of information on financial requirements

You will need information for financial requirements for your section if you are involved in:

- the preparation of budgets relating to your own area
- the monitoring of budgets (i.e. measuring actual revenue and/or expenditure against planned revenue and/or expenditure)
- making periodic projections of future activities and anticipated requirements
- the costing of particular projects, such as the upgrading of computers or the refurbishment of a particular office area
- the costing for capital bids or allocations from the capital budget.

In *all* these cases you will need a mixture of information, both qualitative and quantitative. Your first step, quite naturally, might be to ask staff about the resources they require for a particular activity or project, and then to cost the resources accordingly. However, do be aware that staff may 'lobby' for any and every resource they require! For that reason, if they assert that a particular resource is essential, you should check that their claims are valid. You can validate their requests by obtaining further information from:

- experts in the organisation who can help and advise you
- internal and external suppliers of materials and equipment
- your own colleagues and staff who will be involved in any projects or activities
- past records and data kept in paper files and on computer

- external advisory bodies, external reports and external reference sources.

As an example, a useful check when buying office equipment is *What to Buy for Business* which is, effectively, the equipment buyer's bible. Other user-guides are available on a wide range of items, and details can be found in any office equipment periodical. Standard staff rates of pay can be checked with the local Jobcentre, or by referring to advertisements in the local newspaper over a few weeks.

You will need to analyse your findings – both quantitative and qualitative – to produce your own recommendations. A useful approach is to analyse the quantitative information *first* and then use the qualitative information to modify and inform the decisions you make. This strikes the balance between a purely rational and objective argument and one that includes the needs of users as well.

THEORY INTO PRACTICE

1 Many organisations issue guidelines to managers on the preparation of budgets and provide details of the 'rules to follow' when forecasting particular activities. Check whether such guidelines exist in your organisation, and obtain a copy if you do not already possess one.
2 Find out the timescale over which budgets in your organisation are prepared and how this affects any requests you may make for bids for financial resources.
3 Obtain a copy of the budgets for your own section (both draft and finalised) over the past two or three years, note the changes in each case, and find out why these occurred.
4 If you work for a very small organisation, or in the public sector, you may find that the actual procedure and final documents vary somewhat from the explanation above. In this case, investigate and summarise the main differences you can identify.

An organisation's procedures for the preparation of financial estimates

Your own role in preparing financial estimates may be simply to assist your line manager, or you may be involved in completing certain sections of the projected budget for your own responsibility area. You may also be requested to differentiate between the capital expenditure you require and the consumable items needed. In addition, you may be asked to submit estimates for individual projects or for periodic projections and to include estimates for both income and expenditure.

Your first step should always be to check the guidelines for the creation of budgets, to make sure you understand:

- the rules that apply in your organisation
- the type of expenditure that should be projected under different headings

- any financial limitations that exist in relation to different headings
- the degree of 'mark up' expected on your products, or the breakeven point that applies in a particular situation
- any ratios that are applied as a measurement or 'testing' tool to any projections
- how the budget is compiled and the degree to which changes or amendments are allowed.

In some organisations a system of *zero-based budgeting* (ZBB) is used, rather than *incremental budgeting*. Under ZBB, all activities are completely re-evaluated with each new budget, which then starts with a zero baseline; whereas under incremental budgeting there is an assumption that a certain increase must be added to last year's allocation to allow for inflation. The benefits of ZBB are felt to be as follows:

- ZBB allows for a constant re-evaluation of the allocation of resources, rather than the preservation of the status quo.
- ZBB challenges the assumption that current activities all provide value for money.
- ZBB requires staff involvement and participation at all levels, which prevents managers from setting budgets without the consultation of those who are involved at 'grassroots' levels.
- ZBB encourages managers to rethink their priorities.

Against this, it can be argued that ZBB is time-consuming and often unnecessary. For that reason, many organisations take the incremental approach but also review base estimates on a revolving basis. This is the pragmatic alternative to a full-scale ZBB re-evaluation each year.

Another issue on which you must be clear is the *timescale* under which you are operating. If all project estimates will need four weeks to be processed, or if all capital bids can be submitted only in June, it is important that you know this and operate accordingly. There is likely to be a completely different procedure to follow depending on whether you are submitting a budget forecast or an estimate which will be offset against a particular grant or subsidy. Much depends upon the source of funding in your own organisation and the standard procedures in force. This may also involve understanding the costing procedures in operation in your organisation.

Budgets and periodic projections

Creating the budget is only the first chapter in the budgeting story. Another major activity is the continual comparison of actual against planned activities; i.e. *budget control*. It will be important for you to know:

- the degree to which *variances* will be tolerated
- the degree to which costs are identified as being *controllable* by your section
- whether your organisation operates *flexible* budgets or *fixed* budgets.

The worst scenario is one where there is zero tolerance, no identification of controllable costs, and a fixed budget! In this scenario, there is a case for arguing that your financial estimates ought to err on the side of caution. The reason for this is fairly obvious if we consider each of these factors in more detail.

Variances

Variances can be either adverse or favourable. In a profit-making enterprise, an adverse variance is one that indicates profit forgone, a favourable variance one that indicates extra profit gained. In some organisations, an adverse variance in one area can be offset against a favourable variance in another. Equally, if money is short in one budget area, finances may be *vired* between two budget headings. This means that you can transfer money between different sections of the budget to obtain a balance as the year moves on.

If the degree to which variances are allowed is relatively generous (or even lax), then your financial estimates will not need to be too precise and your submissions can be adjusted at a later date. If, however, you are expected to keep to the letter of your estimates, then you should perhaps consider allowing some 'drift' yourself when submitting the estimates in the first place. Quite obviously, this can lead to a considerable amount of game-playing, with over-inflated estimates being submitted, to allow for a safety margin for those involved in bringing in the project.

(You should note that budgetary control, variances and variance analysis are dealt with in more detail in Element 9.2.)

Controllable costs

It is a fundamental rule of budgeting that managers should not be made responsible for managing costs over which they have no control. For instance, overheads may be apportioned between budget holders and include budget lines for rent, heating, lighting and the salaries of servicing staff. Obviously all of these areas are outside the control of individual managers. Ideally, these lines should be identified as separate from the main budget lines for which the manager is answerable.

Fixed or flexible budgets

The budget is basically a financial forecasting and planning device. As with all plans, however, changes can occur throughout the following year which mean that the plans need to be revised. In the case of budgets, the reason for revisions is usually more specific. A case for flexing the budget is made if output changes and therefore costs also change.

As a specific example, consider the organisation that plans to make 1000 units and sell each one for £10 000. This represents 80 per cent of total production capacity. The Production Manager writes a budget on this basis but, when demand increases later in the year and Sales request that she operates on 90 per cent of production capacity, she readily complies. At this stage her variable costs of production (see below) also increase. It would be totally unreasonable and unfair to criticise the Production Manager for an adverse variance on costs – and reasonable and sensible to agree to 'flex' the budget so that it represents actual, rather than planned, demand.

You were introduced to the concept of game-playing in Chapter 4. Nowhere may you find game-playing more rife than in relation to budgets and targets! Common strategies include the following:

- *deliberately* failing to meet targets in particular areas to avoid a situation whereby the targets are continually increased, year on year
- *deliberately* ensuring that all the money against a particular budget is spent within the year, to prevent savings being made that may be used to enforce a decrease in the amount required in subsequent years.

Budget rules can exacerbate these strategies. For instance, some organisations have a ruling which restricts capital items to a particular figure – say £1000. This is despite the fact that prices may be falling for certain capital items, such as computers. The tendency then is to buy a dearer item than is really required to make sure that the 'rules' are kept.

THEORY INTO PRACTICE

When reading about types of costing systems and methods used in organisations it is important to understand the basic definitions related to costs. Check the definitions listed in Figure 9.1.3 to make sure that you are familiar with all the usual terms, before continuing with this section.

Direct costs – those which are directly incurred by undertaking a particular job. For example, printing 100 reports of 50 pages has a direct material cost of 5000 pieces of paper – if we do not allow for wastage. Equally, the print operator would represent a direct labour cost and any royalties payable would represent a direct expense cost.

Prime costs – the total direct costs for a particular activity.

Indirect costs – *overheads* which cannot be specifically allocated to a particular activity. Examples include rent, rates, heating, lighting, machine maintenance, depreciation and the salaries of service staff.

Product cost – The total cost of the finished product, made up from all its constituent cost elements (i.e. materials, labour and other expenses).

Standard cost – a cost derived from the precise measuring of an activity which is then expressed in monetary terms from an assessment of the value of all the cost elements involved in the activity.

Fixed cost – a cost which is unaffected by changes in the level of production (e.g. rent, rates, insurance, administrative and managerial salaries).

Variable cost – a cost which varies according to the volume of production (e.g. raw materials and direct production labour costs).

Semi-variable cost – a cost which contains both a fixed and a variable element (e.g. telecommunications charges which may include both a charge for the equipment and the line usage).

> **Stepped costs** – costs which are constant or fixed for a particular level of business activity but then jump to a new point if business activity increases. A typical example is wages, where additional staff taken on to cope with new workloads add to the overall labour costs.

Figure 9.1.3 Definitions of costing terms

Costing systems and methods

All costs are concerned with:

- *materials* used in the production of goods or the offering of a service – from the steel used in car production to the paper used by solicitors and accountants
- *equipment* used by production operatives and administrative staff – from lathes to photocopiers, from company cars to computers
- *people* who produce the goods or provide the service and want payment for their labour (you should note that labour may be a fixed cost or a variable cost, and that labour costs include not only the actual salary or wage received but the employer's 'on-costs' of national insurance, pension fund contributions, holiday pay, etc.)
- additional expenses, such as rent, rates, electricity, etc. – normally classed as *overheads*.

Whilst this might seem straightforward, the actual method of allocating costs can cause considerable dissension in organisations, particularly if it is felt to be unjust or unfair. If you feel you are unfairly tasked to meet costs over which you have no discretion, or which are mainly incurred by another department, you may well challenge the figures you are given. Equally, if the financial reports generated obviously give an inaccurate picture of performance then you may object strenuously if you are accused of failing to meet your targets or asked to use such data for future decision making. However, the reason why such problems exist can be seen more clearly if you understand the various choices that have to be made at this stage, namely:

- how the precise difference between direct and indirect costs should be determined
- how to share the indirect costs of services between productive cost centres
- how to share out the overheads between units
- which system of costing to use.

Direct and indirect costs

At first it may seem a simple procedure to determine which costs are direct and which are indirect. In reality, the process can be more difficult. Consider the following scenarios.

- You have arranged for the redecoration of an office. The painters are also redecorating another office in another department, using the same colours of paint. How do they know how much to charge each department? You may well suggest sharing the bill – but what if one office is twice as large as the other? And how do you share the direct labour cost if one office takes more preparation time but the other has more windows and alcoves?

- You are costing the production of a large mailshot and have managed to obtain a job-lot of photocopying paper at a special rate. Your accountant uses a FIFO (first-in, first-out) costing system and insists that the regular price of the main paper stocks must be included in the estimate.
- Three employees are 'shared' between departments on the basis of workload and need. How do you calculate which proportion of their salaries (and on-costs) should be allocated to each department? And what do you do if you find another department always utilises the most junior member (i.e. the cheapest) the most often and is now arguing for contributing less to the costs?

Different organisations will have different solutions to these problems, and you will need to check with your own management accountant how each situation would be dealt with in your organisation – although some of the accounting conventions described on page 693 may help you to second-guess his or her likely reactions! Techniques employed to allocate the cost of materials include standard costing, FIFO, LIFO (last-in, first-out) or calculating the average cost of materials and weighting this in an appropriate way. (However, you should note that in the UK, LIFO is not a valid method for valuing stock for taxation purposes and is therefore seldom used.) Labour costs are always more difficult to determine, and a strict check must be kept on hours worked in various areas and management decisions taken to determine policy in 'grey' areas and to outlaw unfair practices.

Sharing indirect costs

The total indirect costs of an organisation are usually shared or *apportioned* between particular production cost centres. However, again this can present problems.

- Departments or divisions which provide a service (those for reprographics, personnel, maintenance, administration, finance, catering, security) but do not produce revenue will need to 'charge' productive departments for the services they provide. This should be done fairly – so that you do not find that your responsibility centre is charged for services you never use, or use only infrequently.
- Service departments may give a reciprocal service to each other – wages staff use catering facilities and catering staff need to be paid wages! How should these amounts be offset against each other?

Organisations vary in the way they apportion such costs. Costs might be apportioned on the basis of:

- the number of employees (this would obviously be appropriate for, say, the wages office if 500 wages were processed for one responsibility centre and only 20 for another!)

- the area covered (this would be appropriate for maintenance, cleaning and security functions, as it would take longer to provide each service for a large building than for a small one)
- *activity-based costing* (ABC) (this is discussed in more detail on page 682).

In many cases, the degree of difficulty in calculating reciprocal costs for two servicing units means that it is more economic to ignore the whole thing! This leads to a key rule in financial calculations – the time spent allocating finance and making savings should never be disproportionate to the money saved. It is useless spending a whole day to track down £2 if the cost of chasing it was £50.

Sharing overheads by absorption costing

The overheads of the enterprise need to be charged to its specific cost centres. If all the fixed overheads of the enterprise are allocated to production cost centres then this process is known as *absorption* or *full costing*. There should be some attempt, at this stage, to absorb these costs on the basis of a recognised feature which correlates with the expenditure incurred. The usual options are:

- volume of production
- direct cost of materials used
- direct cost of labour
- direct labour hours
- machine hours
- prime cost.

Obviously, each version will give a different outcome for a particular cost centre, and some are more suitable in certain situations than others. For instance, volume of production is useful as a measure only if all the units being produced are identical. In very few cases is there likely to be a direct correlation between prime cost (see Figure 9.1.3) and overheads.

THEORY INTO PRACTICE

Administration is an excellent example of an overhead incurred through the provision of a service. However, in your own organisation, the costs of providing an administrative service must be apportioned somewhere and in some way. You can see how difficult this is, bearing in mind the fact that there is usually no correlation of administrative services with any of the factors mentioned above. Before we examine methods of dealing with this problem, do the following:

a find out whether your organisation operates a system of absorption costing
b investigate how the costs of administrative services are apportioned to production units in your organisation
c discuss the equity or fairness of the system in use with someone who understands how and why it operates.

Sharing overheads by variable costing

An alternative to absorption costing is *variable costing*, where only variable costs are assigned to production cost centres.

In some books you may find this termed, variously, as *marginal costing* or *direct costing*. However, there are dangers with each of these terms. Marginal costing means something entirely different to economists (i.e. the cost of producing one more unit), and direct costing implies that only direct costs are involved in this system, which is not the case. It is therefore safer to think of the alternative system to absorption costing as being variable costing.

The main reason for adopting variable costing is the limitations of absorption costing. For example:

- If goods are manufactured but not sold, then absorption costing will show a higher profit than variable costing. This might come as something of a surprise to the line manager responsible for sales! With variable costing, profits are higher if sales are in excess of production costs, which would seem to the layman to be more appropriate.
- If sales fluctuate then, depending upon the period in which the variations take place, anomalies can occur with absorption costing. In some cases, the situation can occur when profits are shown to decrease even though sales are increasing and costs are unchanged! If a manager is being appraised at precisely this time, it can be expected that some disagreements might ensue!

Needless to say, a management accountant could counter these allegations, add several more arguments against this method and a host of reasons for using it! In-depth debate of this nature is outside the scope of this book. However, note that:

- variable costing *cannot* be used for external reporting procedures under Accounting Standards Committee regulation SSAP9 (see also page 695)
- for managerial decision making, variable costing usually provides the most helpful information.

THEORY INTO PRACTICE

Talk to your management accountant to find out the degree to which variable costing is used in your organisation and the way, specifically, it relates to your own department or responsibility centre.

However, be warned. The subsection above gives only the *basic* facts on this topic. Therefore, unless you have a wish to learn much more about it (or already understand it to a much higher level than is covered by this book), you are strongly advised *not* to challenge your management accountant's views as to which is the most appropriate in your particular situation!

Costing systems

The costing system used in your organisation will depend mainly upon the type of product or service that is offered and the way in which particular goods are produced. This subsection gives a brief overview of the main systems in operation.

Job costing

Job costing is used by garages, builders and suppliers of 'individual' orders specific to particular customers. A bill for car servicing, for example, is divided into sections for parts (materials) used, and the labour cost of the mechanic. The overheads will be absorbed into the mechanic's costs, as will a percentage for profit. Profit on the sale of the parts will be absorbed into their price shown on the bill.

Batch costing

Batch costing can be used by a bakery, a chocolate factory or a firm making clothing or paint. In this case each batch is treated as a separate job. On completion of a batch the total cost can be divided by the total number of items produced to give the average cost of each one.

Contract costing

Contract costing is similar to job costing but rather more complex. It is used widely by the construction industry which costs jobs that may take several years to complete, such as building a motorway, bridge or hospital. Specialist estimators are employed to calculate the cost of each contract over the number of years it will take for completion. In addition, the 'cost' of the project must include *attributable profit* which will be estimated to be fairly recoverable at specific periods. In other words, the accountants will not expect to have to wait until the completion of a 25-year project before any profit is received – and neither will the shareholders! Special care must be taken when costing contracts which are submitted on a tender basis (where the contract is likely to go to the lowest bidder), or where there is likely to be a hefty penalty clause in the contract for non-completion by the specified date.

Process costing

Process costing is used by organisations that produce identical products on a continuous process, such as paper or glass. In this case the total cost of production over a particular period is calculated and then divided by the number of units produced, to give an average cost per unit of production. Issues that must also be considered include:

- abnormal losses (or gains) of output during the production process (these occur when the natural wastage during the production process is more or less than anticipated and result in amounts that must be written off in the period in which they are incurred)
- the work-in-progress at the beginning and the end of each period, and its value
- any by-products that arise as a result of the process (an example would be a firm of chocolate biscuit manufacturers which wraps the chocolate bars in foil and sells any scrap foil to a non-ferrous metal dealer)
- any joint products that are manufactured from the same base material, such as plain biscuits and chocolate biscuits.

Service costing

Service costing is a system used by organisations that produce a service rather than a product. A typical example is a solicitor, accountant or consultant who bills his/her client. The account will be based on direct costs (such as the labour costs), indirect costs (e.g. most overheads) and an allowance for profit. In some service organisations there is still a preference for sending the client a 'one-line' document rather than breaking down the items into specific constituents!

> There has been an assumption so far in this section that every organisation adopts only one type of costing system. In reality this is untrue. Many organisations use *multiple costing* – for instance, where some products are costed by batch costing and others by process costing because the method of manufacturing is different in each case. Others operate a system of *operating costing* because more than one factor must be considered in the costing process. A haulage company would cost a journey on more than one factor as both distance and the amount of freight carried would be major considerations. With a bus company this translates into both the distance and the number of passengers. In the case of an airline, the on-costs associated with airport taxes and landing fees also need to be taken into consideration.

Finding the answer – 'activity-based costing'?

This section has introduced various methods and systems of costing. By now you should have realised that costing is not the exact science that some people make it out to be. Difficulties can occur at any stage of devising the system, as well as during its operation. However, a relatively recent development is an alternative system of costing which aims to apportion costs on a more precise and accurate basis. This system is known as *activity-based costing* (ABC).

With ABC, the idea is to identify the activities that cause costs to occur. These are known as *cost-drivers* as they are the specific activities that cause or 'drive' the costs in the first place. These activities are then selected as those against which the overheads are set, in proportion with the costs, so that overheads are charged more fairly against activities than with any other type of apportionment system.

This is easier to understand with an example. A car manufacturer (e.g. Lotus) makes sports cars for general purchase and usage. It also invests heavily in motor sports and developing Formula 1 cars. These are two separate aspects – or divisions – of the enterprise. However, the activities that drive the costs are entirely different in the two cases. Although a car such as a Lotus is not a routine production car, many aspects of assembly *are* routine, with machines preset, labour trained to operate to standard times, and steady-state raw material purchases. In the case of the Formula 1 team there are fewer, more highly skilled staff, high research and development costs, with each item produced individually and some handcrafted, and publicity costs are higher. There is also expenditure on the Lotus racing team and the back-up crew, plus transportation. Therefore the costs that 'drive' this unit are totally different from those of the other unit. If overheads are apportioned in relation to units of production, then the first unit will bear many of the overheads incurred by the second unit! It is this type of situation that ABC costing seeks to avoid.

In reality, different departments, units and sections of an organisation *each* will be encouraged to identify their own cost-drivers. Once these have been agreed, costs will be apportioned according to these factors. Examples of typical drivers are given in Figure 9.1.4. The aim is to obtain a fairer and more rational system of apportionment of costs than using broad correlation indicators.

Area	Cost-driver examples
Production	Machine hours
	Number of set-ups/readjustments
	Number of orders
Personnel	Number of vacancies
	Number of applicants
	Number shortlisted for interview
Purchasing	Number of orders received
	Ratio of standard to non-standard orders
	Number of enquiries on new suppliers/supplies

Figure 9.1.4 Typical cost-drivers

THEORY INTO PRACTICE

1 Identify the cost-drivers that would apply to your own department, unit or responsibility centre.
2 Find out the degree to which your findings match the system actually in use.
3 At this stage, if there is no match at all – and you are in a position to do so – you may try finding out whether ABC has ever been considered by your organisation and, if not, why not.

Formats for the presentation of financial information and estimates

The formats for financial estimates vary widely from one organisation to another. You may have to use a different format depending upon whether you are:

- bidding for a budget allocation for your section or unit
- bidding for a specific capital item or for investment in a new project
- obtaining authorisation for other expenditure from within your budget allocation.

Budget estimates and allocations

Budgets are generally controlled by a system of responsibility centre allocation codes and expenditure codes. Each responsibility centre is given a specific code against which budget expenditure will be agreed. In addition, each item of expenditure is given a code to enable total costs per heading of expenditure to be monitored and controlled on a centralised basis.

As an example, we will assume that each administration unit of an organisation is classed as a separate responsibility centre. In this case, Sales Administration may be A01, Marketing Administration A02, Purchasing Administration A03, and so on. The codes for expenditure will include a variety of factors but are usually subdivided under different headings. An example is shown in Figure 9.1.5. The two codes will be combined on authorisation documents to ensure that the expenditure is correctly logged. Thus, general hospitality catering organised by Sales Administration would be identified by the code A01/501. Ensuring the codes are entered correctly is extremely important for monitoring and control, and this aspect is covered in more detail in Element 9.2.

Figure 9.1.5 Sample budget expenditure headings for non-labour costs

General overheads

301	Electricity
302	Gas
303	Water
304	Fuel oil
310	Insurances
320	Rent
321	Rates
331	General equipment hire and leasing
341	Telecommunications – rentals
342	Telecommunications – calls
351	Cleaning materials
352	Security equipment

Administration expenses

361	Postage
362	Stationery
371	Computer software
372	Photocopying – equipment/maintenance
381	Office equipment
382	Office furniture
391	Computer equipment
392	Computer maintenance

Travel

401	Car mileage
402	Car hire
403	Taxi fares

410	Rail fares
421	Air fares – UK
422	Air fares – overseas
431	Accommodation – UK
432	Accommodation – overseas
441	Subsistence – UK
442	Subsistence – overseas

Catering

| 501 | General hospitality |
| 502 | Staff functions |

Entertaining (customers)

| 550 | Entertainment – UK |
| 551 | Entertainment – overseas |

Health and safety

601	Protective clothing
602	Protective equipment
603	General uniforms
604	First aid
605	Awards and presentations
606	Suggestion scheme awards

Training and development

701	Personal development requirements
702	First aid/health and safety training
703	Internal courses
704	External courses

Marketing and promotions

801	Promotional literature
802	Advertising
803	Display materials
804	Promotional items/gifts
810	Exhibitions
811	Conferences
812	Seminars

Budget submission forms are likely to require the inclusion of codes for each item of expenditure required. However, they will also require the costing of any labour that is to be used, with a percentage increase required for 'on-costs'. Again there will be specific budget headings for labour – usually subdivided under basic salary (and grades, in some cases), bonuses, commission, performance-related pay increments, overtime, and additional allowances. Temporary and casual staff are usually classified under a different heading from permanent staff because the on-costs will be less (temporary staff are not part of a pension scheme, for instance, and if they are hired from an agency there may be no on-costs at all).

As an example, we will assume that the Sales Administrator has been asked to submit a budget estimate linked to her unit objectives for the coming year against the expenditure headings identified in Figure 9.1.5. Overheads are not included at this stage, her task being to identify expenditure that her unit will incur. A simple format for such an estimate is shown in Figure 9.1.6 on the facing page. However, you should note that, depending upon the policy in operation in the organisation:

- justification for certain resource bids may be required in a separate document (see below)
- there may be a more complex format which includes details of the previous year's allocation and justification required for any increase
- projected expenditure may need to be subdivided further on a month-by-month basis to assist and inform cash-flow forecasting.

It is quite feasible that the estimate may go through a variety of revisions before it is finally accepted. Much depends upon the degree to which it links with organisational expenditure targets and cash-flow projections.

The National Audit Office report *Employer Compliance Reviews*, published in 1997, identified that 41 385 companies out of a total of 54 156 checked by the Inland Revenue were deducting too little tax or national insurance and making mistakes when calculating expenses and tax on company cars. A total of more than £290 million was recovered in underpaid tax, national insurance, interest and penalties. Most of the mistakes found by the Inland Revenue were in the employees' favour!

Many organisations use customised software packages for budgeting purposes and the estimates may be submitted on forms designed to link with the control system in operation. In other cases, spreadsheets are used to calculate and estimate particular projects – particularly when these include an estimate of both revenue and expenditure. In this case both the format and the formulae are often preset and figures which must be included to cover on-costs and overheads may already be included or determined in the organisational guidelines.

In many cases, such spreadsheets are a numeric version of a *breakeven analysis* where the total costs (i.e. fixed plus variable costs) are compared with the projected sales revenue to identify the sales volume at which a project would become profitable. The advantage of using a spreadsheet for this purpose is the ability to undertake a variety of 'what if?' calculations, to estimate the likely profit achievable for different levels of sales in relation to the effect increased sales would have on the variable costs incurred.

THEORY INTO PRACTICE

If you are not familiar with using spreadsheets then this is an area of your personal development you should address promptly. The ability of spreadsheets to simplify budget forecasting, to estimate projections and to make numeric comparisons is such that once you become familiar with a particular package you will throw away your pencil and paper forever! The advantages include the fact that you can vary your forecast almost endlessly, with very little effort, to see the effect on your overall estimate and, if you attach your spreadsheet to your final estimate, the assumptions you made during your calculations are obvious for all to see – without the need to attach pages of explanation.

Capital bids

Most organisations operate on the principle that all major items of expenditure must be included in the overall budget forecast, but specific

Expenditure heading	Expense code	Budget amount (£)	Total budget (£)
PERMANENT STAFF PAY			
Sales Administrator grade PL3	101	14 500	
Deputy Administrator grade PL6	101	11 200	
Administrative Assistants CL5 ×2	101	18 000	
Administrative Assistants CL9 ×2	101	15 000	
Total permanent staff pay			58 700
Plus on-costs @ 20%	103	11 740	11 740
TEMPORARY STAFF/PAY			
Projected overtime	110	2 000	
Seasonal/temporary staff	120	4 000	
Total temporary staff/pay			6 000
Plus on-costs @ 10%	125	600	600
TOTAL PAYROLL COSTS			**77 040**
NON-LABOUR COSTS			
Postage	361	8 500	
Stationery	362	6 200	
Computer software	371	600	
Photocopying equipment/maintenance	372	8 000	
Office equipment	381	3 000	
Office furniture	382	1 000	
Computer equipment	391	2 500	
Computer maintenance	392	400	
General hospitality	501	850	
First aid training	702	150	
Internal courses	703	750	
External courses	704	1 500	33 450
TOTAL NON-LABOUR COSTS			**33 450**
TOTAL BUDGET ALLOCATION			**110 490**

Figure 9.1.6 Sample Sales Administration budget for a particular year

allocations of expenditure against any heading must be substantiated – particularly where these would involve a considerable amount of expenditure. In some enterprises this justification process takes place at the time the budget forecast is submitted, in others applications against particular expense headings may be submitted all year until the money runs out. The authorisation procedure usually differs depending upon the amount of money involved. A scanner costing £300 may be quickly agreed, an electronic filing system costing £3000 would be a different matter, and a new building costing £3 million would require Board approval.

In addition to understanding how you can obtain permission to buy capital items, you also need to make certain that you are clear about the type of equipment covered by this term in your organisation. In some cases it *excludes* items such as carpets and furniture, for instance, but includes equipment. In others, equipment can only be included if it is to be purchased, rather than leased or rented. Additionally you may be constrained by financial limits (both minimum and maximum) for certain classes of expenditure, and there may be a specific number of estimates or detailed quotations you have to obtain.

Quite often, there is a bidding procedure wherein a standard form is completed and detailed estimates of expenditure are attached. The manager responsible for the budget can then compare bids and give them a priority rating. An example of this type of form is given in Figure 9.1.7.

A different type of bid document must be completed if you work for an organisation that can bid for funds from the European Union, from Government grants or even the National Lottery. Such documents are usually quite long and complex. They require not only a full rationale behind the request, but also specific targets to be identified for achievement against which you will be monitored if you are successful in receiving funds.

If you are involved in completing such documents you are well advised to start by photocopying the official documents and practising on the photocopied set. Then, obtain help with anything you do not understand from someone inside your organisation. If no-one can assist you, do not hesitate to ring the issuing office who sent you the form to clarify any headings you do not understand. Incomplete or inaccurately completed bid documents can severely jeopardise your chances of success.

Obtain information on the total value of the fund and the *expected* size of your bid, if you can. There is always a total amount which cannot be exceeded, and going over this may mean your bid is discounted. Often the form designers cover for this by including a section on how the project would be affected if the bid were scaled down. If you state that the project would fold unless you received every penny, you might find your bid is unsuccessful!

Use caution when identifying target objectives you intend to meet and the degree to which you will achieve these. Your performance will be measured and compared with these forecasts, and you may find it difficult to justify an over-optimistic objective.

CAPITAL BID REQUEST FORM			
Department			Unit cost-centre code
Description of item required			
Justification of request			
List of suppliers contacted (attach quotations)	Net price	VAT	Total price (incl. delivery)
Name and address of recommended supplier, and rationale for choice			
Comment by Head of Department		Purchase priority level (1–5)	
Comment by Senior Manager	Authorised Yes/No		Expense code

Figure 9.1.7 A sample capital-bid request form

Expenditure on routine items

Expenditure on routine items must also be authorised at some point, and the forms for this purpose have different formats depending on the sum involved, the type of expenditure and the different types of rationale that may be required. A form designed to include details of expenses on a trip abroad, or an external training form, will be different from the type of form completed for four cups of coffee and a plate of sandwiches for hospitality.

There will, however, be certain commonalities. There should be spaces for a description of the item, the price, the expense code, the signature of the person making the request and the signature of the person authorised to sanction it. For all but the most trivial or common items, you should make sure that you retain a copy of forms you either complete or authorise in case you are asked to provide evidence of expenditure by your auditors. If, at any time, you are concerned that a form does not give you the ability to keep a full record of the reason for the expenditure, then you are advised to keep your own notes on this to ensure that you can supply explanations to support your actions at a later date.

1 Make sure that you are familiar with the formats of all the routine forms for consumable items and the process required for obtaining authorisation for different levels of expenditure.
2 Check that all your own records and supporting documentation would stand full scrutiny by either internal or external auditors if this is ever required (see also pages 695–697 and page 705).

Estimating resource requirements to meet work objectives

The examples of estimates given in the previous section made certain assumptions. In all cases a fixed amount was requested against a particular item of expenditure. In reality, however, you may have to take into account different time spans and different levels of activity. As an obvious example, your stationery budget *may* be such that you require the same amount of paper each month, but it is more likely that this will vary to some degree throughout the year. This is particularly the case if any of your activities are affected by seasonal demand or particular projects – such as the annual sales conference or autumn mailshots.

Estimating your requirements to take account of fluctuations in activity is always advisable – if not essential – to ensure that you have the resources as and when you want them. Moreover, you may need to submit such proposals to your line manager to ensure that there are enough funds left under particular budget headings at the end of the financial year to meet your resource requirements. In addition, as mentioned previously, this may be an organisational requirement to link with the cash-flow forecast.

Assessing work flow

The seasonal variations of work and peaks of demand can usually be identified by considering the main activities undertaken by your department or section on a regular basis. These events are usually determined on a variety of planners and should be incorporated into your budget forecast. From an overall stationery budget of, say, £6000 over a year, this can then be fine-tuned to give a monthly figure which is in line with projected requirements. If you are taking this line, it is usual to try to allow for something to be left at the end for emergency requirements, unscheduled activities or new events.

Assessing project requirements

There is a clear link between assessing and estimating the resource requirements for a particular event and the techniques that were discussed in Chapter 7, such as network analysis. It is suggested that you refer back to Figures 7.1.1 and 7.1.2 (pages 551 and 552) to refresh your memory of this process. In the example given – for a mailshot – resources would be identified under the materials required, the staff needed and equipment utilisation for different stages of the overall task. Obviously, this technique can be adapted to much larger projects, such as organising a conference or seminar, organising a training event or even the total refurbishment and re-equipping of several offices.

The key point to note is that this breakdown is usually ancillary to the main budgeting process under which the total amount of expenditure for each particular type of item must have been identified under its relevant heading.

Profiling estimated income and expenditure

Estimates that are based on projected income and expenditure are not usually one-line items! For instance, labour costs and non-labour costs and expenditure on capital and consumable items are always treated as separate items. However, as you will have seen from Figure 9.1.5 on pages 684–685, it is usual to classify or categorise expenditure by an expenditure code based on particular types of expense in different areas relevant to the business of the organisation.

Estimates of income may not be relevant to your own particular section. If, however, you are involved in receiving income generated from sales, you will need to differentiate between income that is 'routine' and that which is more variable. For instance, if you work for an organisation that obtains any form of maintenance income then this can usually be estimated fairly accurately at the start of the year. Estimating sales income is often based on previous sales plus current projections which take into account the total size of the market and the estimated market share that will be achieved. Finally, you need to be aware of the fluctuations in income which may occur from one month to the next through seasonal factors or through particular projects coming to fruition.

Alternative methods of profiling income are by source or type of sales. Profiling by source is only appropriate for enterprises that have a known and relatively limited customer base – such as a tour operator which deals with 200 travel agents or a public-sector organisation that receives funds from a limited range of sources. For instance, a local authority could profile its income fairly easily into receipts from taxation, government grants, income from investments, and income from sales and services. Profiling by type of sales is more usual for large retailers which, at first sight, would appear to have an impossible task if they tried to profile by individual customer. However, with the development of comprehensive databases linked to customer loyalty schemes, such companies are now profiling more by *type* of customer – which assists the marketing function at least as much as it does financial planning.

Profiling by income source or type of sales assists planning if revenue from a particular area is prone to fluctuate. For instance, if a major capital development bid is justified through income from a steady or growing source, this is much more likely to be approved than if the bid is calculated against a declining or questionable income source.

1 Obtain a copy of the expenditure headings used by your organisation for profiling expenditure, and find out how income is profiled or categorised.
2 Take your investigations one step further by finding out which income sources are growing and which are declining or threatened for some reason, and how this information would affect the success of particular bids for resources.

An organisation's procedures for negotiating financial resources

There may be various routes through which you are expected to obtain financial resources:

- through submitting budget estimates and forecasts
- by submitting requests for capital items and expenditure on consumables
- by negotiating with your line manager or your financial controller.

The actual form-filling procedures and submissions have been covered earlier in this chapter. In this section we will be more concerned with the negotiation aspect of financial resources.

Negotiating with your line manager

If you have studied Chapter 4 in depth, or read Chapter 8, then you should already know a range of strategies for negotiating! Do bear in mind that attitudes to financial resources – and therefore the behaviour of your boss – are likely to be determined by:

- the overall financial situation and financial environment of your organisation
- the attitude of your manager's line manager
- the degree to which finances are tightly (or loosely) controlled in your organisation
- the department in which you work and the degree of justification required for its expenditure
- your own manager's general attitude to his/her staff.

In other words, if your organisation is going through a tough time financially, with cost-cutting measures expected everywhere, this is hardly the best moment to ask for a pay rise for your staff or an upgrade to your computer (although in the right circumstances this could be justified even in times of financial stringency). Even if things are going well, you may have problems extracting resources from your boss if he/she is particularly keen on financial austerity! Usually, the most obvious way to obtain financial resources is by linking the need for these to your line manager's individual targets and objectives and those of your department. Proving, time and again, that you can 'deliver the goods' if you are appropriately resourced is usually better than a hundred speculative arguments and debates.

Negotiating with financial controllers

Negotiating *directly* with anyone in the Finance department may not be allowed by your organisation's procedures, particularly if you work for a large organisation and finance is centrally controlled. However, in a smaller organisation you are more likely to have to justify your requests and actions directly; and, even in a large organisation, you may be called upon to justify or account for your views in writing directly to someone who 'holds the purse-strings'.

The difficulty is often twofold. Firstly, you may not know the person you are dealing with very well and cannot, therefore, decide an appropriate strategy in advance. Secondly, most financial experts are immune to any form of argument or persuasion unless the figures tell the same story. To the average individual, this attitude can be viewed as anything from rationally sound to downright infuriating!

Basically, the attitudes and behaviour of all accountants are constrained by the rules, conventions and assumptions which govern their modes of operation. Knowing and understanding these will help you to assess for yourself which requests for resources are completely 'off limits', regardless of how persuasive you try to be. The main conventions are given in Figure 9.1.8. You are advised to scan this list every time you are scheduled to enter into direct negotiations with your financial controller.

Figure 9.1.8 Learning the language – financial conventions and assumptions

---

Basic assumptions

1 **Business entity**. The accounts are prepared for the business and not for those who own or manage it. This is straightforward for a limited company, which is a corporate entity in its own right, less so for a sole trader who pays all his bills from one bank account!

2 **Periodicity**. The accounts should be prepared on a regular basis and over a regular specified period. This explains your financial year and year-end.

3 **Going concern**. The business is viewed as a going concern, not one that will be sold or liquidated in the near future. This implies that today's resources will be required tomorrow and there is no attempt to measure current business worth or value.

Recorded data

1 **Money measurement**. Only facts and information that can be expressed in monetary terms are included in the accounts. You cannot, therefore, put a value on your staff's skills or commitment

2 **Dual aspect**. At all times the assets of the organisation will equal its liabilities. This is the basis of double-entry booking.

3 **Historical cost**. Assets are valued at the cost at which they were acquired, i.e. the original purchase price. There has been much dissension over this rule, mainly because of the problems of inflation. However, to date, no better method has been found.

---

4   **Realisation**. Revenue from the sale of assets must be entered in the period in which the legal title of the goods was transferred, regardless of when payment was actually made. You may like to note that if your organisation uses the cash-flow accounting method it will enter revenue when the money changes hands. However, this must be done consistently, throughout the organisation and for all purchases and sales.

5   **Accruals**. The financial effects of transactions must be assigned to the accounting period in which they were earned or incurred, rather than the period when cash actually changed hands. This therefore means that there must be some adjustments to cash receipts and payments during a subsequent period.

Ethical and behavioural considerations

1   **Consistency**. Similar items must be dealt with in the same way to enable comparisons to be made easily. This means that the rules and procedures followed in one period must be followed in the next. For instance, items which depreciate must all be treated in the same way from one period to the next.

2   **Prudence**. A cautious view must be taken of all financial transactions. Revenues and profits must never be anticipated but included only upon realisation. Full provision, however, should be made for possible costs and losses. This explains many disagreements between managers and accountants!

3   **Materiality**. Insignificant items and events will be disregarded in the compilation of the accounts. This is why you are not required to do an inventory of your desk drawers at the end of each year!

4   **Objectivity**. The interpretation of accounting rules and regulations should be undertaken objectively and rationally and be free from personal bias and prejudice. This effectively prevents you from interpreting any of the above simply to suit your own arguments.

A businessman who had progressed from market trader to millionaire in less than 5 years was asked why he was so successful in business. He answered by saying that he did sums in different ways from accountants. His accountant regularly told him that to be successful he needed to make a profit of at least 15 per cent on each sale he made to give an adequate return on his investment. He replied by saying he was quite happy to make 1 per cent but to make 15 times more sales than the next man.

This exemplifies the fundamental difference between accountants and entrepreneurs. Waiting to make £1 million on one deal might mean you wait a lifetime but please your accountant. Making £1 on a deal might go against the grain, but doing it one million times has obvious benefits!

Procedures to ensure probity and that audit requirements are met

Accountants are concerned about justifying their actions because of the regulations governing financial reporting. You have already met some of these on page 663, where the requirements of the Companies Act were discussed. Accountants are also regulated by the Accounting Standards Board (ASB) – previously known as the Accounting Standards Committee (ASC) – which reports to the Financial Reporting Council (FSC).

A variety of accounting standards have been published, known as Financial Reporting Standards (FRSs). (Statements of Standard Accounting Practice (SSAPs) are those that were issued by the now defunct ASC.) All members of the accounting profession must comply with these accounting standards, both during the compilation of accounts and when they are undertaking auditing activities, and should follow both the letter and the spirit of all the relevant recommendations. Non-compliance must be identified and stated in the notes to the accounts or in the auditors' report.

Since 1990, compliance with ASB recommendations has become semi-statutory through the Companies Act 1989. Therefore, directors may be asked to provide an explanation for any discrepancies or irregularities which bring into question whether accounts represent a 'true and fair view' of their company's affairs. These may be unearthed by the auditors or the Financial Reporting Panel – which examines company accounts. At this stage, revision of the accounts might be required, if necessary by order of the courts.

At this point you should realise that auditing is in two stages – internal and external. The internal audit is carried out by finance staff who report directly to senior management. They are usually directed to cast an impartial eye over the financial policies and control mechanisms in place, to advise on how these could be improved, and to investigate areas in which savings might be made. In addition they will undertake checks to ensure that the procedures have been followed throughout the organisation.

The external audit is carried out by a registered auditing firm (usually a firm of accountants), officially appointed by the shareholders. In practice, the firm chosen is usually recommended by the directors. External auditing does not mean checking every entry that has been made – which would obviously be too time-consuming. Auditing is usually carried out on a sampling basis, with random transactions selected and 'tracked' across the organisation. Any areas which do not appear completely sound are investigated further.

> Not all organisations need to have a full audit. This requirement depends upon the annual turnover of the company each year, as shown in Figure 9.1.9.

Annual turnover	Requirement
Less than £90 000	Exempt from audit
Between £90 000 and £350 000	Compilation report by an independent accountant
Over £350 000	Statutory audit

Figure 9.1.9 Audit requirements

At the end of their investigations the auditors file their report, which is either *unqualified* or *qualified*. An unqualified report is one which states that the auditors are satisfied that the accounts provide a 'true and fair view' of the company's financial affairs. A qualified report is issued if the auditors wish to express:

- *uncertainty* – because the records are incomplete or because they have reservations about some of their findings; or
- *disagreement* with the accounts themselves – this may be because of factual discrepancies, errors in the financial reports, or non-compliance with the required standards.

The auditors are also constrained by the requirements of the Auditing Standards issued by the Auditing Practices Board – known as Statements of Auditing Standards (SAS) (see Figure 9.1.10). For that reason, they will 'test' the decisions made against these criteria. As an example, SAS 130 links with the 'going concern' convention outlined in Figure 9.1.8 and identifies that the firm must be treated as if it were going to continue in business. (If your boss had sold valuable assets for a song to his brother using the argument that, at that time, he thought the firm was going under, he should hardly be surprised to find that not only his actions but also his motives are questioned by the auditors and result in a serious investigation!)

Figure 9.1.10 The Auditing Practices Board's Statements of Auditing Standards

Responsibility	
SAS 100	Objective and general principles governing an audit of financial statements
SAS 110	Fraud and error
SAS 120	Consideration of law and regulations
SAS 130	The going concern basis in financial statements
SAS 140	Engagement letters
SAS 150	Subsequent events
SAS 160	Other information in documents containing audited financial statements
Planning, controlling and recording	
SAS 200	Planning
SAS 210	Knowledge of the business
SAS 220	Materiality and the audit
SAS 230	Working papers
SAS 240	Quality controls for audit work
Accounting systems and internal control	
SAS 300	Accounting and internal control systems and audit risk assessments
Evidence	
SAS 400	Audit evidence
SAS 410	Analytical procedures
SAS 420	Audit of accounting estimates
SAS 430	Audit sampling
SAS 440	Management representations

SAS 450   Opening balances and comparatives
SAS 460   Related parties
SAS 470   Overall view of financial statements

Using the work of others
SAS 500   Considering the work of internal audit
SAS 510   The relationship between principal auditors and other auditors
SAS 520   Using the work of an expert

Reporting
SAS 600   Auditors' reports on financial statements
SAS 610   Reports to directors or management
SAS 620   The auditors' rights and duty to report to regulators in the financial sector

Auditors often use 'off-the-shelf' checklist packages designed by large firms of auditors such as Arthur Anderson, Touche Ross and KPMG. These provide a list of questions which the auditors can use to 'steer' their investigation and ensure that all the recommended and required areas are covered. This prevents the auditing firm itself being accused of not following specified procedures. These checklists are also used by smaller firms of accountants which may audit small businesses. For instance, Kestrian Publishing Ltd issues *The Really Small Company Audit System* specifically designed for this purpose.

Neither the government nor large established companies are immune from auditing problems. In June 1997, the National Audit Office uncovered a £20 billion 'black hole' in the public finances – mainly caused by unrealistic assumptions on economic growth and forecast savings from tighter controls on tax and benefits to reduce fraud. In the light of their findings, the Treasury had to revise financial forecasts considerably. In the same month, First Choice, the tour operator, admitted that their auditor KPMG had uncovered accounting errors through mistakes in its costing systems. A one-off payment of £8.6 million was required to solve the problem.

THEORY INTO PRACTICE

1 Examine the conventions and assumptions contained in Figure 9.1.8. How many would appear to explain previous disagreements or misunderstandings you may have had with your colleagues in Finance?

2 Obtain a copy of the latest auditor's report either for your own organisation or for a listed public company. Check that it is an unqualified report. You may like to note that the auditor's report is most likely to be the shortest report in the annual documents yet the one accorded the most respect!

3 Check whether your staff who are involved in financial affairs, costings and budget procedures know how to prepare for an auditor's visit, and what to expect. You may like to start by ascertaining whether they keep full and complete financial records for the minimum required period of six years.

Element 9.2
Monitor and control financial resources

For your financial managers, allocating financial resources to your department or responsibility centre is not the end of the story. Of equal importance, in their view, will be your ability to monitor and control those assets so that they are put to good use and not wasted, and so that your financial plans over the year become reality. This is also crucial for your own reputation as a prudent and responsible administrator – let alone for your standing with your line manager or the external auditor!

Chapters 6 and 7 discussed control in relation to systems. Here we will revisit this concept, and examine the methods by which the organisation's financial systems are controlled and your own role in this process.

Your own work role and responsibilities

Element 9.1 introduced the idea of responsibility accounting. Under this concept, only those costs and revenues for which a manager can be held to be responsible should be charged to his or her responsibility centre. This means that, by definition, you should not be held responsible for any costs that you, too, cannot control – such as the organisation's total electricity or heating bill. However, wherever you do have the ability to control the amount spent or determine the quality of service you receive, then you have a responsibility to do your best to keep within your original estimates and budget limits unless there are unavoidable reasons for not doing so.

It may be that, rather than take responsibility yourself for particular budget forecasts or bid targets, you oversee these on behalf of your line manager. In this case, the collection of information and compilation of regular, accurate reports on actual versus planned income and expenditure is essential to good management. You cannot hope to keep a close watch on any financial situation if you obtain only vague or misleading information once every few months. (However, there is a danger in obtaining information so often that you start to ignore it. A bank statement received on a daily basis would be given far less care and attention than one received every month.)

You have a responsibility for monitoring actual events against planned events and noting any variances that occur. As you should have noted from Element 9.1, variances can be either favourable (F) or adverse (A). On a computer printout an adverse variance may be identified by a minus sign or by an entry in brackets; e.g. $-£550$ or $(£550)$.

Variances are usually highlighted in budget performance reports which may, or may not, give reasons for the variances. Your first step on receiving *any* budget report is to check it carefully – mistakes are sometimes made in allocating certain costs to particular responsibility centres or to the correct expenditure code. You also need to check that the items have been entered according to your records and agree with any quotations you have received or estimates you have submitted, and that no unexpected entries have been made. If there is still an inexplicable or unacceptable variance then this needs further investigation.

Refer back to page 675 to refresh your memory on the difference between fixed and flexible budgets. Then check which system is in operation in your organisation. This knowledge may be crucial in determining how to treat or explain certain types of variances.

Scope and limits of your authority relating to expenditure

It is hoped that you are absolutely clear about your own authority in relation to different levels and types of expenditure. If you have your own budget, or manage your own responsibility centre, then this issue is more clear-cut than if you oversee your manager's budget – particularly if he or she is not specific about those areas over which you have complete authority, partial authority or none whatsoever.

You may encounter problems if your line manager regularly travels on business and prompt actions or rapid decisions need to be taken about expenditure issues in his or her absence. If you have a positive and productive working relationship, then this aspect of your job should have been fully discussed; and if you do not have delegated authority for making certain types of decisions, you should at least know to whom you can turn in this situation. In an absolute emergency, you need to obtain advice or guidance from a senior manager. If you then make a rational and informed decision which is the best you could have done at that time, and is in accordance with organisational policy and procedures, the least you can expect is your line manager's support for your actions – and a full explanation if he or she considers you should have done something different. This, at least, will give you guidance for the next time.

An additional area that is well within the scope and authority of senior administrators is ascertaining that the organisation has received value for money from purchased items or service. This means checking that the quality, output and levels of satisfaction from users were as expected. Unless you ask around, you may find that no-one tells you that the latest batch of paper is constantly creating paper jams in the photocopier, that the fax in one office is forever breaking down, and that the temp you hired two weeks ago takes an age to produce one memo. Only if people are *personally* inconvenienced are they likely to report the matter. Keeping a watchful eye on your resources and an ear constantly open for feedback is an essential part of any control system.

To test whether you are fully aware of your own scope and authority in relation to expenditure, ask yourself whether you could cope in each of the following situations.

a Your line manager left the office in a rush on a business trip yesterday morning. Finance are now querying his authorisation for an advertisement for a new member of staff because it will cost twice the amount usually paid.

b A summer temporary worker has submitted a timesheet for more than his contracted or agreed hours, claiming he worked overtime for two weeks. The supervisor for whom he worked is away ill and the temporary employee has returned to university.

c One of your staff colleagues is using twice as many stationery and consumable items as anyone else.

d You recently costed the refurbishment of the office 'to the penny' and had your estimate accepted. The decorators have now contacted you to tell you they made a mistake on their quotation, which must be increased by £200.

e Your organisation has a strict rule that all capital expenditure must be for items over £1000, otherwise the money must be found from the consumables budget. The latter is fully allocated for the year and you were planning to buy a new computer from your capital allocation. You now find prices have fallen and the model you had in mind costs only £750.

Sources of financial data relating to your area of responsibility

Your major sources of financial data will be both internal and external and are likely to be paper-based and computer-based.

Internal sources

The main internal source document will be the budget performance report, which you should receive at least every month – usually by computer printout or on screen to those with a linked PC. An example of such a document is shown in Figure 9.2.1. It is usual for this to give a variety of headings which help you to monitor current expenditure against planned expenditure. If you are fortunate, there will also be a projection section which gives an indication of whether you are on target for your full year forecast. The headings within this document usually coincide with the expenditure headings of your budgeting system (see also Figure 9.1.5 on page 684).

The action that should be taken upon receipt of this document was discussed above, and you should note that your files should contain copies of all internal authorisation and bid forms to substantiate the entries on the statement or report. If you mislay or forget to retain any document it will usually be possible to obtain a copy from the Finance department.

If you are responsible also for revenue-generating activities then there should be a separate report that shows the level of current sales (or income) against the forecast amount. In most cases – in line with accounting conventions – you will find that you are not actually 'credited' with these sales until payment has been made. Organisations selling expensive capital equipment on deferred terms usually have their own procedures for accrediting budget-holders with projected sales revenue.

> Given the dangers of information overload, some organisations issue 'exception reports' to budget-holders. These are similar to the budget performance report illustrated in Figure 9.2.1, but in this case only items with a significant variance are listed. These help managers to save time by using the *management by exception* principle – concentrating on areas that need attention, rather than trying to oversee absolutely everything.

External sources

Obviously your main sources are your suppliers (for expenditure items) and your customers (for revenue items). Copies of quotations, estimates, delivery notes and purchase and sales invoices should always be retained in case there are any queries, and the latter checked carefully before being passed for payment. If there is ever a discrepancy between the amount quoted and the amount charged it is up to you to question the difference and find out why it has occurred. If you have made a mistake (e.g. by bidding for an amount net of VAT rather than plus VAT) then you should always be honest – and then make sure you don't repeat the error.

If the difference is through a miscalculation on the part of the supplier, the action to take will depend upon the reason for the difference, the amount involved and the previous reputation of the supplier. There is obviously a tremendous difference between a small, unavoidable increase and a large one which makes you highly suspicious about motives! At this point you may wish to refer to Chapter 4, pages 394–396 for information on the law of contract and your rights as a consumer. You should also note that detailed information on purchasing and contracts is given in Chapter 8.

Analysing and evaluating financial data

The manner in which financial data are analysed and evaluated tends to become more 'focused' at lower levels in the organisation. The MD or Chief Executive Officer will be most interested in bottom-line reporting in relation to the total income and expenditure for the whole organisation. Departmental heads are principally interested in the facts and figures for their own department, and individual budget-holders are concerned about their own performance and will be tasked with providing explanations for any important variances. In most organisations (though not all!) detailed investigations are confined to those variances which are deemed to be *significant*. This means that someone has to make the decisions about which *types* of variances are important and the degree to which deviations are permitted.

BUDGET PERFORMANCE REPORT

Responsibility centre:
Budget holder:

Date of issue:
Accounting period:

Budgeted item		Current period			Year to date			Full year		Comments
Code	Description	Plan (£)	Actual (£)	Variance (£)	Plan (£)	Actual (£)	Variance (£)	Plan (£)	Forecast (£)	

Figure 9.2.1 A budget performance report (NB: an exception report would give the same information but *only* for items showing a significant variance)

Setting limits for variances

Variances usually occur because:

- the budget target was inappropriate, unrealistic, inaccurate or out of date, and/or
- an unforeseeable event has occurred.

Both types of variances can be considered significant, but in the case of small deviations from budget which could not have been foreseen or controlled it will usually not be cost-effective to investigate in detail.

Significance limits for variances must be set so that performance can be monitored objectively. They may be set by simple common-sense measures based on judgement, experience and the overall level of expenditure being predicted. In other words a £10 deficit on a budget of £50 is far more significant than a £100 deficit on a budget of £1 million. This method of calculating variances is normally known as *estimation*. A more precise figure can be determined by *statistical analysis*. Either way, you are likely to be given a range of possible outcomes which would be considered insignificant, say 'plus or minus 3 per cent'. You should therefore not expect to be overly criticised or praised for overspends or savings within this band. Moving outside the band, however, would be a different matter entirely!

It is *not* the most sensible approach to consider that every favourable variance is good news and the more you can achieve or score on your budget the better. Obviously, savings in one area can always be used to buy additional items you may have thought you couldn't afford, and may even be vired *across* the budget if this is allowed. However, if you *constantly* underspend against your estimates, before too long someone is going to start to query your ability to produce accurate estimates in the first place.

If you work for an organisation where there is zero tolerance on adverse variances, bear in mind that this approach can encourage inflated estimates and budget forecasts to ensure an adequate safety margin!

Variance analysis

Variances can be classified under various headings which help to give an indication of the reasons why they may occur. An investigation should be used to give positive guidance on any corrective action that must be taken.

Forecast/actual operating variance

An adverse variance can occur because of reduced income or increased expenditure on resources. In either case the reason must be investigated by examining, for example, *which* sales failed to achieve forecast levels and why and/or *which* costs exceeded budgets, and whether this was a company-wide trend or occurred only in certain responsibility centres.

Income variance

This can occur because:

- forecasts were overly optimistic, and/or
- volume of sales was not achieved, even though forecasts were realistic, and/or
- the price of the product was reduced for some reason (e.g. to retain competitiveness or to allow discounts and thereby retain volume of sales).

Materials variance

Reasons for a variance in this area include:

- an increase in price without a compensatory reduction in usage
- an increase in usage
- an increase in wastage.

Labour variance

An adverse variance may occur if:

- the price paid for labour is higher than forecast
- productivity is less than anticipated
- more higher-priced labour is used.

Variances are also quite possible on overheads, given that in this area, too, prices can rise, usage can be higher than anticipated and efficiency rates can fall. This is one of the main reasons for all those reminders about turning lights off and not using fan heaters! However, you may be pleased to know that responsibility for this area is not usually passed to the administrator unless you work in a very small firm and are on your own (and therefore the only culprit) for most of the time!

THEORY INTO PRACTICE

Book publishers carry out, for each book they produce, complicated calculations on projected costs and revenue with an estimated forecast for both income and expenditure. Let us assume that:

- all overheads and salaries are classed as fixed costs (this includes the cost of editing the book, sales and advertising)
- printing costs, paper used, binding materials are all variable costs (author's royalties are also a variable cost as they are based on the number of sales).

From this information, brainstorm as many examples as you can as to where and why adverse variances may occur which would affect the operating profit of a publishing company.

An organisation's procedures for expenditure

In most organisations there are strict procedures to follow regarding expenditure. The reasons are obvious, given the requirements of the accountants and the auditors. An administrator has a responsibility not only to follow the procedures, but also to make sure that any junior staff or other colleagues for whom he/she is responsible understand the importance of compliance in this area. The following are very common requirements.

- All financial requests and transactions must be documented. This means confirming any verbal arrangements in writing.
- The appropriate documentation must be completed. This usually means the completion of an official purchase order or internal requisition for resources.
- All documents must be signed and authorised by the appropriate person(s).
- Each type of transaction must be separately and distinctly documented.
- Appropriate expense codes must be entered on all documents, including official orders and invoices.
- Deliveries must be checked for accuracy and completeness.
- Invoices must be carefully checked for accuracy, and also against quotations.
- Payments must be approved only by authorised personnel.
- Details of the amounts spent will then be recorded on the next budget performance report.

In addition, there are likely to be separate procedures to cover areas such as expense claims, petty cash and major capital expenditure items.

THEORY INTO PRACTICE

1 Consider the procedure in operation in your own organisation and note any ways in which it differs from that outlined above.
2 A senior member of staff in your department often fails to conform with specified petty cash procedures. For example, he begs for advances and then neglects to provide receipts to substantiate purchases. Your junior colleague, who is responsible for paying out monies from this fund, is soft-hearted and no match for his persuasive tongue. What should you do?

Formats for recording financial movements

In addition to the budget performance report, which gives only total expenditure against each expense code (see Figure 9.2.1), it is usual for a more detailed breakdown to be available to each responsibility centre. This lists the revenue and expenditure incurred against *each* item under *each* code. Almost invariably these days, these data are entered and stored on computer, using either customised software linked to the financial management system, a basic accounting package, or a spreadsheet.

Ideally, the total of these listings will be linked to the main budget system, so that you can access reports at different levels to provide additional information on any transaction as and when required. The fundamental information likely to be recorded is shown in Figure 9.2.2. The advantage of recording this on any type of accounting package is that the entry is made both in the relevant expenses account and in the relevant supplier's account, which can also be accessed for information. This is because all accounting packages automatically follow a double-entry system. Therefore, when payment is made, the expense account is debited with the payment and the bank account credited accordingly.

When a computerised system is employed, a range of reports can be generated relatively easily. One possible disadvantage, particularly on a networked system, is that discrepancies are immediately visible for *anyone* to see. This information might be sensitive.

Account heading: Expenditure code:					
Date	Invoice no.	Supplier	Net amount	VAT	Total amount
		Total (this page)			

Figure 9.2.2 Example of an expenditure listing

It is important to note that many financial packages do not allow you simply to amend incorrect entries by going back into the account and altering your previous figures. The reason for this is obvious if you consider that many accounting packages provide information that is later audited, and a facility to amend entries would allow considerable manipulation of figures whenever it was thought expedient! Genuine mistakes are therefore usually corrected through an adjustment process, which is then recorded on the audit trail. The latter prints out a record of each and every entry and correction made over a period of time.

An organisation's procedures for dealing with variations to planned income and expenditure

This chapter has already considered in some depth the procedures for classifying variances, the reasons why they occur, and the 'tolerance' levels allowed by organisations. However, the official tolerance levels and the tolerance levels of some of the senior managers in the organisation may be somewhat different. At this stage, therefore, it is useful to take a moment to consider the behavioural effects of budget control systems and financial resource systems on managers and other staff.

One of the most famous studies on this topic was published by Chris Argyris, in *The Impact of Budgets on People*, as long ago as 1952 (see Figure 9.2.3). In the world of finance little seems to change and many of his findings are still pertinent today. Given that other authorities argue that budgets should be motivational and have clear advantages for managers, there appears to be some discrepancy between these views.

In reality, there is always likely to be conflict when using one budget as a planning mechanism, a control device and a motivational tool at the same time (hardly goal congruence for one system!). It is probably for this reason that studies have shown that budget levels which are the most motivational are unlikely to be achieved on a regular basis, and those which are achievable will usually inspire a lower level of performance. This seems to lead to the conclusion that the best type of budgets are those that are demanding, but where small adverse variances are not only tolerated but considered healthy! In other words, the view is taken that it is better to try and to fail than never to try at all.

1   Pressure to achieve budget targets is divisive. It unites employees against management, with supervisory staff under tremendous pressure as the 'go-betweens'.
2   Budgets foster suspicions of management motives behind any actions to increase productivity.
3   Finance staff often feel success is achievable only if they find fault with production staff. The Finance Manager in particular may find that his/her success is derived mainly from an ability to find errors, weaknesses and faults in other areas of the organisation.
4   Errors and mistakes made by line managers or supervisors are frequently made public. This compounds the problem and causes both loss of confidence and demotivation in those under attack.
5   Managers and supervisors may use budgets for their own ends, to give or withhold favours. It is the budget, rather than the budget-owner, that usually takes the blame.

Figure 9.2.3 Human relations and budgets (adapted from Argyris, 1952)

A second key finding is that senior management should encourage their subordinates to view budgets as a tool for information and a performance 'carrot', rather than as a stick with which they can beat the unwary. The problems of budgets being used as a weapon include:

- managers becoming totally focused on meeting budget targets, to the detriment of other issues and ethical considerations
- the tendency to submit the type of forecasts which will 'please the

boss', rather than accurate data – such as low budget forecasts during a period of contraction and high forecasts during a period of growth

- the adoption of deliberate strategies and the distortion of information to ensure actual performance accords with planned performance.

Thirdly, managers are more likely to see budgeting as a positive benefit if they:

- are full participants in the budgeting process and the setting of their own targets
- consider the agreed targets to be realistic, appropriate and achievable
- agree, understand and concur with the areas for which they have designated responsibility
- are accorded the authority to make decisions over their own responsibility areas without interference
- are given the freedom to fail in a particular area *provided* there is evidence to prove that the best attempt under the circumstances was made and that the failure will not seriously jeopardise the future stability of the organisation as a whole
- understand how and why financial data are produced and presented as they are, and there is a two-way development of a common accord between managers and the organisational accountants.

This last point brings us full circle to the rationale behind this chapter – to help you, as a responsible administrator, not only to operate your financial resources system and follow specified procedures, but also to gain a better appreciation of how and why financial systems are designed to operate, and to understand in a little more depth the reasons for any differences in approach which exist in your organisation between the producers and operators and the financial controllers.

THEORY INTO PRACTICE

Study the findings of Chris Argyris (in Figure 9.2.3) and try to establish the degree to which you feel any apply in your own organisation at the present time. If you feel they are applicable, carry out the following task.

Try to identify the degree to which difficulties arise because of any of the following:

a problems with the system itself (lack of participation by managers, unrealistic targets, inaccurate information fed back to managers)
b the way the budget system is related to targets, and the way in which variances and failure to meet targets is handled
c a general lack of communication between the different factions of the organisation
d a combination of all the above.

What steps would you recommend should be taken, or could be taken, to improve the situation?

Comfort your own line manager, the next time he or she is depressed about budgets, by recounting the following story about an MD's strategy for dealing with his budget-holders.

- *Stage 1.* Compare the manager's performance with budget targets. If worse, reprimand manager; if better, say nothing and move to stage 2.
- *Stage 2.* Compare the manager's performance with last year's performance. If worse, reprimand manager; if better, say nothing and move to stage 3.
- *Stage 3.* Compare manager's performance with performance of least-liked colleague. If worse, reprimand manager; if better, say nothing and move to stage 4.
- *Stage 4.* Give manager a lecture on the dangers of becoming complacent.

Remember, in some games you just can't win!

10 Facilitate compliance with legal and regulatory requirements

Element 10.1

Identify and interpret current and emerging legal and regulatory requirements

Throughout the course of this chapter, reference will be made to a number of legal institutions and structures. To avoid repetition, all the relevant information on the basic structure of the legal system and the way it operates is contained in the section entitled 'Overview of the structures and operation of the legal system', which starts on page 737.

Types and sources of legal requirements relating to work practices and conditions

The law permeates almost every area of business life, as the extract from a set of minutes of a Board meeting of a pharmaceutical company indicates (see Figure 10.1.1). All the situations under discussion in those minutes have legal connotations – some of which could have considerable adverse financial implications if the personnel involved are unaware of the legal significance.

---

2 Managing Director's report

2.1 Formal notice of a proposed merger bid had now been received from Rowlands. It was suggested that the proposal should be discussed as a matter of urgency at a special meeting of the Board of Directors prior to any further action being taken.

2.2 Negotiations had begun for the purchase of the building adjacent to the workshops for conversion into an office block.

3 Departmental reports

3.1 **Human Resources**
... The majority of the retirements had now been negotiated. However, there remained the problem of Janet Dearing who had reached the age of 60 but who wanted to work on until the age of 65 on the same basis as that of her male colleagues ...

3.2 **Administration**
... Customer Services had received 8 complaints over the past 5 weeks. As the attached schedule indicated, most of these were minor and had been dealt with satisfactorily. However, one complaint required further attention. The local Friends of the Earth group had complained that the company was polluting one of the local rivers with industrial waste ...

3.3 Accounts

Some of the outstanding debts had become a matter of concern. All the internal procedures had been exhausted and it was recommended therefore that the Board look into the possibility of legal actions against certain of the debtors ...

3.4 Production

... (as part of the section on health and safety issues). On 20 August, one of the operatives received acid burns to his hands when a container of chemicals was knocked off a workbench. He was not wearing the standard protective gloves. No hospital treatment was necessary ...

3.5 Marketing

3.5.1 ... There were some rumours circulating that Sankeys were planning to produce and market a new form of indigestion tablet called 'Solvit'. If so, it could easily be confused with the company's range of indigestion tablets, 'Solvall'.

3.5.2 Recent market research had indicated that company products would sell well abroad, particularly in the EU. The team were anxious to explore this possibility ...

3.6 Purchasing

... a consignment of plastic containers from Murphys was found to contain at least 20 damaged items. The suppliers had refused to accept liability because they maintained that the fault was that of the road haulage firm. The road haulage firm denied that the goods were damaged by them ...

Figure 10.1.1 Extracts from the minutes of a Board meeting

Even though many organisations have their own legal departments or retain the services of a solicitor, individual managers and administrators can benefit from knowing how the law affects their area of work. At worst this can save them from personal liability; at best it can enhance their reputation in the workplace as someone who is able to give preliminary legal advice to avert a possible problem or to facilitate an important initiative.

Prior to 1066 there existed only a very primitive legal system, with a proliferation of local courts. After the Norman Conquest, however, the ascendancy of the King's courts over the local courts began to take effect (even though the process took about 300 years to complete) and nowadays the English court structure is almost completely centralised – although no less complex.

The two sources of law upon which the courts can draw are case law and statutory law, both of equal importance. They can be used either individually or together and cover all areas of either civil or criminal law, the most significant of which are outlined on page 742.

Non-statutory requirements

Case law and the doctrine of precedent

Most systems of law have their origins in ancient customs and UK law is no exception, based as it is on the oral customs of the Anglo-Saxons. In the twelfth century, the Norman judges incorporated these customs into a more formal system of law in the medieval royal courts, and a record began to be kept of the decisions made in each individual case. When the courts were called upon to decide similar issues in subsequent cases, they reviewed the earlier decisions and, if one was found that covered the same area, they applied the same decision.

As a result, large areas of UK law have been developed by basing decisions on past cases. Thus, for instance, if your company is in dispute with an employee over a dismissal, your legal advisers may be able to argue your case by looking back at similar cases over a large number of years and using the decisions in those cases to defend your actions.

One example of this procedure is *Lewis v Motorworld Garages Ltd* [1986] ICR 157, in which Mr Lewis was demoted without warning, lost his office and had his pay structure altered so that he took home less pay. He nevertheless continued to work for the firm even though he could have regarded the treatment as being sufficient to allow him to claim a breach of his contract. Over the next few months he was persistently and unfairly criticised and threatened with dismissal. When his employer gave him a final warning without any real reason, Mr Lewis eventually left and claimed that he had been 'constructively' dismissed; i.e. the breach of contract on the part of the employer was such that he was entitled to treat himself as being dismissed and that the dismissal was unfair. When his case was argued in court, the judge outlined a number of *previous* cases on which he could rely:

1 In order to prove constructive dismissal, an employee must prove that he/she left the employment as the result of a breach of contract by his/ her employer which showed that the employer no longer intended to be bound by an *essential* term of the contract. See *Western Excavating (ECC) v Sharp* [1978] 1 All ER 713.
2 However, there are normally implied in a contract of employment, mutual rights and obligations of trust and confidence. A breach of this term may justify the employee in leaving and claiming he has been constructively dismissed. See *Post Office v Roberts* [1980] IRLR 347, and *Woods v WM Car Services (Peterborough) Ltd* [1981] ICR 666.

(For guidance on how to interpret the information given after the names of the two parties, see page 727).

In making the decision it did, the court, with the help of the claimant's legal advisers, looked back at decisions taken in the cases indicated, which were based on similar facts and covered similar points of law. It is important to note, however, that in many cases, the court is not in a position to decide whether to follow the decision in a previous case: it has no choice but to accept it. This is known as the *doctrine of precedent*, and whether a court is bound by it is usually dependent upon its position in the hierarchy of the courts (see further page 737).

In addition to the requirement that a precedent is binding only on another court of the same or lower status, it will also be binding only insofar as it is a *ratio decidendi* statement. Judgements normally contain three elements:

- findings of fact
- statements of law
- the decision.

Statements of law are known as 'ratio decidendi' if they are based on the facts of the case *and* provide the basis of the decision. Other statements which do not provide the basis of the decision and are, for instance, merely comments on the law are known as *obiter dicta* and as such are not binding on other courts.

Advantages and disadvantages of the doctrine of precedent

There are many advantages to the doctrine. Professor Geldart, a noted legal writer, summarised them as follows.

- *Certainty*. Before you go into court you have at least some guidelines as to the legal points that are to be argued and the cases on which they will be based.
- *Capacity for amendment*. If a higher court disagrees with the decision of a lower court, it may alter or overrule it.
- *Attention to detail*. There are so many cases on virtually every established area of law that there is a strong possibility that at least one of them will apply to the circumstances of the present case.
- *Practicality*. It is argued that basing a decision on known facts and previous 'learned' decisions is preferable to basing it on some untested theory, however persuasive it might be.

The doctrine does, however, have some disadvantages. It can be very inflexible in that once a decision is made, theoretically it has to be followed notwithstanding that it may not have been a very sound decision. There is some room for manoeuvre in that cases can be 'distinguished on their facts'; i.e. it can be argued that the facts of the present case in some way differ from those of the previous cases and therefore warrant a different decision being reached. In addition, as already mentioned, a higher court can overrule the decision of a lower court. Even so, difficulties can occur.

Another disadvantage is that as case law is both so complex and so voluminous, it is sometimes difficult to know exactly what the law is in all areas, and you may find that you have breached it without knowing you have done so. Indeed, the famous jurist, Bentham, called it 'dog's law' – you do something wrong, you are hit and then you realise you have done something wrong!

Another accusation sometimes levelled against case law, and the use of precedents to enforce it, is its inability to respond quickly to new developments. In recent years, for instance, much publicity has been given to the problem of the pirating of videotapes, and there has also been clamour in the press about the need for a law to protect personal privacy. In both instances, case law is of only limited use as neither question has been addressed in great detail in the courts.

Read the following extract from an article which expresses anxieties about the possible legal repercussions arising from the use of the Internet in business.

There seems to be a tendency by users of the Internet to ignore any possible legal consequences accruing from its use. There is, of course, a set of business rules which are followed and which are akin to those applied in any normal commercial activity, but the fact that the Net has been in existence for only a relatively short period means that there is a dearth of legal precedents to call upon. Consequently a number of legal loopholes are being created.

- Copyright violation is difficult enough to control in respect of books, journals and other paper-based documents. In the case of the Internet it is virtually impossible for an author to prevent unauthorised copying – and even though institutions such as the World Intellectual Property Organisation recognise the need for electronic numbering of copyright works, a huge number of people post such work on the Net without bothering to assert their copyright.
- There is also a domain problem. Each name assigned to a computer network and host computer is unique and there are several groups that allocate and control such names. Usually the Net service provider liaises with these groups on the allocation of names, but Net users should be aware that they are not protected against legal proceedings if their allocated domain name infringes upon somebody else's trade name or trademark.
- Since cyberspace is undefined and digital transmission may take place via networks owned and operated by different people in different countries, there may be doubt as to the laws of which country should apply if an illegal act is alleged. What, for instance, would be the legal position, if online contracts were screen-printed to bind users or to limit risk if some countries refused to accept a digital signature as binding? The advertising of goods and services would be equally hazardous in that, in the absence of any pre-agreed contractual arrangement, there would be no certainty as to what the fundamental terms of the contract were; i.e. when and where it was formally agreed.

The situation is being reviewed and the International Chamber of Commerce is taking the lead in the assessment of laws and regulations relevant to business on the Net. Until such regulation, however, the legal difficulties remain immense.

1 Assess the advantages of waiting until certain legal precedents have been established before launching a marketing campaign via the Internet.
2 Consider also what difference there would be in the way in which this article was written if there *had* been a series of cases in which certain legal precedents had been established.

Statutory requirements

Many of the disadvantages of case law are redressed to a certain extent by the use of legislation or statutory law; i.e. law contained in Acts of

Parliament. In Britain, Parliament is the legislative body which may enact any law it chooses (in theory at least – extremely unpopular or controversial legislation is likely to be overruled by a successive Parliament). Routinely, a new law is first presented as a Bill, which has to be approved by both the House of Commons and the House of Lords and also receive the Royal Assent. It then becomes an Act of Parliament (or statute) and as a consequence becomes absolutely binding on the courts.

Acts may be passed to alter the existing law – whether case or statute law – or to create new law. Consequently they can respond far more quickly than case law to social and economic developments. When, for example, there was a public outcry over the attacks on children by certain breeds of dog, Parliament was able to pass a Dangerous Dogs Act which imposed conditions on the ownership and control of such dogs. Case law would have developed much more slowly.

There are various types of statutes. A *consolidating* statute is one that gathers together several Acts on one topic and re-enacts them so that all the statute law on that topic can be found in the same Act. A *codifying* statute involves the enactment of the *whole* law on a particular subject – and thus normally includes what was also case law on the subject (e.g. the Employment Protection (Consolidation) Act 1978). *Statute law revision* embraces the reprinting of old Acts with a view to omitting obsolete sections.

Legislation of the European Community

Prior to 1972 it was a well-established doctrine that Parliament had supreme legal authority. However, the European Communities Act 1972 has eroded that authority to a certain extent by providing that any enactment of the UK Parliament is subject to the *directly applicable* legislation of the Community. If a provision is 'directly applicable', any individual in the UK can enforce that right in any member state without the need for further legislation by the UK, and – significantly – any Community legislation that is inconsistent with UK legislation must be given precedence.

Since the EU is concerned primarily with economic and commercial matters, the effect of this legislation has been most marked in the areas of business and employment law, one interesting example being that of *Macarthys Ltd v Smith* [1980] ICR 672, in which a female employee was taken on as stockroom manager. She then discovered that her male predecessor had been paid a higher salary than her. There was no-one else in a similar post with whom she could compare herself (a requirement of the UK Equal Pay Act 1970) so she claimed equal pay with her predecessor. The Court of Appeal held that the provisions of the Equal Pay Act did not allow her to do this and the case was therefore referred to the European Court of Justice. It was held that Article 119 of the EEC Treaty, which required members states to ensure and maintain 'the application of the principle that men and women should receive equal pay for equal work', applied in the present case and Mrs Smith was therefore successful in her appeal.

The primary sources of Community law are the Treaty of Paris 1951 and the Treaty of Rome 1957. These treaties set out in broad terms the objectives to be achieved but leave most of the details to the *Commission* and the *Council*. The *European Parliament* is a directly elected body which exercises its consultative and advisory functions through standing committees dealing with specialist topics. Its formal opinion is required on many proposals before they can be adopted by the Council.

- The *Commission* is the executive body of the Community and consists of Commissioners appointed by mutual agreement of the member governments. It is responsible for the formulation of policy, and although it acts collectively, individual Commissioners specialise in particular areas such as agriculture, transport and social affairs. It initiates and drafts most Community legislation and puts its proposals before the Council for enactment.
- The *Council* is the Community's decision-making body. It agrees legislation on the basis of proposals put forward by the Commission.

EU law-making powers

The Community instruments which may be classified as legislation are as follows.

- *Regulations*. These are designed to ensure uniformity of law through the member states and are therefore of general application, binding in their entirety and directly applicable in all member states without the need for further legislation. They confer individual rights and duties which the national courts of the member states must protect.
- *Directives*. Unlike regulations, directives do not have immediate binding force in all member states. They merely require the national Parliament to make whatever changes are necessary to implement the directive within a specified time. Important to note in this context is the Social Action Programme adopted by the Council in 1974, which produced a series of directives between 1974 and 1979 that constitute the main body of Community labour law:

  – the Equal Pay Directive
  – the Directive on Collective Redundancies
  – the Equal Treatment Directive
  – the Transfers of Undertakings Directive
  – the Social Security Directive
  – the Directive on Insolvency.

- *Decisions*. These may be addressed either to a member state or to an individual or institution. They are a formal method of communicating policy decisions and they are binding on those to whom they are addressed.

- Somewhat surprisingly, perhaps, EU regulations are not concerned solely with major issues. For instance, the Prince of Wales has appealed to vegetable consumers to 'adopt' one of the thousands of vegetable varieties which are threatened with extinction because it is no longer legal under EU regulations to sell their seed. Examples include the Silsden Bomb cabbage, the Lazy House French bean, the Rat's Tail radish and the Tiger Tom tomato.
- Other member states are by no means always willing to accept EU legislation without argument. A German lawyer who wanted to practise his profession in Italy had to take his case to the European Court of Justice when, despite an EU directive which laid down a general system for the recognition of higher education diplomas awarded on completion of professional education and training of at least three years' duration, the Milan Bar Council suspended him from pursuing his professional activities on the grounds that he had contravened his obligations under an Italian law by pursuing a professional activity in Italy on a permanent basis.

THEORY INTO PRACTICE

1 Consider the *disadvantages* of the direct applicability doctrine.
2 Consider the implications of the following extract from a newspaper article – assuming you have some responsibility for the cleanliness of inland waters.

'Although the UK has more than 400 beaches recognised as satisfying EU directives, inland waters do not get this blessing. In December, a House of Lords select committee concluded: "The implication must be that no UK inland waters presently meet the criteria". The truth is that many may well do so, but the Department of the Environment chooses to interpret the EU bathing water directive as not requiring inland waters to need any designation.'

Types and sources of regulatory requirements relating to work practices and conditions

Delegated legislation

Sheer volume makes it impossible for Parliament to deal with all the proposed legislative measures. As a consequence, much use is made of *delegated legislation* – laws passed by a body to whom Parliament has given limited powers. There are various types of delegated legislation.

- *An Order in Council.* This is the highest form of delegated legislation. In theory this is an order of the Privy Council, but in reality it is usually made by the government and merely approved by the Privy Council (for further details on the role of the Privy Council, see page 739).
- *Rules and regulations.* A statute may authorise a minister or a government department to institute a wide variety of regulatory requirements. These rules are known as *statutory instruments* and are often issued to support or amend an existing statute. For instance, the

Equal Pay Act 1970 contains legislation to the effect that a woman is to be regarded as employed on like work with men:

- if her work and theirs is of the same or a broadly similar nature, and the differences (if any) between the things she does and the things they do are not of practical importance in relation to terms and conditions of employment, or
- if her job and their job have been given an equal value, in terms of the demands made on them through the operation of a job evaluation study.

However, in 1982 the EU Commission successfully sued the UK on the grounds that UK legislation on equal pay contravened EU legislation. As a consequence, a statutory instrument in the form of the Equal Pay (Amendment) Regulations 1983 was passed to amend the Act and to introduce a third situation where equal pay could be claimed; i.e. where a woman is employed on work of equal value to that of a man in the same employment.

- *By-laws*. These are rules made by local authorities. Their operation is restricted to the locality to which they apply.

The advantages of delegated legislation are apparent.

- Delegated legislation saves the time of Parliament, allowing it to concentrate on matters of general policy.
- It can be implemented very quickly and can therefore respond to changing needs much more easily than either statutory or case law.
- It is flexible in that it can be amended from time to time without the necessity for a new statute.

There are disadvantages, however. One is that it creates a vast amount of new law, the number of statutory instruments being issued each year far exceeding the number of statutes.

There are also concerns that delegated legislation takes law-making out of the direct control of elected representatives and places it in the hands of employees of government departments. There has, for instance, been much concern expressed about the number of quangos (quasi non-governmental organisations) in existence, which critics feel wield too much power without adequate checks or accountability. In 1995 the number of quangos had risen to over 5000.

THEORY INTO PRACTICE

Research into the membership profiles of quangos by the Institute of Local Government Studies at Birmingham University revealed certain significant facts. Out of a survey of 1500 members:

- more than half held at least one other similar post, while 10 per cent held four or more posts
- three-quarters of those appointed were male, 60–70 per cent were from the commercial sector, and more than 98 per cent were white.

The researchers were concerned about the possible adverse effects of such a limited profile of membership. However, it could be argued that such a membership results in quangos being run by a small group of very experienced and knowledgeable people, and that enlarging the membership would make it less effective. Consider the merits of both arguments, and possible compromises.

Safeguards

There are some safeguards to prevent delegated legislation from being misused. If, for instance, a minister, government department or local authority exceeds its delegated powers, its action would be held by the court to be *ultra vires* (beyond its powers) and therefore void. There are also several methods of parliamentary control. Some statutory instruments *must* be laid before Parliament and will cease to be operative within 40 days if the House so resolves. Others require a vote of approval from the House. There are also committees in both Houses whose function it is to scrutinise statutory instruments with a view to deciding whether the attention of Parliament should be drawn to the instrument for a particular reason (although it is interesting to note that the last time the House of Lords challenged a statutory instrument was in 1982).

Obtaining information on legal and regulatory requirements

In subsequent sections of this chapter you will be reading about ways of interpreting existing and possible future legal and regulatory requirements. Before you do so, however, it may be useful for you to be aware of the many sources of reference.

Legal textbooks

One obvious source of reference is a legal textbook. Every major branch of the law tends to have a standard textbook which is updated on a regular basis, and which may be worth purchasing if it has an immediate bearing on your work (see Figure 10.1.2). If, however, you work in a very specialised sphere you may find that a specialised textbook designed specifically for legal practitioners may be of considerable assistance – particularly since these are considered to be such good authorities that they can be referred to in court (see Figure 10.1.3).

Administrative law	Wade: *Administrative Law*
Agency	Markesinis & Munday: *An Outline of the Law of Agency*
Commercial law	Goode: *Commercial Law*
Company law	Farrar: *Farrar's Company Law*
	Pennington: *Pennington's Company Law*
Contract law	Treitel: *The Law of Contract*

Employment law	Smith & Woods: *Industrial Law*
Intellectual property	Cornish: *Intellectual Property: Patents, Copyright, Trade Marks and Allied Rights*
Land law	Gray: *Elements of Land Law*
Landlords and tenants	Evans & Smith: *The Law of Landlord and Tenant*
Media law	Robertson & Nicol: *Media Law*
Sale of goods and consumer protection	Macleod: *Consumer Sales Law*
	Dobson: *Sale of Goods and Consumer Credit*
Torts	Winfield & Jolowicz: *The Law of Torts*
	Salmond & Heuston: *The Law of Torts*

Figure 10.1.2 Some standard law textbooks

Bowstead: *The Law of Agency*
Palmer: *Bailment*
Clayton & Tomlinson: *Civil Actions against the Police*
Goode: *Commercial Law*
Palmer: *Palmer's Company Law*
Dicey & Morris: *Conflicts of Law*
Chitty: *Chitty on Contract*
McGregor: *McGregor on Damages*
Rayden & Jackson: *Divorce and Family Matters*
Charlesworth & Percy: *Negligence*
Lindley: *Lindley on Partnership*
Jackson & Powell: *Professional Negligence*
Wilkinson: *Road Traffic Offences*
Clerk & Lindsell: *The Law of Torts*

Figure 10.1.3 Selected practitioners' textbooks

For even more detailed information on both substantive and procedural law, you may on rare occasions have to consult the following practice manuals:

- *Archbold's Criminal Pleading, Evidence and Practice*
- *Stones' Justices Manual*
- *The Supreme Court Practice*
- *The County Court Practice*
- *The Family Court Practice*

Other resources

Useful though law textbooks may be in some cases, it is unlikely that you will find them your only or even your main source of reference should a legal issue arise. They may be intended for a very specific audience – a law student, a human resources manager, a trade union representative, etc., which limits their general usefulness. They may also be published at certain regular intervals over a period of several years and could therefore fail to alert you to any recent and possibly very significant changes in the law. Other sources of information may therefore be of more use.

Legal encyclopaedias

Legal encyclopaedias contain detailed discussions of a particular area of law. They usually have a very detailed index and appendices containing copies of statutes and statutory instruments and – importantly – have loose-leaf pamphlets issued several times a year containing the most up-to-date law. Examples of the most widely used encyclopaedias are listed in Figure 10.1.4.

● British Tax	● Health and Safety at Work
● Banking	● Housing (Law and Practice)
● Consumer Credit	● Local Government
● Data Protection	● Planning (Law and Practice)
● Environmental Health	● Professional Partnerships
● European Patent Law	● Road Traffic
● Financial Services	● VAT

Figure 10.1.4 Legal encyclopaedias

Law reports

It may be advisable for you to know how to access the various law reports that will provide you with a more detailed knowledge of the legal issues in which you are interested. The earliest existing reports are from informal notes made by students from the time of Edward I (1272–1307), although these are not now often cited as precedents in the courts. The process was developed through a series of Yearbooks, and eventually the establishment of the Incorporated Council of Law Reporting in 1865, which now publishes detailed reports of cases heard in the Superior Courts. Several private firms also publish similar reports. These contain both a list and detailed account of cases, with a comprehensive subject index categorising the cases to be found in that particular volume. A list of the most important law reports (together with their *citations* – i.e. the abbreviations used as a reference after every specific case) is given in Figure 10.1.5.

All England Law Reports (All ER or AER)
Appeal Cases (AC)
Butterworth's Company Law Cases (BCLC)
British Company Cases (BCC)
Chancery Division (CHD)
Commonwealth Law Reports (CMLR)
Criminal Appeal Reports (CR App R)
Criminal Appeal Reports (Sentencing) (Cr App R(S))
Crown Office Digest (COD)
English Reports (ER)
Family Law (Fam Law)
Family Law Reports (FLR)
Fleet Street Reports (FSR)
Housing Law Reports (HLR)
Industrial Cases Reports (ICR)

Industrial Relations Law Reports (IRLR)
Lloyd's Law Reports (Lloyd's Rep)
Probate Division (P)
Queen's Bench Division (QB)
Times Law Reports (TLR)
Weekly Law Reports (WLR)

Figure 10.1.5 Law reports and their abbreviations in citations

The amount of reported case law is now so considerable that you will be well-advised, as a starting point, to make use of the several digests available to give you some preliminary information. One example is *Halsbury's Laws of England* which consists of approximately 50 volumes containing the law relating to almost every subject area. The volumes are arranged alphabetically by subject and there is a general index to allow you to find the correct volume. The digest will give you the relevant case law and the statutory law and will also refer you to any useful periodicals. Other digests include *Current Law* which includes the Current Law Case Citator and the Current Law Legislation Citator, and the *Empire & English Digest* which is arranged in volumes and subject areas in a similar way to Halsbury's Laws.

Similarly, the simplest way in which to find a relevant statute is to consult *Halsbury's Statutes* or *Current Law Statutes Annotated*. To find a statutory instrument, either consult *Halsbury's Statutory Instruments* or refer to the original government documents published by HMSO.

THEORY INTO PRACTICE

Select one legal issue which, from experience, you know may affect your own work – or that of the area in which you work.

a Using *either* one of the books listed in this section *or* another up-to-date law book on an appropriate topic, write no more than a paragraph on your findings. Include the title of the book, its author and publisher, its date of publication and the relevant page number.
b Consider whether you found the information of *practical* rather than merely *theoretical* use in the solving of the legal issue you have selected.

Interpreting legal and regulatory requirements

Finding your basic source of reference is often merely the first step in a more complicated process. *Understanding* what you find can be somewhat more testing, particularly since the law is not straightforward. Many of the concepts have developed over several years, and each time they are addressed, the more sophisticated and complicated they tend to become. Look at the following passage taken from the Employment Protection (Consolidation) Act 1978 – Part IV: Redundancy payments: Death of employee:

22(1) Where an employer has given notice to an employee to terminate his contract of employment, and before that notice expires the employee dies, the provisions of Part IV of this Act shall apply as if the contract had been duly terminated by the employer by notice expiring on the date of the employee's death.

22(2) Where the employee's contract of employment has been terminated by the employer and by virtue of s.90(3) a date later than the relevant date as defined by subsection (1) of that section is to be treated as the relevant date for the purposes of certain provisions of Part VI of this Act, and before that later date the employee dies, s.90(3) shall have effect as if the notice referred to in that subsection as required to be given by an employer would have expired on the employee's death.

The first paragraph seems pretty straightforward, but the second may need deeper consideration. Interpreting such a statute requires precision and depth of thought. A perfunctory reading and hasty interpretation can cost you and your organisation dearly. However, this fact has been recognised not only by practitioners and legal researchers but also by the courts themselves. Consequently, over the years, a number of 'rules of interpretation' have been developed.

The courts can take three differing approaches to the problem of interpretation:

- *The literal rule*. Here, the words of a statute are clear and unambiguous and they must be followed 'even though they lead to an absurdity'. Thus if the words are clear, no interpretation need take place.
- *The golden rule*. Here, the words of a statute are not clear and the court must apply this – or the mischief rule (see below) – to ascertain the intention of Parliament. Thus in *River Wear Commissioners v Adams* [1877] it was held that the whole statute should be construed together, giving the words their ordinary meaning unless to do so would result in 'some inconsistency, absurdity, inconvenience or repugnance'.
- *The mischief rule*. This rule applies where a statute purports to remedy a particular 'mischief' which hitherto has gone without remedy.

THEORY INTO PRACTICE

Consider the advantages and disadvantages of each method of interpretation.

General rules and principles of interpretation

Unless the literal rule described above is followed, the courts tend to observe the following principles:

- They must always attempt to ascertain and give effect to the intention of Parliament.
- They may not look into the 'background' of a statute to assist them. They cannot therefore refer to Parliamentary debates, although in order to establish the mischief the statute seeks to remedy, they may look at reports of commissions such as the Law Commission.
- Where there is ambiguity, penal statutes should be interpreted favourably for persons accused of crimes.
- A major change in the law can be effected only by clear and positive words. In the absence of such words, the courts will presume that no such change is intended.
- In assisting understanding, words should be added or subtracted no more than is absolutely necessary.
- Ambiguities as to particular words may be resolved by the following rules of construction:
  - *Ejusdem generis*. Where a number of words, all of similar meaning, are followed by one of doubtful meaning, then that word should be interpreted as having a similar meaning to the others. For example, if a list included a number of occupations all relating to hospital work and then added 'or any other person', the last phrase would be interpreted as relating only to people working in hospital-related occupations – and not, for instance, to an estate agent or agricultural worker.
  - *Expressio unius est exclusio alterius*. Here, the mention of one word in itself rules out a contrary meaning. For example, in *R v Immigration Appeals Adjudicator ex p Crew* [1982] a statute included the word 'mother' and was thus interpreted as having excluded the word 'father'.

Such rules, however, are of more use to the courts than to individuals. You need to be able to interpret a legal requirement in such a way that it is understandable to you and to those in your organisation who expect you to give them a reasoned summary of it. Consequently, Figure 10.1.6 gives certain *practical* rules of interpretation.

Rule 1: *Read the statute at least three times. Then read it again.*
Each reading should produce a more complete picture.

Rule 2: *Pay close attention to 'ands' and 'ors'.*
The meaning of a statute often depends on which clauses are joined by an 'and' and which by an 'or'. When clauses are joined by an 'or' it means that the conditions in at least one of the clauses must be present but not in all. When clauses are joined by an 'and' the conditions in all the clauses must be met.

Rule 3: *Assume all words and punctuation in the statute have meaning.*
Sometimes statutes can be internally inconsistent. However, courts presume that all words and punctuation *do* mean something and you should do the same.

Rule 4: *Interpret a statute so that it is consistent with all other related statutes if possible.*
Courts will attempt to reconcile a number of different statutes and it is wise therefore for you to ask yourself whether any interpretation of the statute you have made makes it inconsistent with other statutes.

Rule 5: *Interpret the statute so that it makes sense and does not lead to absurd or improbable results.*
Courts will try to make sense of a statute – so should you.

Rule 6: *Track down all cross-references to other statutes and sections.*
Do not ignore cross-references. If you do you may miss some crucial information.

Figure 10.1.6   Practical rules of interpretation

THEORY INTO PRACTICE

Consider which of the rules of interpretation you might have to use when interpreting the following extract from the Employment (Protection) Act, which outlines certain exclusions from the right to redundancy payment.

Except as provided by s.92, an employee shall not be entitled to a redundancy payment by reason of dismissal where his employer, being entitled to terminate his contract of employment without notice by reason of the employee's conduct, terminates it either:

a   without notice, or

b   by giving shorter notice than that which, in the absence of such conduct, the employer would be required to give to terminate the contract, or

c   by giving notice (not being such shorter notice as is mentioned in paragraph b) which includes, or is accompanied by, a statement in writing that the employer would, by reason of the employee's conduct, be entitled to terminate the contract without notice.

The importance of cases that interpret statutes

Some statutes are so complicated and subject to so many slightly different interpretations that you may need to refer to the cases in which those statutes are discussed, before you fully understand them. There are two ways in which you can do this:

● Check the notes accompanying the statutes reproduced in the annotated volumes of *Halsbury's* or *Current Law Statutes Annotated*.

● Check the *Current Law Legislation Citator* which is usually published once a year. Its index lists all statutes and statutory instruments, and refers you to cases that have cited the relevant legislation in the year or years with which the publication is concerned. For example, if you were trying to interpret the provisions of the Town and Country Planning Act 1971, you could turn to the *Citator* and against each of the sections of the Act you would find further references. Against s.246, for instance, you would be referred to: *Strandmill v Secretary of State for the Environment; South Buckinghamshire District Council v Secretary of State for the Environment* [1988] 2PLR 1; *Young v Secretary of State for the Environment*, The Times February 26, 1990 (CA), etc. Reading these cases should clarify the statute for you.

- Check the *Law Reports Index* which cites cases that have dealt with statutory law.

THEORY INTO PRACTICE

The decision by the House of Lords in *Pepper v Hart* [1992] 3WLR 1032 allows courts to refer to *Hansard* (which publishes the speeches of the promoter of the legislation and any debates carried on in the Houses of Parliament) whenever there is an ambiguity in the piece of legislation under consideration. Consider why that should make the interpretation of the wording of a statute any simpler. Consider also any possible inherent dangers in this approach.

If you are unsure about what a word or phrase means you can look it up in a law dictionary, or in the multi-volume publication *Words and Phrases* (Butterworth), which defines the more common words and phrases to be found in statutory law.

It is also possible to seek some assistance from the statutes themselves, most of which have a definitions section – although in some cases the definitions can be as confusing as the statute itself. For example:

- 'In this Act, except so far as the context otherwise requires ...'
- '... act' and 'action' each includes omission and references to doing an act or taking action shall be construed accordingly'
- 'effective date of termination' has the meaning given by s.55(4) and (5)'

Interpretation of cases

No matter how important a statute or statutory instrument may be, the way in which it has been applied by the courts in reaching a decision in a particular case is often of even greater significance. You should therefore know how to interpret case law. Most case reports are divided into:

- the headnotes
- the names of the solicitors and barristers involved
- a list of the case law and statutory law referred to in the case
- the arguments of counsel (i.e. the legal representatives of both parties)
- the judgement – which contains a statement of the facts, a statement of the legal issues involved, the decision made or the order given, and the reasons for doing so.

Headnotes generally consist of a short summary of the facts, what the parties were trying to obtain, the legal issues involved, and then a number of paragraphs giving the ruling and a brief summary of the reasons for the decision. There is usually a mention of the previous case law followed, overturned or distinguished.

The paragraphs in the headnotes will follow the sequence of the judgement and usually make reference to the appropriate page or pages of the judgement. Note also that most law reports letter their pages A–H in addition to the page numbering system. Consequently if you want to refer to one point only in the judgement you could be referred in the headnotes to 124B, which would not only give you the relevant page (124) but also the section of the page (B).

Consider a case reference such as *Western Excavating (ECC) v Sharp* [1978] 1 All ER 713. It consists of five items:

- Western Excavating (ECC) v Sharp – the names of the parties involved
- [1978] – the year the case was reported (round brackets would mean it was not reported)
- 1 – the number of the volume of the law reporter in which the case report is to be found (this number is not always necessary)
- All ER – the law reporter that holds the case
- 713 – the page number.

Identifying emerging legal and regulatory requirements

The law is vast. You have only to look at the legal periodicals published on a regular basis to see that each one contains descriptions and summaries of both substantive and procedural legal developments, whether they be new cases, new statutes or merely new interpretations of existing provisions. Using out-of-date reference material is therefore unwise and sometimes dangerous. In addition, the higher up the managerial ladder you climb, the more you will be expected to *anticipate* any changes in legal requirements affecting the business – and to prepare yourself and others for those changes.

Some of the changes you may hear of indirectly, particularly if you work in a specialist area. You may attend a meeting of your professional institute and hear a reference to some proposed legislation that may affect the way in which the profession operates. You may pick up a local or national newspaper and read an article which either condemns a particular working practice or proposes its reform – and realise that if there is sufficient media and political pressure, this suggestion may eventually be given a more concrete form in the shape of a statute, a statutory instrument or a by-law. Television documentaries and news bulletins also give you an indication of what types of issue may sufficiently concern the government of the day to impel it to take some legal action.

However, obviously there is a considerable difference between the level of knowledge you will gain from those sources and the knowledge you will need if you expect your organisation to take notice of your advice on any possible changes required. Fortunately there are several sources available to assist you. Mention has already been made, for instance, of the importance of legal digests, most of which are not regarded as static documents and are updated at regular intervals. *Halsbury's*, for example, is updated with loose-leaf editions each month and with single-volume supplements each year. *Current Law* also has monthly paperback editions called the *Monthly Digest*, which include case summaries of the latest cases and a list of statutes and statutory instruments referred to in the cases summarised in that particular edition. In addition, several publications cater to the need to keep up to date by offering a loose-leaf compilation of recent developments in a certain field. Examples include a series of publications on:

- company law
- family law
- immigration law
- personal injury litigation
- road traffic
- the law of education
- the law of food and drugs.

The following publications are in loose-leaf format:

- Shawcross and Beaumont: *Air Law*
- Clarke, Hall & Morrison: *Children*
- Palmer: *Company Law*
- Harvey: *Industrial Relations and Employment Law*
- Hill and Redman: *Law of Landlord and Tenant*
- Woodfall: *Landlord and Tenant*
- Kemp and Kemp: *The Quantum of Damages*
- *British Tax* (encyclopaedia)
- Simon: *Taxes* (encyclopaedia).

Possibly of even greater significance to you, however, are the law reviews and other legal periodicals which are almost always produced on a monthly or quarterly basis and are bound only at the end of each year. These comment on any recent changes in the law. See Figure 10.1.7 for a list of the most important of these.

- *Cambridge Law Journal* (CLJ) is a quarterly journal containing articles on all areas of the law, generally of an academic nature.
- *Criminal Law Review* (Crim LR) is a review containing articles and the latest case law on substantive, procedural and evidential law.
- *Modern Law Review* (MLR) is a monthly review containing articles on all areas of the law,
- *Law Quarterly Review* (LQR) is a quarterly review containing articles on all areas of the law.

- *Local Government Review* (LGR) is a review containing articles in administrative, public and local government law.
- *Public Law* (PL) is a journal containing articles on public and administrative law, such as judicial review.
- *Estates Gazette* (EG) is a weekly gazette containing articles on planning and land law.
- *Law Society Gazette* (LSG), *New Law Journal* (NLJ) and *Solicitors' Journal* (SJ) are weekly gazettes containing articles on all areas of law.

Figure 10.1.7 Law reviews and other periodicals

There are many more journals that cover more specific areas of law, such as *The Journal of Business Law*, *The Journal of Environmental Law*, *The Journal of Child Law*, *The Industrial Law Journal*, and *Income Data Services Briefs, Bulletins and Supplements on Employment Law*.

Nowadays many members of the legal profession make use of an automated legal research system known as *Lexis*. This contains almost all reported cases, regulations, law review articles, commonly used treatises and practice manuals. All the information is stored in a central computer with terminals connected to it by phone lines. Because it is updated so regularly, it is an ideal source for checking any new developments. It is costly, however, and most public law libraries do not offer it as a service.

Types and sources of specialist advice

Useful though all the sources of reference mentioned in the last section may be, it is highly probable that, when faced with a legal problem, your first thought may be not 'Where can I find the relevant information?' but rather 'Is there anyone I can ask about this?'.

It is often more important – and certainly safer – to know what specialist advice is available on various aspects of the law rather than to rely on your own sketchy knowledge of the law. Obviously, if the point of law in question is highly technical – or could have grave repercussions for the organisation – the advice of legally qualified experts such as solicitors or barristers should be sought. However, in some cases you may find that you are expected to make some preliminary enquiries before you take any further steps. The same reasoning applies if you do not have an immediate problem but merely want to check on some point of law which you feel may affect your area of work.

Your first source of reference may be close at hand. If you are working with experienced colleagues, one of them might have faced a similar situation and have some knowledge upon which you can draw. In a larger organisation you may also have the benefit of specially trained or qualified personnel to assist you. The Human Resources Manager should be conversant with employment law, the Sales Manager should be aware of the sale of goods and consumer credit legislation, the Health and Safety Officer should be able to advise you on matters relating to safety, and so on. One difficulty here, however, is your ability to trust absolutely the advice given. In certain cases – such as information given by a specially trained member of staff – you should have few doubts; in other cases your trust should be less absolute.

THEORY INTO PRACTICE

Consider how you would try to verify any information given to you by experienced colleagues about which you may nevertheless be unsure. Consider also what you would do should you find the information to be inaccurate or misleading.

Sources outside the organisation

Consulting a solicitor or barrister can be extremely expensive, and may also be unnecessary if all you require is some information that you feel might be helpful rather than advice on a potentially high-risk and immediate problem. Other outside organisations can offer you advice which is either free or at least much less costly.

Depending on the type of organisation for which you work, you may be able to take advantage of its membership of various bodies, part of whose remit is to offer legal advice to its members. Examples include:

- Association of British Chambers of Commerce
- International Chamber of Commerce
- London Chamber of Commerce
- Association of Independent Businesses
- Institute of Management
- Confederation of British Industry
- Institute of Directors
- National Federation of Self-Employed and Small Businesses.

The Department of Employment and the Department of Trade and Industry (the Financial Service and Companies Division, the Overseas Trade Division, the Small Firms Service) may also be able to offer advice or to refer you to a more appropriate source. In very specific circumstances, the advice of bodies such as the Monopolies and Mergers Commission, the Registrar of Companies or the Land Charges Registry may also be sought. Other external organisations address more specific problems.

The Advisory, Conciliation and Arbitration Service (ACAS)

ACAS is set up as a body independent of the Department of Employment. Its functions include the following:

- *Collective conciliation.* Where a trade dispute exists or seems imminent, ACAS may, at the request of one or more of the parties or on its own initiative, offer its assistance for the purposes of conciliation or mediation.
- *Individual conciliation.* ACAS has a statutory duty to attempt to conciliate in cases brought before tribunals by individuals claiming

unfair dismissal or denial of employment protection rights, including sex and race discrimination.

- *Arranging arbitration.* ACAS may arrange arbitration for an actual or anticipated trade dispute if one or more of the parties request it and all parties consent to it.

In addition, however, ACAS is empowered by section 213 of the Trade Union and Labour Relations (Consolidation) Act (as amended by the Trade Union Reform and Employment Rights Act 1993) to 'on request or otherwise, give employers, employers' associations, workers and trade unions such advice as it thinks appropriate on matters concerned with or affecting or likely to affect industrial relations'. This power covers general advice, specific replies to queries, in-depth surveys and projects, holding conferences or seminars and the publishing of advisory booklets.

Current ACAS advisory booklets include a general *Employment Handbook*, and individual booklets on job evaluation, introduction to payment systems, personnel records, labour turnover, absence, recruitment and selection, induction of new employees, workplace communications, the company handbook, employment policies, employee appraisal, redundancy handling, hours of work, appraisal-related pay, health and employment, effective organisations, supervision, employing people in small firms, and discipline at work.

> It is interesting to note that the Chartered Institute of Arbitrators, which offers the services of trained arbitrators, is now a fast-growing alternative to the use of ACAS in this respect.

Codes of practice

ACAS is also empowered to issue *codes of practice*, which are becoming increasingly important given that they attempt to interpret relevant (and often complex) legislation and give practical advice on how to put that legislation into effect. A code of practice is not law in itself, so a person will not be liable for its breach. However, a breach of its terms may be used as evidence against an employer in any proceedings before a tribunal. Existing codes of practice cover disciplinary practices and procedures in employment, disclosure of bargaining information, and time off work for trade union duties and activities.

> In 1987, ACAS submitted the draft of a revised and greatly expanded code of practice on discipline and dismissals, but the then Secretary of State refused to approve it. It was therefore subsequently published in part as the ACAS handbook *Discipline at Work*, which did not need ministerial approval.

The Health and Safety Commission and Executive

The Health and Safety at Work Act 1974 set up a Health and Safety Commission and an Executive. The Commission is under a duty to:

- assist and encourage all the purposes of the general provisions of the Act

- encourage research and its publication
- encourage safety training
- ensure wide dissemination of advice and information, particularly to those practically concerned in this field
- prepare and propose regulations.

Like ACAS, the Commission is empowered to approve and issue suitable codes of practice. A code of practice now exists with regard to safety representatives and committees.

> The use of codes in health and safety law has been extended further by the six new sets of EU-inspired provisions which came into force on 1 January 1993. The regulations are short but contain extensive practical advice, either in the codes themselves or in the accompanying guidance notes (see further Chapter 2).

Other external sources

The usefulness of other relevant sources of specialist advice depends very much on your area of work. For instance, in the following list the first four sources will be of interest if you work in sales or exports, the fifth to the ninth will be of interest if you work in administration or finance, and the last four of interest if you work in research, and so on:

1. Consumer Credit Trade Association
2. Office of Fair Trading
3. Export Credits Guarantee Department
4. Hire Purchase Information Ltd

5. British Franchise Association
6. Data Protection Registration Office
7. British Insurance & Investment Brokers Association
8. Equipment Leasing Association
9. Finance Houses Association

10. Copyright Tribunal
11. Patent Office
12. European Patent Office
13. Performing Rights Society.

THEORY INTO PRACTICE

1. Consider the legal problems underlying the issues discussed in the extract from the set of minutes reproduced as Figure 10.1.1 on page 710. Think of at least one source of specialist advice you think it would be necessary to consult on *each* of these issues.
2. Select two sources of specialist advice (either mentioned in this section or from your own personal knowledge) which you feel would be most useful in your area of work. Contact them and assess the results of your findings under the following headings:
   a   what legal advice they were able to offer
   b   how such advice could be of specific assistance to you.

Communicating legal and regulatory requirements

It is sometimes said that the most highly qualified and knowledgeable people are the least able to communicate what they know to others. The law is a complex discipline which can be difficult to understand and – on occasions – even more difficult to explain. You are already aware of how to interpret legal and regulatory requirements (see page 722). You must also be able to transmit that knowledge to others.

As with all forms of communication, you have first to determine the make-up of your audience – whether, for instance, you are providing information for the Board of Directors or a group of junior staff. It is unwise, of course, to assume that one group necessarily knows more than another simply because they are part of the senior management team. You may find, for instance, that the new recruit straight from university or college knows considerably more about the legal repercussions emanating from, say, the Employment Protection (Consolidation) Act or the Wages Act than does his or her more experienced colleague. The canteen assistant is much more likely to be aware of legal regulations on the preparation of food than is the Managing Director – and so on. Another important point is to be aware of the mental barriers that may obstruct your attempts to communicate complicated information. Junior staff may not be conscious of the need to pretend to a knowledge of a certain issue; senior staff may feel unwilling to admit to the same lack of knowledge.

THEORY INTO PRACTICE

Assume that you work for an organisation that manufactures bottled mineral waters and imports certain specialised makes from the USA. One of your responsibilities is to make members of the organisation aware of relevant legal developments. Some problems have arisen which make you realise that many staff, both junior and senior, do not have a clear understanding of even the basic principles relating to defective product liability, and you therefore draft out the following notes for yourself which outline the general legal position.

'Under pressure from the EU, there has been a change in the law relating to consumer protection. The Consumer Protection Act 1987 covers industrially produced consumer goods, including electricity but excluding agricultural products and game, unless industrially processed. Liability is no longer based on fault; and when damage is caused wholly or partly by a defective product, liability is strict and can fall on anyone in the chain of supply, from the manufacturer, through the middleman, who contributes to the making of the product, to the person who packages, carries or installs it or who puts his name or other distinguishing feature on it. Also liable is the importer who sells, hires, leases or distributes the product, even though he may not be able to export his claim to a foreign supplier. Liability cannot be excluded by contract, notice or otherwise.'

Consider how you would explain to (a) the Managing Director and (b) the production staff the law in this area and its importance to the work of the organisation.

Methods of communication

In legal communications it is rarely a good idea to communicate the information verbally. Despite all the many advantages of such a form of communication, these are outweighed by the need to have some written document that can be used as a reference and can be up-dated at regular intervals as the law changes. Much depends on the organisation for which you work and the formats you are expected to use, but the generally recognised forms of such communication include:

- the summary
- the report
- the memorandum.

THEORY INTO PRACTICE

Assume that you have just been appointed as the Manager of the Human Resources department of a local authority. The previous manager was on sick leave for many months before she eventually retired on the grounds of ill-health, and no temporary replacement was appointed. Consequently certain legal requirements have been either overlooked or not sufficiently well implemented. Of particular concern to you is the fact that some of the senior staff appear to have little knowledge of the law relating to maternity leave and other maternity rights and its possible effect on their dealings with staff.

1 Research the current law in this area and prepare a brief *summary* for your own use, including the sources you used.
2 Consider what action you would take to ensure that the legal requirements are being met, and how you would communicate them either in *memo* or *report* form to the relevant staff.

The legal memorandum

You should be aware that there exists a more specialised form of legal communication, normally referred to as a legal memorandum. Although the primary function of such a memorandum is to provide you with an easily accessible record of what you understand of a particular legal issue, its secondary function is to allow you to communicate the results of your research to others in a format that is particularly relevant. The headings used are:

- Facts
- Issues
- Conclusion
- Reasoning

and are arranged in such a fashion as to imitate the four primary elements contained in most judicial statements. If, for instance, you wished to draw the facts of a certain court case to the attention of a senior manager, because you felt that it might be of some significance in his or her dealings with trade union officials, the legal memorandum could be the most effective way of recording that information. Figure 10.1.8 gives an example.

LEGAL MEMORANDUM

To:

From:

Date:

Topic: Report on *Noone v North West Thames Regional Health Authority* [1988] IRLR 195 (CA)

Facts

Dr Noone was born and obtained her initial qualifications in Sri Lanka. She applied for a vacancy as a consultant microbiologist with the Regional Health Authority and was one of three candidates interviewed by the Advisory Appointments Committee, whose function was to select a candidate on the basis of 'suitability'. The qualities considered by the committee were training, qualifications, experience and personality. Despite having better qualifications, experience and publications than the successful candidate, Dr Noone was not appointed. She complained that she had been discriminated against on the grounds of race.

Issues

The first step for the court to decide was whether there had been an act of discrimination. The second step was to decide whether there was any positive evidence which supported the allegation that it was discrimination on racial grounds.

Conclusions

In the court's opinion there was sufficient evidence to entitle it to reach the conclusion that there had been racial discrimination.

Reasoning

1 Of the three candidates, only one was Sri Lankan. The other two were English.
2 Despite Dr Noone's superior qualifications, experience and publications, she was placed third by all the members of the panel.
3 Evidence given by one of the members of the panel indicated that she was looking for someone who would 'fit in' with the existing establishment. It could be concluded therefore that the panel felt Dr Noone would not 'fit in' because of her Sri Lankan background.

Figure 10.1.8   A legal memorandum

Recommending ways of complying with legal and regulatory requirements

Although the report and the legal memorandum are the two most obvious formats to use when making recommendations about legal and regulatory requirements, a less detailed document – the information sheet – is equally useful when recommending ways of complying with the legal issues. Figure 10.1.9 shows an example of such a form.

Name of organisation . . . .

Information sheet no. . . . .

Heading:

| Content: | Action: | By whom: | By what date: |

Signature:

Title:

Date:

Figure 10.1.9 An information sheet

The advantages of such a document are that:

- it is more user-friendly because it can summarise in broad outline the contents of a more detailed document
- it can be constructed in such a way that it highlights any action to be taken, by whom and in what timescale
- it can easily be updated should the law change – particularly if it is in loose-leaf format
- it can be useful as a training aid in staff development sessions.

Note that the compiling of the information sheet is only the *start* of the procedures you should take. Ensuring compliance with those procedures is another stage in the process (see further page 747).

THEORY INTO PRACTICE

Select a recent case which you feel is of relevance to your area of work or that of your colleagues – and one on which you feel your organisation should take some action. You may like to look at legal issues that have a particular significance for your organisation, or choose an issue of general importance (e.g. health and safety, employment law, consumer protection).

1 Compile a legal memorandum outlining the facts of the case and the issues it raises.

2 Compile an information sheet (using either the example in Figure 10.1.9 or your organisation's format if there is one) summarising the law for the rest of the staff in your organisation, and incorporating your recommendations for ensuring compliance with it.

Overview of the structures and operation of the legal system

This section outlines the basic structure of the legal system and ways in which it operates. The contents are divided into:

- an outline of the court structure
- application of the doctrine of precedent in the courts
- the major categories of law over which the courts have jurisdiction
- court procedures.

The court structure

The English court structure has four basic levels, as shown in Figure 10.1.10:

- Inferior Courts (the county, magistrates and juvenile courts)
- the High Court and the Crown Court
- the Court of Appeal
- the House of Lords.

Within this structure, unfortunately, there is no clear division into criminal and civil courts, nor a division into first-instance and appeal courts.

Magistrates courts

The magistrates courts' *criminal* jurisdiction extends mainly over summary offences (i.e. minor offences that are capable of being dealt with quickly) – all of which are statutory offences. However, they also have some jurisdiction over *indictable* offences (more serious offences triable only in the Crown Court) as in certain limited circumstances an accused person may choose to be tried and sentenced by the magistrates even though the alleged offence is an indictable one.

The *civil* jurisdiction of these courts includes:

- the recovery of certain debts, such as income tax, electricity and gas bills
- domestic proceedings, particularly in relation to non-payment of maintenance
- the granting of gaming and liquor licences.

Juvenile courts

Children under 14 years and young persons (14–16) generally have their cases 'heard' (not tried) in a juvenile court. The court may order the

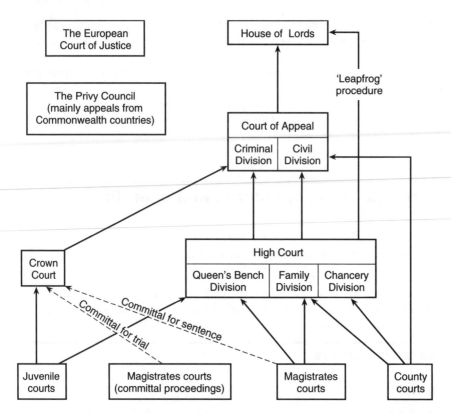

Figure 10.1.10 The English court structure (arrows indicate paths of appeal to higher courts)

detention of a child or young person in a community home where this is necessary for the protection of the public. It may also make a supervision order placing him or her under the supervision of a probation officer, a hospital order or a guardianship order.

County courts

County courts decide civil actions involving relatively small sums of money. Their jurisdiction is entirely statutory, so that if in any matter statute provides no jurisdiction then none exists. A court is presided over by a circuit judge who usually sits alone without a jury.

The Crown Court

The criminal jurisdiction of the Crown Court concerns all cases above the level of magistrates' courts. The more serious cases are tried by High Court judges and the less serious by circuit judges. The court sits with a jury of 12, although a verdict can be reached on a 10–2 basis. When hearing appeals from magistrates' courts, the court may allow the appeal, reduce the sentence, or increase the sentence up to the maximum that could have been imposed by the magistrates' court.

The High Court

The High Court is divided into three divisions:

- the Queen's Bench Division has both criminal and civil jurisdiction; i.e. it deals with contract and tort actions, commercial matters, etc. It also exercises a supervisory jurisdiction over the lower courts and can make certain orders to compel them to exercise their powers properly or restrain them from exceeding their jurisdiction.
- The Chancery Division's jurisdiction includes trusts, mortgages, bankruptcy, company law and partnership and contentious probate business.
- The Family Division deals with defended divorces, wardship, adoption, guardianship, legitimacy, disputes concerning the matrimonial home, and non-contentious probate business. It also hears appeals from magistrates' and county courts on family matters. The head of this Division is known as the President.

The Court of Appeal

The court is split into civil and criminal divisions. The head of the civil division is the Master of the Rolls, the head of the criminal division the Lord Chief Justice. Appeals are normally heard by three judges, but certain cases may be heard by two and occasionally a full court of five judges will sit for a very important case. A majority decision is sufficient. An appeal takes the form of re-hearing the original case by drawing on the judge's notes and the official shorthand writer's transcript, and by listening to arguments from counsel. The court may uphold or reverse the decision in whole or in part, and may alter the amount of damages, make a different order as to costs or, if new evidence is discovered, order a new trial.

The House of Lords

The House of Lords is the final court of appeal for all internal cases. Note, however, the *leapfrog* procedure which was introduced to avoid there always having to be two appeals – from the High Court to the Court of Appeal and from there to the House of Lords – and which under certain circumstances allows an appeal directly from the High Court to the House of Lords.

Note here the role of the Judicial Committee of the *Privy Council*, which consists of the Lord Chancellor, the Lords of Appeal and Privy Councillors, all of whom have held high judicial office, together with people such as Commonwealth judges. It is not strictly a court at all, but a committee that advises the sovereign. It hears appeals from the ecclesiastical courts, from disciplinary bodies such as the General Medical Council, and from courts in the Channel Islands, the Isle of Man and certain Commonwealth countries.

Article 177(3) of the Treaty of Rome affects the jurisdiction of the House of Lords by providing that a court of an EU member state against whose decisions there is no judicial remedy under national law *must* refer certain questions to the European Court for a preliminary ruling, and having obtained the ruling is *bound* to follow it. The questions concern:

- the interpretation of a treaty
- the validity and interpretation of acts of the institutions of the Community, or
- the interpretation of the statutes of bodies established by an act of the Council of Ministers.

Look back to page 715, if necessary, to remind yourself of the EU influence over UK legislation.

The European Court of Justice

The European Court of Justice is a court of first instance from whose judgements there is no appeal. Its jurisdiction includes:

- actions brought against member states either by other member states or by the European Commission on the ground that treaty obligations are not being fulfilled
- actions brought against EU institutions by members states, private individuals or corporate bodies
- disputes between the EU and their employees arising from the employees' contracts of employment
- rulings on the interpretation of treaties.

Tribunals

In addition to the more traditional court structure, there are also a series of statutory *tribunals*. These are specialised courts established by statute to deal with disputes between government agencies and individuals, or between two individuals in a less formal manner than is normal in a court.

- Social security tribunals hear the claim of a person refused a social security benefit.
- Rent tribunals fix fair rents to be charged by landlords.
- Lands tribunals determine disputes concerning the amount of compensation payable when land is purchased compulsorily.
- Commissioners of Income Tax hear appeals by taxpayers against assessments made by the Inland Revenue.
- Industrial tribunals have jurisdiction over employment matters, such as unfair dismissal, redundancy pay, equal pay, sex or race discrimination, etc. An appeal can be made to the Employment Appeal Tribunal (EAT) and from then on to the Court of Appeal and the House of Lords.

The main difference between tribunals and the ordinary courts is that tribunals consist of both lay and legally qualified personnel. In industrial tribunal hearings, for instance, the panel usually comprises a legally qualified chairperson together with two lay members, one representing the TUC and the other the CBI.

The advantages of tribunals are that they:

- are able to specialise in a particular field using people who have the appropriate expertise
- are relatively informal and therefore not as threatening as the more formal courts
- are less expensive
- are able to act more quickly than the courts.

Given, however, that the traditional court system still exists and must therefore be deemed to have some advantages over the tribunal system, consider what you think may be the *disadvantages* of the use of tribunals.

Application of the doctrine of precedent in the courts

Look back to page 711 for a discussion of the way in which the doctrine of precedent in the courts affects the extent to which decisions in earlier cases must be followed in later cases of similar facts. The following list indicates the ways in which the doctrine is applied throughout the court system.

- Although not bound to do so, the European Court of Justice *generally* follows its own decisions as precedents.
- The House of Lords (HL) is not bound by any decision of a UK court – even a decision made by itself. It is, however, bound by certain decisions of the European Court of Justice.
- The Court of Appeal's Civil Division is bound by HL decisions and by its own earlier decisions. However, there are certain exceptions:
  - It must not follow one of its own decisions which is inconsistent with a later decision of the House of Lords.
  - It will not follow earlier decisions arrived at through want of due care.
- The Court of Appeal's Criminal Division is bound by HL decisions and *in general* by its own decisions. However, because, generally speaking, more is at stake in a criminal case than in a civil case, more latitude is given to the court in allowing it to deviate from its own earlier decisions.
- Divisional Courts are, in civil matters, bound by decisions of the HL, of the Civil Division of the Court of Appeal (CA), and by their own earlier decisions. They are not obliged to follow a CA decision which is inconsistent with a statute or HL decision.
- The High Court is bound by the HL, CA and the Divisional Court of the same Division.
- County courts are bound by the HL, CA and the High Court.
- Although the Judicial Committee of the Privy Council is not strictly bound by its own decisions (normally regarded as advice), in practice it will rarely depart from them.

Major categories of law

UK law is divided into criminal and civil law, the former being broadly concerned with the punishment of the individual, the latter with the compensation of the victim. Criminal law is regarded as a wrong done to the state, and prosecutions are usually commenced by the state (although they can on occasion be brought by a private individual). Civil actions may be commenced by anyone who seeks compensation for a loss that he or she has suffered.

The major categories of the *criminal law* include:

- offences against property – theft, fraud, etc.
- offences against the person – assault, homicide, kidnapping, sexual offences, etc.
- terrorist offences
- drugs offences
- public-order offences
- road-traffic offences
- firearms offences
- contempt and perjury
- obscene publications
- official secrets
- trade descriptions, consumer protection and food offences
- tax evasion.

The major categories of the *civil law* include:

- administrative
- bankruptcy
- commercial
- computers
- constitutional
- contracts
- companies
- discrimination
- employment
- environmental
- equity, probate and trusts
- evidence
- family, divorce, domestic relations
- health
- intellectual property
- landlords and tenants
- media
- prisons
- property
- public utilities
- tax
- tort.

Tort law includes negligence, assault/battery (normally arising from negligence), libel and slander, trespass, false imprisonment and malicious prosecution.

> Criminal and civil hearings have different standards of proof. In a criminal trial, the prosecution must prove the accused's guilt *beyond reasonable doubt*. In a civil case, the plaintiff must prove his or her case on the *balance of probabilities*.

Court procedures

The higher the level of a court action, the more complicated the procedures are likely to be. If you take a case to a tribunal the procedures you have to follow are deemed to be informal. If, on the other hand, you are involved in a county court or High Court action, the procedures are much more formal, even rigid. To illustrate this point, given below is a brief outline of the steps you (or more usually a solicitor) would have to take should you be involved in a civil case taken to the High Court or a county court.

Pre-trial High Court actions

Before a case is heard there are certain actions that must be taken. These are often begun by *the issuing of a writ*. However, in situations where the material facts of the case are not in question but the interpretation of a particular Act or set of documents is disputed, it is less expensive and more usual to seek the ruling of the court via an *originating summons*.

To issue a writ, the necessary form must be obtained from the Central Office of the Supreme Court or from a district registry. The plaintiff must then complete the form, two copies of which must be registered with the Supreme Court and a fee paid. One signed copy is retained by the court while the second copy is sealed and returned to the plaintiff. This copy becomes the *writ in action* which must then be *served on the defendant* within four months of issue. The defendant must acknowledge the writ and indicate whether he/she accepts liability or intends to defend the action. If at that stage the plaintiff considers there is no valid defence, he/she can then apply to a Master for summary judgement under Order 14 of the Rules of the Supreme Court.

The *pleadings* are an interlocutory stage before the trial, whereby certain matters of contention can be resolved before the case comes to court. The first pleading is the *statement of claim*, which is sent by the plaintiff to the defendant detailing the material facts of the case, outlining any alleged injuries and losses, and stating the remedy sought. The defendant must then submit a *defence*, repudiating each allegation made. Should he/she fail to answer any allegation, the court will accept that allegation as proven. The plaintiff may reply to any new matters brought up in the defendant's defence, but only in exceptional circumstances may the defendant reply with a further pleading – known as a *subsequent pleading*. He/she can, however, submit a counterclaim to which the plaintiff must reply. The final stage is the *close of pleadings* which occurs 14 days after service of the reply.

Next, the *discovery and inspection of documents* involves each party providing the other with a full list of the documents that each holds relating to the case. Both parties can then inspect the other party's documents, other than those marked 'without prejudice'.

Next comes the *summons for directions* which the plaintiff must take out within a month of the close of pleadings. At the hearing of the summons, the solicitors of both parties will appear before a Queen's Bench Master who will direct on:

- the adequacy of the pleadings
- whether there is to be a jury
- whether, if there has not been a discovery and inspection of documents, an *affidavit* is necessary (i.e. a sworn written statement by either or both parties disclosing all relevant documents)

- whether it is deemed necessary for either party to answer *interrogatories* (i.e. formal written questions submitted by one party to the other)
- the time of the trial.

Finally comes the *setting down of the action for trial*. The plaintiff files two sets of documents with the court, including the writ, the pleadings, all orders made on the summons for directions, and certain legal-aid documents if relevant. The case is then entered in the appropriate list of cases waiting to be heard.

High Court proceedings

When the court action commences, certain set procedures are followed.

- The plaintiff's counsel outlines the case using the pleadings. He/she will call and examine witnesses and submit any relevant documents as evidence.
- The defence counsel may then cross-examine the witnesses.
- The roles are then reversed, with the defence counsel putting his/her case and the plaintiff's counsel cross-examining. The plaintiff may also be given the chance to further address the court at the end of the defendant's case where the defence counsel has raised a matter that appears to negate the case.
- After this preliminary stage, the counsels again outline their arguments to the court, the defence counsel being allowed to speak first.
- A judge will then deliver a *judgement*, although he/she may *reserve judgement* if the issues require further consideration. If there is a jury the judge will summarise the arguments and direct the jury on points of law. When the jury returns with a verdict the judge will then deliver judgement.
- After the judgement the successful counsel will ask for costs to be awarded, although if either party wishes to appeal they can ask for a stay of execution at this stage.

County court procedures

The plaintiff must first obtain from a county court a request form which should be completed together with two copies of the *particulars of claim* (i.e. an outline of the claim) and returned with the appropriate fee. The court will then register the claim, issue the plaintiff with a *plaint note*, and issue a *summons* to the defendant requiring him/her to appear in a specified court at a specified time. The defendant will then have 14 days in which to admit the claim, submit a defence or make a *counterclaim*. A fixed date will then be given for a pre-trial review so that any matters that can be settled prior to trial will be agreed before a district judge and a date fixed for the trial. The procedure at the trial itself is similar to that in the High Court.

THEORY INTO PRACTICE

1 It has been estimated that, although there are about 35 000 High Court actions each year, only 10 000 get to the 'setting down' stage and only about 2500 actually get to trial. The main reason for this, of course, is the expense involved and the time it takes to bring a case before the court.

This problem has been recognised to a certain extent by the introduction of small-claims courts and industrial tribunals. Depending on the nature of your work, select one of these and research the procedures involved in taking a claim to it.

2 Read the following extract from a letter sent to you by a friend:

'... I've almost decided to take the plunge and open my own florist's shop. A shop unit has become available in the new precinct and I think I can raise just about enough capital to buy it. I want to trade under the name "Flowers Unlimited" – but I'm open to any other suggestions! I haven't thought too much about staffing but I'd like to have at least one full-time assistant and a part-time Saturday assistant – possibly someone still at school looking to earn a bit of extra money. I've done a bit of homework already and found out the names and addresses of some supposedly reputable suppliers of flowers, shrubs, etc., but I haven't actually contacted any of them yet – probably because I have no idea about the sort of agreement they may want me to enter into with them. I don't want to be restricted to dealing with only one supplier – nor do I want to be in the position that they can leave me stranded without anything to sell without my being able to do something about it.

You were always a bit of a legal expert. I don't suppose you'd like to give me a few legal pointers would you? I'd like to know a little about the questions I should be asking a solicitor – and to be able to understand the answers I get – before I make my final decision ...'

a Research the areas of law to which you think you should draw the attention of your friend. Summarise them, together with a list of the appropriate sources of reference (e.g. cases, statutes, regulations. etc.).

b Compile a list of questions you think it would be advisable for him or her to ask a solicitor.

Element 10.2

Maintain compliance with legal and regulatory requirements

Types and sources of legal requirements relating to work practices and conditions

The degree of importance attached to any legal requirement is, of course, directly related to its relevance to the work of the organisation. If, for instance, you have little to do with Sales you would probably be unlikely to need to know much about the Trade Descriptions or Consumer Protection Acts; unless you work in Finance you might find the information contained in the Finance Acts far too specialised to be of any real assistance, and so on. On the other hand, some legislation is relevant to every member of an organisation, employment law and health and safety legislation being two obvious examples.

1 List those employment law statutes in Figure 10.2.1 which you feel are directly applicable to your own area of work – or may have been in the past. Outline at least two examples of the way in which any of your work practices have been adapted or introduced in order to comply with the legislation.

2 If possible, repeat the exercise in respect of any other statute relating to your own particular specialism – finance, consumer rights, etc.

General
Terms and Conditions of Employment Act 1959
Contracts of Employment Act 1963
Redundancy Payments Act 1965
Contracts of Employment Act 1972
Employment Agencies Act 1973
Employment Protection Act 1975
Employment Protection (Consolidation) Act 1978
Employment Acts 1980; 1982; 1988; 1989; 1990

Discrimination
Disabled Persons (Employment) Act 1944
Race Relations Acts 1965; 1968; 1976
Equal Pay Act 1970
Rehabilitation of Offenders Act 1974
Sex Discrimination Acts 1975; 1986
Disability Discrimination Act 1995

Payment of wages
Payment of Wages Act 1960
Wages Act 1986

Trade union rights
Trade Union and Labour Relations Act 1974
Trade Union Act 1984
Trade Union and Labour Relations (Consolidation) Act 1992
Trade Union Reform and Employment Rights Act 1993

Figure 10.2.1 Major employment law statutes

Types and sources of regulatory requirements relating to work practices and conditions

Statutory instruments can affect work practices to a greater extent than can statutes, simply because they are more numerous. They also tend to contain the more up-to-date law, given that one of their main purposes is to supplement the statutory law on the topic in question. For instance, although Figure 10.2.1 lists a number of important statutes, these are supplemented by a frequently changing list of almost equally important statutory instruments, such as:

- Employment Protection (Recoupment of Unemployment Benefit and Supplementary Benefit) Regulations 1977
- Equal Pay (Amendment) Regulations 1983
- Industrial Tribunals Extension of Jurisdiction (England and Wales) Order 1994
- Industrial Tribunals (Constitution and Rules of Procedure) Regulations 1993
- Race Relations Code of Practice Order 1983
- Rehabilitation of Offenders Act 1974 (Exceptions) (Amendment) Order 1986
- Sex Discrimination and Equal Pay (Remedies) Regulations 1993
- Social Security (Unemployment, Sickness and Invalidity Benefit) Regulations 1983
- Transfer of Undertakings (Protection of Employment) Regulations 1981.

THEORY INTO PRACTICE

As part of your administrative duties you may be expected to keep your boss informed about legislation relating to both state and occupational pensions. Research (a) the major relevant statutes and (b) the supporting statutory instruments (SIs). Consider why you think the SIs have been introduced to supplement the original statutory legislation.

Monitoring compliance with legal and regulatory requirements

Only very inexperienced managers ask their staff to carry out certain activities and expect that to be the end of the matter. In modern offices there are heavy demands upon staff time, and some staff cannot be relied upon to remember to carry out all the work allocated to them, without any reminders. Some staff tend to have selective memories, particularly if what is asked of them is difficult or time-consuming. Consequently, methods of monitoring what they do assumes considerable importance. This is particularly the case when the work involves compliance with legal or regulatory requirements, given the serious consequences of non-compliance (discussed in the next section).

The ideal managerial approach is to incorporate *monitoring* into an overall action plan which covers not only the planning stage but also the control and review stages, to ensure that what has been planned is actually being carried out within the required period of time. During the control stage, there is a choice of several traditional strategies:

- personal supervision of the key activities
- regular meetings
- assessment of individual performance
- reliance on certain appointed bodies to carry out the monitoring for you.

Personal supervision

The simplest method of monitoring actions taken is to make a personal check on them. Such supervision is easier, of course, if you are in control of staff who work in the same geographical area as yourself – particularly in an open-plan office. It is also useful if you are desk-bound most of the day. It is less easy to supervise in such a fashion if your staff are scattered and you are at your desk for only short periods; although you can make use of your powers of delegation to ensure that, if you cannot supervise the work directly, one of your deputies can.

Regular meetings

Effective channels of communication are essential in any system of monitoring. If, for instance, you have regular meetings with your staff, very important information – such as that relating to major legal requirements – can be made a standing item, either on every occasion the meeting is held or, say, at the first meeting of every month. Much depends here, of course, on a good meetings secretary who has systems in place to enable him or her to include that item automatically on the agenda on the agreed dates.

If the legal requirement in question is one that has only recently begun to affect the work in your area, you may consider it necessary to hold a series of meetings, all pre-arranged at regular intervals over a certain time period, at which the same topic is discussed repeatedly until you are sure that everyone is aware of what the requirement entails, and its considerable importance. When the series of meetings come to an end, staff should be almost conditioned into complying with the requirement in question. Even so, regular follow up meetings are advisable.

Assessment of individual performance

Monitoring the work of a group can be very effective. However, since groups comprise a number of often very different individuals, it is also necessary for there to be an element of individual monitoring in most areas of work if you want to be completely sure that important legal requirements are being followed. In such cases you must be aware not only of the depth of staff knowledge but also their reaction to having to comply. Some people may genuinely not understand what is required; others may understand only too well, but choose not to comply. In the former case, you can always arrange additional training or ensure that the member of staff concerned works alongside a more experienced and knowledgeable colleague. In the latter case you are faced with a more difficult problem.

THEORY INTO PRACTICE

As Senior Administrator in the Sales department of a large manufacturing organisation you have been faced with a number of complaints about your staff which may have legal repercussions.

a One of your best sales staff, who consistently achieves the highest targets, has been accused by one customer of making misleading statements about the goods on offer, which is in breach of the Trade Descriptions Acts 1968 and 1972.

b A similar complaint has been made about a local newspaper advertising campaign which has been planned to extend over a two-month period and about which your Managing Director has received a letter from the Director of Fair Trading asking for further details under the Control of Misleading Advertisements Regulations. The campaign itself is being spearheaded by the Marketing Manager and her team.

c One junior member of your staff cannot seem to grasp the intricacies of the credit arrangements he can agree with customers and tends to confuse them so much that they are unwilling to enter into any agreement at all. He is also rather remiss about letting customers know about their rights to a 'cooling off' period.

Once alerted to all these problems, you carry out the following actions:

a You discuss the problem of the making of a misleading statement with the salesman. He is contrite and admits to 'stretching the truth' on some occasions in order to close a sale. With a winsome smile, he promises to be more careful in future.

b You send a long memo to the Marketing Manager asking her to rectify the situation so that the campaign can continue without any further problems.

c You talk to the junior member of staff and discover that he has very little idea of what the legal situation is with regard to the granting of credit. You agree with him that he should attend the next in-house training course.

Somewhat naively, perhaps, you feel that the problems are now resolved. Within a matter of weeks, however, it is brought to your attention by a memorandum from the Managing Director that, despite your initial actions, the complaints are persisting.

1 Consider what control measures you would institute to ensure that the problems were resolved.

2 Consider the action you would take to ensure that someone who is not within your direct chain of command – such as the Marketing Manager – but who has the power to make your job harder or easier, does in fact comply with certain essential legal requirements.

3 You have a feeling (nothing more) that your top salesman, despite his assurances to the contrary, is going to continue to feed clients with less than truthful information – only in future he may be more careful to avoid your finding out what he is doing. Determine the action you would take to check that he is doing what you ask.

Reliance on other bodies

Compliance with some legal requirements is considered to be so important that the monitoring function is not left solely to individual managers. You may, for instance, work in an organisation that has centralised monitoring systems in place to check on the preparation of tax returns for the Inland Revenue and the company accounts for the Registrar of Companies, the appointment or re-appointment of auditors, and all other related financial matters. Similarly, if you work in all but the smallest of organisations you will probably be familiar with the role of the safety committee and its representatives in relation to health, safety and welfare matters. (Look back to Chapter 2 for further details about their activities.)

In such circumstances your role is to act as that of liaison officer, in that you must first of all familiarise yourself with exactly what information is required, on what time scale, and how regularly it must be provided. You may then be expected to monitor the activities of your staff in the preparation of that information by using one or all of the procedures already discussed. The role has both advantages and disadvantages. One advantage is that the onus is not solely on you to monitor compliance with the legal requirements in question. One disadvantage is that you are reliant on two groups of people – the checkers and the checked – carrying out their roles effectively while you have little control over one of those groups.

Consequences of non-compliance with requirements

Statutory requirements

Whether you have management responsibilities at present or hope to become a manager shortly, this topic should be of the utmost interest to you. The most obvious consequence of non-compliance with a legal requirement is that you will be in breach of the law and may have to face one of a number of legal penalties (including, in extreme circumstances, a sentence of imprisonment).

In this context an important legal concept for you to recognise is that of the *doctrine of vicarious liability*, which imposes upon an employer the liability for the torts (i.e. wrongful actions) committed by an employee during the course of employment. Thus an employer, who had no direct involvement in the accident, was held vicariously liable for the actions of one of his employees who had ignored the safety rules laid down about the driving of vehicles in the factory grounds and had negligently injured a fellow employee. The doctrine is applied quite rigorously in that, even if employees are doing something forbidden by the employer, they will still be acting in the course of employment if they are doing their authorised work – albeit in an improper way. Consequently a bus driver who had been forbidden to race other buses, but continued to do so and eventually caused a collision, was nevertheless still held to be acting in the course of his employment and the employer was therefore liable.

Indeed, an employee may be acting within the course of his/her employment even though he/she has acted fraudulently. A clerk with a firm of solicitors fraudulently induced a client to convey two cottages to him, which he then resold before absconding with the proceeds. The solicitors were held to be vicariously liable on the grounds that, by allowing him to perform conveyancing transactions, they had given him apparent authority to act as he did. It is little wonder that employers take the law seriously!

There is a considerable amount of case law on the subject of what constitutes work carried out 'during the course of employment'. Although decisions in such cases are largely questions of fact, Lord Lowry gave the following guidance on what could or could not be included in that definition.

- An employee travelling from his/her ordinary residence to the ordinary place of work is not in the course of his/her employment (unless obliged to use the employer's transport).
- Travelling in the employer's time between workplaces, or in the course of a peripatetic occupation, will be in the course of employment.
- Receipt of wages (although *not* simply a travelling allowance) will indicate that the employee is travelling in the employer's time and for his/her benefit.
- An employee travelling in the employer's time from his/her ordinary residence to a workplace other than the normal workplace, or on peripatetic work or to the scene of an emergency, will be in the course of employment.
- A deviation from, or interruption of, a journey in the course of employment (other than a merely incidental one) will take the employee out of the course of his or her employment.
- Return journeys are to be treated on the same footing as outward journeys.

Non-statutory requirements

Unless you are the owner of the business in which you work, you will not be personally affected by the doctrine of vicarious liability. However, as a manager – and probably a manager who wishes to develop a career – your career prospects will not be enhanced if you or one of your staff involve your employer in any financial loss emanating from your non-compliance with a legal requirement.

Non-enforcement of contracts

In some cases, non-compliance with a legal requirement can render contracts unenforceable. The law of contract demands that a valid contract should comprise certain elements:

- a valid offer
- a valid acceptance
- some 'consideration' passing between the parties (normally a sum of money).

It also demands that:

- both parties should intend to create a contractual relationship, and that there should be no mistake or misrepresentation as to what the contract actually entails
- both parties will carry out their part of the agreement.

If any of those elements are missing, the contract can be considered either *void* (unenforceable) or *voidable* (enforced by the 'innocent' party if he or she chooses to do so).

However, both parties must also have a 'capacity' to enter into a contract. Minors, or people with a form of mental incapacity, or drunkards, are not considered to have the capacity to understand their obligations under a contract, and therefore most contracts they enter into will not be binding on them or the other party. Similarly, companies and corporations that do not comply with certain statutory regulations may also on occasions be considered not to have that capacity.

If, therefore, you decide to set up your own business and wish to choose a business name that is different from your own, but you fail to comply with the requirement that you must register that name with the Registrar of Companies or you breach the regulations relating to the way in which it can be displayed and publicised, you may be guilty of a criminal offence. However, you may also find it difficult to enforce any *contract* you have made while your business is in breach of those regulations as you may be considered as being technically incapable of entering into that contract.

Imposition of fines

A more common form of financial penalty is that incurred through the imposition of a fine because of non-compliance with a legal requirement. The instances in which such fines can be imposed are extremely numerous. Nevertheless the following example should give you some indication of the types of breach that could result in this penalty.

Suppose, for instance, you decide to form a limited company with a Board of Directors to satisfy the requirements of the Companies Act. You are responsible for the annual preparation of a set of accounts which must give a 'true and fair view' of the state of the business. If the accounts do not comply with the Act, you (and any other directors who have approved them and who have either known that they do not comply with the statutory requirements or have been 'reckless' as to whether they do so) are liable to be fined. You will also be fined if the accounts are delayed. If you fail to provide the necessary tax returns you will be liable for interest on the tax paid late.

Payment of damages

In certain circumstances, an organisation that fails to comply with legal requirements will be expected to pay damages to the injured party. This arises through the awarding of damages by a civil court and covers many breaches of the law, including:

- breach of a commercial contract
- an act of negligence, such as an accidental but careless personal injury or damage to property
- occupiers' liability
- defamation (i.e. slander or libel).

A similar situation can occur if any consumer rights are breached. If you are engaged in manufacturing or production you have to be aware of the law relating to the sale of goods and the rights of the consumer. Any breach of the law in this area tends to result in claims for damages, particularly in relation to defective product liability. The Consumer Protection Act 1987, for instance, provides for such claims in respect of death, personal injury and loss or damage to property, including land. (For more detailed information on remedies, see Chapter 8, page 658.)

Payment of compensation

Compensation is a form of damages – often paid to a person who has suffered a breach of obligation, such as during the course of his or her employment. If, for instance, you intend to employ a workforce you must ensure that you comply with an extensive range of health and safety regulations and employment law rights, and if you dismiss someone unfairly or are found to have discriminated against an employee on the grounds of race, sex or disability, you may be asked to pay compensation to the injured party. Section 68 of the Employment Protection (Consolidation) Act 1978 lists the remedies for unfair dismissal as:

- reinstatement or re-engagement, *or*
- an award of compensation.

The award of compensation is made up of several elements:

- a *basic* award which is dependent on the employee's length of continuous employment, his/her age and the amount of weekly pay he/she earns (up to a statutory maximum fixed annually)
- a *compensatory* award which may take into account:
  - loss incurred by the employee up to the date of the industrial tribunal hearing (e.g. loss of income)
  - future loss (e.g. if the ex-employee has not yet found another job or has obtained one at a lower rate of pay)
  - loss of accrued rights or pension rights
  - loss due to the manner of dismissal (e.g. if perhaps the manner of dismissal could be said to have affected the employee's future prospects).

The combination of all those sums can add up to a considerable financial loss to the organisation!

> The situation can be exacerbated if the claim is for sex or race discrimination, in that a tribunal is empowered to award additional damages for injury to feelings.

Imposition of an injunctions

In some cases of a breach of a legal requirement, the result will be the issuing of a court injunction preventing you from carrying on with either part or the whole of your business, the financial consequences of which can be very severe. One example is the issuing of a prohibition notice by an HSE inspector if your premises do not comply with the requirements of the Health and Safety at Work Act. Similarly, if you are found to be in breach of the 1988 Copyright, Designs and Patents Act, the copyright owner can stop infringement by injunction (a remedy which would cost you dear given that it may stop you from trading), as well as claim damages.

In some instances you may also be expected to comply with what is known as the doctrine of *specific performance*. If so, despite your protests, you will be expected to carry out your part of an agreement even if previously you have refused or felt yourself unable to do so. Thus, if you agree to supply someone with some goods and then fail to deliver them, a court may insist that you do so no matter what difficulties you may face.

THEORY INTO PRACTICE

1 The doctrine of specific performance is rarely applied to a breach of a contract of employment (i.e. one between employer and employee). Consider the possible reasons for this.
2 From your own experience at your workplace, think of at least three activities which may carry certain specific consequences should the law be breached. List those consequences and state what precautions are in place to prevent the law being broken in those areas.
3 Research the financial penalties that may result from:
   a failing to register with the Data Protection Register
   b the wrongful use of a trade mark
   c giving advice on credit terms without a licence from the Director of Fair Trading
   d not complying with the Fire Precaution Regulations 1992.

Meeting obligatory requirements for information

Given that the consequences of non-compliance can be very severe, it is imperative that the preparation of all information relating to any obligatory legal requirements is given a high priority. One of your aims should be to ensure that all information relating to relevant legal requirements is as readily available and as user-friendly as it is possible to make it.

THEORY INTO PRACTICE

1 Read the following extract from a leaflet which outlines, in a somewhat confused and repetitive form, the legal position in relation to patents. Then consider how you would summarise it so that even the most junior member of your staff can understand it.

A patent is a collection of monopoly rights which gives the patentee the exclusive right to exploit the invention for a given period of time. It is a right to stop others, a positive right to exploit an invention not being necessary. If the invention has been made by an employee in the course of employment, the employer owns the invention and may apply for a patent to the Patent Office with the inventor's consent. Alternatively a joint application may be made, or the employee may apply, in which case the grant will be subject to the employer's interest. Once granted the patent covers the UK and is in force for 4 years although it can be renewed annually for a further 16 years. A patent must be a patentable invention which is capable of industrial application. It must not have been made available to the public anywhere in the world by written or oral description, by use or in any other way. An invention involves an inventive step if it is not obvious to a person skilled in the art, having regard to state-of-the-art knowledge. Examples of non-patentable inventions include scientific theories or mathematical methods, literary, dramatic, musical or artistic works, playing a game or programming a computer. Since most inventions are made by company employees, the question of rights to the invention are important. The law provides that an invention made in the course of employment shall belong to the employer, but it also establishes a statutory award scheme to compensate employees for inventions made on behalf of their employers which will ensure a fair share to the employee having regard to the benefit derived by the employer. Any contract term which diminishes the employee's rights in law is void.

2 Consider how you would monitor any information circulated to staff to make sure that it contains the most up-to-date information.

Allocation of responsibility

A sensible policy is to draw up a list of all legal requirements affecting your own sphere of responsibility. Then, if you are not going to carry out the work personally, make a named person responsible (and accountable) for preparing the information and despatching it to the correct person or organisation within the prescribed period of time. (It may also be useful to have a second named person to whom the task can be delegated if – and only if – the first person is unavailable.) The next step is to draw up a precise list of instructions detailing what has to be done and by what time. You may also find it necessary to include in that list a report-back procedure, again within a specified time limit, which obliges the person to whom you have delegated the task to confirm that he or she has completed it. Thus the onus is on that person to be proactive in the preparation and circulation of the required information.

What you also need to do, however, is to keep a check on the overall situation. If you work in an area in which there are many requests for such information, you may feel that the use of a straightforward planner – daily, weekly, monthly or yearly – will be of considerable assistance. If you display the information in a public area, you have the advantage of reminding yourself and other members of your staff of the ongoing situation.

THEORY INTO PRACTICE

Assume that you work in the Human Resources department of an organisation which has a large staff turnover because of the seasonal nature of the work, and because it employs family members of service personnel at a nearby RAF station who are required to be transferred to other stations at regular intervals. In general, 10–15 new full-time employees are taken on every week. During the summer, about 20 seasonal workers are also taken on each week – generally for a 10–15 week period.

After two embarrassing instances in which employees have claimed that they were not given their written terms and conditions of employment within the statutory period, your Managing Director has asked you to draw up a planner that is capable of detailing the information necessary to record the starting dates of all new members of staff and the dates on which they received their written terms and conditions. Some of the seasonal workers are not regarded as employees but as self-employed workers; others are part-time workers.

Research what the law says about the issuing of terms and conditions of employment to new employees, and consider how this would assist you to draw up an accurate planner.

Consequences of failing to provide obligatory information

The major legal consequences of failing to provide obligatory information have already been outlined in the section relating to the consequences of non-compliance with requirements:

- the possibility of contracts being rendered unenforceable
- the imposition of fines
- the payment of damages
- the payment of compensation
- the possibility of an injunction being served which can effectively stop trading.

Again, however, you have to be aware of the further consequences if, as a manager, you fail to provide the information. Managers and senior administrators are not expected to involve their organisations in costly lawsuits – or in loss of business. If you do so, you will possibly find yourself subject to disciplinary proceedings. This will result either in a written warning or in dismissal, and any claim you make for unfair dismissal is unlikely to be regarded sympathetically by an industrial tribunal in those circumstances. There are many advantages in achieving managerial status – improved promotion prospects, more interesting work, increase in status, higher salary. The corresponding disadvantage is the accountability that goes with it.

THEORY INTO PRACTICE

1 Assume that you work in the Accounts department of a large organisation and are responsible for a small team that concentrates in the main on trying to maintain cashflow by ensuring that customers pay their accounts on time. Outline the *internal* procedures you would initiate to make sure that:
   a   the customers are credit-worthy
   b   they are fully aware of the terms and conditions of payment
   c   the staff know what credit facilities they can allow
   d   there is a check on non- or late payers.
2 Assume next that, despite your many precautions, some customers still owe money.

a Draft a letter offering them a final opportunity to make payment.

b Research and summarise the actions to be taken should you then wish to follow the procedure for debt collection, both through the county court and the High Court.

c Research the remedies that may be available to you through the courts.

3 It has been argued that legal restrictions on business organisations are now so extensive that they are stifling economic growth and allowing foreign competitors an unfair advantage. Consider to what extent you agree with this argument, with particular reference to any legislation affecting your own organisation.

Index